Red Tape and the Gospel

William Paton (1886-1943)

Red Tape and The Gospel

A study of the significance of
the ecumenical missionary struggle
of William Paton (1886-1943)

by
Eleanor M. Jackson

'One who never turned back but marched breast forward,
Never doubted clouds would break,
Never dreamed, though right were worsted, wrong would triumph,
Held we fall to rise, are baffled to fight better,
Sleep to wake'

Published for the Paton family
by Phlogiston Publishing
in association with
The Selly Oak Colleges,
Birmingham

Photoset and produced by
Alan Sutton Publishing Limited.
Printed in Great Britain
by Redwood Burn Limited
Trowbridge & Esher.

Contents

Foreword

The publication of works of scholarship for which there is only a relatively small market at a price which that market can be expected to pay is nowadays a notoriously difficult exercise. It has been made possible in this case by the readiness of Dr Eleanor Jackson to spend long hours shortening her original thesis; by the generous co-operation of several persons and institutions (and especially of the Selly Oak Colleges and of my brother Professor Sir William Paton), and by the happy accident that the printer's office occupies part of my over-large parsonage.

The result is that the family and friends of 'Bill' Paton and students of the missionary and ecumenical movements have access to a full-dress study of his life and work; and that when the immediate demand is met, the remaining copies will be held for the future by the Selly Oak Colleges, where there is a Lectureship founded in his memory.

I am very grateful to Bishop Lesslie Newbigin and to my brother for reading the proofs, which it has not been practical to send to the author in South India; and to my brother also for help with the index. For the mistakes that remain I must myself accept responsibility and crave forgiveness.

I like to think that in our camaraderie as in our practical efforts those responsible have been imbued with a little of the mixture of faith, humour and inventive determination with which throughout his life William Paton confronted daunting tasks.

The passage from 'Asolando' by Robert Browning on the title page was quoted of William Paton by his friend Nathaniel Micklem.

Gloucester   DAVID M. PATON
Autumn 1980

To my family and friends
who have shared the suffering involved in the writing of this biography

and

to the family and friends of William Paton
who have shared their experience of his sufferings with me.

Introduction to a theological biography

There are many epithets of virtue used to describe William Paton, such as 'missionary statesman' and 'ecumenical pioneer', and many sincere laudatory tributes have been penned since his premature death in August 1943, for Paton was undoubtedly on the side of the angels. However, it is proposed in this biography to use a different theological substructure from that employed in hagiography. On the other hand, this will not be an orthodox biography, in the sense of a discussion of Paton's progress from birth to death and of his importance in his milieu and times. Instead, emphasis has been placed on those events in his life and aspects of his thought which illuminate the development of the ecumenical movement. It is possible to do this without distorting the pattern of his life because his progress from the Student Christian Movement and the secretaryship of the Student Volunteer Missionary Union to the International Missionary Council via experience in India as secretary of the National Christian Council of India, and from the I.M.C. to the ministry of the World Council of Churches in process of formation (W.C.C.F.), from a theology orientated solely towards mission to one which embraced social questions and the problem of the Church, is mirrored by the development from the undenominational ecumenism of the international youth movements to the interdenominational co-operation of the movements which formed the W.C.C.F., which was spurred on by the drive for Christian unity in the mission field. The fact that Paton reflected the trends in ecumenical history so exactly should not disguise the extent to which he moulded the organizations for which he worked by the impact of his personality and his prodigious capacity for hard work and travel. Nevertheless, although this book would not stand comparison with G.K.A. Bell's monumental Life of Randall Davidson (Archbishop of Canterbury, 1903-1928), and the assessment of the Church of England which Bell achieves in those pages, it will be demonstrated how, by using Paton's life as a yardstick, one can assess the ecumenical movement, or that part of it which has manifested itself in organizations with specific aims, salaried officers and study programmes.

One presupposition axiomatic for a study such as this is that history is not comprised of a sequence of ever-recurring events, nor is it controlled by economic forces and impersonal social upheavals, but that it is the medium within which God acts to effect the salvation of mankind. This is why the wanderings of an obscure Middle Eastern tribe of shepherds who finally settled between the River Jordan and the coastal plains of the Levant are more significant than the rise and fall of the mighty civilizations of Egypt, Assyria and Babylon. It is not merely that the story of God's relationship to man has a historical context, in that God incarnate in Jesus of Nazareth

9

lived and died between two definite dates and that his crucifixion is an historically verifiable event, but that the whole of history is given meaning by God's intervention. The problem of much 'heilsgeschichte' theology is that it speaks in general terms of God's judgments in history, and relates these to the central act of redemption in the life and death of Jesus Christ, but it offers no guidance as to how these principles are to be related to the ordinary events of history. Meanwhile, historiography as practised today has become secularized to the extent that vain efforts are made to write 'objective' history, whereas the great historians of the nineteenth century wrote from the standpoint of distinct political convictions and a belief in the evolution of man from barbarity to the glories of Victorian civilization. Only Marxist historians remain the exception to this tendency, integrating the study of history with an acknowledged ideological standpoint. However, since one must establish criteria on which to select events for an historical narrative and interpretation, the advantage of using a 'heilsgeschichte' technique is that it combines both theological presuppositions for the interpretation of history, and one's observable personal bias, and provides a positive alternative to a sterile recitation of the 'facts' by which an objective assessment can be made by another standard.

It is the aim of this work to examine the life of one man by historical and theological criteria, that is, to use an historian's technique, such as the study of contemporary documents, interviews with those who knew William Paton and comparisons with other theologians and church leaders, to make a historical reconstruction of his life, and to advance various hypotheses to explain certain features of his life; but also to use a theological interpretation to explain the significance of this life. To avoid writing church history which has no correlation to secular history, considerable efforts have been made to trace Paton's secular contacts and to establish that his influence extended beyond the bounds of church assemblies and congregational worship to the corridors of power in colonial governments and to the camps of aspiring nationalists in the third world, although in the closing years of his life he was particularly concerned with helping the powerless: refugees, prisoners of war, persecuted Jews, and other minority groups. Theological criteria are also necessary to understand Paton's motivation for a life devoted to evangelism, his stand on socialist and pacifist principles when these were very unpopular in England, and his tendency to stampede people into church unity. His death raised theological questions in their most acute form: why did he die at such an inopportune moment for the organization of ecumenical co-operation and before he could contribute to the reconstruction of Christian life in Europe after the war? The various answers which his family and friends produced will be discussed at the end of this book.

Paton himself used the fact of the missionary expansion of the Protestant churches to the Far East, India and Africa in the nineteenth and twentieth centuries and the growth of indigenous churches in these countries to argue for the existence of a divine as well as a human nature for the universal Christian Church, but in general Paton's writings are not the product of systematic or abstract theology, but are a practical exposition of orthodox Christian theology, or a description of the practical application of missionary principles in the contemporary situation in the Far East. Paton laboured under the belief that he had a good second class mind and was good at explaining other people's ideas but not at creating his own. Therefore, it is very difficult to construct a theological analysis of his writings. It is more important to analyse the significance of what he did. For example, he wrote relatively little on the important transition from missionary society dominated evangelism to church-based mission, but he was responsible for greatly increasing the representation of the younger churches in ecumenical structures and policy-making bodies so that at the I.M.C. meeting at Tambaram in 1938 European and American missionaries were outnumbered by representatives of African and Asian churches.

As an historical event, Paton's conversion is difficult to date, or explain. Working backwards from hints in his letters, Spring 1905 would seem the most likely date, but why a healthy, high-spirited, even-tempered eighteen year-old enjoying rugby, rowing and classics, and university life generally should suddenly be able to relate in a personal way to the death of Christ, and feel that God loved him and died for him, redeeming him from whatever sins his teenage conscience convicted him of, and changing his future if not his present character, is something which it is more logical to attribute to the grace of God than any psychological cause. It was the first manifestation of the Holy Spirit in his life. In the years at Oxford, with his strict adherence to the Student Christian Movement's regimen of daily prayer and Bible Study, he sowed the seed of his spirituality which was his main strength, and is vividly described by those who knew him well. However, his early ambition to be a missionary to China was frustrated. Although he described his work in India as going round encouraging missionaries who were being overwhelmed by the problems they faced, and who were unable to lift their eyes above their particular patch of the field, the opportunities for direct Christian witness became increasingly rare, as his administrative burdens increased. So much of his life exhibits this tension between spontaneity and bureaucracy, that the title of 'Red Tape and the Gospel' was adopted to express this tension. The spirit and the organization remain an unresolved problem in many facets of Christian life today, because an effective church cannot function without both. Occasionally both forces pulled in the same direction. It is extremely difficult to decide whether Paton's impatience at the slow progress towards church unity in South India arose from his perception that the disunited Church could not cope with the demands made upon it by the influx of converts in the 'mass movements' of sub-castes, whose desire for baptism he attributed to the Spirit, or whether his business management sense was affronted by the over-lapping and duplication of resources in church-structured education. As a secular extension of this, Paton became very concerned from about 1935 onwards about the way human freedom was being eroded by mass society and by state control both in totalitarian and non-totalitarian states, and he cast the Church in the role of protector of human freedom because of the Christian evaluation of the dignity of man which it should uphold.

Apart from the work of the Spirit, it should be possible to show something of the scope of the Gospel in the wide variety of Paton's activities, whether he was studying the effect of shari'at law on would-be converts from Islam, and the difficulties of Coptic Christians as members of a minority Church; or arguing that to refuse to evangelize the Jews was to treat them as inferior, not good enough for the gospel; or collecting evidence to harass the government of India about the opium trade; or rescuing German missionaries from internment camps; or getting the British ambassador in Moscow interested in the peace aims discussion (1943). Paton worked on the principle which was summed up in the Message of the I.M.C. meeting at Jerusalem in 1928, that the Christian Gospel was true for all, or it was not true at all. Either he had to throw all his energies into world mission or there was no point in being a Christian at all, because the Gospel would only be a relative truth, or truth whose very nature he was denying by selfishly failing to share its benefits with others. There is a beautiful evangelical simplicity about the logic of this position, that if the Gospel is true, it is true for all, and it will be shown how Paton applied this principle in his work.

There were occasions in Paton's life when one can argue that God's will was done against his inclination. Paton went to the W.S.C.F. meeting at Mysore in India in 1929 expecting to be invited to succeed John Mott as chairman of the W.S.C.F. He then let it be known that he had declined it because of pressure of other commitments. However, there is nothing in the Minutes of the W.S.C.F. executive and business committees, when the new appointments were deliberated, to suggest that Paton's name was ever considered, and Robert Mackie gives very good reasons why it was not. In 1928 Paton was 42, with a son who would shortly be a student himself. He presented a fatherly image, albeit a greatly respected one, which the members of the W.S.C.F. were in revolt against. The W.S.C.F. had now 'come of age' and was handling its own finances, making its own appointments instead of accepting Mott's nominees, and had attained a certain maturity in its awareness of political and social problems in their world context. In many ways Paton had become something of an anachronism in the W.S.C.F., but he must have very much wanted to become chairman to distort the truth in this way. Whether he was attempting to save face with his family or not, he was prevented from taking a false step, just as it was ultimately much better for him that Tatlow blocked his accession to the General Secretaryship of the S.C.M.

In many respects the pattern of events in the development of the ecumenical movement is a depressing one. Because those involved were human, and did not live up to their own high standards, one finds vested interests obstructing the merger of the movements which eventually formed the World Council of Churches. One finds clashes of personality holding up vitally important projects, and an overall lack of imagination on the part of the average missionary society secretary or church member that was stultifying. Fortunately the climate gradually changed. When Paton organized the Religion and Life week in St Albans in 1942, Dr Craig remembers that at the first meeting held to discuss the proposal when the chairman, who was the Dean of the Abbey, invited questions, a lady arose and asked: 'Mr Dean, can you please tell us whether we ought to regard the Presbyterians as schismatics or heretics?' She was greeted by a roar of laughter. Yet it was still a great ecumenical event to have a Presbyterian minister preaching in the Abbey. Paton was involved in pioneering work, setting new precedents with every conference he organized, but the period 1904-43 was in no sense a glorious age, nor a golden missionary period nor even a time when the issues were simpler. This biography will have failed if it evokes any nostalgia for the past.

When David Paton heard of his father's death he guessed that someone would start to write a 'Life' of his father almost immediately, so he wrote to his brother William giving his ideas on how it should be done, including the instruction:

> 'Daddy was a very human person underneath the international big shot covering, and I deeply hope that this won't be covered up if a memoir is written, partly on personal grounds and also because I think it is rather irreligious to present the leaders of the Church or any other human beings for that matter as inhuman and sinless'. (26.8.43)

It is important to reconstruct Paton's character both as a guide to understanding the mass of documentation which survives and as a means of explaining his reactions in certain situations. However, although Paton was a very consistent person, throughout his life he grew and matured, continually developing his ideas in new directions. Certain facets of his character remained constant. The poem by Robert Browning was quoted by Dr Micklem to sum up Paton's character and in particular the way he would battle on 'not easily daunted by adverse circumstances' as Dr Boyd said when describing how he raised money for the India Colleges' Appeal in the 1930s. The effect of Paton's conversion was to make him a naturally religious person. Many whom I have interviewed have echoed Professor Paton's description of him as 'a simple, near transparent, rock-like person, profoundly unself-conscious and always operating in some sense in awareness of his Maker — he had a trust which generated trust'. It may be the basis on which students caught his passion for mission, and were persuaded by him to sign the declaration: 'It is my purpose, God willing, to serve as a missionary overseas'. Boyd recalls his 'quietly powerful influence' securing missionary candidates, and Kathleen Witz, who went through much anguish of spirit before she could make the decision to volunteer, remembers his helpful, sensible counsels and his encouragement. Yet there is much evidence that Paton was very reticent about the things closest to his heart, he did not 'wear his soul upon his sleeve' as one of my correspondents expressed it. Like John Calvin, he has only left hints in his letters about his conversion. He never wrote a proper account of it as Canon Raven did.

The Revd Alan Booth has written one of the best general accounts of his character as it struck him in his student days.

> 'There was nothing sentimental or 'pious' in the bad sense about him, but one of his attractive features was a certain sort of adolescent mischievous delight which he took in moving about the corridors of power, and, he felt, influencing events. He had some of this responsibility always as a missionary statesman and more particularly of course in the war years when his responsibilities to the I.M.C. in relation to governments were very considerable. He was not above a certain boyish boastfulness and name-dropping but at the same time he was a man of very great wisdom and far-sightedness. He combined a certain evangelical simplicity of faith with a real appetite for handling events and people and manoevring committees'.

A student contemporary of Paton's, The Revd A.J. Haile, remembers his 'buoyant and eager personality, his deep bass voice, and broad grin and hearty laugh marked him in any company . . . his self-confidence was never offensive'. In the S.C.M. Paton was an endless source of practical jokes, as William Temple was, but he was less happy when the joke was on him. The food at the S.C.M. camps was always awful, and Paton had an enormous appetite. On one occasion he was seen sneaking a second helping of ham. When he rose to give out the notices, the tent was rent with cries of 'Ham, ham' for several minutes, much to his annoyance. His family probably saved him from any incipient tendency to pomposity in middle age by their ruthless teasing.

Dr Payne describes him as 'sturdy in build, clear-headed, determined, a most able organizer, but a very friendly and human person'. His closest friend, Bishop L.S. Hunter, recalls: 'William Paton's contemporaries forgave him his forcefulness because he was so obviously first class and worked hard, but there were occasions when he was a little too ruthless and at meetings sometimes a little too compelling, but he was right at the heart of the early days of the ecumenical movement'. Sir Kenneth Grubb writes of Paton's abilities, comparing him with Churchill, under whom he worked during the war. Seeing so much of both men, he concluded that Paton lacked Churchill's patience. 'He did not suffer fools gladly, and he did not gladden fools'. Paton did in fact have endless time and patience with students, Mrs Paton's 'lame dogs' and with anyone not incarcerated in his own opinions, but even with the fools he had the happy knack of making them laugh with him, so that he had very few enemies, if any. He certainly enjoyed the amount of influence he had with politicians, civil servants and journalists. From 1917 he used to report regularly to Lambeth Palace in the same way that Anglican diocesan bishops returning from abroad did. David Cairns remembers as a young man going to see Paton in his London office, and, greatly daring, related a dream that he had had of Paton answering two telephone calls at the same time, one from the Archbishop of Canterbury, the other from the Archbishop of York. Paton looked a bit sheepish and indicated the telephone which he had just put down. 'As a matter of fact', he said, 'that was the Archbishop of York'.

Paton was very much hindered by his reputation. William Temple could make anyone feel at ease with him, however obscure they were; Paton was less successful in doing this. Robert Mackie never felt at ease with him in spite of a long association when he was General Secretary of the S.C.M. Kathleen Bliss felt she was not popular with him, and I think this was because she did not fit into any of the known categories into which he placed women. Paton could be diffident and nervous in feminine company because he was afraid of the supposed female tendency to emotional outbursts. Mrs Pym relates how on one occasion at Swanwick the camp-site was flooded so that Paton had to inform the women who were sleeping in the ballroom of the hall that they must move out for the rain-soaked men. Even though she accompanied him, he was apparently terrified of the situation. When she became the first woman chairman of the S.C.M. General Committee in 1917, he informed her that the task was too much for a woman. His initial protective view of the weakness of women must originate from his family experience as the older brother of five sisters. Paton learnt to work with women in India (1922-26) where he encountered a number of remarkable pioneer women missionaries, educationalists and doctors, such as Dr Shonie Oliver, who later worked for the N.C.C. of India at his suggestion, Ethel Gordon, a rural expert, and the heads of the women's colleges. With his secretaries he could be kind and paternalistic, while he was tactful and courteous to his sons' girlfriends. A small band of women, Mrs Pym, Lorna Southwell and Mrs Hunter, and one or two others, were life-long friends, but they were all exceptional women by any standards. According to Mrs Hogg he simply ignored the wives of colleagues. If one compares Paton with Garbett and Lang, who were both bachelors and ill at ease with women, one is struck by the fact that Paton, despite his eminence, never suffered their loneliness and depression, and was much more blessed with friends of both sexes. This capacity for friendship was often at the root of a successful partnership in mission.

It cannot be denied that Paton 'looked the part'. His physical presence inspired confidence, even if he was once likened to a pocket battleship. He was about average height, (5′ 10″ approximately) stocky in build and tended to wear suits of dark or light clerical grey to the office (the correct garb 1930-43) and a round, pork-pie hat which he put on his head absolutely straight. He had a nautical gait and rolled along looking as though he was strung up by his braces. He usually took stairs at a run, and appeared somewhat untidy. His idea of an ideal holiday was to walk twenty-five miles a day, preferably in beautiful scenery, though he once dragged the party out in the pouring rain, saying that even if one could not see the mountains, it was worth it to feel them behind the mist. Unfortunately, Paton's wife could not share these holidays because after having six children, she had anaemia, and she had been led to believe, quite wrongly, that since 1906 she had a weak heart. She also had a retiring nature and did not like going away at all.

Paton's courtship of Grace Mackenzie MacDonald, whom he won in spite of bitter parental opposition from both sides, had all the elements of a great romance. They fell in love at first sight, as she was coming downstairs in her father's manse and he was arriving as the visiting preacher. To break up the relationship, her parents arranged for her to work as a private secretary to the future leader of the Independent Labour Party, Ramsay MacDonald. So Paton was forced to haunt Transport House or the pillar box where Grace MacDonald posted her employer's mail. Since etiquette forbade that they should meet alone, and he was not admitted to her house, he hired a hansom cab for an hour's drive every Thursday afternoon. Eventually her father relented sufficiently to perform the marriage ceremony, but it was several years before Mrs MacDonald would speak to her son-in-law, convinced as she was, that her daughter had 'married beneath her'.

Grace Paton not only provided Paton with the emotional stability of a happy marriage and a family life which he so much cherished, for she had a gift for home-making, but she influenced him subtly in a number of ways. She was suspicious and sceptical of ecumenical organizations, feeling that they were all committees and no action, when there were desperate social conditions at home and abroad which ought to be tackled. She was shy and awkward in large gatherings, and hated the formal receptions in India, but she organized a canteen for workers both during the General Strike and during the war. She induced Paton to consider social questions, and in 1916 wrote a very lively and scathing account of the government's statutory responsibilities for children, called 'The Child and the Nation'. She supported him in his pacifist stand, but in 1918, as a result of a new religious experience, almost a 'conversion', she found herself better able to express her faith as a member of the Church of England. This was a shattering blow to Paton because it was an experience which he could not share, and because it introduced a religious barrier into their life. In some respects it was easier for him when she became a Roman Catholic in 1936, but the ecumenical harmony of their home was only achieved after much soul-searching. It is surely not a coincidence that both steps were taken either during or after a very long absence of Paton from home. Mrs Paton was very lonely, and had to bear a great burden of responsibility for the family when he was away for months on end, and catholicism, whether Anglican or Roman, was a great support for her. She was also a genuinely mystical person, which Paton was not. It is significant that when they met Gandhi, Gandhi particularly asked to see her again, not Paton, probably because he perceived these depths in her. She read herself into Anglo-catholicism and Roman Catholicism, the one following logically from the other, but one reason for her abandoning the Church of England was that she felt it was ignoring social questions and was not sufficiently involved in practical social work. The 'last straw' came when she heard Dean Henderson deny, by implication, the doctrine of the Real Presence in the sacrament, which was a cornerstone of her faith. The Paton family were all intensely loyal to each other, and would tolerate no criticism of a member of the family, so that it was the hostile reaction from many of Paton's acquaintances which forced him to be reconciled to the position. Family loyalty outstripped theology. Shortly after Paton's death, Mrs Paton encountered one of her parish in St Albans, who made sympathetic noises about her bereavement. Mrs Paton replied that her consolation was the certainty that her husband was in heaven. According to Roman Catholic teaching, since Paton was a heretic, this was not possible, and the lady was shocked:

'What? Not even a short spell in Purgatory?' she replied.

A question of some difficulty is that of Paton's health. Most of his colleagues were amazed and shaken when he died comparatively young, since they had always believed that he enjoyed robust health. However, if one consults Appendix C where his illnesses are listed, it will be seen that after 1936 his health deteriorated. His chest became weakened by successive attacks of pneumonia, a crucial factor in the question of surviving an anaesthetic. He was also overweight by today's standards. He died after an operation for a perforated ulcer from post-operational pneumonia and shock. He would have stood a better chance of surviving if he had taken more care of his health, but he tended to shrug any illness off as being of no consequence, keeping a stiff upper lip and declaring that he was perfectly fit when he was not. The ulcer might be attributable to stress and overwork during the war, and to his habit of dashing out of the office at lunchtime, eating his lunch and dashing back inside fifteen minutes, which he kept up for years. I tried to pace out the distance he walked, and could not do it in under fifteen minutes, apart from the time allowed for eating a meal.

Although the story that Paton's parents sent him to his first day at school wearing a kilt must be regarded as apocryphal, an important element in Paton's character was the fervour with which he supported all things Scottish. He celebrated his 'Scottish-ness' with more emotion than accuracy, as might be expected from one born in Brixton, but his marriage to Grace Mackenzie Macdonald brought him a rich dowry of Highland traditions, so that one of his sons declared to me with pride that there was not a drop of English blood in his lineage. He went to great lengths to procure oatmeal in Scotland for porridge, but his Scottish accent could only be detected as a blur when he preached or broadcast.

This biography has been in preparation since December 1972 when the Paton family first gave their blessing to it. Without their help and encouragement, it could not have taken the shape it has, apart from the inestimable value of having access to Paton's most private letters, which have revealed many otherwise unknown facts. Canon Paton, Mrs Montefiore and Professor Paton have been particularly generous with their time and hospitality, and very honest and frank in their conversation, and I am enormously indebted to them. All the people whom I have interviewed have been very kind and helpful, often putting me up for the night when I had to travel a long distance to meet them, or arranging for me to meet other friends of Paton's. Three chapters were written in 'Croftlands', Dr Mackie's home in Lanarkshire, where I was able to retreat from the distractions of Birmingham, and where his advice was continuously available. I am grateful also to those whom I interviewed who helped me with the rest of my train fares. Kathleen Bliss has been a most helpful collaborator, since her work on J.H. Oldham overlaps much of mine. Kathleen Witz was one of several people who wrote to her friends to try and find more people who had known Paton. My debt to Miss Morden is also very great. A complete list of all whom I have interviewed will be found at the end of this book.

Several people could not meet me, but sent long and detailed letters containing their recollections, which have proved most useful. I am particularly indebted to Miss Carol Graham, who worked with Bishop Azariah for many years; the Revd A.J. Haile, a student friend 1907-12; Mrs Hudson, a friend of the Paton family who lived in St Albans; Dr Charles Ranson of Connecticut, U.S.A.; the late Miss Standley, an I.M.C. assistant secretary; and the late Canon Max Warren, formerly of the Church Missionary Society (C.M.S.)

I must also acknowledge with gratitude the assistance which archivists and librarians have given me, often extending privileges to me which the ordinary library user does not enjoy, such as the use of an office, and endless cups of coffee. I am particularly indebted to Dr van der Bent, Librarian of the World Council of Churches, who first suggested that I should write a biography of William Paton, Paul Jenkins and his colleague Herr Ninck of the Basel Mission archives, and Miss Frances Williams of the Selly Oak Colleges' Library.

It is unlikely that this book would have progressed very far without the help and advice of my tutor, Professor Hollenweger, who has written so many letters on my behalf, and has forced me to work systematically and thoroughly.

It would have taken many years longer to write the original thesis without the grants which enabled me to study full-time in Heidelberg, Geneva and Birmingham. For this I am indebted to the World Council of Churches for a scholarship October 1972 - Christmas 1973, to the Department of Education and Science for a grant 1974-1975, and to the Deutsche Gesellschaft für Missionswissenschaft for a grant towards travelling expenses, the first time that the society had made a grant to a non-German. The Selly Oak Colleges have generously paid for the essential photocopying of documents, which have been added to the ecumenical archive centre now established there. They have also supported Canon Paton and Professor Paton when they kindly arranged for this book to be published.

My own friends have generously put me up in Oxford, London and Geneva when necessary. Roswith Gerloff, Neville and Carleen Richardson, Steve and Mary Rennie and Diana Shorey in particular have rescued me from some desperate situations. Finally, my family have nursed me back to health after the four operations which I had to have during the period of this research and have helped in innumerable ways, not only by checking and typing parts of the thesis, but by keeping up my morale. To all these people this work is dedicated, because without them it would not have been possible to write it.

Chapter 1
Paton's Apprenticeship in the Christian Faith

'Send up a shout, and let the glory out'. An exuberant bunch of high-spirited undergraduates sang as they swung through the mellow medieval passageways of Oxford in the heady years of student evangelism when the British Colleges' Christian Union was created.[1] From Constance Padwick's graphic description of Oxford 1893–1896 to the university world which Paton discovered in Autumn 1904, it would seem that little had changed outwardly, for Paton's voice was soon added to the racket which another generation of students in the 'pi squad' were making.[2] Yet within its brief history the British Colleges' Christian Union (B.C.C.U.) had already developed considerably since it was founded at the Keswick Convention in 1893 to link together twelve Christian Unions flourishing in different universities and to prepare the ground for the presentation of the missionary challenge of the Student Volunteer Missionary Union.[3] An ebb and flow in its influence was already discernible, but Paton plunged in at high tide when John R. Mott had shaken Oxford on missions in 1904 and 1905, and the S.V.M.U. had already held its biggest Quadrennial conference to date, involving 807 students, at Edinburgh in January 1904.[4] Already a change in the movement's self-understanding had led to a change of name at the summer conference held at Conishead in 1905. Oxford 'undergraduates' objected to being classified as 'students' in the nomenclature 'Student Christian Movement'[5], but were overruled because the movement was becoming more catholic and more democratic.

It would be difficult to over-estimate the importance of the Student Christian Movement (S.C.M.) in terms of its influence on Paton's generation of church leaders and evangelists, while its organisation, spirituality and theology are extremely significant for an understanding of the processes of evangelism in the twentieth century. Its membership of the World's Student Christian Federation gave it both an international context for its development of Christian apologetic and enabled individual students such as Paton to contribute to the world-wide movement. However, although the W.S.C.F. and Paton's specific contribution to it will be considered within this chapter, the development of his ideas on social questions and international relations will be deferred for consideration in later chapters.

Unfortunately there are considerable problems endemic in any discussion of the S.C.M. based on original sources. The documentary evidence is extremely meagre because the S.C.M. archives were flooded in the Second World War, and were neglected from 1952 until they were removed to the Selly Oak Colleges' Library in March 1975.[6] Their fragmentary nature means that one must be careful in drawing general conclusions lest what survives is not representative of trends in the movement as a whole, especially as almost all the surviving material emanates from Tissington

Tatlow, General Secretary of the B.C.C.U./S.C.M. from 1903-1929. If the paucity of the material relating to Paton were an accurate indication of the role which Paton played in the S.C.M., one would conclude that he was a relatively obscure member of S.C.M. staff compared with Malcolm Spencer, the first social studies secretary, or Martyn Trafford (1875-1910) whose memoranda were a seminal influence on the theological colleges' department of the S.C.M. Yet oral sources suggest that this was not so.

Therefore the evidence of the surviving members of the S.C.M. assumes a particular importance. A complete list of those whom I interviewed is to be found at the end of this book. Their help was invaluable in reconstucting Paton's contribution to the S.C.M. and they patiently criticized many of the hypotheses advanced in this chapter. The spirit of former Student Volunteers and secretaries of the S.C.M., now nearly all octogenarians, was in itself striking evidence of the power of the S.C.M., especially in those whom one might characterise as 'spicy saints' and in the two people who were so close to eternity that its light was suffused in their presence. Yet R.L. Pelly (Bible Study Secretary 1911-14) was so torn by self-doubt that his observations were particularly shrewd and free from presuppositions.

Finally, there are certain general features of student life throughout this period which must be borne in mind. The first is the great difference between students of 1904 and 1976. There were then only 44,000 students engaged in any form of higher education in Great Britain and Ireland, a figure which remained constant until 1939, but which is less than half the annual intake into British universities today. Almost without exception English students were drawn from the middle and upper classes, since apart from 30,000 places made available by the government for ex-servicemen in 1919, there were virtually no government grants and few scholarships. Secondly, the competition for university places was far milder than for arts subjects today (the majority of students studied arts subjects, law or medicine). It is still remarkable that the S.C.M. could count 10,000 members in 1914, and doubtless its influence on the uncommitted made its outreach still wider. There were, however, no national student organizations then, such as the National Union of Students, founded by S.C.M. members in 1923,[7] nor were the denominations supporting a nationwide network of chaplains to students as they do today. There is sufficient evidence in the S.C.M. archives to show that the churches were largely negligent of the student population until the S.C.M. forced their attention on the campus situation (c.1908-1910), yet at the same time S.C.M. was strong enough to guarantee that it would act as an inter-denominational pastoral agency. Tatlow was responsible for maintaining this ecumenical situation. He dissuaded church leaders who proposed to send ministers on to the campuses, in forcible terms and with good reason. The average Christian Union secretary already had so much to do that visitors from every church and missionary society would have obstructed the existing student work and worship. The exceptions to this were the Baptist Student Federation, the University Women's Camps and local 'Churchmen's Unions' and 'Free Church Fellowships', though of the latter it should be said that there were so few non-conformist students at Oxford and Cambridge that they all automatically knew each other.[8]

Another distinction which must be made between 1904 and 1976 is that the S.C.M. which Paton knew bore no resemblance to the movement which bears the name today.[9] In its organisational structure and its missionary outreach, but not in its theology or its relationship to the churches, it was closer to the present U.C.C.F.

(formerly Inter-varsity Fellowship), whose member bodies today call themselves the Christian Unions of the particular universities which they serve. In this book 'Christian Union' will be the normal appellation not of a non-denominational Evangelical student group, but of the university S.C.M. societies, since that was the name they then bore. The exception was Cambridge, where the Cambridge Inter-collegiate Christian Union, the first Christian union to be formed (1877) and the first to affiliate to the B.C.C.U. (1893), repudiated the national S.C.M. rather than yield to pressure to elect its committee and to broaden its membership to include non-conformists and non-Evangelical Anglicans.[10] The significance of this schism will be discussed later.

Students in the Oxford Intercollegiate Christian Union (O.I.C.C.U.) seem to have had no problem fitting in daily prayer meetings, missionary study circle meetings and perhaps Bible Study or social study meetings every week, apart from the larger meetings with outside speakers. Dr Micklem relates how it was always possible to get a group of students together to provide an audience for an S.C.M. travelling secretary. He did not expect to be very successful in arranging a meeting for Robert Wilder, the American evangelist, because 'New College were a rather sickish lot'. However he browbeat a sufficient number into coming, and smoothed things over with jugs of steaming mulled claret. Robert Wilder took no notice of this, but spoke straight off about Jesus Christ and was heard with respect. It seems that student life then was generally more leisurely, except at the 'new' redbrick universities based on the great nineteenth century industrial metropoles where students had to commute from home or lodgings to lectures, were burdened by a crowded lecture time-table and had no student unions. Oxford in 1904 pulsated with the gentle rhythm of academic life based on an eight-week term and occasional explosions of student high spirits: Paton himself was able to spend hours at rowing, tennis and rugby, apart from less commendable pursuits such as elaborate practical jokes and 'ragging' of other students.

Obviously, in considering the effect on Paton of the S.C.M. both as student and staff member, the most important single instance is its agency in Paton's conversion. It is futile to speculate on what he might have been if he had not suddenly felt the love of God to be so real to him that he was compelled to struggle against what he considered to be his sinful nature and to commit himself to Christ, whatever the consequences for his life. Paton did not leave more than a few clues as to the nature of his conversion, but from his contemporaries' remarks it would seem that it was an extremely profound experience, which might be described as the discovery of his natural religious self, and a transformation of his purpose in life. His children describe his religious faith as something as natural to him as breathing, unforced, unselfconscious and sincere. This was always characteristic of him because Dr Micklem, Canon Pelly and A.J. Haile, who came to know him c. 1907-8, noted his earnestness but never realised that he was a convert, he seemed so at home in the Christian faith. Paton's reticence is reminiscent of that of another theologian in the 'Presbyterian' tradition, John Calvin, who in all his writings only alludes to his conversion twice.[11] Lockhart's discussion of Cosmo Gordon Lang's conversion experience at Oxford is valuable for purposes of comparison because Lang also came from a Scottish Presbyterian background,[12] though he did not adopt the faith of his fathers as Paton did, and also was a more subtle and highly strung character, a lawyer and not an evangelist.

If one person can be named as being the principal instrument in Paton's conversion, it is the Revd. Frank Lenwood, whose position as tutor in New Testament

Greek at Mansfield College, with pastoral responsibility for non-conformist students, conceals the full extent of his influence. Lenwood and his sister Maida were involved in the highest councils of the S.C.M., contributing an abundance of new ideas. For example, Lenwood was the originator of the plans for a permanent conference site in 1908. They were also irresistible evangelists and recruiting agents for the S.C.M. Lenwood had many of the qualities of Robert Wilder, the founder of the S.V.M.U.; a gift for personal relationships and evangelism among students, but not Wilder's rigid Evangelical views and literalist interpretation of the Bible.[13] After an extended tour of China and India Lenwood offered his services to the London Missionary Society and worked in Benares 1909-1912. He was then recalled to work for the London secretariat of the L.M.S. Paton described his first encounter with Lenwood when he spoke at Lenwood's memorial service in 1934.

> 'I shall never forget as long as I live my first touch with him. I got the usual circular inviting undergraduates to some form of pious meeting, and had scornfully tossed it into the waste-paper basket. Next day I got an invitation to come to breakfast with Frank Lenwood — he had got hold of my name, as he did of all of us — and that was the end of that. I cannot describe the kind of spell he cast over those of us of many denominations at Oxford. One of the things was that he always set us to work. Psychology was new in those days, but he was perhaps giving us a chance of expression for all the impressions he was making on us. No one ever got near Frank without being made to do something.
>
> One of the first things he did was to set us to prepare for a campaign by Mott. . . . He turned us out into the Free Church camps for school-boys . . . most of all he turned us into the little villages around Oxford. Many ministers today turned their hands first to the aweful task of preaching the Word of God because Lenwood made them do it . . . man after man well known today in Anglican and Free Church societies . . . first conceived the very idea itself to go abroad because Lenwood saw something in him. . . . He would not leave them alone until they had made up their minds in the presence of God what they ought to do'.[14]

This may be a reference not only to Paton's own conversion, but to the forces which drove him to sign the S.V.M.U. declaration. Paton's conversion can be dated with reasonable certainty to the Easter term 1905, but evidently he was not alone in his experience. There is no evidence apart from this passage as to when or how he discovered his vocation to the ordained ministry. The other great influence in his conversion was a layman, John R. Mott, and so many of the S.C.M. members adopted lay professions that it is unlikely that Paton was guilty of the fallacy exhibited by the undergraduate who burst into a tutorial at Oxford and said to his tutor: 'Sir, I've just discovered that I believe in God. Oughtn't I to be ordained?'[15]

It is more probable that Lenwood got him involved in a lay preaching ministry until he realised himself that this was his vocation. There is much documentary evidence that Paton regarded the ministry as a high calling, and it is significant that he allowed his wife to teach their children as much Anglo-Catholic doctrine and practice as she liked, but his own orders must never be called in question.[16] In 1933 Paton wrote to the Revd J. Banninga that:

> 'I am quite clear that I do not claim to be a sacrificing priest and if an Anglican claims to be a sacrificing priest, and denies that my ordination

22

confers on me the powers to do the things which his ordination confers on him, I entirely agree, adding, of course, that I do not want to do the things which he claims to be able to do'.

From Lenwood Paton derived his scrupulous adherence to 'the Morning Watch', as the practice of private prayer and reading early in the morning was called, his practice of reading the Greek New Testament every day and his love of Scripture, but he distanced himself from Lenwood's nineteenth century 'liberal' theology and heterodox view of the Incarnation.[17]

In an S.C.M. scrapbook of newspaper cuttings about Mott's 1908 campaign, there are pictures of a young man with an extraordinary fixed stare of judgement and courage. When he was older it became a 'bulldog look' similar to that which Churchill possessed. For this reason people with whom he stayed found him terrifying and forbidding. In Oxford the S.C.M. used to hire the schools for him, which he used to fill night after night with 800-1,000 awestruck students. He had no rhetorical tricks and despised the emotional appeal of other freelance evangelists. He was totally unlike Moody and Sankey with whom he is often compared. He was very sincere and his appeal was principally ethical. Talks were entitled 'The Fight for Character', 'Temptation' and so on. Dr Micklem recalled his constant refrain: 'Give your hearts to the Lord Jesus and your lives to his service', but this was not meant in an introverted, pietistic way, but as a response to the Lord's challenge to get out into the world and face the challenge of the young nations emerging in the Far East, the ancient cultures untouched by Christianity, and the poverty and deprivation of the uneducated and the unevangelised. Mott thought in continents and could communicate this vision. He conveyed an impression of great power not only by his words but by his superb physique. The gauntlet he threw down made the students like Paton who picked it up feel like champions. For perhaps twenty years after his conversion, Paton consciously or unconsciously modelled himself on Mott.

Both Mott and Lenwood possessed in abundance the quality of 'manliness' of which there was a cult in the S.C.M.[18] It appears to have originated in the tours which the 'Cambridge Seven', all well-known athletes, made in 1885 when they volunteered for service in China,[19] and was perhaps re-inforced by the public school mythos on the one hand, and on the other, the obvious requirement in pioneering days that missionary candidates should have considerable physical stamina. However, it is difficult to understand why it was necessary to make such a pronounced 'man to man' appeal, even going to the extent of excluding women from meetings. (Mott addressed the men's Christian Union at the new Birmingham University while the Women's Christian Union gathered downstairs to pray for the success of the meeting. Even in 1928 the S.C.M. found it difficult to persuade Mott to address mixed audiences.) However, this method was effective in reaching aggressive athletic men like Paton, who in turn incarnated this ideal in such a way that it formed a potent part of their own appeal. In 1917 Paton received a request for advice on prayer from a woman student who was more convinced 'if a man like Mr Paton' advocated prayer, than by other women.[20]

There is, of course, no such thing as a 'typical' conversion experience, yet his experience was indicative of a new trend in the S.C.M. This emerged from Paton's intervention in the controversy over the Aim and Basis of the S.C.M. from 1910-12. One can also see that Paton himself made this connection between his own experience and that of other students and applied his growing theological awareness to the issue. Paton, Lawson and E. Murray Page, who were both S.C.M. secretaries, and a 'senior friend', Kingsley Williams, were so disturbed by the official report produced by the 1910 S.C.M. Commission on the Basis that they went away together for the week-end to discuss the question, then produced a very significant memorandum. Their desire was, they said, to speak on behalf of the newly-converted freshman, (of whom Paton is clearly the archetype), whose position is very different from the members of the General Committee of the S.C.M. 'Our plea is for the little child who is just beginning theological thinking who is suddenly plunged into the tossing currents of modern thought'.

There are, they say, two classes of converts, those to whom the Incarnation is central from the first, and who move from that to the idea of redemption as a fact affecting them, and from there to an experience of Christ, which is the pattern exemplified by Neville Talbot's experience; and those who come to know Jesus as their saviour and then work out the meaning of the Incarnation. The second group have no theological language. They know that Christ makes the difference and no other allegiance works. God is in Christ as He is nowhere else, but they feel like the fishermen on Lake Galilee. They cannot articulate their wonder — they are only aware of a relationship which means everything to them.

'Theology we take to be the articulation of all that is involved in and meant by the spiritual facts which are the foundation of Christian life and faith. This articulation may be more valuable but it is not more Christian than the faith of those without theological formulation. We plead for the little child against the philosopher. A belief such as his implies a belief in the divinity of Christ and does not differ much from the worship of the Church. We have no personal objection whatever to a declaration which includes a statement of belief in the Deity of Christ — such in fact is our own belief, but it is a belief to which we have come not as the necessary antecedent of devotion to our Lord, but as a God-given consequence of it'.

Although the S.C.M. must have a Basis which is eventually accepted personally by all members, and not consigned to the archives in the care of the General Secretary, as the one element of permanence in a vanishing world, nevertheless the primary aim of the S.C.M. is evangelism. It does not exist to regiment converts. So they stated that the Christian life is a progressive one. An attitude of faith and the theological expression of it must come *pari passu*, but under no circumstances should the genuinely converted be excluded because they lack the vocabulary to express their faith, or have various intellectual difficulties. There is a danger otherwise of giving the Christian Unions the impression that orthodoxy is more important than faith, and that the S.C.M. is a quasi-church requiring credal confessions of the newly converted.

> 'We believe that faith in the uniqueness and absoluteness of the revelation
> of God in Christ is of the *esse* of Christianity. But in our experience that
> interpretation put on it by the convert is only reached after many years of
> theological thoughts'.

Tatlow tried to suppress this pamphlet, labelling it as a 'manifesto' and a 'bomb', but Kingsley Williams resisted this. Paton admitted that some of the wording was infelicitous, but no less so was the official report which calumniated the Scots for a genuine theological difficulty, calling their reluctance to sign 'slackness'. He was prepared to withdraw the statement but maintained that their side of the discussion should be put, perhaps anonymously, with a covering note from Tatlow so that the party spirit which he detected there would be removed.[21] He wrote:

> 'There is one thing I feel strongly. We do stand for a position regarding this whole matter which is not primarily or in many cases ultimately a question of Christology at all, but of what you might call religious chronology. We think (all of us) that a man can make a pact of full surrender to Jesus Christ, can know that he is absolute for his religious conscience without being able to go to the highly metaphysical statement that he is God, still less 'my God'. I should personally admit that the Logos doctrine and what Denney[22] calls a 'full' Christology is logically implied in that religious consciousness. I'm not prepared to make the second year man say so if he doesn't yet think so and has an accurate sense of language. This is rightly the crux of what we think'.

Significantly, by the time the Commission on the Basis met in December 1912, not only had Paton and his friends been put on the commission (from April 1911), but Tatlow had absorbed the whole of Paton's argument including his argument that his ideas were fully consonant with the intentions of the S.V.M.U. pioneers who first adopted a Basis in 1895 and revised it in 1902 for the B.C.C.U.[23] He blithely plagiarised Paton's ideas as the basis of his introductory statement to the commission.

It is clear from this document that Paton's conversion began as an intense sense of redemption combined with the beginning of a personal relationship with Christ. This faith he possessed without any theological instruction or any Christian inherited tradition; rather he had slowly and painstakingly worked out for himself the meaning of his experience. For Paton's parents had observed the conventions of the day in making their children say their prayers, and in sending them to chapel three times on Sunday; but although the girls had to walk at least a mile in each direction, instead of using public transport because of the Sabbath, the maids still had to work as usual. James Paton was an elder in the Presbyterian Church, which improved his social standing, and it is an admitted fact that spiritual leadership was not required of elders in the Presbyterian tradition.[24] There were no family prayers, no teaching of the children and nothing in the home of genuine religion according to his sister, Mrs Kingsley Smith. There is no question of his mother educating him in foreign missions, she says, whatever she may have claimed later when he was a famous missionary statesman.[25] It would seem that it was the effect of Paton's conversion which caused him to regard his childhood as dull and uninteresting, something which he rarely mentioned in conversation; whereas from his sister's recollections he would seem to have been a happy and healthy child energetically learning music and games. His relationship with his parents was then remote and formal, for the Paton family were not given to displays of affection.

Paton's attitude in 1910 was clearly very catholic, since he wished to include in the fellowship of the S.C.M. all who believed they had a personal experience of Christ. His categories unconsciously reflect those of William James,[26] so that it is not surprising that he appeals to I Corinthians 3, and insists on 'faith in the uniqueness and absoluteness of the revelation of God in Christ'. Paton rested his case not only on his own experience but on the Gospel narratives in which those who encounter Jesus and decide to follow him, rarely confess him to be divine immediately. His position is very 'Protestant': faith precedes theology and inspires it, being something intimately related to his personal experience, which he must work out for himself, and not receive from the hands of another, whatever the authority such an intermediary would claim in the S.C.M. or in the Church.

That Paton's conversion experience continued to be of paramount importance to him can be seen in his reaction to his wife's decision to join the Church of England while he was in India 1917-18. From the letters which he wrote to her it is clear that he first searched within himself to see whether he could also become an Anglican, but he had too much knowledge of Anglican malpractices in India for that to be possible, apart from his abhorrence of a state religion and the manifestations of its support for the war.[27] Then he reconciled himself to her decision as he came to understand that she was committing herself to a new understanding of God, rather than to the Church of England. In the ecumenical climate today it is difficult to appreciate the enormity of the step Grace Paton was taking. In an undated letter he wrote:

> 'My darling, your letters are inexpressibly dear to me. I was so glad to hear what you said about your finding God again, nothing will make me believe that you ever lost Him, but that you have gained a new experience of Him fills me with joy. You are more of a sacramentalist than I am, but I am getting more of one, and I don't think we shall find that our re-thinking has divided us. And you don't think I am so smallminded as to be amazed at your becoming catholic. You have far too much Presbyterianism in you ever to lose that side, and it is only that foundation which makes the catholic side safe'.

In another letter he wrote:

> 'I have the feeling that you have been almost exclusively swayed by the help you have received from confession and the Eucharist and the saintly character of old Severton. I don't suspect him or anyone else of proselytism and I think I understand your mental sequence. Let me beg you to remember that confession and the Eucharist as administered by a good old man in a country parish is not the Church of England.
>
> If it is God's will for you, it is His Will that you face the whole thing. I can very well conceive that it may be His Will and if it is, it will not be I who hinders you . . . while frankly I don't want you to join the Church of England unless you really must, my feeling on the whole thing is one of rejoicing really because you have come nearer to God and realised his love and Grace'.[29]

The effect of Paton's conversion can be seen not only in his attitude to the S.C.M. and his personal relationships, but also in the theology of his first book, a collection of essays which he edited under the title of 'The Missionary Motive'[29] An S.C.M. study book, it was the product of discussion among the contributors, so one may justifibly assume that the views expressed by H.A.A. Kennedy in his chapter 'The Missionary Motive in the Mind of St. Paul' and by the Revd P. Brereton in the chapter 'The Missionary Motive in the Conversion of the Roman Empire' reflect something of Paton's theology. Apart from a number of errors caused by the contingencies of large-scale generalisations, which the scholarship of that generation would not have condoned, there is a marked tendency for which the editor must be held responsible. Kennedy's essay paints a mistakenly grey picture of the Jewish religion of Paul's day. There is no mention of the liberal school of Gamaliel, but only of the legalistic, exclusive aspects of Judaism, which were not normative before A.D.90, and of the transforming effect of Paul's conversion. Kennedy maintains, in the teeth of the evidence, that the early church was preserved by the Spirit from serious cleavage and discord. The chapter reflects conventional Victorian Protestantism, the conversion experience of members of the S.C.M. and the unity of the S.C.M. more accurately than the New Testament Church. Brereton makes the same mistake, probably because of the traditional deprecatory attitude of classical Greek scholars for the philosophy and culture of the Koine Greek period. In other words, as with his interpretation of his family background, Paton was sanctioning the presupposition that one's pre-Christian existence is one of unmitigated darkness. The sense of a compulsion to evangelize was also Paton's, as the authors claim it was Paul's and the early Church's. They ignore the 'Johannine' growth in the faith which was the experience not merely of Origen and the Cappadocian fathers but surely of many humbler Christians in sub-Apostolic times.[30]

Paton's own contribution contains a central passage which is significant:

> 'It is enough for us to know that at the end of every one of the muscle fibres into which the main nerves of the missionary enterprise branch there is a human soul, much like ourselves, standing in as real need of God as we do. The knowledge of the redemption of Jesus Christ, and nothing less than that, will surely fill us with a longing to give the news of that redemption to all for whom it was wrought'.

He argues that the eternal motives of God are valid in every age, but in Jesus Christ he has revealed himself to man.

> 'The Incarnation, Jesus's mission to men, is the ultimate source of the motive for missions. In the person of Jesus Christ one sees the fullness of God and realises what is in man. Thereby one knows that He is for all men. It is because Jesus the Son of Man has taken all manhood up into Himself and revealed the possibility of a redeemed humanity that we can never be content to leave any of the families of men without the knowledge of the divine purpose for them . . . we do not deserve our salvation and cannot repay Him, but we can give our own lives that the redemption be made known to others. Power to do this comes through the Resurrection'.[31]

It is clear from this quotation that Paton's conversion experience has led him to a missiological formulation of the implications of the Incarnation. He has extended the implications of his experience to the point where he sees all mankind redeemed in a fuller humanity. Paton does not take a severely penal view of the Atonement, but merely emphasizes the total unworthiness of man and his debt to God, which Kennedy places as the root of St. Paul's experience of God. Redemption seems to mean for Paton the realisation of a new person in Christ, which is a revealed gift and is not due to any human merit or perspicacity.

One could write at much greater length to demonstrate this point from Paton's apologetic writings. Suffice it that Paton's conversion was central to the theological formulation of his faith. The question of whether he was troubled by intellectual difficulties admits of no categorical answer, but it should be noted that Paton had already achieved a steady growth of faith and the theological expression thereof before the debate caused by either the claims of science or of Marxist philosophy really came into the ascendant in British universities. Discussion of his understanding of mission must be deferred to another chapter.

Paton's conversion has occupied so much of this chapter not only because of its effect on him, but because it was symptomatic of a new trend in the S.C.M. Before

1904 the overwhelming majority of students joining the B.C.C.U. came from Christian homes and their conversion was a confirmation in their own language of a pre-existent reality for them. J.H. Oldham's father, for example, was a freelance evangelist after his retirement from the Indian Army. Neville Talbot's father was a bishop.[32] William Temple had a set of vestments made for him as a child and played at being bishop in his father's palace. R.L. Pelly was once confronted by a crusty old bishop who conveyed his disapproval of the S.C.M. by saying: 'Mr. Pelly should honour his father and mother'. They were well-known Evangelicals. Because they had intellectual resources not available to Paton and those like him, they took a great deal more for granted. Consequently, after 1910, there was not only fresh debate about the Aim and Basis of the S.C.M. but it became necessary to change the emphasis of conferences to include lectures on Apologetics, Christian Doctrine and Bible Study; to appoint first a Bible Study secretary and then an Apologetics secretary; even to start apologetics study circles in some universities though some considered this dangerous because it would encourage unprofitable philosophical speculations on the part of students, and would deflect them from mission studies. The effect of this influx of first generation Christians was to produce in the S.C.M. an atmosphere as different from the former situation as was produced in British universities when there ceased to be a majority of students from university or professional backgrounds. Bishop Hunter considers that Paton's greatest contribution to the S.C.M. was to broaden it out, and this is an example of how he did it. The first category of students would have become 'good chaps and Christian gentlemen', even if they had not listened to the S.C.M. but the latter would not have had any Christian connection at all.

The impact on the S.C.M. can be seen in the shock given to the carefully formulated 'Interdenominational position of the S.C.M.'[33] It was futile observing the proprieties of the different denominations, avoiding any infringements of church discipline and concentrating on the common evangelical faith when students were entering the movement who had no idea what these lines of demarcation were, or which church they should join. Consequently it was argued that the S.C.M. was a type of church (Talbot) or an 'ecclesiola in ecclesia' (Kingsley Williams); while those who advocated that as in the Theological College Department, church membership should replace the 'Basis' of the S.C.M. as a solution to the problem, lost the argument. The ultimate effect was that the churches and the missionary societies received an injection of new blood which had revolutionary effects, for example, as shown in the various crises in the Church Missionary Society, particularly in 1914 and 1922. This suggests that an accurate description of the S.C.M. would be 'praeparatio ecclesiae', since the weight of the evidence is that most graduates from the S.C.M. became active members of their churches. Tatlow and senior members of the S.C.M. were disappointed that they did not see a nationwide spiritual awakening, as in the early years of the S.V.M.U., but it seems reasonable to suppose that the reason why so many church leaders involved themselves in the S.C.M. was because they could see the benefit of such a harvest of students.[34]

The continuing impact of the S.C.M. on Paton can best be described by discussing the significance of what can broadly be termed its spirituality, theology and experimental organisation. The last mentioned has particular importance because so much of what Paton and his friends created in the I.M.C., the W.C.C. and other ecumenical organisations reflected their experience in the S.C.M.

It is almost a cliché among the former secretaries of the S.C.M. that the spirituality of Paton's generation was moulded by 'the morning watch, Bible Study and Baslow', and that this set them apart from succeeding generations. Paton caught the habit of regular prayer from Lenwood, and in spite of the testimony to the contrary from some of those whom I interviewed, earnestness and sincerity in prayer would seem to have been an abiding characteristic with him. He even tried to instil it into his children when he was in charge of them.[35] The atmosphere produced by prayer is very well reflected in the pages of Tatlow's 'History of the Student Christian Movement'.[36] In circulars to S.C.M. secretaries and C.U. office holders one finds frequent exhortations to prayer, and in the period 1910-14, the decline in prayer as a universal practice among S.C.M. members is held responsible for the failure of certain projects. The term 'morning watch' was abandoned in 1914, before the war broke out, but it would have been impossible to maintain during the war. Prayer was a subject regularly treated by speakers at S.C.M. conferences and meetings. The S.C.M. was driven to produce its own collections of prayers, which proved very popular and continued to be compiled for succeeding generations.[37] It was therefore natural for Paton to conclude 'The Missionary Motive' with an exhortation to prayer: 'Let us in the spiritual solitude which is inseparable from every supreme choice take courage in the thought of the noble band of men and women of whom we have read . . . '.

The principal effect of these prayers was to reinforce the sense of dedication of S.C.M. members. Intercessory prayer for the spread of the Gospel predominated. The S.C.M. central offices produced the 'Terminal Intercession Paper', which was a list of things to pray for on each day of the term and was widely used in the 'daily prayer meetings'. Although administrative confusion occasionally meant that Christian Unions did not receive the paper until mid-term, nevertheless it was an important factor in creating solidarity and fellowship among students, and in educating them in prayer. Paradoxically, although it was the prayer life of the S.C.M. which held together such diverse mystics as Herbert Kelly, S.S.M. and his brethren at Kelham, H.F. Hodgkin, the Quaker missionary in China, and Neville Talbot, the actual content of prayers uttered by the S.C.M. seems to have been practical rather then mystical, as for example in the prayer which formed an essential part of the preparations for the S.C.M. Quadrennials. It is significant that when Oldham had virtually withdrawn from the work of the S.V.M.U. to work for the Continuation Committee of the World Missionary Conference, he wrote to Tatlow asking to be kept informed of the work of the S.V.M.U. so that he could pray for it at the specified time.[38]

Written in 1915, Dr H.E. Fosdick's book 'The Meaning of Prayer' contained the quintessence of S.C.M. theology of prayer. It is a typical study book, with questions at the end of each chapter tactfully couched in the impersonal pronoun for students to discuss. However it is not only about prayer; though it constituted a powerful apologetic for the practice as a natural function of mankind, and as an essential part of one's filial relationship to God. It is also a book of prayers arranged in such a way as to illustrate the main point of each chapter, e.g. one not only reads about the difficulties people face when praying, but one is led to spiritual exercises to resolve these problems for oneself. The book reflects a weakness of the S.C.M. generally, in that there is no mention of corporate prayer. Miss Witz and Canon Pelly both remarked that before 1922 the S.C.M. members thought in terms of the individual, without having any appreciation of the significance of the community. For example, sin was always described in personal terms: the individual's pride, impure thoughts, 'slackness' and so on, and never in terms of the hypocrisy, corruption and jingoism of society. Similarly the slogan 'We are the social problem', which emerged from the Liverpool 1912 Quadrennial, meant 'each of us is responsible for social degradation in England'. This was in its turn the natural outcome of nineteenth century Protestantism with its over-emphasis on the individual.[39]

Martyn Trafford invented the practice of Theological College Department retreats. He would select about ten students from various theological colleges, always so that he could match students from colleges with a heavy academic emphasis with the semi-monastic communities of the Church of England, and the Evangelical colleges. William Temple led one of the first retreats, setting a high level of spirituality expressed in quiet walks in the countryside and common intercession and Bible Study.[40] It is inexplicable that Paton's name does not appear in the lists of participants at the retreats, although Miss Sinclair recounts that he was present. Trafford also prepared a number of memoranda justifying this development, which contributed to the S.C.M.'s self understanding. The theological significance of the spirituality of the S.C.M. lies in the emphasis placed on an intimate personal relationship with God, the way in which a sense of God's leadership was sustained, and the unity which it inspired in the movement. Paton was so much influenced that he ensured that there was a real element of prayer in the proceedings of I.M.C. conferences and that the N.C.C. of India meetings were preceded by day retreats; while the secret of his friendships with Evangelicals and the Oxford Mission fathers was probably the kinship in the spirit of prayer which he gained from the S.C.M.

When the General Colleges Department of the B.C.C.U. turned from agressive expansion to a policy of consolidation, Bible Study was singled out as the most effective means of doing this. In 1899 it had been decided not to appoint a Bible Study secretary in order to keep the organisation simple. The choice of text-books and their use remained very haphazard in spite of the success of the study circle method as applied to Bible Study. Numbers were estimated at 5,000 students involved in study circles, a figure which remained constant until 1906. In 1906, however, it was estimated that more than a fifth of these students were not C.U. members, which complicated the issue. Paton probably joined a circle in 1905.

From about 1898 the S.C.M. had found it necessary to produce its own text-books. These were a type of commentary in which a scholarly approach was combined with a devotional attitude. Achieving this balance created much controversy. Tatlow opposed the tendency to give a 'best thought for the day, and warmth for the students' souls'. He resisted Garfield Williams' demands for even simpler books as tending to produce students of the 'keen and sentimental C.I.C.C.U. type'.[41] The original text-books were produced by S.C.M. secretaries, but later the S.C.M. commissioned 'senior friends' to write them. In 1908 a standing committee was formed to keep surveillance over the production and use of text-books, to which Paton was elected in June 1912. Text-books in fact created as many problems as they solved. There was always a tendency for the group to become too dependent on them, in the case of Bible Study substituting them for the Bible. Lawson, a travelling secretary, wrote to Zoë Fairfield, Tatlow's assistant, that the text-books only help those who already have a strong faith, and take the authority of the Bible for granted. Men with real problems are not helped.[42]

In 1909 a conference of officers heard Winifred Sedgwick and Martin Houlder announce that Bible Studies were a kind of fetish among Christian Unions. Judging by the evidence of Zoë Fairfield's 1908-10 report, this must have been the women's

C.U.'s because the men's C.U.'s displayed a distinct lack of enthusiasm. The conference decided that apologetics lay outside the scope of Bible Study circles, and unsympathetically declared that people should read up on Christian doctrine for themselves. It was not until 1911 that a separate sub-committee for apologetics was formed.[43]

A continuing refrain is the difficulty of finding competent students to lead Bible Study circles, since they need not only a firm faith of their own, but also the ability to lead rather than to dominate discussion and to help students in their difficulties. Various schemes were discussed 1908-12, but the situation was not properly resolved until Paton, R.L. Pelly, and later L.S. Hunter pooled their resources, first to organise a 'women's Bible school' at Swanwick in April 1912, and then, since that was so successful, joint Bible Study, mission study and social study conferences at Swanwick 1913-14 at which the future leaders of circles received intensive training in how to lead a circle and in the actual contents of the Bible, for about ten days. Bible Study in the summer conference programme, usually led by T.R. Glover or D.S. Cairns, both well-known scholars, served the dual purpose of enthusing the average student and introducing him to a particular book. Una Saunders revived the question of a Bible Study secretary in October 1908, but it seems that three years of comparative decay were allowed to elapse before the means were found to appoint a new secretary.[44] R.L. Pelly was approached, and accepted even though his health was so shattered after he gained a first at Cambridge, that he had to go on a long sea voyage to recover. His first reaction after an inspection of the mens' colleges was to declare that circles were conspicuous by their absence. Few would admit that Bible Study was helpful, yet 'Bible Study ought to be giving one such a realisation of God and such a vision of Christ as would electrify all other departments. This is simply not happening'. The most important thing was to recover belief in the possibility of great results through Bible Study. Pelly also wanted to encourage private study. There is a hint that the weight of the previous years' failure was preventing the healthy growth of Bible Study because a group of Swiss students at the 1912 Quadrennial drank in all that he could tell them, and applied it to their home situation with such success that Pelly took note of what they were doing as being an important lesson for the British S.C.M.

Although 'higher criticism' was blamed for much of the decline in Bible Study circles,[45] the transition from a literal acceptance of the verbal inspiration of the Bible in 1900 to a reverent attitude tempered by modern scholarship in 1920 was achieved with remarkably little heartbreak, considering the gravity of the question. There are agonised letters from individual students in the archives, and the S.C.M.'s flexible attitude was used as grounds for dissension by Evangelical churchmen hostile to the S.C.M., but on the whole the transition was effected as Tatlow describes it in 'The History of the Student Christian Movement', and was characterised by moderation throughout.

It is significant that the earliest surviving fragments of Paton's writings concern biblical expositions. His attitude was probably always that of this letter, written in the 1930s:

> 'We (Mott and Paton) went to the Abbey this morning and listened to the usual earnest and half-baked admonition, this time from the deacon, Somerville . . . all about the Church again as usual. If only these persons would sit down (or alternatively kneel down) in front of a good chunk of Scripture, try to understand what it says and then try to interpret that to the

people, we should get something to chew and think about, as I got last
Sunday from an ordinary Scots minister'.[46]

There is no evidence that Paton ever held fundamentalist views, but he so
saturated himself in Scripture that its authority became paramount, and in any
argument, as with Henry Carter or James Parkes over mission to the Jews, he hurled
the authority of the New Testament in their teeth. His love of the New Testament
would stem from his relationship to Christ and his sympathy with Paul. His high
standards of Bible Study he derived from the S.C.M. because for all the criticism of the
circles, it is clear that it was a crucial element in the life of the S.C.M., even though it
did not achieve parity with mission study until 1912. If the desired standard was not
achieved, still the ideal was there, and provided a stable point of reference for
generations of students.

D.S. Cairns included in his letter of condolence to Grace Paton a description of
his first encounter with Paton.[47] Paton was then an exuberant teenager. He remembers
him sitting in a boat on Coniston Water singing and jollying along a company of
newcomers to break the ice. That would have been Paton's explanation, but in fact he
was really doing it from sheer vitality and youthful happiness. This was the beginning
of Paton's friendship with D.S. Cairns and is, it seems, a recollection of Conishead
1905. It is typical of Paton that, although a newcomer himself, he is putting others
at ease.

The summer conference of the S.C.M. had a special significance for many
reasons. The B.C.C.U. had been born in a tent at the Keswick convention, first when
it was decided to have a special tent for students, and then to have a camp for students.
Matlock Spa in Derbyshire, Conishead in the Lake District and Baslow, a small village
near Chatsworth, are all famous 'beauty spots', and in the glorious summers of the first
decade of this century there was no danger of the camps being ruined by adverse
weather. The peregrination of the camp was due to rising costs, and in the case of
Baslow (1907-10) practical difficulties in securing enough beds in the village for
women, ferrying them morning and evening to the camp-site, and laying on water at
the camp. Miss Bretherton recalled that it was very amusing to see church dignitaries
come down to earth when faced with living in a cottage or tent without servants.
Tatlow describes how the atmosphere in the camps held these eminent visitors for days
after they had delivered whatever talk they had been invited to give.[48]

Between 600 and 800 students attended each camp. After 'The Hayes', Swanwick,
was acquired in 1911, three separate conferences were held, which brought the number
of students involved each summer to 1,200. It is difficult to appreciate the novelty of
camping, which was not then an established recreation, or to realise that students then
were not able to get vacation jobs or travel cheaply as they do today. This made the
summer conference experience more exciting; and the S.C.M. sensibly provided
sports facilities for surplus energy. 'Sports Day' became one of the notorious high-
lights of the camp. For the women from training colleges, it was virtually their only
opportunity to meet members of the opposite sex. All students found it of great value
to meet students from other universities though this encounter was less effective than it
might have been, owing to the custom of each men's C.U. having its own tent.

Those who remember Baslow speak with awe of the atmosphere in the great
meeting tent with 800 students bowed in silent prayer.[49] Apart from the fact that the
summer conference was used to ratify the major decisions of the S.C.M. executive, to
change the constitution, to elect the committee members for the next year, to discuss

the budget, or rather to hear about the need for persistent fund-raising, and to receive the annual report; the camps were also exploited as a means of winning support from hitherto hostile dons and clergy, as a milieu in which to convert half-hearted students. The officers' training conference was important for training the coming year's C.U. office holders. These gatherings made a profound impact on the policy and theology of the S.C.M. For example: after Conishead 1906 the Free Church representative on the T.C.D. committee composed a circular on the implications of the conference.[50]

He declared that the conference was in the highest degree inspiring to all. They were granted a fresh vision of themselves, of the world and of God. The value of this lies in the permanent direction it gives to life. It was a time of searching, with meetings that made self-examination inevitable and unpleasant, but with a real sense of communion. Whether that remains or not it is impossible not to feel that prayer for oneself and others will not open some gateway to God. It is necessary to have a sense of corporate unity and at once the power of the Holy Spirit is inwardly manifest. The hobgoblin of denominationalism had been overcome by agreement to recognise their differences.

This document demonstrates the most important function of the summer conferences: the transmission of the vision. The speeches from the main speakers were almost invariably on a Christological theme, the question of living a Christian life, or the missionary imperative. There was always a particular effort made to get overseas students to camp, and this enhanced the sense of the international scale of missions. The strong sense of corporate identity in the Spirit is significant. It underpinned the conviction Pelly and Micklem received, that there was nothing they could not do, if it was God's will. Students changed their lives because of this vision, so that it is not surprising that certain aspects of the camps came to be interpreted as manifestations of the Spirit. For Paton the experience would mean that his faith would be confirmed and nourished, his high spirits would be consecrated, and his powers of leadership developed, since he was camp manager at the post-war Swanwick conferences.

There was no fixed S.C.M. theology beyond that expressed in the Aim and Basis of the movement which in 1904 had as its kernel: 'I desire in joining this Union, to declare my faith in Jesus Christ as my Saviour, my Lord and my God'.[51] Even that, although accepted by four-fifths of the affiliated Unions, was more honoured in the breach than the observance, as successive reports show, including those of Paton in 1911, 1912 and 1913. Generally, the formula was kept on file in a C.U.'s minute book, and endorsed every year by incoming officers, although there were always cases of people being elected who were subsequently found not to accept it, and of strong Unions such as Edinburgh and St. Andrews defying all the blandishments of the S.C.M. headquarters to get them to accept it. In order to achieve some sort of uniformity, it was held that all C.U.'s affiliating after 1901 must maintain an exact verbal copy of the Aim and Basis adopted at the summer conference, and any union abandoning it subsequently, was held to have disaffiliated itself. The whole situation demonstrates the fluidity of theology in the S.C.M. The controversy over the Aim and Basis is being taken as an illustration of the theology of the S.C.M., although Miss Bretherton and Miss Witz believe that its roots were political, not theological — the inevitable result of having such strong characters as Talbot, Lenwood and Wilder on the committee, around whom opinion polarised.[52]

There was fear among senior S.C.M. members that any theological discussion would divert students' attention from evangelism. Therefore Tatlow and other members of central staff tried to play down the issue and got the Commission of 1910 to produce a very 'safe' report against a change in the Basis. One reason motivating Tatlow seems to have been the desire not to attract hostile criticism from other member organisations of the W.S.C.F., although in 1913 Tatlow instructed Paton to report to the W.S.C.F. that the British S.C.M. was never healthier than when it was debating the Basis. They were not suggesting that continuous debate was conducive to the movement's health, only that when there was peace over the question it should be the peace of those who are satisfied and know why they are satisfied.[53] Mott took a hard-line view that the Basis should be a test of orthodoxy and that all spirituality should result in orthodox church membership or it was dead. Paton, Lawson, Murray, Page and Kingsley Williams, whose minority report has already been quoted, objected, declaring that orthodoxy which was slavish adherence to the letter and was not spiritual was dead. Yet according to Tatlow's survey of June 1909, most C.U. secretaries wanted a formula so that they knew where they stood, and had a safeguard and a common bond. The Basis was also considered a challenge to men to think things out.

Paton's friends' objection to this final point as Paton formulated it in a letter to Tatlow has already been discussed, but they had strong theological objections, as well as disagreements on tactics. Briefly, these could be classified as those which stated that the old Basis was uncatholic because it contained no reference to God, but verged on 'Jesusolatry', and those that it contained too mature a Christology which blinded students to Christ's humanity. They intimated that students signed the Basis without properly understanding it. The ideal Basis would be accepted by all in Christ by faith, which was an objective power sanctifying man, and not an emotional outburst. The new Basis which they proposed was quite different: 'I desire in joining this Christian Union to surrender my life to God through Jesus Christ, my Lord and Saviour'. Theological principles were more important to them than questions of the expediency of the debate. They declared that concerning the W.S.C.F., the British S.C.M. had a duty to show them that evangelical fervour was not the same as timid orthodoxy — a Christian need not wear his head in a theological sack. It is no coincidence that Paton and several British students played a leading part in the revision of the W.S.C.F. Basis in 1913 and 1920. However, as in 1901, it was the women of Edinburgh University who proposed an acceptable compromise at the 1913 summer conference: 'In joining this Union I declare my faith in God through Jesus Christ whom as Saviour and Lord I desire to serve'.[54]

The idea of 'serve' was found to be more acceptable to students than 'surrender my life'. Lorna Southwell wrote to Tatlow in July 1913 that she had not originally agreed with this, but had heard Paton muttering Greek to himself in a meeting, and had discovered that he was translating servant as 'doulos' which also meant 'slave'. She then thought of the New Testament texts involving this word and thought it more appropriate because of, for example, the text 'no man can serve two masters'.[55] Miss Underhill, later Paton's co-editor of the I.R.M., wrote from India that she could remember the debate at Matlock Spa in 1901 and she gave thanks to God that students were now prepared to sign a statement which implied a much greater degree of commitment to life service.

There is no doubt, even in Tatlow's account, that Paton had a decisive effect on the theology of the S.C.M. by forcing this debate on the S.C.M. headquarters. He shared responsibility for resolving the problem of combining a statement of personal faith suitable for the newly converted, with a theological enunciation of the S.C.M.'s principles. A statement of the doctrinal position now preceded the actual declaration which the student made. This distinction was further refined in the revisions of 1922, 1928 and 1952, and was only abandoned in 1974. In view of Paton's objections to the theological nature of the pre-1911 Basis of the S.C.M., it is significant that the trend of the national movements which presented the emendations which they had made to their 'Aim and Basis' formulations to the meeting of the W.S.C.F. at Lake Mohonk in 1913 was away from credal statements and towards an expression of the way to live a Christian life; in other words, away from a formula which required an intellectual assent and towards one based on the Christian experience of the student.[56] In both the cases of the S.C.M. and the W.S.C.F., the 1913 solutions were a 'halfway house' to church membership and selfunderstanding on the part of the student. This development prepared the way for the admission to the W.S.C.F. in 1926 of the Russian S.C.M. in exile whose basis of membership was membership in the Russian Orthodox Church. The tendency was for S.C.M. theology to become more catholic and inclusive with regard to members, and more trinitarian. The only dissension was from the London Inter-Collegiate Christian Union led by Walter Seton, a former treasurer of the W.S.C.F., who had nearly gone into schism, but was appeased byWilder.

Paton summed up the position of the British S.C.M. when he opened the discussion on the Aim and Basis of the W.S.C.F. at the W.S.C.F. meeting at Lake Mohonk:

'The controlling membership must be in the hands of redeemed men and women. Therefore the British basis challenged the student in his fundamental attitude to Christ. It is not a theological test, but that of a relationship to the person of Christ. It puts a tremendous spiritual weapon into the hands of the secretaries and the community when properly used'.

It should be noted that however elastic the situation was with regard to ordinary members of the S.C.M., a much higher standard was expected of the leadership.

Some idea of the S.C.M.'s attitude to theology, as well as of the theology of the S.C.M. can be seen in the memoranda which Martyn Trafford produced on the theological colleges' department. His memorandum on 'The Theological College Department and the Truth of Chistianity'[57] is also significant for its relevance to Paton's experience. He begins with the perplexities and doubts of the present generation of students, who can no longer accept the Basis without question. The urgent need for a re-statement of faith is the task of the theological colleges.

> 'The theological colleges ought to be turning out men who, because they have come through the storm themselves, or at least are fighting their way through fearlessly, can effectively help through word and pen, those who are beaten down by it'.

The theological colleges must be convinced that the search for Christian truth is part of the work of the S.C.M., instead of which they think that it is pre-occupied by missions.

Also in 1910, but after the World Missionary Conference at Edinburgh in August, he produced a memorandum on the significance of the theological colleges for the unity of the church. This is mainly a plea for ecclesiology to be taught in Free Church colleges, instead of neglected as at present, and for an end to the type of discussion at summer camp which ends with ordinands of the respective denominations concluding that the others are 'jolly good fellows', and not taking this happy fellowship further, so that they could examine the real issues which divide them. He suggested a complete programme for the T.C.D. based on the concept of fostering unity, which all who saw the vision at Edinburgh should take seriously. These memoranda were discussed at the September 1910 executive meetings, at which Paton was present, and were accepted as major policy documents. Their implementation was more difficult, as the reports of successive T.C.D. secretaries show. Nevertheless, it must have been due to Paton and his colleagues that Trafford's vision was not lost in the ecumenical evangelical work from the theological colleges after Trafford's premature death in 1911.[58]

Therefore the significant points about the S.C.M.'s theology are the reluctance with which older members discussed theological issues even when Paton's generation were not prepared to have theological principles sacrificed to expediency; the flexibility on non-essential questions and the insistence on a basic Christological minimum. After 1910 there was a broadening out of theology, as it became more trinitarian, more catholic and more comprehensive, although it is wrong to accuse the S.C.M. of losing its missionary fervour. Gradually contact with Christians of other denominations was causing an interest in ecclesiology to grow, and a greater appreciation of the importance of the theological issues at stake in the problem of church unity. This coincided with the birth of the Faith and Order movement in 1910. Significantly, Trafford was breaking down the prejudice which left theology to flow in narrow denominational channels, regarding it as a threat to evangelical faith. Instead theology was to be a means of apologetics, of interpreting the faith, which was Paton's experience of its use.

Finally, one must consider the experimental and ecumenical nature of the S.C.M.'s organization. Its significance lies not only in its existential value, but in the way in which S.C.M. methods were copied by later ecumenical organisations. The original principles employed by the S.C.M. are clearly exposed by the controversy over the Cambridge Inter-Collegiate Christian Union because, contrary to popular belief, the issues at stake were political and not theological. Paton was precipitated into this long drawn-out crisis which culminated in the first Evangelical secession from the S.C.M.. Cambridge Evangelicals had been meeting together since Moody's campaigns, and were proud of the tradition of 'The Cambridge Seven'. The CICCU was affiliated to the B.C.C.U. in 1893 and produced a number of outstanding early leaders, but was causing Douglas Thornton anxiety in 1898, because of its lack of sympathy with his ecumenical policy for the B.C.C.U. It became progressively more Evangelical, reversing the tendency of the B.C.C.U. to a more catholic membership. High churchmen were 'papists', but nothing was done to draw in non-conformists. In fact it is surprising that Paton was a member. The O.I.C.C.U. was regarded with particular scorn in spite of its successful evangelism of Oxford students and the active support of younger dons like Temple. R.L. Pelly, president of the CICCU 1907-09, was sent to evangelize it. Meanwhile, there had grown up in Cambridge a number of dons who had been to Swanwick, and non-Evangelical Anglican S.V.s who would not join the CICCU. Power was in the hands of a self-perpetuating group who were not members of the university. From 1907-1910 great efforts were made by Pelly and his successor Bellerby to reconcile the CICCU to the S.C.M., but such moves always floundered because the committee resisted any attempt at democratic government, and countered with charges that the S.C.M. was losing its evangelical fervour. The correspondence reveals a great deal of unsavoury politics. Paton's contribution was to urge a broadening out of the membership. He was involved in the negotiations to bring together the excluded high churchmen, the non-conformists and the Swanwick campers. He pledged himself in December 1909 'to put in a lot of spadework' to get members for the new S.C.M. body which was emerging, and he was a signatory to the historic letter circulated to the S.C.M. to explain the split from the non-Evangelical viewpoint. It took two years for the dust to settle, 15 out of 100 S.V.M.U. members in Cambridge resigned, but in the end the S.C.M. in Cambridge emerged as a strong, catholic and democratic body.[59] The primary principle of the S.C.M. that it was an organisation of students run by students for the benefit of students was maintained. In 1979 such a principle does not seem revolutionary but in 1910 it was, when students were very definitely 'in statu pupillari' as Tatlow was always reminding his correspondents. Tatlow had the gift of remaining close to student opinion despite his age and in any argument on the executive committee, he would always support a student member against a secretary. His correspondence reveals the great pains he took to see that all the committees had a representative cross-section of students of different faculties and denominations. He fought hard to obtain the release of ordinands of all denominations to be S.C.M. secretaries, and it was the opposition of Methodist church administration and not a 'tendenz' in the S.C.M. which prevented Methodists being adequately represented.[60]

The S.C.M. study circles were unique. J.H. Oldham and his generation spent much time selling the method and the text-book to the churches.[61] For students they were a new method of study because the seminar method had not been evolved. A lecture system prevailed in redbrick universities, while instruction was by tutorials at Oxbridge. The summer conferences were a refinement of the Free Church camps for schoolboys,[62] which were held each August at Matlock, West Runton (Norfolk) and Bridport in Devon with students, including Paton, as camp leaders. The importance of the summer conference as a method of evangelism, of increasing spirituality and as a meeting point for students, missionaries and churchmen cannot be over-estimated. Above all, the organisation was as flexible as it had to be with the changing demands of students and the perpetual shortage of funds. A whole generation of church leaders was educated in S.C.M. methods, and later reproduced them in the adult ecumenical movement, as will be shown later in this book.[63]

Paton was bombarded with a whole range of ideas and experiences, but there always remained the solid devotional practices on which he nourished his faith. In the S.C.M. he was subjected to an ecumenical fellowship, catholic and inclusive, whose value must have been underlined for him by the CICCU controversy. His growing powers of leadership were developed. From 1910 he was introduced to the bureaucratic side of the S.C.M. when he first became a member of T.C.D. committee. Previously, of course, he had held office in the O.I.C.C.U. One can justifiably ask if the S.C.M. was not an élite, and too rarefied in atmosphere. The fact that Paton fitted in although he came from a less affluent background and had no family tradition of church ministry, shows that it was a broadly based élite.

It is difficult to estimate the importance of the W.S.C.F. for the British S.C.M. and for Paton. Robert Mackie has asserted that while Tatlow was General Secretary of the S.C.M., the W.S.C.F. was very much his private concern, which the ordinary student was not concerned about, except to hear the occasional address on the subject, and to meet students representing other national organisations at Swanwick or the

Quadrennials.[64] In fact it was not until 1908, more than a decade after the founding of the W.S.C.F., that the W.S.C.F. launched 'The Student World' as its own magazine, whereas British students had edited their own paper, albeit with several changes of name and editorship, since 1897. It is therefore safe to assume that Paton was unaware of the developments in the W.S.C.F. described by Eric Sharpe in connection with J.N. Farquhar's influence at the W.S.C.F. meeting at Oxford in 1909. However, in 1905 the W.S.C.F. was claiming 100,000 members in 40 countries. In the W.S.C.F.'s first decennial report it was claimed that the W.S.C.F. bound people of different nations together more strongly than they could be bound by treaty or alliance, that it was nurturing future national leaders, and that it was extending Christ's kingdom throughout the world: the possibilities were limitless. What could the Federation not expect as an answer to prayer?[65]

The histories of the W.S.C.F.[66] which have already been written indicate the strength of this international friendship: Lawson's comment on the W.S.C.F. meeting at Constantinople was:

> 'The conference at Constantinople rather reminded me of the gathering at the Tower of Babel. Our Christian hearts were warm but we could not understand what the other fellow was talking about'.

The conference, which was Paton's first experience of the W.S.C.F. and the world outside Britain, was significant in ecumenical as well as international terms. A good relationship was established with the Orthodox churches, since Mott had secured the blessing of the Phanar, and henceforth the W.S.C.F. was able to spread its influence into the Orthodox countries of the Balkans and Greece. For Mott had succeeded in convincing the Orthodox authorities that no proselytism was intended, but only the spread of the Kingdom of God. This meant that the W.S.C.F. ceased to be a pan-Protestant organisation with a sprinkling of Roman Catholic members and a very few Russian members. Paton's reaction to Orthodoxy can be gauged from his reaction to Roman Catholicism as typified by High Mass in the Peterskirche in Vienna.

> 'The music was sublime. I was impressed in a way by the ceremonial, but I can't get away from the feeling that it isn't specifically Christian. Perhaps it is prejudice, but there does seem precious little connection between the actual historical Last Supper, and the ceremony on Easter Day here, I'm willing enough to allow for historical development, but I think that the essential character of the brotherhood is gone. Still, I think the service did me good'.[67]

The effectiveness of the Constantinople conference was also restricted by the arrangements for accommodation. Delegates were scattered all over the city. The British Secretaries were very disappointed that because of this they were unable to meet any foreign women students.[68] The British delegates also thought that the addresses were facile and misdirected, even though they accepted that other national S.C.M. movements had not yet evolved as far as the British S.C.M. Evidently Mott's address did not impress when he laid down the aims of the meeting. He had declared that the purpose of the meeting was to make visible, real, attractive and impelling the great plan of the W.S.C.F. which embraced the whole student world. The conference was necessary for communication since no-one can know every development since the Oxford meeting. The conference would reveal 'a larger Christ' and a 'larger Kingdom of God' because some people have a small Christ and imagine that he has revealed himself fully to their nation or communion; yet Christ requires all the nations of the world in order to reveal himself fully. His other address was on 'Processes by which we may realise the answer to Our Lord's prayer that we may all be one'. The motto of the W.S.C.F. from its earliest years was the phrase 'Ut omnes unum sint',[69] and probably the most important result of the conference was the manifestation of Christian unity there. Ruth Rouse claims that the conference marked a turning point in the ecumenical history of the Federation because a resolution was adopted to the effect that in future no student, whatever his church allegiance, could be refused membership of any national movement affiliated to the W.S.C.F. if he adhered to the Basis of the Federation or the national equivalent of the Basis in his country.[70] This resolution had profound implications for the development of the ecumenical movement, but also caused great problems for the W.S.C.F. in Eastern Europe, where Slav and German, Serb and Croat student groups were reluctant to create one movement, especially in areas of strong communal feeling.

The value to Paton of the international and ecumenical character of the W.S.C.F. can be seen in this extract from an article which he wrote in the W.S.C.F. meeting at St. Beatenberg in 1920:

> 'I link with this (the international and interdenominational character of the W.S.C.F.) something to which a convenient name cannot easily be given — the inclusion of different religious and devotional outlooks, the older and the more modern, the liberal and the conservative. . . . One observed a great tolerance and desire to understand in the attitude of modern and conservative to one another. The memorable discussion on the Cross sprang from the determination of one man not to gloss over, but to probe and understand what seemed to him real differences, and it issued in a wonderful sharing of outlook and conviction on the central facts of our faith, on the part of men and women of the most diverse training and environment. This spirit is necessary in the Federation. The only path of progress lies in the fearless facing of differences and believing in a truth which transcends them'.[71]

Two examples will suffice to demonstrate the impact of the W.S.C.F. spirit upon national movements. Paton's comment to his wife in the letter that he wrote during a W.S.C.F. committee meeting, that he was sitting between a Chinese and an Indian, seems innocuous until one reads Ruth Rouse's account of the dramatic impact on race relations in the U.S.A. which the Lake Mohonk meeting had. Although the American movement had four black secretaries, there had been no national meeting at which black and white students had been represented. The arrival of the W.S.C.F. insisting on complete integration, especially at meals, and on delegates being chosen without discrimination from all races in the United States, set a precedent which the Y.M.C.A./Y.W.C.A. in America exploited by holding a number of mixed student conventions and the first black student convention in the following year.[72]

Secondly, there was the meeting between representatives of the British and German S.C.M.s in December 1919. Tatlow, Paton and Zoë Fairfield had dissuaded Mott from trying to call a committee meeting of the W.S.C.F. immediately war ended as Karl Fries advocated. Instead this small meeting took place at Kastel Hardenbrock on 31st December, 1919 which resulted in a virtual reconciliation after much difficult discussion, although still no German students came to the Glasgow Quadrennial in

1921. There were Austrian, Hungarian and German students at St. Beatenberg, which was important not only because of the need for reconciliation, but because the meeting saw the founding of European Student Relief to give a proper organizational structure to existing spontaneous efforts by national movements (within the Federation) to alleviate the poverty of the destitute students of central Europe of whom there were large numbers in Europe. When the programme came to an end in 1925 the organization was switched to a means of providing cultural exchanges and activities to increase international understanding. Therefore it would be difficult to under-estimate the effect of the W.S.C.F. on its participants in terms of their growing understanding of international problems and of the ecumenical nature of the church. The full impact of this on Paton will be seen when his ecclesiology is discussed, because of the peculiar significance which he attaches to its universal nature.[73]

The first decennial report, which was quoted above contains the following significant sentences: 'Who can measure the Federation's power as an apologetic? What can limit its influence against the forces of evil and against the influence which would oppose the progress of Christianity?' In other words, the very existence of the W.S.C.F. was seen as proof of the validity of the Christian faith. Mott was already using this argument in the book which he wrote about the W.S.C.F. in 1898: 'Strategic Points in the World's Conquest'.

At its crudest, this argument resembles the advertisment for a particular brand of nylons 'One million women can't be wrong', i.e. '250,000 students can't be wrong'. (250,000 was the number of members claimed in 1913: it consists of the sum total of the affiliated movements' members).[74] At a more profound level, it is a demonstration of the universal relevance of the Christian Gospel, a tangible sign of the truth as they understood it. For the W.S.C.F. had as its fundamental aim:

> 'creating and building up reasonable and vital faith to enable students to confront their problems, in generating and guiding the spirit of unselfish service and raising up true Christian leadership'.[75]

Even when the Watchword 'the evangelization of the world in this generation' ceased to be common currency, the aim remained. The W.S.C.F. was only responsible for evangelization among students, but its existence facilitated exchanges of staff members between member organisations, which were in some countries such as India, China and the U.S.A., the Y.M.C.A./Y.W.C.A. organisations. It also facilitated evangelistic speaking tours, and its secretaries were continually being invited to address large audiences of non-Christian students as in Russia, Latin America and so on. Other methods included sponsoring Bible Studies and conferences.[76] In this respect there was no difference between the aims and policy of the W.S.C.F. and the British S.C.M. although there were in fact considerable theological and organisational differences between affiliated movements, and Paton resisted moves to give W.S.C.F. secretaries greater powers to encourage conformity or 'harmony'.

In both the British S.C.M. and the W.S.C.F. Paton was at the centre of controversies which were variations on the conflict between spontaneity and bureaucracy: effective presentation of the Gospel and organisation. The clearest illustration of this is the controversy over the Aim and Basis in both movements, and the question of leadership of the movement being defined by it. Both organisations conveyed a vision of a wider application of the Gospel than in terms of personal salvation, and both had a crucial formative influence on generations of students and future church leaders.

Chapter II

'The Moon turned to Blood in our Generation': Paton's Work for the Student Volunteer Missionary Union

The title of this chapter is not merely Paton's best remembered joke, a parody of the Watchword of the S.V.M.U.: 'The evangelisation of the World in this generation'. It is also a shrewd piece of hyperbole to explain the intoxicating student vision of the Gospel being preached to every nation, which aroused so much missionary enthusiasm from 1893-1925, and whose force was not completely spent until 1940.[1] Probably more frequently than in the S.C.M., Paton experienced in the S.V.M.U. an unresolved conflict between the spontaneity of the spirit, inspired by the vision of world evangelisation, and the demands of organisation, including in this case the selection procedures of missionary societies. The former is well illustrated by the motivation of volunteers and the changing theology of the S.V.M.U., the latter by the recruitment and selection procedures of the societies which Paton investigated. Paton's work with the S.V.M.U. from 1911-21 is particularly significant because of his efforts to implement the policy of integrating the missionary interest with the general S.C.M. endeavour, thereby anticipating the transition from specialist society-based mission to mission as the responsibility of the whole church. Paton's appointment, activities, and his reflections on the significance of his work underline the theological significance of the S.V.M.U.

One should remember that the S.V.M.U. was always the senior department of the S.C.M., and its secretaries could influence the entire policy of the S.C.M. This was largely because of the early history of the S.V.M.U. as the parent organisation. Created as a result of the persistent prayers of Robert and Grace Wilder, children of missionaries in India, nourished by association with the Y.M.C.A.'s summer camps at Northfield; organised by the students themselves, who toured the colleges with their message for a few months before they sailed for the Far East, the S.V.M.U. was brought to Britain by Robert Wilder and British students who visisted Northfield.[2] It became in Britain the organisational expression of a spontaneous reaction which had been stirring British campuses since seven first-class athletes left their Cambridge laurels to go to China in 1885. From the correspondence of Louis Byrde, who acted as the first S.V.M.U. secretary while still at Corpus Christi, Cambridge, one can see how the idea was sown in the Scottish Universities 1892-94.[3] In the first year, 1892-3, 500 students enrolled, most of whom hastened abroad as soon as they had completed their studies. A heady missionary romanticism swept the universities, which might be compared with the idealism of the Children's Crusade. In fact, 'Romantic missionary enthusiasm' was the phrase by which this phenomenon was acknowledged in the report presented to the S.V.M.U. Quadrennial in 1900.[4] However, although there were 1,000 student volunteers in 1895, the churches were failing to respond to the S.V.M.U. challenge and the missionary societies were so unenthusiastic that the students began to wonder if they had misjudged the need. Nevertheless, it was decided to hold a conference in Liverpool in 1896 for uncommitted students and to appoint an education secretary to organise systematic mission studies for Volunteers. The immediate result was to stabilise the S.V.M.U., to recruit a second generation of students in place of the pioneers who sailed in 1894, and to create conditions to favour the growth of the B.C.C.U.

In America the S.V.M.U. remained very closely linked to the Y.M.C.A.,[5] but in Britain Douglas Thornton set various moves afoot which brought the S.V.M.U. much closer to the mainstream churches and ensured that instead of becoming a specialist missionary agency for recruiting students, the S.V.M.U. diffused its message to a wider cross-section of students and had an extended power base within the churches from which to draw support. The creation of the Theological Colleges' Department after the Birmingham conference of 1898 meant that a department was set up which counter-balanced the S.V.M.U. to a certain extent in the embryonic organisation of the B.C.C.U., but at the same time it gave the S.V.M.U. the necessary entrée to the colleges and the means of cherishing the theological students who became volunteers.[6] The magazine of the S.V.M.U. was taken over by the B.C.C.U. and its name changed from 'The Student Volunteer' to 'The Student Movement' in 1898. The financial appeals made by Tatlow in 1900 indicate that the integrated organisation now consisted of four departments, each with its own travelling secretary, with one woman secretary in addition.[7] The S.V.M.U. was the only one of those departments to be solvent, even though it had the largest budget of the four, because its specific aim attracted more financial support. Committed student support, measured by the numbers volunteering, fluctuated. The S.V.M.U.'s leadership were disappointed that the peak figures of 1893-4 and 1897-8 were not sustained. In fact it was recognised that the principal effect of the S.V.M.U. Quadrennial of 1900 was to strengthen the college Christian Unions, rather than the S.V.M.U. bands.[8]

The figures compiled by the S.V.M.U. must be accepted with reservations. There is abundant documentary evidence surviving to suggest that more than a little optimism was employed, in view of the reluctance to accept that a student volunteer was withdrawing, and of the need to use the figures for propaganda. However, if the error recurs consistently, then the figures are still reliable for indicating the general trend of membership. For example, starting from a small proportion in 1893, the number of women volunteering increased steadily, to achieve parity in 1910.[9] Although the student population increased by 10,000 with the creation and expansion of the 'new' universities 1900-1904, the number of volunteers did not rise proportionately. The number who had sailed by 1904 was 904, representing 60% of the total number of those who had volunteered. In spite of all the efforts of Tatlow, Paton and other S.V.M.U. secretaries, to prevent missionary societies rejecting volunteers, usually on alleged medical grounds (20-30%),[10] or to dissuade volunteers from dropping out, this figure remained constant over many years. In 1904 there was actually a decline of more than a third in the number of male student volunteers in colleges. It would seem that the ebb was reversed in 1906, the year Paton joined the S.V.M.U., when there was a marked increase of volunteers after the Conishead camp. It should be noted that this ebb and flow imitates that already observed in the S.C.M. itself, probably because other converts like Paton required about a year's interval between signing the S.C.M. Basis of membership and signing the S.V.M.U. Declaration. (The reverse procedure never occurred because signing the Declaration was held to imply assent to the Basis.) In 1908 there were 3,121 Volunteers, of whom slightly less than half had already sailed. This, then, was the size and shape of the S.V.M.U., and the framework of the struggle between the missionary inspiration of the volunteers and missionary organisations, against which the theological significance of the S.V.M.U. and Paton's contribution to it should be considered.

The impulse behind the volunteers can be characterised in various ways. There was an indefinable heroic quality about the S.V.M.U. endeavour which was epitomised in the signing of the Declaration, but there was also an impersonal element, as though a movement of irresistible force was sweeping the campuses like a mighty wind, whose advent people could hear and feel, but not see, and which was therefore attributed to divine causation, in spite of the contemporary secular influences also at play. It also created a backlash. Miss McNair cannot have been the only student repelled by the very success of the S.V.M.U. and by being told that she ought to join the S.C.M., who later accepted an invitation to a college overseas.[11] Four of the principal factors in the S.V.M.U. will be examined to define this spirit, namely the motivation of those signing the S.V.M.U. declaration, the theology of the S.V.M.U., the fate of the 'Watchword' and the findings of the missionary commission of 1918.

The difficulty in unravelling the competing ideas motivating S.V.M.U. members lies in the fact that there was never an S.V.M.U. 'orthodoxy', but a continuous dialogue on the issues involved. Significantly, the S.V.M.U. gave up attempts to answer the question of why earlier generations of Christians had not responded to the obligation to evangelize, and simply got on with their own work, basing their primary argument on an interpretation of the command of Christ recorded in Matthew 28 v 18 to 'go and make disciples of all nations' as an individual, personal responsibility. Robert Speer,[12] speaking on the moving of the Holy Spirit in the present missionary outreach to the 1900 Quadrennial, argued that if Christ cannot save the world, he cannot save a single soul. Therefore, if He has saved that soul, then He has put that soul under bonds to pass His salvation on to the whole world. He quoted St. Paul's dictum: 'Woe to me if I preach not the Gospel', The Spirit of God will teach man that he is called to this. There is a need to revive a passion for Christ at the root of all endeavours. This is an accurate summary of the motivation of many volunteers.

The central motive was the desire to spread the Kingdom of God by bringing the good news of Christ's resurrection to all. Paton wrote that the Church has within the hope of the Kingdom of God on earth the consummation of that hope by the students' imagination, by understanding it in their own hearts and by their experience of new life as the earnest of the new order. They know that the world is not subject to the same experiences as they were, but is in the grip of materialism, the evil effects of the economic situation and of world-wide movements which the Church has to grapple with or be overwhelmed. Is not the situation a call to come to the help of the Lord against the mighty? Students need to be so certain of the Kingdom that nothing can quench this faith.[13]

The psychological and the theological seem to be somewhat confused in this passage in Paton's first book, written in 1913, but he is expressing a fundamental cause of S.V.M.U. motivation, that because God has intervened in their own lives, and caused them to range themselves on the side of the Kingdom, then they must share this experience. Paton's argument is self-vindicating. The given-ness of the experience is also the rationale for its practical consequences. One might call it 'realised psychology' of conversion. Such was the force of the love of God that grasped the student volunteers that they felt impelled to share it with all races in the family of man. Student volunteers were expected to begin by witnessing to their fellow students. The main aim of the S.V.M.U. bands in colleges was to draw attention to their experience and challenge other students with the love of God. As far as Paton was concerned personally, D.S. Cairns recalled the following incident:

> 'I remember once when we were discussing the change in thought from the days when the great missionary motive was the salvation of the heathen from the universal damnation which many believed they were all doomed. I said to him:
> 'What would you put in its place as a motive force?'
> He looked up at me and said 'Who loved me and gave Himself for me'. Bill was in all my knowledge of him so averse to conventional pietism and so wholesomely reticent in the most sacred things that the words came with revealing force'.[14]

The question is whether members of the S.V.M.U. ever believed that 'the heathen were destined to perish in the flames of hell', although more than one speaker at a Quadrennial threatened that that would be the fate of those who refused to take the Gospel to them. From the surviving records all one can say with certainty is that C.T. Studd's generation, who sailed before the founding of the S.V.M.U., did believe that the heathen were perishing. The incipient racism in this attitude was criticised at the 1900 Quadrennial, when Alexander Connell declared that they were too quick to despise other races, who may come to give better witness to Christ than they do. Another speaker, R.T. Campbell, even detected a healthier Christian attitude, which recognised that heathendom may have something to teach us.[15] However, persisting even until the I.M.C. meeting at Tambaram in 1938, which was attended by many former Volunteers, the tendency prevailed which considered the great religions as having no future, if they were not actually rotten to the core and in a state of decline. According to Bishop Woods, this was an enormously comforting thought, because it meant that Christianity was bound to prevail ultimately. In spite of this, the resurgence of Islam was monitored as it occurred in Africa.[16] For example, the 1900 Quadrennial received a telegram from eight Volunteers in Cairo: 'Islam defies your king'. Frequently it was said that one must evangelise the tribes of Africa before Islam reached them and slammed the door on the Gospel.

How eschatological the S.V.M.U.'s expectations were will be discussed in the context of the 'Watchword'. There was a lively sense that the hour of redemption had arrived in the changed world situation, which represented a unique opportunity for missionary effort. Advances in transport systems and communications made missionary journeys easier than before, while the work of scholars and linguists meant that more was known of anthropology and language to enable the Gospel to be communicated. The leaders of the S.V.M.U. appreciated the significance of the Japanese victory over the Russians in 1904, which inspired an upsurge of nationalism in the Far East. The network of contacts established through the W.S.C.F. was used to study the conditions of students abroad. An explosion in the demand for higher education was occurring, stretching missionary staffs to the point where they had no time for personal contact with the students. The extension of western scientific subjects to the Far East had been accompanied by enthusiastic demands for rationalist and humanist philosophy. The S.V.M.U. challenged students to respond by taking the Gospel as well as teaching or medical skills to these mushrooming colleges. Another version of this argument, which Paton frequently used, was that commercialism and exploitation were the only aspects of western civilization known in many places, especially where colonial empires had been created by force, and it would be a crime not to introduce the moral force necessary to mitigate these evils. As far as I know, there was no suggestion that the S.V.M.U. might tackle these economic evils directly before William Temple addressed the 1912 Quadrennial and because he revolutionized S.V.M.U. motivation and theology it is necessary to consider his speech in detail.

Temple argued that the laymen and not the professional missionaries were taken as being representative of Christian people, and that as English society was half-pagan, many Englishmen were witnesses against Christ. Not only were slums created in England, but they were also appearing in India, the result of human sin and greed. Therefore the action of the individual conscience or the individual philanthropist will not avail against these conditions. It is a question of collective sin bred by collective social systems. Students must stir up governments at home and abroad, give up their own social privileges and root their lives in Christ. He also asserted that the salvation of England was dependent on the evangelisation of the world, and was not to be viewed separately. In short, the English were in peril of God's judgment and were exporting their sin.[17]

The implication of much theology written and spoken under the auspices of the S.V.M.U. was that conditions overseas were the equivalent of hell. Appeals were made on behalf of the millions of women enslaved in non-Christian countries by forced labour systems, child-marriage or prostitution, the outcastes in India and the starving peasants everywhere. In some respects the motivation of the students who responded resembled that of those who support Christian Aid and the various development agencies today. Undoubtedly many volunteers would today be found going out as part of Voluntary Service Overseas, Peace Corps and U.N. programmes, instead of working for missionary societies, then the only agents in the field. In this context one should note the valiant efforts of students to raise money for missions, selling books, going without meals and so on. One volunteer was considered an apostate by his friends for buying a packed lunch for a train journey, instead of saving the money and making his own sandwiches. This austerity had the added importance of training volunteers for the hardships of the mission field.

Paton was forever insisting that the real power of the S.V.M.U. lay in its use of the declaration which volunteers were called on to sign.[18] 'It is my purpose, if God permit, to devote my life to missionary service abroad' was a refinement of the earlier version 'It is my purpose, if God permit, to serve as a foreign missionary'. It was changed because, as Miss Hewat argued in her minority report of 1919, there was an inbuilt student resistance to the concept of being a foreign missionary, but not to the idea of service, which would cause a student to brood for days and finally, after much prayer, to sign. The anguish which such a decision caused can be demonstrated from this letter which Neville Talbot sent to Tatlow in 1908.[19]

> 'I feel rather in doubt as to what the condition "If God permit" in practice generally comes to — I mean, what is generally expected of the S.V.M.U.? Does the Union really expect an S.V. to get off as soon as he can, health permitting? In my case does it mean my settling now to sail after my first curacy? There is always a good deal of difference between what a statement

means on paper and what it means in practice . . . I suppose it is right to make these calculations about oneself — it would be foolish on my part not to have some expectation of being asked to go back to Oxford for a bit after my first curacy as a don in orders . . . if some sides of me are drawn to 'having a go' in Oxford, others are quite as truly relieved by my coming to a decision which would foreclose that possibility. Besides, if I am going abroad, I had better get off soon as I am already 28 . . . if the S.V. had not been brought into my life I should be content to keep the general intention to wait for a particular call . . . '.

Talbot had an additional obstacle to overcome before he could sign. He was to be the first Anglo-Catholic volunteer to sign the Declaration, he involved his father, the Bishop of Winchester, and his circle, including the S.P.G. candidates' secretary, Bishop Montgomery, (in speaking at S.C.M. conferences), and with his help Oldham and Tatlow persuaded Anglo-Catholic missionary leaders to participate in the World Missionary Conference in Edinburgh in 1910. The fact that he could break out of his narrow High Church upbringing under the stimulus of the S.V.M.U. was of great significance for the entire ecumenical movement. There were even a few Roman Catholic volunteers.

It seems that Paton's strength lay in the sanity and practicality of his counselling when he was helping students overcome these difficulties. Miss Witz appreciated this when she finally decided to sign in 1916, since he dispelled the doubts created for her by the mystical attitude of other volunteers, who regarded the moment they signed as sacred, a high point in personal devotion, as Mrs Hogg described it to me. Despite the footnote on the S.V.M.U. cards repudiating the concept of the Declaration as a pledge, many Volunteers did consider it as a pledge, marking a special calling, which may be why Micklem discovered that ordinary S.C.M. members were considered second class Christians by the rank and file of the S.V.M.U.. Paton refused to pander to this mystical approach. Instead, he used to ask: 'Is there any reason why you should not go abroad?'

These conflicting trends in the S.V.M.U. were epitomised by the controversy in 1919 over whether the original volunteers had regarded their action as a sacrifice. Arthur Davies, then principal of St John's College, Agra, maintained that the S.V.M.U. only had life in it because it was a definite call to sacrifice and that it would perish if it became a goodwill exercise. S.V.M.U. members should be committed to the simple life and renounce good salaries.[20] His statement was challenged at the missionary commission hearing on this subject by Miss Craig, who maintained that students should be told the facts of missionary life, but it should not be presented to them as a sacrifice, being no more of a sacrifice than primary school teaching. Tatlow insisted that Douglas Thornton never used the word, he simply got on with the job which cost him his life.[21]

Strong non-theological factors were also at work in the student body. Undoubtedly many volunteers would have gone abroad anyway, as civil servants in the colonial administration, enjoying limited contracts, better salaries and more frequent furloughs. There is no evidence that Paton would have done this, in spite of Miss Sinclair's assertions in her biography of Paton. One attraction must have been the knowledge that so many other volunteers would be sailing out at the same time, and working in the same areas. In 1904 343 S.V.M.U. members in China appealed to students in Britain to come out and join them. Some volunteers were influenced by the fact that their friends had volunteered, although unfortunately it is not known whether Paton's two closest friends at Oxford committed themselves to work in China before or after he did. Some credit must be given to the S.V.M.U. secretaries, whose personal qualities and efficient organisation were a factor in inspiring volunteers and in holding them together during the long years before they could sail.[22] Nevertheless it can be demonstrated that one student generation was more susceptible to the missionary appeal than another. Given that the appeal remained consistent in its content, then the sociological factors within each student generation must have influenced the degree of motivation in students. It would be interesting to correlate the numbers volunteering for the colonial service with those sailing under missionary auspices. Another constant factor was the refusal of the S.V.M.U. leadership to countenance emotional appeals for volunteers, or to allow instantaneous decisions.[23] Students were not allowed to hand in membership cards at missionary meetings, but were expected to think and pray for long hours before signing.

The most significant correlation is between the numbers volunteering and the state of world peace. During the Boer War 1898-1902, and in 1915 before conscription was introduced, there was a dramatic slump in numbers. A number of volunteers decided their primary duty was to crush the evil they believed was incarnate in the German empire, and volunteered to fight. Their deaths further depleted the number of volunteers sailing.[24] This suggests that the same devotion to duty, idealism, desire for sacrifice, zeal to defend a righteous cause and disregard of danger and discomfort were in this generation of students exploited both by the S.V.M.U. and by the political propagandists who inflamed public opinion against Germany, and by the government whose recruiting officers had to turn away volunteers in 1914. Therefore theological and sociological factors must have been very closely interwoven, but what was a valid response to the divine command in one generation would not catch fire in another.

The motivation of the volunteers has been discussed at length because it illuminates the theological significance of the movement. If the members of the S.V.M.U. were correct in their assessment of the situation and their duty to obey the command to take the Gospel to all nations, then one must concede that the S.V.M.U. was an example of 'heilsgeschichte', of God's intervention in the lives of individual and the life of the Church. However, in their interpretation of the implications of signing the S.V.M.U. declaration, unconditional obedience to the commands of Jesus to leave everything, including one's family, to follow him, was not demanded of volunteers. It was considered to be a daughter's duty to stay at home and nurse her aged parents if circumstances required her to do this. A dependent relative, illness or debts owed for one's education (as there were no grants) were interpreted as being evidence that it was not God's will for that person to go abroad. According to Micklem the phrase 'if God permit' covered a multitude of reasons. In these circumstances Paton and other S.V.M.U. secretaries advocated work to promote missions at home. After the 1912 Quadrennial Tatlow received a moving letter from a former volunteer about how the conference had helped her reconcile herself to work at home, since she now realised how much work there was to be done in England.[25] The position of candidates' secretary was for Paton, Agnes de Sélincourt and Lettice Shann a pastoral one because volunteers could present a great variety of personal problems, and it was considered to be one of the S.V.M.U.'s functions to hold people to their original purpose. Marriage, on the other hand, was classed as a distraction, and was frowned upon. Many missionary societies did not allow their candidates to marry during their first tour of duty, but Paton seems to have slipped through the net before the English Presbyterians imposed this rule. He was fortunate that Grace Macdonald was as enthusiastic as he was.

In a fascinating letter in which Paton managed to propose without actually writing the words, he informed her that he had both won the Williams scholarship, which would enable him to finish his studies at Westminster College, but also that he had accepted the position of S.V.M.U. secretary. 'You know that I have to be a missionary — we've talked about it. Could you stand the climate in South China? I have an awful dread you might be too delicate — then I would have to disappear out of your life'.[26] Not all volunteers had Paton's strength of character to make such a renunciation, but the S.V.M.U. were gaining a man so convinced of his vocation that he was prepared to give up the woman he loved. Because of his total commitment Paton was prepared to use the S.V.M.U. declaration to challenge students to volunteer. The reaction was not always what he expected.

In a discussion of the policy of the S.V.M.U. in relation to the S.C.M. in the General Report of 1913/14, Paton wrote that the claims of the S.V.M.U. ought to be pressed more. There must be a great number of S.C.M. members who have never heard of it because he is always having to explain it at great length. Eight years ago, when he became an S.V., there was no question of not joining the S.V.M.U. — it was the obvious thing to do if one wanted to become a missionary. Now becoming a missionary and joining the S.V.M.U. seem to be considered separately.

> 'Of course we ought not to conceal from ourselves the fact that there may be some fundamental weakness in the S.V.M.U. which may render it ultimately a hindrance to the cause of missions, in which case it ought to be scrapped. I feel that our immediate task is to push the S.V. idea, to get the thought of decision and of the real and potent claims of the missionary vocation before the members of the S.C.M. If this were done more strongly, surely some of our present difficulties would be at an end'.

This plan was aborted by the outbreak of war, and when the S.C.M. was revived, the relationship between the S.C.M. and the S.V.M.U. underwent a profound change, with a consequent theological development. So the mature expression of Paton's experience of how the declaration should be used comes as the final point in a complete survey of S.V.M.U. policy which Paton was commissioned to produce in April 1921.[27] Paton argues that the declaration can be used more extensively than to recruit for the S.V.M.U. Though it might hardly be fair to expect the entire membership of the Christian Union to become volunteers, its spiritual life would improve if each faced the challenge even if they then decided to do social work at home. The weakest point of the Christian Union is that it is not doing enough to call students to service. The note of vocation must never be lost. In this way Paton made the challenge of the S.V. declaration inseparable from the more general commitment to Christ of every Christian Union member.

The practical and theological importance which Paton attached to the declaration is significant when one comes to consider the use made of the 'Watchword' of the S.V.M.U. in Britain; 'The evangelisation of the world in this generation'. The fact that the Watchword should have been used for such a brief period (1898-1904) in Britain, but then should have proved such a troublesome ghost for Paton and his colleagues to exorcise is indicative not only of the distinctive S.V.M.U. theology of mission in

Britain, but also of the importance of theological discussion in the S.V.M.U. As the history of the 'Watchword' has already been fully discussed by Tatlow and by Denton Lutz in his Ph.D dissertation,[28] it is only necessary to comment on the more significant points as they relate to the main themes of this chapter.

The first point is that the Watchword was only adopted in Britain in 1896 after considerable controversy, as S.V.M.U. members were not satisfied with Mott's explanation in 1894, and rejected it.[29] A new generation of volunteers accepted it at the conference in 1896 because those who formerly objected had already sailed for the mission field. Even then the intentions of conference were unclear. In 1906 those who testified to a meeting held to debate the continued use of the Watchword, disagreed in no uncertain terms about the Watchword's meaning and value, in particular its eschatological significance. Louis Byrde, a founding member of the S.V.M.U., maintained that the early volunteers had understood its primary significance as being grounded in the second coming of Jesus, but complained that it concealed the need for more volunteers. Ruth Rouse, an 1896 volunteer, denied this, but said that there was a note of urgency in the Watchword which was a substitute for belief in the second coming for many.[30] C.W.G. Taylor probably came closest to the reason for the Watchword's short-lived appeal when he declared that although there was a very close relationship in the students' minds at Glasgow in 1894 between the Watchword and the second coming, it had declined as a force as the years went on. In support of this came a letter to Tatlow from E.H.M. Waller repeating complaints that the Watchword was pre-empting God's purpose by demanding that He fulfil it. Waller asserted that the S.V.M.U. did the thinking for the missionary societies and that they ought to move forward to find a new policy more appropriate to the changing relationships between East and West in 1906. Obviously Waller felt that the former S.V.M.U. eschatology was deficient in the face of rising nationalism in the East.[31]

The eschatological element in the interpretation of the Watchword seems to have been valued as injecting urgency into it, but it unfortunately led to speculation as to how long 'a generation' was, and when they might reasonably expect the Watchword to be fulfilled. Oldham put his evidence to the committee in the form of two letters to Tatlow in which he argued that in spite of frequent denials the Watchword is regarded as a prophesy. He recalled that in 1899 the S.V.M.U. executive had consulted former members to ask if they thought it would be fulfilled by 1929, and that many thought it would be fulfilled by 1936, and that now they were so confused that it would be better not to discuss the Watchword at the Quadrennial, but sort out an interpretation privately and present it to the Quadrennial for acceptance. He would recommend dropping the Watchword altogether if it were not for the danger that they might thereby lose the thing for which it stands, the note of urgency, and the missionary obligation.[32] A.G. Fraser was so moved by this note of urgency that although he did not become a volunteer, he reduced his personal expenses from £400 to £80 per year. He held the Watchword responsible for a great awakening of missionary interest in England and thought this ought to be maintained somehow, if not by the Watchword.[33]

As the years unfolded and no dramatic wave of conversions occurred, the Watchword was reinterpreted in an attempt to rationalise this eschatological impetus. Mott, who was continually being forced to change his interpretation, began the trend in his book 'The Evangelisation of the World in this Generation' in 1899, when he defined 'in this generation' as meaning that this present generation of students are responsible for the evangelisation of their contemporaries.[34] A further implication drawn from this was that this generation of students must undertake the evangelisation of the world, not a future generation nor people living in more favourable circumstances. Oldham was again to be found stimulating the demythologising tendency, while arguing that the urgency must be preserved. Paton's own criticism of the 'Watchword' can be inferred from the introduction to 'The Missionary Motive', where he states that with all the methods of modern missionary organisation, there is a danger that God may be forgotten; that 'in our insistence on the crisis and opportunity of the present time, we shift the ground of missions from the eternal love and mercy of God to the temporary exigencies of a single race or generation'.

It may not be entirely co-incidental that this rationalisation of the Watchword and its decline occurred across the years when the impact of New Testament criticism was first felt in the S.C.M., and that Wilder, the champion of the Watchword, was also the most conservative and most literal of the entire S.V.M.U. in his interpretation of the Bible. New Testament criticism was most damaging to the fundamentalist ideas on eschatology. There were suggestions that a similar slogan to the Watchword be found to express the need for social reform, but none was ever found, although Temple thought that 'Thy kingdom come' would satisfy both. Again it should be noted that the Watchword declined in proportion to the rise in concern about social conditions. Recollections of the Watchword seeped into the subconscious of many church leaders before the First World War. The eschatological note re-emerged most dramatically in the Archbishop of Canterbury's closing peroration in his address to the Edinburgh World Missionary Conference in 1910:

> 'The place of mission in the life of the Church must be the central place, and none other, that is what matters . . . it may well be that, if that come true, there be some standing here tonight who shall not taste of death till they see the Kingdom of God come with power'.[35]

In spite of the protestations that the Watchword was a great incentive to prayer, it became clear to later generations of volunteers that it was not endowed with any supernatural powers, and it would probably have gone the way of all slogans much sooner if it had not been for the affection in which Robert Wilder was held, so that great tolerance was shown for his fanatical devotion to it. He could never understand why the Watchword was so much more effective in America. Oldham considered it a matter of national temperament, the Americans were enthusiastically in favour, the Germans irreconcilably against, and the English and the Scots stood between the two wasting an unnecessary amount of time in the colleges arguing about it. Lenwood, Paton's mentor, never accepted the Watchword, but in minutes of 1901, 1906, 1909 and so on was to be found strongly arguing for its relegation. Undoubtedly the controversy, the detailed exegesis to which each word was submitted, and the pluralism of interpretation which had to be permitted, robbed the Watchword of much of its inspirational force among British students. Oldham's letter of November 1906 is inadvertently damning:

> 'At Conishead this year scarcely a single speaker came near the real issue. Personally, I think that the Watchword is capable of intelligible explanation but experience seems to demonstrate that nine people out of ten fail to understand it'.[36]

Oldham continued by protesting against what might be considered a literalist interpretation. He comments that Mott had run into difficulties with the phrase 'the world', by saying that it meant that there should be one missionary per 50,000 of the world's population. Not even one missionary to 1,000 would be adequate if they could not speak the vernacular sufficiently well, as three out of four missionaries cannot, nor understand the prejudice against foreigners, and so on. The answer would be to Christianise the native language and thought, but this would take more than a generation. The most detailed calculations of the forces needed to evangelize the world can be found in a series of articles written by G.T. Manley in 'The Student Volunteer' in 1897. 100,000 men would be needed to lead the native churches in this campaign of which Britain's share would be 33,000 or one in every 300 Protestant church members. The total number of British Volunteers 1892-1940 did not exceed 5,000, but before this credibility gap could be exposed such strong theological objections had been made to the idea of calculations, especially by Dr Warneck, that figures disappeared from S.V.M.U. literature.[37]

Objections to the Watchword often focussed on the hasty evangelisation it seemed to imply. For this reason the missionary societies were hesitant or critical about its value. Miss de Sélincourt raised the same point as Oldham when she wrote to Tatlow in 1909 that it was no use preaching at people. Evangelisation meant more than letting people hear the Gospel. The fundamentalist view was that evangelisation meant conversion. Warneck's criticism led to a modification: to the presentation of the Gospel to all people, but subsequently the idea of 'christianisation' was raised. Tatlow thought this would cause worse problems of exegesis, while Lenwood and others objected that the Watchword focussed attention on the means to an end, not the idea. i.e. 'christianisation' itself.[38] Periodically doubts were raised as to whether it expressed God's will anyway.

In 1919 the Watchword was still printed on the back of the S.V.M.U. Declaration forms, and the would-be Volunteers was invited to ponder on it and bring all the decisions of daily life into conformity with 'this great ideal', by prayer and by study. Nevertheless, when Paton conducted a survey into the efficacy of the Watchword on behalf of the S.V.M.U. in 1919 he discovered that it was a dead letter. Consequently the S.V.M.U. decided to abandon it, provided that the missionary ideal was sufficiently emphasised in the new 'Aim and Basis' of the S.C.M., and that there was strong representation of the S.V.M.U. in the new constitution.[39] The changed world-view of the ex-servicemen students and the new rising generation meant that Paton merely administered euthanasia to a dying concept. In 1906 S.K. Datta, the Indian travelling secretary of the S.V.M.U. 1906-8,[40] had explained to the S.V.M.U. how the Watchword was resented by Indian Christians, who saw it as an insult to their national aspirations. By 1918 the demand for an independent Indian Church was much greater so that Manley's call for European leadership would have been intolerable. Datta's protest indicates the most serious weakness about the Watchword, that it did not allow for the growth in the appreciation of the nature and purpose of the Church in the S.V.M.U. Thirdly, the secular hinterland of the Watchword had been destroyed by the war, for although slogans were very popular in the infant advertising profession and in political propaganda before 1914, slogans had been so misused during the war that the genre itself had lost all currency.

Tatlow summarised the decline of the Watchword succinctly when he answered a query from Charles Flint in 1922. He wrote that the Watchword had not been used for 14 years, having been killed by the secretaries of missionary societies and senior friends in 1902-8 because they felt it gave the impression of superficial methods of evangelism.

'When people began debating what one meant by 'evangelism' and what was the length of a generation, the Watchword was ineffective. Students have no interest in watchwords now . . . the missionary driving force of the S.V.M.U. comes from different sources. William Paton was fond of pointing out that the real power of the S.V.M.U. lay in the Declaration . . . if the use of the Watchword is a criterion, then the S.V.M.U. declined 1902-8'.[41]

In fact in Britain the Watchword was valuable because it gave S.V.M.U. speakers an arresting statement to explain to critical students, but when its symbolism ceased to be effective, or to relate to the theology of the S.V.M.U., then it had to be dropped, Robert Wilder notwithstanding. Possibly the Watchword was responsible for some of the impulsion of the 1896-1898 wave of volunteers, but since the degree to which it inspired students is not measurable, so its real significance must be in the degree to which it reflected S.V.M.U. theology.

Both the theological presuppositions of the S.V.M.U. and its ability to channel the missionary spirit in effective structures for evangelism at home and abroad were severely tested by the First World War, although Paton had isolated malignant long-term problems before 1914. According to Tatlow, the missionary retreat held at Swanwick in the first week of January 1916 was the turning point in this crisis in the S.V.M.U. Certainly it should be compared in importance with the Matlock Spa conference of 1909 at which the S.C.M. systematised its policy on social questions for the first time.[42] The organising committee confronted the problem that many religious people appear to believe devoutly, but see no need for missions. The introductory pamphlet the committee produced began with the premise that since the numbers of volunteers have remained constant every year except for the war, but the membership of the S.C.M. continued to rise: 'There has been a certain failure, in spirit and imagination, a lack of simple devotion to the Kingdom of God, or this could not have been'. It is not that the claims of social work have reduced the number of volunteers because an S.V. who is blind to industrial life in England and its miseries is not likely to be a good missionary in India or China. There are enough students in the S.C.M. to provide ample volunteers for work at home and abroad. The problem is that there are too few dedicated to the Kingdom of God.

The harm is being done by a superficial knowledge of other religions, especially when a student realises the achievements of truth and beauty in other religions.

'The all-pervading idea of progress and evolution reinforces this restraint and many who do not suspect themselves of any disloyalty to Christ have unconsciously or half-consciously drifted into the position where they do not really believe in the final and universal message of the Gospel of Christ'.

The war was a compelling reminder that it was going to be a more difficult task to win the world for Christ than they thought. There were great practical difficulties in the crippled and depleted colleges and churches. Therefore this retreat was being held to wait on God.[43]

This pamphlet is a sign that the S.V.M.U. and the S.C.M. were rethinking their theology radically. It may be that it was at this retreat that Tatlow is remembered as having a terrific argument with some of the students because he would not abandon his belief in the progress and evolution of man towards the good, since this was virtually an article of faith for him.[44] The report of the retreat reflects this problem. Uncertain of God's purpose for foreign missions, the life and thought of the movement had become more complex than in earlier days. The war and social work made it less easy to be certain of one's vocation. The theological experience of the retreat was described as re-learning Christ's uniqueness. This is the message which it is worth taking to the world, the assurance of God's unconquered love, and of new life in Him. There is nothing new in this, but it came to them with new force when they had studied the missionary situation in different parts of the world. The work of foreign missions springs from the essential nature of the Gospel itself. Those who come to know God are debtors to men to make Him known to them. This is not simply to be done on an individual basis, for the Christian nations are in the debt of the non-Christian nations. Whatever the practical problems in a world organised for war, the Kingdom of God can only be served by spiritual methods. For students now the first great need is to know Christ, to study, to pray, to strive to understand the world and to rediscover their faith in the Holy Spirit. Death, the dying to oneself, has to be faced or one's faith will never be strong. No radical new policies or programmes emerged but this quiet, strong inner re-examination of the rationale of the S.V.M.U. bore fruit in the revival of the S.V.M.U. after the war, the spirit having been nourished by subsequent retreats and by the corporate thought and prayer of the S.V.M.U. executive.[45]

It is the theological shift which is important, particularly the questions raised about the progress of man, and the concomitant suspicion of the theology which found good in other religions, but which present Christianity as the fulfilment of 'lower' religions. Such a 'liberal' attitude had legitimised tolerance as well as understanding of other religions. The S.V.M.U. was forced to return to a basic apologia for missions. Probably they were also fighting a tendency to regard mission as a specialist interest, just as one might have an interest in social problems as an 'extra' to the Gospel. Having been confident of the power of the Lord to turn the world to Him, they had been confident of their own power of evangelism, but the war had shattered their expectations. So they went back to the heart of the Gospel as they saw it, the unconquered love of God for men. This turning back to the austerity of the purposes of God in the face not only of a decline in mission, but also in the shadow of the terrible effects of the war, is identical in essence to the experience of Paton's future friend Hartenstein, then an artillery officer on the western front, and of Koechlin and Karl Barth in their parish work.[46]

The other important difference is the emphasis on the obligation of groups — the S.V.M.U. as a whole, the Christian Unions, Christian nations and so on. There is markedly less reference to the individual. This should be seen as a corporate sense of mission and prayer which had been achieved and not as an agglomeration of S.V. members, the sum total of individual achievement.

While Paton was still in India in November 1918, the first meeting of a 'missionary commission of the S.C.M.' was held, the first to be held for over seven years. This commission acted in a way similar to a Royal Commission, summoning S.C.M. staff to submit their views in writing, receiving evidence from a great many individuals, and from the new regional councils of the S.C.M., and co-opting to their number such experts as they thought could help. Paton was elected secretary of the Commission, so it is reasonable to assume that he wrote the final report, although unfortunately it is not possible to disentangle his ideas from those of the chairman, J.H. Oldham, or from those arising from group discussion.

Apart from questions of policy with regard to overseas students and students enlisting for social service or government positions, the commission concerned itself with the question of 'the message' and its urgency, since they considered it vital that students be enabled to clarify their thoughts about the message. At present many students appeared to believe that a missionary was engaged in obtaining intellectual assent to a series of propositions about God, such as the doctrine of the Trinity, instead of regarding missionaries as concerned with the facts about the nature of God's human life.[57] (This is a revealing lapse into patripassianism: the S.V.M.U.'s theology was predominently Christological.) Objections to the S.V.M.U. and missionary societies were to be examined in detail.

The S.C.M. also had on file an angry letter from its former Bible Study secretary, now serving with the Y.M.C.A. in Cologne.[48] L.S. Hunter demanded that the S.C.M. should pull itself together. The sort of things it had been doing and saying were not going to be adequate to the situation, such as 'the social slop which passes as fellowship, the moral subtlety begotten of pacifism, the pseudo-broadmindedness and so on'. Four years of war have 'put the clock back'. The immediate need is to prevent the world becoming hell. 'The tactful evangelism of the Student Movement House seems ridiculous from here'. The S.C.M. has been led astray by pacifists and pantheists and recherché enthusiasts to the point where it cannot gauge the situation correctly. Chatterjee, an Indian of whom he thinks very highly, doesn't think, he says, that the S.C.M. has been as uncompromising on moral issues as it ought to have been. Hunter thinks that no church gives thoughtful Christianity, least of all the Church of England. They, the S.C.M., must get a creed they believe in. The commission uncovered widespread and grave criticism of the churches. There was a great unwillingness to perpetuate denominational differences on the mission field, as students suspected the missionary societies were doing, as well as disseminating a narrow party theology.[49]

The heart of the matter was that 'one religion was seen as being as good as another'. Christianity was not seen as a dynamic revolution. Very great intellectual doubts seem to beset students on a scale unknown before. All the S.C.M. secretaries reported this, whether they attributed it to a hazy knowledge of other religions culled from overseas students, or to a preoccupation with the League of Nations idea. Grace McAulay wrote that it was no longer a question of what students think, but why they don't think. They have no knowledge of conditions in other countries, very little knowledge of the League of Nations, but a vague inarticulate feeling that the future lies with internationalism. There is great uncertainty of religious truth, with very few students perceiving the central problem to be the nature of God because they are focussing their attention on the person of Christ. There was a general reaction against any type of absolute in theology or ethics. In fact, had the word been invented then, the S.C.M. secretaries would probably have used the word 'permissiveness'. Indifference to the S.V.M.U.'s message sprang not only from intellectual doubts but also from frivolity flowering as a reaction to the war and the influenza epidemic of 1918-19. Affluence and ambition created as a result of the government's reconstruction programme also played a part. There was even a tendency among students in the North of England to take the attitude to the problems of people overseas that 'the government should do something'. The idea of personal commitment was not attractive.

To counter these tendencies, the following lines of apologetic were suggested. 'The Christ of our experience' should be the central idea. He is seen as the expression of God and of the character of man, the complete and ultimate revelation, summing up all truth. This, it was said, did not mean that other religions were false, nor that historic Christianity enshrined the one element of truth; Christ is not the monopoly of any race or age, but he is the whole revelation, and one can work out one's problems by the principles of truth in the Gospels.

The main burden of the report is the need for drastic reform and revitalisation of the S.V.M.U. education procedure, the importance of working among foreign students and the need for closer links with the missionary societies so that the S.V.M.U. can assist in making up the losses in the mission field due to the war and can respond to the need of 'orphaned missions', in the former German colonies. The position of women is treated with great seriousness. Boards should not allow the present unfair situation to continue. Students will demand equal pay for women. The report nevertheless closed in typical Mott vein:

> 'There is nothing that the movement cannot do, if it will lay hold of the strength of God and forget itself in the glorious cause of Christ and his Kingdom'.

It should be clear from the above examples of the theology of the S.V.M.U. that the movement was responsive to theological developments and to the needs of apologetics discovered from experience in the universities and the mission field. There was a flexibility and pluralism within a basic christological framework which made it impossible to hold the movement behind any one slogan for more than a few years. Yet this did not diminish the evangelical fervour of the movement, even though a radical revision was necessary to meet the spiritual reverberations of the first World War. The theology of the S.V.M.U. was designed to interpret the S.V.M.U. experience and message and therefore should be seen principally as an expression of the Spirit and not as a justification for its structures, unless one counts the Watchword as part of the S.V.M.U. establishment. There the very liveliness of the discussion crushed all attempts at regimentation. It would, however, be a purely personal opinion that the theology of the S.V.M.U. was as educative for Paton as the formal instruction which he received in Westminster College, Cambridge.

The theology and the structure of the S.V.M.U. cannot be separated into water-tight compartments, not simply because of the tension between spontaneity and structure, but because several important organisational changes were made as a result of changing ideas on mission. Paton was appointed missionary study secretary originally with responsibility for channelling the interest in mission aroused by the Edinburgh World Missionary Conference, but inevitably he was caught up in organisation when he became Central Volunteer secretary in 1911. It was intended that when he returned from India in 1918 he should devote his energies to improving the S.V.M.U. study programme, but in fact he became involved in the organisational reforms of the S.V.M.U. and the missionary societies. His interest in the S.V.M.U. did not diminish when he was assistant general secretary of the S.C.M. from 1914-17. He was tireless in speaking to S.V.M.U. bands, composing memoranda, compiling minutes and organising retreats. A summary of his work for the S.V.M.U. not only explains much about Paton but also reveals the strengths and weaknesses of the S.V.M.U. organisation.

The 'job description' for an S.V.M.U. secretary was supplied by J.H. Oldham and Malcolm Spencer.[50] Oldham envisaged a secretary who would hold office for at least five years instead of the usual two-three years, and would not only develop policy in relation to the colleges but would be a volunteer himself. He should feel personally responsible for recruiting. He would implant the idea of mission in the colleges and deepen their spiritual life since Lawson considered that the problem was at root a spiritual one. Oldham then quoted from a letter of Lawson's: 'In theory we may believe in the Kingdom of God, but we have no real knowledge of the King'. Oldham's own conclusion was that two men and a woman were needed for a period of years because: 'everything comes back to the question of whether we who were given the vision and the call are prepared to hold on in unwavering faith until the divine will is fully realised'.

If Tatlow's letters to the generous donor of Paton's salary, Charles Flint, were to be taken at face value,[51] then Paton was the S.V.M.U.'s first choice and they were lucky to secure him. He was wanted for an 'important job in China', but on the S.V.M.U.'s 'urgent solicitation', the English Presbyterian missionary board had agreed to release him for three years. Only the second part of that statement is true. Other correspondence reveals that two other men were approached first, and that Spencer supported another candidate, but was overruled.[52] Paton, however, only accepted after much soul-searching and some financial bargaining, since not only his future work, but his marriage was in balance. He had no private means so could not accept much less than he would get as a probationer minister if he was to have a hope of marriage.[53] His agonising is revealed in a long letter to 'Miss Macdonald'. It is also clear from the letter that he was offered a position working among students in Oxford on behalf of the Presbyterian Church.:

> 'This S.V. thing is a big affair. The post doesn't exist yet but has been formed . . . in view of the importance which people think the S.V.M.U. will have after the World Missionary Conference, so that the main thing needed would be the solid thinking out of a policy. I feel somehow, although the offer came as a shock, and I can't say that I want the job, that I've got to take it. You know the kind of feeling. I think it is right, don't you, to attach importance to these intuitions . . . I've always worked on that line in the past. I've heard from one of the S.V. exec. that they've been thinking over my name for six months, and that makes it a pretty imperative call . . . '.[54]

Tatlow professed to having scruples about holding a man back from the field, but Lenwood wrote from Benares that it was arguable that an S.C.M. secretary in London was doing more by his work to spread the Gospel, although vicariously, than a missionary overseas.[55]

When Paton began to tour the colleges he composed a memorandum of which he wrote 'the substance is founded in inexperience and the phrasing doubtless smacks of zealous haste'. Nevertheless he exposes the principal problem of channelling and sustaining the S.V.M.U. impetus. He defines the aim of the S.V.M.U. as being to get men and women to face their vocation and to assist such as have decided upon a missionary calling to prepare for their work. The main recruiting agent is supposed to be the individual volunteer, but instead it has become the travelling secretary, missionaries and the home influence.

> 'We undertake a singularly grave responsibility in asking students to sign the S.V.M.U. declaration. Many of them have years of college life ahead . . . we urge the claim with eloquence, we put them on the roll and swell the year's

total. They receive literature and join a mission study circle perhaps, and an S.V. Band if they are fortunate, but most bands are Laodicean. Their prayer is uninformed, lifeless and of little faith . . . so the early fervour and missionary vocation fades away. Possibly they go if a vacancy is offered'.

Paton continues by saying that the S.V.M.U. has to meet a huge volume of just criticism, but the greatest criticism is just a huge sniff. S.V. members are considered slack and unbusinesslike. If volunteers are not progressing in missionary knowledge they will invariably fall away. The voices of the world's needs are insistent enough, and China is far away. Thinking and living ought to be missionary. There are four things a volunteer ought to think about: theology (even in small doses), non-Christian religions, sociology and missionary shop whereof the text-book is the Edinburgh World Missionary Conference reports. The main thing is private study with perhaps S.V. band meetings twice a term.[56] In other circulars, Paton is concerned about the isolated volunteer, who must be got to Swanwick at all costs. Paton's task was not difficult in Oxford and Cambridge which each had an S.V. band of over a hundred members, but in Scotland and in some of the newer non-residential universities, it was a case of a struggle for existence. Paton always strove to support the missionary candidate as much as he could and organised retreats, camps and circulated S.V.s with lists of separate missionary posts for which they could apply with this end in view.[57]

In some universities and colleges the relationship between the S.V. bands and the C.U.s was difficult because the former were so strong and pre-occupied with mission that they were a competing sphere of influence. Paton worked for the integration of the two bodies by requesting the bands to bring the missionary need before the whole Christian Union, and for the Christian Unions to make a concerted drive to get more recruits than the colleges are producing.[58] If they work together they will find it easier than they anticipate. In 1912 he wrote that all the work of the Christian Union ought to lead to the idea of vocation so that the S.V. appeal does not come as a sudden jolt to a man. Missions ought to be to the forefront of prayer meetings.

Paton took this idea of co-operation in colleges a step further by working for the integration of the S.V.M.U. into the S.C.M. in order to capture the entire S.C.M. for mission to make each Christian Union responsible for the missionary appeal. Constitutional changes in the S.V.M.U. executive and the S.C.M. in 1912 and 1919 did bring complete integration of the national structure. One can see in this a microcosm of Paton's later work to make the Church the missionary agency of the Gospel rather than leaving power in the hands of the traditional missionary societies. Circa 1913 A.J. Haile, Nathaniel Micklem and Paton produced a joint document on the missionary policy of the S.C.M. in response to a general feeling that there was no clear policy for the S.V.M.U. Reviewing past policy, they concluded that at first the S.C.M. had been entirely devoted to mission, raising up potential volunteers. Then the S.C.M. developed its own interests: evangelism, social questions and so on, and the missionary interest declined. The S.V.M.U. had remained distinct until, in an attempt to make the General Committee of the S.C.M. responsible for mission, a foreign missions sub-committee was formed to deal with general questions of missionary policy. Consequently the General Committee contrives to delegate the entire discussion to the sub-committee, which is composed entirely of S.V.M.U. members, while taking away its executive power. This is intolerable. Either the General Committee must discuss missionary questions, or hand everything back to the

S.V.M.U. Micklem found the arrangement wasteful and futile. If the General Committee really performed its function the S.V.M.U. would shrink to 'Bill and a typist'. Paton's comment was that the situation was highly unsatisfactory but if the S.V.M.U. ceases to recruit, it ceases to exist, and he returned to his theme about the importance of the S.V.M.U. declaration. The question he raises is whether the machinery can be made to fit the need. It would be significant if it could be proved that the reasons for the decline in the number of volunteers discussed above was not changing motivation but inefficient machinery for channelling the missionary impetus. It is even more significant that they consider that the ultimate in effectiveness would be the minimum of administration — 'Bill and a typist'. Yet I do not think that it was any lack of confidence which caused this self-criticism of the S.V.M.U., but rather a practical response to the call for penitence made at the 1913 Swanwick to those who were such inadequate[59] servants of the missionary ideal. There is already tension here between the 'red tape' and the Gospel.

Paton's greatest contribution may well have been in the relationships he fostered between the S.V.M.U. and the missionary societies. These had been carefully cherished for a decade and now encompassed the ecumenical spectrum. Every Quadrennial and summer conference had seen distinguished visitors from the societies who came to give addresses and lingered on enjoying themselves afterwards.[59] The S.V.M.U. must have first become aware of its power to influence societies when, rather than lose the S.V.M.U. candidates, S.P.G. agreed to send delegates to the Edinburgh conference even though 900 members signed a petition in protest against such a dangerous step. In 1911 a significant development was the return home of an S.V., Henry T. Hodgkin, to be secretary of the Friends' Foreign Missionary Association. Lenwood followed in 1912, becoming the secretary of the London Missionary Society, and several S.V.s returned from the field to the central office of the Church Missionary Society in 1910, though the effect was negated by the mass resignations of 1914.[60] The revolution which shook the C.M.S. in 1922 was, I suspect, arranged in Annandale. In short, the S.C.M. had friends in the organisation of the main missionary societies, except the C.M.S. There is not space in this chapter to rehearse the complaints of the C.M.S. about the S.C.M., but the correspondence reveals the difficulties elderly administrators had in understanding the aspirations of students who were breathing a different theological climate, and the impatience of the students at the unfair treatment traditionally meted out to women candidates.[61]

The informal relationships became institutionalised by degrees, encouraged by Paton. The United Council for Missionary Education arose from the common interest of the S.V.M.U., the S.C.M. and the missionary societies in the production of cheap editions of books suitable for the layman and for group study. One publisher would be used, but the edition would bear the imprint of the U.C.M.E. or the different societies and be marketed through the missionary societies' own bookshops or the S.C.M. By 1914 some divergence of interest had arisen which eventually led to the establishment of the S.C.M. Press, but the missionary titles remained the responsibility of the U.C.M.E. Paton first participated in the committee when he found himself in the chair at a meeting in a luxurious hotel in Hindhead in March 1914. He became convinced that the U.C.M.E. ought to receive all the backing possible, though he comments with irony on the predominance of women at the meeting. The meeting agreed that present lists of titles omitted the subject covered by Paton's book 'The missionary motive', which he considered significant, and therefore wrote it. Paton was a member of the U.C.M.E. whenever he was working in England until his death in 1943.[62]

Another committee which had been formed in 1908 under the inspiration of J.H. Oldham, who was its secretary, was the Board of Study which exercised a general ecumenical oversight over the methods of training missionaries. Since so many of these had passed through the S.C.M., that body was well represented, and in due course Paton came to participate in this, too.

As a result of the S.V.M.U. crisis and the effect of the war on the missionary societies, a joint 'recruiting committee' was set up in November 1916 under Paton's chairmanship, to consider a memorandum written by him. It concerned the problem of recruiting and training candidates who were being called up from college, the acute shortage bound to result from the war and the need to put the case for Christian missions with renewed vigour. One of the practical courses of action adopted by the committee was the production of literature for the Y.M.C.A. huts in France, and steps were taken to liaise with chaplains to locate and encourage men who were thinking of working abroad after the war. Canon Guy Rogers was the key figure in this.

In December 1916 Paton composed a significant memorandum on the attitude of societies to candidates, in which he incorporated many common complaints, such as the tendency to submit candidates to a schoolroom regime. He questioned whether societies were not recruiting Europeans for positions which could be filled by the indigenous people. Methods of interviewing were criticised, a subject Paton examined exhaustively in 1919. In fact Paton was working very hard to get the committee to think out the long-term implications of recruitment during the wartime lull. The Baptist Missionary Society at least treated Paton's memorandum seriously; discussion on it began immediately.[63] The S.C.M./S.V.M.U. was never in any sense a missionary society, but always referred volunteers to the society of their denomination. It consistently refused involvement with individual projects, such as the Christian University of China. Tatlow performed an inestimable service to the development of Christian unity on the campuses by his insistence that missionary societies worked through the S.C.M. instead of organising their own student work. Christian Unions then requested missionaries on furlough as speakers from the societies, but there was never any question, because of Tatlow's firmness, of having competing societies doing a 'milk round' of the universities. Instead, the S.C.M. asked boldly for S.V. members as S.C.M. secretaries, as they did in the case of Paton, R.D. Rees, R.O. Hall and so on, or employed returned missionaries as members of staff, such as Agnes de Sélincourt and Lettice Shann. Some societies, such as the L.M.S., made generous grants towards the finances of the S.V.M.U. in recognition of its value to them, even at times of financial difficulty.[64] In 1916 Paton became the S.C.M. representative on the C.B.M.S., which meant that the S.V.M.U. had an important opportunity to influence the growth of ecumenical co-operation between the societies (and prepared Paton for his work with the I.M.C.). The recruitment committee became a sub-committee of the C.B.M.S. in 1919, which Paton saw as the best way of maintaining contact between the S.C.M. and the societies, instead of relying on personal friendship, as before. At times the discussion between the S.C.M. and the societies was extremely frank and critical, as when Paton organised a joint meeting in October 1919 on recruitment. The S.C.M. had sharpened its views as found in the 1917 missionary commission with the most recent reactions from the colleges. K.T. Paul was also invited to be present to put the view of the churches in India, who wanted missionaries who would sympathise with Indian aspirations, and share the life of the people.

'When there is no vision the people perish': in the S.V.M.U. before 1921 there was a remarkable sense of vision which gave impulsion to the whole movement, and which had a wider influence first on the S.C.M. and then on the new ecumenical missionary committees and the missionary societies themselves. This vision, however was not for more than a limited number of volunteers clothed in the ambiguous symbolism of the Watchword. It was anchored to earth by Paton's favourite weapon, the Declaration. It consisted rather of an experience of the love of God which evoked a response of dedication to the work of sharing this experience, not with the heathen in danger of the flames of hell, but with men and women groping towards national identity, demanding western education and paralysed by a poverty not of their own making. It was due to the power of this vision that the S.V.M.U. judged its own success by religious and not secular criteria, and renewed itself by repentance and not by resolutions in committee. For example the circular letter which Paton sent out in September 1913 contained the following typical analysis:

> 'All of us who were at Swanwick in July and who met under the S.V. tree or in the tent or the hostel, felt the disgrace and sin of past failure, especially in view of the falling off in numbers, and felt that there was no new 'dodge' to be found as a remedy for it all but we know God was there and that we must pray as never before'.

The machinery and methods of the S.V.M.U. are significant because they were necessary to sustain the motivation of volunteers and transform it into hard mission fact: the evangelisation of the students, self-preparations for mission, and the arousing of the S.C.M. to its missionary obligations. It would have been an important step if the organisation could have been reduced to 'Bill and a typist', but it was healthy that the S.V.M.U. was working for its own abolition. The missionary interest of the S.C.M. was never sufficiently stable to allow this, but the whole weight of the evidence in this chapter should point to the way in which the S.V.M.U. was the soul of the S.C.M. The changing nature of the S.C.M., the effects of the war and the new theological insights arising from the dialogue on social questions meant that the S.V.M.U. became less of a specialist agency, an élite within an élite, and more an educational force within the S.C.M., a process encouraged by the growing interest among students on international questions.

Paton's role is difficult to summarise. He was a volunteer himself and shared each volunteer's anguish, as well as being a mine of practical information about missions. He nursed the S.V.M.U. through some of the most difficult years of its existence, and saw it flourish again after the First World War. His appointment coincided with that of a Bible Study secretary and a social study secretary, these three, being known, according to Canon Pelly, as 'the three wise men'. The 'wisdom' he brought to the position was balanced by what he learnt of evangelism while working for the S.C.M. and was fully tested in the tension between the growing spirit of the S.V.M.U. and its organisational problems.

Chapter III

From Pacifism to Political Realism: Paton's Convictions in Two World Wars

During the persecution of Christians in Carthage in 249 the bishop, St Cyprian, counselled his clergy to keep their heads down and not to court persecution.[1] Paton acted in a similar way when he faced imprisonment and physical ill-treatment for his pacifist principles during the First World War. In fact his position is highly significant because he was never an idealist, nor held absolute pacifist views, nor in any way equated pacifism and the Christian faith. Instead one can observe a consistent maturation of his thought until, in the Second World War, he became on the one hand the champion of the right of pacifists to broadcast on subjects other than pacifism, and on the other hand, the outspoken enemy of fascism, involved in civilian defence duties and proud of his sons and daughter in the armed forces. Paton was never afraid to espouse unpopular causes or hold dissenting political views,[2] but he was fortunate that the S.C.M. was one of the few forums for discussion between pacifists and serving soldiers. Even so, evidence will be brought to show that Paton paid a price for his principles: the only explanation for his fall from grace as heir apparent to Tatlow in the S.C.M. secretariat would seem to be Tatlow's prejudice against pacifists, and he found the exile in India without his wife hard to bear especially as there was no foretelling when the Manpower Act would be repealed, and the danger of conscription removed.

Much of the evidence of this chapter is circumstantial or fragmentary, resting on a handful of letters in comparison with the thousands from which the two preceding chapters have been built up. Without Grace Macdonald Paton's letters to her father or one crucial letter from Tatlow to the English Presbyterian Church authorities, this chapter would have resembled a crime detection novel rather than serious history. As it is, the background to Paton's action is more than usually important, and the reader must decide whether a consistent interpretation of events provides a better hypothesis than that of a random coincidence of dates.

Tatlow prefaces his chapters on the S.C.M. in the First World War by remarks to the effect that the S.C.M. was oblivious to the dangers of war until war was declared, and that very few of its members had thought of the implications of war and peace, but simply accepted the government's explanations at face value and responded to the call to arms with the same overwhelming enthusiasm as the rest of the population, with the exception that whereas 60% of male students volunteered, 70% of the S.C.M.'s membership did.[3] In fact, according to R.L. Pelly and N. Micklem, their contemporaries were oblivious of all political issues, invariably voted Conservative and accepted Tatlow's oft-stated position that political subjects had no place on S.C.M. platforms because students were minors and not entitled to vote. This position was slowly eroding under the impact of the women's suffrage question and the S.C.M.'s new interest in social problems and the possibility of government action to alleviate poverty.[4] Private meetings were arranged between S.C.M. secretaries and Labour leaders, though of course Paton had already met his wife's former employer, Ramsay MacDonald.[5] Nevertheless S.C.M. members were political babes in August 1914 and so were swept along by the mass fervour.[6]

Paton's position was therefore exceptional, not only because his wife influenced his socialist political allegiance but because his religious convictions were in harmony with his politics. Unlike the Social Democrats in Germany, the Independent Labour Party under Ramsay MacDonald opposed the war from the outset, if not always consistently, refusing to condone the clash of capitalist empires, and emphasizing the international brotherhood of man. This was the position of William and Grace Paton, who loathed Lloyd George and all that he stood for almost as much as they did Winston Churchill.[7] In the years of Paton's nascent political awareness, his mentor was Principal Skinner of Westminster College, now a keen supporter of the S.C.M. and a frequent speaker at summer conferences.[8] There is good reason to believe that a letter dated 20.9.14 and written in reply to a letter from Paton, reflects not only his views but also Paton's and demonstrates the derivation of Paton's convictions.

Skinner wrote that it was absolutely clear to him that Christianity was opposed to war as such, and all this talk about fighting to advance the Kingdom of God or peace was sheer self-delusion. War never opened a door for the Gospel . . . it was wrong for any Christian minister or candidate to become a combatant in this war or any other. There was a dilemma of applying two standards, but the only answer was a lame one, that those who see the Christian ideal in its purity will refuse to fight while not condemning those who can and do with good conscience. Two points stood out:

> 'First, what you yourself mention: that the Church, by her supine acquiescence in the policy of which war is seen to be the natural outcome, has got fatally compromised and must hack her way out with the rest of the nation.[9] That, however, is no excuse for telling lies by picking out those elements of the war which bear a moral significance and saying it is a just war. The other thing is that lesser goods like civil liberties which can be maintained by fighting — it is possibly God's will that we should preserve these by force. Possibly God is trying to teach us that we have reached that stage of civilization where nothing can be achieved by armed force . . . what the situation ideally demands is a reconstruction of Christian society on the basis of universalism'.

After rejecting other religious institutions as being incapable of inspiring such action, Skinner concluded: 'Quietism is too much a parasitic force. Could the S.C.M. do anything?'[10]

Skinner's dilemma should be compared with that of W.H. Dyson, the T.C.D. secretary, who had the misfortune to be canonised by Tatlow, but who represented much of the anguish of the S.C.M. in a very different way. Dyson had served for six years in the Officer Training Corps, then resigned in 1913 because he 'didn't know if it was the right thing'. Now the fact that he possessed certificates of proficiency in arms weighed heavily on him. War in the abstract seemed immoral to him.

> 'But in the present situation it is not so clear. We seem to be fighting in a life and death struggle with barbarous militarism which would be nothing short of appalling if it were to overcome Europe. We stand to gain nothing

for ourselves but safety through war. If it is ever right to go to war it is right now. Either one uses force or one leaves one's own weaker ones undefended'.[11]

He added that it may seem ridiculous to Tatlow for him to give up the T.C.D. secretaryship for Salisbury Plain, but he would be grateful for his advice. Tatlow managed to quieten what Dyson called 'that delicate mechanism which we call conscience', helped by the fact that Dyson was turned away from the recruiting office in October 1914 on the grounds that sufficient officers had already been enlisted. Dyson began work as T.C.D. secretary in an atmosphere in which he found it 'appallingly difficult' to get people excited about anything like systematic study, mission study and the church instead of war.

> 'It is above all things necessary that everyone should be trying to lead the best life at this time. A deep spiritual life is the only real anchor of faith in such time, and the only preventative of 'jingoism' and 'bellicosity' '.

Dyson obtained his commission a year later when the theological colleges were closing down as they emptied of men, and he died of wounds behind the German lines in July 1916.[12] Significantly, one of his closest friends was one of the Forrester-Paton brothers, a leading pacifist.[13]

Skinner's appeal for the S.C.M. to do something about the confusion, rather than leaving it to the individual conscience in a quietistic way, found a response because three months later the S.C.M. held a retreat for 120 people at Baslow on the lines of the Matlock Spa conference of 1909 and the missionary retreat of 1916 discussed in preceding chapters. The theme was Christianity and war, and produced very serious discussion between pacifists and non-pacifists, led by Temple, whose radical approach set the level of theology attained. Paton spoke on the meaning of the Cross in the present situation, but unfortunately there is no record of what he said. The theology of the Cross was the keynote as all present acknowledged their guilt for the war situation. It was almost as though they anticipated the Stuttgart Declaration of 1945,[14] though I do not think anyone then could imagine the horrors of modern warfare or the anguish of the human soul, revealed by the poetry written in the trenches. This is remarkable considering that the majority of those present probably shared Dyson's view that German aggression expressed in the unprovoked attack on Belgium was the cause of the war. Instead they saw the Cross as revealing God's nature and method of overcoming sin with love at an indescribable cost. They thought it was possible for them to share God's nature and in the same way overcome the hatred and sin of war by absorbing the sin and suffering of the war and transforming it by love. There were differences of opinion concerning the use of force but all were agreed that 'war could never be lightly entered into by a nation, that taken as a whole it was "the devil's work" '. The spiritual unity among students created by the W.S.C.F. was seen as the pattern of the work of the Church among the nations.[15]

The experience of this retreat, and the consensus achieved, should be associated with the capacity of the local Christian Unions to keep going even when the majority of their members disappeared to war or to prison, and their places at university were taken by 18 year olds, women and overseas students. One Christian Union underwent five changes of treasurer in one term as one man after another enlisted but still the fifth treasurer to resign could report that its affairs were flourishing, and that as an S.V. he felt more committed than ever, thanks to Mr Paton's guidance. Nearly all the wartime

S.C.M. secretaries were at the retreat, so it is reasonable to assume that it formed part of the inspiration behind their heroic labours. A similar crystallisation of faith and courage in the S.C.M. is found in the letters sent to the London headquarters on scraps of Y.M.C.A. paper from serving soldiers 'somewhere in France' or in Mesopotamia, usually with requests for books, 'The Student Movement' and often with donations and exhortations to keep the S.C.M. going as everything it stood for suddenly seemed vitally important. On its side, the S.C.M. executive sent a regular newsletter to all its members in the forces and the universities similar to that sent out in the Second World War which McCaughey quoted in 'Christian Obedience in the University'. Tatlow seems to have realised very quickly that Lord Kitchener was the only leader of any military competence, and propagated his sombre prediction that the war would be long and difficult, probably lasting four years. Consequently, the S.C.M. publications display none of the optimism of the secular press in England and Germany, the which political judgement coincided with the theology of the Cross worked out at the Baslow retreat. The retreat did not solve the participants' difficulties, but it is significant how many of their names appear in association with Temple's in the radical Christian newspaper which he edited, or among the group of writers behind the 'Papers for Wartime', whose importance is acknowledged in the standard ecumenical histories,[16] as members of the Fellowship of Reconciliation and as workers in the Y.M.C.A. in France and Mesopotamia. Therefore it would seem that Skinner's plea for action was partially realised by members of the S.C.M.

C.F. Angus wrote to Tatlow while sailing out to India in January 1916 that the ship's company made him realise how small a part of the country felt any sympathy with the S.C.M.'s sense of the sin of war. On the other hand, Danish missionaries who were taken on at Gibraltar told him that a group of twenty German conscientious objectors had been shot. It would seem that C.F. Angus' diagnosis was correct, especially when British attitudes hardened in 1916. Robert Graves the poet and other serving soldiers have written of the growing gulf between them, with their understanding of trench warfare and its unspeakable suffering, and the civilian population who did not wish to listen to descriptions of conditions at the front, nor showed sympathy for the wounded, but continued in their blind prejudices and their frenetic search for distraction in the austerity of war restrictions on consumption.[17] This gulf seems never to have existed in the S.C.M.

Among S.C.M. members, though not among the general populace, the prevailing attitude was that there was little point in fighting a war, as they believed in defence of a just and democratic society, if there was no place for conscientious objectors. One dissenting voice was 'W.W.' of Aberystwyth University.

> 'There is a certain amount of a dangerous form of pacifism here (which to some extent, I'm sorry to say, percolated the C.U. committee), the sort of 'conscience won't let me' sort of business, which won't let a fellow defend the country but which doesn't hinder him staying in college and getting a degree . . . while the other man spends a couple of years in khaki. I can understand the man whose conscience won't let him fight, but drives him to the R.A.M.C. and Red Cross or the same sort, but this other just nauseates me'.[18]

This letter is an isolated example of the animus against pacifists instigated by older men and former suffragettes.[19] The virulence of women in their letters to the press, and the onslaughts on men they saw out of uniform in the streets are perhaps an hysterical reaction to the fears of the first total war, but those least touched by suffering and furthest from the theatre of war seem to have been the most bellicose. Secular historians quote sufficient examples of clergymen who claimed that God was on the Allies' side and that Jesus was an Englishman for there to be no necessity to call evidence to support Paton's contention that the Church was fatally compromised.[20] In contrast, the S.C.M. was much more united and tolerant of differences of conviction in a truly ecumenical way, although some very significant tensions did exist, and the S.C.M. was under very great pressure from outside organizations and individuals.

I have not found any letters to support Tatlow's claim that certain principals of theological colleges tried to pressurise him into having recruiting officers present at Swanwick. He maintained the strictest neutrality, allowing neither recruiting speeches nor anti-war demonstrations, but he was hypersensitive to accusations that the S.C.M. was a pacifist body.[21] In a typical letter to a Mr Shakespeare, he rejected this as unfair. Like all church bodies, it has a few pacifist members, chiefly Baptists and Congregationalists, large numbers of C.U. branches have no pacifist members at all, so it is obvious that it is the Free Church colleges which are producing them all. The S.C.M. has decided that its platform must not be used by its pacifist members for any propaganda, and on the one occasion when an attempt was made to break this rule, the S.C.M. officer present ruled the speaker out of order. Tatlow contrasted the small percentage of pacifists in the S.C.M. with the 10,000 S.C.M. members in the trenches, and his final shot was that if there seemed to be a large number of pacifists in Mr Shakespeare's church, he should remember that it was one of the smallest in Great Britain.[22]

This letter is very odd for many reasons, and it is unfortunate that with so many letters lost from the archives, one cannot reconstruct the true situation more completely. Nevertheless it should be noted that of the S.C.M. secretaries, as opposed to members, those who were pacifists came from all the mainstream churches. Paton and Donald Grant were Presbyterians, R.D. Rees (conscripted in 1917) was a Methodist, and Holtby of the Manchester Inter-Collegiate secretariat was an Anglican. Neither does Tatlow acknowledge the large part Friends had played in the S.C.M. since its founding, which meant that many Friends were still associated with it, such as H.T.Hodgkin and Lucy Gardner, who were prominent in the founding of the Fellowship of Reconciliation, and A.P. Gage the Welsh Intercollegiate secretary, who, like Holtby, was imprisoned. The C.U.s most affected by pacifism were in Scotland, where presumably the majority of students adhered to the Church of Scotland. In Edinburgh 70% of the C.U. committee were pacifist at one stage. Tatlow was very emotionally involved in this question: he told one correspondent that if the S.C.M. had adopted a pacifist position, he would have resigned. It is indeed questionable whether in either the contemporary letters or the 'History' published in 1932,[23] Tatlow represents the admixture of views in the S.C.M. accurately.

To conclude this discussion of the S.C.M.'s varying reactions to war, it is worthwhile to note in detail the report entitled 'The S.C.M.: its Responsibilities and Problems During a Third Year of War'. According to this report, in 1917 there were 25-30,000 students in Great Britain and the S.C.M. now has 200 branches serving them. There was a tremendous number of women and even some 16 year-old men in the Christian Unions. They are encouraged to study and to surrender themselves to Christ as Saviour and Lord, to consider the nation's need and prepare themselves for citizenship. Letters are quoted from servicemen begging the students not to 'let the S.C.M. slip', but to keep it going on a world-wide basis and to approach more nearly the evangelisation of the world. A military chaplain is quoted as saying that if the S.C.M. had existed a hundred years ago, they might not be 'out here' now. It is up to civilians to keep the torch of civilization burning.

An appeal for £6,500 per year follows, it being necessary even to keep the reduced staff of 16 (cut from 25) in the field. Otherwise the work in the colleges may collapse. (By 1917 so many S.C.M. members had been killed that the generous contributions from officers' salaries had dwindled away.)[24] Yet in contrast the German Student Christian Movement is reported as doing much better, with a larger income than in peacetime. Although one does not wish the D.S.C.V. (as the German Student Christian Movement was then known) to be worse off, the British S.C.M. should do better.:

> 'We learn that the D.S.C.V. is holding on to Christian ideals. They know very little about the cause of the war. They are amazed when told of the atrocities in Belgium. What will their reaction be when they discover the truth? Meanwhile we are glad that there are Christian Germans. The D.S.C.V. is a spot of light in a dark country.'[25]

It is remarkable that amid soaring inflation, shortages and rationing of every kind, restrictions on travel, compressed university courses and the emotional strain of the war, the S.C.M. continued to function as normally as possible. There was no obsessive preoccupation with the questions of war and peace. Study circles continued, with the S.C.M. publishing new titles for the circles including in 1915 'The Child and the Nation' by Grace Paton, about the million normal children living in conditions of deprivation, and the local government's obligation to help them. The S.C.M. executive, meeting in London in October 1914 in order to save money, instead of at Swanwick, resolved that 'it was our simple duty to go on working away at our ordinary work. The Student Movement must of its very nature always look to the future; we have our duty to the days to come.'[26] This was to be done in penitence, steadfastness and humility, and in fact was done. The S.C.M. perhaps did not fully realise the significance of what it was doing at the time, both for its existing members and the post-war generation of ex-servicemen, but the fund for post-war operations, the missionary commission, the recruiting sub-committee, and much of the planning of the Reference Committee all date from the time when the war was threatening to be a shattering defeat for the Allies, and unrestricted submarine warfare had caused stocks of many vital food commodities in Britain to be reduced to less than two weeks' supply.[27]

Articles in the 'Student Movement' urged students to discover on their knees whether their vocation was as a soldier or a missionary or at home, but Paton's thoughts were not cast in such black and white hues. He explained to his son, Michael, how he felt in the First World War when he accepted the argument that only relatively few individuals could attain the moral condition of non-resistance in the face of aggression.

> 'Here you come to the real crux. When I was a pacifist that was where I stood; I didn't deny that the British cause in 1914 was a just cause, and I

still think it was. I tried to believe that in some way (which I was never able to discover, and got more and more unhappy in the process) one could bear a witness of love and all the rest of it alongside the action of one's fellows in the State who were acting up to their own conceptions of duty. My fundamental reason for deserting pacifism was that I found it unreal, far too much a matter of words. I found among men who were fighting and getting killed at least as real a 'love' for their enemy as I found myself or among pacifists. I found it to be intolerable to be in the position of saying to others; 'Yes, you must act up to your lights, it is a just war and if you see things that way it is right for you to fight.', while I was profiting by their sacrifices . . . '

'As against sharing in the suffering of others, as against taking a part in the establishment of justice without which there can be no stable state in the world, he has to be so sure of God's call to him at all costs to witness to the absolute ideal of individual Christian conduct that he will weaken the forces of his country and even help the total cause of injustice. Still, I cannot deny that there are some called to that stand, because I know them. They are a reminder that the law of suffering love is ultimate, and that one must let one's actions be judged by no less a standard if one is a Christian. But it ought to be remembered that a pacifist so long as he lives in the world is as truly involved in the sin of it as the fighter.'[28]

None of this uncertainty shows in an article which Paton wrote for the 'Student Movement' in 1914 on the effect of the war on mission. Paton begins with the problem of mission finance in war, particularly for the Continental missions, whose organisation is as world-wide as the war itself. However, the issues go deeper than practical re-organisation. The springs of war are found among the Christian peoples and the strength of religious feeling has been thrown powerfully onto the side of the different armies so that many are asking if Christianity is proving inherently unable to sustain national life. Can Christianity be considered a religion for all mankind any more? Not only are those hostile to the Christian faith voicing this doubt, but many Christians are having to struggle for faith in the face of the war. If it is argued that there is no such thing as a Christian nation, that there are nations whose population is partly Christian, but it is unfair to regard all the actions of such nations as the direct product of Christianity, these doubts are not assuaged. It is no answer to say in effect that Christianity is an individual thing because the East demands a religion not only for the individual but as the basis of a new civilization.

'Must we not in truth confess that our civilization, our society, our corporate life, are not Christian? We must do more; we must acknowledge in this great world tragedy a call, not only to a purer, more earnest individual following of Christ, but a consistent, persevering effort to work out Christian faith into the body politic; to achieve the hope of the redemption of society, to make not only individual hearts, but all the bonds and ties which unite human beings one to another, instinct with the spirit of Christ. If we say that we have a Christian society we stand condemned. If we say that there can be no Christian society but only Christian men and women, we confess ourselves futile, but if we try to learn our lesson and resolve to work our faith out into all the relationships of life, then indeed will the Lord have turned the curse into a blessing for us.

'In this comprehensive effort after a Christian society, the East must help. It is unthinkable that the peoples of the West should by themselves work out a completely Christian society, and then export it to the East . . . it is only as all those in every land, who own the Christian loyalty and fellowship, work out their faith continually into the whole of life, claiming ever larger and larger areas of life for their Lord, that the perfected Christian society becomes possible'.

Paton debunks the attempts that had been made to justify Christianity by pointing to the well-being of Western society. These are now discredited as the rottenness of our own society is revealed to us. The Christian missionary enterprise is forced back to the 'final verities of our faith'. It is not Christianity but Christ whom they must preach in the faith that where men are drawn to him, there are the seeds of Christian society. Problems which require an urgent answer include that of race. The war proves that the world has become too small for one race to remain uninfluenced by the events in another land. Then, the 'magnificent offer of service' from thousands of men who volunteered for war compares poorly with the sort of sacrifice which most Christians think is good enough for their master. The tremendous crisis ought to cause a radical reassessment of one's Christian commitment. The war could prove as much a stimulus to the growth of the Christian Church as the early persecutions.[29]

In this article Paton has correctly gauged the impact of the war on Christian missionary apologetic, since the outbreak of war held by many non-Christians in the East and in Africa to expose the weakness of Christianity. His idea of comparing the response to the call to arms and the call to missionary service was taken up and further developed by R.D. Rees, the S.V.M.U.'s executive's chairman. Very close parallels were drawn, which substantiates the assertion made in the previous chapter that this generation was peculiarly susceptible to such appeals, and that the S.V.M.U. and the government were alike exploiting them. The passage quoted is particularly interesting for revealing Paton's view of the propagation of Christian society. Paton's article should be compared with the series of lectures which Temple delivered to American theological students in 1915 under the title 'Church and Nation'.[30] Temple's answer to Paton's questions is to point out the limited, fallible nature of nations — even though divinely sanctioned, they are a natural growth — and to urge service to the Church, which although fallible as well, does participate in the divine reality. He reluctantly confesses that the idea of international fellowship within the church was an ideal and not a reality. Like Paton he compares the difference between the enthusiasm for war and the lack of commitment of Christians to their Lord. Paton and Temple were moving in the same milieu and their great friendship may date from this time or earlier, but who influenced whom at this point is impossible to determine.[31] Temple prefaced his lectures with a statement of support for the Government's war aims, which, while he does not exonerate Britain for part of the overall responsibility for the situation, would nevertheless be unacceptable to Paton. The ideas Paton touches on are more completely worked out in J.H. Oldham's book, 'The World and the Gospel', written for the U.C.M.E. in 1916. It is an attempt to restate the Christian message now that war has revealed the rottenness of society and to construct an apologia for the church in the mission field.

Conscription was introduced in England in January 1916 because of pressure from the French and for political reasons, and not because there was a shortage of volunteers. From a military point of view, it made possible the prodigal waste of lives in 1916 but otherwise there was no discernible change in the pattern of the war in

Europe. Social pressure and prejudice received the sanction of the law; as far as pacifists were concerned, the difference was between the discrimination to which any minority group is subjected, for example the early Christians, and the legalised persecution such as when every Christian was required to sacrifice. When the first Military Service Act was passed, 55 Members of Parliament voted vainly for an amendment to preserve freedom of conscience, on the grounds that the Act represented the final erosion of human rights, which began with the emergency powers assumed by the Government under the Defence of the Realm Act (1914).[32] The appeal tribunals set up under the Act were composed mainly of tradespeople of little education and no sympathy with the 'shirkers' brought before them.[33] Quakers and others were confronted by tribunals dominated by the representative of the War Office, who was always present to 'advise', and ignorant of their own powers to grant exemptions.[34] Some cases were even dismissed unheard. A conscientious objector whose case was dismissed was held to be a member of the army and was treated as a deserter if he did not henceforth obey orders. Even without this legal fiction there were cases of men being illegally kidnapped by the military police and sent to France from where Philip Snowden, M.P. intervened in the cases brought to his notice to save the men from being shot. The term 'conscientious' was not defined by law, but was held to apply only to absolute religious convictions, not ethical or political beliefs, but even Friends of long standing and high local reputation were being imprisoned.

It seems that the popular opinion prevailed that conscientious objection was used as a cloak for 'shirking'. This prejudice countenanced the appalling physical mistreatment of pacifists. Only the 'Manchester Guardian' gave any publicity to their sufferings, and to the basic principles involved. It seems that the aim was to inflict upon pacifists treatment worse than they would receive in the war, in the same way that workhouses were made so austere that the poor would only seek refuge there as a last resort before death. In vain Philip Snowden and others argued that in treating conscientious objectors in this way the British Government was behaving no better than the German government, whose 'militarism' and 'Prussianism' were supposed to be the cause of the war.[35] This was also Grace Paton's view, while in the Second World War Paton often declared that one could not claim to defend democracy and freedom if pacifists, however small a minority they might be, were denied fundamental human rights. In the First World War, 16,100 known pacifists opposed government measures in varying forms. 175 evaded the Act. Nearly 4,000 accepted non-combatant service in the Friends Ambulance Brigade or the Royal Army Medical Corps.[36] 6,261 were arrested of whom 94% held out although 267 were discharged on medical grounds. Others refused the army medical as they did not recognise the army's authority over them, or else because they thought it would be an easy way out, since they were patently medically unfit. 900 were given work under the tribunals directly, while the Pelham Committee and the War Victims Relief Company found alternative work for others, though under such harassment from the tribunals that regardless of their skills the work found for pacifists was menial or agricultural and did not provide a living wage for a man and his dependants. A Central Relief Fund organised by Ramsay MacDonald ensured that the families of those imprisoned did not starve, but many were brought to penury. The systematized brutality is evidenced by the 71 deaths caused by the conditions of imprisonment which would have done a fascist regime credit.[37]

It is in this context that one must study Paton's pacifist stand, and what it cost him. His father-in-law, David Macdonald, sent Grace Paton the manuscript of a book which apparently contained some criticism of pacifists. She replied that he was not fair to pacifists:—

1. They don't want to be let off saving their country — but it is made as hard as possible for them, given that they won't join the Army. The R.A.M.C. is barred to them, and the Friends' Ambulance Brigade and the Red Cross have enormously long lists. This is a fact. Many of the people serving in them are not Quakers. I myself know several.
2. Bill is quite prepared to go to prison for conscience's sake.
3. It isn't fair to judge pacifists if you do not know any. The press is out to discredit them.
4. While the Government is at liberty to imprison or shoot them, it is thoroughly un-British and beastly behaviour to bully them and torture them to make them give up their principles. I had always understood England was supposed to be fighting against that sort of thing. The men themselves don't complain but it makes one ashamed of one's nation.[38]

According to Grace Paton, writing to her mother before May 1916, Paton had received assurances from the authorities of his church that for the purposes of the Act, he was a parson, and Tatlow would argue that he was indispensable to the work of the S.C.M.[39] Tatlow was consulted on several occasions by Randall Davidson because he wanted to discover what the German government's policy was (students who had taken the 'zweites Examen' were exempt)[40] in order to argue for the exemption of British students. In France ordained ministers were called up in the initial mobilisation in 1914, and Boegner's autobiography describes the chaos this caused in parishes. It became clear that united church action would be required to make representations to the government when the failure of the Earl of Derby's recruitment scheme meant that the government would shortly introduce the first of a series of Manpower Acts to conscript all classes of men. Consequently the S.C.M. called a conference of 83 theological students from 29 colleges to discuss the possibility of obtaining consideration for theological students who felt called to continue their studies. Letters of support were received from a further 19 colleges. Tatlow reported the consensus of opinion and the resolutions of the conference supporting the students who wished to serve the nation as ordained ministers to Randall Davidson who was pessimistic, and with justification.[41]

The S.C.M. secretaries belonging to the Free Churches were in an anomalous position. They generally served, like Paton, for a period between the completion of their theological studies and their assignment to a congregation. Anglicans, on the other hand, were ordained first and were given a nominal charge — Tatlow described the usual arrangement as half an hour a week assisting at a service. Paton apparently felt the ambiguity of his position acutely, and after speaking to him, Tatlow wrote to the most appropriate person he could think of in the English Presbyterian Church. Significantly, the confidant of Randall Davidson begins by saying that he does not know whom he should be addressing re Paton's ordination. He is clearly embarrassed by the fact that because of his work for the S.C.M., Paton's ordination had been delayed longer than usual. Yet, he argues, the Student Movement involves a cure of souls which any minister might envy. By comparison Paton is taking far more services than Anglican secretaries, and yet is worse off, Tatlow is more discomfited by the likelihood that Paton will be called up while the ordained Anglican secretaries will not, and in fact have been told by their bishops that they are to remain at their work for which they were set apart.

> 'I know that there is an additional factor which may cause confusion, in that Paton is a pacifist . . . I always thought it somewhat misleading that so prominent a Student Movement man as Paton should have been a pacifist. It rather gives the impression that the bulk of the membership is pacifist, which is not the case, and therefore on this ground I am not particularly keen that there should be any conflict on this subject associated with him, especially as it does not seem to me to be fair to our own men who are with the army to allow the impression to get abroad that the Student Movement is a pacifist affair.'

Tatlow concludes with a request that steps be taken to arrange Paton's ordination. Not only does Tatlow employ powerful emotive images such as the views of the S.C.M. men at the front. His distaste for pacifists is obvious. He seems less worried about the prospect of Paton languishing in prison or being physically mistreated then the blow to the reputation of the S.C.M. if Paton was arraigned before a tribunal. The letter also contains implications that some pacifists were 'shirkers', although it is the opinion of Principal Graham that only the deepest convictions would have sustained men through such inhuman treatment.[42] Whether Tatlow means to imply that a leader of the S.C.M. should have more sense than to be a pacifist, or that pacifists should not be appointed to leading positions in the S.C.M. is not clear.[43] His animus against other pacifist S.C.M. leaders will be discussed shortly.

Paton's own account of his ordination comes in a letter to his wife written on his journey to India in October 1917.

> 'The Presbytery ordained me as a minister before I left, the S.C.M. being my charge. I had had this in mind for a long time, but did not raise the question formally until I had been for several years in the movement and could make out a strong case. It is a great thing for the movement to be recognised in this way and it is very gratifying for me, and I felt more and more that the status of licentiate, when it extends over one year, is quite anomalous: The Presbytery went thoroughly into the constitutional question through a special committee and eventually decided to ordain forthwith, no reference to Synod being necessary.'[44]

It seems very strange to write such a letter to one's wife even though she was 'baby-bound' in Cornwall. One can only conclude that the decision was made so suddenly that he could not write beforehand, even though he was writing daily to her on his journey from Cornwall where she settled to be out of the air-raids, to Southampton via London, in the manner prescribed for all lovers by Oscar Wilde.[45] The decision to go to India came as a result of an invitation from the Indian Y.M.C.A. who had operated such an exchange scheme before. Nevertheless the date of Paton's sailing, as with the timing of his ordination, falls so close to the date when he would probably have been conscripted that it cannot be entirely fortuitous.

Paton had been working for the Y.M.C.A. since 1916 when he began work in its central office in London, reorganising the religious work, dealing with a certain amount of administration and touring the army camps, visiting the Y.M.C.A. huts and canteens and speaking to the men. In this he was doing no more than other S.C.M. secretaries or W.S.C.F. workers such as R.L. Pelly, Dora Ivens, S.K. Datta and Rena Carswell. According to his wife in letters to her father, he got very keen on this, although in his letters to Tatlow he expressed his exasperation at the inefficiency and dilatory attitude of his colleagues. He conducted a lively correspondence with Dora Ivens, who was posted to France and complained to sympathetic ears of the inadequacies of a charity run by countesses and invalids.[46] The Y.M.C.A. was filling a vital role, providing facilities such as canteens, libraries, small shops and club rooms in the complete absence of any such provision by the army. Much of the work was highly experimental, developed as a response to the soldiers' spiritual needs, but the staff were hopelessly overworked and over-burdened with unaccustomed responsibilities. By mid-1917 Paton was apparently spending three-quarters of his time with the Y.M.C.A., though this is hard to credit when he was doing so much travelling for the S.C.M. with their decimated staff. So in some respects the invitation to go to India was not inappropriate though it was convenient.

The question of what would have happened to Paton if he had not been ordained, nor gone to India, would have remained speculation if it were not for the experience of Donald Grant, Scottish Inter-Collegiate secretary. His position was identical to Paton's since he was a licentiate of the Church of Scotland. In 1916 representations to a military tribunal secured him exemption as a probationer minister, but in April 1918 a civilian court sentenced him to imprisonment as a persistent conscientious objector just as he was about to start work as Irish Inter-Collegiate secretary. Tatlow maintained that the transfer was because he was not intellectual enough for the Scottish universities, but Grant thought the General Committee had made this decision on the grounds of expediency because of criticism of his life-style. Donald Grant was blamed for the less formal life style of a number of students in Scotland, even though this was a national trend. Thompson of Cambridge was similarly censured by Tatlow. Tatlow complained that Grant was the only pacifist who could not be defended on the lines of 'Yes, so and so, although he is a pacifist, does identify himself with the sins of the world'. Grant, like Murray, the English travelling secretary, was accused of being a womaniser, though with the number of women in the universities, it would have been difficult for him to avoid the company of women, and both were scrupulously careful to have chaperones with them when visiting women. In fact all Tatlow's allegations were completely unfounded, I am assured by members of the S.C.M. who knew them. Tatlow's unjustified accusations must spring from his dislike of their pacifist principles, apart from the way in which they offended against S.C.M. standards of 'manliness' discussed in the first chapter.[47] Paton's conduct was above reproach in this respect, but he was vulnerable in another way.

His position in the S.C.M. had become far from secure. This was in contrast to what he knew to be Tatlow's attitude in 1913. He had accepted the position of Assistant General Secretary of the S.C.M. only after much anguish, facing up to the vision of China's needs.[48] Tatlow could then write to Connell of the Foreign Mission Board of the English Presbyterian Church asking for Paton's release on the grounds that a man with several years' experience of the S.C.M. was urgently needed to understudy his work and halve his burden. He even went so far as to say that if he broke down tomorrow, Paton was the only man in the S.C.M. who could take his place.[49] This statement is reinforced by another three paragraphs of argument. If Paton was considered so indispensable then, the question then arises why Tatlow prevented him being given a permanent appointment on the S.C.M. staff in 1917 when his contract expired. Tatlow convinced Paton that he was mistaken to ask the General Committee for this, and his appointment was only renewed for another five years. This would be less significant if, at the same General Committee meeting, Hugh Martin, a Scottish Baptist minister, had not been given a permanent appointment as Assistant General Secretary, and Zoë Fairfield, the other Assistant General Secretary had not insisted on being given a permanent appointment when she was first appointed in December 1912. As Tatlow was urging Paton to take on more Y.M.C.A. work, one might infer that he was being 'edged out'. Finally, there are a series of letters which Tatlow wrote to representatives of missionary societies on the U.C.M.E., which contain severe criticism of Paton and transgress the standards of loyalty to a colleague one could have expected in Tatlow.[50] It should be said in mitigation that all the S.C.M. secretaries worked themselves to the point of collapse in 1917-18, and Tatlow's judgement was on several occasions warped by nervous strain and fatigue. Many people whom I have interviewed regarded Paton as Tatlow's natural successor, though it has also been suggested that Tatlow did not want a Presbyterian to succeed him. To comprehend the full implications of the predicament of a pacifist it is necessary to read Bertrand Russell's memoirs, since he lost his lectureship at Trinity College, Cambridge, as well as being fined £100 under the D.O.R.A. laws.

Paton sailed to India under wartime restrictions, with J.N. Farquhar for company, whose influence on his theology will be discussed in the next chapter,[51] and with a group of S.V.M.U. members whom he quickly organised into a daily prayer meeting. He was in India for thirteen months, returning November 1918, but from his vivid letters only those incidents are chosen for comment which illuminate his pacifist principles. The Sinclair biography contains a description of his work for the Y.M.C.A. which it is not necessary to repeat here.[52] In some ways it seems a contradiction that men with pacifist principles should be found working among the troops as Y.M.C.A. secretaries, but there do not seem to have been any instances of friction because of this. In India an important feature was that many of the Y.M.C.A. secretaries were Indian Christians, some Syrian Orthodox, some from families recently converted, and therefore did not have the status of English officers, as the chaplains did. Paton also observed that the Y.M.C.A. drew educated Indians, who refused to work for the missions. From them he gained a profound insight into Indian nationalist aspirations. Paton was a perceptive observer of the racial tension in India, but his contact with the soldiers must have also had an important influence on him. However, on the voyage he was already reconsidering his convictions:

> 'What has been gradually coming home to me is that there is something far more in the God-Man than I have ever got to and I often feel myself on the edge of a new understanding which yet eludes me. I am moving more to the old idea of vicarious suffering and trying to combine that with our pacifist thought and Christ as bearing the sins of the world in a . . . . . suffering love. I am reading the New Testament continually with this thought in mind, I feel that some of the passages are rather overlooked by our modern people, that something lies buried there and only thoroughly put by the old Evangelicals.

> It has come home to me in talking with soldiers and Indians about Christianity. If you are up against it, you soon find out that if all you have, as an outwardly way of confession is a series of truths about God, that He is Love etc. grips you . . . The oldfashioned man would say 'Jesus died for your sins, you need forgiveness, without him you are lost. I can say 1) and 2) but not the third ?(word illegible) If sin is that sense of the intolerable plight men are in without ?(word illegible) as well as the glory of having Him, that old chap had it and we haven't. 'Be ye reconciled to God' is what I have simply got to tell them. I believe they are not reconciled, I can see it all around me, but I haven't got the sense of urgency which should be there'.

He confessed that he doubted if one could ever get 'the realities' into a system, but his letter was not to be taken as one of woe and doubt rather than spiritual assurance. Really he is finding more and more in the New Testament and the person of Christ.[53]

Although it is somewhat incoherent, this letter is important for showing how Paton, confronted with pacifism on the one hand, and the demands of his work, particularly among Hindu soldiers, on the other, is forced back to a re-assessment of his understanding of the New Testament and the meaning of Christ's suffering.

The moral conditions, and the living conditions of the soldiers horrified him. In Bangalore there were 12,000 British troops and 7,000 Indian troops on leave from Mesopotamia, with three Y.M.C.A. secretaries. The only facilities for the troops seemed to be the licensed disinfected brothels. Paton protested in high circles about the official subsidising of vice, and the attitude that vice does not matter but disease does. Decent men in command he thought, were ignoring the situation, while the young soldiers, whatever their good intentions, were being corrupted.[54]

Paton was very conscious of the rigid censorship. Often his only source of news such as the Russian withdrawal from the war was 'The Challenge' newspaper which was sent to him from England. When he heard that the Manpower Bill (under which he would have been conscripted) had been withdrawn, he wrote that he was trying to get to the Nilgiri Hills, Poona and then Ceylon and home.

> 'These are awful days and I pray that they may end soon. The war cannot last for ever, and we need to believe that God is in it all somehow. It gives Him pain far more than us, and that is something to dwell on these days'.[55]

Paton wrote that in India both among the troops and when visiting missions and speaking on evangelistic campaigns, he became much more aware of the meaning of sin and forgiveness.[56]

Reference has already been made to Paton's reaction to his wife's conversion and entry into the Church of England.[57] He considered very hard whether he should also become an Anglican, but was deterred by the spectacle of the Anglican Military chaplains whom he met and the whole panoply of the national English religion.

> 'You know that I am not an Anglican, not because I don't love the sacrament of Holy Communion, but because I never feel that the Anglican one is honest and truthful. . . . . If the Eucharist were Anglicanism I could be an Anglican (except the High church theory of the sacrament which is materialist), but there is far more in it than that and you feel that as much as I do. Pacifism finds a strange soul in the Anglican snobbery and Erastian-ism which are awfully prevalent, the state idea of religion and all that is very common. I could never find myself in that gallery, my experience of

Anglicanism out here has rather hardened me. The bishops are admirable and the chaplains are the limit. Even the missionaries connive far more than any other to the alliance between their missions and the Raj and all that I cannot agree with'.[58]

In July he wrote that

'The Cowley fathers have a window to victory draped in flags and say mass for victory. We Presbyterians are not so lofty, but I have yet to find a Presbyterian minister who would put flags on his communion table. I am not being bitter but violently put off. They think that communion can be turned on with a certain purpose, like a water-tap'.[59]

The importance of these comments is not only their significance for reconstructing what Paton believed about the sacraments, but also because they clearly show the obstacle which the nationalist and anti-pacifist spirit of the Church of England was for Paton; he could not reconcile himself with its pretensions nor join his wife in its worship. It is idle to speculate on what would have happened if he had become an Anglican, but Garbett wrote in 1943 that had Paton been an Anglican, he would have been one of the archbishops.[60]

William and Grace Paton's critical attitude to the British government has already been noted. At its inception in December 1914, the members of the Fellowship of Reconciliation, who at the first few meetings were almost exclusively former and present members of the S.C.M., were not critical of the government. The group which came together for prolonged meetings of prayer every week was concerned that the positive testimony of pacifism, which must not be isolated from social and industrial questions, should be worked out, apart from the need to back up conscientious objectors. A journal was issued called 'The Venturer' and much of its way of working was derived from the S.C.M., though Principal Graham claims it was pure Quakerism.[61] The initial conference in Cambridge was attended by 130 people including the Patons, and 2,000 people had enrolled before the July conference at Swanwick in 1915. By 1918 it had achieved a membership of about 8,000 distributed among 165 groups and branches. Lucy Gardner, a Birmingham Friend, was the first honorary secretary, but in the autumn of 1915 the first full-time secretary, the Revd. Richard Roberts, was appointed. H.G. Woods considers that the ecumenical significance of its executive committee lay in the way in which Anglican and Free Church ministers were content to have a Quaker layman, H.T. Hodgkin (the chairman of the S.V.M.U. 1900-1905) in the chair.[62] Temple participated with them in some of their discussions but generally, H.G. Wood writes, the pacifist position was an embarrassment to the group producing the 'Papers for wartime'.[63] Like Paton, Hodgkin's views underwent some modification, from being Tolstoyan to the position of the S.C.M. pacifists, that if men felt it was their duty to join up, then they must do it. If on the other hand more people were seized with the desire to live redemptively, there would be results. A defeat by Germany in this spirit would be a victory such as Calvary. The Fellowship distanced itself from the politics of the anti-war groups, but co-operated with them in organizing relief for the victims of the government's measures. Early in 1917 their offices were raided by Scotland Yard and everything removed, but Hodgkin's enormous physical bulk so intimidated the police that the documents were returned. However, legal action was taken against them for undermining morale, and mobs broke up many of their open air meetings. The real subversion lay in their examination of social problems and their pamphlets and book written as a series 'The Christian Revolution'.

In 1942 Paton sent a letter of resignation to Artingstall of the Fellowship of Reconciliation in these terms:

> 'I still believe in the Christian ministry of reconciliation, but I have for a good many years past ceased to believe that it follows from this that it is always and in all circumstances wrong for Christians to resort to war . . . . I was one of the earliest members of the F.o.R., but I am not one of those whose mind has been changed merely during the present war. For several years before this war broke out I had become convinced for a variety of reasons, with which I do not want to trouble you, that the position which I had formerly held was untenable morally . . . . I still hold that the deepest duty of a Christian is the task of reconciliation and I still put that as more important than the use of compulsory force. I now recognise that the place of compulsory force is real and necessary and that only disaster can follow upon a failure to recognize this. Nevertheless I still hold that when force has done its necessary work the task of reconciling and rebuilding remains.
>
> 'If it were clearly understood that this was my view, I should not feel it necessary to resign from the Fellowship, though I deplore the efforts which I see associated with the Fellowship, in the direction of negotiating with the enemy.[64] If, as I anticipate, someone holding my view can no longer be a member I should be grateful if you would take my name off the list'. (3.12.42)[65]

In order to trace the development in Paton's views, it is necessary, unfortunately, to make certain assumptions. There seems no reason to suppose that he was not possessed of the enthusiasm for the League of Nations prevalent in Anglo-Saxon ecumenical circles, as he followed the debate in the Life and Work movement closely. In India he met Gandhi several times, Gandhi's chief Christian apologist, C.F. Andrews, was a respected friend, but though Paton was sympathetic to the moral and theoretical force of Gandhi's non-violent methods, he was exasperated by the amount of violence which inevitably broke out as a result of non-cooperation demonstrations, for which he held Gandhi responsible.[66] David Paton remembers sitting between his father and C.F. Andrews at a meal at the Birmingham S.C.M. Quadrennial of 1937 while Paton belaboured Andrews about this. He thought the British tendency to repression equally deplorable. It is significant that in the many comments on Indian affairs which concluded almost all Paton's letters, there is very little idealism. He was becoming what might be called a political realist.

It was the naked evil of fascism, particularly the organised brutality in Germany, which caused him to revise his views radically, chiefly because of the experiences of his close friend and colleague Karl Hartenstein, the India secretary of the Basel Mission, whom he first met in 1928. Hartenstein came from Pietist circles in Baden-Wurtemberg, but entered the Christian ministry because of his traumatic experiences as an artillery officer 1914-18 and because of his grief at the suicide of his brother. At first he welcomed Hitler's seizure of power in 1933, but he was very quickly undeceived. Cultivating the German hinterland of the Basel Mission, he wrote penetrating reports about the implications of the German Church Struggle, and was himself interrogated by the Gestapo in 1934.[67] He would have told Paton what fascism really meant before the Paton household became a staging post for German refugees, probably even before the Röhm massacre, the significance of which

Paton fully appreciated. Secondly, Paton's friend T.Z. Koo of the W.S.C.F. was a patriotic Chinese, whose heroic struggle to overcome his anger against the Japanese moved the Tambaram conference.[68] Japanese aggression in China must have also influenced Paton as he saw it through the eyes of his friends there. Hence the paragraphs in his letter to Michael Paton:

> 'Further, and this I feel much more now than I did, because the whole ideological business has got so complex and evil, the pacifist position lands you today unless you are very clear-eyed in the most curious semi-political positions. Not many people will deny that the Nazi plan for the world is a bad show — vide Poland, Czechoslovakia, etc.' passim. It is not easy for the ordinary decent man to believe that the consequence of the Christian religion is that little nations ought to be left to suffer; that does not sound very noble, it breathes a different atmosphere from the Sermon on the Mount. So you find pacifists — notably of the Peace Pledge Union variety[69] — slipping into a sort of defence of the other people on political grounds. I even know cases where the pacifist passion made a man more or less anti-semite — he was so keen to show that Hitler really had such a strong case and that if only we had behaved differently it would all have come right . . . .
>
> 'This, then, is the dilemma, and no serious ethical action is ever free from some measure of tension. If you fight, you have to do things which are most certainly not 'loving', you may have to kill men and cause intense pain, you have to blockade etc. etc. If you take the other line, you consent to do nothing (and it really does come to that) to advance the reign of law in the world, and you say to every aggressor, Come on and be at ease. In political life pacifist action can never be anything but weakness to law, and it is always in fact allied to the craven forces of finance and the like.[70] I used to think war could be abolished by disarmament; I now see that you cannot abolish arms unless you establish law, and that you may have to fight to establish law'.

Paton disliked the Oxford Group Movement intensely, and one of the things he must have found particularly obnoxious was the shady political activities it was involved in in its attempt to reconcile Hitler.[71] It would be a perfect example of his thesis in the letter above.

Paton was not involved very much in the preparations for the Oxford conference of the Life and Work movement on 'Church, Community and State', except to contribute the material contributed to Tambaram on 'Christianity in the eastern conflicts', but he was the secretary of the section on 'The Universal Church and the World of Nations'. With the chairman, John Mackay of Princeton, he had helped the section's drafting committee to formulate the report. As secretary, Paton addressed the plenary assembly on the problems: either to take majority decisions, coming up with platitudes, or to do what they have done, which is the honest thing. The Church is not going to be any weaker in its witness for facing its own weakness. Mackay described it as 'teamwork without compromise'.[72] The whole report can be found in the report of the Oxford conference: 'The Churches Survey their Task'. The report of Paton's section resembles an early Faith and Order report, inasmuch as all the varying degrees of Christian opinion are recorded from absolute pacifism advocated by Charles Raven, to the view that there are occasions when a Christian must take up arms to prevent his neighbour being oppressed or martyred. There were many who agreed with Temple that there were times when a Christian must take risks for peace, even if his hands also become bloodstained.[73]

Although the question of whether another war was imminent was the burning topic of the day, in public opinion as well as in the Church, the section wisely set the debate within the framework of the responsibilities of the universal church. Dr Visser't Hooft describes the difficulties he had, chairing the sub-section on war, where the chief protagonists were conducting themselves as though in the House of Commons, because the British delegates apparently dominated the debate in a manner completely disproportionate to their numbers.[74] Members of other sections thought it amazing that any consensus at all was possible, and how much this was due to Paton's sympathy with both pacifists and non-pacifists one cannot say. His hand can be seen in the report, in the emphasis on the significance of the world-wide presence of the church, the responsibility of older churches to help younger churches especially in time of war, and the responsibility of all Christians to attempt to reduce tension by combatting racism, protecting minority groups, and influencing public opinion towards reconciliation. The report is very practical in spite of the doctrinal preface asserting the churches' common faith. Paton's thoughts on the importance of international law and arbitration between nations, have already been quoted. The report deals with the necessity for states to surrender part of their national sovereignty if the League of Nations is to be revived, and castigates the tendency(which was very pronounced at the Stockholm conference in 1925) to invest in the League of Nations aspirations which rightly should be found in the expectation of the Kingdom of God.[75] Lord Cecil, Britain's ambassador to the League of Nations for many years, and Professor Max Huber, an expert on international law, who subsequently became president of the Red Cross, stated the case for the League of Nations. In the plenary session debate they were most strongly supported by the representatives of Eastern European countries and Spain.

Professor Lauga of France warned against the pharisaism of praying for one's enemies when all were accomplices in sin, and in need of pardon. It was this conviction firmly set out in the report, which marked the progress since the first World War, and presaged a better spirit between the churches in belligerent countries in the next war, instead of both sides trying to fasten guilt for the war on the other side. It may have been a point absorbed from the pacifists, though the passage emphasizing the horror of war would not belong to their case exclusively, but there were still many members of the section who felt that in certain circumstances war was the lesser of two evils. The chief value of the work of the section, and of the report itself, is the positive attitude taken to what the churches could do in the face of war, rather than being a negative condemnation of war and a demand that the churches abstain from the issue. This is consonant with Paton's remarks in his letter to Michael Paton It was also recognized that there could be no peace without social justice. The important feature about the report is that it managed to say so much that was constructive and yet not foreclose any of the possibilities for dialogue.

Paton possessed the rare distinction of being one of the few British people not deceived by the Munich settlement.[76] Perhaps his observation of the Japanese in China made him realise that appeasement was impossible as a political reality, apart from the moral issue of betraying Czechoslovakia. When war in Western Europe did break out, Paton was immediately confronted with the issue of pacifism in England, mainly as incarnated in the person of Charles Raven, the Master of Christ's College,

Cambridge. Raven had had a shattering experience of trench warfare in the first World War and had been growing progressively more pacifist over the years, traversing the same ground as Paton in the opposite direction, except for the fundamental theological differences between Paton and an amateur biologist and ornithologist much respected in scientific circles, a charismatic Christian apologist who held students at Swanwick in the 1920s spellbound, and the best sort of 'liberal' Anglican whom Barth castigated for his 'natural theology'.[77]

Raven was an outstanding broadcaster, whether on bird-watching or the Christian faith, but in company with a number of other 'well-known pacifists' such as George Macleod, Donald Soper and Archie C. Craig, was banned from broadcasting on any subject. Not only was pacifism not to be broadcast, which would have caused very great offence to the public, and in theory at least, undermined morale, but no-one associated with it was to be heard. W.D.L. Greer and Alan Booth, who were then the General Secretary and Assistant General Secretary of the S.C.M., became indignant about the implied infringement of the right of freedom of speech, but without, they thought, eliciting any response in the offices of such church dignitaries as Paton.[78] Indeed, it is clear from Smyth's biography of Garbett that neither Garbett (who was chairman of the B.B.C.'s advisory committee on religious broadcasting) nor his biographer realized the full implications of the issue at stake.[79] Eric Fenn, who had been Oldham's adjutant at Oxford and Dr. J. Welch, his superior in the Religious Broadcasting Division of the B.B.C., nearly resigned over the issue. Professor Fenn still thinks that they should have done, instead of which he trusted Garbett, who talked him out of resigning, 'to do something about it', which unfortunately in Garbett's terminology merely meant dropping a word in someone's ear at the Athenaeum, and was totally ineffective.[80]

The issue was an extremely complex one, so much so that the principal letter in which Paton expressed his views to Fenn on the subject is appended to this book as it is virtually impossible to summarise or quote from it satisfactorily. To begin with, in spite of the strong religious principles of Lord Reith, the founder of the B.B.C., the Religious Broadcasting Division was in a very weak position, in the internal power struggles of the B.B.C., just as the Religious Affairs Division of the Ministry of Information would have been abolished without the patronage of Kenneth Grubb. The resignations of men as good as Welch and Fenn would have greatly damaged it, without influencing the Foreign Office, who, it eventually transpired, after much correspondence between Paton and the B.B.C., were the power behind the prohibition.

The other point which it is important to note is that broadcasting procedures were very different from today. Vernon Sproxton, who entertained me at the B.B.C., was amazed at the inflexible procedure of scripting everything and getting it passed by various committees in the higher echelons of the B.B.C. There were no 'spontaneous discussions' and once, when a well-known Methodist churchman began to pray ex tempore, he was cut off.[81] With this degree of control it would have been perfectly possible to censor any talk for pacifist sentiments. Secondly, and related to this point, is the fact that the B.B.C. was much less independent than it is now, and in wartime acknowledged that it was a vehicle of government propaganda (this was the argument used by the B.B.C. to resist pressure to allow religious broadcasts in German).[82] It was argued that it was a contradiction for those actively opposed to government policy of winning the war to broadcast on this medium.

Indeed Paton refuted Fenn's claim that the ban was analogous to the stifling of the Confessing Church in Germany, because there the issue was that they could not speak at all, whereas the issue here was the pacifists' right to broadcast on pacifism, a negative thing.[83]

At one stage of his correspondence Paton threatened to bring the whole wing of the Church out against the government and the B.B.C. if the policy was not eased, and in fact it became apparent that younger men, who had not been the centre of controversy, even if they were pacifists, were allowed to broadcast on other subjects. Paton was annoyed that 'the broadcast Church', as he described it, should have lost the services of some of its finest apologists, but he admitted that they were not irreplaceable. However, there the matter rested after a very curious crisis. The B.B.C. carried the rule to extremes by refusing to broadcast performances by the Glasgow Orpheus Choir. There were questions in the House of Commons, and Churchill delivered himself of the opinion that it did not matter what a man's convictions were if he was playing the fiddle. What carried weight with the B.B.C. was that Vaughan Williams wrote to the B.B.C. forbidding them to broadcast his next symphony, which they had commissioned, unless they revised their policy. Raven, however, remained under the ban until the end of the war, which intensified his feeling of isolation.

Raven's biographer, Canon Dillistone, writes that Raven felt that the ecumenical movement had by-passed him, and left him out. This is curious, because Raven was involved in the 'Cloister Group' which he, Bartlett of the Fellowship of Reconciliation, Temple and Paton set up in a similar way to the Peace Aims Group, which is discussed later in this book.[84] An informal collection of friends attempted a dialogue between pacifists and non-pacifists to which they all attached some importance. They met at Christ's College several weekends a year and it is difficult to see how anyone who could secure so much of the Archbishop of Canterbury's time (as Temple then was) could claim to be left out of the ecumenical movement. The group did not have the same links with American and Continental churchmen as the Peace Aims Group did, nor the same access to government sources of information, but it was nonetheless a significant ecumenical study group, and should have done much to lessen the isolation of pacifists and to improve understanding within the church. It came to an untimely end when Canon Raven suffered a very serious heart attack in 1943, followed shortly by the death of his wife, who had triumphed over wartime restrictions to entertain the group, and the death of Paton himself.

The group did not often discuss pacifism per se, though its members were concerned that pacifists should not be victimized, but in May 1943 the following discussion took place:

> 'William Paton spoke to a letter of his drawing attention to the question which would arise in the structure of peace. Pacifists and non-pacifists could agree to differ about the war, but they thought they would differ sharply about the peace. The question ought to be thought out now. Henry Carter agreed. The meaning of the term 'negotiated peace' had to be considered. It was agreed that the subject should be taken up at the next meeting.
>
> Percy Bartlett spoke of a concern for joint effort regarding the tragedy of the whole war situation and the problem of an early and righteous peace. It was not a question of appointing a day of prayer or a set service of inter-

cession or of drawing up forms of prayer; or making lists of people willing to pray. Many were already deeply exercised in prayer. And yet something further was wanted to spread a quiet movement through the Church, a sense of unity in intercession for the power of God to be made known in peace. William Paton reminded the group of the fellowship of prayer meeting years ago in the Jerusalem Chamber under the leadership of Bishop Donaldson, and of their agreement on basic themes which had stood the test of time.'

Considering the disfavour into which Mott and Oldham fell in 1917 in Germany for allegedly becoming tools of their governments when they were supposed to serve an international organization, the I.M.C., it is surprising that as far as I know Paton was not criticised for his broadcasts to Germany. These openly served British propaganda ends by their savage attacks on Nazi policy, even if they appealed to the better nature of Germans who, Paton accepted, were living in the first country to be occupied by Hitler.[85] Two examples of this are the broadcasts delivered on a date about 14th July, 1941, and 'St George and the Dragon' dated 27th July, 1941, both of which were designed to counter German propaganda that Germany was leading a crusade against Bolshevism (the dragon) to save Christian civilization, and to deny accusations that Britain was turning Bolshevist, since one did not need to depart from one's theoretical opposition to Communism to sympathise with an invaded country. Paton points to the demise of law in Germany, the treatment of the Jews and the murder of old people as the abnegation of Christianity, whereas in England serious planning is going ahead to remove social injustice. (He meant the preparations for the Welfare State.) The hearts of all decent men are hardening against the Nazi tyranny.[86]

'Fighting talk' such as these broadcasts reveal how far Paton had moved since 1914. Talking to young lads with problems of conscience he could be gentle and sympathetic, but there is little doubt that with the ardour with which he threw himself into fire-watching duties, with his pride in his sons and daughter in the forces, that he was now a 'combatant'. In a sense it was a triumph of realism over abstract principles, though Paton was never an idealist. From his years as a pacifist in the First World War, he gained a better understanding of the meaning of suffering and the importance of the witness of a minority to an alternative way. He conceded to Michael Paton that there were people who had a God-given vocation, as they thought, to pacifism, and he respected their viewpoint just as he respected the Oxford Fathers' vows of celibacy, though he commented to Grace that it would never do for them! The crux of the matter lay in his understanding of the Sermon on the Mount. A man steeped in the New Testament, he could not accept the pacifist exegesis of isolated texts, which he felt were contrary to the essence of the New Testament. One sees also a general sharpening of Paton's mind, 1914-18, and increased lucidity in expressing himself. The most significant thing ecumenically was that he could create a meaningful dialogue with such absolute pacifists as Raven and Bartlett, yet confront Nazism with such propaganda.

Chapter IV
From Farquhar to Kraemer: The Development of Paton's Understanding of the Christian Message to Non-Christian Peoples

Paton was a prolific writer, producing books and articles almost with the frequency of Simenon or Agatha Christie; so that it is possible to compile a bibliography of 21 books and 94 articles, though it is by no means certain that this list is complete. Two books lay in embryonic manuscript form at the time of his death. Almost all were written very hastily to meet a specific request for study material, and all might be termed 'popular', being designed for the intelligent layman or the student. From four of these books in particular, 'Jesus Christ and the World's Religions' (1916, revised 1926); 'Alexander Duff' (1922), 'A Faith for the World' (1929), and 'The Faiths of Mankind' (1932), it is possible to glean the development of Paton's thought on the content and implications of Christian mission. By this is meant his understanding of non-Christian religions, his apologia for the missionary Christian faith and his treatment of the question of the approach to other faiths.

It is necessary to say at the outset of this chapter that no-one has ever claimed that Paton showed any originality of thought, though he thought none the less deeply for that. He had the distinction of being a Presbyterian, so that he had been given a thoroughly theological training at Westminster College, Cambridge, which made him less susceptible to 'liberal' theology than his Anglican and Methodist colleagues and contemporaries were.[1] It will be one of the aims of this chapter to describe the unique eclecticism of Paton's essentially othodox theology.

Paton's views on the relationship of theology to faith and religious experience have already been discussed in this book with reference to his contribution to the debate on the Aims and Basis of the S.C.M. Throughout his life Paton consistently subordinated theology to faith and religious experience, as is demonstrated by his remark that Emil Brunner (whom he esteemed highly) had benefited from his association with the Oxford Group Movement because he had 'got some religion' from them.[2] The effect of a secular world outlook and the criticism of modern humanists and rationalists are given due consideration in 'A Faith for the World' (1929),[3] as might be expected after the emphasis on their significance at the Jerusalem meeting of the I.M.C.,[4] but are scarcely mentioned in 'Jesus Christ and the World's Religions' (1916), which is the only book in which 'animism' and primitive religion are fully discussed.[5] It was always Paton's unshakeable conviction that men are basically religious, however they may try and fill the void in their lives, by which he means that they have a belief in the existence of higher powers, a will to worship them and a sense of dependence on them. In 'A Faith for the World' Paton draws much on Rudolf Otto's 'The Idea of the Holy', but feels bound to defend his view against Huxley and against the view that religion is one stage in man's evolution.[6] In 'The

Faiths of Mankind' (1932), he is more preoccupied with the question of who or what man is than what religion is, but it is still for him part of man's essential nature. This presupposition was natural to a man to whom religious faith and the habits of prayer and worship were an integral part of his life, and who had seen so much of India's religiosity. He admits that there have been men apparently indifferent to or oblivious of the claims of religion, but such people are blinded by ignorance or prejudice. Some sort of consciousness of the numinous or craving for religion is, in Paton's views, the common factor in all mankind. Therefore, there can be a universal response to the universal claims of the Christian faith. Because of this conviction of Paton's, it is more logical to discuss his writing on secularism in connexion with his books and lectures on social ideals and social action.[7] This distinction is merely for convenience, and is not germane to Paton's thought in which the theological expression of his faith gave muscle to what he was doing and praying.

Theology was something which Paton enjoyed. He is remembered for having spent whole evenings, sitting by the fire, smoking, and discussing the theology of Karl Barth with a friend. He once went to great lengths so that he could spend the three hours he had between trains, in a Zurich station waiting room, discussing theology with Emil Brunner. Unfortunately, he worked under such pressures that he never had the time or the opportunity to write a scholarly work. It is, of course, open to question whether he had the ability to produce a scholarly work, yet if one had only the evidence of his many 'Penguin' paperbacks to judge him by, one would conclude that Bell could never have produced such an outstanding biography as 'Randall Davidson'.[8]

Although the books by Paton under consideration in this chapter vary in length between 90 and 247 pages, there is every reason to think that they all were written in the fashion he related to A.C. Craig, when asked by him how he could write book after book when carrying such a load of administrative and propagandist work.[9] 'The recipe for my books is (a) scissors and paste (b) being content with a 70% mark, and (c) a dash of bluff now and then.' Craig comments: 'I think that reply gives the clue to three things in his make-up (a) industrious reading by virtue of which the scissors and paste were well used; (b) a lack of inhibiting self-regard; (c) the kind of blithe insouciance of a man who knows that he will never make anything if he is afraid of making a mistake, and who therefore pushed along with a given bit of work without a sidelong . . . glance.'

Craig's summary is an exact description of what were essentially impressionist works, with broad, sweeping brush-strokes, to convey the outline of the subjects. In the books under review in this chapter, however, there is a very great deal of repetition and a heavy reliance on the speeches, sayings and definitions of other works, especially in 'A Faith for the World'. There are also instances where what has appeared as a quotation in 'Jesus Christ and the World's Religions' appears almost word for word in the text of 'A Faith for the World' without quotation marks.[10] The footnotes and references are sparse in places, but by the time he came to write 'The Faiths of Mankind', this had improved. As with all S.C.M. study books there are suggestions for further reading. In 'Jesus Christ and the World's Religions', these come at the end of each chapter. At the end of the chapter entitled 'Christianity the Universal Religion' he simply puts 'THE BIBLE'. Since all Paton's books were written for very specific purposes, inevitably the content has suffered under the constraints of the format. With the possible exception of 'A Faith for the World', his books were written for 'the home front', and not for the non-Christian. His purpose was to provide a Christian apologetic for the interested inquirer, who has perceived his need of 'the sacred', and to educate the ordinary ill-informed Christian. 'Jesus Christ and the World's Religions' begins with the statement that:

> 'A diffused knowledge of the subject combined with some misapprehension as to the nature of Christianity has produced in many quarters a kind of nebulous tolerance of everything which calls itself religion, which is different from the attitude of Christian scholars who treat other religions sympathetically but remain convinced of the supremacy of the revelation of God in Christ.'

In the second edition of 1927 a further motive is adduced: that in the upheaval and social change in the East, which has been accompanied by the eclipse of Western prestige (which Paton prophesied in December 1914 in his article for the 'Student Movement' of that month); Christians 'owe to the world the supreme duty of faithfulness to the truth, studied and grasped with sincerity and honesty and preached in love.'

In 1928, when he wrote 'A Faith for the World', Paton was less convinced of the continuing success of Christian missions, since in spite of the missions' great record, it is still an open question whether the Church will respond to the missionary call with the ardour and abandon that is demanded. He is uncertain whether mission will prove to be the task of the whole Church or of a tiny enthusiastic minority. In the book he proposes to justify world-wide mission by showing that the Christian faith, in comparison with other religions, is the universal faith which the world stands in need of, and that it is useless to accept the uniqueness of the Christian faith without its concomitant challenge to action. The book systematically deals with the main themes of the Christian message and the principal tasks of the Christian mission as defined by the I.M.C. meeting at Jerusalem, and in fact is an attempt to present the findings of the conference in the guise of apologetic. Paton remarked in letters to his wife in 1918 and 1936 that his main role in India seemed to be 'going round encouraging disheartened missionaries'.[11] This book is encouragement for Christian workers. It is interesting to contrast its confident note with 'Rethinking Missions', the controversial American analysis of mission written in 1932.[12]

'The Faiths of Mankind' is a more subjective work than 'Jesus Christ and the World's Religions', and as before, Paton makes no pretence of impartiality if that means, as he defines it, to write without conviction of what is true. But he hopes that this position is not incompatible with honesty and fairness in stating a position with which one disagrees. Again he is engaged in apologetic. The other book, 'Alexander Duff', a biography of the first Church of Scotland missionary and a pioneer educationalist in Bengal,[13] is in essence an apologetic work on missionary education in India. Paton is, however, aware of the limitations of the apologetic method.[14] His final word in 'The Faiths of Mankind' is that ultimately the reasoned arguments of this book and others, and the power of reason itself will avail nothing because what is required is faith, faith in a living God. This is a slightly different emphasis from the closing pages of 'A Faith for the World', which ends with a gentle exhortation to prayer, even in the simplest language, because it is the basis of world mission.

The final qualification which one must make in any assessment of Paton's writings is that although he himself was not a systematic theologian, he had a high regard for those who were, and did much to provoke and stimulate theological discussion. The most notable example of this was the encouragement he gave to Hendrik Kraemer to write 'The Christian Message in the Non-Christian World' for the I.M.C. meeting in Tambaram. This involved finding a salary for Kraemer while he wrote it, and taking the decision to permit him to write double the amount commissioned, which meant that someone (Nichol MacNicol) had to be found to produce a summary of it, and to help Kraemer write readable English.[15]

Paton's lack of original thought, the subordination of theology to his faith and religious experience, the purpose of his writings as Christian apologetic and the way in which they were tailored by a specific format and for a specific type of reader, are all factors to be weighed in this assessment of Paton's writings. When due consideration is given to these factors, one can see more clearly the extent to which Paton's thought developed and was influenced. However, there are also fragments of Paton's writings of 1909-1911, which give some indication of the point from which he started. All four pieces are studies in various Bible passages, a point which substantiates what has already been written in the second chapter of this book concerning the centrality of the Bible to Paton's work.[16]

'So each of us shall give account of himself to God' (Romans 14 v 12) is the text Paton chose for exposition for a sermon or an essay, and began by contrasting the sense of the futility of life with the actions and judgment of God in the history of Israel. The Resurrection is a sign of His power no less than the Exodus, and happened out of God's holy purpose of love. There are difficulties with other faiths. The Hindu considers the world an illusion, which is a question of an escape from reality. Stoicism is equally criticised. Paton declares that Jesus instead loved life, and was not a monk, but saw life as at the school of God (which is an idea which Farquhar frequently used).[17] If one asks 'What is there in it for me?' the answer is: a difficult time with no ease again. 'Our actions are done in a world in which God is active and therefore real'. He concludes 'Nothing is so real and awful a thing as the purpose of God in Christ'.

One can appreciate how an understanding of God as acting and judging in history would provide a spur to mission. The fragment is pregnant with the differences between Christian faith and other religions since in this outline there is nothing to suggest the ontological character of God's existence, and the high value placed on action is the antithesis of the Hindu and Buddhist idea of passivity.[18] The emphasis on God's judgment differs from contemporary ideas of progress and evolution which were inspiring such optimism in 1909.

Only two pages survive of a commentary on the Greek text of the Book of Revelation which Paton seems to have been writing for his fiancée (Rev. 1 v 3 - 2 v 9).[19] He begins by criticising Schweitzer's 'dropping of bricks'. 'They (Schweitzer and Co.) allege that Christ's teaching is all 'Interimsethik' whereas it is obviously only of that character in the very smallest degree'.[20] Paton seems to have missed the point or not to be interested in why the Jews of that period had 'put God far away with lots of intermediaries', just as he fails to understand the significance of apocalyptic. Instead he states that Jesus accepted angels and the rest of Jewish apocalyptic belief only as a framework. His followers gave apocalyptic its ethical content.[21] He thinks that Grace is right to consider Revelation very individualistic. Unfortunately his feelings get the better of him, and the commentary is transformed into a love letter. What he has already written indicates his sympathy for young churches. The most important comment is on a phrase in 1 v 9 which he translates as 'the witness borne by Jesus' and infers from that that we bear witness to Him and with Him. We are all bound up in the same act as He and it is practically the Gospel. This is very significant in view of the fact that members of the S.V.M.U. at this time believed that they went out to the East with a very definite message. For Paton, not only is Christ the Gospel, but he shares in the proclamation of it.

'The tree of knowledge and the tree of life' is a thirty-six page essay on Genesis 3, but apart from the fact that it establishes that Paton was prepared to use all the resources of German scholarship to argue that different traditions have been merged into a very complex story in a manner very radical for the S.C.M., there is little which has any bearing on his subsequent writing. His dependence on Gunkel and Wellhausen is interesting, especially as he not only discusses their conclusions derived from form criticism, but also their theology. His own exegesis leads him to defend a view of the place of reason in man and the necessity of consecrating one's reason to God's service if it is not to be a vain thing.

However, it is his essay on 'St. Paul's missionary methods' written circa 1911 which is most significant because so many of his later themes are present in em-bryonic form. He begins with the assertion that 'to us the importance of Paul the missionary should be greater than to any of the generations that have intervened between him and us'. He deduces this from the similarity that he alleges exists between the first century A.D. and the first decade of the twentieth century, such as the loss of any desire for liberty since men were living in large political units, and the decadent syncretistic religious clime. Oblivious of 'the tumult and bustle and weariness and disquiet' of this world, Paul preached the cross of Christ, with his eyes fixed not on the kingdoms of this world, but the kingdom of God. The preaching of the word of God was his principal method and the supreme duty of the missionary. Instead of a detailed discussion of Paul's theology, Paton asserts:

> 'Paul was the first to assert the significance of Jesus as Redeemer. The older preachers, it is true, taught that Christ died for sins, . . . but they confined themselves to preaching judgment near at hand, and the return of Jesus as Messianic judge. Paul, on the other hand, gave highest place to Christ crucified: having convinced his hearers of their sins, demonstrated in their ignorance of God and idolatry, he would appeal to their consciences and thence lead them to the cross of Christ, as the power and wisdom and love of God'.

His second approach Paton deduces from the speech Paul gave to the men of Athens,[22] when as well as his usual tenets of Christ the resurrected and the judge, he stresses their own religious experience of a God whom they do not know and the elements in their own history and philosophy which point to Him.

> 'Paul has laid down no more valuable principle than this, and none that is bearing more fruit in our time. It may fairly be said to be a condition of success in modern missions among the civilized peoples of the East, that missionaries shall begin with native ideas of God and lead thence to the true God whom they are groping after in ignorance. We must seize upon national thought and tradition and atmosphere, and develop these so that they blend with the Christian revelation. It will be a practical point to educate Indian and Chinese children in their own sacred books, and bid them dig deep in the lore of their national sages and seers. It is a thought

which should reduce us to deep humility, that the fullness of Christ is to be apprehended not by the Jew alone, nor by the Englishman nor by the American, but by the whole race of the sons of men. We need to be wary how we thrust upon our Eastern converts anything that is solely of ourselves and not of Christ, for it is their own Christ whom they must find'.

It would be valuable to know whether this was written before or after the papers of Commission IV of the World Missionary Conference were published, in which Farquhar's ideas of such an approach to the Hindu achieved a prominent place, though Paton expresses the thought more boldly than the Report of the Commission did. Eric Sharpe explains how Farquhar introduced what was a revolutionary idea into the commission, though similar views were expressed in some of the answers to the commission's questionnaire.[23] Farquhar subsequently toyed with idea of using readings from Hindu scriptures in place of the Old Testament, but eventually rejected the idea because he thought the milieu of Hindu culture was not sufficiently consistent with that of the New Testament and because the same quality of relationship between God and Israel was lacking in Hindu scriptures. However, both he and Paton clearly take the principle of maintaining research in the ancient cultures very seriously. There is no indication that Paton was yet aware of the deracinating effects of conversion to Christianity on Indians, or of the propaganda of the Congress party that to be a good Indian one should be a loyal Hindu.

The universal claim of Christ to all men is a recurring theme in Paton's writing until the time of his death and was one of the most important principles to him.

Paton argues that since Paul never worked miracles to stir people to faith, but because he had compassion on the suffering, so one can defend medical missions against claims that they are an unworthy attempt to trap the hapless sufferer into belief in Christ. Medical missions exemplify the spirit of him 'who went about doing good'.[24]

Paton then describes the care with which Paul built up the young churches, getting them to encourage and support one another. This is also a missionary method: the young church in itself, especially as converts often have to give up their entire family to be Christian. In the difficult question whether missionaries should press caste Hindus to be baptised at the cost of their losing caste, he calls on St. Paul's practice to support the view that the primary work is not baptism but the pioneer work of evangelism, to arouse people from their sinful state. Baptism is a further stage when the convert realises the responsibility involved. Similarly baptism is not to be pressed on the caste Hindu, but is a privilege to which he might aspire if found worthy. In later life, when Paton was much exercised by the problem of providing adequate pastoral care and education for the hastily baptised members of the 'mass movements' he modified this view, which is typical of the practice of Presbyterian, Baptist and Lutheran missions.[25] In 'Alexander Duff', he stresses Duff's pioneer work in converting high caste Indians, who were almost the first in North India to become Christians, but sympathises with the Hindu protests that Christianity was breaking up families.[26] However, Paton denies that Paul sought to lighten the burden and whittle away the precepts unnecessarily. Paton uses the part Paul played in the controversy at Antioch over the question of Jews and Gentiles sharing the common meal to demonstrate that however easy the approach to Christianity may be made, the essential principles remain, for caste may not be tolerated in the Church.

Paton asserts that Paul had no conscious 'missionary method' or policy which he was following, because all was swallowed up in his desire to preach Christ crucified. The methods have to be forgotten in order to be used:

> 'Let us look round upon the religious world today. We see and hear of countless schemes, policies, conferences about missions and missionary methods, the social problem, the supply of men for the ministry. We live in an age when in a pre-eminent degree method has been carried into the sphere of religious activity. Are we strong enough to forget these methods? There is much idle talk about the number of missionaries who would be required to evangelize China in a given space of time . . . and even stopping short of such vulgar irreverent things, have not all of us fallen into the temptation of seeing how much we can do by our skilful free thought and management in God's cause? Not by might nor by power, but by my Spirit saith the Lord God. Let Paul teach us to forget everything but Christ. True we must lose sight of it in the magnitude of the spirit which is our real strength and the exceeding brightness of the vision which is before us'.

Paul's real missionary method was his faith, using the 'unbounded power of God'. 'Today, in a world of unparalleled opportunity, when ways open out before us on every hand, we are called to see the vision and believe that the miracle will come to pass'. Paton's firm belief is that with God nothing is impossible. His sentiments on the expendable nature of missionary organization echo a refrain in the writing of Roland Allen, who even wrote a book: 'Missionary Methods: St. Paul's or Ours' along the same lines, although there is no evidence to link him and Paton in any way.[27] In spite of the fact that Paton spent most of his working life in missionary administration, there is no reason to believe that he ever ceased to consider missionary methods to be only of relative significance before the all-consuming power of faith in the Gospel.

It is interesting that c1911, Paton was so critical of the excesses Mott had encouraged concerning the plans for 'The evangelisation of the world in this generation'. To Paton, human calculations are almost blasphemy, and have no relevance to the fact that God has chosen to wait for men and to inaugurate the kingdom in his own time by his own power alone.

One indication of the way in which Paton's thought evolved is the development in his ideas on the value of other religions. This was a subject of much controversy in missionary circles where the fear of syncretism was always lying under the surface of any debate, and it is important to appreciate Paton's position in view of the way the debate dominated the I.M.C. meeting at Jerusalem in 1928.[28] In his preface to 'Jesus Christ and the World's Religions', Paton stated his determination to take other religions at their best rather than in the instances where they had deteriorated into superstition and depravity, but his theme is the lack in other religions, their gaps in theology and ethics and the way in which Christ fulfils all. So, for example, he seeks to find good in some of the primitive taboos which could protect their users from stronger neighbours, or in the system of caste for giving the caste member security and assured social status, even if the misery of the millions of outcastes makes the abolition of caste essential. (In fact across the span of these books under review, Paton's evaluation of caste grows progressively more positive.) In the case of Islam he follows Temple Gairdner in describing the strong reality of the Islamic brotherhood as a rebuke to Christians for tolerating racial discrimination.[29] Curiously, though, he nowhere acknowledges Gairdner's work. Inevitably he finds an inner contradiction, a failure to encompass human existence, a negativeness or an emotional lack in other religions which shows that the Christian message, Jesus Christ himself, is the sole means by which the sinner can be forgiven, the soul assuaged and the intellect satisfied. Paton's position is logical given the centrality and uncompromising nature of the Gospel to him, but it is questionable how much impact this method of diagnosing the problems which the patient has with his health and then prescribing a cure for them would have on the 'patient' himself.

Paton describes the rise of Islam as a corrective to the loss of certain truths which had become overlaid by theological discussion and controversy with heretics in the North African church in the seventh century. It is typical of his method that he praises the early life of Mohammed and then criticized him for his polygamous marriages in later life. He detects a 'curious lack of moral definition in the Muslim idea of God'. There is a law governing outward acts, but if a good Muslim believes himself in need of forgiveness, forgiveness from Allah is a matter of mood. It is the duty of men to submit to the will of Allah without really knowing what he submits himself to.[30] In contrast to this the Christian missionary must demonstrate the love of God by practical acts of love in providing hospitals and schools, and by empha-sising the character of Christ. He repeats Gairdner's assertion that Christian apologetic must face up to the theological difficulties for Muslims in the doctrine of the Trinity and so on. The limitations of his view of Islam are obvious, for example, in describing Islamic mysticism.

Paton confesses to awe in the face of the piety of so many myriads of people in India. His attitude is a paraphrase of Jesus' demand that the righteousness of his followers must exceed that of the scribes and the pharisees.[31] In discussing caste he condemns the effect it has on individual initiative while failing to realise that it is possible for a whole caste to take action and change their status by more rigid observance of the cultic laws. He is unaware of the provision for intermarriage between certain sub-castes and his analysis on the question of the sacredness of the cow is not only wrong, it is not even common sense.[32] He tries to give a picture of all the different shades of worship which Hinduism has absorbed into itself, but does not discuss the important position of holy men, whether as teachers or ascetics. It is characteristic of Paton's happy outlook on life that he castigates the Hindu view of life as an illusion to be escaped from and the Hindu concept of karma, and of God as too impersonal. The figure of the suffering servant has a strong hold on the Hindu imagination (a point Stanley Jones used to dwell on in the 1920s),[33] but Paton rightly detects that the principal stumbling block is that Jesus is not just another teacher nor another saviour or incarnation of godhead, but that there is no other name by which one may be saved, and that the Hindu finds these exclusive claims intolerable. Paton quotes Ram Mohun Roy's approval of Christian ethics,[34] saying that the problem with Hinduism is that there is no concept of sin and the need for forgiveness, only of offences against the ritual laws.

Paton's main source of his description of Hinduism was J.N. Farquhar's 'Crown of Hinduism' which is analysed and discussed in Eric Sharpe's dissertation 'Not to destroy, but to fulfil'.[35] It was considered somewhat avant garde when it appeared in 1915, but it became a standard work, whose basic premises about the positive value of Hinduism as a *preparatio evangelica* were accepted by the majority of Anglo-Saxon missionaries until the Second World War, although it can be argued that A.G. Hogg of the Madras Christian College had demolished Farquhar's arguments intellectually in his writings. Compared with two other books propagated by the S.C.M. in 1910, S.K. Datta's 'Desire of India', and Godfrey Phillips' 'The Outcastes' Hope', Hinduism is much more favourably assessed by Farquhar and Paton. It should be remembered that at the time of writing Paton had not been to India. In 1917, his letters to his wife show that he was fascinated and appalled by his visits to Hindu temples. A remark in 'Alexander Duff' is significant: 'He (Duff) is not the only man in whom these huge shrines, memorials as they are of the religious quest of mankind, have aroused mingled horror and loathing'.[36]

Grace Paton once wrote to her mother saying that they never passed by the local shrine across the road in Calcutta without sensing an evil presence there. Therefore in India Paton was forced to modify his theological position in the light of his experience of Hinduism. There is no denying that both Paton and Farquhar considered that the force of Hinduism was spent, as all the traditional religions were bound to decay, though he criticised Duff's conclusion that modern science and philosophy, which were undermining Hinduism among the educated classes in India would themselves act as a preparatio evangelica by teaching rational thought.[37] Instead he saw that the void created by these forces might be unsatisfactorily filled by humanism, theism, or excessive patriotism. However, as we have seen, he also espoused the Mott doctrine of unparalleled opportunity in the Far East with the expansion of western university education there.[38] It was not until Paton faced the intellectual challenge of the nihilist ideology of national socialism c1935 that he came to agree with Kraemer that traditional Christian religion would also perish, but that nothing could quench the Christian message or destroy the claims of Christ. For this reason he never claimed that the Allies were defending Christianity in the second World War, for in the event of a Nazi victory Christ would go underground, but the ideal of a Christian civilization would be lost.

The results of Paton's search for the spiritual values in other religions in 'Jesus Christ and the World's Religions' are uneven. The range is from his sympathy with Buddhism, which is so profound that it is clear that if he were not a Christian, he would be a Buddhist, and can be attributed in part to the fact that he was writing in 1916, when his pacifist convictions were under attack, to his condemnation of the religions of Japan:

> 'Religiously, Christianity has everything to give Japan. The Japanese religions have failed to make God known to men. Shinto with its combinations of nature worship and religious patriotism has never given men a worthy revelation of the Divine, and the average Buddhist knows more of superstition and the hope of a material paradise than he does of God. There is a popular saying in Japan 'one inch and all is dark' indicating the dim twilight in which Japanese religion moves. That sure hold upon God which enables a man to tread his way through the perils of life unafraid and to maintain a steady trust in the love and power of an unseen Father, has never come to Japan'.[39]

One hopes that Japan's position as Britain's ally in the first World War was immaterial to Paton when he wrote that although the Japanese reverence for the Emperor was very dangerous, and constituted the greatest obstacle to Christianity in Japan, nevertheless Christianity could purify this patriotism and place it in its proper context, that of the Kingdom of God. In his subsequent writings, Paton was very much more critical of Japanese patriotism, but this will be discussed in Chapter VI in the context of the gradual 'politicisation' of his appreciation of the significance of oriental religions.[40]

Paton tended to find direct connections with Christian teaching in other religions, such as Nestorian Christian influence in the case of Japan, and so on. He drew parallels with Buddhist ideas on the saving intercession of the boddhisattva, which modern scholarship in comparative religions has, Professor Margull says, shown to be untenable.[41] In this Paton was merely following his contemporaries, and since he had so little opportunity to read the original texts, or do his own research, it is not surprising that he was so dependent on the findings of European scholars. Actual acquaintance with Buddhism of the southern school caused Paton to revise his favourable estimate of it, as he wrote to his wife in 1918:

> 'I have no use for Buddhism in practice. As in India, religion is a community affair. The national movement is galvanising Buddhism with a kind of life . . . But it hasn't got the necessary religious guts. It is fatalistic and anti-Western'.[42]

Paton's appreciation of non-Christian religions in 1916 rested on his admiration for the human endeavour and the deep sincerity which their adherents bring to them, and not on any approbation of their theological or ethical merits, except that he acknowledges that at the time of their creation, they were an advance on contemporary religious standards.

> 'No-one can follow even so cursory a sketch of the great non-Christian religions as that which we have concluded, without being touched by the splendour and the pathos of man's age-long search for God. Whether one thinks of the great souls in whom the divine flame has burned most brightly; or of the innumerable multitudes who have lifted their eyes to the heavens and believed after some manner in a God; one cannot resist the impression that man's nature longs for the Divine and will never cease from the quest until it is satisfied . . .
> But when we have made this frank acknowledgement, does it not remain true that these religions have all failed? What kind of God have they given men in the end? . . . It is a picture of broken lights; nowhere does there shine out the clear radiance of a perfect faith. God has not left Himself without witness, but in His real nature He has never been revealed'.[43]

It is, of course, open to question whether Paton's search for the values in other religions sprang more from his desire to be fair to his fellow-men than from any theological convictions about the extent to which God has revealed himself to men of other faiths. Although he nowhere states the criteria which he is using in his search, it becomes clear from his exposition of the Christian message in the closing pages of 'Jesus Christ and the World's Religions' what these criteria are. He begins by making the contentious statement that no other religion except Christianity has made steady regular advances to draw in all classes and races of people; only Christianity can claim to be a faith for all mankind. No other faith contains such an explicit and concrete revelation of God as there is in Jesus Christ. Anticipating the I.M.C. meeting at Jerusalem he writes that the Christian message is Jesus Christ, who is rooted in historical reality, not myth. The moral standards which he taught have not been equalled in any other teaching, nor the costly means by which God forgives men and reconciles him to himself. Paton was a man for whom the pursuit of righteousness was fundamental, combined with the demand he made for social justice. His reaction was similar to Queen Victoria's,[44] and inevitably a religion was inadequate in his eyes if it did not teach a sense of moral responsibility beyond the reaches of one's friends and family. A religion must be capable of bringing new life to man. In his opinion, only in Christian faith is death completely vanquished. Only Christianity is simple and straightforward in its fundamental attitude towards God.

In his writings Paton gradually devotes more and more space to the question of human rights, using the status of women as a criterion by which to judge other religions. He does acknowledge improvements in China and is sentimental about the Hindu ideal of the housewife and mother, but he considers that in spite of this ideal in Hinduism, and especially in Islam, women are treated as sex objects with consequent damage to themselves and the nation. In view of the complete revolution in Paton's attitudes to women described in the first chapter of this book, it is interesting that he should attach so much importance to the question of women's rights.

The question of criteria must have become clearer to Paton after he wrote 'Jesus Christ and the World's Religions' because he changed the format of his approach to the subject in his later books. From a geographical description of the religions of various lands, he adopted a thematic approach. He admitted that the weakness of this latter approach was that then only Christianity was treated as an organic whole, and he also has difficulty dealing with the founders of the great religions. However, it did make it easier to dispel the 'guidebook to interesting religions overseas' impression that can so easily creep into books using the format of 'Jesus Christ and the World's Religions'. It makes it more difficult to discern whether his attitude to the value of other religions had changed. The assumption which he made in these later books is that there are 'gut questions' of men everywhere, with which they wrestle, and that the theologies of the different world faiths are constructed in order to answer particular expressions of these questions, for example that of suffering in Buddhism. Paton's approach reveals the questions which have caused him to wrestle until he found the most satisfying answers in the knowledge of the love of God in Jesus Christ, but it does not solve the problem that men of other religions may not be concerned about these questions which Christianity answers at all.

Paton's first question is that of who man is, and the assessment of man in relation to God in the main religions. For him, no religion is adequate which, like Hinduism, denigrates human personality and which cannot sustain it in tribulation. A religion in which man is described as naturally good, whose moral acts are simply those of maintaining the right relationships in society (the classical idea of 'pietas' is what he means) is inadequate for him. Similarly he finds Islam as much lacking in the moral imperative as Confucianism, because while absolute submission is required from man, there is no comparable sense of the righteousness of God, to that in the Judaeo - Christian tradition. According to Paton there is no unselfish morality in Hinduism nor in most of the Buddhist tradition either, because any virtuous act is a means of improving one's own fate, not the other person's. Buddhism inculcates admirable qualities of gentleness and compassion, and attempts to solve the terrible problem of man's suffering by preaching the way of ending desire, the cause of all misery. The deficiency, Paton declared was to be found in the complaint a Singhalese made to him, saying that there was no provision for the salvation of the lay person. Only through the religious celibate life could one achieve perfection (which naturally did not appeal to Paton). Paton supports the scholars who consider Buddhism and Confucianism as being in their pure form, logically at least, atheist or agnostic, and while he admires the honesty of this position, it is not sufficient for him. His conclusion is that not only must the human personality find sufficient expression in religion, but it is necessary to find personality in God as well, or the whole attempt to find an underlying unity in the world is nonsense. A personal God must be both immanent and transcendent, because men turn away from a God who is depicted exclusively in one of these concepts. God has to be both in the world as its life and beyond it as its maker and judge.[45]

A thread running throughout Paton's books, to which every discussion on the relationship of God and man returns, is the radical nature of sin which stands between God and man. Paton is not interested in speculating on how this situation arose, simply saying that it is the experience of the saints that confronted with God's righteousness, they are conscious only of their unworthiness. Although he does not say as much, from what has been written in the first chapter of this book about Paton's conversion, it will be seen that one may reasonably infer that this was also Paton's own experience.

The traces of Victorian confidence in the stability of the world, which may be detected in odd phrases in 'Jesus Christ and the World's Religions', are absent from his later books; instead he diagnoses in the climate of the 1920s a great search for the power to renew the emerging nations: 'to give India moral biceps' as he describes it.[46] Indeed in all three books (that is, excluding 'Alexander Duff') there is much emphasis on the tensions between the upholders of the traditional forms of the world religions and the younger generation with their vigorous nationalism and their increasing knowledge of western education. However, in 'A Faith for the World' (1929), he shows equal concern about the effect of confused sex ethics in the west, over which the Church itself is divided, and the doctrines of economic determinism. In a thinly veiled defence of William Temple, he rebukes the attitude which would keep religion 'a poor tame thing' and would object to a bishop speaking out on a point of foreign policy which had already occurred to most people anyway.[47] Christians need to bestir themselves because to many Christianity seems no better than the crumbling faiths of the East. This leads him, in 'A Faith for the World', into a critical discussion of the divine community and the way in which it is only partially reflected in the contemporary church, particularly with reference to the persistence of racial discrimination in the church. His approach is similar in 'The Faiths of Mankind', where the vital questions are again those of man and his world, his relationship to God, sin, suffering and salvation, and the 'good life', by which he means the relations of man in society and the need for criteria by which to judge society. The great weakness of his long exposition of the Christian view of sin is that he does not relate it sufficiently to the problem of evil, which he dismissed in a brief paragraph. Since the problem of evil is a major stumbling block for Christians and non-Christians alike, this is a very serious omission. There are two possible reasons why he did this, either that it was no problem for him, or that he found it a problem, but wanted to avoid a semi-philosophical discussion. The omission reinforces the argument that he did not succeed in asking the right questions in relation to non-Christian religions and not always the right questions in relation to the Christian faith.

What is significant in this summary of his argument is that the search for spiritual values in other religions has caused him now to turn to the most obvious manifestation of the Christian presence, the Church, where the non-Christian would expect to find the spiritual wealth of Christianity displayed. It should be remembered that these criticisms of the Church were made at a time when, as secretary of the I.M.C., he was presiding over the beginning of the transition from a situation where missions and churches co-existed to the concept and practice of the mission of the church.[48]

It is evident, therefore, that the search for appreciation and understanding of other religions has thrown Paton back on the value of the Christian religion, not in a defensive way, but as the more constructive method of evangelism. Farquhar's writings mark a change from the policy of missionaries in India of condemning the worst aspects of Hinduism (which was much resented) to a tendency to comment sympathetically on the good aspects of Hinduism, but to argue that an incomplete, partial perception of the truth should give way to the fullness which Christ represents.[49] Paton's habit of quoting Hindu hymns and Chinese poetry as being appropriate to the worship of God in 'Jesus Christ and the World's Religions' was not original, nor was his belief that the only thing lacking in the beautiful Northern Buddhist myths of saviours suffering in order that mankind might be released from suffering, is an historical foundation. However, in line with the developments at the Jerusalem meeting, which are reflected in some of Farquhar's writings, was the idea of concentrating on the Christian message, preferably in as much of a non-western garb as possible. The very change in scheme of Paton's work was bound to emphasise the differences rather than the continuation between the Christian faith and the non-Christian religions, but it should be noted that the parallel with the working of the Jerusalem meeting cannot be too closely drawn because within the section on 'The Christian Message' there were sub-sections on the Christian approach to the various religions, with an end product which is very similar to the conclusions of 'Jesus Christ and the World's Religions'. (Also, Paton prefaced 'A Faith for the World' with the remark that although the book owed everything to the Jerusalem meeting it was a commentary on the general principles behind the Jerusalem findings rather than a report.)

When he came to write 'The Faiths of Mankind' in 1932, Paton confessed that the book was wrongly named, because it was the Christian faith which he was concerned with. At the end of this book he records that there is considerable justification for the view of Barth and his disciples that one should not talk of non-Christian religions at all, because they are in a totally different category from the Christian faith. Yet this did not cause Paton to revise his view that if we believe that God made man in His own image, then it is natural that he should, through his ceaseless creativity, using a long line of seers and prophets, prepare the way for the Gospel in the hearts of men.

> 'To say that men are rebels against God is not to say the whole; there is that in their hearts that longs for the Father. True, the gift of God in Christ is always far more than the expectation of man, Christ is more than the fulfilment of a human quest, but He is that fulfilment, and believing this we need not anxiously look for traces of early Christian influences where we find some faith in the hearts of men which seems almost to suggest our own'.[50]

It follows from this, he writes, that the Christian task is not to press the claims of a rival religion against those of others, and in fact Hindus and Muslims, particularly in India where the communal question is involved, will not be content to exchange one religion for another.[51] Christianity is not a religion in the sense that they formerly understand it at all. 'On God's side it is the revelation of Himself in the sublime act which is the giving of Himself by Christ: on man's side it is the humble acceptance of forgiveness and sonship in a fellowship of those who through Jesus believe in God'.

Whereas the S.V.M.U. used to publish the needs of those who were without Christ as a motivating power for mission, for Paton in this book it is faith in the loving purpose of God which is the decisive factor in inspiring mission. Love and gratitude to God through Jesus Christ are at the root of Paton's motivation here, rather than the strict command to obey his will, which was often the note in S.V.M.U. addresses. As before, the emphasis is on the divine intention rather than any responsibility an individual might feel for the heathen who were perishing.[52] It is important to note that whatever the shortcomings which Paton finds in the non-Christian religions, he never suggests that their adherents are more liable to divine judgment than Christians are. It is also striking that Paton's principal concern is with the state of men everywhere, whether they are enslaved by fear of the supernatural as in the animistic religions of Africa, or living in intolerable social conditions because a metaphysical system pronounces this as their lot under the laws of Karma, or their punishment for sins in a former existence, or treated as inferior in every way because they have the misfortune to be female. His severe judgments on the metaphysical systems of these religions are tempered always by his consideration of the human element. Yet it will not be knowledge of the need of others which will convince men of the demands of world mission, but faith in the loving purpose of God. One of the severest criticisms made of Kraemer was that he left too little place for human reason in his system.[53]

Paton prefaces 'The Faiths of Mankind' with a cautionary note:

> 'If we find, as we shall, that the best imaginings of man fall immeasurably short of His own gift, that will fill us, not with a sense of our superiority as Christians, but with a new sense of the majesty of the Gospel'.

As a postscript to this investigation of the value Paton placed on other religions, one must mention that he used the same tactics in dealing with the criticisms of religion brought by modern science. He praised some of the qualities which scientific research induces in the human character, but he subjects science to the same criticisms that, for example, it does not provide a common basis for life, but leads to an aristocracy of educated people. One will probably find the finest flower of civilization among scientists, but their values will not support everyone. Mankind is impatient of the temporal as the final sphere about which one can have any certainty. In Paton's view, a scientific explanation of the world is no substitute for a spiritual one. This does not mean that Christians will not have to take the challenge of science very seriously, and correct the abuses in the organised Church it reveals.

Two factors combined to ensure that Paton wrote nothing further on the subject of non-Christian religions after 1932: his increasing pre-occupation with the political significance of religions such as Islam and Shinto and their effect on world events and universal human rights, and the development of his ideas on the Christian Church as something much more than a means of evangelism. There is also the inescapable fact, as far as I can discover from interviewing Miss Sinclair and the Paton family, that Paton only wrote books when asked to do so by the S.C.M., the U.C.M.E., or the Religious Book Club, and not because he was the victim of a sudden inspiration or a burning passion to express something. Consequently, the reason why there is no sequel to 'The Faiths of Mankind' may simply be that no-one wanted him to write such a book. In November 1943 Nicol MacNicol wrote to Grace Paton saying that for her husband's sake and for C.F. Andrews' sake, he had agreed to complete the biography of C.F. Andrews which Paton was writing at the time of his death. Paton was much closer to C.F. Andrews than he himself was, so he would like to see the material which Paton had collected. Unfortunately Mrs. Paton must have told MacNicol that he could keep Paton's notes or manuscript, because no trace of it survives in the family papers, but had Paton written this biography, he would not have been able to avoid discussing Andrews' sympathy with Hinduism.[54] It is impossible to detect Paton's work in MacNicol's book.

The transition is marked in a pamphlet which Paton wrote for the C.B.M.S. in 1933 or 1934 entitled 'The New Era in Missionary Work: the Next Steps' which is a consideration of the theological issues raised by the contemporary economic crisis. However, there is one passage under the heading 'Evangelism' which is very revealing.

> 'The challenge to the missionary's own Christian thought and life comes from two directions; he shares to some extent in that general blurring of the outlines of the redemptive message by the secular and humanist temper of the time, and he is likely, especially if he is of the sensitive and sympathetic type of which the best missionaries are made, to take something of the colour of the religion around him, at least in its higher manifestations. Only the people who sit at home can talk big and bold about the evils of 'syncretism'; the more intimately a man tries to understand the minds of those with whom he is dealing, the more certainly he will risk agreeing with them! We must find ways of helping missionaries far more effectively than we now do to penetrate even more deeply into the meaning of the Christian Gospel, and into the true understanding of the world crisis, social and intellectual, for which that Gospel is the divine answer. There is need that the best work now done by the relatively few leading minds should be mediated to the missionaries and that they should be helped . . . to avail themselves of special studies . . . '.[55]

Among Paton's papers at the time of his death was also an outline for a book on missionary policy which is as radical a departure from his earlier work as the sketch which Bonhoeffer left behind is from his. Economic planning, a new system of ethics for secular world, and the need for a means of translating ideas on the new post-war order into evangelism, seem to be his principal concerns. There is absolutely no mention of non-Christian religions, only of the effect of defeat on the young people in Germany and Japan. For Paton the Church must now address the secular world, not men of other religions.[56]

One would be able to deduce from Paton's writings the influence which Farquhar had on him, even if he had not written to his wife in October 1917 that he and Farquhar were the only missionaries travelling first class to India, and that he is consequently seeing a great deal of him and that he is gaining a great affection for him.[57] With Kraemer the reverse is true. In the absence of any published work of Paton's reflecting Kraemer's theology, one is dependent on the evidence in the correspondence between Paton and Kraemer and eye-witness recollections, such as the Bishop of Worcester's recollection of seeing Paton having a terrific argument with one of Kraemer's critics, Kagawa of Japan, hotly defending Kraemer's book to him. Reading the correspondence, it is clear that not only was there a deep friendship between the two men, but a very considerable degree of theological sympathy.[58]

Hendrik Kraemer was Paton's antithesis. He was a solitary individual who could not accommodate himself to other people's views very easily, and who had no 'school' as Barth had, even though he became Professor of Mission at the University of Leiden. He had a brilliant, original mind, and was capable of very intense and passionate thought, as Dr. Visser't Hooft accurately described it, tempered by what Paton felt to be his own greatest lack, years of experience as a missionary and an apologist in the Dutch East Indies. His wise counsels were important in the Javanese and Balinese field, both in practical evangelism and in the study of the Islamic and primitive beliefs of these areas. He had a very difficult life, attended by several nervous breakdowns, the worst being in 1932. One can see how suffering has shaped his work (and may have prepared him for his courageous resistance to national socialism in Holland). He always lived on the brink of a crisis under terrific strain, so could never be detached and relaxed in what he did. Yet his letters breathe a gentle spirit of Christian charity and charm and there is no mistaking the warmth of his friendship with Paton. An excellent biography of him has been written by Dr Van Leeuwen, which has been translated into German. Paton probably met him originally at the special meeting for Continental delegates held in Cairo before the I.M.C. meeting at Jerusalem in 1928. In the following years Kraemer produced a number of papers for the I.M.C., chiefly on the younger church in relation to its environment, before he was commissioned at the I.M.C. meeting at Northfield in July 1936 to write a book on the witness of the Church in relation to the non-Christian religions. Paton's role in encouraging Kraemer to write this book, 'The Christian Message in a Non-Christian World', is described in the sixth chapter of this book, as well as the repercussions in I.M.C. circles. The monumental nature of Kraemer's theology is such that it is easier to state his entire case and then compare it with Paton's theology rather than take it point by point.

Kraemer's central and most controversial concept is that of 'biblical realism', a phrase he uses to express the idea that the Bible is a human, historical record of God's self-disclosing revelation in Jesus Christ and His sovereign acts to bring salvation to His people. (His description of God at work in history is close to the modern understanding of 'heilsgeschichte', and is an improvement on Barth and Bultmann's tendency, whether consciously or unconsciously, to denigrate history.) The Bible is not primarily a record of religious experience and ideas, nor an account of 'the pilgrimage of the human soul towards God'. He asserts that the only way to maintain Christian revelation as the one way of truth is to isolate the Gospel message from the whole range of human life so that it forms a radical discontinuity with what has gone before. Christ does not perfect what has gone before, and although he may fulfil man's longings, he stands in opposition to all that reason or religion may provide. It is, therefore, not a question of finding the 'religious values' in other faiths, as was advocated at the Jerusalem meeting, because Christ is the crisis of all religions, even the defective historical Christianity. This means that there is no possibility of natural religion, for although men may live lives acceptable to God, they do so not as a result of anything good in their religion, but as a result of God's grace, which cannot be confined to any historical phenomenon. There can be no standard apart from the Christian revelation, but the difficulty is that man has an imperfect understanding of it. Kraemer draws a sharp distinction between the eternally true Christian revelation and historical Christianity, as he does between the idea of the Church and its actuality. Through modern scholarship we now have a great deal of information about other religions, but we cannot be 'objective' about them because that would imply that there was another ultimate standard besides Christ. The Christian attitude should be one of scrupulous honesty and diligence to the facts of the Christian revelation and the religions of mankind so that one must try sincerely to understand the other's viewpoint. Any sort of superiority on the side of the Christian is intolerable. The missionary should be marked by his intellectual integrity, his ruthless self-criticism of his own weak faith and his humility in approaching other religions. Evangelism is the task of the Church and the newly-converted, not the Western expert, though the humble individual will always be a useful servant.[59]

The scheme of Kraemer's work is interesting, as compared with that already discussed in Paton's books. He begins with the world crisis in east and west, non-Christian religions and the Church; then states his understanding of the Christian message as revelation and as practised in the Christian ethic; he examines the attitudes to non-Christian religions among contemporary theologians, and the problem of natural theology, which he considers both Barth and Brunner have approached in the wrong way, the justified search for points of contact with other religions, though ultimately the only point of contact is the personality of the missionary himself; and then he discusses the non-Christian religions themselves. A substantial amount of the book is devoted to the missionary approach to the non-Christian religions in terms of the indigenisation of the Christian Church, the extent to which it should adapt sociologically to the people around, with the adoption of specifically national institutions, such as the ashram in India, and the worship, witness and ministry of the Church.

Kraemer's analysis of the problem of the human aspirations in a non-Christian religion, the beautiful and good spiritual creativity outside the Christian revelation, and the known discontinuity of the Christian revelation form part of the underlying assumptions of Paton's later books. His emphasis on the human dignity of the worshipper, for example, is fully justified by Kraemer. Kraemer is even more severe than he is against any suggestion of superiority or racism on the part of the missionary; there is an obvious parallel between the emphasis the ex-secretary of the S.V.M.U. places on the personality of the missionary, and what Kraemer writes about the importance of the missionary's personality. (Kraemer was very profoundly influenced by Mott when he was a student.) Kraemer's evaluation of the significance of the Bible was consonant with what Paton believed, stated in a more sophisticated way. In fact, the discussion of Paton's criteria in searching for spiritual values in other religions shows that Paton was unconsciously doing what Kraemer describes as the abandonment of 'impartiality' and the use of the revelation in Christ as the ultimate standard. Paton found in Christ a full appreciation of man's humanity, the condemnation of racism and the subjection of women, a means of knowing a personal, loving God, the father of Jesus Christ a promise of new life and so on, and

98

then searched for these things in other religions. Kraemer manages what Paton fails to perceive is necessary; a proper justification of this method. By 1930 approximately, Paton had abandoned the search for 'spiritual values' and so would presumably have agreed with Kraemer's condemnation of this method. Paton did not possess the scholarship which Kraemer had to analyse other religions for himself, and therefore fell into the traps his contemporaries were ensnared in. However, when he had some personal experience of non-Christian religions, his attitude became less sympathetic, as has been shown, and closer to Kraemer's position. Like Kraemer, he freely recognises the human aspirations which Christ satisfies, which were expressed in the convert's former religion, but he denies that Christ actually fulfils the metaphysical structure itself. Since Paton is writing a popular apologia for mission he does not articulate this as clearly, or as fully, as Kraemer. In his later writings Paton also separates the Christian Gospel from historical Christianity, which he criticizes severely, and wishes to reform. In this he stands alongside Kraemer. In fact, there is much to be said for the argument that Kraemer's work takes to their logical conclusion a set of ideas which Paton also shared.

Paton's proximity to Barth will be discussed later in this book. It is not a mere coincidence of ideas that Barth and Paton produced the same theological and political onslaught on national socialism in the Christian Newsletter series of books in 1940. Kraemer provides a link between the two. Neither Paton nor Kraemer could be described as Barthian, but in the division between 'liberal theology' and the followers of Barth, they were definitely on his side of the fence. Kraemer in fact went through a similar experience to Bonhoeffer and Brunner to achieve his independence of Barth, and his criticisms of Barth were very much resented by Barthians. The major difference between Kraemer and Paton on the one hand, and Barth on the other, is that the former were always primarily concerned with evangelism.[60]

What can one say about the presentation of the Christian Message which is always the climax of Paton's books? It was always colossally sincere, but never original. It possesses a certain credal character in its simplicity and catholicity. One could infer much about his character from the priority which he gives to the idea of atonement and forgiveness, to reconciliation of man with God and to the ethical nature of the Christian faith, but everything is predictable from a man who had undergone a conversion experience in the days of the evangelical revival of 1904/5. It would not be very fair to judge Paton's theology by such brief statements from one who never claimed to be a systematic theologian. However, one such statement on the means of presenting the Gospel to the India, written as a discussion paper in 1919, is appended to this book.

The final question is whether Paton's books achieved their purpose. It is the consensus of all the people whom I have interviewed that they served their purpose, though only 'Jesus Christ and the World's Religions' was a best seller, with sales of more than 50,000. They were an effective apologetic for missions to the half-Christian students, vaguely fascinated by the mystery of the orient, and they provided useful ammunition for S.V.M.U. members trying to convert others, and faced with the argument that the existence of other religions invalidated Christianity's claim to be a universal religion — the sort of half-baked tolerance very prevalent in England. Paton's uncompromising stand was probably more acceptable in the inter-war period than it would be now because youth was then searching for absolutes in fascism, socialism and religion, and was then sufficiently idealistic to die for these absolutes in the Spanish civil war. Taken as examples of a particular genre in a particular era, Paton's books on other religions were better than most and at least they helped to pay the housekeeping bills.[61]

Chapter V

'My Beloved India!': Paton's Work in India, 1921-43

A boycott of all civic functions organised in the Prince of Wales' honour during his visit to India, civil disobedience and riots, and massive government repression with the outlawing of the 'Khalifat volunteers',[1] greeted the arrival of the Paton family in India at the end of October 1921. Race hatred was intense, inflamed by the massacre of 379 Indian demonstrators at Amritsar in April 1919 by General Dyer's troops and by the subsequent travesty of justice when Dyer was not condemned by the Commission of Inquiry, but was given £26,000 raised by public subscription and had his actions approved by vote in the House of Lords.[2] The Montagu-Chelmsford reforms of 1918 were proving almost impossible to implement because of the lack of co-operation between the British and Indians. Even in the churches tension was running high.

In this atmosphere Paton began working for the national Y.M.C.A. of India, arguing the case for independence for India in his letters home and mediating between the Y.M.C.A. supporters and the disapproving officials in the Indian army and the Home Department of the colonial government.[3] Paton was continuing his work in India 1917-18, no longer as a visiting S.C.M. secretary, but on a permanent basis, since he did not anticipate that it would prove to be a preface to his work for the National Missionary Council of India. Since this episode in his life was so brief and since it is fully discussed in the Sinclair biography, Paton's work for the Y.M.C.A. is not analysed in this chapter although two points are worthy of note. Firstly, Paton's mandate to develop the Y.M.C.A. work among Indian students was given at a time of transition, when Indian higher education was being reformed radically. Previously organised on the 'external board system' in a way similar to the present University of London external examination system, it was being replaced by a unitary residential teaching type of university to which missionary colleges could be affiliated, but at the cost of following prescribed university syllabuses. Paton travelled India investigating the situation to see how the Y.M.C.A. could help students by providing hostels, halls, recreation centres and so on. He also observed what pressure the new system was putting on the missionary colleges, already in straitened financial circumstances without the burden of finding better qualified staff and new equipment. Secondly, in his letters home he comments on the good will shown to the Y.M.C.A. by Muslim and Hindu university staff and administrators who instructed him on how to extract government grants for the hostels. Paton was convinced that their cordiality was the result of their admiration for the ethical nature of Christianity and a tacit recognition that an equivalent moral influence would not be forthcoming from any other source.[4] It is significant that he could gain such sympathetic co-operation from highly educated Muslims and Hindus.[5]

Paton's relationship to India was a passionate one, his concern lasting until his death, since even in 1942 he was assisting the midwives of the Church of South India, and was playing a small but not insignificant part in the attempts to mediate between the British Government and the Congress party. All the best facets of his life and work can be seen in his involvement with India: his skill at supporting new, imaginative methods of evangelism, his diplomatic arts, his sensitivity on the racial question and sympathy with the longing for independence of a colonised people, and his ability to communicate ideas and set up the minimum of bureaucracy to execute them. However, in the compass of one chapter it is only possible to discuss the more outstanding features of Paton's work, and those which demonstrate the growth of ecumenical co-operation and new insights into the nature of mission. Thus Paton's championing of the then neglected medical missions, which led to the appointment of a medical missionary to the staff of the National Christian Council, and the vast amount of work he did for Christian literature in India can only be briefly mentioned. Many things, significant in themselves, but less important in the wider ecumenical context, are omitted altogether.[6]

Certain motifs or strands of thought are common to all Paton's work, making it a coherent whole. The most significant was his determination that responsibility for evangelism and worship, welfare and education in India should be transferred from mission structures controlled by mission boards overseas to the Indian church, whatever its weaknesses and shortcomings — what today might be called the decolonialization of the church. This process can most clearly be demonstrated by describing the work of the new National Christian Council, which replaced the former National Missionary Council. The radical revision of educational policy which he engendered through the Lindsay Commission was also directed to this end, since Christian education as a method of Christian mission was demonstrably a relative failure. Instead, Christian education came to be seen as the building up of the Church and the means of training a future generation of leaders. Paton found in India also the practical application of his belief that the Christian Gospel was bound to result in the social uplift of the people and the leavening of society, as in the gradual emancipation of Indian women, the literacy programmes and rural development. Paton's thought on social questions will be discussed in a later chapter.

A second theme is the concept of missionary freedom and freedom of worship. Paton's views changed a great deal over the years as a result of his experience in India and the Middle East, culminating in his confrontation with fascism. The most fundamental questions of the relationship of missions to a colonial government or a foreign power became in Paton's work in India a paradigm of the problem of Church/State relations which Paton and his friends had to face in so many different contexts.[7] Another recurring theme was the inter-cultural and inter-racial problem in which Paton's overwhelming personality was more of a problem than any prejudices he might have had. Transmitting the Gospel across racial and cultural barriers is a problem so relevant to our present society that Paton's experiences are discussed at some length. Finally there were the 'nuts and bolts' of ecumenical co-operation, the patient diplomacy to achieve a working partnership between the denominations, solve ancient controversies and unite the churches. Fortunately Paton's views were not so controversial, and although he did not live long enough to see the inauguration of the Church of South India, he could claim some substantial successes in the field of ecumenical co-operation.

The Secretary of the National Christian Council.

It must have seemed extraordinary by any standards that within three months of arriving in India Paton had been appointed the first full-time secretary of the National Christian Council of India, a new ecumenical project which would be the equivalent of the Conference of British Missionary Societies, but included a 50% membership of Indian Christians themselves. The National Missionary Council of India, Burma and Ceylon (N.M.C.) which it replaced, was born in 1912 as part of the continuing repercussions of the World Missionary Conference held in Edinburgh in 1910. John R. Mott's visit to India in 1912 was decisive, as Micklem remembers from seeing his feats of chairmanship there. The intermittent regional inter-denominational or confessional conference of the kind held since 1868 gave way to regular national conferences on a variety of subjects of mutual interest.[8] From 1919-21 a valuable survey on village education was compiled as a result of this co-operation but by 1922 it was apparent to many that the N.M.C.'s machinery was no longer adequate for tackling India's problems.

The proceedings of the first two days of the N.M.C.'s eighth meeting at Poona in January 1922 illustrate this point well, as J.H. Oldham commented:

'The Council on this occasion realized the futility of the whole pro-ceeding. Some of the keenest minds were alive to this before they came. It is rather surprising that the provincial councils and the National Missionary Council should have survived so long on their existing methods of work. Nothing else is possible without an executive force. We are not a day too soon in making a change. Without it there would have been a bad breakdown of missionary co-operation in India'.[9]

Oldham, who was present as a secretary of the I.M.C., had discovered that at the beginning of 1922 the N.M.C. had 18 sub-committees on various topics, such as education, women's work and so on; most of these could not meet until the evening of the council meeting, and consequently proposed meaningless and innocuous resolutions for adoption by the Council. Alternatively, a group who lived comparatively near each other would produce a report, only to have it rejected because it was only relevant to one particular set of conditions. For example, at Poona the report on higher education was laughed out of court because it was manifestly the work of four Madras missionaries.[10] One reason for reform of the N.M.C. was that the problems of communication in a such vast and diverse country as India were crippling research and discussion. Missionaries might enjoy holidays together in Assam and the other hill areas, but since Indian pastors and mission employees were not included in these arrangements (which they resented), there was no Indian participation in the missionary gatherings in the hills.[11] The N.M.C. was not doing enough to counter the isolation of missionaries. Hence Paton's extensive travels when he became secretary of the N.M.C. Secondly, as Paton commented, as far as research was concerned: 'The sending of questionnaires to busy missionaries only provokes an outburst of bad language, which is not good for the missionaries'.[12] This situation also precluded much preparation for conferences. Communications with the mission boards and the C.B.M.S. in London were no better, as the misunder-standings and muddle after the Poona conference showed.

The N.M.C. succeeded in embracing most Protestant missionaries, although women were unfairly excluded by the rules of membership[13] and it is clear that the N.M.C. never commanded much support from Indian Christians, even K.T. Paul being very critical. S.K. Datta wrote to Oldham in November 1920 complaining that the N.M.C. was a failure, cumbering the ground, because under its present devious secretary it was an instrument of reaction. The only hope, he said, was for a new secretary imbued with Oldham's spirit to come out straight from England.[14] Part of this antagonism sprang from the antipathy and suspicion of the Y.M.C.A. harboured by the more conservative missionaries, apparent when K.T. Paul and S.K. Datta were nominated for the new N.M.C. staff, described (to use the term anachronistically) as a 'sell out' to the Y.M.C.A. Indians.[15] The Y.M.C.A. was organised by Indian nationals themselves, which is significant not only because of Paton's Y.M.C.A. background. An additional advantage the Y.M.C.A. had was not being dependent on the brief hours that over-burdened missionaries could snatch from their work; it had a fulltime staff little older than the people they worked among. The natural social cohesion of students as a class meant that the Y.M.C.A. organisation could command a greater loyalty to its aims and ideals than the N.M.C. could. However, I do not think that the polarisation of educated 'Y.M.C.A. Christians' not belonging to any church and on the other hand, mission/local Church Christians, was ever a problem of the proportions it was in China.[16]

Oldham had, in his short time in India before the Poona conference, correctly divined the causes of disquiet among Indian Christians. Therefore he anticipated the Indian Christians' demand that there should not be a great strengthening of the N.M.C. organisation while it remained primarily a mission and not a church body.[17] In response to this, the Council changed its name to 'National Christian Council', and passed a resolution that in future at least one half of the members of all provincial Christian Councils and the N.M.C. itself should be Indians, directly appointed by the churches. Although it should be remembered that at this time reforms were being introduced so that secular legislative assemblies were required to have a larger proportion of Indian members,[18] this was a revolutionary step, the beginning of a transfer of power and responsibility from European and American missions to the churches in India. In the official minutes it was hedged about with a reassuring paragraph that: 'In no circumstances will the Council commit the churches or missions to any attitude or course of action without their consent'.[19] The churches and missions in India are to decide missionary policy in India and the N.M.C. will only act with their consent, keeping in mind the primary purpose of evangelism. A resolution was also adopted calling for an All-India conference of Indians and missionaries, a matter of great importance in Indian Christian opinion.[20]

A committee was appointed to work on the question of the representation of each sub-group, and the proportion of church to mission representatives in each case. Paton saw this as 'the mobilising of the whole of the Christian forces of India'.[21] Banninga wrote to Warnshuis that it was clear to the majority of those present that there had to be such a change because of leading Indian opinion, but that Anderson (the former secretary) seemed to him to have grave doubts about involving so many Indians. He described it as 'pathetic' to see some of the men who had been leaders go through agonies at seeing the whole atmosphere change. Like Paton, Banninga, of the American Mission at Madura, was experiencing his first N.M.C. meeting. Although there was such a hostile reaction from the home boards, it is clear that without this change the support of Indian Christians would never have been won.[22] As it was, K.T. Paul was not convinced of the sincerity of purpose of the council until the Poona resolutions were ratified at the meeting at Ranchi in January 1923.[23]

Although it would be dangerous to generalise about a 'generation gap' at the Poona conference, nevertheless, the age factor was of importance in reforming the N.M.C. structure and providing for better Indian representation. Controversy was caused by the proposal to create a five-man executive force and to invite specific people to fill these positions as they were established. Dr Banninga commented that if Oldham had not been at the Council, it would have chosen a completely different team, with long experience of India.[24] Fortunately the Metropolitan of India (Bishop of Calcutta) and the Bishop of Bombay backed his suggestions as to whom they should invite to fill the new executive positions. As might be expected, a strengthened central organization received more support from Anglicans accustomed to centralized structures of church government than from more 'congregational' churches. The bishops who supported the plan at Poona were also those who supported the consecration of Azariah of Dornakal, the first Indian Anglican bishop, in 1912. After initial strong objections, the Anglican Home Boards reverted to their custom of giving local bishops discretion in the handling of funds, and supported the scheme most consistently.

Oldham's strongest 'argument' was the guarantee he had extracted from the Canadian boards to pay for the scheme. Oldham wanted a concrete budget to present to the Canadian boards. One has only Oldham's testimony to the enthusiasm of the Canadians, but the Canadian missionary representative at Poona endorsed the scheme, although in 1924 the Canadian boards refused to contribute anything more substantial than their prayers. There were those at Poona who questioned the wisdom of relying on one region alone,[25] and this point was much debated at the Ranchi meeting the following year. The Anglicans declared that the scheme was worth trying anyway, even if it was necessary to start in a small way. In fact the N.M.C. did not find five salaries, as planned, but built up the organisation from a secretary loaned from the Y.M.C.A. (Paton).

This question of financial sources affected the discussion concerning the appointment of the first Indian secretary. The nomination of S.K. Datta is significant for showing the seriousness and openness of the whole debate. S.K. Datta had been reported as promulagating very radical criticisms of missions in Canada, which had caused great offence in missionary circles there.[26] It was therefore felt that his name would banish Canadian support for the scheme, but recognizing Datta's calibre, the N.M.C. decided nevertheless to approach him. Datta would have lent credibility to the N.M.C. as no-one else would have done, but he was doubtful if it was the right position for him. Instead he became private secretary to Lord Lytton, Governor of Bengal, and then a member of the national legislative assembly.

The other Indian nomination was not controversial. A.C. Mukerji of Benares, a layman and an adviser to the L.M.S., offered to give his two years' furlough to getting the scheme started. In the event his commitments to the L.M.S. prevented him actually working for the N.C.C. The N.C.C. had to wait until October 1924 before Miss Ethel Gordon of the United Free Church of Scotland, who was an expert on village work, could be released to fill one of the positions envisaged at Poona. J. McGee of the famous model village at Moga, also a Presbyterian, managed to do a great deal of the N.M.C.'s work on rural education in his spare time until she came, as this was one aspect of missions which Paton could not handle. Eventually a young and energetic Indian, P.O. Philip, who was a Syrian Orthodox, joined the team in 1926, the first of a succession of Indian secretaries.

Paton's presence at the Poona conference was marked by his being appointed minute secretary and by his contribution to a reduction in tension and formality by organizing a 'Presbyterians v The World' volleyball match. The conference then took on much of the atmosphere of a Swanwick summer conference. However, Paton was scarcely known except by a few influential leaders and Oldham himself.[27] His experience of India was very limited and his knowledge of missions mainly confined to what he had learnt as study secretary of the S.V.M.U. He had barely completed two months' work for the Y.M.C.A. when he began working out six months' notice, so it is hardly surprising that the official minute reads:

> 'The Council realises the great sacrifice that is demanded from the Y.M.C.A. if Dr S.K. Datta and Mr W. Paton are set free for this work, but it is in the interest of the Christian movement in India as a whole that they venture to ask the National Council of the Y.M.C.A. to make the contribution of those who through their special experience of inter-denominational and international work in the Y.M.C.A. are peculiarly fitted for the service they are desired to render'.[28]

It was, of course, true that very few administrators outside the S.C.M./- Y.M.C.A. had any experience of ecumenical work, which was why their secretaries were so much sought after. However, Paton made it quite clear to Oldham when his name was first suggested, that he had a moral obligation to work for the Y.M.C.A. which he could not lightly discharge. Mrs Paton felt very strongly that Paton was not treating the Y.M.C.A. at all fairly,[29] as well as harbouring deep distrust of Oldham's schemes. The fact that Paton wrote to Oldham in April 1922 saying that 'I have a great deal more confidence now in the practical ability of the whole scheme than I had', suggests that at one point he shared some of her doubts.[30] The Metropolitan and other senior churchmen put very great pressure on Paton to accept, and even wrote to Mrs Paton putting their case for the N.C.C., which alarmed Paton lest she should think that he had arranged this. It was not only K.T. Paul's advice which swayed him finally, but the entreaties of Mrs Anderson, anxious about her husband's continued breakdown in health. Anderson resigned immediately because of his ill health and his impending furlough, but the fact that he opposed the plans for the formation of the N.C.C. gave substance to the belief that he had resigned in protest, thereby causing a crisis in the C.B.M.S. because of Baptist agitation. When Maclennan reported the rumour to Paton in India, he tackled Anderson, who declared that it was a lie and wrote a letter home stating that he resigned for health reasons.[31] The letter was dated 5.4.22, by which time much damage had been done because of the impression given of a 'fait accompli', of decisions being inflicted on India by a small coterie without the consultation of the 'constituency'. In fact, Paton took over the secretaryship of the N.M.C., the new position not being created until it was ratified at the N.C.C. meeting in 1923.

Paton's first year was a difficult compromise between keeping the old machinery running until the changes could be ratified, without allowing his belief in the new scheme to commit him too far. The significance of this acceptance of the position lies in the fact that he was effectively turning from youth work to missionary administration though at 35 it would not have occurred to anyone in the 1920s that he was too old for student work. Yet in many ways it was a logical progression in his career. One of the arguments Oldham used in defence of his appointment was that Paton had been found worthy to be appointed as Kenneth Maclennan's successor as secretary to the I.M.C., had not Maclennan recovered his health. There is also a mysterious letter from Miss Gollock, then assistant editor of the I.R.M., which seems to be a reply to an application by Paton for the position of part-time study secretary of the U.C.M.E., a position which would seem to be incompatible with his work as study secretary of the S.C.M.[32] So it cannot be said that this move was entirely unpremeditated. Many criticized the appointment on the grounds of Paton's lack of experience, but it could be said that he brought a fresh mind to the problems, unembittered by any unfortunate mishap in the field, often said to be the cause of young missionaries losing their confidence. Paton retained, as his writings show, a healthy respect for all who had actually laboured on a mission station, but he kept the ability to envisage missionary strategy in terms of all India, Burma and Ceylon, and not simply as the problems of one particular field. Gradually he won the confidence of the older missionaries by his quiet diplomacy, since he took care not to exceed his mandate. Yet he was successful in creating his own style as the first full-time secretary of the N.M.C. The situation was similar when he became a general secretary of the World Council of Churches in process of formation sixteen years later, when doubtless his previous experience proved useful.

It was hardly Paton's place to explain to the mission boards at home the plans of his new employers, but eventually that was what he did, in a breakdown of communication which demonstrates the gulf between missionary administrators in London and innovators in India. MacNicol, who championed the scheme among missionaries in India, and Paton, were agreed that it had been a mistake to entrust Oldham with the task of explaining the situation to the C.B.M.S. Oldham proceeded to China to catalyse a similar development in the N.C.C. of China, leaving the C.B.M.S. with no more information than the official minutes of the Poona meeting. Societies felt that they were being shepherded into policies and budgets which they wanted to consider without having made any prior commitments. Letters received from missionaries contained nothing to suggest that they were in any way convinced by the proposals. Paton perceived this as soon as Oldham left India and set about personally wooing the lukewarm.[33] He and MacNicol organized a barrage of favourable letters home. A further cause of difficulty was the poor impression given by the leader of the C.M.S. delegation, who was present at Poona as a guest. Cyril Bardsley failed miserably to convey his own professed support of the scheme to the C.B.M.S. Maclennan eventually wrote to Oldham that it would be a miracle to get the proposals past the boards: 'but we live in an age of miracles' he concluded. Oldham's friends regretted the twenty page letters which he sent defending his actions because, as Paton said, even in twenty pages he had not explained the situation clearly and objectively.[34] Oldham made his first documented threat to resign:

> 'The outlook is so dark that one ceases to worry. Our only hope lies in a resurrection. The whole movement of missionary co-operation is either on the point of collapse or we shall witness a spiritual miracle which will be an assurance that great things lie ahead in the future'.[35]

However, the I.M.C. secretaries, Lenwood of the London Missionary Society, the Anglicans and the Friends carried the day, and even the Wesleyan Methodist Missionary Society was dissuaded from its threatened secession from the C.B.M.S. When the boards understood the situation in India, they even found sufficient money to carry the N.C.C. through until the North American boards could be persuaded to send a contribution. In all questions of missionary co-operation the problem of finance looms large. In 1922 drastic retrenchment was necessary for many societies, and it was always difficult to persuade them that money and man-power expended on projects not showing a direct evangelistic result in terms of the numbers baptised etc., was not wasted. Since 1880 the greatest response to the Gospel had come from the 'scheduled castes', the lowest strata of Indian society; and whereas much had been done to improve the social conditions of these peasants, fishermen, weavers, tanners and so on, the self-sufficiency of the Indian Church was impossible of attainment. Some Indian Christians resented the new doctrine of economic independence of the Church because they had previously benefited from the societies' generosity, and now suspected they were using this as an excuse for withdrawal. They did not connect it with 'swaraj', Gandhi's ideal of self-deter-mination. Paton was probably right to identify another factor in the opposition as being due to the fact that the Poona resolutions represented a more advanced stage of thinking than conservative missionary circles could accept. Gradually, as Paton's correspondence with Oldham during the years 1922-24 reveals, distrust for the N.C.C. melted into active co-operation.[36]

In a book entitled 'Red Tape and the Gospel', it is essential to consider the degree to which Paton harmonized the conflicting forces in his routine work, and produced a creative organization which in its day appeared as an exciting ecumenical experiment, which was of lasting value to India. In 1923 the journal 'The East and the West' published Paton's apologia for the N.C.C. in an article entitled 'The National Christian Council of India'.[37] He describes the developments outlined above, but adds that the Indian Christians objected to the racial proportionate membership on the grounds that it should not be necessary to specify what race a person should be. They dropped this objection, however, when they saw that the percentages were designed to ensure what they most wanted to do, to participate. In explaining the new staffing arrangements, he describes three conferences which he attended in December 1922.

At Beas in the Punjab representatives of all Christian colleges and most high schools met under the auspices of the Punjab Representative Council (the regional organization of the N.C.C.) and the N.C.C. The conference was called to discuss the changes which the University of the Punjab was proposing to introduce, which made it doubtful whether missionary establishments could meet the required standard. It was decided to concentrate on maintaining the quality of Christian education by creating one union college at Lahore in place of the existing colleges and to set up two intermediate colleges elsewhere. As the missionaries were too busy to work out the details, this would be done by the N.C.C. staff. The conference was considered to be so representative that no difficulties were anticipated in getting the necessary missionary approval.

The second conference was at Moga, in the Punjab which even representatives from South India managed to attend. It concerned rural education and, in particular, the teaching methods necessary to prevent adults from lapsing back into illiteracy.

The third conference on theological education dealt with the question of how to make Serampore College more efficient, since 25 staff were teaching 100 pupils. Paton concluded the article by expressing his belief that there was a great spirit of fellowship and happiness at the conferences, which was symbolic of the new relationships. The plans for the N.C.C. will not fail as this is the Spirit of God.

Paton's contribution to these conferences was in their preparation. The preceding May he travelled round the Punjab collecting information and assembling figures on the number of pupils involved, the percentage who were Christians, the consensus of missionary opinion on the problem and so on, all of which was preparation which no-one in the teaching profession had time to do. He also took the opportunity to visit non-Christian educational establishments in order to furnish a comparison. Hence his strong views on the subject of providing education in the Christian colleges which would provide not only for the nourishment of a student's academic abilities, but also his spiritual potential. Yet Paton was careful not to assume the role of an expert himself, but to see that information was at the disposition of those who needed it. Neither did he convene conferences for their own sake. He frequently utilized the regular gatherings of the Christian Councils, as when he toured West India and then attended a conference held by the Bombay Christian Council. There his suggestion that the Ahmednagar Training School be supported by all the missions instead of only the American Marathi Mission and the United Free Church of Scotland as at present, was carried unanimously, with a resolution that an enlarged council should address itself to a more ideal system of training for rural teachers and plan a new community middle school for this.[38]

Paton not only exercised strict principles as to the educational usefulness of a conference, but insisted that the ephemeral exhilaration at a conference must not make one oblivious to the necessity for hard work on the 'follow up' programme. (This was an old S.C.M. refrain.) Hence his asperity when he criticized Mott's plans for an N.C.C. of Western Asia and North Africa:

> 'I wonder if Mott realises the inherent difficulties of carrying out large co-operative schemes in practice after the thunder and dust of his conferences have passed away . . . and I would not care to be in the shoes of the man who had to take on the North Africa and West Asia business'.[39]

In addition there was the ever-pressing question of whether the conference would be money well spent. Paton wrote a strong letter to Oldham which illustrates this point clearly. Writing of Mott's proposal to spend a few days in January 1926 in India, he says that he has talked to the Metropolitan and they have decided that it is impossible to make plans for the future without money. Since Mott and Turner (secretary of the Federal Council of Churches' Foreign Missions Board) have not explained the situation to the boards, he will have to go himself in January 1926. He lists the other factors which would diminish the effectiveness of a conference besides the prohibitive cost and concludes that the N.C.C. should be left to get on with the job. Therefore he has cabled Mott not to come.[40] Meetings of the N.C.C. were supposed to occur at biennial intervals, but were somewhat more irregularly spaced for financial and climatic reasons.

Another effective instrument in Paton's hands was the periodical which he edited. It was resolved at Poona to accept the offer of the Methodist proprietors of the 'Harvest Field' and make it the journal of the N.M.C. It was re-named the

'National Christian Council Review', and a subsidy set aside for it.[41] In two years Paton increased the number of subscribers from 404 to 910 with a gross circulation of 1,200 so that production costs were covered and the subsidy greatly reduced. This achievement is indicative of the journal's growing influence as well as Paton's energy in promoting it. As a journal it resembled the I.R.M., but Paton used it to pursue definite campaigns, for example to publicise the campaign to control opium growing, writing a series of articles between 1924-26 connecting the Indian problem to the League of Nations' inquiry which Bishop Brent and other church leaders were involved in. Similarly he publicized the findings of the C.O.P.E.C. conference held in Birmingham in 1924,[42] and turned missionary attention to social and economic reform. Subscribers all over India could be kept informed of developments in other fields. Through the Review and the N.C.C. machinery Paton conducted an intensive survey into the effects of the opium trade and the colonial government's vested interest in it in response to a request from the N.C.C. of China, with whom he consulted at every stage since it was in China that the most diabolical effects of the opium trade were felt.[43]

The review was printed in English. The Indian Literature Fund evolved from the Christian Literature committee, which had virtually collapsed when the Y.M.C.A. suddenly withdrew in 1921, and from the literature survey sub-committee of the N.M.C. A fund was set up to subsidize the publication of books and pamphlets in the main Indian languages, most work being done in Tamil, Telugu, Marathi and Malayalam. When Paton took over the administration with Griswold in January 1923, 30 books in 13 different languages were scheduled to appear in 1923, most being on Biblical themes. This number steadily increased to meet the demands of the mass movements, which were still occurring in this period as a whole village, a sub-caste or a large family unit would decide to seek baptism, for there was a lack of suitable literature for the newly converted.[44] The minutes of the N.C.C. meeting at Calcutta in November 1926 show that there was conflict over the question of the proportion of works in English to works in the vernacular which should be printed.

On a regional basis, increasing ecumenical co-operation led to shared use of mission and church presses, as missions experimented in producing simple, practical literature for rural communities. In 1936 it was agreed that one of the most imaginative pieces of evangelism was the Christian bookshop in Benares. One bookshop with four Christian workers seconded from different missions is symbolic of the problem.[45] It is estimated that literacy among Indians stood at 10% of the total population of India from Lord Curzon's reforms in 1900 until independence in 1947. This was because in spite of major educational reforms in 1918 and 1935 and an increase in the actual numbers of student places, the rate of expansion barely kept pace with the population growth, and because it was the Indian middle classes who exploited the educational system, demanding a high standard of western education with the result that resources were spent on higher education, not primary education. If this assessment is correct, and it is supported by secular historians,[46] then the debates among those participating in the N.C.C. literacy work are doubly significant because the emphasis was on providing simple reading material in the vernacular for the newly literate or the barely literate. Financial backing was given to the efforts to establish a simplified script on principles pioneered in China.

In the late nineteenth century and early twentieth century Muslim scholars and politicians were much exercised as to whether they were living in an infidel state in which they were deprived of freedom to practice their religion or not. Most Muslims inclined to the latter view until 1914, convinced that the British were protecting them from Hindu domination. However, there was great suspicion about western education as traditional Islamic customs prevailed, and it was only at the end of the 1920s that Muslim children began to take advantage of modern education.[47] Dr Zwemer, the American evangelist, nevertheless found enthusiastic Muslim audiences wherever he preached. It was then discovered that there were no resources available to cultivate the ground which he had broken: of the total missionary force in India, estimated at 5,000 Protestant missionaries in 1924, only 12 were engaged in work among Muslims. Almost total ignorance prevailed about the Koran, Islamic culture and the sacred languages in use, Persian and Arabic. Paton did much to drive home the implications for evangelism of the deplorable situation and to initiate measures to remedy it.

His pungent comments are contained in a letter to Oldham, written July 1924, urging a change in missionary policy. The mission boards must be compelled to take an interest so that research can be carried out and people set aside for the work. Consequently the Society for the Propagation of the Gospel found two missionaries, one of whom they had already found to be unsuitable for conventional missionary work.[48] Means were found for the establishment of the Henry Martyn School of Islamics. This school was always very small with 6-12 students at any one time, but a well-qualified staff provided intensive courses in Islamic religion and language. Paton did much of the fund-raising and gave much advice. Yet when one considers the work being done at this time among Muslims in the Dutch colonies, one can only conclude that a great opportunity was lost, especially if Muslim converts had been made in sufficient numbers to witness against the evils of communalism in the way that Indian Christians were doing to the Hindu community.

Paton's work was not always creative. He had to fight a rearguard action to prevent the N.C.C.'s work being sabotaged, even when this meant for example, refraining from chairing the N.C.C. subcommittee on education lest the opposition be further alienated.[49] Paton might have justified the centralizing tendency in ecumenical co-operation which he by the nature of his position represented, by pointing to the successful functioning of the N.C.C. machinery and the growing interest in the I.M.C. in India. The latter can be demonstrated quite simply from the preparation and 'follow up' for the enlarged I.M.C. meeting at Jerusalem in 1928.[50] The former is more complicated, but it is hoped that by the end of this chapter, its success will be clear.

Paton considered that the value of the N.C.C. lay in its practical, unpretentious programme, and the way it got on with the job in contrast to the great schemes and controversy of the N.C.C. of China.[51] The N.C.C. of India seems never to have aroused such antagonism as the N.C.C. of China, which may well be due to the way in which it was quietly inaugurated, and to Paton's own personal style, his ability to communicate with Evangelicals and to make jokes with difficult personalities such as Urquhart of Calcutta. The N.C.C. of India suffered from the financial problems endemic in all ecumenical organizations, with the additional difficulty that Paton could not tap private donors in the way in which the I.M.C. or the C.B.M.S. could, but was dependent on the mission boards and the church in India, who were either reluctant or unable to contribute. Paton wrote heated letters on the complete failure of the American boards to reform their cumbersome structures and allow prompt payments, rather than sending them a year late, if at all.[52] If S.K. Datta or K.T. Paul had accepted the position they were offered in 1922, there would have been no means of paying them, and the only reason why Paton was not asked to take a lower salary in 1923 was the N.C.C.'s concern for his five children. Paton wrote to Maclennan at the close of 1924 expressing his appreciation of the C.B.M.S. contribution, which exceeds the American effort, but hoping that a further Rs16,000 will be found. At this time Paton was anxious lest the deficit on the N.C.C. finances would not be cleared, and that there would be no means of sending him on furlough in 1927. However, he went on furlough in 1926, and used the time to raise funds energetically.

While Paton was in London, he was invited to become the 'third secretary' of the I.M.C. Consequently he returned to India alone, leaving behind the family whose two halves he had united (the children who had been left behind in England with those who had been born in India or taken there as babies.) Then Maclennan's illness and Oldham's decision to go to Africa with the Stokes-Phelps commission necessitated his return to London. The N.C.C. reluctantly agreed to surrender him in the interests of the wider ecumenical movement, sending him on his way with a florid testimonial: '. . . to these, Europeans and Indians alike, who have been brought into contact with him in the course of his work, he has endeared himself by his transparent sincerity, wide sympathy and genial temperament'. However, he probably would not have gone if it had not been for K.T. Paul's insistence. He still contrived to spend the winter season in India four times between 1928 and 1938.[53]

The Future of Christian Education in India

The danger in citing the educational reforms enacted as a result of the findings of the Lindsay Commission as an example of the transition from missionary dominated evangelism to church-based indigenous activity is that one can blur an even more fundamental theological problem. This is why a reassessment of the missionary situation, similar to those produced by the missionary society delegations which inspected the field in 1922, was no longer a sufficiently radical solution. More than an adjustment in the balance of responsibility was required. It has been argued by Dr Karl-Heinz Dejung that painful economic necessity in the face of the contemporary worldwide economic crisis was the cause and catalyst of the crisis in missionary thought represented by the 'Laymen's Inquiry' and the 'Lindsay Report'.[54] Curiously, since he does not seem to have heard of the 'India Colleges Appeal', he is surprised that missionary administrators were so little impressed by it that they did not implement the Laymen's Inquiry. In fact, as Paton was to demonstrate throughout the 1930s, when people were convinced of the importance and urgency of a project, they would make great financial sacrifices, even in wartime.[55] It is rather the case that the whole basis of the Christian faith within the ecclesiastical establishment was being undermined, and confidence in missionary activity was one of the first casualties of the upsurge of 'secularism' which the I.M.C. meeting at Jerusalem sought to confront.[56]

Apart from the significance of both these reports for the reconstruction of a theology of missions and for the practical administration of the institutions of missionary outreach in India and the Far East, it is a striking fact that virtually all Paton's friends and colleagues with whom I have corresponded have cited the report of the Commission on Christian Higher Education in India (the Lindsay Commission) as one of his greatest achievements.

The published report pays a warm tribute to Paton's work in preparing the ground for the commission and for technical assistance.[57] It is difficult to determine how much of his accumulated wisdom about India lies within the pages of the report since it was almost by accident that I discovered how much influence Miss McNair had had. This complicates the question of comparison of views. Yet if Paton exerted the full range of his diplomatic talents to promote the Lindsay Report, his attempts to suppress, or to contain the effects of the Layman's Inquiry also beg important questions. In the same way that Paton had led a retreat preceding the meeting of the N.C.C. in 1924 on the spiritual meaning of evangelism, the central issue with which these commissions were called to grapple was not primarily that of a more efficient redeployment of assets to achieve a more effective missionary outreach, but, as K.S. Latourette wrote, that of the need for a fresh outburst of life in the Church.[58]

The idea of a Commission on Christian Higher Education in India was formulated at a three day conference of missionary educators and Indian Christians, held at Agra at the end of January 1929 with Paton in the chair. Resolutions were passed expressing concern at the relative decline in the quality of Christian education, which must be raised to its former pre-eminence so that the Christian colleges could provide future leadership for India and for the Church. Radical criticism of the relationship of Christian education to secular education, now in the ascendant, was demanded. Implementing the report might require sacrifice and heartbreak in the interests of co-ordination of effort. A small but weighty commission should be appointed by the C.B.M.S., the F.M.C. of North America and the N.C.C. of India. These resolutions were approved at Poona when the N.C.C. met in March 1929 and an appeal was launched for finance since the N.C.C. had no resources to spare. S.N. Mukerji, Principal of St. Stephen's College, Delhi, and S.K. Datta were nominated by the N.C.C., who also appointed what was in effect a liaison committee to assist the Commission. The C.B.M.S. approved the idea and appointed Canon Arthur Davies, a former Vice Chancellor of Agra University and doyen of the C.M.S., who subsequently made a large donation to the Commission's expenses and Nicol MacNicol, who had succeeded Paton as secretary of the N.C.C., but who was an influential older missionary and Presbyterian theologian. The C.B.M.S. raised some of the necessary money, while Paton found the rest from private donors. From America Dr William Adams Brown and Dr Hutchins were appointed. The I.M.C. persuaded Professor Oscar Buck of Drew University, New Jersey to act as secretary to the commission, and Paton was successful in persuading Dr Lindsay, of Balliol College, Oxford, who later founded Keele University on then revolutionary lines, to act as chairman.

The Lindsay Report therefore owed its inception to the concern of missionaries and Indians with the state of Christian education in India. Originating in India, it was a representative international cross-section of educationalists, who did not neglect Continental missions, because they consulted Dr Larsen, an eminent Danish teacher, and included the work of the Basel Mission in their survey. Paton's influence can be seen in the choice of British members, while he was present at the meeting in the U.S.A. at which nominations were made for the American members, and he forced the N.C.C. to justify its choice so that he could defend it in England.[59] Since at least half the commission were his friends and mentors, his indirect influence must have been great, but in India he was careful to protect the commission's reputation for impartiality by keeping out of its way.[60] Undoubtedly the work of the commission benefitted from the international approach, both because of the interplay of ideas from different cultural backgrounds, and because each member thereby became aware, almost for the first time, of how typical of a particular national culture each institution they visited was.

The Commission's formal terms of reference were practically identical to those envisaged in the Agra resolutions, namely: to review the field of service open to Christian colleges under the present conditions, to ask how they contribute to the building-up of the Church, and to investigate their effectiveness as a Christian influence upon the population. However, the Commission had complete freedom to adopt any additional terms of reference it saw fit. It was decided to exclude all Anglo-Indian and English colleges from the survey, but Miss McDougall, the principal of the Women's Christian College Madras, insisted that the original decision to exclude women's education be repealed.[61]Schools of all denominations except the Roman Catholic Church were included, even the schools of the autonomous churches of St. Thomas.

The maximum expenditure of the Commission was fixed at $ 15,000, with the Indian colleges providing free hospitality. Unfortunately an additional £400 was required because travel in India proved more expensive than anticipated. In contrast, when Paton wrote to Lord Irwin to inform him of the coming of the Lindsay Commission and the Laymen's Inquiry, he drew attention to the latter's access to unlimited funds (the affluence of the Laymen's Inquiry rankled with many missionaries),[62] its importance as an influence on American public opinion and the fact that it had Mott's backing. It should also be noted that the Laymen's Inquiry embraced China and Japan, and was not confined to questions of higher education.

The limitations of the Laymen's Inquiry, as the Commission of Appraisal of Foreign Missions is always known, were largely due to the fact that it originated in America independently of the mission boards, and remained an American endeavour, with disastrous results for the theology and methodology of the report. In January 1930 a group of Baptist laymen invited Mott to address them on his impressions of the missionary situation after his world tour. Faced with falling income and a crisis of confidence in mission they decided that a thorough survey of theory and practice of mission was necessary. Doubtless Mott delivered one of his 'crucial hour of decision' talks, but for once he elicited a response which he was completely unable to control. Just as the legislative, executive and judicial wings of the American government are supposed to operate completely independently of one another, so the Baptist laymen and six other groups embracing Episcopal, Methodist and Reformed traditions, elected a commission completely independent of either the boards or the F.M.C. Professor W.E. Hocking of Harvard University agreed to act as chairman, and wrote most of the final report, but Professor Rufus Jones of the Society of Friends seems to have had a strong influence, which is significant in view of his association with the Jerusalem meeting of the I.M.C. Three women, and an assortment of businessmen and educationalists were added. Since they had a handsome grant from Rockefeller, who had initiated the Mott lecture, they were financially independent of the mission boards. The I.M.C. acknowledged the calibre of the Commission, whose members should not be considered less intelligent than the Lindsay Commission, even if their experience was unrelated to mission.[63] The idea of a fresh approach was a good one, even if in this instance such negative results were produced.

One cannot but feel sympathy for the American colleges in India, who completed questionaires for both commissions and were visited by both within twelve months. Perhaps this is why both commissions were so impressed by how harassed and overworked the European educational missionaries were (or Paton had impressed it upon them). The Laymen's Inquiry were surprised that all the questionnaires were returned. In addition they sent the 'Fact Finders', a team of sociologists, into the field to prepare reports for them before they sailed. It was their discourtesy which caused the Bishop of Rangoon to write in a vein echoed by others;

> 'I hasten to add that of course I drew a sharp line between Lindsay and
> Co. and the Fact Finders. If all commissions were like the former, we
> should find commissions more tolerable than we did, and the Fact Finders
> were a great trial. I would rather sleep without mosquito nets than face
> them again, and Oh the time we wasted'.[64]

Although the six preparatory volumes of the Laymen's Inquiry contain useful summaries of the evidence presented to them from people with a variety of viewpoints, the final report bears scant reference or no reference to those with whom the commission disagreed. For example the work of S.P.G. among the Karens, for which the Bishop of Rangoon would have been responsible and which impressed Paton on a visit in 1922, is not mentioned, only the work of the American Baptists; and the N.C.C. does not receive the acknowledgement it deserved. Paton wrote to Hodge, now the secretary of the N.C.C., in February 1932, saying that he wished the Americans were more enthusiastic about the N.C.C. and would go home and say so.[65] Paton also had a curious correspondence with Galen Fisher of the Institute of Social and Religious Research, which provided the 'Fact Finders', who had reported that the Fact Finders 'were annoyed by what they called the open contempt of Mr Hodge for them'.[66] Paton declared that Hodge has helped the Fact Finders far too much for this to be true, and is most anxious to help. Hodge also lavished a great deal of time on the Hocking group when it arrived. Yet little or none of this is reflected in the report, which leaves one to suspect either a failure of communication in India or antipathy to the N.C.C. There is certainly little trace of current ecumenical thinking in the Laymen's Report.

Paton himself concealed his initial antipathy, which arose from a misunderstanding. He thought that the Institute of Social and Religious Research would be responsible for the whole inquiry, and that they would not produce an interpretation of the facts which would be in any way superior to any other interpretation. He perceived at this stage what would be the commission's greatest difficulty: embracing the Indian churches in the survey; a problem the Lindsay Commission avoided by including Indians in the Commission. Paton considered that the success or otherwise of missions should rest on the question of building up stable native churches, difficult though they are to understand.[67] He did not realise until later that the Laymen's Inquiry would be undermined by its inability to define the concept of the church even in terms of Christian fellowship, apart from any ecclesiological terms they might employ. He did express a certain premonition before the event. In a letter dated November 1931 he wrote:

> 'I want to say how serious I regard your warning about the possible
> religious and theological angles of the Appraisers. You, of course, know

Hocking well and we are quite clear here that it will be he who dominates
the Appraisers' Commission's theology. Oldham and I are quite prepared
to believe that he may take a line so radically opposed for example, to all
that the new crisis theology is standing for, as to precipitate a split in the
mission throughout the world'.[68]

Paton was alarmed by Hodge's reports that the members of the Laymen's
Inquiry, particularly Mrs Hocking, had been unduly influenced by Mahatma
Gandhi, lest they advocated syncretism.[69] Hodge reported that Hocking thought
sympathetically of Hinduism but considered that it lacked the necessary moral fibre
to regenerate India. Paton and Hodge tried to increase the Laymen's Inquiry's range
of contacts by paying the expenses of distinguished Indian laymen so that they could
travel to meet the commission. The Lindsay Commission on the other hand, gave full
weight to the experience of the kind of Indian convert who was most vehement at the
Jerusalem meeting about the need to make a complete break with all one's former
religious habits.[70] Possibly, in trying to cover so vast a field, the Laymen's Inquiry
did not allow itself sufficient time to reflect on the theological implications of their
recommendations.

Against this background of preparation for the Commissions, and in the context
of the civil unrest and turmoil which greeted them in India in 1930-32 when the
Congress Party was at the height of its influence,[71] one must assess the theology and
the practical recommendations of the two reports. Their impact on both the international missionary movement and on the development of the theory of mission was
considerable. The Laymen's Inquiry set out to adopt a 'typical' layman's approach.
They denigrated the word 'theological' and the accepted metaphysical jargon for
expressing religious truths, but then proceeded to write their own theology in order
to explain the reasons for mission. Latourette credited them with re-introducing
theology into mission, and indeed it was a courageous enterprise.[72] Unfortunately
they were unable to transcend the 'liberal humanitarian mid-West Protestantism' of
their background although in Dr Boyd's opinion: 'They did not write such awful
stuff as they were supposed to have done'.

Mission was defined as a natural instinct which one could as well try to suppress
as goodwill between nations. Mission was not seen as a divine imperative, as the
Lindsay Commission assumed it was. However beautiful some of their abstract
definitions in the opening four chapters of the report are, they would not inspire a
missionary to travel thousands of miles to the other side of the world to labour for a
lifetime at a task for which he will receive no thanks. (Though it must be said that
many of the missionaries whom I have interviewed have been very reticent and
modest about their ideals, giving the impression that they arrived in India almost by
accident.) The report has a chapter on Christianity without mentioning the person of
Christ as Christians believe he leads men today, and the word and concept of
eschatology are lacking, even in a report written in 1932. In fact the report is an
anachronism, showing no signs of the contemporary missiological debate. Nevertheless the commission was not seduced by the broad horizons of the 'Social
Gospel',[73] but did try to distinguish between secular and Christian efforts to better the
human condition, and to draw some useful lines on the vexed question of the
involvement of missionaries in politics. Here caution prevails, and the report
approaches the conclusions of the Lindsay Commission, that if an educational or
medical project is to be conducted as part of Christian mission, it must be of a

standard not only comparable with non-Christian institutions but surpassing them. All in all, these chapters exhibit an interesting conflict between the Commission's need to establish basic theory , and the principles which are known today as 'cost effectiveness'. Subsequent to the report's publication, there were attempts made to divorce the four chapters of theology from the rest of the report, but Hocking was undoubtedly right, as Paton reluctantly came to see, in refusing to separate the theological presuppositions from the practical recommendations.

The Lindsay Commission began not with theological presuppositions, but with the practical realities of the situation. They were careful not to become so radical in their proposals as to advocate the unacceptable. This would only result in discrediting a policy which they could not change. No proposals were made without careful consideration of what agencies could best implement them. In their ecumenical spirit, they ignored many of the denominational vested interests and were oblivious to the fact that by taking each case on its merits they had recommended the closure of every single Methodist college. Such pragmatism meant the absence of heady flights of theology. Their guiding principles only emerge in the course of the discussion. They formed their impressions by listening to Indians and non-Indians, experts and people from the wider Christian community at one conference, then sounding out these ideas at the next conference and reformulating them until a definite pattern emerged:— the form in which they appear in the report. In addition, they consulted many individuals and garnered questionnaires. This process may explain a certain repetitiveness about the report as well as its simplicity and readability, while it protected them from mounting their own hobby-horses.

When Christian higher education began in India in the mid-nineteenth century, the pioneering missionaries intended that the colleges should train leaders for the Christian community, but their primary purpose was to provide an uplift to the mind and character which would serve as a 'praeparatio evangelica'. This was not merely to be an academic training, nor a bonus to improve the career prospects of Christian children, but a living demonstration of Christian fellowship into which non-Christians could be drawn. Now, the exception of the women's colleges notwithstanding, the commission found that this high ideal of first class education and Christian fellowship was disappearing under the pressure of the university examination system and agreed syllabuses, the insatiable demand of non-Christian students for education and the colleges' need to enlarge their classes in order to remain financially stable, and the lack of teachers which made the employment of non-Christian staff inevitable. (The Commission accepted Miss McNair's submission that the percentage of Christian to non-Christian staff and students made a vital difference to the effectiveness of the school.) The colleges were becoming too large for personal contacts between staff and students and teaching was stultified by the requirements made by the government in exchange for grants-in-aid. The Commission also gave much consideration to the effect of western education and lamented the lack of education in Indian culture and history. When they sketched out a new model syllabus, they placed Indian history as the linch-pin. They were equally doubtful of the value of western denominational theology, and hoped that a new accent could be achieved in the union theological colleges which they advocated.

As in the Laymen's Inquiry, they deplore the colleges' tendency to isolation from the Indian community, and the effective isolation of pupils from their families. Many missionaries dreamed of a Christian university on the lines of those created in

China, but the Lindsay Commission decided that it would be better for the Christian colleges to be integrated into the secular universities, provided that they did not thereby lose their Christian character. The commission were very critical of the other fashionable alternative: that of Christian hostels attached to the secular universities, and laid down strict principles by which they ought to operate. Both Commissions were aware that education in India touched only a minute percentage of the population, but devised different solutions. The Laymen wanted the resources spread more broadly, with intensive efforts to improve rural education in the villages. The Lindsay Commission suggested a totally new type of education to suit rural needs, and stressed the need for literature for the newly literate. Christian village ashrams and village workers could be a valuable means of rural education and evangelism. The Lindsay Commission saw great potential in the rural programme of the Y.M.C.A.

The Lindsay Commission dealt sensitively with the question of the tension involved when a Christian college must evolve patterns of co-operation between Christian and non-Christian staff, and yet must maintain its Christian purpose. The role of the Indian Christian teacher is deemed to be of crucial importance. It is recommended that not only should all the staff participate in evangelism, but that a much more democratic system of government be introduced, so that Indian Christians can influence policy and possibly even staff appointments. Indians will work out the actual content of Christian education. The basic principle is that Christian education should form the mind to receive the Gospel by breaking down its prejudices and developing the qualities necessary to sustain faith. It has to be a defence against syncretism, materialism and anti-Christian tendencies which originated in the west. Christian colleges will regain their reputation by service to the community. Since the relationship between teacher and student is such an important educative influence, the commission proposes drastically curtailing the number of students to 250 per college, and strengthening the staff. Important suggestions were made for a national college of research and for linking existing research bodies to the colleges and the churches.

The chapter on theological education, the work of William Adams Brown, was one of the least successful in the report, yet until the Lindsay Report no ecumenical, coherent, systematic scheme of theological education embracing all India existed. Each denomination trained men as it saw fit, some in colleges, some attached to working clergy, but with no uniform standard. Vernacular theological education hardly existed except in small evangelical colleges with no academic standards. The Commission not only made general recommendations for union colleges and for improving both the financing and the academic standards of the colleges, but also gave each college it visited a detailed confidential report for its own use. Finally, the Commission looked to the generation of young men and women to whom an inter-denominational appeal could be made for them to serve the Indian Church. It saw the S.V.M.U. as a sign that the right young people could be found, without whom limitless financial resources and impeccable administration would be worthless.

The Lindsay recommendations have been elaborated in such detail not only because they indicate the theological principles behind the report, but also because Paton spent the next ten years of his life implementing the report. He organized the English end of things, engaged in his habitual disputes with Warnshuis about the American side, and raised the necessary finance with the 'Indian Colleges Appeal'.

He had the pleasure of seeing the fruits of his work in a very tangible form when the Tambaram meeting of the I.M.C. in 1938 was accommodated in the newly-opened buildings of the Madras Christian College. Plans for new buildings were made in 1908, but nothing concrete was achieved until the appearance of the Lindsay Report in 1932, when money was found for building to begin in 1935. As the Commission recommended, it was a federation of smaller colleges. He also laid the foundation stone of Kinnaird College, when it got its first purpose-built buildings as a result of the India Colleges Appeal.[74]

Paton worked hard to 'sell' the idea of acting on the Lindsay Report to the mission boards (Warnshuis' caution and maladroitness almost sabotaged his efforts in America).[75] By September 1931 he had condensed his thoughts into a three-page memorandum, which he circulated, defining the areas on which decisions had to be taken. He insisted on the necessity of change, not only as something desirable, but as a necessary prerequisite to prevent students being abandoned to the forces of secularism. The difficulties in achieving the required co-operation were enormous. In the same month he was writing that the C.B.M.S. had agreed to recommend to the boards the acceptance of the Lindsay Commission's principle that ultimate responsibility for education be transferred from the boards to the field. The C.B.M.S. was also making proposals on how to do this. It was 'grasping the nettle' of how Indian Christians would be given control of the colleges by reducing the proportion of missionaries on the governing boards of colleges and phasing out non-Christian Indians.[76]

It is interesting to turn to the archives of a missionary society to see how the report was received. For example, S.P.G.'s general secretary, Canon Stacy Waddy, had a considerable correspondence with Paton. He wrote to one bishop in India that the society took the report very seriously, not because they wanted to make decisions but to offer guidance. He thought it unlikely that S.P.G. could arouse support for the colleges as they were then constituted, but an appeal could be made on the basis of a radical remodelling of the colleges. He wanted to see the church in India running the colleges instead of the London boards. A generation of young men were sent out to India by the societies, who took the Lindsay Report with them as their Bible.[77]

Although the Lindsay Report was sold out within two days in London, there was endless arguing over distribution in America. The Boards in America were slow to take responsibility for the child the I.M.C. had fathered on them, mainly because they considered that the proposals were too expensive to be implemented. Nevertheless, by February 1935 Paton was writing to Warnshuis to express his admiration for the success of the appeal in America.

The progress of the implementation of the report can be traced through J.Z. Hodge's fortnightly letters to Paton. Paton himself visited India and stirred things up in 1935-6. The problem lay in getting an effective machinery set up, such as was eventually achieved in the 'Central Committee of Education' which was a standing committee of the N.C.C., in getting the support of leading missionaries, and in allaying fears that it was all an Edinburgh House plot to take over missionary education in India. Very few colleges were actually closed because of the storms of protest which rose whenever closure threatened a particular college. Dr Boyd's theory is that the planned colleges of extension and research were simply a way of finding a use for what would be obsolete colleges. He maintains that they never got the money from the missionary societies to implement the changes, but the colleges did definitely change from being a means of evangelical expansion controlled by the missions to a means of upbuilding the church. He felt that the Lindsay Commission's emphasis on research was misplaced, obscuring the importance of influencing students. The Lindsay Report had its uses in the conflict with older missionaries, and was a tremendous boost to the women's colleges, previously regarded as an inferior species. In July 1936 Paton dispatched £16,000 to India as the first installment of the appeal, and Hodge responded by writing that the Christian colleges would always be grateful for his 'splendid advocacy, unwavering faith and sheer hard work'.[78]

Unfortunately, the results of the 'Laymen's Inquiry' were quite different, for there seems to have been no question of a 'follow-up', nor of the implementation of its proposals. Instead one must ask: to what extent did the Laymen's Inquiry split the international missionary movement and alienate its supporters? There are some grounds for thinking that Lundahl, the Swedish secretary of the Northern Missionary Council was right: only those who wanted an excuse for leaving the I.M.C. did so. It must be remembered that a fierce controversy over the I.M.C.'s Department of Social and Industial Research was raging at the same time as the controversy over the Laymen's Report.[79]

Paton was not initially hostile to the Laymen's Report, but he was critical of the sensational serialization of the report in the American press before the mission boards had seen it. This maladroitness caused widespread resentment, and an onslaught from Robert Speer, a conservative Evangelical and a good friend of the I.M.C.[80] Paton feared that the valuable practical suggestions in the report would be lost in a wave of condemnation, and he regretted that the report tended to divide people along the fundamentalist/liberal line. He sympathized with Mackay's views in the article he commissioned from him for the I.R.M., where the transcendence of God and recent Continental theology are emphasised, but he held that unless there was widespread unrest, nothing should be done.[81] In another letter written at this time, he said: 'A great deal of the report is really very mediocre and I cannot help feeling that the discussion now going on all over America would not have been sowed solely by the intellectual merits of the documents. This, however, is a wicked and ungenerous thought'.

Oldham was a personal friend of Hocking, so on his own admission his criticism was less severe. With his love of long memoranda, he wrote several on the issues raised by the Inquiry, but it was in a letter to Lerrigo, the irate secretary of the American Baptist Foreign Missionary Society, that he wrote that the report was irrelevant: it matters what God does, not what we do. In his correspondence with Speer and the secretaries of the English societies, he summed up the British position accurately: that they welcomed the challenge of the report but profoundly disagreed with it. Discussion in England proceeded along other lines: firstly to face the economic crisis and secondly the implications of the I.M.C. meeting at Herrnhut in 1932. Paton and Oldham had to deal with another outbreak of the theological conflict between Scandinavia and America. Paton had particular difficulty defending Mott, whom Westman of Sweden declared was compromising and losing his grip. Paton denied this, but said that allowance must be made for the fact that he was 70 and would have to retire sometime. He resisted demands for a statement from the I.M.C., saying that the Laymen's Inquiry had nothing to do with the I.M.C. anyway.[82]

In America there was no possibility of containing or suppressing the report, for after it had appeared, the 'Christian Century' continued to stir things up. The 'faith missions' such as the Christian Medical Alliance and the China Inland Mission not only broke off relations with the I.M.C. and the F.M.C., but exploited the report to gain more members. In March 1933 Mott and the I.M.C. officers held a consultation with the boards. All the major denominations were represented, but there was not always agreement between co-denominationalists as to the effect the report was having on rank and file church members. It was felt that people were using the Inquiry as an excuse to suspend their contributions. Only the Methodist Episcopal boards endorsed the report, the rest repudiated it.[83] At another conference secretaries of two of the boards confronted the members of the Inquiry, and tried to get them to substantiate their accusations by naming the missionaries supposedly guilty of misconduct, and the allegedly ineffective schools and hospitals, but the members of the Inquiry were evasive or exonerated the missionaries of the boards to whom the secretaries belonged.

The reaction in India was significant. P.O. Philip wrote that the Laymen's Report was not as sensational as he expected, and not very exciting.[84] The Indian newspapers greeted it with enthusiasm. Conversely, as the Lindsay proposals began to take effect, and it was clear that the Christian position was being strengthened, the attacks in the Press grew fiercer. As Paton told Philip, Hindu opposition was bound to be aroused by the improvements in Christian education.

Certain conclusions are inescapable. It would be easy to dismiss the Laymen's Inquiry as not worthy of serious study. Inevitably, it is the product of amateurs, more accustomed to the tangible results of business deals than the years of patient labour needed to establish the Christian Gospel in a hostile environment, who compounded their misunderstandings by alienating the agencies who could have helped them. Yet the report is important as a symptom, not a cause, of the widespread unease concerning missions, and of fears that missionary sincerity was being misinterpreted as cultural imperialism. Their report was seized upon by those looking for battle, who were less than scrupulous about the weapons they used. Reading Paton's correspondence, one sees the agitation of a diplomat embarassed by a show of naked force. One suspects him of glossing over real frictions and of concealing facts for the sake of ecumenical harmony. Reaction to the American theology of Hocking and Rufus Jones may have caused him to throw himself firmly onto the side of dialectical theology. He was undoubtedly afraid that it would jeopardise the implementation of the Lindsay Report, which had been prepared with a thoroughness typical of his own way of working, and which displayed similar pragmatism. Not only did he convert it to bricks and mortar — he rejoiced that it was another stepping stone towards an independent Indian church. The Lindsay report was not a magic formula, only to be recited to dissolve the objections of conservative college principals, and money-paring mission finance boards. Yet the Lindsay report is still something of which Paton could justifiably be proud, as one of the best things he did for India.

Freedom of worship and the right to evangelize: Paton in the Eastern conflicts

Paton first became involved in the questions of missionary freedom and freedom of worship when the N.M.C. was trying to cope with the practical consequences of the expulsion of German missionaries from India in 1915. Important principles were involved, including the relationship of missions to government, and the principle for which Paton fought so long and so hard, the 'supranationality of missions'. In handling the question of alien missions at all levels in India and in London, Paton became a very skilled missionary diplomat, while the I.M.C. achieved a status of importance in the secular world which it would not otherwise have had. Precedents were set both for the rescue operation necessary from 1934-36 when the German missions were forbidden to export currency and for the much larger global operation necessary during the Second World War, which is discussed in another chapter. In some ways the situation was a paradigm of the problem of church/state relations and the importance of an ecumenical united front when dealing with government policy.

When Paton became secretary of the N.M.C., he inherited an extraordinarily complicated situation, with which he was not wholly unfamiliar, judging by his sympathetic comments on the plight of the Basel Mission in his letters home in 1918.[85] Paton would have learnt from Oldham, Hodgkin and Lenwood of the fierce battle which the War Emergency Committee (which superseded the Continuation Committee of the World Missionary Conference) and the British Churches fought to prevent German missions being completely eradicated by the Treaty of Versailles, and to stop the licensing of all missionaries, whatever their nationality, in a fashion which would have been completely incompatible with Christian principles of religious freedom.[86] These efforts were tragically misunderstood in Germany, where the 'caretaker' arrangements to maintain German missionary work were interpreted as an imperialistic take-over by the Anglo-Saxon missions. So the task of the staff of the I.M.C. and the N.M.C. of India was not only to wear down the colonial government until German missions were allowed to return, but also to reconcile their former friends and colleagues. The German missions committee, a sub-committee of the N.M.C./N.C.C., handled all questions of finance.

There was no general internment order issued by the War Office until 1915, but some colonial governors were too zealous, and anticipated the London government by arresting and interning missionaries. In the Gold Coast (Ghana) the governor ignored the order until forced by public pressure to give way in 1916. In India, public opinion was provoked by the behaviour of young German missionaries in Ranchi, and the Bishop of Chota Nagpur found it very difficult to help Stosch and his colleagues of the Gossner mission when he visited them, because they were convinced that Germany would win the war and then the roles would be reversed.[87] Some missionaries were paying the penalty for a cultural exclusiveness and sectarianism, which had not endeared them to their Anglo-Saxon neighbours; others had been less than discreet in discussing the war with their Indian pupils, and yet others refused financial assistance when it was offered to them. It remains a difficult question to decide, whether missionaries can claim a privileged position as compared with ordinary expatriate civilians, especially when matters of security are concerned. Oldham himself was convinced that a few Basel lay missionaries had been guilty of seditious activity, and that the government had adopted the right course.[88] War hysteria and frustration at being separated from their lives' work, as well as recollections of the humiliation of being arrested by black troops, produced the allegations of 'atrocities' from the German and Swiss missionary boards. The British government did over-react, even if the German government had set a precedent by forcing the Baptist Missionary Society to leave Cameroun after the signing of the

Treaty of Berlin in 1885.[89] A few German women missionaries were, at the urging of the N.M.C., allowed to stay in India.

From the correspondence in the S.P.G. archives, it is clear that there were numbers of missionaries and British residents as well as the government of India who did not want or expect the German Missions to return. Unfortunately there were at least two cases in 1922 of English missionaries circulating critical and libellous reports about the methods of the German missions, which caused anger in Basel and embarrassment for the N.C.C., and a further complication for Paton to deal with.[90]

After the Lake Mohonk meeting of the I.M.C., when a motion was adopted rejecting the charges of sedition against the German missions, there was a concerted effort to break down the British government's prohibition. Oldham and Paton became involved in a scheme whereby individual German and Swiss missionaries were allowed to return, provided that they worked under the supervision of a British or American society. There was still great difficulty getting visas, which Paton had to overcome in India, but a trickle returned, senior missionaries who benefitted from the scheme by acclimatizing themselves to the changed situation in India. Younger missionaries were sent to the Selly Oak Colleges, Birmingham, for the first time, for language training. Paton and Oldham got very annoyed about what they castigated as 'a petty policy of pinpricks', though Paton eventually decided that the government's reluctance stemmed from economic and not political considerations.[91]

The Basel Mission had pioneered a scheme popularly known as 'the Basel Industrials'. In the early years of mission to Muslims in India, converts faced terrible economic pressures and often lost their employment (under traditional Islamic law conversion rendered their property forfeit). So the Basel Mission founded craft industries and factories to employ Christians. These factories must have been among the first to be seen in India and Africa, and became a means of social improvement and Christian influence, as they had a mixed work force. They were highly successful, and their profits financed the missions, though there seems reason to believe that employment in them became part of the age-old pattern of patronage in India and that the Basel Mission expended much money training and sending out technicians and businessmen to run the concerns. The Basel Mission deserves credit for making such a response to a social problem in the mid-nineteenth century, but unfortunately the 'Basel Industrials' became an asset so valuable that the colonial government became very sensitive to its obligations under the Treaty of Versailles, and very reluctant to see the Industrials under 'alien control'.[92] So the Basel Industrials were vested in a 'Commonwealth Trust' and were thereby made immune from confiscation to pay for German war debts. The financial situation for German missions in India deteriorated so much that it became necessary to raise mortgages on mission property, which was often in desperate need of repair, and then redeem the mortgages by the profits on the Industrials. This plan failed because the Industrials, in the harsh economic climate, did not make the anticipated profits, but in Africa incurred so much debt that a subsidy from the Indian plant was necessary. The Basel Mission wanted the Industrials back, and a proper financial settlement, especially as German traders were allowed to operate before the missionaries returned. Negotiations lasted from 1928 to 1935, with Paton visiting Basel to explain the complicated legal situation in 1928 (twice), 1929, and 1935, but the society lost its connection with the Industrials completely. One suspects that the 'right to free enterprise' was at stake rather than the 'freedom of missions', but Paton judged the situation correctly:

not merely bureaucratic incompetence but deliberate procrastination motivated the government's dilatory replies to Paton and the other N.C.C. secretaries. Paton concluded that jealousy of the Basel Industrials was prompting Calcutta businessmen to press the government to exclude the Basel Mission.[93]

As pressure increased for the return of the German missions, and the Basel Mission, the government of India retaliated by driving a wedge into the ranks of the Basel Mission by insisting that before there was a return, the Basel Mission must make a settlement with the Kanaresischer Evangelische Mission (K.E.M.), whose unhappy history is an example of a mission's capacity for self-inflicted injury. When 'alien' missionaries were excluded from India, and with them the Basel Mission's staff, a young Swiss doctor, Pierre de Benoit, visited the field and was so anguished at the inevitable withering of the Basel Mission's work, that he managed to find enough enthusiastic French Swiss missionaries to re-occupy the former Basel field of South Kanara. Oldham put pressure on the British Consul in Berne to get visas for Dr Pierre de Benoit and his colleagues; and the N.M.C. persuaded the government of India to continue the government grants to the schools and clinics which they had formerly granted to the Basel Mission, and a proportion of the income from the Basel Industrials. This caused a great deal of acrimony in Basel, as it exacerbated the tension between the Swiss Reformed and the Baden-Würtembourg Evangelische supporters of the Basel Mission.[94] The government ministers declared they were protecting the K.E.M. from going under to Basel and the Basel Mission was convinced that the K.E.M. was keeping it out of India. Paton had great difficulty in separating the two issues of the K.E.M. and the nationality of the Basel Mission, and its right to be a society 'recognized' by the I.M.C. In London Oldham laboured patiently to bring the two sides together. In 1925 the financial situation of the K.E.M. became so acute, because it had no independent constituency in Switzerland, and could not develop one in competition with the Mission Suisse Romande, that serious negotiations for a reunion began. In the annals of the Basel Mission it is written that the affair ended amicably,[95] but in fact when the Basel Mission returned to Kanara in May 1926, half the former K.E.M. missionaries, joined the L.M.S. rather than work for the Basel Mission. To a certain extent this episode demonstrates the need for strong international missionary co-operation to protect missions from government interference in their internal organisation.

The most important principle being contested in the aftermath of the first World War was that known as the supranationality of missions. The Treaty of Berlin had recognised this principle, which did not really become an issue until the outbreak of the first World War. Then Oldham wrote an exceptionally sensitive letter to Dr Richter of the Berlin Mission on 9th September 1914 summing up the whole dilemma of a missionary who shares whole-heartedly the aspirations of his combatant fellow countrymen, yet is bound through Jesus Christ to his brethren in the 'alien' missions, whose loyalty was also to the Christian Church.[96] If he did not possess that loyalty, and were not able to pledge himself to strict neutrality as an officer of the I.M.C., he would resign. Unfortunately the initial cordial and sympathetic relations between British and German missionary leaders became strained to breaking point when Oldham broke off relations with Basel in February 1917, and Lenwood and Hodgkin had great difficulty bringing about a reconciliation in 1919.[97] Mott lost the trust of the German missionary circles when he accompanied the American mission to Kerensky's government in 1917 at the personal request of President Wilson.

Nevertheless it may well be that he allowed his support of the British to become known before then, since in 1915 he was writing to Tatlow in strongly partisan terms.[98] If the principle of the political neutrality of missionaries and of a higher loyalty to Christ was so difficult to maintain without misunderstandings in I.M.C. circles, it is not surprising that it was difficult to induce governments to recognize this principle, and refrain from treating missionaries as potentially disloyal elements.

For this reason the position with regard to the French, Spanish and Portugese Empires was very difficult. Non-French missions were never allowed to return to French Cameroun (formerly part of German Cameroun). In common with other predominantly Roman Catholic empires, adherence to the Roman Catholic Church was interpreted by the colonial government as a necessary part of loyalty to that government. To be Protestant was to be disloyal, and natives who were Protestant were likely to rebel. This suspicion was heightened by the I.M.C.'s investigations into the slave conditions of Africans engaged in forced labour in Portugese Africa. Paton tackled the problem in 1940 by approaching the Roman Catholic hierarchy in Lisbon and by supporting the tiny Protestant churches in Portugal and Spain.[99] The problem was less acute in French territories because of the work of the Paris Evangelical Mission, which also worked in the British Empire. However, Paton was most successful in the Belgian territories where he could rely on Monsieur Anet of Brussels to smooth things out with the Belgian government, and give advice on the best procedures for Protestant missions in Belgian territories.

A second question is that of the position of missionaries in relation to other civilians. Missionaries in China were 'protected' by the 'extra-territorial' rights of all Europeans in China, which had been wrung from the Chinese after successive 'Opium Wars' and were much resented.[100] Missionaries could not unilaterally divest themselves of these rights although many wished to. Many of the younger missionaries in India were much troubled by the nature of the pledge of loyalty they were obliged to give the government, which they feared made them government agents in the eyes of Indians. L.P. Larsen, an outstanding Danish missionary, resigned from a school in Madura in 1930 rather than be compromised by the District Collector's demands. Paton himself looked forward to the independence of India as the only permanent solution to the problem.

The government devised a system of licensing missionaries, which was designed to ensure their loyalty to the colonial government and their neutrality in Indian politics. It is necessary to examine the nature of the system to understand the complexity of the question. In essence the system was half bureaucracy of a very time-consuming kind and half gentlemen's agreement, which meant that it broke down when those involved were not gentlemen. Paton used to boast that apart from the Keithahn case, there had never been any friction between government and missions because of the system, and that no applications ultimately failed. This was not true, as his own files reveal,[101] and Continental societies found the three to six month wait for visas very aggravating. The system eventually resembled the Schleswig-Holstein question of which it was said in 1863 that the only people who knew who was the rightful duke were Prince Albert who was dead, a German Professor who was mad, and Palmerston, who had forgotten the answer. By 1938 only Paton understood the process, and when he raised the question of a revision by the India Office, he received a very apologetic letter which made it clear that they no longer understood the procedure and that the government of India had now proceeded so far with devolution that it was impossible for them to recommend changes. Tracing the operation of the system from 1922-40 through thousands of letters in the I.M.C. files,[102] one can appreciate the colossal amount of time Paton expended, writing letters, interviewing people, lunching with senior civil servants and even in approaching the Viceroy. The provinces of India sometimes had to be dealt with separately. Some were under princely rule, others under direct colonial rule, all with varying degrees of autonomy, and they often adopted different attitudes to missionaries. It may not be a coincidence that Paton had most difficulty with administrators in the Madras Presidency, and with junior rather than senior officials.

The cumbersome procedure was first invented in September 1921 by which a foreign (i.e. non-British) missionary had to be invited back to the field at the urging of local missionaries, who had to be able to show that his services were indispensable to the welfare of the people and the continuance of the mission. Then enquiries had to be made to show that there were no objections on the grounds of security:— in 1920 an American couple who had the misfortune to bear the name Hartmann were told that their very surname would inflame public opinion. It was alleged also that they had been guilty of 'indiscreet conversation' on their former term of service. It was this procedure which took six to nine months. When a missionary went out as a private individual without the support of a mission he had also to deposit the cost of his return fare with the government and give a personal undertaking of loyalty to the government.

Both Oldham and Paton considered that the one valuable point in the system was that the government was forced to recognize the value of missions. The revised agreement concerning the admission of alien missionaries to India of September 1921 began with a preamble negotiated by Oldham and sustained by Paton through subsequent revisions until 1939:

> 'Appreciating to the full the value of the work done in the past by missionary and other philanthropic societies and organizations, His Majesty's Government and the Government of India cordially welcome their co-operation in the future in furthering the moral and material well-being of the peoples of India'.

In this revision the original clause of May 1919 excluding foreign missionaries 'for a period to be defined hereafter' was amended to five years from the date of the revision, except that a provision was made in 1923 for individuals to return under the aegis of British societies. In November 1926 these instructions were superseded by a more detailed system for missionaries from 'recognised' societies. For a missionary society this meant that the C.B.M.S. or the F.M.C. recommended it as a body whose good faith and stability could be guaranteed. Non-British societies had to give an undertaking that:

> 'All due obedience and respect should be given to the lawfully con-stituted government, and that, while carefully abstaining from political affairs, it is its desire and purpose that its influence, in so far as it may properly be exercised in such matters, should be so exerted in loyal co-operation with the government of the country concerned, and that it will only employ agents who will work in this spirit'.

This formula is an interesting indication of the common aims in the relationship between missions and government in India. It did not change in the subsequent revisions of procedure, but that required from individuals did.[103] Memorandum C, as it was known, contained an additional sentence, which changed subtly from 1919 to 1925. Initially it read; 'I undertake, if engaged in educational work, that my influence shall be exerted to promote loyalty to the government in the minds of my pupils, and to make them good citizens of the British Empire'. It became; 'I undertake to do all in my power to promote goodwill and understanding between the people and the government of the country and to make those in my care law-abiding and good citizens'. This was, apparently, more acceptable to the missionaries' consciences, and indicates perhaps, the effect of the missionaries' sympathy for the mounting demand for self-government.

Complications arose concerning the re-entry of missionaries to India for a second tour of duty. The local administration insisted on treating American missionaries as foreign missionaries instead of according them the privileges of British missionaries, as had been originally intended. Missionaries also had to give a pledge of loyalty and a 'no objection' certificate when they applied for a visa for a second visit to India. Since by 1930 candidates had only to show they belonged to a 'recognised' society or give an independent undertaking, this produced the situation where it was easier to get a visa for a first journey than a second. Paton interpreted the requirements in 1922 the same way as Oldham did, that American missionaries should be allowed to proceed to India without special inquiry being made, unless there was reason to believe that they were 'disloyal' on a previous term of service. The N.M.C. could not make enquiries about all the American missionaries in India and therefore the F.M.C. should, in exceptional cases, satisfy the government.[104] For American missionaries it was basically a question of providing a means of identification.

Paton's repeated efforts to simplify the process and iron out anomalies were met in many instances by the sort of correspondence which caused him to write to Oldham:

> 'I am very glad to read what you say about the question of German missionaries, and I have for some time been of the opinion that we can't with Christian self-respect much longer assent to have this important issue handled by unimaginative and prejudiced asses like Knapp (Sir Arthur Knapp). There is not the slightest doubt that Government will be far better advised to trust your council and mine and so get some restriction on the sending out of undesirable men, than to risk being forced into a general lowering of barriers'.[105]

C.F. Andrews was one of those who were urging the N.M.C. to fight the issue in the courts to see if the government had any basis in law for their action. The 'system' was basically a gentleman's agreement since it hinged on a man's word and his society's guarantee. This was clearly a solemn matter to them. With the true impartiality becoming to a gentleman, Paton had to point out to Warnshuis on several occasions that societies were 'recognized' irrespective of whether they were ecumenically minded, observed comity agreements and were in contact with the I.M.C. or not. Similarly, the N.C.C. could do nothing when a society disowned a missionary and wanted him removed from the field. Only a missionary whose society had collapsed, or whose financial support was very questionable, would find that when he applied to renew his visa, that he had been removed from the Memo. A category to Memo. C category.[106]

The conference of the N.M.C. at Poona in 1922 passed a resolution to dispel the misunderstanding about the undertaking which, it stated, recognised the legitimate requirements of government and the apolitical nature of missionary work, but denied that such an undertaking would then make the missionary into a government agent.[107] It was precisely at this point, that missionaries would not provide positive political support for the government, which caused the Keithahn case in 1930 to take on such a grave aspect.

The Keithahn case, which much exercised Paton's diplomatic talents 1930-31, can be viewed from many angles. Essentially it was a failure of the system because of the obstinacy and partisanship of the local district collector, but for Keithahn himself it was a personal tragedy, as his letters show; and a very damaging incident for the 'crack' Madura mission. Paton considered that too much protest was made over an utterly exceptional case, but all the principles of co-operations between missions and government were threatened, and while it eventually became clear that the district collector, Hall, had exceeded his authority, he was not dismissed or discreetly transferred, but continued to make life very uncomfortable for neighbouring missionaries.

Keithahn was a young missionary on his first tour of duty, acting as vice-principal at the American College at Madura. Unfortunately, he was not popular with the senior members of staff because of his progressive views; but there is general agreement that he was a good teacher, and had an excellent relationship with the students, whose political views he sympathised with, even wearing khaddar and staying for periods at Gandhi's ashram. It was there that he met an English Friend, Reynolds, who, judging by his letter to Paton, was politically naive, but had a large Indian following.[108] With typical American hospitality, Keithahn extended an invitation to this pacifist whom he hardly knew, and whom the District Collector regarded as a dangerous agitator because he had recently delivered a petition to the Viceroy on behalf of a group of Indian nationalists. As the Friend was English, the Collector could not proceed against him unless he broke the law. A few months later Reynolds came to Madura, and stayed overnight. Unfortunately all the senior members of the mission were away, having left Keithahn in charge. He invited Reynolds to address a small group of senior students and later accompanied him to the station. There a 'spontaneous' political demonstration broke out among Indians who had heard that Reynolds was in the district. Keithahn could not escape, and was garlanded and feted as well. In the ensuing crisis with the District Collector there was only one American, Dr Banninga, to support Keithahn.

The District Collector pressurised Keithahn into believing that for the good of the mission he should leave India, and that if he did not go voluntarily he would expect the mission to dismiss him. Dr Banninga attempted to mediate, but was confronted with the demand that the mission should disown Keithahn, or lose its grant-in-aid for its educational work. The mission complied, too readily in Paton's opinion, and Keithahn disappeared on a tour of China and the Far East.[109] This made the mission's position very weak when Hall denied all this, and said that the mission had expelled Keithahn. Paton spent several months establishing the facts. Hall provoked the attention of the American boards and the I.M.C. by circulating a letter demanding that the missionaries should actively work against the Congress party,

and support government propaganda. When issuing the threat concerning government grants-in-aid, he said that the Madras government required missions to be
responsible for the political views of Indian pastors. The Boards were most anxious
to know if this was the case.

Paton tackled the question on all levels, the India Office in London, the
Viceroy, at this point a noted Christian, Lord Irwin, the Madras Government, and
the recalcitrant District Collector. Only the latter refused to co-operate, and
absented himself from his office when Paton visited Madura. On all other levels
complete agreement was reached, culminating in an open letter from Paton to the
government, and a reply, both of which were published, as a means of publicly re-
establishing the principles involved, and quietening the storm raised in America
against the British colonial government.[110]

Paton countered the government view that Keithahn left voluntarily, though he
admitted that technically they were right. He established the right of appeal from a
district collector to the provincial government, which, of course, is what the Madura
mission failed to do. Paton even persuaded the mission to invite Keithahn back, the
which invitation he deemed it expedient to decline. However, Paton was involved in
the case because of the general principle at stake, rather than because of the injustice
to Keithahn, with whom initially he had little sympathy. It was made quite clear that
the government had no desire to hold the missions responsible for the views of
Indian Christians. The question of political neutrality only arose here if an Indian
wished to use mission buildings for political purposes. Neither were grants-in-aid
dependent on the nationality of the missionaries, or positive political propaganda by
them. One cannot help sharing Paton's view that the mission lacked guts in failing to
stand up to Hall when he exceeded his authority. Yet clearly it was easier for Paton
to take a tough line than the principal of the Madura Mission, since he could use the
threat of bringing the full weight of the international missionary movement into the
arena to protect any mission which was unfairly treated, with all the embarrassing
publicity for the government which this would entail. He had already used this tactic
successfully 1927-29 to prevent the government acquiring the Basel Mission's
hospital at Calicut by compulsory purchase.[111] At the back of every missionary's
mind must have been the danger of becoming too closely identified with the colonial
administration. Paton was also aware of the precedent set for the days when India
would be self-governing. One can also sympathise with Keithahn, whose fault was
that he was too decent and self-sacrificing, and that the mission, being divided over
his progressive views (which according to Bishop Hollis and Bishop Newbigin, were
muddled and inconsistent), did not support him as they should have done.

According to Paton's biographer, this was the end of the case, a notable
diplomatic triumph for Paton on behalf of international missionary co-operation.
Unfortunately the surviving papers belie this. Hall continued to harry missionaries,
on one occasion demanding from returning American missionaries an undertaking
far in excess of what was required under Memo 'A' and in another instance, sending a
circular on the obligation of missionaries to arm themselves and resist any uprising
by the natives. He once banned a missionary from preaching for four weeks. Paton
had to restore calm in missionary circles after both these indiscretions. He also
encouraged Keithahn to re-apply under Memo 'C' when he wanted to return to India
after his marriage in 1934 which he did, and he is still working in India today. In the
other cases of missionaries against whom the authorities took action, it was a

question of the missionaries being heavily involved in political activities after resigning from their societies.[112]

When Paton reviewed the system in 1936 with the intention of renegotiation, he met with complaints about the bureaucratic delays, but not protests over a question of principle. His own views on the relationship of government to missions had changed subtly by 1936, when he wrote 'Christianity in the Eastern Conflicts'. He was now more concerned with the freedom of the Church rather than the rights of missionaries, particularly in the countries of the Far East. One pertinent conclusion he came to, which is significant in view of his work in India, is that there is nothing in the Christian faith which leads one to say that as of right a British or American missionary should be free to proclaim the Gospel to another nation. What is crucial is that the nationals of that country should be free to evangelise their fellow country-men. This paragraph is clearly the crystallisation of his experience in India:

> 'A foreign missionary in a country ruled by a foreign power different from his own has to be bound by the necessities of the case, which obviously include an abstinence from open indulgence in political activity . . . It is perfectly possible to show a sympathy with the objectives of a national government without overstepping the bounds which are proper to such a case. The foreign missionary whose nationality is the same as the dominant power, is placed in a rather different situation. The fact that he is of the same people as the rulers will pre-dispose him to agree with them and see things as they see them; he will, therefore, have to watch his actions with peculiar care lest he allow his national sympathy to estrange him from the Christians of the land with whom he is working. Because missionaries of other nationalities are precluded from public statement, it is the more incumbent on him not to be silent in the face of grave injustice'.[113]

Leonard Schiff made the interesting comment on this question that as a British missionary one simply carried on one's political interest as if one were at home. The difficulty about making any protest was that British missionaries were so divided among themselves. It was a very artificial situation for the non-British missionaries. However, the N.C.C. did very occasionally issue a statement or a call to prayer in the event of a national crisis. Missionaries could speak with a united voice when they could not speak as individuals. It is significant that there was widespread missionary protest at the execution of two men whose appeals had been pending for five years in 1942. Considering the conservative politics of most missionaries, it is hard to imagine them inciting anyone to rebellion.[114] However, so much of India's problems sprang from the fusion of religion and politics that their separation in the conditions imposed upon missionaries by the colonial government was probably a good thing. It gave the missions more freedom to experiment in education and social recon-struction or in the setting up of ashrams. The system was a reasonable one; it is merely reprehensible that it took so long to evolve properly and that so much anguish was caused to German missionaries who were excluded for far longer than was necessary. When the formation of the N.C.C. was being strongly criticised, it was said that the problem of German missions alone would justify its existence. As far as Paton was concerned, the system reveals his ability as an administrator and diplomat. He learnt how to use red tape to tie other people in knots and even to construct a noose for them to hang themselves in when they were hindering the work of the Gospel.

A cynic might observe that in the international missionary movement's terms of reference 'freedom of religion' meant 'freedom to convert others', but in fact the debate, to which Paton contributed much thought, seems to have arisen as a reaction to the criticism of missions in India, and in particular to Gandhi's strictures. Fears for the future of Christian missions and for the Indian Christian minority in a country increasingly torn by communal warfare were combined with more fundamental questions about the individual's right to pursue the religious faith of his choice. Paton became more and more concerned not only about the intolerable position of men and women attempting to leave Islam in traditional Muslim countries, but also about the demands being made on Christians in the Far East to conform to the state religion under the guise of patriotism.

Criticism of Christian missions in India was no new phenomenon, but the campaigns of the Arya Samaj[115] and the complaints of nationalists received new impetus when Gandhi, whose moral reputation and sanctity were unassailable, also voiced his objections to 'proselytism'. Consequently, when Paton managed to arrange to visit Gandhi in April 1924, one of the questions he asked was about his views on the work of Christians in India.[116] Gandhi began by saying that he had always felt that if Christians were merely out to proselytise, they would fail, but that if they would preach and practise Christ's spirit of unselfish and loving service, they would bring incalculable good to India. Paton asked what his objections were to a man reaching the point in devotion where he wishes to be baptised; Gandhi replied that this was for a man himself to decide, leaving Paton with the impression that he thought that missions were out for numbers and that he did not realize how Christians deplore the kind of activity which was described as 'proselytism'. Paton concluded that a campaign was necessary to show what the true Christian objective is, since the air was rent with the tumult of Hindus trying to convert Muslims and vice versa and Christianity must not be confused with this kind of 'communal aggrandisement'.

Paton had not expected Gandhi to adhere so rigidly to Hindu customs, but was impressed by his reverence for Jesus Christ and what he felt was personal knowledge of Him. His simplicity and genuine love of poverty, the ordering of his life and the atmosphere of his abode, the qualities which had won him a unique place in the hearts of India's people were the aspects Paton chose to emphasize in his letter, not Gandhi's political and religious opinions. Paton's descriptions of subsequent visits to Gandhi are less uncritical.[117]

It seemed that at the 1924 All-India united conference on religion some measure of agreement had been reached on the subject of conversion by representatives of India's religions (the Metropolitan of Calcutta represented the N.C.C.) as expressed in the resolutions of the conference but although Gandhi accepted the terms of the resolution in a private meeting with members of the C.B.M.S. held in Edinburgh House in 1931, publicly he provoked very great controversy.[118] He denounced medical and educational missions as unfair methods of proselytism among the sick and the young, repeating the oft made allegation that converts were provided for in missionary budgets at so much per head. He had no objection to genuine conversion, except that someone undergoing such a religious experience should not change his ancestral religion, but become a better Hindu. India's religion is sufficient for her.

Paton entered the fray through the traditional medium of his generation, the correspondence columns of 'The Times'.[119] His argument was that Gandhi was the victim of a false philosophy, that using one's country's own food and clothes is dependent on one's perception of truth, whereas missions commend Jesus Christ to all men without trying to get hearers to become like them. The doctor and teacher are trying to get their witness across and give life to the people as an integrated whole act. The Church of England Newspaper supported Paton:

> 'Mr Paton renders conspicuous service to the cause of truth by emphasizing the point that Mr Gandhi has not made any attack on Christians, neither has he spoken of driving the missionaries out of India. According to Mr Paton, Gandhi has been saying things like this about proselytism for years. It is a challenge to missionary work, but it is not to be mixed up with fantastic charges whose intention is political. No medical missionary expects someone to change their faith if they are cured, but people start asking about their motivation. Gandhi misses the point because he thinks we stand for a superior civilisation — we crave forgiveness if our pride has offended'.

Explaining the controversy to S.K. Datta, Paton wrote that he wanted to deny that Gandhi is a threat to Christian missions. Gandhi's view is grotesque, to which C.F. Andrews agrees. True and full religious liberty includes the right of foreigners to conduct religious activity provided that they do it decently and lawfully. In 1933-34 Paton had to organize another offensive in the 'Times' because of allegations by Sir John Thompson and Sir Henry Page Croft that large numbers of churchmen in India had anxieties about reform in India and that a British withdrawal would lead to the disappearance of Christianity in India, as in Russia. So a letter was sent to the 'Times' composed by Paton and Thompson of the M.M.S. and signed by Stacy Waddy of S.P.C., R.L. Pelly, Holmes Davies, A.G. Hogg, Holland, G.E. Phillips of the L.M.S. and several other missionaries from India welcoming the prospect of an Indian government because then the confusion between the British Empire and Christianity would cease.

The controversy involved Paton in reading a paper to the East India Association in June 1931, which attracted favourable comment from Sastri, also in London for the Round Table conference, as Gandhi was. Paton represented Gandhi's view as being that it was not a question of legal disabilities being introduced for converts but that it was morally wrong to disturb another's faith, this being the same tolerant view held by many an English gentleman. Datta's reply to Paton is highly significant:

> 'None of you so far as I can see has emphasized what to my mind is fundamental. It is only when we Indian Christians in India feel that the Christian work carried out in that country is our own work that it will be possible for us to take effective action. I would like to be in the position to say to Mr Gandhi that as an Indian I shall stand for the liberty of Christian work being carried out. I do hope that the question of the status of Christian missions is not going to be bracketted with safeguards for European commerce'.[120]

The meeting between Gandhi and the members of the C.B.M.S. which Paton chaired (8.10.31) was notable for revealing the distance between the two parties which was greater than Paton had supposed. Gandhi had begun by telling Paton that the misunderstanding between them was temporary, misrepresented by the press. To him all the great religions are true to a greater or lesser degree and all are descended from God. One is attracted to religion in the same way that one is attracted to a rose by its scent. He admitted the indirect good of missions in awakening him to the evils of child marriage and untouchability, but one does not need to talk about God to untouchables. Wilson of the B.M.S. wanted to know if Gandhi excluded all preaching. Is it not right to take them the highest thing we know? Gandhi replied that it must be left for God to speak to man. They should teach God through the religion the people have already got. That is the aim of his life, to show God through the life he lives. If they really believed that Christians were sent into all the world to make disciples of all nations (he had declared that he himself had no disciples), why did they invite him to explain his views?

The Round Table conference on the Indian constitution held in London in 1931 was not a very happy context for these discussions, since it was so extraordinarily difficult to separate the issue of conversion from the political head-counting which was going on in certain reactionary Hindu and Muslim sects who were urging separate electorates at the conference for the different religious communities in India. Paton wondered where Gandhi thought the missions would find the money to pay converts, but the situation between the two major religious communities in India was similar to that between the candidates at 18th century elections in England as far as proselytism was concerned. He was obviously right to try and get the issues separated. As a convert himself his sympathy was bound to be with other converts, but he was keen that the N.C.C. should investigate missionary practices in case improper means of evangelism were being employed. Clearly Paton was mystified that such a spiritual man as Gandhi should fail to understand the disinterested motives of Christians. Paton thought that in Hindu ethics, there was no place for the utterly unselfish act.[121] Gandhi thought the missionaries must be in it for something, and the structure of missions whereby so often Europeans dominated Indians, confirmed his worst suspicions.

Paton was a moving spirit in the 'India Conciliation Group' of church leaders, and chaired the 'Round Table Group', which met at Church House in December 1932 in discussions parallel to the secular R.T.C. meetings.[122] He worked closely with Agatha Harrison, who had a position financed indirectly by Gandhi to liaise between him and all the groups interested in him and in the situation in India. Through her he met Mrs Nehru and her doctor. Realizing how ill she was he put it to the India Office that she ought not to be allowed to die without seeing Nehru. It may not be a coincidence that Nehru was flown from his prison cell to see his wife after she went to a sanatorium in Switzerland (where Paton also saw them. He was shattered to find that such intelligent people were so bitter against the British).[123] It was in a letter to Agatha Harrison that Paton gave the final expression to his relationship to Gandhi. Dated 16.6.36, the tone is quite different from that of his first meeting with him.

> 'There is no escaping the fundamental difference between him and us. He doesn't believe that any religion is more than one of several approximations to the truth. We believe that while Christianity in any given form is full of human frailty, there is in Jesus Christ the fullness of the Godhead, salvation for man, peace, joy and strength. Believing this, it is totally impossible for us to refrain from the presentation of the Gospel to all mankind. This does not prevent people like myself from recognizing the fundamental altruistic views of Gandhi's own movement. We wish him well'.

However, Paton declares that the mass movements began before Dr Ambedkar brought politics into it and are moved by the spirit, not by political motivation. Why can't Gandhi see this?

In 1920 Paton jotted down notes for a paper entitled 'A plea for a fresh study of mission to the Muslim world'.[124] He emphasized the missionary societies' neglect of the Muslim world in spite of its political importance and the unrest among the western educated young, but only in terms of the opportunity for evangelism and not the difficulties for converts, except to declare:

> 'No religion is so firmly wedded to the use of force to compel assent as Islam. The Christian view on the other hand is of society as a thing to be redeemed into the form of the Christian ideal by the witness, service and if need be by the suffering of the Christian society'.

The present collapse of the Muslim world view, which had created a possible receptivity to Christianity, is caused by the military eclipse of Islam. It is the political implications of the situation which have attracted Paton's attention, not the question of human rights. It would be interesting to know what Paton's reaction was to a more radical paper by J.N. Farquhar, also written in 1920,[125] but applying the same criticism to Christianity. In the present revulsion against all that is not Indian, missions are denounced on racial and political grounds. To Indians, it seems the final insult to a subject people to attempt to convert them from the Indian religion. One must have patience and sympathy with this attitude and seek solidarity with the nationalist struggle, but at the same time encourage Indian Christian leadership and theology.

The decision to hold the I.M.C. meeting at Jerusalem attracted a great deal of criticism from local Arab leaders, which may be why the subject of proselytism was discussed, but without any important conclusions. The subject of religious freedom was fully discussed at the Williamstown meeting of the I.M.C. in 1929 as a result of concern about the legislation on religious education in state schools in the United States and because in a test case in Egypt an Egyptian woman had been denied the right to join the Christian church.[126] This was serious because there were every year a number of girls educated at mission high schools who wished to become Christians, but the ruling meant that the traditional Shari' at law, whereby they could be forcibly married to Muslims to keep them in the faith, was upheld. In Iraq and Syria different questions relating to missionary freedom were being discussed by the Mandates' Commission of the League of Nations, and the situation in Turkey was causing the American missions there grave disquiet.

Apart from the measures adopted at Williamstown, Paton became himself a one man team of investigation into the question of freedom of religion. From this period until the outbreak of war made communications with the Far East impossible, Paton lectured, wrote, spoke, preached and made representations to government about the principles and facts of freedom of religion or its absence in certain countries. Since his work frequently repeats the same themes, only a small cross-section is considered here.

Much of Paton's work was delivered to students, starting with the S.C.M. Quadrennial held in Edinburgh 3-9.1.33. when he spoke on 'What is the Muslim World?', of which no record survives. He spoke at the joint W.S.C.F./I.M.C. conference held in Basel in August 1935 on the subject, and again at the S.C.M.

Quadrennial held in Birmingham 1-7.1.37., but his ideas developed and crystallised as a result of his participation in the preparatory studies for the Oxford Conference on Church, Community and State (C.C.S.) and his observations when he circum-navigated the world in preparation for the third world missionary conference 1935-36.

In the paper for the Oxford conference[127] he claimed that there was possibly greater tension on the issue in the East than in the West, and he found that there were three main influences at work which threaten the religious freedom of the 'nascent' Christian churches, namely nationalism, dogmatic secularism and the problem caused by the canon law of Islam. Nationalism is involved in the fear of the foreign influences associated with the indigenous churches and its effect on children. In Japan the Shinto cult is controversial depending on whether it is religious or an act of veneration for national heroes, but in either case the clamour is likely to grow that Christians are unpatriotic, while Christians on their part cannot accept that the Emperor or the state is an absolute. Some of Gandhi's followers wish to prevent the work of Christian conversion by law. He also spoke of the increasing State control over education to the detriment of religious education. In the East governments with a secularist tendency have awoken to the meaning of education as a means of creating the kind of subjects they want. The Christian teacher faces great difficulties where there are no direct prohibitions but the weight of officialdom is on the side of increasing the patriotic content.

Paton had, in this paper, only just begun an intensive study of the implications of the 'shari'at' law. Where this is in force non-Muslim members of the state may practice their ancestral religion, but not make converts, and they remain second class citizens, tolerated by special concession and not because they have any rights of their own. Since conversion was inconceivable, men are liable to the death penalty for conversion, unmarried women to forcible marriage. Paton then discussed the shades of variation in this situation in the newly emerging nationalist states of Turkey and Egypt and so on. Only a desire to appear modern or the colonial power of a western country over the Muslim country has mitigated the situation. If, however, Europe moves in the direction of totalitarianism this thaw will disappear. Paton's conclusion is that to date there has been little threat to the individual Christian or Christian congregation, but only to those wishing to join the Christian faith. As a postscript he adds that in his opinion foreigners should claim no special rights or privilege to work in a foreign country, and it is entirely up to the indigenous Christians and national governments whether they are to invite missionaries there or not.

It is curious that Paton makes so little mention of the problem of religious freedom in his address to the students at the joint W.S.C.F. and I.M.C. conference held in Basel in August 1935. He talks boldly of the rising nationalism in the East, contrasting its expression in Shintoism in Japan with more democratic forms in China, and explains sympathetically the appeal of Gandhi, because of his 'social uplift programmes' in India, without really explaining how nationalism can be a threat to the church or mentioning the restrictions on the church in Islamic countries. Paton's address seems to have all the background material on the question of religious freedom, without the cohesion which a proper discussion of the problem would have given it.[128]

The theme of the book based on Paton's world tour, 'Christianity in the Eastern Conflicts', is the Christian Church, menaced and yet hopeful, as Paton observed it when he was working on the preparation of the I.M.C. meeting at Tambaram. Here the transition is complete from concern about missionary freedom to a defence not only of the Christian Church's right to evangelize, but to exist.

Paton writes with much sympathy and admiration for the Japanese nation and the tiny Japanese church, which has only been able to grow and evangelize since 1860. Through visiting parts of the Japanese empire, he was able to appreciate for the first time much of the aversion of Indian Nationalists to the British Empire. Yet he was alarmed to see academic standards corrupted, as in Germany, by the desire to create national myths concerning the origins and superiority of the Japanese; and because of the analogy with Germany, he predicted that conflict between Christians and the forces of nationalism and militarism was ahead in spite of attempts by Japanese Christians in influential positions to moderate the ideological excesses, and the consultations between government and the churches. He noted that Karl Barth was being read avidly by many Japanese students.[129] After visiting Shinto shrines and observing the ritual closely and discussing the problem with many Japanese, Paton came to the conclusion that the ceremony was not either religious or patriotic, depending on one's status in the controversy, but that it was intended as something deeper and more absolute than the Japanese understanding of religion, which was seen as something individual and sectarian. The obeisance to the Emperor signified something universally true and of the nature attributed in the West to true religion. Hence the belief among all Japanese that the extension of the Japanese Empire was beneficial to the subject peoples. Paton can see no easy answers to the problems which the Japanese church faces.

Paton is very wary of the common generalisation about Chinese Christians, that they do not comprehend the significance of the idea of the Church, but is forced, after his experiences in China, to agree that it is true. Large numbers of Christians have no connection with any organized body, nor any ideal of the Christian community to sustain them in the almost inevitable persecution, which having already begun in Manchuria, will follow the Japanese conquest of the country. In his estimation of the situation facing the Chinese church he adheres to the prophecies of T.C. Chao in which he sums up the future of the Chinese church in the word 'martyrdom'. Yet the evangelistic opportunity is boundless, as Chinese students search for God.[130]

Paton barely mentions the issues of freedom of conversion and freedom of religion in India because his attention is caught by Nehru's analysis of the problems of India, which he agrees with, and by the phenomenon of the secular and 'scientific' attitude of many young Indians. He is merely concerned to defend the Indian Church against Gandhi's accusations, and to state that the Hindu position, tolerant of all religions, can admit that no one religion is so superior that people should adhere to it irrespective of their natal religion.

Instead, he devotes much space to a detailed discussion of the Church and the Protestant missions in the Near East. Their position is the most critical of all the members of the universal church. Either they face the overwhelming disabilities of the traditional Islamic law or they are crushed under the demands of very potent nationalism as in Turkey. While Paton is very pessimistic about the possibilities of evangelism, he sees much value in the educational work done in the various Islamic countries and emphasizes the significance and importance of kindling new life in the ancient churches, rather than creating new churches. The problem is that these churches have been subjected to a second class existence of inferior rights that they do not possess the confidence to evangelize. Paton is also able to perceive the social, as opposed to the religious strength of Islam. In many points he follows the lead of Temple Gairdner and Hendrik Kraemer, though much of the section is taken from an unpublished paper by D.B. Macdonald.

Paton's reflections on the countries he visited are arranged thematically, one chapter being entitled 'Church, Community and State', the connection with the Oxford conference being that the Church in the East is threatened by the same manifestations of a totalitarian philosophy of the state, although in the East Christians only form a very small proportion of the state. The great movements of nationalism and communism in the East pose an equal serious threat to the Church because they claim the whole man: men and women are prepared to die for them. The Church is also greatly handicapped in the East because almost everywhere it is seen as a foreign import, even as exhibiting the same superiority as the foreign power. Paton's concept of the Church is discussed elsewhere, here it is sufficient to state that Paton was convinced that as a matter of truth, not of expediency, the Church should be as close in spirit and life to the community as it can be. As an expression of solidarity with that community, Christians will be found serving it in education and medical work since this is a spiritual work, and an integral part of the work of evangelism.

> 'The gravity of the situation in which the Church finds itself today in more than one land lies in the fact that the state is denying the truth about the nature of life and of mankind, and trying to impose a false orthodoxy of its own. If it is true . . . that man is essentially one to whom God speaks, the child of God intended to find himself in the world as a fellow with others in doing the will of God, then it is not true that there is no call on him higher than that of his nation, or that he is the result of the economic inter-play of forces, or that he is what his race and blood are and no more. The Church needs not to organise opposition on such matters; its very existence and the fellowship and interior life which it enjoys are hostile to all such sub-personal or merely biological views of man'.

The Church in the eastern lands stands as a witness to the universal, not the national as the norm of fellowship, however sympathetic Christians may be to national aspirations. For this reason it is seen as a potential threat by certain national leaders. If active persecution has not yet broken out, nevertheless the Church, because of the very nature of its existence in the eastern conflicts, is experiencing difficulties in evangelism and education, whatever ways round particular laws may be invented. No justifiable ground for complaint such as 'proselytism' or 'denationalising influences' should be tolerated in the church. Whatever restrictions the Church may accept in its methods of work, denial of the freedom of worship is unacceptable. The key to the problem of the pressure of the state on the Church lies in the deepening of the life of the church. 'It is fatally easy to become so engrossed in the detailed work of securing legal toleration for Christian activity as to lose that dynamic redeeming power which is the final charter of the Christian society in the world'. If martyrdom is much talked about in East and West, it should be remembered that the word means 'witness' and that there is no witness except out of life, the authentic life of the Spirit.[131]

Paton's assessment of this situation facing the Church in the East is noticably more pessimistic than his earlier views, or the views expressed to the Birmingham

S.C.M. Quadrennial in 1937.[132] His understanding of the position of the Christians in every land is unchanged, it is only his emphasis on the political realities of the situation which change a little. Otherwise he displays a consistent reticence on the question of martyrdom and persecution. He almost always defers to the judgment of Christians in the country concerned, since they are nationals of the country, and they will be those who will suffer for their faith. 'God speaks to this generation' was the title of the conference: it involves criticism and repentance within the Western nations, a response in service overseas and finding the means to make real the concept of the universal church, for in the East for many Christians the way of Christ is leading straight to the Cross in terms of literal martyrdom, as T.C. Chao said.

At Tambaram the subject was taken up by the section devoted to consideration of the relations between Church and State. The conference report began with a positive appreciation of the position of the State, but then proceeded to delineate the exact limits to which the State might go and the essentials of religious freedom in worship and education of its members for the church. It also outlined the right to associate with other churches, and the principle that churches should come to the support of a persecuted church. The grounds for such claims were to be found in the obligations of men as children of God and the Church as the Body of Christ, which obviously is not recognised by a non-Christian government. Therefore, the Church should use arguments which would appeal to the state. One of the most 'startling revelations', the report of conference found, is the degree to which these rights are denied all round the world. The question then examined was how the Church could live under such restrictions and inch its way towards a more relaxed situation without compromising the Christian faith. Finally, the report stressed the responsibilities of the Church towards the care and protection of minorities and refugees (two of the principal responsibilities of the post-war World Council of Churches).[133] Formal studies of the question of freedom of religion did not start until the end of 1943, under Warnshuis, but had Paton lived, he would undoubtedly had much to contribute.

It is significant the way Paton's thoughts have moved from considering the position of the individual convert and the right of an individual to decide his own faith, to the position of the churches and their right to evangelize, and finally to the demand for solidarity of all churches with their persecuted brethren and the positions of Koreans and Manchurians, or any Christians who are determined to resist the total demands of an absolute state. Missions have become irrelevant, without any particular right to exist, but the Church as the Body of Christ is the rock on which all else is attached.

An independent Church in an independent State

In considering Paton's contribution to the establishment of an independent church in an independent state, one has the distinct impression that Paton did not succeed in the work of reconciliation to which he set himself because he tried to be all things to all men, and ended up being too radical for many of the members of the missionary societies and too paternalistic for many Indians. His gaffe at Tambaram might have been due to his age when confronted with the rising generation of Indian churchmen, for he was at least facing in the right direction, and must have had something to do with the decision to throw so much of the I.M.C.'s slender resources into a study of the problem of 'older and younger' churches. One must remember also that Paton was a highly political animal, — if one had no other sources, it would still be possible to reconstruct the history of the British withdrawal from India from his letters — and that he had one foot in the world of colonial administration and secular politics.

Interesting though such a study would be, there is not space in this book to reconstruct Paton's political commentary on events in India. Only a few documents can be selected to give the flavour of his participation in the questions at issue. Paton seems to have begun to write a book in April 1919 entitled 'The Place of Missions in the World Today', which may have been a precursor of 'Social Ideals in India' or 'The Highway of God', though I have not managed to find more than the first chapter.[134] Beginning by examining the attitudes to missions in 1919 and the problems which attend the application of Christian principles to the social problems at home, he continues by abolishing the distinction between 'home' and 'abroad' to consider whether Christianity has value and power in the face of the tremendous world problems. Within the British Empire one has the problem, he writes, of the political, social and economic relations of peoples highly developed in the arts of government and more backward races. Previously the imperial idea rested on racial pride and a glamourous interpretation of history which was wholly pagan. Now the idea of trusteeship is being discussed, which is the exact opposite of exploitation.

> 'Now this conception of the 'advanced' nation as trustee for the less advanced springs directly out of the Christian view of life . . . It means that the right of superior force is definitely set aside in favour of a higher law. The duty of the more advanced people to which the care of a less advanced has been entrusted is to develop it, to protect it from aggression, to conserve just conditions of labour and put down oppression, to educate and civilize and train in the political arts, so that when the process is completed the trustee nation may resign the position of trusteeship and welcome the subject people as an equal and fellow in the community of self-governing peoples. This view depends on the Christian idea of the value of human personality and on the Christian idea of service as a more glorious thing than self-aggrandisement. It is an ethical and spiritual idea, and its appeal is frankly to those who love humanity'.

There were many in 1919 who were quite oblivious to the dangers of identifying any particular political idea with Christian ethics or religion and Paton is obviously not exempt.[135] However, it is clear from the examples which he then cites of the principle in operation, that its attraction lies in that it can be used as a bulwark against economic exploitation in the Empire. In India the question is more complicated because of a sophisticated and ancient civilisation. The crunch will come in the question of whether the Montagu-Chelmsford reforms are implemented, bringing devolution of government to the provinces.

> 'The doctrine of trusteeship . . . has been attacked lately by a distinguished American professor as incompatible with another basal principle, that of self-determination. The critic admits that the idea of trusteeship is a moral one, but declares it to be aristocratic and incompatible with the democratic doctrine of self-determination. Is this true? Surely not. It is a matter where the finest character and insight will be needed, but there is no inherent impossibility in passing over from the thought of trusteeship to that of self-determination, when the fullness of

time has come . . . only the clearest grasp of this ultimate goal will free the 'trustee' from the bane of superiority'.

Paton declared that the idea of a benevolent nation is far from the Christian concept of love between equal nations, which is what Christ's teaching implies. The missionary and Christian statesman differ in their function and vocation, but should not differ in ideal or motive. Now is the time to repent.

Paton's article came in for severe criticism from the I.R.M. group, mainly because the theological background was not sufficiently developed, and not because of its political content. It shows the optimism of his character and also his legitimate conviction that Christian principles must be applied to world affairs, a principle still not conceded by many Christians.

It was the degree to which Gandhi introduced a moral and ethical principle into the nationalist party which impressed Paton initially, in the first interview with him which has already been quoted in this chapter. On the same occasion Gandhi told Paton that 'Swaraj is not a thing the British Government can give. It is a thing we must earn for ourselves. If the Government agreed to give us complete Swaraj, and there is no fitness in India for Swaraj, what good is that?'[136] Paton thought that this sentiment was Gandhi's most useful contribution. Paton attributed many of the excesses of the Congress Party to its more flamboyant members, believing that Gandhi could not control them, especially when he was in prison, which is the view of historians such as Michael Edwardes but which M.M. Thomas denied.[137] He was no revolutionary, but believed in an evolution of self-government which he was confident could be worked out by reasonable men of good faith. When such a settlement proved elusive, and he was exasperated by the intransigence of the Congress Party, as well as the stupidity of Whitehall, he came to hold Gandhi responsible for the actions of his followers, and for the riots and deaths. Like many of his contemporaries, he regarded Nehru as a dangerous revolutionary, well on the left of Gandhi, but when he had a two-hour long talk with him in February 1926 he found him frank and charming, but irreconcilable. He wrote to his mother-in-law, Mrs Macdonald:

> 'I don't think public opinion at home has any conception of what is really going on in India, a member of the Viceroy's Council assured me that he had come out with no idea of the truth, thinking that a strong hand was wanted. It is a noticeable fact that Indian politicians now regard all British political parties as being the same. Extreme men hate Labour worse then the other parties because they think they ought to have gone further to meet them'.[138]

Paton found himself agreeing with Nehru that India's problems were not political but economic.[139] Paton thought that he would never carry the Hindu capitalists (who financed the Congress party) to a socialist solution. He appreciated Nehru's stand against communalism, but failed to understand that his secularist stand was motivated by his desire to keep religion out of politics. Paton's sympathies were really with the moderate liberal Parliamentarians who survived from an earlier period of Indian politics, and he failed to realise how little support they had. In all his correspondence from 1921-43 he consistently under-estimated Gandhi's political achievements, while earnestly desiring an independent India if only to stop the confusion between Christianity and the ruling power.

One of Paton's closing comments on a letter of March 1932 is very revealing. His portrait of Lord Willingdon should be compared with that found in Nehru's autobiography, which shows that Paton's fears were well-founded and that Nehru and Paton both had the same low opinion of the intelligence of the Indian Civil Service.[140]

> 'I had a talk a few days ago with Lord Willingdon and . . . I was deeply disappointed. I think he has got cold feet before starting. He seemed to me to have been got at by the die-hards in this country. He was convinced that the Congress were going to turn down Gandhi's recommendation (I hope he feels more cheerful about it now) and was inclined to think that martial law might have to be introduced at an early date, felt Lord Irwin had exalted Gandhi in a dangerous way etc. etc. etc. I gave him as vigorously as I could the opposite interpretation of events. Lord Lothian came in while I was there, and I was delighted to find that he takes a very sound view of the whole situation, and between us we tried to cheer up the Viceroy-elect. It is a little discouraging to find a man of his years approaching so difficult a task with an initial hopelessness'.

In view of this Paton thinks it is particularly important for people to relate their prayers to India. In November 1932, Paton wrote to Forrester Paton that he had seen a long private letter from the Viceroy (still Willingdon) in which it was clear that he would not budge before the civil disobedience campaign was called off, which Paton thought a totally unreasonable demand.[141] Significantly Paton laments that it is not easy to get public interest in India (Nehru thought even the 'Manchester Guardian' was lacking in this respect). Sometimes Paton's influence on the Viceroy was less direct. Given the privilege of showing the Viceroy the Tambaram conference and introducing him to delegates, he took the opportunity to make a few comments, while envying Mott for escorting the Vicereine, a very attractive and intelligent woman, whom he schooled in Indian politics. When Irwin (after 1936 Lord Halifax) moved to the Foreign Office, having met Paton in India, he invited Paton to keep him informed of Indian opinion. Paton was in constant correspondence with Indian Christians with nationalist views, particularly P.O. Philip, and met Indians with a cross-section of views when they came to London. He was appalled how insulated from Indian opinion British politicians and administrators were, but this was typical I have been told. So he passed on what he could. In his opinion there was a natural and commendable alignment between Christians and those aspiring to national independence and self-government in India and China.[142] He and other church leaders did a great deal to try and prevent the 1942 talks breaking down, and to try and broaden the base of these talks beyond the base of well-known Congress leaders. From his meeting with Gandhi in 1924 he was trying to explain the Labour party's policy towards India, but although he was always aware of the perfidy of successive Conservative governments, he never accepted that the entire system was rotten nor that men of goodwill on both sides could not settle things amicably. Miss Potts, however, has a vivid recollection of the house party at Rydal greeting the news of the emergence of the idea of Pakistan with approval as a solution to the problem of Hindu and Muslim states. Paton was adamant that it would not work, and the birth of Bangladesh has proved him right.

Again, a whole chapter of this book could be devoted to the problem of establishing an independent church in India. Its problems were discussed in my

M.A. Thesis and a specialised bibliography affixed. Since then I have interviewed Archdeacon Mara, M.M. Thomas, Bishop Newbigin and Bishop Hollis, Dr Rossel, Canon Pelly, Leonard Schiff, Mrs C.M. Hogg, Miss Brockway and I received a long letter from Sister Carol Graham about serving the church in South India. Paton's contribution was much the same as his contribution to Indian politics. In the same style of explaining one side's views to the other, there is a notable letter which he sent to Bishop Newbigin on the subject of inter-communion explaining not only his own views, but how far the Anglicans in England would be likely to go. Similarly, in a long and important correspondence with Banninga in 1929, Paton discussed how Anglican opinion at home can be influenced in favour of the 1930 'Proposed scheme of unity', and asks for more material to circulate, while Banninga is engaged in educating missionary opinion. While Banninga was asking him to soften the extreme Anglican reactions, Bishop Azariah was corresponding with him about how the L.M.S. intransigence could be overcome.[143]

The worst problem was that of missionary domination of the church. Dr Rossel gave me a good example of this. He took over from Streckeisen (whose correspondence with Koechlin in Basel is a piece of church history in itself) and found that the warring parties in the Malabar Christian Church were divided between a middle class, educated 'church' faction, and a 'mission' faction financed by Streckeisen. He stopped that, but years after he had been elected to the church council he discovered that everyone hated him because all decisions of the council were being interpreted as 'the missionary wants it'. Elections had become a matter of caste, and were always a landslide one way or the other depending on which way the school inspectors had made the teachers and their families vote. (There are a great many Anglican parochial church councils where one would find a similar situation. The difference is that in England aggrieved parishoners do not resort to litigation.) Bishop Hollis says that he does not think Paton understood the three devils which possessed the churches in India — power, prestige and property. Paton was, however, fully aware of the problem of the domination of the Indian churches by missionaries, a domination which was both organisational and economic. His comments on the racial aspects of this will be considered in a later chapter.

At the S.C.M. Quadrennial held in Glasgow in 1921, Paton spoke on the theme 'The missionary and the growing church'.[144] After justifying the vocation of missionaries because the 'missionary' idea is essential to the Gospel and the experience of Christ valid for all races, he declares that 'no amount of missionaries will convert the world, simply because India, China, Japan and Africa must see and hear the Christian word and spirit spoken and enshrined in Indian lives, by Chinese voices, in the common fellowship of Africans themselves'.

Therefore, the only long-term success a missionary can find is in 'upbuilding a stable, self-directing Church'. There are already highly educated Christians in India, China and Japan so that the missionary must now re-think his position and how to take a subordinate role. This is the burning issue for many an educated Chinese, Japanese, Indian or African Christian, because although it is easy to state the principle of missionary service to the church, it is complicated by prejudices and obstacles from the past. It is a very real handicap that the missionary belongs to the ruling race and a very great spiritual danger to him. The great power and prestige of the ruling class so easily become his own. In a crisis he automatically takes the side of the ruling class. There is also the disparity of salaries, for although a missionary salary is low by European standards, it is high by Indian standards and a very simple life will be necessary to counteract this, though a sincere spirit will be recognized regardless. The funding of the church must be altered so that voting power is not proportionate to the money contributed, which for the Indian is very little. Then there is the problem of helping Indians or Chinese experiment with church life to create a genuine Indian or Chinese church and not an imitation of a western structure. Paton is well aware of the volume of criticism about missionaries, but this does not mean that missionaries should not be there, but this only makes it clearer what their function should be. It used to be the fashion to call students to world leadership (Mott's theme) but now the younger branches of the church call students to service.

The extent to which the formation and work of the N.C.C. of India was an attempt to carry out this transfer has already been discussed. Paton worked both to increase the representation of leaders from the younger churches in the I.M.C., succeeding magnificently at Tambaram in having 55% of the delegates nationals of Asian and African countries, and it is the sincere conviction of Bishop Newbigin that if Paton had lived he would have improved the third world representation at the World Council of Churches. Newbigin feels that the secretariat in Geneva did not see how western the structures of the ecumenical movement were, which produced a certain distortion. Paton might have made the W.C.C. more sensitive to the voice of the Third world in the early post war years.

Paton encouraged numerous I.M.C. studies of the problems of the younger churches, which are listed in the footnotes to this chapter, and reached their zenith in the Tambaram series volumes 'The Growing Church' and 'The Economic Basis of the Church'. For it was Bishop Azariah who drew the attention of the Tambaram meeting to the essential impracticality of the devolution of power in theory from mission to church while the Indian church was so dependent on financial help from the West. The problem of course was, as Bishop Hollis, Bishop Newbigin and R.L. Pelly have explained, that the western churches had superimposed a structure of schools and hospitals on the Indian church which it could not support — it was difficult for converts from the scheduled castes even to support their own clergy — and which represented a source of patronage and employment to educated Indians.[146]

It is possible to argue that Paton's most significant contribution was in steering the re-direction of the I.M.C. from a mission-based evangelism to a church-based one, and to supply so much inspiration on the subject of the universal church, so that the theoretical backing was available for the practical reforms. In India the de-colonisation of church and state proceeded parallel to each other, the Church of South India being created in the same year as national independence, both events after Paton's death. In both the chief stumbling block was economic, though I do not think one can apply the term 'exploitation' to the situation in the church. The noteworthy thing to observe is that in India, in contradistinction to the situation in Africa, the Nationalist leaders have not been mission-educated, and their attitude to missions has been very critical, although the professions have drawn heavily from the Christian communities as in China before 1948 and Japan. Paton's friend K.T. Paul fought a significant battle not only to end the deprivation and discrimination against the Anglo-Indian community but to encourage them to integrate themselves into the Indian community. Paton championed all K.T.'s efforts to avoid a separate Indian Christian electorate, which was very significant for the integration of

Christians into Indian society, with the result that there was little emigration of Indian Christians or Anglo-Indians to England in 1947, unlike the situation which has resulted from the withdrawal of the Dutch or the French from their colonial possessions.[147]

Paton himself did not entirely escape from the sins he castigated in 1921. At Tambaram there was an incident which has no written record, obviously because Paton edited everything, but which Principal Boyd, Sir Kenneth Grubb and Bishop Woods all remember, though with slightly differing details. According to Dr Boyd, Paton, as secretary, had the habit of slipping into sectional meetings 'quietly influencing things'.[148] However, when he should have been making a speech of welcome to guests, Boyd found himself deputed to do it because, he was told, Paton was 'having a spot of trouble with the delegates'. He had 'dropped a ton of bricks' in Bishop Woods' section (which was chaired by Garbett) by delivering himself of some remarks which could only be interpreted as paternalistic. As Grubb said, he had started issuing instructions about what they should be doing in the Indian church and was having to make amends. The same flaw appeared in his efforts for the creation of the Church of South India, according to Dr Boyd. When he received the letter which is quoted extensively in Chapter VIII Boyd wrote back very angrily that Paton's suggestions for church unity were all very well, but impossible to put into practice. Paton could be very authoritative and very British as part of his job in Edinburgh House. He saw the possibilities of reunion very early, but missions would not have found them so easy to put into practice. His mind, Boyd says, saw the dangers of paternalism, but his personality was overwhelming.[149] Cheng Ching-yi's biographer, Jonathan Chao, has explained to me that that was precisely the problem with H.T. Hodgkin and R.D. Rees, that however self-effacing they tried to be, they were such outstanding men that their Chinese colleagues automatically deferred to them. Paton never took jokes about his dictatorial powers very well, probably because they were too near the bone. In another letter home to the secretary of his mission, Boyd said that he wished Paton would stop talking as though to a poor relation. He thought the letter was written in a near panic when he thought everything would be swept away (he received it in 1942) and that the moral demand was meaningless. How could missionaries act together as though there were no differences when the Church of Scotland and the L.M.S. had separate budgets for joint projects?

Of all Paton's efforts, paternalistic or not, to build up an independent Indian church, his mediation in the disputes of the ancient churches of St. Thomas (known as the Syrian Orthodox, though according to M.M. Thomas, they are neither Syrian nor Orthodox), were the least successful. Like footmarks on the sand they left no trace, for the disputes continue today, like the feuds of the Scottish clans passing from generation to generation. Paton's description of the situation in 1931 shows his involvement, and also the lines of division as M.M. Thomas describes them today. For this reason, Paton's letter is given in an appendix instead of being quoted in full here. There are now splinter groups from the main division between those who acknowledge the oversight of the Patriarch of Antioch, and those who do not, those who joined the Anglican Church and later the Church of South India apart from those who belong to the 'Jacobite' Church, those who acknowledge the Pope and those who belong to the reformed Mar Thoma church. The two main independent Syrian Orthodox groups have brought lawsuits against each other concerning the considerable amount of property in the case, which may be why there was the appeal to

Lord Irwin for impartial assessors. It is interesting that Paton was involved, because the other mediators were Anglicans, Bishop Gore, Bishop Palmer and so on. However, the debilitating effect on the Churches of St. Thomas may account for the tendency of Christians in Kerala to vote Communist. M.M. Thomas says that they simply do not associate the church with any political or social view, but find their aspirations reflected in the Communist party.

Whether Paton's contribution to the upbuilding of an independent church in an independent state was sympathetic and apposite, or paternalistic and arrogant, it is agreed that it was very important and valuable. Unfortunately these problems of church finance and colonial exploitation are not amenable to either rational or moral appeals, but Paton did achieve a work of Christian reconciliation which was not entirely without fruit.

When I received the following letter from Dr Marcus Ward, I was inclined to accept his self-depreciatory remarks, that he was writing from hero-worship. Now that this chapter has been completed, one can appreciate why he wrote as he did, why Bishop Newbigin saw Paton as a corrective to much missionary thought which never rose beyond its own patch of the field and as a force against the temptation to become a Sahib, and why Miss McNair, Miss Brockway and Dr Young found him such a pillar of strength. All the problems Paton confronted remain in India to a greater or lesser degree except that mission is now truly in the hands of the Indian Church.

> Dr Ward wrote: 'I went to Madras in 1932 and it was there that I saw and talked with him for the last time alive. The circumstances were highly improbable — a ball at Government House! It was at the close of the old era when missionaries had, and for the most part welcomed the entrée. There came a point . . . in the evening when a group of us were taking refreshment at one end of a colonnade at the side of the ballroom. Suddenly there appeared at the other end — A Presence. "Good Lord, it's Bill Paton" said one. I still recall almost a sense of the memories as W.P. in full clerical evening rig advanced down the corridor, with his slightly nautical gait, conveying the sense of being master of the situation, regardless of all the captains and kings, so to speak. Of the subsequent conversation, chaffing, and hilarity I recall nothing. But the sense of almost over-powering personality remains. There was nothing contrived or self-centred about it. Somehow the impact of the man himself, in control of the situation, adding to the quality of life, and leaving me at any rate a better person'.

Chapter VI
From the Tents at Jerusalem to the Tabernacle of St. Thomas (1928-1938)

When the time came for a 'Message' to be drafted from the third World Conference of the I.M.C., it was not necessary for a William Temple to crouch under a table to write it by candlelight, as he did at Jerusalem, for the conference was housed in the gleaming new buildings of the Madras Christian College at Tambaram. The delegates were, however, enduring the hardship of enforced celibacy, since their wives were quartered at a distance, in Madras, and many of them were ill for several days because of the peculiar climate at Tambaram.[1] The contrast between meeting in Jerusalem, which to them represented the tough missionary assignment to Islam, and the I.M.C.'s visit to the oldest mission field of all, that of the churches of St. Thomas, close to the supposed burial place of St. Thomas in Madras, could be held to represent the movement from the I.M.C' preoccupation with mission per se, to its developing understanding of the mission of the church.[2] Most of this chapter will be concerned with the developing identity of the I.M.C. 1928-38 and the consequent changes in missiological thought. These are conveniently crystallised in the two meetings of the I.M.C. at Jerusalem at Easter 1928 and at Tambaram over Christmas 1938. There are limitations to this somewhat geometric method, of taking two points and drawing a line between them, as Paton himself wrote:

> 'I recognise, of course, as fundamental to the whole matter, that we are setting on foot a movement to which Jerusalem is incidental. We must, however, make full use of the unique importance of Jerusalem in securing the help of the men we want, and I think the plan we have settled on will secure that without at the same time involving us in loading an excessive amount of memoranda on all delegates'.[3]

Although it was the third international ecumenical conference to be held in the 1920s, the Jerusalem meeting of the I.M.C. did achieve a number of ecumenical innovations, including the first united communion service, and marks the beginning of participation by third world nationals in the ecumenical movement on more than a token scale. Paton was not alone in considering that the I.M.C. meeting at Tambaram was the most important for the Christian Church of the three ecumenical conferences held in 1937-38, as compared with the Life and Work conference held at Oxford in August 1937 and the Faith and Order Conference held in Edinburgh two weeks later.[4] Both I.M.C. meetings were significant not only for the international missionary movement, but also for the ecumenical movement as a whole, though both were very nearly cancelled, a fact of significance in itself.

There is a certain pattern to both meetings, perhaps because both bear the imprint of the personalities of Mott and Paton, and because the content of the meetings — the Christian message to the non-Christian world — and the means of expressing it in the modern conflict-torn world, were the same. The nature of the I.M.C. meetings was very different from the S.C.M. Quadrennials. Those gatherings were more of the nature of rallies to evangelise the students and to inspire them with the vision and information of missionary and social work. Numbers were only limited by practical considerations such as the size of the central hall being used or the amount of accommodation available. Only the enthusiasm and the devotional atmosphere were carried over into the I.M.C. meetings, in spite of the fact that so many participants were former or present members of the S.C.M. and sister bodies in the W.S.C.F. Unlike the Life and Work and Faith and Order conferences, the I.M.C. meetings were not, strictly speaking, conferences at all, but enlarged committee meetings. Mott and Paton stuck to this point when the Northern Missionary Council objected that changes to the constitution of the I.M.C. could only be adopted by a world missionary conference, not a committee meeting.[5] The aim in this was that numbers could be restricted to representatives of the national missionary councils and younger churches, officers of the I.M.C. and a few experts. Therefore, in contrast to the Edinburgh world missionary conference, when members were sent by the missionary societies in a ratio proportionate to their expenditure in the field, which gave a total of 1,200 participants, there were 400 delegates at Jerusalem, which represented triple the membership of the committee and 50 leaders of the 'younger churches'. At Madras, owing to the extension of the I.M.C.'s work in Africa and the Far East, there were 471 members.

To trace the hand of Paton in the maze of preparations and administration, is very difficult, which is why a disproportionate amount of space has been given to the conference preparations, where his hand can be more clearly detected. He was ubiquitous, going from one section meeting to another; he was responsible for the administrative and literary work involved in the meetings except for that which appertained to the press officer, and he took the chair at numerous minor consultations which resulted from the fact that various regional organisations such as the N.C.C. of China, were sufficiently well represented to make a meeting worthwhile. Both conferences represent a Herculean labour on his part, since Oldham gave minimal assistance, having been granted leave of absence for the Royal Commission to East Africa (Stokes-Phelps) 1927-28 and having been preoccupied with the Oxford conference 1934-37.[6] In many ways the combination of administration and the advances in missionary thought which the Jerusalem and Tambaram represent a creative inter-play of 'Red Tape and the Gospel'.

It is difficult to appreciate retrospectively how close the I.M.C. came to cancelling the Jerusalem and Tambaram meetings. The decision to hold an enlarged council meeting in September 1927 was taken at the I.M.C. committee meeting held at Atlantic City, U.S.A., in January 1925, and this was confirmed at the meeting at Rättvik, Sweden, in 1926.[7] Oldham, however, had already written to Warnshuis in July 1925 that the British missionary boards were unresponsive to the idea because of their financial difficulties, and the belief that the expenditure would not be justified. On the other hand, the Germans want 'to throw their whole intellectual energies into it', the Swiss and the Scandinavian countries are greatly interested and the Europeans 'are not in a temper at the present time to follow blindly an Anglo-Saxon lead'. He noted the beginning of considerable German preparations, conferences and study-circles, endorsed by the 1925 Bremen missionary conference.[8] In fact one might add that the German preparations were out of proportion to the size of their delegation of eight, which was limited because of financial difficulties and the lack of English-speaking German mission staff. Oldham expressed his own views to Thompson of the W.M.M.S., who acted as a spokesman for the other reluctant missions.

> 'I share your objection to anything in the nature of a conference on world subjects. What I urged on the other hand, was that if there is to be international co-operation at all a meeting of some kind is necessary . . . since it must be held we must make the best of a bad job'.[9]

Oldham found that the Bishop of Salisbury, and other influential members of the British I.M.C. group were very critical, because they did not want a conference which was mere talk. The root of the problem, if one reads between the lines of Oldham's correspondence, was that there were widespread doubts about the future shape and role of the I.M.C. and the direction of international missionary co-operation. It was also felt in Britain that each area of the mission field had its own specialised problems, and that there was little to be gained by making missionaries in other parts of the world listen to them. One is drawn irresistibly to the conclusion that had it not been for Mott's inspiration and German and Scandinavian enthusiasm there would have been no meeting. There was much vagueness about the agenda for Jerusalem as well, but it seems that Schlunk, Richter and Frick found the kernel idea, the Christian message in a non-Christian world. Paton sailed back from India in February 1927 writing an article for the N.C.C. Review entitled 'A plea for unity'. The principal motive in holding the conference for him seems to have been the degree to which it would stimulate church unity.[10]

The choice of Jerusalem was Mott's, because he found the conference on missions to the Moslem world held on the Mount of Olives in 1926 so inspiring. He overruled Missionsinspektor Würz's complaint that the romantic appeal of Jerusalem should not influence the decision. Paton identified a source which he does not name as spreading rumours about the safety of the city, but eventually even the difficulties over borrowing the Kaiserswerth deaconesses' buildings in Jerusalem after the British military authorities had handed them back in 1927 were overcome.[11] The fact that the German missions in Jerusalem acted as hosts sealed the reconciliation of the German missions, while a significant work of Christian unity was achieved in the way in which Russian and Greek Orthodox church dignitaries and religious entertained the delegates. As at Tambaram, the dates of the conference were determined by the advice given on the most favourable climatic conditions.

Much greater difficulties were encountered when a sequel to Jerusalem was planned. The decision to accept one of the pressing invitations for the I.M.C. to meet in the Far East could not be made without controversy. On the table at the meeting of the Ad Interim Committee of the I.M.C. at Salisbury in July 1934 lay invitations from the N.C.C.s of Japan, China and India, supported by letters from individual denominations in the field. The reaction of the meeting was that these invitations were inspired by the belief that an I.M.C. Council meeting in the Far East would help the younger churches in their present difficulties in a time of revolution, and enrich the western churches as well. Paton wrote to Hawkins of the L.M.S. revealing that for him the two most serious considerations were the fact that the I.M.C. had not met in the East since Jerusalem, and that the Council might lose its influence in the East if it did not meet there.[12]

Unfortunately, the I.M.C. committee meeting at Northfield, U.S.A., (October 1935), attempted to effect a compromise which was logical to European minds, but quite unacceptable in the East, namely to hold the conference at Kowloon in the Hong Kong 'new territories'. The Chinese and Japanese delegates at Northfield did not convey the depth of feeling about this at the meeting, so Paton was unprepared for the storm he encountered as he began his world tour in Japan. Some Japanese Christians and the Japanese government interpreted the decision as being actuated by the desire to prevent the conference from being influenced by an Eastern power. Such was the disappointment that the conference was not coming to Japan that Paton was told that had Dr Ebisawa not been a Christian, Japanese public opinion would have required him to commit hari-kari.[13] Paton did his best to shield Dr Ebisawa from any blame for the I.M.C. decision, but left Japan with the impression that it would be as easy for the Japanese to go to China as to Kowloon. In China Paton was very impressed to meet Chinese leaders who said that they would prefer to go to Japan than to a British colony which had all the associations of the opium wars attached to it. The Chinese had also expected to be hosts, and resented not being allowed to choose the venue. Paton saw clearly that no Chinese co-operation would be forthcoming for a meeting which was in China geographically, but not politically. With great tact Paton promised that the question should be re-opened and made discreet inquiries about an alternative centre. He cabled Mott to alert him to the emergency, but did not commit the I.M.C.[14] Eventually it was agreed to meet in Hangchow. The Chinese whom Paton met in November 1935 recognized that the situation in China was deteriorating so much that it might not be possible in three years' time to hold a meeting in China, so some of them suggested India. In the event the N.C.C. of China was forced to concede in November 1937 that hostilities in the Sino-Japanese war had reached the point where it was no longer possible to hold an international conference in China. There was debate as to whether the conference should be postponed or cancelled, but since the idea of the conference was to help the Church withstand the very pressures which caused the war, and since preparations were already so far advanced, it was decided to continue. So the conference came to Tambaram, Paton's sensitivity having averted a disastrous choice of venue.[15]

The doubts about the holding of the conference were voiced by the L.M.S. on financial grounds. In May 1938 the German delegation requested the I.M.C. to consider postponement or cancellation because of the world situation, but agreed to accept the I.M.C. decision. The six German missionaries were very eager to attend, but there was great anxiety lest the six delegates from the mission boards would suffer the fate of the German delegation to the Oxford Life and Work conference.[16] They received their visas and currency only six weeks before the conference, and their presence was one of the reasons why the press was excluded from Tambaram. Paton's correspondence with Bishop R.O. Hall of Hong Kong is very significant as an expression of the doubts surrounding the I.M.C. conference.

> Bishop Hall wrote: 'I still feel you cannot have real participation by China and Japan in an ecumenical conference when a war is on. Theoretically, however, I know the Church must carry out her programme whatever happens in the affairs of men about her. So may God bless you all in India and show us how we may make our full contribution to it all'.[17]

Two months earlier (14.1.38) Hall had argued that the conference should have been postponed, and the Madras gathering converted into a 'What does Oxford and Edinburgh mean for India?' with a similar conference in Africa in 1939. China was in the position of Belgium in 1914, so the 1938 meeting must be different from its original intention. Paton replied that if one postponed the meeting because of the Far East situation, it would have to be an indefinite postponement. (Elsewhere Paton argued that the meeting was not a Sino-Japanese peace conference. The hostilities must be seen in perspective.)

> 'I am certain that a meeting in India with Japanese and Chinese delegates present, as there will be, may well have a gravity and sense of divine judgment such as nothing else could possess . . . It is essential to try and get it out of people's heads that the I.M.C. is trying to interpret Oxford and Edinburgh to the East since that is a very small part of the total aim'.

This exchange of letters shows that the roles had been reversed between Bishop Hall and Paton because in December 1935 it was Bishop Hall who rebuked Paton for saying that one could not expect European delegates to leave Europe on the eve of war, by asking what he thought the Chinese felt, whose country was actually at war.[18] If one considers what a sensitive observer of Chinese opinion Bishop Hall was, one can appreciate the extent of people's doubts. All Japanese Christians and missionaries in Japan would have agreed with him, judging by Dr Axling's letter, written on behalf of the N.C.C. of Japan, but Dr Axeling himself wrote that he considered that there might be an early settlement and that a conference would be a wonderful chance to create a new atmosphere. He believed that the Chinese and Japanese would rise above the situation and work for better days.[19] In fact the Chinese managed to send a delegation of sixty to Tambaram, whose wisdom, dignity and Christian experience made them the outstanding delegation. The Japanese delegation was much smaller, led by the Japanese pioneer of social work, Dr Kagawa, and was rather subdued because of the intolerable moral position their country's invasion of China had placed them in, and their fear of reprisals when they returned home. Nevertheless, to hold the conference in such circumstances after such a long search for a venue was a great act of faith, which marks out the Tambaram meeting from all other ecumenical conferences except the W.S.C.F./- Y.M.C.A. conference in Amsterdam in July 1939.

Paton was appointed third secretary of the I.M.C. at the Rättvik meeting of the I.M.C. committee, and after he had worked out six months' notice with the N.C.C. of India, returned to England in February 1927. Even allowing for the fact that he then had one of his recurrent attacks of influenza, it is surprising that it was not until the end of May that he and Oldham sent Mott the definitive list of topics for study and subsequent discussion at Jerusalem.[20] The correspondence which he and Warnshuis of the New York office of the I.M.C. conducted during 1927 suggests that it was extremely difficult to co-ordinate study plans, and that a certain amount of friction was generated by the Americans putting their own plans into action and then informing the London office. Paton was sceptical about Warnshuis' system of getting groups together to which one person delivers a paper, and one or two others draft statements, nor did he think the standard of the papers he saw was very high. In fact the lack of time and the geographical difficulty of assembling suitable groups made this scheme impracticable in most countries. Hodgkin wrote to Warnshuis vehemently urging him to ensure that young people, particularly those still in college, were involved in the studies, even though one should not be unduly accommodating concerning the conservative theology now gaining ground among them.[21] Paton's inexperience may account for the fact that the majority of the preparatory papers were by Americans, presumably recruited by Warnshuis. For Mott did not repeat his Herculean labours of compiling preparatory reports from questionnaires to form the basis of the conference volumes, as he did for the Edinburgh world missionary conference in 1910. Instead, papers were submitted for the delegates' consideration on the topics chosen for the conference. The most outstanding contributors were Dr. Kenyon Butterfield, Professor de Schweinitz Brunner, who had been conducting research for the N.C.C. of Korea, and also in China and India, and Dr Rufus Jones, an American member of the Society of Friends. The imbalance can be seen in the volume on race relations and Christian mission, where three of the four preparatory papers are by Americans (one a black). Considering the state of race relations in India, or in China, where the massacre of students by British troops in Shanghai had embittered Chinese opinion, a contribution from the Far East would have been relevant.[22] Inevitably the papers gave the impression of a theological 'tendenz' unrepresentative of the I.M.C. and offensive to the Continental delegates, who were so disturbed by what they read before the meeting that a special meeting of Continental delegates with Mott and Paton had to be called in Cairo before the meeting in Jerusalem.[23]

More significant for the Jerusalem meeting itself was Oldham's success in securing the presence at the conference of R.H. Tawney of the London School of Economics, Grimshaw of the I.L.O., Hocking of Harvard, Weigle of Yale, Karl Heim of Tübingen, Kenyon Butterfield, Kraemer of the Dutch Bible Society, working in the Dutch East Indies, Stanley Jones, freelance evangelist in India, Paul Sandegren and S. McCrea Cavert, all of whom exercised considerable influence within the I.M.C. in the succeeding decade.

In the preceding chapter it was said that Paton's primary purpose in his visits to Japan, Korea, China, the Dutch East Indies, Malaysia and India, 1935-36 was to stimulate interest in the world conference and to help lay the foundations of the preparatory work. His description of this tour in 'Christianity in the Eastern conflicts' was written as a preparatory study for Tambaram. After the Northfield meeting of the I.M.C. in October 1935, he expressed the principle on which he thought the preparatory studies should be arranged:

> 'I hope very much that we may escape from the vice to which a great deal of religious work is addicted, namely that of separating thought and action. We are much too fond of carrying out an investigation and then sitting down to discuss how the results of it are to be 'followed up' — this is sometimes unavoidable — but I doubt if there is real advance unless those who have to do the work do the study. It is a very responsible job to get preparation started on the right lines. Hence they should not get hosts of people looking to a series of resolutions to be passed by someone else three years ahead, which they will then (perhaps) 'follow up', but rather a great number of people in every country studying their own problems realistically, sharing their progress as they go along (where the I.M.C. comes in) acting whenever action is called for, and then coming together in 1938 in a world meeting not to pass Utopian resolutions, but to take counsel together as those who have been trying to see the will of God in the concrete situations in which they are set'.[24]

Unfortunately, the hostilities in China made it very difficult to apply this principle. Merle Davis delivered his verdict to the sixth meeting of the Chinese committee on the I.M.C. meeting in Madras that the N.C.C. of Japan was not convinced by the I.M.C.'s arguments for a continuation of the conference prepar-ations, and were only acquiescing in what was being done.[25] This judgment may not be entirely fair since Dr Ebisawa did contribute several articles. In China itself only one of the six environmental studies had been completed because of the hostilities. It was decided that it would be best to make a digest of the previous ten years' studies and to keep a current record of the situation. There would be two lines of approach: the policies and experience of missionaries with response to the economic growth of the church, and the challenge of the new social order and the Christian movement in China. Merle Davis himself was in the Far East because he had converted the Geneva office of the I.M.C.'s Department of Social and Industrial Research (D.S.I.R.) into a travelling caravan, and had been engaged in field studies for Tambaram since 1937. His work can be found in volume IV of the Tambaram series, and for many delegates his work was the most useful preparation for Tambaram. His work did not pass without criticism. Bishop Hall wrote to Paton that Davis was giving the impression in China and Japan that the I.M.C. was more concerned with bringing the thoughts of the West to the East than with the contribution of the East to the family as a whole.[26] Paton apologised to him if this was so and denied that he and Mott wanted to stress that aspect.

Another preparatory volume of essays prepared by Paton independently of the Tambaram series was 'Studies in Evangelism', a symposium of essays on the develop-ments in evangelism. In his book, 'Asia and the Ecumenical Movement 1895-1961'. Dr Weber gives a comprehensive list of the Asian contributions to the Tambaram preparations as part of an excellent discussion of the Asian contribution as a whole. To this must be added the descriptions of the Batak Church in the Tambaram volumes and a series of very sophisticated and penetrating articles on mission in the Dutch East India written by Dutch missionaries whom Paton met on his world tour, which appear to have been circulated in manuscript form. Paton had been fascinated by this completely non-Anglo-Saxon field where such gains were being made in a Muslim environment, though he had long admired the system of liaison between missionaries and the Dutch colonial government.[27]

Preparations in India had a stormy beginning. A breakdown in communications occurred which is hard to explain. It seems that Paton wrote two long letters to J.Z. Hodge explaining the ideas behind the topics suggested for study at Northfield and a pamphlet entitled 'A Five Years' Plan' (the title borrowed from the Congress Party), which failed to evoke a response.[28] Instead he received letters from Alice van Doren, Paton's former colleague in the N.C.C., who was full of ideas for preparing the section on Christian education, and exploiting the talents of people like Stephen Neill, Bishop-elect of Tinnevelly, and P.O. Philips, who was planning to organise the missionaries on leave in the hill stations into discussion groups. Paton wrote to castigate the N.C.C. for its independence, saying that it would be disastrous if each country proceeded along its own lines. He declared that he thought that many missionaries on the field were already using I.M.C. ideas, so it would be unfortunate if they went in a different direction from the N.C.C. Three months later P.O. Philip replied that they had not scrapped any of the I.M.C. work, and were working on section IV, 'The Church and the economic and social environment', Christian education, the question of war and the challenge of the modern state to the Church, especially with regard to what regulations it might introduce on education and the right of conversion. The N.C.C. staff had been strengthened by the appointment of a secretary for mass movements, Whittaker, and a research and extension secretary, R. Manikam, so eventually India made a substantial contribution to the preparation.

There is reason to believe that the notorious questionnaire which Paton compiled originated in a discussion which he had in Shanghai with the members of the N.C.C. of China using a draft by Cash of the C.M.S.[29] However, when the final recension appeared two years later it was much enlarged so that there were complaints that it contained over 600 questions. It is not surprising that delegates in Africa could not answer it. Partly this was the result of the fact that there were sixteen sections to the conference, which is probably the highest number of sections any ecumenical conference has ever had, and these were divided into sub-sections, though some of the lines of division changed at Tambaram. Paton's letters accompanying the questionnaire suggest that the correspondents should only answer those sections which they found relevant to their situation and that their answers should take whatever form they thought fit. Miss Gibson and Hartenstein conducted a long correspondence in an effort to get the questions accurately translated and interpreted in German.[30] A further complication was that the correspondents in the field kept re-formulating the questions, which accounts for the number of recensions.

Dr Weber's comment on the preparations for Tambaram is that one must not allow them to be eclipsed by Kraemer's work 'The Christian Message in a Non-Christian World', and this is undoubtedly right. Important as Kraemer's work was in stimulating thought and debate on the question of the Christian message in a non-Christian world, nevertheless it did not command the exclusive attention of the delegates. Today, Dr Visser't Hooft considers the situation absurd, saying that Tambaram was the only conference at which it has ever been a question of 'Here is your theology, presented to you all complete'.[31] Visser't Hooft was close to Kraemer, his compatriot, now the professor of the history of religions at Leiden University, and he is right in asserting that this was Kraemer's own view of his work, to which he thought the Tambaram conference would simply say 'Amen'; but the I.M.C. organisers did not intend this. How things reached this pitch, and why Kraemer had such a miserable time at Tambaram is an interesting question, especially as it may have been Paton's encouragement which misled him. Since his book has become a classic work of theology since the war, being reprinted as recently as 1969, it has been discussed in detail in Chapter IV as Paton endorsed it personally.

It would seem that the I.M.C. had envisaged a book on the scale of Paton's own preparatory volume for Tambaram, but Kraemer was soon writing to Paton that he was going back to fundamental questions and would need much more space than the publishers would allow him. Paton took the decision to allow Kraemer to write nearly double the intended length, and gave him every encouragement as well as arranging the financial means. He then supervised the publication and distribution of the book. Unfortunately, despite the entreaties of his friends, so Bishop Hall recalled, Kraemer insisted on writing in English instead of Dutch, with the result that his style is often heavy, laboured and difficult to understand. Paton commissioned Nicol MacNicol, as the English-speaking missionary who understood Kraemer best, to assist him improve the English of his book.

Paton insisted that the book was aimed at preparing the way for thorough discussion at Tambaram, and that there would be no question of anyone's views being railroaded through. There were two methods which the I.M.C. could have employed to achieve a theological analysis of the rationale for evangelism. Either they could have contrived the kind of symposium which Oldham did for the Oxford conference,[32] when a group of theologians circulated their writings to each other and then rewrote them until they achieved a common understanding of the problem and something approaching a consensus; or they could select someone capable of writing a book which would provide real 'meat' for the discussion, and a challenge which would not be ignored. This Kraemer did, though it must be said that all the evidence points to the fact that even if 6,000 copies were sold before the publication date in October 1938, few people read the book, and even fewer understood it.[33]

It has been argued that the I.M.C. made a mistake in not appointing a theologian whose views belonged to a majority grouping in the I.M.C., or to a definite 'school', because Kraemer's work came under attack from both the American and Indian liberal theologians such as Pitney van Dusen and A.J. Appasamy and from German theologians susceptible to Karl Barth's influence. For although Kraemer had been profoundly influenced by Barth he was very critical of him for 'not asking the right questions'.[34] As Watson of the American University in Cairo, and others who were influenced by missionary realpolitik wrote: although Kraemer's views were unacceptable to many, they provided a good counter-balance to Hocking. Continental and Scandinavian confidence in the I.M.C. was maintained without the reports being unduly influenced by Lutheran theology, which was the case at Oxford, when the Lutheran doctrine of the 'orders of creation' was far too prominent, and the emphasis on 'German' eschatalogy unjustified in view of the imminence of war.[35] Significantly, both Paton and Kraemer received many letters from missionaries in the field such as Scholten of Tanganika, whose reaction could be paraphrased as 'at last someone has put into words what I have been feeling for a long time, but could not express myself'.[36] Paton himself would accept no criticism of the I.M.C. decision to choose Kraemer, but declared that the protagonists were a good deal closer to agreement than they realized, and even those most opposed to Kraemer should be grateful for the way in which he had stimulated ideas.[37]

If W.M. Horton's reaction in his essay: 'Between Hocking and Kraemer' is a typical reaction, then it is very significant indeed, especially in indicating how the I.M.C. may have stimulated a theological development in the understanding of mission.[38] When he travelled in the Far East in 1932, Horton wrote, he found himself in Hocking's wake, enjoying an atmosphere of sympathetic goodwill which Hocking had aroused in non-Christian religious teachers. He felt the same sympathy, and agreed with the idea that all religious men are natural allies against secularism and materialism. He found no contradiction between his faith in Christ and the unique elements in Christianity, and the hope of inter-religious ecumenism. However, in 1939 he was aware of a great change in his perspective caused by the way in which he has had to concentrate his attention on missions in preparation for Tambaram and also by the new paganism of 'blood and soil' which has arisen. The way in which nationalism has become a religion has made him realize that if one religion is beyond the pale, then all religions are bad because they exalt a limited understanding to absolute truth. Similarly, he saw that two symbols could not be identified, and that Christ was more than a symbol, but was essential reality. He had been groping

154

towards a doctrine of revelation as more than the fulfilment of man's religious aspirations. So he could accept Kraemer's position, especially as he reflected on what he has seen in his travels on the mission field.

Discussion tended to polarise around two of Kraemer's concepts: the radical discontinuity of Christian revelation from everything else that had gone before, and the place of reason. MacNicol and Brunner engaged in much debate in the pages of the I.R.M. on the latter subject, relating it to the understanding of the Jesus of history as the Christ who can only be recognised by faith. Others wished to see reason as a faculty which prepared the mind to understand Christian truth, and others were prepared to concede that reason was irrelevant to conversion, but insisted that it should be employed afterwards to understand what was believed.[39] It is to the abiding credit of Kraemer's work that he opened up the most fundamental questions and did so in the context of mission. Kraemer's criticism of this debate was that the politeness of his critics had prevented them from being sufficiently radical in their objections.[40] The essays published in the Tambaram series are in fact less criticism than elaborations and variations on the Kraemer theme, though it is not clear if that was their writers' aim, and T.C. Chao, for example, caused Kraemer to modify his position somewhat, when he came to restate it in the volume.

Apart from the study preparations which Paton organized, the most important preparations were those for the representation of the 'younger churches'. It is difficult to emphasize sufficiently strongly the importance of the efforts to ensure adequate representation of what is now known as the 'Third world'. Not only did it mean that the voices of Asian and African Christians were heard challenging European views on the relation of the Christian message to the non-Christian religions, and giving a non-Western context to Christianity; but also their presence guaranteed the important theological and methodological transition from viewing evangelism as the work of specialist organizations in the West to considering mission as integral to the existence of the church in whatever land it is set. At Jerusalem, delegates had the experience of being addressed in an African language by the Bishop of Uganda, with a missionary colleague translating. The general policy seems to have been to select 50 individual outstanding churchmen such as Dr Francis Wei, T.C. Chao, Miss Tilak of India, Dr Jabavu of South Africa, and so on, rather than to pressurise the N.C.C.s to elect non-missionary representatives. The lengths to which Paton was prepared to go are revealed in his correspondence with Mott, when he only grudgingly accepts Azariah of Dornakal's plea that he is ill, and refers to the intense pressure that they have been putting on him to come.[41] At Tambaram a more radical policy of election and co-option instead of co-option alone was nearly torpedoed by certain missions who were reluctant to be represented by nationals. A less intransigent line by Paton, and the I.M.C. might have failed to achieve a majority percentage of Asian and African churchmen at the meeting.

Before Oldham phased himself out of the I.M.C., Paton had no first hand experience of Africa, but fortunately Miss Gibson remained with the I.M.C. and continued the African secretarial work. She tackled the problem of making Kraemer's book intelligible to the Africans. It was from East Africa that the idea came of getting all the Africans together on one boat to 'orientate' them, itself a problem because of the segregation practiced by steam companies, and to provide a 'warming up' conference for them in Colombo before they went to Tambaram itself. The Africans were much burdened with a sense of responsibility for going and were very earnest about preparation. Except for Baeta of Ghana, who delighted a bemused Jacques Rossel by greeting him at Tambaram in fluent Swiss German, learnt in Basel, they had not been out of their countries before, so it was arranged that most N.C.Cs should send an African and a European together. Greaves of Kenya was doubtful of this procedure, writing that: 'What they gain in English, they lose in spirituality'. The Africans may have provided an exotic touch for some delegates, but they ensured that African problems were discussed.[42] The Kenyans returned so enthusiastic about the conference that they could not stop talking about it, though both were ill and one nearly died as a result of the unaccustomed climate. Mina Soga of South Africa said: 'My journey out of Africa turned me from a South African into an African. Madras made me a world Christian'.[43]

There is much in the tone of the correspondence concerning Africa to suggest that it was not appreciated in missions in Africa that the I.M.C. office in London was serious when it insisted that Africans should be sent rather than first class missionaries. Couve of the Paris Mission wrote that he thought it undesirable for a West African to meet 'the yellow world in the present circumstances', and it would be very difficult to get permission from colonial authorities for an African to go to the Far East.[44] In fact, the Africans had such an impact on the Japanese, that Kagawa was heard saying that if racism was as bad as that something would have to be done about it. The apathy of some of the Councils, such as the Tanganyika Council, was in marked contrast to the enthusiasm of those chosen to go. One missionary was so enthusiastic that he was prepared to sleep on deck under a blanket to get to Colombo.

The worst problem was the South African delegation. It is difficult to think of another part of the I.M.C. constituency where ecumenical relationships were at a lower ebb. Only three Anglican dioceses had joined the missionary council (b 1934, d 1941) yet the I.M.C. wanted an Anglican at Tambaram. The first list of names which the secretary, du Toit, sent to London consisted entirely of Dutch Reformed ministers. Paton wrote several letters to insist on an Anglican, and in particular, Father Victor C.R., an expert on urban mission. To his amazement Father Victor's brother, the Bishop of Lebombo, whose diocese stretched into Portugese East Africa, was sent instead. The bishop was extremely 'high Anglican', bringing an element to Tambaram which some Continental delegates had never encountered before. It took more letters and the intervention of Kenneth Grubb, a freelance missionary and research worker, to sort out the South African delegation as a balance of white and black, including one woman.[45] Perhaps more by accident than by design, Paton managed to get a number of Anglo-Catholics to Tambaram, introducing a new element to the I.M.C. Archbishop Garbett had never been interested in foreign missions before, but after being persuaded to go to Tambaram was so completely converted that he served as a vice-chairman of the I.M.C.[46]

It seems that the white South Africans and the West Africans resented being made to stop at Colombo for the preparatory meeting. Du Toit was evidently afraid lest the blacks should say too much about the situation in South Africa. At Tambaram Miss Gibson foiled his attempt to muzzle them at sectional meetings. Chief Albert Luthuli and Miss Mina Soga made a deep impression on the conference, as they did when they toured South Africa, speaking to white congregations on their return home. Mott had a special session with the black Africans which greatly pleased them.[47] However, it was decided that an I.M.C. conference statement would do more harm than good. At Jerusalem, Max Yergan, the American black who worked for the South African S.C.M., was present as a reminder of the evils of discrimination, but it was more valuable to have Africans themselves, specially as the delegates were impressed by their serenity and unembittered attitude in describing the situation in southern Africa. Before Tambaram several European bishops had already broken one racial barrier by travelling third class on the Indian railway from Karachi to Madras. However, more is achieved in terms of race relations by the actual presence of an adequate representation from the countries concerned than by formal statements.

In 1927 Mott and Paton did a little judicious wooing of the China Inland Mission to get representatives of the so-called 'Faith Missions' to Jerusalem. These missions were notorious for their refusal to abide by comity agreements, or co-operate with other missions, and for their suspicion of both 'liberal' and 'continental' theology. Warnshuis thought the I.M.C. should not protect them, or negotiate with governments for them, because of their attitude, but Paton's patience was rewarded in that the I.M.C. managed to find a representative sympathetic to the I.M.C. to attend Jerusalem, and in recruiting Kenneth Grubb for Tambaram, Paton established a very important link with the World Dominion Press and the World Evangelization Crusade.[48]

To gain a full understanding of the significance of the presence of German delegates, it would be necessary to contrast the unhappy and strained relationships between the German churches and other ecumenical organizations such as the Faith and Order movement and the excellent relations cultivated by Paton, Oldham and Miss Gibson, which are reflected in the pages of the accounts of both conferences, both edited by Martin Schlunk, 'Von den Höhen des Ölberges' (1928) and 'Das Wunder der Kirche' (1939). It was unfortunate that all the German delegates were accommodated on the same corridor, and were, at both conferences, given less chance to mix with other delegates, but it was a major diplomatic triumph that they were there at all, and an example of Christian amity prevailing over theological differences. To Paton, the presence of such a diversity of delegates was living proof of the reality of the world-wide Church.

Paton's responsibilities at both conferences extended to raising money, assisting with passage money when necessary, arguing with Mott and Warnshuis about publicity arrangements, which he considered should not be vested in Basil Matthews' hands alone, and for enforcing the decision to ban the press from the sessions.[49] The persistence of one correspondent of one religious journal provoked him to write to J.Z. Hodge of the N.C.C. of India: 'I am sorry that people are sorry because we are allowing no visitors, but I should have thought that the reasons were pellucidly clear, that this is neither the Indian National Congress nor the Keswick Convention, but a serious gathering of Christians to do some business together'.[50]

Although it would seem from the ecumenical manoeuvrings preceding the Stockholm Life and Work conference, the Faith and Order conference in Lausanne and the I.M.C. meeting, that the lines of demarcation were firmly drawn between one ecumenical organisation and another; and although the I.M.C. was committed to strict neutrality on confessional issues or matters of church order, nevertheless, as I have shown in my Master of Arts thesis, these distinctions could not be observed absolutely. Therefore it is not surprising that the debate surrounding the Christian Message in the I.M.C. meetings got increasingly theological and unavoidably touched matters of the deepest religious principle. Paton himself was initially sceptical about the value of introducing the subject of 'The Christian Message' in the I.M.C. because he thought that the process would not result in more than a re-shuffling of vaguely conceived ideas. He thought that too much time would be needed to achieve an agreement, that it would be contrary to I.M.C. policy and inevitably dogmatic and controversial. He foresaw 'rocks ahead'.[51] It seems, however, that Warnshuis was responsible for turning the idea of a study of comparative religions into a positive affirmation of the Christian faith, and that Paton had to bow before an unlikely combination of Robert Speer, Hocking's opponent, William Temple, and the German members of the I.M.C.[52]

It is clear from the opening speeches at the Jerusalem I.M.C. meeting that the problem that troubled all delegates was that the distinctiveness of the Christian message had been lost. Speer maintained that there must be no uncertainty, that in Christ there was 'a sufficient, absolute and final Saviour of mankind, a religion with unique values, with the divinely inspired idea of God and the world, and with an absolute, unique and irreplaceable personality in Christ'. The crucial question (with which in fact the whole conference had to wrestle) was how one distinguishes between that which is essential and that which can be adapted to the age and culture. Very profound changes have come over the Christian religion with the disappearance of old values. Especially for evangelism in China, the morality in Christianity must be rediscovered.[53]

Kraemer criticized missionaries for losing a comprehensive view of life and the means of formulating the Christian message so that it could be understood by non-Christians. By seeking to find 'spiritual values' in other religions, the preparatory papers had avoided central issues. Missionaries should have a sense of the glorious mission of the Gospel and an intense longing to discover spiritual values in other religions.[54] His exhortation that they seek the children of God in the world was supported by Karl Heim of Tübingen. There was a great fear of syncretism among delegates, who were alarmed by those prepared to call on all religious minded people in the world to band together against the forces of secularism, and by talk of 'the leavening influence of Christians in society' with which the adherents of the 'social Gospel' spoke of campaigns to redeem society as a whole by social reform pro-grammes.[55] Controversy centred on whether new religious values might be found and preserved from other religions. Apart from the question of syncretism, there was no agreement among converts from Hinduism and Confucianism about whether Christianity fulfilled or nullified their religious past. Canon Quick warned of the danger of falling into the error of Marcion who failed to recognize the God of our Lord Jesus Christ in the Old Testament.[56] The various sections examined the non-Christian religions in detail, because no-one doubted the importance of proper study of them nor the mistakes of former arrogant attitudes to the inadequacies of other religions.

Temple's nocturnal labours, as chairman of the section on the Christian Message, resulted in a statement which was received in stunned silence, because no-one believed it was possible to express an agreement between them all. Significantly, it was based on the Lausanne Report, section II, 'The Church's Call to the World', but it is still a missionary document.[57] It begins by describing the instability in the world and the yearning for social justice. The message to this world is Christ. The Gospel is the answer to the world's greatest need and either it is true for all, or it is not true at all (a phrase which summarized Paton's own theology perfectly). Relentless and exacting self-criticism is demanded for the health of all souls and the missionary movement itself. No religious imperialism can be tolerated, nor any attempt to use the missionary for ulterior ends, even the management of souls in their better interest. The younger churches must be free to express the Gospel through their own genius and racial heritage. The compelling motive is to share God's love, the life which Christ gives. Older churches have been slow to realize their responsibility for evangelism and have not effectively resisted race-hatred, race envy or social envy, the lust for wealth and exploitation. One is still thankful for what has been achieved, but pioneering efforts must continue. This task can only be achieved by the Holy Spirit and by prayer. The message ended with a call to those with the necessary talents to work for a Christian view of life, and to non-Christians (in connection with whom, the spiritual values of various faiths were listed) to look beyond the limitations of culture and historical traditions, to Christ.[58]

The message has been variously described as a call to action and as a call to prayer. It was certainly more than a communique from ecclesiastical diplomats, and it was not an academic judgment on the validity of conflicting theologies. The uniqueness of the Christian Gospel is unequivocally upheld, beside which any valuable contribution from another religion or culture is a relative thing. Awareness of the mistakes of the missionary movement in the past prevented a triumphalist note. The motivation behind the message was to challenge missionaries to fresh efforts, not to console them in their difficulties. Paton took up these themes in his book 'A Faith for the World', which has already been discussed in an earlier chapter. It is unfortunate that it is not possible within the confines of this chapter to discuss in more detail the principles at issue concerning the Christian approach to men of other faiths. Concerning the 'Christian Message' which Temple wrote, it should be remembered that these statements were a relatively new phenomenon in church circles in 1938, and that they therefore seemed more fresh and significant than they do when they are read today.[59]

Paton attempted to justify this method of working when he wrote in the preface to 'The World Mission of the Church: Tambaram, Madras 1938' that:

> 'Unless there is the effort to find agreement in saying something
> together, there is not likely to be in evidence that strong determination to
> understand the other and to be understood by him, and in the tension
> between two points of view perhaps to find a higher truth, which leaves on
> all those who have experienced it an ineffaceable mark'.

He considers that it is not merely a question of good fellowship, but intense contact in an effort to comprehend God's will. Another result is that the less advantaged churches in the west and the east can learn from those more fortunate. He concludes 'There was a drawing together of the whole Christian church in the providence of God, and it has pleased Him to use such instruments as the I.M.C. and the Tambaram meeting to further this process (of unity) . . . It is hard for anyone who has entered even a little into this characteristic modern feature of the life of the whole Church not to feel that here God is manifestly at work, in spite of our weakness and pride, and that the deepest significance of this meeting lies in the place it will hold in that sequence of redeeming action whereby He is leading back His people to be one, even as He and the Son are one'.[60]

From a multitude of letters, it is clear that Paton did see the Tambaram conference as part of God's plan to unite the Church, and that this is part of his redeeming action. This was probably the conviction which sustained Paton's efforts in organizing the Tambaram meeting and was central to the self-understanding of the delegates.

The significant difference between Jerusalem and Tambaram is the degree to which 'The Christian Message' had become 'The faith by which the Church lives', to oversimplify the increased appreciation of the role of the Church, which is, so the report of Section 1 declared, called to warn mankind of judgement unless there is repentance, to speak fearlessly against brutality and aggression, to attack social evils at their roots, to console those wronged and to declare the Gospel at any cost. The Church must become in itself the actualisation among men of its own message. None are more aware of its failings than Christians, but they are constrained to declare the hope of the world. They are discovering that their unity is a fact while their governments are preparing war. In a broken and imperfect fashion the Church is even now fulfilling its calling to be within itself a foretaste of the redeemed family of God. 'By faith, but in deep assurance we declare that this body which God has fashioned through Christ cannot be destroyed'.[61]

The significance of non-Christian religions was judged in this context, but nothing was added to the conclusions reached at the Jerusalem conference. It was recognized that in them were values of deep religious experience and great moral achievement, but Christ alone is the full salvation every man needs. God has not left Himself without a witness anywhere but 'Christ is revolution, he brings conversion and regeneration when we meet Him from whatever point we started'. Therefore, witnesses for Christ must have a deep and sincere interest in the religious life of those to whom they are sent. Following Kraemer the meeting rejected the idea expressed at Jerusalem, that non-Christian religions replace the Old Testament for converts. There is no equality between them and the Old Testament since the Old Testament stands in a unique position as Jesus's Bible.[62]   Instead , the seriousness of the challenge of the 'new paganism' was recognized. Nationalism in its various manifestations was analysed, particularly at the point where in fascist states it becomes a new religion, because in the face of social disintegration, nationalism seems to many to be the only answer. The national community is considered part of the divine order, for which due thanks should be rendered, and which can command the loyalty, service and prayer of its members, but which has become corrupted by sin, especially when it appropriates to itself absolute authority. Communism was divided into two elements. In social terms it stands as a rebuke to Christian lethargy, while in philosophical terms it is completely opposed to Christianity. Scientific scepticism, though acknowledged as often springing from honest but misguided thought, was also added to make up this trilogy.[63]

In his discussion of the Tambaram debate, 'Von Geheimnis der Kirche', Walter Freytag attributes the preoccupation with the question of the Church to the external pressure on the Church, which was not present a generation previously, and this seems to be the most obvious answer.[64] He reports on the difficulties of the churches, whether criticised in India for their disunity, restricted to limited spheres of life in Japan, or rejected as a foreign import. As missionaries they could only preach Christ and marvel that people found their way into it. The Anglicans apparently contrib- uted much here with their insistence that the church be considered God's creation. A better discussion of the question of non-Christian religions than that provided by Paton is found in Siegfried Knak's contribution to 'Das Wunder der Kirche' because it shows how Kraemer's contribution relates to the conference discussions as a whole, but unfortunately it is too sophisticated to be summarized briefly here.[65]

At Tambaram the Church emerged from the timelessness of its battle with the ancient religions and faced the current contexts of the younger churches' problems and the challenge of Western Europe. One might call it a 'stiffening of the sinews'. The Tambaram discussions achieved a good balance between the theoretical considerations of ecclesiology and the practical circumstances of the life of the Church. Frequent allusions have already been made to the relationships between 'older' and 'younger' churches' delegates and to the significant change in the balance of the meetings in favour of the latter. Very delicate diplomacy was needed at all times, as the incident discussed in the preceding chapter, when Paton offended the Indian delegation at Tambaram, shows.[66] The whole question of the 'indigenization' of the Christian Church was hotly debated at both conferences, a Chinese delegate actually giving thanks for the existence of the word 'indigenization', though it is difficult to see anything felicitous about the phrase. Emphasizing the importance of the indigenous church inevitably meant re-thinking the role of the missionary worker. The debate took place at both meetings against a background of minor meetings between nationals and representatives of mission boards aimed at improving relationships.

The preparatory documents for Jerusalem contained much factual information for example, about church constitutions where the balance of power between missionary and church leadership had been re-adjusted.[67] Throughout both meetings ran the idea that the right kind of missionary, highly trained and able to co-operate with the indigenous leadership, would be needed, and welcomed for the foreseeable future, particularly to ensure that no church became solely a national institution, and no longer part of the Body of Church, which in its essence must always be an international fellowship. In the debate there was tension between older missionaries and nationals like P.O. Philip, secretary of the N.C.C. of India, who regretted that the older churches gave so much help that the growth of the young church was hindered. It could spring from the highest self-sacrifice, and yet be harmful because it sapped the recipient of initiative. Wilson Cash pleaded for an end to the dyarchy of church and mission and for the placing of missionaries and nationals on a basis of equality, a controversial point, yet he could say:

> 'The indigenous church must give the foreign workers freedom and not interfere with their business. The matters concerning missionaries' work should be left entirely in the hands of the missionaries'.

He advocated direct links between the churches and the mission boards, but his views would have been totally unacceptable at Tambaram.[68]

It became a generally held view that the home churches would benefit from missions from the younger churches, which would enrich their spiritual life. As Mott said, it was a question of sharing. Paton demonstrated this with the Mission of Fellowship to England he organized in 1932, which was an enormous success, and the post-Tambaram mission to England.[69] The principal implication, an American Baptist said, was that they should pass from paternalism to participation since before God there are no inferior races. It is not a question of which side are the benefactors, but that all are brethren. At Tambaram the racial issue was thoroughly discussed, with reference to the findings at Oxford, but the discussion sprang from the context of colonialism, not from national socialism. Both conferences played an important part in the education of European and American delegates in the realities of the racial situation.

At both meetings there was much discussion of the methods necessary to build up the younger churches and complete the transfer from missionary leadership. At the Jerusalem meeting emphasis was placed on the importance of training leaders, since the uncertain political situation in some countries might necessitate the sudden withdrawal of European missionaries, as had happened in parts of China 1925-27. At the Jerusalem conference, P.O. Philip thought that a similar crisis in India would have a very salutary effect on the complacent churches there, and urged that a larger proportion of control should pass into the hands of Indians, who must prepare themselves for the responsibility. Knak warned of a sinister development which bore a direct relationship to the way in which finance was administered, i.e. the situation in which the pastor is left to feed the flock and the missionary to preach the Gospel. The fierce and urgent discussion threw up the remark from one delegate that if they waited until they had adequate supplies of men and money before they did anything, nothing would ever be achieved. The vision though, was one of patient toil together in the harvest, rather than the flaming horizons of the march into 'unoccupied lands' of Edinburgh 1910.[70]

There was a significantly different note to the discussions at Tambaram which it is worth mentioning briefly here. Bishop Azariah summed it up when he spoke in the debate on the question of the self-support of indigenous churches, a principle which delegates had been forced to admit because of their own experiences and the studies of Merle Davis, was very far from attainment.[71] He spoke against the tendency to regard self-support as an end to be achieved at all costs, even if the work of evangelism was thereby seriously impeded. Resources were desperately needed in India so that the mass movements could be harvested, and yet it was plain that the Indians themselves were too poor to bear the cost. Would the international church shirk its responsibility by insisting on self-support with such rigidity that they would abdicate their responsibility for evangelism? From questions such as this it will be seen that the two chief ideas behind the Tambaram deliberations (the upbuilding of the church and the task of evangelism) were very hard to separate from one another. Freytag's conclusion was that the debate over the question of the indigenous church did not produce a theology of the church or even a critique of it, but was a way of bearing witness to the experience of it. In spite of all the weaknesses revealed by the debate, one could speak of a Church among the nations.[72] This in fact is the paradox of Tambaram, which Freytag hints at, that although the delegates took a long hard look at a decade of devolution and economic changes in the churches, and came to the conclusion that the ideals of self-support and self-government required much modification whether applied in Japan or India; nevertheless they could experience together what they were groping towards. Paton's own reaction to this will be discussed later, in the context of the development in Paton's ecclesiological thought.

Four fields were discussed at Jerusalem which might be brought together under the title of 'missionary strategy', three of which had not been the subject of reports at Edinburgh 1910, and all of which were further discussed at Tambaram, i.e. missions and industrialism, rural missions, race relations and religious education.

According to the introduction which Paton wrote to the fifth volume of the Jerusalem Meeting Report, the problem of industrialism was first discussed at Crans in 1920, and a resolution enjoining the study of industrialism was passed at the Lake Mohonk meeting the following year, but lack of staff prevented any action being taken before the I.M.C. meeting at Rättvik in 1926 (which was the first I.M.C. meeting which Paton attended). Paton, like many of his contemporaries had been influenced by the reports of the C.O.P.E.C. conference held in Birmingham in 1924, which had already run through three editions. He had eagerly read them in India and then had returned to England in time for the General Strike of 1926, when he and Grace Paton became very involved in the welfare activities of the National Union of Railwaymen.[73] In addition to his interest as a factor in tipping the balance in favour of industrial studies, there was also the influence of the Stockholm Life and Work conference in 1925, and the work of Temple, then Bishop of Manchester, for social reform.

Paton's paper: 'Christianity and the growth of industrialism in Asia and Africa', which forms the major part of the fifth volume of the Jerusalem report, is the work of an enthusiastic amateur, though it was compiled from material supplied by discussion groups all over the world and by Grimshaw of the International Labour Organization. It demonstrated to the Jerusalem meeting how much a layman could learn about a technical problem. It is very unfortunate that no record of the discussion at Jerusalem is supplied in the volume, nor survives elsewhere, there being only the addresses delivered by R.H. Tawney and Bishop F.J. McConnell, of the Methodist Episcopal Church in the U.S.A. It may be that the statement adopted by the council sums up not only the main points of the papers given, but also the discussion. Whoever drafted it tried to tread the narrow path between the advocates of the 'social Gospel' and the Scandinavian opposition.[74] It is an interesting advance on the positions adopted at the two S.C.M. Quadrennials which Paton attended on 'Christ and Human Need' (1912 and 1921). The statement began with the conviction that the Gospel of Christ applies to societies as much as to individuals and demonstrated that Jesus was involved with ordinary working people, which implied that the Christian should aim at realizing God's love in society as well as in his own heart. He will, therefore, welcome technological and economic advance provided that they enhance the possibilities for Christian life, and do not enslave people to them. Three fundamental criteria can be used to assess the value of the social and economic system: Christ's teaching on the sanctity of personality, on the brotherhood of men and on corporate responsibility. By contrast to this, the missionaries' frequent lack of sensitivity to the problems of industrialism have been a 'positive hindrance' to the power of the missionary enterprise. The danger from the development of western economic systems in lands previously unaffected by it inspired the consideration of many practical points, and practical suggestions.

Consequently it was decided to set up a bureau of 'social and economic' research and information' in connection with the I.M.C. which would supply missionaries and ecumenical bodies with information and awaken mission boards to the need for specialized workers. Liaison with other bodies such as the I.L.O. would be an important function. The outcome of these plans, and the history of the Department of Social and Industrial Research, finally established in September 1930, will be discussed in the next chapter because Paton had so much to do with their execution.

The reason given for studying rural affairs was that 75-85% of the mission field was rural, and that apart from being the source from which most food was provided, the farmer was in great need of education and technical assistance. The whole rural community must be influenced if it is to achieve reform and accept Christianity.[75] K.T. Paul wrote the account of the discussion, and he comments that the subject was terra incognita to about half the delegates. (Paton himself had become acquainted with the rural education centre at Moga in the Punjab, but consideration of rural questions was the brief of his colleague, Miss Ethel Gordon.) Conequently there were no burning issues or controversies, but simply an exchange of information and a discussion of what could be done to end the way in which missions had neglected rural areas.[76]

The I.M.C.'s statement on rural missions included the sentence, 'It should be the aim of the Church to help correlate all the forces in the fundamental and inclusive task of creating a real Kingdom of God in this natural human grouping that we call the community'. Dr Lo of China declared in the debate that the Church was responsible if people leave the church to find national and social salvation through other organizations. The I.M.C. statement made very specific recommendations as in the industrial report, on the type of projects to be supported. The request that a staff member of the I.M.C. should give full-time service to rural missions was not implemented. The I.M.C. reports are a beginning of the development debate which has become much more of a public issue today, but already the emphasis is on self-help and workers' co-operatives, improved technology and so on, and far removed from any question of charitable donations.

Possibly the most important single issue was the question of forced labour which was discussed in Paton's article and thoroughly debated at Jerusalem. Missionaries were in a peculiar position to gather information about the iniquities of the system, which, like the indenture system in Africa and Fiji, was little better than slavery. At Tambaram, the Bishop of Lebombo produced much evidence about forced labour in Portuguese East Africa, but at a special meeting the problem was exposed as one of great difficulty because Protestant missions in Roman Catholic colonies, where the situation was at its worst, could not achieve the leverage on the colonial government which they could in East Africa. Paton himself was involved in the collection of accurate information and appeals for intervention as in the case of the exploitation of tribesmen in New Guinea whom the German missions there were powerless to protect.[77]

Consideration of economic questions at Tambaram followed from the question of the self-support of the younger churches, according to the account by Carl Ihmels.[78] It is interesting that as director of the Leipzig Mission he accepts the importance of missions working with government for general economic improvement while writing scathingly of an unsuccessful American attempt to revive the 'Social Gospel'. Stanley Jones was responsible for the compromise whereby it was stated that individual conversions were only adequate when the individual went out to tackle society's problems. Therefore the section attempted to work out characteristics of the new order for which the Church should strive. The Church's role was seen as an educative one in many circumstances. Ihmels records the problem for the German churches since the state removed the Church's opportunity for service. In the mission field there was no provision of state welfare, so the German delegation envisaged sending out Church social workers.

The difficulty of comparing Jerusalem and Tambaram on this issue is that at

Tambaram the discussion was conducted much more on the lines of concepts of ministry and the role of the laity as they would be exercised in industry, in farming communities and so on. There was much less consideration of the role of the Church in relation to international welfare agencies, possibly because these, for example the I.L.O., were no longer new, or because they were collapsing under financial strains or the threat of war.

Religious education was a subject which featured in an important position on the agenda at both conferences, but the developments at Jerusalem have been very ably dealt with by Canon Dillistone in his biography of Charles Raven, whose influence was both accidental or spontaneous, depending on one's interpretation of events, and profoundly affected the thought of the Council; so there is no need to repeat what he says here.[79] Paton encouraged Raven to produce his lecture in book form, but otherwise had little to do with the question in the 'follow up' because it was Oldham's special interest at the time.[80] Much could be written about the discussion of religious education in the I.M.C., but it is certain that this subject will be adequately treated by Kathleen Bliss in her forthcoming biography of Oldham.[81]

The importance of the Jerusalem and Tambaram meetings for the growing awareness of racial problems in the ecumenical movement has already been adequately discussed in the preceding chapter. The great advantage of the I.M.C. discussion over that conducted by other ecumenical movements (excepting the W.S.C.F. and the World's Y.M.C.A.s) is that those who were discriminated against were present, outnumbering the privileged. At Jerusalem the cultural implications of various racial situations were fully discussed for it was recognized that here was the supreme challenge to Christianity, to the faith that asserted that all men were children of God; and that the failure of the Church to make an adequate stand on racial issues was driving more and more potential converts to Islam, for even missionaries in the past had not been free from prejudice.

The discussion on international affairs at the two conferences was wholly different, reflecting the changed international situation. At Jerusalem there were reports on the situation in various countries, such as that of Dr Cheng Ching-yi, whose speech 'Days of Vision', on the relation of the Christian hope to national aspirations in China, was so provocative that D.W. Lyon tried unsuccessfully to tone it down before publication, and S.K. Datta's speech on 'What is moving in the heart of India today'.[82] There was no attempt to discuss the world-wide developments, as was done at Tambaram under the title of 'Church and State'. The only such discussion concerned two controversial resolutions which caused much heart-searching. In the final session, a declaration against war was brought, to the effect that Christian mission must transcend race and class divisions, that war was the foremost hindrance to the triumph of the spirit of truth and peace, that peaceful means must always be sought to overcome international problems and that alternative attitudes created war. This was the final, almost meaningless agreement after much drafting and re-drafting and opposition from radical pacifists. It was symptomatic of the age of disarmament talks and the Kellogg-Briand pact. The second issue concerned the loyalty of missionaries in countries at war with their home government, and their rights in peacetime. They should have full freedom or give a pledge of loyalty to the colonial government. It is essential that they should retain the trust and goodwill of those to whom they are preaching. The whole context of this resolution has been discussed already, in the chapter preceding this.

   The situation at Tambaram was very different, since serious thorough studies on the subject of Church and State in the Far East had been conducted, and appear in the Tambaram series, volume VI, edited by K.G. Grubb, who was an expert on Latin American affairs and the problems of Protestant missions in Roman Catholic countries. The topic, he admitted, did not dominate proceedings, as at Oxford, and was based on the practical experience of members of the I.M.C., not the findings of scholars. However, the conference did, it is clear from many statements, absorb the Oxford findings, and measure them up against the Far Eastern situation, where, according to Grubb, after great expenditure of life, wealth, and talent in the missionary enterprise, the younger churches through dangerous conflicts with the state seemed to be denied freedom of development. The problem has not caught the imagination as the plight of Christians in Russia has, but their predicament is no less real. The question was one of where to make a stand, and how to unite the Christians of the country in that stand.

> 'Certain missionaries, especially in times of war, would consider that there are aspects of cultural penetration that are fully justifiable for them. They would maintain that they are bound to commend the cause of their country as well as the message of their Bible. Indeed, it may be difficult for them to resist political pressure that may be put on them in times of crisis'.

This situation, Grubb commented, would lead to expulsions and suspicion on the part of the local church. This is a very perspicacious prophecy of the developments in India, Tanganyika and Cameroun where there were national socialist missionaries, whose internment was a source of much difficulty for the I.M.C.

   'It must be recognized that persecuted minorities often develop into persecuting majorities and that quite small groups of Christians sometimes manifest an intolerance of spirit which is only rescued from becoming an intolerance in action by lack of power'. Hence the declaration of the Oxford findings against compulsion as a means to secure religious changes. Grubb's comment is still relevant concerning the manifestation of sectarianism. The conference, however, proceeded to state what they considered were basic rights of religious freedom and the various means by which the state was trying to curtail the growth of the Church, for example, by prohibiting 'proselytism'.[83]

   To Knak, in his survey of the debate, the most important principle established at Tambaram was the separation of church and state. The conference was not concerned to formulate a theology of church and state relations, but to work out the practical implications, starting with a consideration of the Biblical injunctions. Knak gives the debate on religious freedom in great detail, and points to the close relationship between the theme of this debate and the question of the church and international order, which was handled by another section.[84] As at Oxford, there was no agreement on the role of the Christian in the time of war, but only on the position of the missionary and the joint action which the churches ought to take for the relief of suffering caused by war. However, what is significant is the way in which delegates from countries at war with each other refused to allow the situation to break their fellowship in Christ. This was only achieved at great cost, as T.Z. Koo revealed in his address to the meeting.

> 'During the past few months, I have often asked myself the question whether my faith as a Christian will stand this strain or will it break under

it? Every time the same answer came back to me with inexorable clarity: 'Your Christianity will break under the strain if in your life as a Christian you place loyalty to your country before loyalty to God. Only if you have learnt to love God more than you love your country will your Christianity stand the strain of war'.

He called upon all followers of Christ to place social justice above purely national interests and to cease the kind of spiritual laissez faire which he found in the United States of America. He evolved an understanding of suffering love in which one regarded one's opponent as part of oneself and worked for his good. Yet Christ did this and was crucified for it.[85] 'Obedience to the cross' was no abstract theological phrase for the delegates, but an imminent reality. The Japanese Christians in particular were vulnerable to persecution, so the Chinese were not alone in their agony. Paton's reactions to the problem can be seen in his book 'Christianity in the Eastern Conflicts'.

I have already discussed the contribution of the international missionary movement to the ecumenical movement in my M.A. thesis. The specific contributions made at Jerusalem and Tambaram should be fairly clear from this chapter already. Paton wrote in an article in the I.R.M. entitled 'The Madras Meeting and the Ecumenical Movement' that one must get away from any idea of the conference being a means of interpreting the Oxford and Edinburgh conferences to the East. Rather it was a question of the missionary movement bringing the challenge of evangelizing the unreached masses into the heart of the ecumenical movement. The I.M.C. meetings, it is clear from other articles published in the I.R.M. on Tambaram, were responsible for giving a world dimension to the ecumenical movement.[86] The debates about church union were more intense at both conferences than anything recorded in the annals of the Faith and Order movement, because the practical consequences of disunity were so serious for the younger churches. Paton himself felt that great steps could be made towards an ecumenical church through the I.M.C., but only God could save the proposed W.C.C. from being a reshuffling of the ecclesiastical status quo, or an institution for academic research. The proposal made by Hodgkin that the Jerusalem meeting should consider changing the structure of the I.M.C. from an umbrella organization representing N.C.C's or mission boards to a federation of churches was too radical for its time, but his proposals, and similar I.M.C. ideas will be considered in due course in the context of the formation of the World Council of Churches.

The most radical and most significant contribution of the Jerusalem meeting is shrouded in a veil of silence. Canon Dillistone's sources for his account of the united communion service at Jerusalem in which an Anglican bishop and an Anglican priest helped to administer a basically Presbyterian rite are impeccable, but nothing survives on paper, perhaps because the matter was too controversial.[87] It was certainly the first occasion at which such a thing had happened, since Bishop Brent declined the requests that he celebrate communion for the Lausanne Faith and Order meeting, and the controversial Kikuyu celebration was basically an Anglican rite.[88] Paton also assisted in the service which was the high point of the Good Friday and Easter Sunday devotions which the delegates shared. Both Jerusalem and Tambaram worship showed great imagination in that the former was arranged around Easter in Jerusalem, and the latter around Christmas. Eric Sharpe has written an account of the Tambaram worship in his biography of A.G. Hogg, though he exaggerates Hogg's contribution.[89] His was by no means the most imaginative address. United worship, however, was the most important feature of the I.M.C's contribution to the ecumenical movement, and far outweighs all the things which were said about the importance of Christian unity.[90]

Finally, it is necessary to draw together all the different ways in which Paton was involved in these conferences. One could never say that they were 'his' conferences, in the way that Sundkler writes of Söderblom and 'his Stockholm conference'. It is nevertheless worth quoting Schlunk's portrait of him at Jerusalem: . . . 'ein Schotte, breitschultig und gedrungen, am liebsten die kurze Pfeife im linken Mundwinkel, mit einer Aussprache, die oft ebense schnell wie undeutlich war. Er hatte den Schalk in den Augen winkeln, und seine Worte waren oft von frohem Humor durchzogen. Immer aber wußte er zur Sache zu reden, und in der Kenntnis der indischen Mission and ihre Missionare war er unübertroffen'. It amazed him how much Paton and Warnshuis did for the conference, often beginning when the delegates went to bed.[91]

For Jerusalem, Paton was responsible for the study preparation in spite of his initial doubts about the theme 'The Christian Message'. He was much involved in fund-raising for it. He mediated with the Continental delegates at their preliminary meeting in Cairo and overcame their reluctance to participate in a conference with 'liberal' theologians. He lost the battle over appointing an independent press officer, a long and sordid struggle not worth discussing here. He was heavily involved in the day to day running of the conference as the ad hoc conference standing committee minutes show, and he was editor of the eight volumed conference report, which he produced very rapidly after the conference (published in September 1929) in defiance of the more cautious approach of Warnshuis. With Oldham he shared the burden of organizing an effective 'follow up' to the conference.[92]

At Tambaram, by an act of faith, he managed to avoid cancellation and got a representative body of missionaries and churchmen there. Otherwise, he was responsible for as much organization as at Jerusalem. The outbreak of war prevented an effective 'follow up' and the volumes he edited were virtually given away in the end. But above all he kept before the I.M.C. the fact that the conferences were not an end in themselves, but a part of the continuing work of evangelism on a world-wide scale, and the search for Christian unity.

Chapter VII
Cultivating the I.M.C. Garden:— Paton's Day to Day Work as I.M.C. Secretary

In considering the two world conferences which Paton staged, his work in organizing the rescue of 'orphaned missions' and his efforts to improve Christian education in India, it is easy to overlook his more mundane work as an I.M.C. secretary, which continued year after year as he patiently cultivated the interest in the international missionary movement and channelled the impetus behind the world conferences and the special appeals into the on-going activities of the I.M.C. This work was essential to the growth and development of world evangelism, but was unspectacular and unsung.

The scope of this work involved such a multiplicity and diversity of activities on behalf of the I.M.C. that it is not possible to do more than select four of the most significant aspects of his work which together constitute a picture of the way in which he cultivated the I.M.C. garden. By assessing the impact of these activities it is also possible to build up a picture of the degree of commitment to the I.M.C. which existed across the world. In this context, the financial situation of the I.M.C. is significant because the extent to which individuals and organizations were prepared to find the financial means for the I.M.C. to continue is an indication of their commitment to it. Paton could wring money out of a stone, and had a genius for making a small amount of money go a very long way, but there were limits to his ingenuity, and in the hostile economic environment of the depression and the associated ills of the inter-war period, the I.M.C. was at times fighting for its survival. In considering Paton's work in extending the constituency of the I.M.C. to include the Continental missions and nationals of African and Asian countries on an unprecedented scale, and his editorship of the I.R.M., one is seeing a side of Paton's character which was creative and also demonstrates his ability to work in partnership with others. In discussing the financial problems of the I.M.C. and the Department of Social and Industrial Research, one is seeing Paton the enabler, who could find the means for others to do the work. The D.S.I.R. was in fact one of the most original and controversial achievements of the I.M.C., contributing as it did to an understanding of the deeper issues of urban and rural mission and of the practical problems of 'younger churches'. However, in supporting it without explaining the project sufficiently to the Scandinavian members of the I.M.C., Paton nearly lost the more conservative wing of the I.M.C.

Paton did not compose great policy-making documents for the I.M.C. in the way that J.H. Oldham did, neither did he make 21 page long letters of resignation into analyses of strategy as his colleague did,[1] although he did write an article on 'The future of the I.M.C.' in 1927 which was much discussed.[2] He struck much more closely to the letter of the policy mandates of the I.M.C. meetings than Oldham, but it is clear that he had great influence in the framing of such resolutions. For example, at the Herrnhut meeting in 1932, a very keen interest was taken in the whole question of evangelism. Paton interpreted this as a reaction to the protest of the Scandinavians against what they considered to be the missions' undue absorption in institutional work and social advance, but also as a response to the despair of their contemporaries of economic or political salvation with a return to the search for God. In writing to Hodge he upheld the Herrnhut decision to concentrate more on evangelism and to let Oldham study the non-religious philosophies which are undermining Christianity, but he also states his conviction that systematic study of evangelistic method is necessary in order to understand the nature of evangelism and the reason why evangelism in some areas of India for example, has been so sterile.[3] The study of methods of evangelism was authorized at Northfield and played an important part in the preparations for Tambaram. Paton edited a collection of essays on the subject in 1938 and undoubtedly he influenced the I.M.C. decision to sponsor such a study. One could cite other examples of this influence.[4]

The four examples chosen illustrate Paton's ability to harness his administrative abilities and prodigious capacity for hard work to the task of evangelism by means of international co-operation. He was proud of this, remarking to his family when he came home in the evening that he had 'filled up three secretaries today', i.e. dictated so many letters and memoranda that three secretaries had been kept busy all day. He dictated letters at a very steady 120 words per minute, with no pauses for thought, no alterations and no halt between letters. According to Miss Morden, he never asked how a task was being done once he had handed it over to a colleague, he simply assumed it would be completed as quickly as possible.[5] His colleagues and secretaries found this very encouraging. They also appreciated the fact that if they made a serious mistake he would put it right without reproaching them, and take the responsibility for the error on himself.

Expanding the I.M.C. constituency in Europe and Asia

Much of Paton's work in involving the representatives of the 'younger churches' in the work of the I.M.C. has already been described in connection with the delegations to the meetings at Jerusalem and Tambaram. His work in encouraging the growth of Indian leadership in the churches in India has also been described. An amusing example of the educative pressure necessary to achieve this can be found in his account of a talk he had with the Rev R. Mercer Wilson, the general secretary of the Religious Tract Society, who was about to sail for India and who wished to appoint someone to supervise the production of literature, especially in Marathi. He wrote to Hodge concerning this:

> 'I must warn you that Mercer Wilson is a person with no knowledge of India; that he has not got past talking about natives, and that it seemed to him quite strange when I suggested that he should try to find an Indian for his new job. I agreed of course that it must be a competent man, and that I would not defend putting in a man who could not do the job, but I urged that *ceteris paribus* an Indian should be preferred'.[6]

Getting nationals appointed to such posts was one way of involving a wider cross-section of the Christian community than representatives of European missionary societies. The formation of new national Christian Councils was another, because as in the cases of the restructured N.C.C.s of China and India, 50% of the members were nationals, not expatriates. Sometimes the government of the country concerned was the I.M.C's best ally, as for example when the Chinese government decreed in 1928 that the heads of all educational institutions must be Chinese. This brought to the fore the generation of Chinese Christian scholars who played such an impressive role at Tambaram. It is difficult to appreciate in the post-war period of rapid travel at popular prices how much time would be lost by an Asian Christian coming to Europe for an I.M.C. meeting, nor how much that would cost. If certain well-known church leaders had responded to more than a fraction of the invitations they received, they would never have been able to carry on their work in their diocese, circuit or school. When Paton was planning the post Tambaram visitation he also had the problem of finding national church leaders who could communicate to European audiences. He had to deal with a certain type of prejudice on the C.B.M.S. which created the demand for 'fruity' speakers, 'the more coloured the better', who would appeal to congregations because of their exotic character. Paton declared with some exasperation that it was a privilege to receive Christians from Asia, and that this sort of attitude was intolerable.[7] Paton was endeavouring to weave together the European base of missions, the European churches and the Christians of the Far East and Africa. His tours of India and the Far East were very significant for the question of expanding the constituency of the I.M.C.

Paton describes an incident on his tour 1935-36 when he was entertained in a Chinese restaurant by Japanese Christians in Manchuria, who also invited two Chinese pastors. He may very well have been the only European present, but he writes of the insensitivity of the Japanese to the grievances of the persecuted Chinese, in their attempts to create a festive occasion. The incident is also remarkable for demonstrating the outreach of the I.M.C. In counselling the Manchurian and Korean Christians, Paton advised putting friendly pressure on the Japanese Christians to intervene with their own government rather than looking to European intervention, which would probably be counter-productive.[8]

The I.M.C's Latin American constituency grew as a result of Mott's tours, but Paton was responsible for drawing Kenneth Grubb, explorer and evangelist among the Indian tribes of Latin America, into the activities of the I.M.C. Through Grubb Paton could also reach the fundamentalist missions of the World Evangelization Campaign and the World Dominion Press.[9]

Despite tension between the I.M.C. and Life and Work over the creation of the D.S.I.R., Paton accepted responsibility for organizing the so-called 'Fifth Section' of Life and Work, which was supposed to cover the Far East and Africa. This administrative arrangement was the first organisational link between two ecumenical movements which later formed the World Council of Churches. The secretaries of the N.C.Cs in effect became the corresponding members of Life and Work. This was an important development because Life and Work and Faith and Order failed to invite more than a handful of Chinese and Indian Christians to the world conferences of 1925 and 1927.

Although Dutch missionaries in what is now Indonesia maintained strict independence from the I.M.C. and did not form a National Christian Council, Paton, Warnshuis and Oldham enjoyed excellent relations with the officers appointed by the Dutch missions to liaise between them and the colonial government. He was very impressed by what he saw on his tour of the Dutch East Indies arranged through their good offices.[11] The corresponding development at the home base of these missions was due entirely to the energy of one woman. In 1930 the wife of a former mission 'consul', Baroness Boetzelaer van Dubbeldam, was elected to the Ad Interim committee of the I.M.C. She immediately attacked the problem of making the I.M.C. less Anglo-Saxon, and carried out a personal survey of the relationships of the various member missions of the Netherlands Missionary Council, and some of the German missions based in North Germany, in order to assess the Continental interest in the I.M.C. On several occasions she arranged for Paton to meet the Netherlands Missionary Council of which her husband was chairman, and she was responsible for two highly successful I.M.C. meetings at Kasteel Hemmen, in 1937 and 1939. In her, Paton had an invaluable friend and ally. He managed to keep in touch with her through Dr Visser't Hooft during the war, but her death in July 1942 robbed the ecumenical movement of one of its most ardent spirits.[12]

The I.M.C's constituency in Germany was slow to expand after the acrimony caused by the First World War dissolved. Paton's principal contact was Schlunk of Tübingen, but in the 1930s he is to be found encouraging the younger generation of missionary administrators such as Walter Freytag (senior), and Gerhard Brennecke, whom he first met through the S.C.M. and to whom he sent the I.R.M. free of charge. When negotiation with the German Government was necessary, Siegfried Knak of the Berlin Mission was Paton's contact, and though Paton grew a little impatient of his position when Knak appeared to have been seduced by Nazi propaganda in 1940, he never really lost faith in him because he appreciated Knak's efforts to protect the German missions from government interference. He could not develop his contacts with the German churches very far through the missions because they only encompassed a very narrow section of the German church and the universities. Similarly the D.C.S.V., with whom he had contacts through Robert Mackie and Hanns Lilje, never had more than 1,000 members, a tiny fraction of the entire student population. Missionaries were not usually graduates, in spite of the existence of chairs of mission at the universities, and missionary societies tended to be the fruit of pietist circles. Therefore the I.M.C. could not penetrate very far into German church life, even though Paton regularly attended the annual Bremen missionary conferences. There was nothing he or the I.M.C. could do to improve the situation, especially since National Socialism made the word 'international' a term of abhorrence. Although some German students did attend the joint W.S.C.F./I.M.C. conference in Basel in 1935 its impact on them seems to have been limited.[13] It has to be admitted that the German missions were under-represented in the I.M.C. numerically, but since Schlunk always insisted that it was very difficult to find participants with sufficient command of English and since the missions were so straitened financially, probably they could not have improved their representation even if they had been allocated more places. The appointment of Dr Otto Iserland to the staff of the I.M.C. was a great encouragement, but it was unfortunate that apart from the I.M.C. collaborators involved in the International Christian Council on the Approach to the Jews, he was the only non-Anglo-Saxon staff member.

This situation contributed to the strained relations between the I.M.C. and the Scandinavian missionary societies which made up the Northern Missionary Council. For when Iserland visited the Scandinavian capitals shortly after taking up his appointment, he was able to improve matters immeasurably simply by listening to their grievances and explaining misunderstandings.[14] In particular, he placated Professor Torm of Denmark, who had been a thorn in the side of the I.M.C. since he was excluded from the I.M.C. meetings at Rättvik in 1926. Yet despite the success of his visit Paton only visited Oslo and Copenhagen for two days in the period 1927-38 and Warnshuis once. The Scandinavian societies could justly complain that the I.M.C. ignored them since until the Herrnhut meeting in 1932 they had only two representatives to cover the four countries, and although the societies were very small by American standards, they did cover vital fields in South West Africa, Assam and the North West Frontier of India, Manchuria and parts of China which were barely touched by other missions. If the I.M.C. had taken more care to cherish their relationships with the Scandinavian missions, it is possible that the Lutheran World Federation would not have been so successful in fostering the growth of confessionalism during and after the Second World War.[15]

Warnshuis seems to have guarded North America jealously as his province. There are several surviving sequences of correspondence in which he was attempting to stop Paton building up support for the I.M.C. in America by a visit. It is as though he thought there ought to be a comity agreement to cover North America. It irritated him that the Canadians bought the London Office's publications, not the New York office's. It is therefore very difficult to decide how much credit ought to be attributed to Paton for the interest in the I.M.C. in America.[16]

Therefore, although during Paton's tenure as secretary of the I.M.C. the outreach of the I.M.C. was extended and its constituency roots in Europe driven much deeper, nevertheless in certain vital areas the I.M.C. failed to take the initiative and important opportunities were lost. However, there can be no doubt that as a result of Paton's activities, particularly his ceaseless travelling, the I.M.C. became a truly world-wide movement.

The International Review of Missions

One of the most effective and successful aspects of Paton's work for the I.M.C. was his editorship of the International Review of Missions, which he inherited in 1927 from Oldham. In many ways his policy as editor reflects his earlier experience as the editor of the National Christian Council Review, but with certain important differences. He ceased to wage specific campaigns as he had against the opium trade in India, and he strove to give the journal an international appeal. Regrettably, Miss Sinclair does not discuss the question of Paton's editorial policy in her biography of him, since as associate editor of the I.R.M. from November 1939 until his death, when she carried on alone, she would have known what his policy was. Unfortunately owing to the lack of editorial comment in the I.R.M. and the fact that he rarely felt obliged to defend his decisions in his correspondence, it is very difficult to reconstruct that policy. One is forced to rely almost exclusively on his correspondence with his co-editor, Muriel Underhill, who succeeded Georgina Gollock in 1927, and with K.S. Latourette, who headed an 'I.R.M. Discussion Group' in the United States.[17]

Paton's initiation into the I.R.M. took place earlier than 1927, because from October 1919 until some point in 1921 he was a member of an experimental discussion group which aimed at producing papers for the I.R.M. as a kind of exercise in 'collective theology'. From the surviving records it is possible to see how great Paton's influence was, and conversely, how the discussions affected his book 'The Highway of God' and several articles which he wrote in the period 1919-21. The group's method of working is significant because it presaged the groups which Oldham directed as part of the preparations for the Oxford Life and Work conference in 1937, and some of the ideas behind the 'Christian Newsletter', in which Paton was again involved.[18]

. The group decided to wrestle with the problem that however successful missionary methods might be, they would be in vain if the theory behind it was not true. Even in 'Christian' countries there was widespread distrust of organized Christianity because of ignorance and faith unreconciled with the new knowledge of the last century. Paton emphasized repeatedly in the discussions that the fundamental issue was the reconciliation of man to the world in which he lives. He believed that many young American missionaries were going out who had very little faith, and did not even believe in the historicity of Christ. The I.R.M. was widely read on mission stations, but one wonders how effective this policy of Christian apologetic to missionaries would be. Paton talked of a similar problem in the colleges: one cannot persuade students to give their lives to missionary service unless they believe in Christianity. Although the group were agreed that living experience and personal religion were central to the series, Paton insisted that readers must be helped to distinguish between the essentials and non-essentials of the Christian faith, and that the historical Jesus could not be proclaimed without theological interpretation to make him intelligible to those listening. Paton thought that the starting point should be the Cross 'because people are very much up against the problem of evil'. And also that 'the love of God is something you can rest on'.[19]

Paton wrote the first two papers which the group considered, though these were not published first in the series. Contributions invariably came in for heavy criticism, occasionally being rejected altogether as in the case of D.S. Cairns' paper of December 1919. It is interesting that Oldham appears to have drawn out his colleagues, and refrained from imposing his authority as editor on them. Paton tried to repeat this experiment in 1927 and 1930, but found it was very difficult to get people together.[20] However, in 1930 he managed to form an editorial advisory committee. Paton may have derived from this experience his policy of introducing a certain amount of theology into the I.R.M. inasmuch as he regularly published articles by Emil Brunner, and allowed much space to the debate on secularism which followed the Jerusalem meeting of the I.M.C. Paton's standpoint in this debate was entirely consistent with his published works on mission. As in the 'Christian Newsletter' one finds the occasional devotional article.

Paton had a long and hard struggle to keep to the policy of an annual survey of the entire mission field. It was composed from missionaries' reports, which were supplemented with a certain amount of statistical information and shrewd political comment. Paton's correspondents sometimes questioned the amount of political comment, which was an innovation on his part. Oldham had merely tended to weight the survey with material about Africa. Paton took the view that the gravity of the political climate in which the missions were working deserved such comment.[21] The annual survey required a very great deal of research by Paton's co-editor, and was a very great labour to get to press. Robert Mackie confesses that it was the only part of the I.R.M. which he read, and he was probably not the only person who found the survey the most interesting part of the I.R.M. Also popular were the

'Quarterly Notes', a sort of current affairs supplement on the state of missions in various key areas, which many missionaries used as the basis of their intercessory prayers. In the economic crises of the 1930s the notes became too expensive to produce, as the actual length of the I.R.M. had to be cut down, so Paton fought a long battle to save them, getting a generous donor to subscribe the cost of each issue.[22]

One revolutionary aspect of the survey was Paton's determination to include the work of Roman Catholic missions in as impartial a way as possible, and for this he consulted a Roman Catholic expert, usually Father Houblou. Considering the difficulties which Protestant missions had because of the unscrupulous practices of Roman Catholic missions in India, and the problems of Protestant missions in Roman Catholic colonies, this was a remarkably tolerant view.[23] Miss Underhill had doubts, after complaints in 1931 from Carr of the Zenana, Bible, and Medical Mission (ZBMM) about the Roman Catholic section of the survey being written by a Roman Catholic, as to whether they should continue to treat Protestant and Roman Catholic missions as being of equal value. Miss Gibson was terrified that some of the Evangelical missions would leave the I.M.C. on this account.[24] Paton defended this policy in 1936 on the grounds that one can learn much from Roman Catholic missions. They rightly stressed the importance of the spiritual life and religious vocations in mission, though he was not suggesting that monasticism was necessary in all cases.[25]

Paton only produced one decennial survey, a policy he took over from Oldham of summarizing the main trends of the preceding ten years of mission, though one was due in 1943. He was proud of the fact that he had managed to produce a much more concise and compressed survey in 1933, as compared with the Oldham-Gollock survey of 1923. (The I.R.M. first appeared in 1912 as part of the continuation of the work of the Edinburgh World Missionary Conference.) However, it was Miss Underhill who did most of the research for the decennial survey and to whom the credit should go. The whole policy of surveys and quarterly notes was very beneficial from the point of view of serving missionaries and planners because it was a means of conveying the universal scope of missions and the international implications of problems, such as Shintoism in schools. Related to this is Paton's plea for help from the Ministry of Information during the war to get information on international affairs to missionaries when the normal channels of communication were severed and it was difficult to send the I.R.M. abroad.[26] During the Second World War, the annual survey became an important summary of the progress of the operation to rescue the 'orphaned missions'.

During the period of Paton's editorship the balance of articles in the I.R.M. changed very little, in spite of all Paton's efforts to get new, non-British contributors.[27] According to the analysis made of the years 1934-38, 43% of the articles were by British contributors and 25% by Americans, though obviously they were writing about the whole spectrum of missionary problems and successes, from all parts of the world. About 8% of the contributions were from German writers, but this was compensated somewhat by the reviews of German works and the articles on German theology which Oldham, Hartenstein and others provided. When Paton was travelling in the Far East, he commissioned articles from missionaries and nationals, but frequently the article had not been written a year later.[28] To say that he maintained certain academic standards conveys the wrong impression, but he did reject articles which were sentimental, inaccurate or unexceptional. It is interesting to compare the I.R.M. with a periodical like the Evangelisches Missionsmagazin, published by the Basel Mission in Basel and Stuttgart, which is so much more theological and was written almost exclusively by the Basel-based missionary administrators and by the senior missionaries in each area. The I.R.M. was in a different class from the 'house literature' produced as propaganda for the home constituency by the missionary societies; and before the Second World War it could claim a unique place in the realm of missionary literature as an international specialist journal, in spite of the preponderance of British writers.

It was in an attempt to rectify this, that Paton began a close liaison with K.S. Latourette in June 1933 in an attempt to find more American contributors. Unfortunately he was never able to establish a similar working arrangement with anyone on the Continent, although the I.R.M. was much in demand in the mission houses, as Betty Gibson discovered when she visited Germany. The women missionaries, whose work was kept strictly separate and was almost invariably among women in the mission field, complained that the I.R.M. never reached them, because the male directors did not pass it on. She had great satisfaction in arranging subscriptions for the women's departments of the main missionary societies. Perhaps it was the different format of the continental missionary magazines which made it difficult to get contributions, for there was no difficulty in translating articles in the I.R.M. office.[29]

In February 1943 Paton received a request from America to make the I.R.M. suitable for pastors. Paton's reaction was to write that it seemed to him hopeless to make the I.R.M. popular in this sense. After all, no-one else in the world was doing what the I.R.M. was doing. A change of policy would disturb the I.R.M's regular readers. He himself is encouraged by the number of American pastors who do read it anyway. The I.R.M. is not a ready map for congregations but a challenge to the best intellects.[30] Paton never lacked confidence in his editorial powers.

When Paton took over the editorship the circulation of the I.R.M. was beginning to decline. It continued to do so, because Paton could not find new subscribers to replace those who withdrew their subscriptions as a means of economising in the worsening economic climate. At the same time the cost of paper and printing rose, forcing Paton to reduce the number of pages in the I.R.M. and to apply for a subsidy which was usually about £400 per annum although it was claimed that about £220 of this was to offset adverse exchange rates between Britain and America. Paton halted the decline in December 1934 when the circulation increased from 2,595 to 2,630 and the sale of single copies from 685 per annum to 786. Warnshuis had been very active in increasing sales in America, but no other member of the Ad Interim Committee ever approached Baroness van Boetzelaer's feat in finding 100 new Dutch subscribers in 1930. The subsidy was justified in terms of the importance of the I.R.M. for dialogue within the I.M.C., and for conference preparation. Before both the Jerusalem and the Tambaram meetings a 'double issue' of preparatory documents was produced, for which Paton extracted a subsidy from conference funds.[31]

No other part of the ecumenical movement produced a comparable journal for more than a few years, so there is nothing with which one can compare it except possibly the 'Student Movement' and the 'Student World', which are much less specialized in their appeal to students. Paton did not hesitate to give space to his critics, such as Professor Torm, and to minority concerns, such as the problems of Protestant Missions in Belgian Congo, when he felt that an important principle was at stake.[32] In short, the I.R.M. was an instrument in Paton's hands for the general development of the I.M.C. constituency, and a vehicle of communication for I.M.C. policy as well as a means of educating missionaries in the wider scope of missions and the deeper theological issues involved.

As a postscript to this, one interesting feature of his work as editor is the extent to which he delegated responsibility to Muriel Underhill and then to Margaret Sinclair. Muriel Underhill had experience as a missionary in India with the Zenana and Bible Mission, and had been a keen supporter of the S.V.M.U. Her views by no means coincided with Paton's, as for example in her criticism of C.F. Andrews. She was a very shy and diffident person, but she could take the initiative, as when she refused to go to Tambaram on the grounds that someone had to stay and look after the I.M.C. office and then quietly raised £1,000 for new evangelistic work being done by the younger churches.[33] Miss Sinclair had a very different background in publishing and came to the I.M.C. after six years with Life and Work in Geneva. She was very outspoken and stood up to Paton when he was throwing his weight about. It annoyed her that he would pirate her ideas for the I.R.M. without acknowledging them. Her judgment in matters of art or the theatre was highly valued by the Paton family. The I.R.M. thus remained the fruit of a remarkable partnership.[34]

Paton's attempts to solve the problem of financing the International Missionary Movement

The significance of the economics of the ecumenical movement has already been thoroughly discussed in my M.A. thesis, when it was demonstrated how important the availability of finance was in shaping the character of the ecumenical movement. While the popular thesis that church unions are inspired by financial exigencies is not tenable, nevertheless, it is undeniable that much of the influence of Mott, Paton and Oldham, and certain of their contemporaries, resided in their ability to raise great sums and to organize ecumencial finance on as sound a basis as possible. In many respects the I.M.C. is a special case, whose finances bear more resemblance to that of missionary societies then comparable ecumenical organizations. Yet the problem of attracting contributions for an organization whose work is less tangible than that of an ordinary church or mission is the same. It would in fact be impossible to explain the growing points of the I.M.C. structure without some reference to the significance of the I.M.C's finances. Much is revealed about Paton's character and methods of operation from a study of I.M.C. finance. In complete contrast to his life-long failure to balance his family budget, which occasionally made him rather depressed when he considered that his children's combined scholarships amounted to more than his salary, he displayed remarkable persistence, prodigious energy and considerable financial acumen in a decade-long battle to eliminate the I.M.C. deficit, only for the outbreak of war to destroy all his careful arrangements, and impose new burdens on the I.M.C. budget.[35]

The odds against Paton and his colleagues succeeding were very great. In the period under consideration, 1928-1939, contributions to missionary societies slumped in the Anglo-Saxon world and fell slightly in Scandinavia. There is no doubt that the savage attack on the I.M.C. budget by members of the Committee of Reference and Counsel of the Foreign Missions Conference of North America on

September 27th 1928, at a meeting at which Warnshuis was not present, was motivated by the fact that the income of American missionary societies in 1928 was 25% less than in 1927. There were objections to the decision of the Jerusalem I.M.C. meeting to increase the I.M.C. budget from $27,000 to $40,000, especially as 70% of the I.M.C. budget had hitherto been found in America. Estimating their contributions as $27,000 of the new budget, the representatives of the American boards proposed to send $20,000, thereby precipitating a financial crisis in the I.M.C. Paton found this exasperating, because of the presence on the Committee of Reference and Counsel of some of the American delegates to Jerusalem, who had presumably voted for the increased budget.[36]

On another occasion, Lundahl tried to persuade Paton to accept a reduction in the Swedish contribution, only to receive a letter from Paton arguing that Europe and Great Britain must make up the shortfall in the American contribution because the Americans would do the same if the roles were reversed, and the level of missionary giving in Europe and Britain declined in a comparable fashion. He notes that it is very hard for people to accept that there has been a decline in missionary giving in North America.[37]

Through the C.B.M.S. the system of allocating the British contribution among the British member societies was to ask for 39 shillings per £1000 of expenditure.[38] However, in spite of the reduction in the I.M.C. budget and therefore in the quota in 1934, it was observed that owing to the loss in income in the societies, this would no longer serve as a means of meeting the entire quota. It is, therefore, all the more extraordinary that despite the worst effects of the economic depression being felt in Germany, the German societies steadily increased their contributions to the I.M.C. This continued to be the pattern even during the war, although after 1934, owing to the prohibition of foreign exchange, the money had to be banked in Germany, and used there. The I.M.C. financial system was based on the principle of the national councils levying an agreed proportion of the budget from their member societies, and therefore there was no way of avoiding the consequences of a decline in the societies' income. Paton noted an improvement when the societies pledged themselves to contribute fixed sums instead of a percentage of their incomes, but this merely left the societies totally unable to respond to special appeals for specific causes. No amount of goodwill from the smaller societies in Britain and Scandinavia could produce money where there was none.[39]

Paton frequently observed ruefully that when a society was trying to cut its expenditure, its contribution to ecumenical projects or international missionary co-operation was the first victim. This short-sighted policy was particularly irritating because in so doing the societies were undermining their own best chances of successful evangelism. An example he cited was the crucial research work by the D.S.I.R., which was an essential preparation for successful evangelistic work in the Copperbelt in Rhodesia (Zambia). However, when he was appealing for the Madras conference, the secretary of S.P.G. told him it was impossible to help with every missionary bishop pleading for funds. Lack of conviction about the fundamental usefulness of I.M.C. work was at the root of the problem, apart from a natural distaste for giving money to write off a deficit.[40]

The main problem, however, was the complete failure of the American societies to appreciate the work which Oldham was trying to do for Africa. This lay at the root of much of the tension between Warnshuis and his colleagues in London, and affected the financial situation very profoundly. It must be stated in fairness to Warnshuis that many of the British missionary societies had given priority to China in their appeals to the churches for money and missionaries. Africa was a very undeveloped field, to which men with practical abilities rather than intellectual talents were sent. It was Oldham's genius to perceive the importance of the future church in Africa, and of Africa as a continent and gradually to persuade missionary societies and the British government to devote more resources to Africa. Oldham's first leave of absence in Africa was financed by the surplus from an I.M.C. conference on Africa in 1926. The American missionary societies were much more emotionally committed to China than the British societies, while Warnshuis himself had laboured for many years as a missionary in Amoy in the pioneering days when a missionary had to do everything virtually single-handed. Kathleen Bliss is undoubtedly right to see also in the furious exchanges of letters about finance a basic conflict of personality between Warnshuis and Oldham, in which Paton defended Oldham almost invariably. For example, Warnshuis wrote to Paton in the 1928 financial crisis that he could not defend Oldham, or raise money for his salary, when Oldham was in Africa, and no-one knew his future plans. Paton replied that this should be obvious: Oldham was merely implementing the policies adopted at the Jerusalem I.M.C. meeting. However, this was peculiarly difficult for him to do in relation to Africa because unlike other areas, such as China and India, there were no national Christian councils with whom the I.M.C. could work. Oldham had to be both I.M.C. and N.C.C. in relationship to colonial government in Africa.[41] In fact, in the decade up to the Tambaram meeting, Mott, Oldham and Paton did much to rectify this situation, with the formation of councils in Tanganyika, South Africa (1934) and the Near East and North Africa (1924), for which they had to raise considerable sums of money privately and from missions.[42] The results as far as the representation of Africa in the I.M.C. is concerned, have already been discussed in the context of the Tambaram meeting.

A further source of tension can only be described as a suspicion of another nation's interests. The American missionary societies were full of high-minded abhorrence of 'colonialism' as typified in the British Empire, and mistakenly believed that Oldham's work was only of value for the British Empire.[43] This was another reason for their reluctance to support I.M.C. work in Africa financially. There was criticism of the fact that two of the three I.M.C. secretaries were British and were based in London, though Paton was at pains to point out that either Oldham or he himself was absent from Britain at any one time, and to pass on the view of the C.B.M.S. that the C.B.M.S. derived no special benefit from the presence of two I.M.C. secretaries in London. In October 1928 there were criticisms of the expenditure in London on the maintenance of Edinburgh House by the American members of the I.M.C., which Kenneth Maclennan deeply resented; his rebuttal of these criticisms was relayed anonymously to Warnshuis by Paton.[44] It does not seem to have been appreciated that the American I.M.C. office benefitted from the fact that Mott's salary and expenses were met privately and did not appear on the budget. While it was surely a healthy situation when Paton and Warnshuis could write to each other so frankly, nevertheless the prolonged financial crisis which so alarmed Paton, was acerbated by tension between British and American societies, based not only on a failure of communication, but also lack of a common understanding of priorities.[45] The task of raising money as well as that of administration would surely have been easier and more successful without these tensions.

The divergence between the methods of budgeting and financial administration of different missionary societies, and between the Committee of Reference and Council and the C.B.M.S. has already been sufficiently discussed in the context of the problems which the N.C.C. of India encountered in extracting finance from the mission boards. Paton and his colleagues inevitably encountered the same problem with reference to I.M.C. central finances. A problem closely allied to this, which persists in the problem of raising funds for the W.C.C., is that the I.M.C. officers had to be careful not to impinge upon the missionary societies' financial constituency. They had continually to be finding 'new' money to supplement the amount contributed directly by the national councils. This was done in a great variety of ways, as is evident from the documents relating to efforts in 1927 to raise the 'Third Secretary's' salary and the expenses of the Jerusalem conference. Oldham took the somewhat unconstructive attitude that with regard to issues as complex and important as these involved in the Jerusalem meeting, he could not very well explain them by letter and had no time for interviews with people because he was leaving for Africa shortly. In spite of that he managed to raise £7-800 from sources in Scotland. The Bishop of Leicester invited Paton to his diocese, where the encounter with the 'Third Secretary' himself produced donations from a meeting of another £800. Lord Maclay contributed £1,000, the largest single donation. Bishop Temple sent a list of aristocratic names to be tapped, but could not help personally, because of his own appeal.[46] This in fact was a recurring problem, that of having to compete with many other good causes making claims on the benevolent aristocrat or industrialist, whose income was shrinking in the financial crisis of the decade 1928-38. Paton did have certain never-failing patrons, such as the Forrester-Patons, and Canon Arthur Davies, who was also much involved in the counsels of the I.M.C. However, Paton rejected the principle that the Third Secretary should be paid by a special fund, insisting that the Rättvik decision be upheld, that the secretary's salary be found from the central budget.[47] The inherent weakness of this situation was revealed as early as November 1928, when so many individual donations proved to be unique efforts, that Oldham submitted his resignation, because of the 'gentleman's agreement' that if the salary of one of the secretaries failed, he should be the one to go. (It is interesting to note at this juncture, that Paton was prepared to scour England, raising his own salary, but that Oldham would not condescend to this.[48]) The whole situation demonstrated the problem of finding sources outside those on which the missionary societies drew, and the instability of the budget which depended so much on individual donations. To some extent this situation was inevitable, given the difficulty of finding resources for an international organization when national organizations were in desperate need of finance, and when etiquette demanded that there should be no public appeal for the I.M.C., a thing which Paton himself rejected as a solution.

Apart from these 'internal' factors which made the finance of the I.M.C. so difficult, factors which derived from the nature and structure of the I.M.C., its member councils, and their member bodies, there were almost overwhelming odds facing the I.M.C. in the shape of the external economic situation. There had already been a slump following the end of the immediate post-war boom, in 1922, when Germany was so badly affected, but this had less impact on missions than might be expected because of the ban then existing on German missionary work in the British

Empire, which obviously reduced German missionary expenditure. No country escaped the effect of the 1929 crisis, when the stock market in New York crashed in October, to be followed by a series of related crashes. The failure of the Austrian Credit-Anstalt in May 1931 brought financial collapse to central Europe, while the following September the Bank of England went off the gold standard, and in 1934 the United States revalued the dollar to little more than half its former worth. The loss of confidence in currencies used in international transactions was only one degree less serious for the I.M.C. than the erosion of investments and the decline of the real value of the I.M.C's income. In 1933 the I.M.C. cut back the number of secretarial staff drastically, and all the remaining staff accepted a 15% cut in their salaries, thus saving $4,000, but still leaving a deficit of $6,000. The most disturbing element was the recurrence of these crises, which no government seemed able to control. In March 1938, the Swiss missionary societies were so badly hit by the devaluation of the Swiss franc that they could only send half their promised contribution to the Tambaram budget. Among Paton's correspondence on finance one frequently finds letters in which he attempted to evolve elaborate schemes to defeat the effects of the poor exchange rates, which Warnshuis had to point out were neither logical nor legal. One can, however, appreciate Paton's exasperation in transmitting the correct amount to New York on one occasion, only to be informed that there was a discrepancy, which eventually proved to have been caused by the falling value of the pound while the money was in transit.[49]

Another policy adopted in an attempt to reduce the I.M.C. vulnerability was the so called 'domesticating of the budget'. This was akin to the principle of self-support among the younger churches and implied that each country would endeavour to raise the costs of I.M.C. expenditure in that country. So, for example, the cost of sending the British delegates to Jerusalem was farmed out among various agencies while the I.M.C./C.B.M.S. concentrated on raising the travelling expenses of the Chinese and Japanese delegates. This policy was never very successful because the British societies could never meet the cost of the I.M.C. operation in London even though the I.M.C. rented rooms from the C.B.M.S. at a non-commercial rate. Half the London expenditure had to be sent from America, and delays and difficulties involved in doing this caused constant friction between Paton and Warnshuis.[50]

Paton admitted to Mr and Mrs Flint that the Williamstown meeting was held in America because of the influence of American money. Presumably the same would be true of the Northfield meeting of 1935. There was much controversy within the I.M.C. as to whether it was financially possible to accept the invitation of the Moravian community to meet in Herrnhut in 1932, but when Paton had overruled Warnshuis' objections to imagined austerities in the Moravians' homes, the meeting proved to be not only one of the most successful I.M.C. meetings, but also one of the most economic.[51]

It has already been shown in Chapter V how considerations of financial expediency were not allowed to influence the N.M.C. of India's choice of staff, when they voted to appoint S.K. Datta at Poona, a man very unpopular with the Canadian boards, who were expected to provide much of the money for the N.M.C. Nevertheless, I.M.C. policy was dictated by the availability of finance, which made staff appointments possible, or prevented them, and not by those who had access to financial resources exerting undue influence except where there was evidence of inefficient administration of those resources, as in the case of the N.C.C. of South Africa. This is consistent with what was discovered in my M.A. thesis, that in no case had the Americans threatened to withdraw financial support of the W.C.C. because they disapproved of its policy.[52] The predominantly western influence in the I.M.C. was sustained for a much simpler reason than ecumenical power politics. With the high cost of travel from the Far East, it simply was not possible to pay the fares of representatives of the younger churches to come to I.M.C. committee meetings in the west, unless the cost could be shared with a missionary society who had invited a church leader to visit England.

If the odds were stacked so high against the I.M.C., whether because of the weakness of the I.M.C.'s internal organisation or because of the contemporary economic crises, one can gain a better perspective on the nightmarish aspects of the I.M.C. financial predicament by comparing it with that of other ecumenical organizations. The S.C.M. was in continual difficulties after 1922 when the effects of expanding so rapidly to meet the post-war expansion in the universities began to be felt at a time when senior friends were suffering from the beginning of the 1922 slump. Many promising S.C.M. projects, such as the training colleges' secretary (1922-24) or the secretary on industrialism (1922-24) perished through lack of finance to provide a successor to the innovators of projects. S.C.M. finances were always on a knife edge in spite of the extent of their operations, but somehow Tatlow was always able to secure new money to pay off old debts.[53] The W.S.C.F. was in a much more precarious situation as a study of its finances reveals. As Dr Visser't Hooft says in his memoirs, there was a time when the W.S.C.F. was simply his desk in Geneva, because there was no money available for another salary.[54] Miss Sinclair relates how all the Life and Work staff in Geneva were on one month's notice because there was no guarantee that it would be possible to pay their salaries at the end of the month. The importance of Oldham's transfer of allegiance to the Life and Work movement in 1934 was significant not only because his organisation of the study preparations for Oxford, but because he brought his financial abilities to the Life and Work movement, and found the sum necessary to finance the Oxford conference.[55] He did not, however, manage to see that Eric Fenn's salary as the secretary responsible for the Oxford conference 'follow up' was continued even for the initial two years envisaged.[56] Even in 1932, when the I.M.C. went through one of the most severe financial crises ever, in which the budget was reduced by a fifth, the situation was nothing compared with the parallel crisis in Life and Work.[57] Miss Sinclair could not believe the degree of financial security she found when she came to work for the I.M.C. in 1940. She found it much less exciting. Undoubtedly, the relative degree of financial stability which the I.M.C. enjoyed was a key factor in giving it seniority and an 'established' reputation among ecumenical organisations.

It is important to realize from the extent of the Paton correspondence on financial matters, how much of Paton's time and energy was drained away by the necessity to be constantly raising money. At one point he was raising money for the I.M.C. central budget, the D.S.I.R. separate budget, the International Council on the Christian Approach to the Jews (I.C.C.A.J.), the Lindsay commission followed by the India Colleges Appeal, the Christian Literature in India fund, and the Mission of Friendship, apart from helping individuals find scholarships and so on. Large single donations, such as Edward Cadbury's contribution to Tambaram, were far outweighed by thousands of letters requesting much smaller sums.[58] Considering that overwork was one of the major factors contributing to Paton's premature death, one cannot but regret the necessity for him to spend so much energy raising money. Another question is whether Paton's relationships with his colleagues were soured by financial problems. However, it seems that the conflicts between Paton and Warnshuis owe more to differences of personalities and principles than to the financial problem which merely gave content to the disagreements. Yet Paton got very exasperated with Merle Davis over financial matters in 1939 because of what he considered to be the latter's irresponsible attitude.[59] The effect on Paton himself is impossible to measure. It cannot have been calculated to give peace of mind to a man with financial commitments such as Paton's, to have been continually worried about the future solvency of the I.M.C., even if Oldham's preparedness to resign if necessary removed the immediate threat to his income. Elisabeth Montefiore has described the cuts in salaries as being the final blow which made it impossible for him to manage on his salary for all his wife's economizing. Nevertheless, he and his wife maintained a quiet confidence that 'the Lord would provide'. It makes Paton's achievements for the I.M.C. the more remarkable when one considers that he was constantly harassed by financial problems, whether personal or belonging to the I.M.C.

Paton's achievements for the I.M.C. are remarkable. Eventually, after a decade of struggle in which he not only had to balance the central budget, but also to provide the means to hold the Tambaram meeting, the deficit was eradicated in 1939. The budgeted expenditure of $40,000 in 1928 rose to $42,000 in 1932, but after that fell steadily to $35,000 in 1939. The deficit was more intractable, fluctuating between $10,000 in March 1933, $969 in December 1933 to $2,000 in 1936 and $5,000 in the winter of 1937-38. The I.M.C. was marginally in credit in January 1939. A concomitant of this achievement was that the essential work of the I.M.C. was preserved. In spite of the doubts about the financial position which were raised with regard to the I.M.C. meetings at Jerusalem and Tambaram, these meetings were held. 'The Third Secretary' was retained until he could no longer be prevented from resigning properly in 1937. Financial problems never prevented there being a very good relationship with the C.B.M.S.

One positive benefit is that the financial difficulties of the I.M.C. forced its staff and committees to discuss very much more thoroughly their strategy and their priorities. Oldham had to account precisely for his visits to Africa. The Herrnhut meeting had to produce constructive results, because there might not be another opportunity to meet. Committee meetings of the I.M.C. became much less frequent than was originally intended, a development which some members of the I.M.C. approved of. In fact, when one compares the I.M.C. budget with that of a secular organization, such as the I.L.O. or the League of Nations, one is amazed that so much could be achieved by the I.M.C. on the proverbial shoestring. Whether one is considering the position of the German or the Scandinavian societies, or the efforts made by the N.C.C's of India and China to contribute something, one is impressed by the extraordinary tenacity of those involved in what appears to human reason to be insuperable difficulties — the weakness of having to depend so much on America and Britain for finance, and the vulnerability of the system to the contemporary international economic crises. The whole of this discussion on the financial problems of the I.M.C. demonstrates that it is possible to run a highly effective and esteemed international organization on a shoestring.

The Department of Social and Industrial Research.

Without question, one of the most audacious experiments the I.M.C. ventured upon, and financially the most precarious, was the creation of the Department of Social and Industrial Research in Geneva. Few I.M.C. projects encountered more criticism before being accepted as a success, even though it has been shown in the previous chapter how invaluable its field work was to the Tambaram meeting. The idea of such a department was adopted at the I.M.C. meeting at the Jerusalem meeting, but there was a long gestation period until the first directors were appointed in September 1930. Several attempts were made to abort it or smother it at birth. Paton was involved throughout, convincing Mott and a doubtful Oldham of its viability, refusing to allow the Life and Work movement to swallow it up in its own research department, the International Social Christian Institute, and defending it against all comers.[60] It was perhaps less an affair after his own heart than the Lindsay Commission was, and he was less successful in raising financial support for it, but it was no mean achievement to keep it going during the financial crises of the thirties, and the principles behind it were identical with his own. The existence of the D.S.I.R. was also a provocation to other ecumenical movements, and therefore affected the course of discussions about the integration of the I.M.C. with other organisations.

Discussion at the Jerusalem conference on rapid industrialisation, migrant labour, and all the social evils which accompany the commercial exploitation of primitive societies, although reinforced by a monumental essay from Paton on the subject, revealed that neither the younger churches nor the missions were sufficiently well-prepared or accurately informed to be able to respond to the problem adequately.[61] The I.M.C. was already employing freelance researchers such as Professors Herbert Butterfield, Schweinitz de Brunner and K.S. Latourette, but as individuals working on individual projects.[62] The proposal to create a bureau involved a much more permanent institution, whose first task would be to define the areas where research was most needed.

The delegates from the 'younger churches' had been the most enthusiastic in their support for the proposal. Baron Boetzelaer van Dubbeldam admitted later that his initial opposition had been overcome by the younger churches' delegates' arguments.[63] Consequently a resolution was passed entrusting the I.M.C. officers with the responsibility of formulating detailed plans for the department. This, being interpreted, meant that Paton applied his mind to the scheme and in a series of letters and memoranda, produced a blueprint.

It is difficult to trace the exact sequence of Paton's ideas because two important letters are almost certainly wrongly dated, but it is typical that Paton began by considering the possible budget, which he placed at £1,500, and how to raise it. Only then did he begin to think out the principles at stake.

> 'If there is to be brought to bear upon the social developement of Asia and Africa in the new day any measure of the Christian influence and spirit', he wrote, 'it will lie with the missionary movement to bring this to pass'.[64]

He argued that the existing Christian movements for social reform were concerned entirely with conditions in the West, and could not provide the information the younger churches needed for understanding conditions in their own countries. Accurate information was the first pre-requisite for negotiating effectively with governments. Knowing that the success of the department would depend on the personalities of those engaged to run it, he emphasized in his letters the interest H.A. Grimshaw, an eminent sociologist, the chief of the Native Labour Section of the International Labour Organization, had shown in the I.M.C. since Paton had persuaded him to attend the Jerusalem meeting.[65] Paton hoped that the contact with Grimshaw would prepare the way for full co-operation with the I.L.O., since he divined correctly that Grimshaw would like to have worked for the I.M.C., had his health permitted. In fact, his condition became so much worse after Jerusalem that he was admitted to hospital in Geneva, and then to a clinic where he died a few months later.[66]

Although other members of the I.L.O. staff gave their support and encouragement, there was inevitably some delay before an equally good potential leader of the department could be found. Initially, Paton wanted Miss Agatha Harrison, author of the study into child labour in Shanghai, to be appointed, since the I.M.C. had no women executive officers.[67] Then he realized that since there was no Continental member of the I.M.C. they must find one in Europe. Eventually in May 1930 the search ended when J. Merle Davis was approached. He had resigned from the Pacific Institute of Social and Religious Research at Honolulu, but unfortunately to secure him, Mott had to offer him a disproportionately high salary.[68] Paton had meanwhile found the man to counter Continental suspicions that the department would propagate the 'Social Gospel'. Dr Otto Iserland had been a Marxist trade unionist and then taught economics at a university in Japan. In Japan he had become a convinced Christian, and at great financial sacrifice to himself and his family, had studied theology. Paton was adamant that his appointment was independent of Davis's, that he was not to be Davis's personal assistant.[69]

An equally fortunate move was the decision to rent offices in the new office block, being built by the Y.M.C.A. in Geneva. The Life and Work movement also took offices there, and Dr Ehrenstrom attributes the friendly relations which eventually prevailed between the two movements to Iserland's proximity on the floor above and to the fact that he spoke German while they were sharing the same coffee-making facilities.[70] The rent was very reasonable, but Paton made it a condition of their participation that the organization should not be compromised by the presence in the same building of a group such as 'World Religious Peace'. In this he was anticipating criticism that the I.M.C. was taking a syncretistic approach.[71]

Paton submitted his ideas in the form of a memorandum to a group of interested people in London in June 1929, and to the I.M.C. meeting at Williamstown, U.S.A., in July 1929.[72] One of his strongest arguments which he used on these occasions was that projects such as the investigation conducted by the I.M.C. office into the Kenya Forced Labour Ordinance in 1919 had had to be abandoned because neither time nor staff could be spared in the face of more urgent work. This was a problem which Paton must have encountered himself, as during the years 1927-30 he tried to investigate by correspondence such questions as the League of Nations' proposals on sleeping sickness, the 'liquor trade and native races' question which resulted in a C.B.M.S. delegation to the Colonial office, the question of mandated territories, and he later supported various people who were investigating the plight of White Russian refugees in China and child slavery.[73] The D.S.I.R. must have relieved Paton of a certain amount of work which he would otherwise have done, while Warnshuis' work on religious freedom was also transferred to the D.S.I.R. Paton envisaged a minimum of two staff members, one normally resident in Geneva, the other frequently travelling, and that in addition a member of the I.L.O. was prepared to give sufficient honorary help who would be known as 'honorary technical adviser'. The D.S.I.R. would be of considerable help to the I.L.O. in gathering material not normally accessible to it, and in return the I.L.O. would make its expertise available to the church. The travelling officer would gather information and communicate it to the churches in other parts of the world where it was relevant, and also stir up the emerging Christian social conscience to action in regard to industrial problems. All this would be part of an endeavour to build up a 'Christian world view' and a 'Christian sociology'.[74]

With various amendments, additions and redrafts, this scheme was accepted at Williamstown, but not without incurring some criticism. The D.S.I.R. came into being in September 1930 and began to create its own style of work. Since it was decided to answer attacks on the D.S.I.R. by good work, not by an elaborate theological defence, the department's programme will be considered before the various attacks on the D.S.I.R.

Merle Davis began by interviewing a great many 'interested parties' as to what the most important subject for investigation would be, and eventually conducted a survey of conditions on the African Copperbelt, which missions in Northern Rhodesia, Southern Rhodesia, Belgian Congo and the Union of South africa had requested. By some astute diplomacy, Merle Davis and an excellent team of sociologists and economists, two missionaries and a Jewish consultant, managed to win the co-operation of the Union Minière du Congo and the Anglo-American companies operating on the Copperbelt so that the team had access to the plant and could talk to managerial staff and to workers.[75] The main question was how, given that economic development and industrialisation could only be regulated but not reversed, the social and moral evils which followed industrialisation in South Africa could be averted from the new mines and factories of the Rhodesias and the Congo. The report, when it was written, was an important influence in the decision of the C.B.M.S. to set up a United Mission to the Copperbelt. The emphasis of the report was, nevertheless, more on what the Christian Church should be doing in industrial areas than on what European missions should do.[76]

Another successful programme which involved two years' field work was the Bantu Cinema Project, sponsored by the Carnegie Trust, to discover what effect this new medium had on the African mind and how it could be most effectively used in rural uplift programmes, prevention of diseases and so on. The department's team worked very closely with government welfare agencies and missions, and at the end of their experiments produced a number of films for general use.[77]

Two reports exist of the D.S.I.R's first two years' work, the one a formal submission to the Herrnhut meeting of the I.M.C., the other a more frank assessment of the situation which Iserland gave to an informal meeting held in Edinburgh House a few months before the Herrnhut meeting. Since, from independent sources, it can be established that Davis and Iserland conducted an intensive public relations exercise at Herrnhut to justify the D.S.I.R. it seems that the latter report is more likely to be an accurate appraisal of the situation.[78] Iserland confessed, in the informal discussion, to having tried and failed to make a study of the social and industrial work which missions had done, and to disappointing results in his attempts to contact missionary societies in Europe. This he attributed to their inability to follow up anything new in a time of financial recession. He found it difficult to make contact with other offices of the League of Nations, apart from the I.L.O., and friendly relations with other Christian organisations had not led to any active co-operation in research. One paragraph of the minutes of this meeting suggests that the D.S.I.R. had attempted to take policy decisions outside its competence because no principle about this had been established. Action should only be taken after consultation with the officers of the I.M.C., because, as Oldham pointed out, the D.S.I.R. is a research institute and its protection lies in that fact.[79]

It is immediately apparent that the department was very flexible in its programme, tackling the most pressing questions in the field while building up a base for co-operation with similar bodies in Geneva. The lack of enthusiasm in Germany was balanced by the enthusiasm among mission secretaries in London, Belgium, the Netherlands and Switzerland (especially the Mission Suisse Romande). It must have had an impact quite disproportionate to its size, because of the calibre of Davis and Iserland, and the practical revelance of their work. Its involvement at these two levels, in Geneva and in the field, must have been an important step in making the I.M.C. more international and less Western. Significantly, when a choice had to be made, between facilities in Geneva and cheaper accommodation elsewhere, Davis ran the office from a houseboat in Kashmir, as his memoirs record.

The department was run on the proverbial shoestring. Money was extremely difficult to raise. Because the same sort of suspicion attended the D.S.I.R. in the minds of conservative churchmen as is associated today with the W.C.C's programme, it had a separate budget, and depended on special contributions from individuals apart from a small regular income from the I.M.C. offices in London and New York, which had been authorized by I.M.C. committee meetings, and grants from charitable foundations for specific projects. Paton tapped some most unusual sources, including the old subscribers to Miss Rouse's salary before she retired from the W.S.C.F. Providing funds from two offices caused great confusion because the New York office was supposed to send funds to London and Davis complained about the London contribution being delayed. The D.S.I.R. was severely affected when Britain came off the gold standard in 1931.[80] There was a none too amicable correspondence between London and New York concerning the financial arrangements. Paton wrote to Warnshuis that he thought it was his obligation to raise half the budget, though he did not manage that in 1932: 'Most of us regard it as very fortunate indeed that I got as much as I did, as it came from sources which do not normally give to missions, and that I raised it by myself, without any help from the missionary societies, and made every effort not to interfere with their normal givers. There is steadily increasing interest. If we can get through these few years and the department will be patient, we can ultimately place the thing more securely and broadly'.[81] It has already been noted that part of the difficulty was due to the fact that Davis did not recognise that he was responsible for raising a proportion of his salary. Paton did not want responsibility for Davis' salary to be transferred to New York lest he lose control of the situation.[82]

In spite of the complicated arrangements evolved to counter the effect of the weakness of the pound, the deficit mounted, reaching £1,137.15s.11d. in 1953 (the total income was £4,000 per year). Severe retrenchment was necessary, which was the reason for moving the D.S.I.R. from Geneva. Iserland had earlier been forced to abandon the department's quarterly newsheet and cut back on the office secretarial staff. Iserland solved the financial problem by resigning in 1936 because he became a Roman Catholic, before he had to be asked to resign because there was not the wherewithal to pay his salary. It is regrettable that the D.S.I.R. should have been so very restricted in what it could achieve by lack of finance.

The Life and Work movement faced similar difficulties in maintaining its Institute, which was one of the arguments for a joint institute. It seems fairly clear that even after the Institute was strengthened by Schönfeld being seconded from the German Evangelische churches in 1928, Paton did not trust the Life and Work movement to work efficiently or in such a way as would serve I.M.C. interests. Warnshuis interpreted the appointment of Schönfeld as a last effort to save what remained of the Stockholm idea. Paton replied:

> 'There is no doubt that our action at Jerusalem had caused the Stockholm people to take their own bureau very much more seriously, and I hope now to explore very fully with them the possibility of co-operation'.[83]

This comment might be considered an example of Paton's arrogance if it were not for the abundance of evidence in support of his judgment. The Revd P.T.R. Kirk, secretary of the 'Industrial Christian Fellowship' and honorary secretary of the British section of Life and Work objected very strongly to the existence of the D.S.I.R., and caused much trouble for Paton in England. One does not, unfortunately, know how representative his protest was of the views of members of the British Life and Work section, though part of Paton's annoyance with him undoubtedly sprang from the threat he posed to Paton's patient wooing of the members of the Christian Social Council.[84] The whole incident is illustrative of the vigilance of ecumenical organisations against 'ecumenical poaching' on what was felt to be their territory.

At a meeting to inform members of the Christian Social Council of the plans for the D.S.I.R., Kirk tried to raise the whole question of co-operation and would not accept Paton's assurances, trying to probe the whole character of the I.M.C. department's structure, which Paton told him bluntly was not his concern, nor that of the other people assembled.[85] Using slightly more diplomatic language, he wrote to the Bishop of Salisbury, a vice-chairman of the I.M.C., to elaborate his personal views:

> 'I have been at pains to study the Stockholm Bureau at first hand. I welcome unreservedly the foundation of it, and hope that it will do fruitful work. It is I think, qualified to render a service in regard to problems in Europe and America, but there is nobody on its staff who had any knowledge whatever of the problems emerging in Asia and Africa. This is simply not open to denial by anyone who knows the facts. Moreover, while I acknowledge the gifts of Dr Keller, I frankly do not regard him as a suitable head of a bureau of this kind, and while it is not my business to question the wisdom of Stockholm in putting him over their bureau, I am unalterably opposed to committing to his ultimate charge the study of problems in the mission field and the guidance of action in regard to them.[86] As I have said, I have refrained from making any comment of this kind when it could be quoted, but if the Stockholm Committee, without, it seems to me, lending their minds to the thoughtful consideration of the very urgent problems to be faced in the mission field, persist in claiming

> the world for their parish, it will be necessary to speak with plainness on this question of knowledge and efficiency.... In writing to you in this way I do not wish to appear uncharitable and captious.... we propose in our bureau to deal with a part of the whole area with which we are already intimately connected. I think the Bishop of Winchester should be reminded that the body to which he refers as the Continuation Committee of the Jerusalem Conference, the I.M.C., dates back in one form or another for seventeen years, and has a certain established position in the missionary world. At the same time, so far as I as secretary can speak for the I.M.C., I have given the most positive assurances.... that we will co-operate with the Stockholm Bureau to the limit, using the same office, combining so far as we can in the use of staff, and above all in any approach to the home field.... Cannot these assurances be accepted so that we may get on with the work instead of wasting time in these futile arguments about responsibility?'[87]

The second paragraph summarised the I.M.C. position. As senior ecumenical organisation, they were affronted by the unreasonableness of the 'take-over' bid, as they interpreted the Life and Work argument. Having very practical ends in view, they were not prepared to sacrifice them in an act of union. When one contrasts the style of the work of the Stockholm Institute with its international seminars and conferences with Merle Davis' caravan roaming the industrial plains of Africa and Asia, one must acknowledge the strength of Paton's position.

Significantly, Paton's opinion was shared by missionary circles in Germany. Paton received a long letter from Professor Schlunk of Tübingen in June 1928, urging him in the name of German missionaries to keep the bureau independent. He has heard that Söderblom has suggested that the I.M.C. should simply add a man to the Stockholm Institute. Paton was interested that it was the German missions who took this line in spite of the widespread support in Germany for Life and Work.[88] Perhaps as a final comment one should quote Bell's letter to Oldham concerning the proposal for the I.M.C. to be responsible for the fifth section of Life and Work's representation: 'I quite realize that the I.M.C. has everything to give and very little to gain from such co-operation'.[89]

If there was friction with the Life and Work movement, there were doubts in the C.B.M.S. One doubter was Oldham. Writing to Hickman-Johnson he explained that he had nothing to do with the founding of the D.S.I.R. because he was in East Africa. His doubts sprang from the practical difficulty of setting up a research institute, but the choice of personnel reconciled him to the idea. He was impressed because he was finding among laymen an increased interest in the I.M.C. because of the D.S.I.R.

> It is increasingly clear to me that the only way in which we can respond to the demands of the world situation is by greatly broadening the circle of those who are interested in the work of the church overseas. Spiritual revival is the only thing which can achieve this, but until this happens the D.S.I.R. may be God's way of reaching those untouched by present methods of appeal'.[90]

The most intransigent opposition to the D.S.I.R. came from the Scandinavian mission councils, whose reaction to Oldham's views would be that even if Oldham conceded that spiritual renewal in man was the sine qua non of mission, he was overemphasising the social environment of missions and was in danger of dissipating Christian forces of evangelism in social work.[91] The degree of scandal which was felt among the Northern Missionary Council repays careful analysis because it is indicative of an important development in the understanding of the approach to mission. Whatever the conflict over personalities and representation, their objection was basically theological. Much of the scandal was unnecessary, had the I.M.C. not neglected its Scandinavian constituency so much, as had been argued earlier in this chapter. This generalisation is true for many aspects of I.M.C. policy, if one considers the mass of I.M.C. records.[92]

The protest from the Norwegian Missionary Council was based on fears that the action of the I.M.C. was exceeding the original mandate of the Edinburgh Continuation Committee, by doing the work of a missionary society directly instead of being a bureau of information and counsel. Secondly, while social work may be an auxiliary ministry, the present tendencies have led to the obscuring of the Gospel. The missionary movement and missionary administration have been influenced by 'modernism', so that those who hold the 'biblical view' are very distressed at the degree of rationalisation. The 'social Gospel' is anathematized, and contrasted with the correct motivation for mission, the ultimate victory of the Kingdom of God, which gives missionaries boundless confidence.[93] However, it is clear both from the documents laid before the I.M.C. and from the other sources, that the real source of disquiet was caused by the situation in China, where two major Norwegian missionary societies and the China Inland Mission had withdrawn from the National Christian Council of China, which the Norwegians identified with the I.M.C. and where Norwegian missionaries were working in the main field of American missionary effort, and consequently where the 'social Gospel' was most influential. A frequent Danish and Norwegian complaint was that the I.M.C. tendency would cause young people to volunteer for social work, not for mission. Further causes of friction were their hospitality to the Chinese representatives on the I.M.C., and the I.M.C. support for the excellent work of Reichelt's Christian monastery for Buddhist monks, which they eventually disowned, and general I.M.C. neglect and under-representation.[94] Paton's response was to invite Professor Torm to write for the I.R.M. In the article which appeared in October 1930, Torm maintains that while of course a missionary must be concerned to mitigate social injustice, especially when it is the result of western civilization, there is no such thing as a social content of the Christian message. It is no part of the Gospel to create a Christian sociology. He disagrees with Tawney's speech at Jerusalem supporting the creation of the D.S.I.R. by the argument that the Church must regain the former position as a leading cultural influence. The Church is a 'little flock', not a conquering force. He attacks Paton's contention in 'A faith for the World', that it is an important task for the Church to consider the implications of social questions, because it is dangerous that the East should think that Christianity has no social message, but the Communists have. (Paton was close to the controversial W.C.C. slogan 'Let the world write the agenda' (for the Church)). Torm cannot understand Paton comparing the Church with Communism. The Church must proclaim its message irrespective of the prospects of victory or defeat. Obviously the Christian must love his neighbour and protest against injustice, but he must not provide a social alternative to this injustice. The command for Christians to be obedient to temporal authority shows clearly Christians are not to become involved in political and social reforms. Paton has clearly rejected New Testament eschatology by his attitude when he says he cannot understand people who say there should be no social improvement until after the Second Coming. Torm concludes: 'And this difference (concerning eschatology and social questions) is so fundamental that an insistence on an attempt to solve the social problems from the side of the central organisation might endanger the unity and co-operative work of the Protestant Church'.[95]

Paton cannot refrain from his editor's privilege of reply to this. In an 'editor's note' he declares that he has much sympathy with Torm's view that social evil is sin, and that the Church is a 'little flock', but he cannot see why it is right for local organisations and individuals to combat social evil, but not international organisations. Torm has misunderstood Tawney in thinking that he meant by 'Christian' sociology the enunciation of a particular social programme. In fact it is the question of taking the radical meaning of the fact of Christ and asking what its implications are in life and thought. The D.S.I.R. will not impose a common social theory on anyone. The plans for it arose from the particular need in Asian churches for information on exploitation and industrialisation.

A compromise was reached in a paper which Dr Siegfried Knak of the Gossner Mission prepared as a 'Supplementary explanation' of the D.S.I.R. In it he repudiated the 'Social Gospel' which he asserted was once the prevailing conception in I.M.C. circles. (In this he was surely mistaken.)[96] However, he answered the argument that Jesus was not interested in the improvement of social conditions, so his followers today are not to take them as a primary concern, by saying that Jesus was not a missionary going to a people of another culture who would misunderstand his message if he were silent on the social evils of the day. He stood in a quite different relationship to his hearers, who would have failed to understand him if he had spoken of social conditions. But 'we come as foreigners to these foreign peoples and even more as debtors burdened with guilt'. The missionary cannot avoid being a disciple of Christ and a representative of European civilisation. This civilisation has brought so many evils in its train to the East, which are destroying the souls of the East, that missionaries must combat by word and deed these non-Christian western influences. The African miner cannot possibly understand the Gospel of love if the missionary ignores his suffering and hunger. The missionary movement is continually under the judgment of God because of this situation. The D.S.I.R. is necessary so that missionaries can judge how far they should be involved in social and economic problems.

Knak's paper marked the consensus of opinion in the I.M.C., and coincides with Paton's own views. Coming from a German missionary administrator, it was more acceptable to the Scandinavians, and is significant as marking the abandonment of neutrality on the part of the missionary for involvement in industrial and social problems, not merely as the outworking of individual compassion, but as providing the rationale for the D.S.I.R's work to provide data for intervention with governments, as the work on narcotics for example, shows. Tawney's idea of submitting sociology to the theology of the presence of Christ was perhaps too radical for all members of the I.M.C., but it is very significant that Paton should have justified the D.S.I.R. in the light of it. In studying such things as African concepts of marriage, the D.S.I.R. was influencing Christian ethics as well as pronouncing on a fearful missionary problem. The department was intended to increase missionary impetus and was also an important means of keeping theology and mission together, for as with the Lindsay commission the emphasis is on solid research being made available to a wider field. However, geographical proximity was not sufficient to bring about closer ecumenical co-operation, as the I.M.C. and Life and Work fiercely defended their own concepts and provinces.

In studying the development of the D.S.I.R. one sees many of the I.M.C.'s problems in microcosm. It should be clear, however, that the I.M.C. was a living growing organisation, whatever its financial problems, and that Paton had a catalysing influence on it.

Chapter VIII

Missions in Wartime (1939- 45)

It is possible to describe the significance of the international co-operation involved in maintaining the work of missions during the Second World War solely as a practical relief operation to rescue the starving and stranded European missionaries, to alleviate the conditions of those interned and to encourage the development of native leadership. Paton however claimed, with justification, that the whole system was a manifestation of the universal church on a remarkable scale, developing the theme in talks and articles so that the theological significance of the situation was clarified. The spiritual quality of the unbroken friendship between Paton and Hartenstein and the attitude of the other German missions directors must also be considered because it inspired Paton to write to the Under-Secretary of State for India: in September 1939: 'This kind of fellowship is one of the most hopeful and practical things in the world'.[1] The fact that there was no barrier of suspicion and doubt to overcome made missionary settlements during and after the war totally different from those which characterized the aftermath of the First World War. This fellowship had its roots in the Tambaram meeting and gave a cutting edge to Paton's proposals of the question of a united church in India.

There were complicated political overtones to the position of the governments involved, concerning delicate questions of Church-State relationships. Paton exerted his influence on a wide range of issues from preventing the exploitation of missionaries as agents of propaganda to cultivating the favourable opinion of neutral countries. Having wrested from the British government an acknowledgment of the supranationality of missions, the principle was then sabotaged in some countries by flagrant confessional empire-building when certain of the Christian denominations exploited the weaknesses of 'orphaned' missions to extend their own influence. The issues this raises must be discussed since there is reason to believe that the I.M.C. may have inadvertently contributed to this unecumenical situation. Finally, Paton, Koechlin, Bishop Neill and others unwittingly, or with full knowledge of the facts, propagated a number of myths which it is necessary to demolish.

Even before one can discuss the significance of the action to save missions cut off from their hinterland, one must concede the extraordinary range of practical problems with hostilities affecting five continents. The I.M.C. and the German missions had had a dress rehearsal, which proved of great importance, when German missions had been prevented from exporting currency from Germany in 1935-36.[2] Therefore they had already introduced stringent financial economies, while encouraging the self-sufficiency of semi-autonomous churches. Unlike the war period, when a number of factors hindered the normal functioning of missions, the problem was confined to financial restrictions: German missions found it increasingly difficult in 1934 to obtain foreign exchange from the German Treasury. Eventually all currency exchanges were forbidden unless they were for the export of German goods or the propagation of German cultural and political influence. Various ingenious schemes invented to link mission finance with that of German trading companies proved incapable of realisation. The missionary administrators in Germany were well aware of the danger of compromising the neutrality of their missions within the British Empire.[3] Towards the end of 1936 Knak managed to extract concessions from the Treasury, but to Paton and the secretaries of British societies anxious to help, it seemed realistic to treat the emergency on both a short-term and long-term basis, considering any money raised in Britain as a gift rather than a loan and envisaging tactical redeployment of mission personnel to make a permanent reduction of staff possible. It is clear that both these presuppositions are relevant to a situation of war. The German Missionary Council did not accept Paton's view, but after much correspondence a compromise was achieved which is an interesting example of international missionary co-operation.[4] An Emergency Fund was established in London from which payments were made for the support of German missions. At the same time the exact equivalent was deposited in a German account, but since no foreign body was allowed to invest money in Germany, it was only by a 'gentleman's agreement' that this was known as the I.M.C. account, and was used for I.M.C. expenses in Germany. Later by agreement the money in the German account was used to purchase a property in Berlin and the rents accumulated to the I.M.C. as interest. Amazingly, the property was unscathed during the war, sold at a profit in 1946 and the I.M.C. debt settled.

Non-German missions were considered to have a collective responsibility to ensure the continuance of the work of the German missions, so proposals were made for the long-term support of those missions, the cultivation of indigenous leadership and financial support, the employment of German missionaries by other missions, and for similar societies taking over the work in a way similar to the pattern of temporary supervision used in the First World War. As far as can be judged from the I.M.C. India correspondence, individual Germans did find new employment with other Continental missions, and there was a drastic reduction of projects, but as far as I know, no mission actually took up the work of a German mission during this period.[5] Most British societies were suffering acute financial embarrassment themselves anyway. The exercise undoubtedly deepened Anglo-German missionary understanding.

When war was declared in September 1939, the I.M.C. had already evolved a contingency plan, in consultation with German missionary leaders, which Paton wasted no time in putting into operation.[6] The problem of maintaining the normal functioning of German missions and helping interned German missionaries and their families became much more difficult after the fall of France in April 1940, and the loss subsequently of financial aid from Holland, Belgium, Denmark and Norway. Paton acted swiftly to ensure that missionaries from these countries were not treated as enemy aliens though they could technically be considered as such, since their home governments became Nazi-dominated.[7] A stream of protests failed to move the British government over the position of Finnish missionaries in South Africa and China, with the result that American rather than British I.M.C. contributions had to be used to help them. The I.M.C. won the respect and tolerance of the pro de Gaulle governments in the former French colonies, but experienced great difficulty in contacting and aiding missions in pro Vichy colonies even though it was possible to obtain a little money from Vichy France until the country was completely occupied in 1942. Probably the most complicated and tragic situation was that of the German missionaries handed over by the Dutch colonial authorities in the Dutch East Indies for internment in India, whose families were sent to enjoy an ambiguous custody in Japan. When a Dutch ship transporting 400 passengers, including 36 interned missionaries, to India was sunk in January 1941, the I.M.C. and Dr Visser't Hooft had great difficulty establishing the losses (approximately 200 passengers and 18 missionaries) and communicating the news to their families.

Not only was relief necessary on a global scale, but communications were extremely difficult owing to the battle of the Atlantic, and the circuitous routes via Sweden and Lisbon which had to be employed. Paton managed to get mail sent through diplomatic channels, through the good offices of the Ministry of Information, but even then a letter to Westman in Uppsala could take three months to arrive and the Post Office refused, during 1941-42, to send the I.R.M. to Sweden on the grounds that it was too heavy. Maintaining a flow of accurate information was one of the primary concerns of the I.M.C. From the figures collected an overall picture of the numbers involved can be built up, which is appended as a table at the end of this book. Fortunately, through his neutral correspondents, Paton had access to the figures published in the Evangelische Missions-Zeitschrift, edited by W. Freytag, and to the German Missions' Yearbook. In the January issue of the I.R.M. the 'Annual Survey' evaluated the position of the 'orphaned missions' in each field, though as the figures given tend to be cumulative, it is sometimes difficult to assess the amount of new money coming in each month.[8]

As a result of America's late entry into the war, the New York Office of the I.M.C. was especially favourably placed to help the 'orphaned missions'. The major part of the funds needed were raised in America by Warnshuis. The I.M.C. London office lent Miss Gibson to the New York Office in 1940, but she returned in October 1940 because of her father's fatal illness. A great deal of correspondence was generated as an efficient system was gradually evolved,[9] though not without friction. The various psychological gambits that Paton and Warnshuis concocted in order to raise money are interesting: for example, stressing the degree of self-help among the British churches, whom the Americans insisted on helping, often unsolicited and to their great embarrassment, and Paton's tactic of challenging the Americans to make greater sacrifices that the British. Norman Goodall describes the American side of the operation in his biography of Warnshuis.[10]

Paton expended a great deal of time raising money for the orphaned missions, pressing for appeals on their behalf to be broadcast on the B.B.C. The most important single step was the large grants made by the Scandinavian and Dutch governments in exile to their missions. Forrester-Paton made the first donation of £250, which it took Koechlin several months to find a use for. Reading between the lines of the Paton-Koechlin correspondence, it is evident that certain circles in the German government were much embarrassed by the action to save German missions within the British Empire.[11] Probably because of government pressure, missionary circles in Berlin appeared reluctant to accept financial support. Koechlin was initially very annoyed when Hartenstein sent a letter to various contacts in the field via Basel concerning the German government's decision to allow money to be released from Germany in February 1940. Then he was counting on the Basel Mission's own censor, a young pastor in Bern, or Koechlin himself to stop the letters, instead of transmitting them to the field. (This was the Basel Mission's self-imposed system of censorship.[12]) It was, of course, impossible for money to be transmitted from 'the enemy' to British colonies.

Paton was continually petitioning the Treasury in order to extract the maximum possible amount of currency exchange. In this field he became an acknowledged authority, consulted by other ecumenical organizations. In the colonies the governments continued their grants-in-aid to institutions formerly run by the interned missionaries, but it is certain, as Koechlin admitted, that had all those interned been free for the duration of the war, neither the Continental missions nor the Allied churches could have supported them.[13] As it was, virtually every mission drastically reduced its budget in 1940, irrespective of whether the younger churches could shoulder the burden or not. As Paton explained in his correspondence with Professor Westman, he was acting on the presupposition of an Allied victory, because he was in a position to see, as the neutral churchmen could not, the firmness of resolution of the British to win; but if, in spite of that, the British Empire fell, there would be no future for missions anyway, as the evidence of the Nazi persecution of the German churches proved.[14]

The simple facts of this vast system of missionary co-operation seemed pregnant with theological significance to Paton. The article which he wrote in early 1942 at Visser't Hooft's behest entitled 'The Churches help each other', is typical of his thought.[15] Basically, he found that the situation was one of hope: 'The facts show that beneath the many words that have been spoken about the growth of a universal Christian society there is a reality of life'. He continued by describing the vast scale of missionary enterprises in peacetime, involving a contribution from the churches (including the Roman Catholic Church) of £18 million, and the response made by churches in Sweden, Switzerland, the United States and the British Empire to enable a skeleton staff to continue to 'hold the fort' during wartime. However, he comments that it is no less remarkable that the young and relatively weak churches of Asia and Africa have helped one another in a way undreamt of in the last war. He quotes figures, but emphasizes the 'sacrifice and passion' behind the collection of such sums.

> 'Money is not everything, but when it is given in this way it is in a sense sacramental; that is to say, it expresses and is the vehicle of a spiritual reality. Surely this is proof of the reality of a Christian solidarity in the world, this evidence of a commitment to one another across the bounds of race and nation, means something for the future of world order'.

As Paton says, it is the two-way flow of money which is significant, as opposed to the usual one-way flow in missionary finances. It is tangible proof of a spiritual reality. Paton's empirical approach is rather evident here, but it saved him from sentimentalism. Secondly, Paton is presupposing the existence of this fellowship as a God-given reality, of which mutual aid is the expression, not the cause.[16] This conviction he elaborated fully in a small book written for the C.B.M.S. in October 1939 under the title 'The Hour and its Need'. In this book Paton argues strongly against the suggestion that missions should be discontinued for the duration of the war, on the grounds that:

> 'It is plain that to maintain, much less extend, the labours of the mission-
> ary movement in the face of all the obstacles, financial and other, of the
> present time, is so difficult as to be impossible if judged by ordinary
> reasonable and prudent standards. But it is here that we return to the
> realisation that what we are about is not an ordinary human enterprise,
> however noble, but is nothing less than obedience to the manifest call of
> God . . . if the evangelisation of the world is the will of God, then it cannot
> be postponed to a more convenient season . . . we have no right or power
> to offer less than the full Gospel, the Lord Jesus Christ in his fullness, who
> knows no Kingdom without a Cross . . .'

Paton has in fact preceded this paragraph with a considerable argument *ad
hominem* about the contribution which the continuing world-wide Church can bring
to the search for world peace and international law, with its commitment to fight for
the protection of minorities, human rights and racial tolerance, and its encouragement of international federation and political union. However, he writes, the Church
is not a well-managed zoo of nationalities and races, nor an international professional
organisation, but a universal response of those obedient to God's call, hence the
compulsion to evangelism in wartime. The significance of the 'orphaned missions' is
to be understood within the framework of the question of the nature of the Church.
He declares that the dislocation experienced in the last war with the internment of
missionaries and currency restrictions caused the missionary movement to be vitally
concerned with the issues of war and peace. His account of the events of 1914-1919
omits any mention of the bitterness engendered by the consequences of the Versailles
treaty. Reviewing the prospects at the new outbreak of war, he pins his faith on the
twenty-five year old I.M.C. and N.C.C. structures, especially on their experience of
the 1935-36 crisis. 'The problem is therefore more one of providing pastoral care
than providing funds' (A prophetic statement, since the missionaries whom I have
interviewed who were ill-treated by the Japanese bore their sufferings with Christian
fortitude and forgiveness and amazing good humour, whereas missionaries interned
in the hill stations of India succumbed to bitterness and boredom.[17])

> 'The kind of action . . . is nevertheless in the nature of ambulance work
> and we have to ask ourselves whether there is any light that the missionary
> enterprise can shed on the problem of creating a better international order,
> namely that 'The Church comes into the arena with something more than a
> hope of ideal unity to be built up out of national entities. It tells of a unity
> given to men by God'. Despite the fact of sin . . . 'the unity of which the
> Church is a missionary in the world is declared by the Church as real in the
> purpose and act of God. It is not lifted up as an ideal for human aspiration,
> but declared as a fact of experience'.

In the book Paton warns of the danger to the Church if it be seduced ideologically as in 1914-1918, and connives at the tribal religion of the kind which
flourished along with the patriotism and camaraderie of war. He recommends
prayer and penitence, even on the part of those who think they are fighting a just war,
as the only means to defeat this heresy. The world fellowship of the international
missionary movement will remind the belligerents that the Church is not an aspect of
national culture. These thoughts explain the cryptic message to Archbishop Eidem at

the end of a letter to Westman:

> '. . . assure him of the continued ecumenical spirit of British Christian-
> ity. He and you will understand that in our judgment an ecumenical
> Christianity does not mean that we fail to appreciate the demands made by
> the present juncture that our nation should fight to the uttermost. We
> remember also that there is a Kingdom of God'.[18]

The theological link between the ideas and emotions expressed at the Tambaram
conference and the motivation to rescue the missions is clearly demonstrated in the
book, though 'Tambaram' is not invoked to justify the connection.

The relationship of missions in wartime to the reality of the universal church has
been treated at length because it shows that the phrases of sympathy in the letters on
purely practical matters spring not from politeness, but from deep conviction. So
Koechlin wrote to Paton concerning the organisational changes within the Basel
Mission, prefacing the letters by the sentence: 'Let me simply say that I am thinking
of you day by day, night after night, and that the fellowship in Christ proves to be
stronger than ever. I do not need to say more'.[19] It is clear that the strength of this
fellowship lay in the way in which it was theologically and spiritually interpreted.

The most remarkable example of the spiritual heights reached by those involved
with the orphaned missions, came in the letter Hartenstein wrote to Paton immediately after resigning as India Secretary of the Basel Mission, when he was expecting
to be called up to fight for a regime he detested.

> 'Tambaram nine months ago is like a bright star of God's promise, a
> signpost of the communion and fellowship by all Christian churches of the
> world. But now darkness has come upon us and nobody knows when the
> holy but terrible will of God will be changed again to mercy and love . . .
> My dear friend, I have to say nothing else than my whole-hearted thanks
> for all you have done for us during the last thirteen years we were co-
> operating, for all the friendship and confidence, for all the trust and love
> you have shown me personally in difficult times and questions . . . And
> now we have to go the way into darkness. We are not alone on this way.
> Jesus Christ is being with us. And if the day comes when the light of God
> and His mercy will shine again upon our peoples and churches, then do
> remember, my dear friend, if I am still alive, that there is a friend of yours
> in whose heart all the spiritual heritage of thirteen years of missionary
> work does not fade away . . . I shall remain a man of Christian mission in
> spite of all that will come upon us during the following years . . . The Lord
> may lead us on his way and protect us in His grace'.[20]

Paton was extremely moved by this letter. He discreetly showed it to highly
placed government officials to remind them of the calibre of the 'enemy', and to his
missionary and ecclesiastical colleagues to foster fellowship. Finally he published the
contents in 'The Hour and its Need' as evidence of the triumph of Christian love in
wartime. He replied in one of his rare handwritten letters, sent via Koechlin, who
sent on a translation:

> 'your letter . . . incarnates the whole spirit of our ecumenical fellowship
> in Christ. Surely we are right in feeling that this fellowship is eternal . . . I
> have always felt to you a special warmth of affection, because I feel that we
> see things in the same way, though you are more Barthian than I, and have

the same sense of humour. You do not need me to say that I will do all that I can to preserve the work of the German missions. We move in dark and terrible days but whatever may happen I shall always be certain of your friendship in Christ and you can be certain of mine. I am glad that Tambaram was not just an ordinary conference, but one called under the shadow of war and full of the sense of God's judgment and love'.[21]

It is interesting that both men interpret the missionary situation as being under God's judgment, and use the motif of light and darkness. Yet Christ is there. The degree of commitment to mission is also characteristic of both men.

Finally, it is important to consider the significance of the argument Paton employs in a statement he drafted in 1941 on closer co-operation in India, when he was attempting to stimulate discussion about a united church.[22] As usual, his theology arises from an empirical situation — in this case the war and its straitening effect on missionary budgets. He declares it may be that the entire economy of the West is being re-cast. It is the duty of Christian men to discern the signs of the times. 'We must seek so to plan that whatever power it may please God to release through mission work of the Church shall not be hindered by our lack of readiness to hear and alertness to change'. The churches must act together so that the basic needs may be met as completely as possible. Grateful though one is for the existing structures of co-operation, there are sharp limits to the possibilities for advance. Therefore, he argues that what is needed is the simpler, more radical structure of a united church. The progress in negotiations so far suggests that there is agreement in matters of faith, and while he does not underestimate the importance of the differences in order which remain, action should be taken in virtue of that agreement so far as it extends.

The whole document is a simple and practical one, discussed seriously by the C.B.M.S., but much criticized in India, according to Boyd, as was shown in the discussion on the independence of the 'younger churches' in chapter V. The translation of practical exigencies into an ecclesiastical context is a theological move, but although Paton's document is intended to stimulate discussion, one is left wondering if it was not an over-simplification of the problem to reduce the argument to such practical terms.

The principal significance of the situation of the 'orphaned missions' lies in the light thrown on the question of Church and State relations. The political ramifications are in fact extremely complicated, but can be exhaustively documented from the archives of the I.M.C. London and New York offices, the Basel Mission's papers, and the government records now accessible in the Public Records Office in London. During this period Paton drew on every ounce of political influence that he had. He exploited a vast range of governmental contacts in the India Office, the Colonial Office, the Foreign Office and the Ministry of Information, departments which occasionally met to plan joint policy with regard to missions, and sometimes interpreted the situation differently from one another, as their records and internal memoranda show.[23] However, only significant incidents can be mentioned. The question is whether Paton succeeded in establishing relations which were close enough for effective co-operation, but not so close that missions could be compromised. Two features present themselves at once, firstly the difficulty caused by the governmental tendency to act first and reflect afterwards, when confronted by private protests from Paton or a public outcry, and secondly, the manoeuvring necessary to induce the government to take positive action, for example to acknowledge the principle of the supra-nationality of missions. The effect of Paton's work was to present a united front to the government. His appreciation of the weakness of Protestant missions when confronted with the argument of 'political exigencies' from government officials was more than justified by his apprehension of the more favourable treatment accorded to Roman Catholic missions. The question of the relationship of Protestant and Catholic missions under colonial governments involves the question of religious freedom which cannot be adequately discussed in this book. Here it is sufficient to say that careful study of the Foreign Office files leads one to say unconditionally that Paton's observation was right and that this was due to the Vatican's power as a sovereign state to use diplomatic channels to protect its missions. Paton's own standing in government circles is well summarized in the notes on his visa application in 1940. A Foreign Office secretary noted:

'McCann is trying to find out what useful purpose the Ministry of Information hope this Protestant missionary's visit to Catholic Portugal will achieve'.

Underneath came the reply:

'He is, I think, the authority to whom the M.O.I. refer Protestant missionary questions. His objective is to meet other Protestants'.[24]

What the I.M.C. hoped to achieve from its liaison with the British government is clear in the contingency plan developed at the Kasteel Hemmen meeting of the I.M.C. in August 1939.[25] It was proposed that Koechlin should act as intermediary between the I.M.C. and the German missions, that in countries where missionaries might be interned the N.C.C.s should be asked to accept responsibility for such action as might be advisable, in consultation with the self-administering churches; that money should be raised for missionaries when they are not interned; and that Clause 438 of the Versailles Treaty be re-affirmed. (This was the clause which prevented the confiscation of missionary property to pay a nation's war debts. In Australia and India the I.M.C. had never succeeded in getting the German mission-aries' personal property returned to them, and Paton was concerned lest they lose their private belongings again.) A Foreign Office Minute of 19.9.39 notes that 'The meeting (of Foreign Office, India Office and M.O.I. officials) agreed to a proposal of the I.M.C's representative to have some negotiations eventually with a representative of German Protestant Missions, probably in Switzerland'. Koechlin agreed after a bombardment of letters from Paton, since he was reluctant to compromise the Basel Mission's reputation for loyalty by dealings with Germany, and when the scheme became known in Germany, he was overwhelmed by letters from Germany. He laid down stringent conditions that he should only correspond with Hartenstein, that his name should not appear in any German publications and that what he was doing should not be exploited for German propaganda. Similarly, in England, Paton was his sole correspondent for missionary affairs.

The same minute of 19.9.39 also records the principal point of interest to the Foreign Office, that a wholesale deportation or internment should be avoided because of the great offence caused by such a policy in the First World War in neutral countries, particularly the United States. It would be better to leave them to carry on. This point was also argued in letters to the Foreign Office by Cardinal Hinsley, Paton and Maclennan.[26]

An undated memorandum, found in the Ministry of Information papers, reveals the degree to which the Ministry hoped to stimulate church leaders to produce suitable propaganda. However, on 12th September 1939 the Minister of Information addressed a meeting of church leaders at Lambeth Palace to whom he confessed that the churches per se cannot be used as instruments of propaganda, because the Church in its essential nature is ecumenical and supranational. Instead he concentrated on outlining the kind of contacts he hoped to develop. It is interesting that the I.M.C. had succeeded in communicating its aversion to a propagandist role. The following day the Minister composed a memorandum, eventually placed in the hands of the missionary societies, to the effect that the Ministry of Information does not consider it possible to utilize the missions as agencies of propaganda and obviously the societies would be unwilling to accept such a role.[27] He declared that he attached great importance to their normal functioning, especially in the field of native education. Therefore government departments would be well advised to give exemption from military service. It was important to supply missions with information on the war in Europe (this was a point Paton insisted on at this time) and to avoid bad publicity such as resulted from the treatment of German missions in the last war. It had been suggested that discrimination should be employed in order to release anti-Nazi Germans (a policy which Paton was urging, both for missionaries and refugees).

Finally, the Minister, Lord Hailey, the Under-Secretary of State for India, Findlater Stewart, Maclennan, now working for the Ministry of Information, and representatives of the missions met to discuss the entire situation. Partly at Paton's request the whole meeting was minuted in great detail, in order to serve as a basis for further negotiation. Cash of the C.M.S. drove home the point that if the government wanted educational establishments maintained at their present strength, there would have to be concessions on the question of conscription.[28]

Paton urged that although German missions were in a political sense 'enemies', they wanted to maintain links with them. He did not deny the necessity of internment, but it would be right to distinguish between the Nazis and Confessing Church sympathisers. The latter were much harried by the Nazis, for example in Calcutta. The missions had not recovered from the 1931 depression so far as bearing the burden of other missions is concerned. He re-inforced what Cash said by underlining the 1914-18 policy. He said that they had no doubt that the government would abide by Clause 438.[29]

From the Ministry's papers, one can see how the Ministry researched the last point and conceded it. On 20th September, the 'Missionary War Emergency Committee' met for the first time, consisting of an M.O.I. representative, members of the C.B.M.S. and Paton. Paton seems to have dominated the proceedings at subsequent meetings judging by the sheer volume of matters which he was dealing with:— travel permits, censorship of the I.R.M., his proposed trip to America (delayed until February 1940) and so on. The minutes are in fact a very valuable source for the mechanics and principles of the whole operation. The societies were very persistent in pressing their case with the Ministry, and the closest consultation is evident. The meetings became less frequent as the war proceeded and principles were established. It is significant that the missionary societies won recognition of the positive value of their work. For example, in response to a query about the legitimacy of fund-raising for missions in wartime, Viscount Halifax wrote to Paton that it was the desire of the British Government that services rendered by Christian missions should continue. He himself was convinced that the support of foreign missions in wartime was an essential part of the Church's witness. He would regret people deserting this 'universal Christian obligation'.[30]

The War Emergency Committee was also very concerned about the follow-up for Tambaram. The Ministry of Information helped with the purchase of paper for missionary publications and extra clothing coupons for missionaries having to buy tropical outfits.[31] The Foreign Office recognised that relationships were very much the result of good relationships fostered by the C.B.M.S. during years of co-operation with the colonial governments. Nevertheless, it seems that a certain amount of pressure was necessary to hold the various government departments to their commitment to allow missions to maintain their staffing strength. There was not only continual difficulty about lay missionaries, who dared not return to England for furlough lest they be called up, though it should be recognised that the British government's policy stands in marked contrast to that of the French and German governments, who conscripted ordained men.[32] The C.B.M.S. could never obtain as many passages for missionaries as it wanted, and explanations that all available berths had to be used for troops were not accepted. R.R. Williams, later Bishop of Leicester, remembered Paton's anger when he had to return the list of missionaries awaiting passages to Paton with only a fraction permitted.[33] It was impossible for non-C.B.M.S. societies to get passages at all. The mission work suffered irreparably from the decision of the M.O.I. not to allow single women to sail, as the rigours of being in a torpedoed ship were considered too great for women, and thus they became liable to conscription in 1942, much to the annoyance of societies who feared they were losing their women candidates permanently. The Ministry, however, could not be moved.

Although the Ministry of Information representatives denied any desire to exploit missionaries for propaganda purposes, nevertheless it is clear from the documents under consideration that the M.O.I. wished to discreetly publicize the good works of the government with a view to influencing neutral opinion. The India Office on the other hand, was reluctant for anything to be known at all. In the end, the departments approved a letter which Paton sent to 'The Times' in October 1939 about the steps being taken to preserve the orphaned missions.[34] In his letters to his various I.M.C. colleagues Paton also defends the government line on internment. Paton's loyalty must have been of some considerable importance to the government, owing to his independence and influence, because in an inter-departmental exchange on the subject of granting parole to missionaries, Dibdin wrote to Frampton of the Home Department of the Government of India, saying that he would be grateful for information so that they can protect Paton from going too far in his denials.[35]

The question of parole was fraught with difficulty, and misunderstandings appeared on all sides, some deliberately fomented for political ends by certain German papers. In India and West Africa in general, it is true to say that the colonial authorities interned all aliens first, on their own initiative, and not on orders from London, and then discriminated in individual cases. In Ghana the Basel Mission hospital at Agogo was sequestrated and used as an internment camp. After a few months the women missionaries were allowed to return to work in a few cases and part of the hospital was re-opened. In Nigeria the Foreign Secretary intervened to obtain the immediate release of Roman Catholic missionaries, in order that Vatican opinion might be placated.[36] In East Africa the authorities were more cautious, in Tanganyika even discriminating between missions which were held to be predominantly Nazi and those which had been strictly apolitical.[37] In Cameroun it was a year before the governor considered internment necessary, when, as he told the new Praeses, Raaflaub, after the war, he was brought evidence that a Basel Mission evangelist was corresponding with an illegal German organisation in French Cameroun, and he faced strong pressure from his chief of police to intern all Basel Mission personnel, including the Swiss.[38] The case of India, however, is the most interesting. As soon as war was declared, J.Z. Hodge and Bishop Azariah travelled to the centres in South India where most assistance was needed to arrange affairs on a war-time basis. The N.C.C. successfully petioned for the release of seven key missionaries, including Stosch, director of the Gossner mission, who was trapped in India while on a tour of inspection. Then during December 1939 and January 1940 Sir Malcolm Darling travelled to the internment camps on behalf of the Government of India and reviewed each case. This he seems to have done in such a sympathetic and imaginative way that his visits were not only administratively successful, but were also of pastoral value. The Basel Mission particularly appreciated the steps he took to secure treatment for two severely ill missionaries who were subsequently invalided home to Germany. The Home Department consequently telegraphed London that of 876 enemy nationals interned, 474 had been released, including 325 out of 333 Jews interned, 110 of the 133 missionaries interned and 39 'others'. In the critical month, May 1940, when England faced invasion after the fall of Holland, it was reported to the India office that 123 out of 130 German missionaries were still at their posts. In December 1940, under a new internment measure all enemy males were interned unless they had been in India for more than 15 years (virtually an impossibility for missionaries unless they came out before 1914) or were one of the seven exempted missionaries.

The Government, in close co-operation with the I.M.C. and the internees, had worked out what they thought was an acceptable form of parole, taking wording suggested by Leipzig missionaries in Tanganyika, and employed there. It was virtually identical to the Memorandum 'A' declaration, requiring a person on parole to promise not to engage in political activity, not to take up arms against the government of the country and to obey government orders. Paton and others had been insistent that the formula should contain nothing which a patriotic German could not accept. The whole operation was nearly jeopardized by J.Z. Hodge declaring in October 1939 that those released would have to forswear National Socialism, and by Bishop Sandegren making a similar much publicized statement while he was on furlough in Stockholm.[40] Paton was exasperated by articles in the Berliner Missionsberichte of January 1940, repeated in 'Die Junge Kirche', that German missionaries were imprisoned simply because they were German 'because the missionaries are German men and women they have to bear Germany's fate and the hate of England against everything that is German'. He wrote to Koechlin to refute this as being untrue when so many missionaries were still at work: 'I am not concerned with German official propaganda, which is quite conscienceless, but it is to me a very serious thing when our own missionary colleagues write this kind of stuff. I hope you can do something to represent the truth'.[41]

It is unlikely that any missionary was immune to Nazi influence. Apart from those who eagerly embraced the party line, and constituted themselves chaplains to the German settlers in the British colonies, such as Praeses Ittmann of Cameroun, all missionaries had to belong to local 'German culture' groups or the actual party branch. They were vulnerable to pressure from German civilians abroad: in a notorious case Koechlin and Paton were asked to advise on, a Basel Mission press manager was blackmailed into reading the proofs of the local party magazine.[42] They were afraid lest their families be victimized, if they perceived the darker side of Hitler's 'New Order'; but those who had rarely been home since 1933 probably did not. These pressures undoubtedly intensified when the question of parole came up, so that Paton saw his hard-won concession being sabotaged. Koechlin and Paton corresponded a great deal on this point as Koechlin tried to interpret the reasons of those who refused parole. Paton replied:

> 'The other question you raise is whether German missionaries may not feel that they are being separated from their brethren, and being allowed freedom while others are in adversity. This, of course, they must settle for themselves. I should have thought that men who believe themselves called of God to the work of a missionary would have regarded it as the supreme call to them that they should continue their work of evangelisation and ministry to the local church unless they were absolutely prevented from doing so. I do find it a little difficult to sympathize with the view that a man who is set free to do the work to which God has called him should consider it better to be imprisoned out of deference to the opinion of his fellow German. I quite understand that men might feel that, but I do not find it easy to understand how they can act like this or feel in this way if they are really and wholeheartedly committed to the missionary purpose. Forgive me if I write rather strongly, but it is a little disconcerting when we have been working for the release of German missionaries on the grounds of the supranational character of Christian missions in the world to find men who would rather give up that task for the sake of national feeling'.[43]

A more satisfactory piece of Koechlin-Paton diplomacy with the Government of India concerned the repatriation of men too sick to remain abroad, but who might in Germany recover and be called up. This was a risk which Paton persuaded the government to accept, but the question of conscience arose, if the missionaries had once given their pledge not to resist the government in India. With typical British ambivalence, it was agreed that this meant not resisting the government when they were in India, as opposed to the British government in Europe.

Contrary to his policy in the case of P.O.W.s, Paton never argued the case for humane treatment in the hope of reciprocal treatment of British nationals, but nevertheless when an Egyptian ship, the Zam Zam, was torpedoed while carrying, among other passengers, an exceptionally large contingent of American Lutheran missionaries going out to man the 'orphaned missions' in East Africa, Knak managed to secure their release from Germany, which was remarkable.[44]

Kraemer sent Paton an article by Knak, which may have been the one which he considered 'fairminded'. It did, however, conclude: 'It is a matter of gratitude that the I.M.C. has pleaded as much as it could for the German missionaries, though it could not achieve much as it liked. It left nothing untried to withhold the British Government from unnecessary cruelty and interference with money help for the mission field, on which is the greatest need . . . the unity of those who feel bound to preach the Gospel in the world, continues in this time of war' (Kraemer's translation).

The whole question of internment, parole and repatriation was one which demanded much patience and diplomacy. It was hard for Paton to appreciate the effect of home conditions on missionaries and for nationals of neutral countries to appreciate the need for national security. It is now known that the amount of espionage in the British Empire during the war was minute compared with the amount perpetrated in Europe. However, in 1940 the possibility of a fifth column seemed very real. A greater risk was the amount of disaffection in India which might be fomented. There was something of an illogicality in Paton's position that he accepted the government's view that missionaries and ministers could not be exempted in the general internment in view of their nationality, but objected to their refusing parole because this was not offered to all Germans. In correspondence with Warnshuis, however, Paton insisted that it was the I.M.C's aim not to get missionaries out of internment who do not want to come out, but to prevent the government interning them in the first place.[45] There were some awful blunders in individual cases, some of which even the I.M.C. could not do anything about, but most internment camps were healthy and the treatment humane.[46] I told Herr Göttin who was in Indonesia, how internees in India had complained of having to prepare vegetables, and his reaction was that he and those imprisoned with him would have been glad of vegetables to prepare. The main hardship was loneliness, so Paton tried to arrange for missionaries to be interned in pairs, to work together as prison chaplains.

These questions, and those of currency exchange, passages for missionaries, exemption for lay and ordained missionaries, the continuance of missionary schools and hospitals, and the government's acceptance of the neutral stance of all missionaries were questions on which the I.M.C./C.B.M.S. was able to extract considerable concessions from the government, though not to the extent they would have wished. There are no reliable figures on the number of missionaries who refused parole: in India virtually all accepted, in Ghana the governor disagreed with the whole policy and had them shipped to the West Indies before there was a chance of introducing the policy, but in East Africa in some countries as many as 50% refused. In spite of this setback, the principle of the supranationality of missions was established within the British Empire, though Paton doubted whether it was established in German missionary circles, and therefore expressed his doubts to Westman confidentially about whether German missionaries would be re-admitted to the British and Dutch Empires immediately after the war.[47] Whether his suspicions about the German missionary mentality were accurate (he considered Siegmund-Schultze and Freytag exceptions) — his pessimistic forecast about the future of German missions was unfortunately prophetic. However, certain precipitate governmental actions also placed the principle in jeopardy.

The storm broke in mid-August 1941 when two American ladies were refused visas for India. When Paton was informed he wrote back to the India Office:

'I am very sorry to hear of the desire of the Government of India to exclude from India all Lutheran missionaries. I suppose they realized this includes all the Swedes, Norwegians, Danes and Finns and one of the largest American societies. It seems to me a proposal to create the worst possible impression in America and it may be taken as certain that every effort will be made to get the decision reversed. It is in fact a gross piece of religious discrimination, based doubtless on ignorance of Lutheranism and on a vague idea that all Lutherans are in some degree pro-German . . . '

To the Secretary of State for India, L.S. Amery, he wrote in no less uncertain terms. The American Lutherans have been extraordinarily generous towards orphaned missions. 'It will seem to them a most extraordinary return for self-sacrifice of a unique kind'. Although it involved severe criticism of the Government of India's intellectual capacity, the argument that all Lutherans are dangerous and pro-German seems the only reason, preposterous though it is, for the action. He begged Amery to intervene for the sake of Anglo-American relationships.

Amery did so, in a flurry of telegrams, but meanwhile Warnshuis established that it was the Passport Office in New York, not the Home Department of India, which was operating this ban. Finally Warnshuis got the case taken up by Knudson, a senior civil servant with the ear of Secretary of State Cordell Hull. Paton passed this information on to the India Office, that the Lend Lease contract was threatened because the civil servant responsible for the Lend Lease programme was a keen Lutheran (and a friend of Roosevelt's) — a situation which amused him enormously, but not the India Office, who immediately revoked the ban on Lutherans. It transpired that a Norwegian Lutheran had been the victim of an unpleasant accusation and interrogation and had written to Andreas Helland of the Augsburg Seminary, Minneapolis, about it which resulted in an indiscreet article in a Lutheran magazine. Paton read the India Office a lecture on the folly of judging all Lutherans by one printed paragraph, when they have supporters in high places.[48]

A somewhat similar situation arose in November 1940. Paton heard from Canon Needham of Australia that missionaries had arrived from New Guinea, some in handcuffs; 16 were Lutherans and had joined the Nazi party. He promised to investigate and then appeal to the Federal Government of Australia, because he could not understand how missionaries could involve themselves in politics to the cost of their missionary vocation. Then an earlier letter of his arrived explaining that the 16 party members had been telling the natives that the government would be over-thrown and then a better German government would be instituted. Dr Theile and he cannot in conscience ask for an appeal to be made to the government. It would be wrong to draw public attention to the situation which had developed in Lutheran missions. He simply wants Paton and Warnshuis to expedite the sending of American Lutheran replacements.[49]

Given this as a background it is perhaps possible to understand the extra-ordinary hold which a rumour gained, that German missionaries had met the Japanese invaders and guided them inland along the main roads. Former missionaries to New Guinea in England explained to Paton that the geography of New Guinea did not admit of this, but the Australian government announced that henceforth only British citizens would be acceptable as missionaries in New Guinea. Two years of correspondence ensued as Paton tried to discover the truth and get the ban lifted. The debate was futile because the Japanese occupied most of the island.

One should perhaps end this discussion on the question of the supranationality of missions by quoting a letter of Paton's to the Reverend Jesse Arrup of Canada.

> '. . . All of us who are belligerents, as, thank goodness, you are, are in constant danger of becoming too nationalist and forgetting the claims of the universal church. I believe that if we can go through this war and at the end of it still say that the main work of the Continental missions, including that

of the Germans, has been maintained, not of course at full strength, but in being, it would be a tremendous fillip to the whole Christian cause'.[50]

As a commentary on this one should remember that the Scandinavian view in 1940 was that the Provisional Committee of the W.C.C. was too full of belligerents to be effective. Fortunately they were mistaken.

The influence of confessional ties in the predicament of 'orphaned missions' is complex and all-pervasive. Paton was most involved with the situation in Tanganyika, though letters written by Bishop Manikam in 1945 reveal that it was an important factor in India also. Predictably, the Gossner mission at Ranchi, storm centre in the First World War, was also a problem in the Second World War, though after reading vast quantities of letters, I incline to the view that the character of the Indian Christians in that particular congregation had as much to do with the problem as the confessional question. The best documented and discussed case is that of Lutheran missions in China, which Jonas Jonson has written about in his admirable book 'The Lutheran Missions in a Time of Revolution. The China Experience 1939-51'. China was not within Paton's province, but the book is to be commended for the general factors which emerge. After discussing his thesis with Dr Jonson, I am certain that exactly the same situation existed in Tanganyika, and all Paton's attempts to stop confessional empire-building failed.[51]

Briefly, the situation was as follows. There had been very considerable Nazi activity among the 2,500 German settlers in Tanganyika but Knak had toured the field in 1936-37 issuing stern warnings to the missionaries not to get involved in this, but they could not fail to observe that recalcitrants who did not join the party were arrested as soon as they returned to Germany. There were parades and in 1939 a boycott of Jews was organised. Consequently internment measures were severe when war broke out. Paton's argument that interned missionaries should have a say in the future organisation of German missions in Tanganyika fell on deaf ears. Paton was incensed that Catholic missionaries were still at large, working under other nationals, so in December 1940 the governor agreed to a similar scheme for German Protestants. This failed because 50% refused parole (after the war one admitted, because he was blackmailed) and most of the rest were known Nazis. There were 78,412 African Christians under the care of German missions, now left with a staff of 10 where previously 48 women and 91 men had worked. The largest remaining mission was the Universities' Mission to Central Africa which, including Zanzibar, had 37,425 converts followed by the C.M.S. with 7,450. The Augustana synod had only 1,667 converts, but 30 missionaries as compared to the C.M.S. staff of 33. The Tanganyika Missionary Council attempted to sort things out by dividing the field among adjacent missions, principally the C.M.S. and the Augustana Synod, which was not a member and made life so difficult for the secretary, an extremely good missionary, Langford Smith, that he resigned. The Augustana Synod then built up its empire, since the L.W.F. provided the bulk of the aid to these missions, and the balance could not be held by the individual Scandinavian missionaries who were brought in. From C.M.S. missionaries' letters, it is clear that the German missionaries' action in ordaining Africans in 1939 to take responsibility did bear amazing fruit in some areas, and independent congregations worked very well on their own. As in China, there was conflict between the long-serving missionaries and the new Lutheran recruits from America. The I.M.C. found it difficult to co-operate with the

L.W.F. over the relief to orphaned missions, despite Miss Gibson's diplomatic skills.[52] No overall strategy or planning seems to have been attempted, and if it were not for the resilience of the African pastors and the 70 year old German pastor Priebush who was allowed to continue his ministry, it would be a depressing picture. The Church of Sweden commissioned a report in 1944 from Harald von Sicard which bears out this analysis.[53]

Paton also encountered denominational mistrust when raising money. The American Baptists for example, were asked to support other Baptists, otherwise they would not have contributed; yet their secretary, Lerrigo, was ecumenically-minded and slipped a handsome proportion to the I.M.C. without strings. Paton was forced to 'twin' churches — Canadian Presbyterians to the Paris Mission, for example, Episcopalians to Episcopalians. This system of aid undoubtedly raised the denominational consciousness of churches, as much as their awareness of the universal church, Jonson argues. Paton had difficulty in co-operating with Bishop Aasgaard, who took responsibility for Norwegian Lutherans, and with other Lutheran secretaries. Orphaned missions clung to their original denominational allegiance, making the task of missionaries who went to their aid very delicate. In fact, denominational questions appear as a blight across the whole of the spectrum of the orphaned missions.[54]

The ecumenical myths about orphaned missions are manifold. It should be clear from what has already been written that Bishop Neill was quite wrong to write to Paton that all the missionaries were sympathetic to the Confessing Church.[55] Koechlin had continual difficulties with Nazi missionaries. Equally, the entire fabric of missions was not maintained. Paton more or less admits this in certain of his letters, already quoted. With the ban on the sailing of single women, the British missions could barely survive, and it is clear that as the numbers of missionaries replacing the internees was so much smaller, only the key stations were maintained. Koechlin and Streckeisen conducted a prolonged correspondence on the state of the Basel field in India, and the shortcomings were of great concern to both men.[56] The problem was not one of old-fashioned missionaries employing out-of-date methods in the German missions but of the younger men coming out imbued with national socialism and views on the inferiority of the non-European races. In India, native leadership was strong before the war. The withdrawal of the missionaries did not improve it. And so on.

Therefore, the conclusions that one can draw are that the situation allows of no generalisations except that the I.M.C. and its associates were held together by a vision of the universal Church, which they had experienced at Tambaram, and which political difference could not destroy, but in each field the problem was different. The principle of the supranationality of missions was difficult to establish in such a way that it was unquestioningly put into practice. As far as Paton is concerned one can learn much about his vision, his craft when dealing with politicians and civil servants and his great sympathy in dealing with the missionaries themselves. It is an open question whether his patriotism did not blunt his judgment at times, but at least he was aware of the danger, and held up an ideal of the universality of mission, only to become very frustrated when others could not live up to this ideal.

Chapter IX

The Plain Man's Theologian Looks at Social Questions

Before the phrase 'the social Gospel' became alternatively a battle cry for those committed to pursuing social justice as a necessary part of the Gospel, or a term of abuse to outraged Scandinavians protesting against supposed Utopianism, Paton had adopted the phrase to describe the relevance of the Gospel to society. His precise definition changed in successive books and lectures, since he first used the phrase in 1919, having perhaps read the seminal work on the subject, 'The Theology of the Social Gospel' by Walter Rauschenbusch.[1] He echoes some of Rauschenbusch's presuppositions and phraseology, though he never subscribed to the idea that one could build the Kingdom of Heaven on earth by human means. Therefore in 1939, when he gave the 'Beckly Social Service Lecture', he was treading a delicate path between the Scylla and Charybdis, described in Chapter VII in connection with the D.S.I.R., not because he believed that this represented a sensible compromise which appealed to his practical soul, but because he sincerely believed that this was the best answer which he could find in the Bible.[2] Whether judging Hinduism, Buddhism or Christianity, Paton rejected a religion so full of heavenly ideals that it was no earthly use. For Paton it was intolerable to speak of the love of God in giving His Son to be crucified without finding in that Gospel a concomitant challenge to action in society. Paton's thought on social questions developed and modified itself over the period 1914-1943, but in it he was always striving to find a theological basis for his observation of society and his reforming views. He seems to have been attempting two things: first he sought a theological explanation for social evils, secondly he applied Christianity as the remedy for man's misery.

It should be remembered that Paton was always a profoundly religious man and always used a religious framework of reference, a point already discussed in the examination of his ideas on mission. Therefore, to some extent the absence of any religious motivation to reform society was equivalent to secularism, though he appears to have made no semantic distinction between secularism and secularization. It would be an anachronism to compare his definition with that of Harvey Cox.[3] Paton was principally concerned with the effect of this secularized world outlook which he found among Christians and non-Christians alike, namely, the tendency to divorce religion from life and to hold politics, religion, one's personal life, social concerns and so on, in separate compartments, not allowing one to influence the others. His protest was against anything which would limit the application of the Christian faith to certain sectors of life alone. Presumably he would therefore be as opposed to the classical Lutheran teaching of the 'two realms', which was so prominent at the Oxford conference, as he was to the totalitarian political philosophies which relegated religion to the citizen's private life alone.[4]

Throughout this discussion of Paton's writings on social questions, one can see the effect of his intense pre-occupation with the motivation of individuals to tackle society's evils, to follow the teaching of Christ and so on. No less important is what one might call the inner dynamic of society, though he does not use that phrase. Consequently depersonalized forces, such as economic pressures, are never insuperable obstacles, and in discussing such things as the weight of tradition in India, which smothers new agricultural innovations, he gives the impression of seeing tradition as the accumulation of human customs, not impersonal law.

As with Paton's thought on mission, his view of social problems and their causation is completely integrated. Bad factory conditions are bad factory conditions whatever country they are found in. He does not condemn racism in one country without pointing also to its insidious position in England. He tells missionary candidates that if they will not help overseas students in Britain, how can they expect to love the people they will meet in India? The sea voyage will not miraculously change their outlook. Churchmen concerned about foreign missions must also campaign for social justice at home, while the view that one cannot help those overseas while there is such suffering and deprivation at home (the 'charity begins at home' syndrome) is equally intolerable.[5] The appeals which he made 1919-21 for students to devote their lives to social work are as strongly worded as his appeals for missionary candidates, though increasingly missionaries were involved in relief work and rural reconstruction, literacy programmes and so on, so that the distinction was being blurred.[6]

Ultimately, Paton traces the attitude to social problems among Christians to their concept of the Kingdom of God, and therefore Paton's understanding of the Kingdom of God must also be considered. It is better to take Paton's thought on social issue and secularism as an integral part of his total theology, rather than to compare it with his contemporaries' work, for example, with William Temple, who was a great influence on him. R.H. Tawney, the L.S.E. economist, was a personal friend, whom he consulted for technical questions, and who helped with the establishment of the D.S.I.R. It is more difficult to assess Reinhold Niebuhr's influence. He and Paton met frequently after 1930, but Paton was not caught up in the 1936-39 wave of enthusiasm for Niebuhr in the S.C.M. Niebuhr's influence on Paton was probably more political than theological.[7]

The paper which Paton delivered at the Lake Mohonk W.S.C.F. meeting under the title 'The social problem and its call to students to enter social service as laymen or experts in specialized forms of social service' was significant not only as his first known utterance on the subject, which itself had only been on the W.S.C.F. agenda since 1909, but also because it is a theological analysis of the question.

> 'There falls upon all who have realized the meaning of that fabric of organised sin which is called the social problem the command (which is denied) to a life of love of holiness. This is a duty which does not wait until students leave college but derives from their first awareness of sin. Secondly, they are called to social action which requires careful thought. The kingdom of Selfishness is not going to fall down because we shout, and we shall find as good brains defending it as we can muster on our side'.[9]

Paton went on to speak of the service which can be given in private, unofficial ways, such as educating public opinion, which is actually very difficult work. In England there were two types of help to be found, the leisured classes helping the less fortunate, and self-help by those suffering from social deprivation. The defect of the former is that it gets interpreted as 'superiority' and is resented. It is better to join the Independent Labour Party and the Women's Labour League, since students cannot join a trades union. (There was no National Union of Students until 1923.) These are socialist bodies but they are not anti-Christian, as on the Continent, so one can bring one's Christian faith to it. There are adult schools, the Workers' Educational Association which are 'brotherhoods' and an excellent opportunity for Christian service, provided that one goes in order to learn, not to teach. Secondly one might find one's vocation in administering State welfare services and preventing the growth of 'officialdom' by infiltrating the administration with a Christian spirit. In the discussion after the paper was given, Paton explained that in Britain the S.C.M. had the choice of encouraging men to administer palliatives or praying for a new social order. He concluded 'I have no doubt that the strongest and holiest movement for the regeneration of society is among the labouring classes'.

Since in the discussion students there were castigated for treating the servants without consideration or regard to their welfare, as they rushed out to work on 'settlements', one may assume that the meeting of W.S.C.F. students represented the privileged classes, and in this context Paton's remarks were very radical.[9] In describing 'the social problem' as 'sin' Paton is echoing the Liverpool 1912 Quadrennial message that students (and all the other 'haves' in society) are responsible for the misery of others, not the poor themselves, and that they have created the system which oppresses the poor. Paton connects this realization with the fundamental insight of the convert into his own sinful nature and identifies the pursuit of personal holiness with service to the community not by an individual act of charity, but by joining a socialist political party or by becoming a professional social worker. 'Sin' was a powerful word in Paton's understanding of man's relation to God, since his view of the reconciliation between God and man was built on classical Evangelical lines. To describe the Labour Movement as 'holy' is an extraordinary tribute to it.

In 1939, delivering the Beckly Lecture, Paton criticized much of Christian social and international thinking because it lacked 'a realistic recognition of the terrible fact of human sin'.[10] It has been unfashionable in some quarters to use the word 'sin', but people seem nowadays to be willing to recognize the thing, though still shy of the word. To Paton the contemporary world is full of proof of the Biblical understanding of man as a creature capable of good impulses, but also corrupt and unable to do what is right. 'Human sin is both an individual and corporate thing. It clogs the operation of the individual's desire to do better, it lies as a miasma over the society of which he is a part'.

On the other hand, by taking the fact of sin seriously, as Paton terms it, one can escape from the heresy of regarding the world as being in the grip of fundamentally intractable, mysterious forces, a modern equivalent of 'The Furies', which one endeavours to placate by calling them 'The Kindly Ones'. In contrast, Paton declares that 'We stand outside this world of darkness, for we have learnt that all things were created by the eternal Word, who is Christ Jesus. We know, in the Pauline phrase, that it is in him that the whole universal order of things 'consists' or holds together'.

However, in 1939, Paton rejected more emphatically than in his earlier writings on social questions, the idea that the conversion of the individual would lead to the reform of society, or that there was any value in the phrase 'If only men would realize . . . ' In 'Social Ideals in India' he wrote of the significance of the mass movements in India, where perhaps first a family, then a subcaste, then a whole village seek baptism and a new way of life.[11] He rejected the idea of individual conversion and reform as unrealistic in Indian society. When he gave the Beckly Lecture he formulated the theological corollary of this, condemning the idea of removing social evil by the conversion of individuals.

> 'Life is corporate, and corporate life is not merely the aggregation of an infinite number of separate atoms. There must be a corporate redemption, a bringing into the system of life of the same power of recreation which remakes individual life'.[12]

To Paton it was not simply a question of illuminating the misguided and selfish, or of reorganizing society but of saving men from their sins and remembering 'on pain of our own spiritual death' that we must make some effort to share what we enjoy. The same rationale inspired the S.V.M.U. conviction that spiritual death awaited those who ignored their responsibility to evangelize the world.[13]

It seems logical that the reason why Paton was so uncompromising in his condemnation of social evil was that he had such a strong view of man's sinfulness and of his need for redemption in society and in his soul. Without giving examples of his polemic against particular evils of which he was well acquainted, such as the forced labour system, it is worth noting a general statement:

> 'We have allowed our industrial development to outstrip the growth of the Christian conscience, and whole areas of our national life have been befouled and degraded by an unchecked commercialism. Even today we are living in a social system which denies to masses of human beings the rights of manhood and womanhood and we have acquiesced in these things. Too often the organized fellowship of Christians has turned its back on the problem, or has even allied itself with the powers of the existing order'.[24]

Therefore, he says, the Hindu was becoming convinced that 'Christianity was just like other religions, good in its ideals but without any power to help me to realize them'. If this were true, then Paton would have to look elsewhere to find the power to redeem the world. However, the Christian social conscience is gradually being awakened, and after a period when it was content to administer palliatives against the worst abuses, now it is demanding a new order of society based on the principles of Christ in spite of the almost herculean task this involves, and the forces of evil hidden in humanity which it must overcome.

It was observed in Chapter IV that Paton judged the effectiveness of other religions by their ability to inspire moral conduct and social reform. A parody of the sort of questions he asked would be 'Can Confucianism give the Chinese the necessary moral fibre to tackle China's problems?' It is obvious that he is not afraid to apply the same question to Christianity, and it should be noted that in two of the books under consideration in this chapter, 'Social Ideals in India', published by U.C.M.E. in 1919 and 'The Highway of God', written jointly with Kathleen Harnett in 1921 for the S.C.M., he continues this method of examination.

Paton called his attitude to sin 'Biblical' and 'realistic'. Whether or not one agrees with him probably depends on one's own temperament because he is dealing with the question of the fundamental nature of man and his need for radical redemption which tends to be a matter of belief rather than reason.[15] Paton maintained that it was the view of man which pre-determined one's view of God, but it seems that in Paton's own theology there was some considerable degree of his view of God influencing his view of man, since he is judging society by standards of righteousness which he perceives in Christ, not in Christian society. (He is emphatic that missionaries in undeveloped countries must scrupulously avoid preaching a concept of Christian civilization as found in the West). It is Christ whom they must preach, not any particular blueprint of society.[16] This is a position which he thought out for himself, since it has been shown in Chapter II that he rejected the 'hell-fire' theology of the previous generation of Victorian churchmen, and contemporary Presbyterian teaching had not saved its adherents from moral complacency.[17] In a broadcast of July 1942 he still maintained this position.

It is significant that, unlike many of his contemporary churchmen, he can describe sin as the result of individual and personal vices — gambling, alcoholism, promiscuous sex and so on, — but also as a corporate fact to which individuals contribute — bad housing, exploitation of the poor, repressive colonialism. Yet he insists that it is within the power of the individual to pit his will to do something about the situation, and that the body of the redeemed in Christ, the Church, can tackle the problem with the assurance that they are doing God's will.[18] Being a realist, however, he would add that some problems require government action for which the Christian must agitate (hence the significance of joining a political party), though laws and the removal of bad social conditions will not automatically provide the environment for humans to be kept from sin. It must be admitted that a case could be made out for attributing Paton's view of the radical nature of sin to his common sense, not any particular theological insight, rather than to a combination of the two.

Writing of the new community spirit from the members of the Christian Church united a common spiritual conviction and life, Paton declares that the Indian Church contains the social dynamic which India needs.[19] Otherwise Western civilisation will be a curse to India. This 'social Gospel' represents the message of Christianity to India. He had earlier in this book, 'Social Ideals in India', argued that Christian concepts were making a radical difference to the practice of caste and racial barriers in India, and that new economic structures were following in the wake of the outcaste movements into the Church. However, the 'social Gospel' in the context of the book, does not mean that a social programme is to be identified with the Christian faith (in a notorious example of this, an American speaker at the Stockholm Life and Work conference identified prohibitionism with the coming of the Kingdom of God).[20] It is the Christian fellowship, united across racial and cultural differences of background which is the 'social Gospel' to India, torn with communal violence. It is this new kind of fellowship with God and with man which makes it possible to call Christianity a social religion. The idea that 'Christian principles' must be applied to social questions, or that conversion means accepting set beliefs about Christ and living a new life, is less than the whole truth. It is a question of a new relationship to God.

> 'The insistence of the New Testament writers upon love as the essence of the nature of God and as the supreme standard by which all human action is to be judged shows up the importance of this aspect of Christian life . . .

we are given in Jesus Christ a vision of the nature and character of God which is utterly adequate and complete for the needs of man, and He tells us that God is love. . . . The Christian God is a God of love and the Christian life should be a life of love. To know and love the true God carries with it the necessity for loving our brethren also, and if we cannot love our brethren whom we have seen, we cannot very well love God whom we have not seen'.

From this point he argues the importance of the Christian community as it existed from the beginning, introducing a new social principle of love cutting across all the divisions of society. The Christian task, therefore, is to spread this fellowship rather than any package of abstract ideas about God.[21]

It has been necessary to quote Paton at such length in order to establish precisely the context of his use of the term 'the social Gospel'. By rooting it firmly in the nature of Christ and the Christian community's attempt to reflect this nature, he avoids the temptation to equate the 'social Gospel' with any purely human endeavour, nor does he fail to set the Church over against the world and its standards and ideas of progress, which are the two principal points of criticism in the Oldham/-Visser't Hooft discussion of the 'Social Gospel' written in preparation for the Oxford conference of 1937.[22]

By 1921 Paton had become aware of the dangers involved in the question of the 'social message of Christianity' and by implication, in his own apologetic. In a chapter in 'The Highway of God' on the recent upheavals in China (on which he and his co-author take a conservative line, severely criticizing Sun Yat-sen), he discussed the problem for the exponents of Christianity in China. The general cry in China is for power to overcome national and social evils, corruption and moral weakness. Christianity can do this but:

'Christianity is a social gospel and in it is power for the healing of national wounds. . . . Yet in the anxiety of the preacher to extend the visible bounds of the Christian Church, it is easy to preach, almost unconsciously, a rather cheap, superficial version of this social Gospel'.[23]

The effect on Chinese minds would then be that Christianity is primarily an inexpensive cure for all national ills, with a resulting disillusionment in the more perceptive hearer. He also quotes a Chinese scholar sympathetic to Christianity, but agnostic, who rebukes politicians in China for trying to use the Christian Gospel against the Japanese and the Communists, whom Jesus also came to save. Paton concludes that it is necessary to present Christianity as the answer to the student's question: 'Is it the truth?', not as the solution to all the country's ills.

The final chapter of 'The Highway of God' is an exposition of the significance of the Cross. In discussing the basic equality of all men, the writers insist that this is because of the value that God sets on each soul, and not because of any intrinsic value the members of various races might have, which might make them equal on their own account. It is God's treatment of man which erases the difference, and makes one's fellow man a brother in Christ without any national or cultural label as a barrier. Hence the affinity of Christianity with the Labour movement in the West — an optimistic statement for Paton and Harnett to indulge in.

In seeking the truth between the two extremes of treating Christ's message as entirely 'other-worldly', and of limiting it entirely to this plane of life and social principles, Paton and Harnett declare that the ultimate values of the Christian life are eternal, but time is a preparation for eternity and the Christian's duty is to create in this world an order of society animated by the power of the world to come. The Christian is bound to seek ways of expressing the love of God by service to mankind and in fellowship with other Christians.

These rather cryptic remarks are to be found in an elaborated form in a paper 'Age-Long Principles and Modern Life', published in the I.R.M. in April 1920, after it had been discussed by the I.R.M. group.[24] In this article Paton attempts to answer the question 'Is there any spiritual principle on which human civilisation can be securely based?' This principle must be capable of translation into the plans for economic and political reconstruction which are being discussed at the moment. The alternative is chaos. Christians will turn to the New Testament and the life and teaching of Christ to see if they can find enlightenment there, but they often fail because of the difference between the Palestine Jesus knew and the twentieth century. However, if the New Testament is treated as a classical expression of the Christian spirit rather than a law book, then principles may be discovered which, if accepted, could save society.

The first is Christ's insistence on the supreme value of human personality because all men are loved by God as His children, whether they recognize this or not. To those who do recognize it, is given a standard superseding the values which the world maintains. Secondly, there is Christ's example of self-sacrifice and love in the service of others. Thirdly, there is the principle of fellowship in God with one's fellow men. This common life is not a voluntary society of people with common aims, but a divine society which moulds its members and is implicit in the central Christian experience of God. These principles, however, have been largely ignored in modern society, even in the section which calls itself Christian, because even if it is perceived that the Christian approach is revolutionary in the true sense, there is no sign that the Church is trying to turn the world upside down.

Paton continues by applying these principles to the contemporary industrial situation. He interprets the Labour movement as striving against the dehumanizing forces in industry, which, in an un-Christian way, were treating men as machines. 'The application of the principles of Christ to this situation involves the cordial admission that Labour is right in its main contention, and that a state of society which rests on the supremacy of profits and places the rights of human personality below money-making, stands self-condemned and can only lead to anarchy and social dissolution'.

The principle of service is similarly denied in modern industrial society in the pursuit of private profit. The worker cannot feel he is serving the community, he is only creating profits for his employer. This should be contrasted with the attitude of those in 'the professions' who do have the satisfaction of feeling that they are providing a community service. Class distinctions are also a standing challenge to the Christian way of life and the situation has been worsened by the extent to which the Church has identified itself with one particular class. It therefore seems an irony to say that the answer lies in the Church. However, inasfar as the Church is true to Christ, it contains within it the seeds of social health.

> 'No other spiritual principles but those of Jesus Christ challenge the
> world's attention today . . . the prophetic word is both 'Repent or ye shall
> all likewise perish' and 'Repent for the Kingdom of Heaven is at hand'.

It is questionable whether one can replace the profit motive by the professional's job satisfaction; and whether Paton has thought sufficiently deeply about what the alternatives to private profit in industry are. However, it should be appreciated that Paton had no technical sociological knowledge, and that in 1921 there had been no experimentation in public ownership in Western Europe. Paton objected less to profit making than to profiteering at the expense of the workers.

It is difficult to appreciate how radical Paton's views were, because the Labour Party has become respectable and trade unions are now a power in the land. Temple caused continuous controversy by being a member of the Labour Party and by making similar pronouncements.[25] The working classes had only been enfranchised in 1918, and their conditions were terrible, as Grace Paton's book, 'The Child and the Nation' revealed, yet the Labour movement was subjected to vilifying attacks and as Paton said, its altruism was ignored.[26] The principles which Paton elucidates are firmly grounded in the New Testament, though he skims over the question of a prophetic community. It is questionable whether he is successful in avoiding the identification of Christian principles with one particular socialist programme. This is because he is more concerned with the practical course of action which a Christian should take, than with constructing a philosophical system of Christian social ethics. He does not question whether society ought to be saved — in 1942 in his anti-Nazi propaganda, he was much more circumspect — and the implications of New Testament apocalyptic are therefore without significant influence on him.[27] He argues that Christians must apply a divine, not a human standard in judging the world, industry and so on, but he does not consider the question of God's judgment, except in that final text. Considering Niebuhr's injunction that Christians should stand to the left of the politicians and to the right of the theologians, it seems that he does not quite achieve the latter position in this article.[28]

In his Beckly Lectures Paton addresses himself to the problem which he does not treat adequately in the 1920 article, the reason why Christians are so uncertain and confused about the claim of social work upon the Christian.[29] Summarizing the controversy over the 'social Gospel' and the Scandinavian reaction described in Chapter VII, without placing any particular nomenclature on the two positions, he declares that the difference is due to a fundamental difference in the respective understanding of the bearing of the Christian Gospel on human society and their understanding of the Kingdom of God. He describes 'The Anglo-Saxon Protestant' position as the belief that the structure of human society should be altered to conform more closely to God's will, because whether the Kingdom of God refers to a phase beyond this life or not, it is relevant to this age as well. Involved in this is the recognition that many of man's actions are determined by his social conditions which may reduce him to an unfair struggle not only for existence but also for virtue. Therefore men allowed themselves to speak of 'building the Kingdom' and 'establishing the Kingdom of God on earth'. For a moderate statement of the opposing position he quotes the document read by the German delegation at the I.M.C. meeting at Tambaram.[30] From this, Paton picks out the most significant statement as being: 'the Church has not to bring into force a social programme for a renewed world order or even a Christian state'. The Christian must give himself to all works of compassion and fight evil wherever he finds it, in this view, but he will not join in planning for a Christian state. Such action will not be a way of realizing the Kingdom even in the smallest degree because one's Christian ideals for society will be disappointed. It is obvious from Paton's war-time activity in various 'Peace Aims' and planning groups how little he shared this view.

He summarizes his own beliefs because he says there is not time to discuss his position on Biblical and theological grounds fully. To Paton, the Kingdom of God is always something which, in accordance with New Testament teaching, God brings in and that even the action of good men cannot effect. But this concept of a final transforming action by God must not undermine one's perception of His present reality and activity in history. Human affairs are in God's hands, and He is moving them towards their consummation. Secondly: 'No emphasis upon the second coming of our Lord — and I must confess that those who are most dogmatic on this matter seem to me to study the Bible somewhat selectively — ought never to obscure the supreme and joyful fact that he has come already'.

Therefore one must apply his teaching, for example on money, where far too much has been said about stewardship and not enough about the dangers to the soul of possession of wealth. Since we live in a mass civilization, we must address ourselves to the system, not merely the individual, and strive to make it conform more to the mind of Christ. Thirdly, Paton launches an attack on all forms of utopianism and on the identification of any system of life and social organization with Christianity, in the terms described earlier in this chapter. Fourthly, it is wrong for those privileged in wealth, education, comfort and so on, to stand by while others are deprived of these. Christ's injunctions on this score are unmistakeable.

It can be seen from this lecture, from Paton's handling of the concept of the 'Social Gospel', from the way in which his thought is influenced by what he believed to be Christ's teaching, and from his diagnosis of the sinful nature of man and society, that Paton's thought on social questions is firmly grounded on theological presuppositions and anchored to a view of God's transcendence, not man's innate perfectibility. This sets him apart from the 'liberal' theology of the twenties, and much of the reforming idealism of the time, while demanding from him what was for his day and class a radical political stance.

Paton's thought is essentially a response to the social conditions of his day, and not an attempt to impose a Christian master plan on them, nor an attempt to construct a 'Christian sociology', as V.A. Demant and his circle were doing. There is no indication that Paton ever read the works of F.D. Maurice or Charles Kingsley by comparison with whom he is a well-intentioned amateur. However, he did tackle the question of social injustice, even if the time, energy and resources at his disposal were limited.

When Paton arrived in India in 1917 what struck him most forcibly was the difference between English society in which industrialism and Protestantism had relegated religious practices to a discreet and unobtrusive occupation of a minority, and the great religious festivals of India.[31] Paton strenuously denied the popular belief which he says many educated Indians advance, that the West is 'materialistic' and the East is 'spiritual'. Nevertheless it is clear that Paton is beginning to diagnose in the India of 1917 the causes of 'secularism' and its manifestations, since in 'Social Ideals in India' and 'The Highway of God' he discusses the effect of the breakdown of caste regulations and some customs under the pressure of modern travel and urban life, and the spiritual plight of sceptical students, whose faith in their traditional religion has been undermined by a modern Western scientific education and the influx of humanist writings into India.[32] Paton evidently believed then that the absence of religious belief was like a vacuum because he discusses the forces which might replace religious faith, such as patriotism and nationalism, which, naturally, he considers inadequate. However, it was not until the I.M.C. meeting at Jerusalem that the subject was given any systematic treatment, and was described as being a positive thing, rather than the absence of religion.

Just as the Jerusalem meeting was the first international missionary meeting to consider the 'Christian Message', so it was the first to tackle the question of 'secularism', to articulate the alarm of Christians and to assess the seriousness of the phenomenon.[33] The importance of this debate is reflected in the article written by David Gill for the I.R.M. in July 1968, the detailed examination given to it by Karl-Heinz Dejung in his dissertation, and the inevitable reference to it in ecumenical histories, although, as has been shown in Chapter VI, many other features of the Jerusalem conference could claim equal significance. The impact of Rufus Jones' paper to the plenary session was such that, according to Paton, delegates flocked to the sectional session on the subject.[35] A year later he was complaining that 'the menace of secularism' was now the latest missionary 'gag', a deplorable development because the catchword was preventing serious thought on the problem.[36]

The impression which I received from the Jerusalem correspondence was that the decision to ask Rufus Jones to prepare a paper on the subject was almost accidental and was inspired by concern about the appeal of humanism and dialectical materialism among the educated élite. In view of Paton's great reluctance to see the I.M.C. study the 'Christian Message', because he was sure that Christians from such diverse theological backgrounds would not be able to come to any agreement for a statement, it is surprising to find, in a letter quoted by David Gill, that a year before Rufus Jones' paper was written, Paton was considering the question of a preparatory document on secular civilization.[37] This letter was written at the behest of the I.M.C. Committee for Emergencies to explain what was meant by 'secular civilization'.[38]

In this letter Paton argues that it is not sufficiently recognized that among educated men in the East the same alternative to traditional religion is appearing as has been prevalent in the West, what is being loosely called 'the spirit of secular civilization', and that therefore they ought to see what spiritual values were to be found in it also.

His attempt at a definition of the phenomenon is significant. 'Materialism' he says, is inadequate; it is much more than that, though it draws its strength from this present world. It owes much to scientific research and definitions of 'reality', to standards of empiricism (Paton does not use that word, but that is what he then describes), and to much that is commendable in scientific method. In its prevailing mood of pessimism and melancholy it bears a close resemblance to modern art, which is also concerned to portray things as they actually are, and for their own intrinsic qualities of beauty. It is this combination of art and science, with the added benefit of service from unselfish and faithful men in East and West (he was referring to the 'Servants of India Society', which he much admired).[39] There is also a certain unrestrained rejoicing in the immanent world and its potential which at times becomes crude 'materialism'.

In this very suggestive letter, Paton has captured the spirit of the age very well. Significantly, he finds much that is positive in the trend already, in 1927. In his article 'What is secularism?' he finds much more that is positive:

'. . . many of the elements in the secular movement are perfectly good in
themselves — education for instance is a good thing, so is the emancipation
of women, so is social progress in the different forms in which it is being
advanced throughout this whole great area; so is the study of natural
science. . . . I do not pretend, of course, that secularism in India or Egypt
or Turkey is not aided, as secularism in Germany or England or America is
aided, by the natural man's antagonism to God, the attraction of the world,
the flesh and the devil. We shall, however, make a great mistake if we are
content merely to denounce the secular movement and do not realize that
its strength lies in its positive assertion of some things that are good in
themselves'.[40]

In 'A Faith for the World' (1929) Paton also acknowledges that the Christian
must be grateful to the secular movement for ending the wars of religion, and the
persecution of heretics, for producing the Voltaires and the Humes, who 'stand
between those days and ours', and that it is ruthlessly destroying all that is false and
insincere in religion, bringing about the twilight of the gods.[41] In the I.R.M. article
he wrote:

'We have to examine humbly the criticism of religion made by the
movement of God's spirit. In so far as even the Christian religion has
become tied up with ideals that are alien to its truth and simplicity, has
become legalized or superstitious, loading on men's backs burdens that are
no part of the yoke of Christ, we may look with certainty to see the secular
movement eating into it in just the same way as it has eaten into the ancient
religions of the East'.

It is clear that it is a short step from this position to that enunciated by Kraemer
in 'The Christian Message in a non-Christian world' that Christian religious practice,
where it is equivalent to that of other religions, will be swept aside, and only the
Christian faith will survive (to over-simplify his argument somewhat).[42] Kraemer
was at Jerusalem of course, and in the succeeding years before the writing of the
'Christian Message in a non-Christian world', studied the question of secularism.[43]
As a result of searching for the values in secularism, which was basically an
application of the same principle and method which had been employed with regard
to the non-Christian religions, following the example of Farquhar, Paton came to
realize the principal defect of secularism, and to evolve a new definition. This second
definition even seems more appropriate than the first, but it is interesting that a
similar effect overtook those who studied other religions sympathetically, that they
came to a new understanding of them as well as evolving a more radical critique of
them (W.H.T. Gairdner's work on Islam demonstrates this point very well). As
David Gill says, this correlation of methodology as applied both to the non-
Christian religions and to secularism would be a good area for more detailed study.
The definition current at Jerusalem was that of Rufus Jones, and is very similar
to that used 30 years later by Charles West at a Bossey consultation, as David Gill
points out. 'Secular' was defined by Jones as being 'A way of life and an interpretation of life that include only the natural order of things and that do not find
God, or a realm of spiritual reality, essential for life or thought'.[44]
Paton condemned this type of secularism as being the divorce of various facets
of life from their centre and from him in whom all things cohere. If there is a
conception of God it reduces him to a misty immanence or a bare transcendence,

devoid of the personality we have come to know and love through Jesus Christ. It removes the 'thought of the spirit of God, dwelling in men, so that external law can be transformed into indwelling love, and the continual adaptation of moral principle to changing and developing need'.[45]

One of the most disturbing aspects of secularism, he finds, springs from the attitude it sponsors whereby each part of life, religion, politics, art, science, business, education and so on, is placed in a sealed separate compartment and never be allowed to influence any other aspect of life.

> 'This then is secularism — the separation of the departments of life from the centre to which they belong, so that they become kingdoms in their own right, self-dependent, acknowledging no common suzerainty. Business then will be business; art will be for art's sake; education will solve the mystery of human life in its own strength; the chemist's crucible will be a sufficient test of all reality: and then religion becomes a little department of life with its own petty interests, its own peculiarly odious separatisms, its own professional jargon. The heart of secularism is the divorce of religion from its proper task, and it is here that some of us have come to look for the centre of the world's evil'.[46]

He concludes that the noblest elements should be integrated into a religious interpretation of the world if they are to survive at all, but he warns against the supposition that a world without religion would simply be a world without beauty and passion, superstition and sectarian warfare. It would be a world of unredeemed confusion, disillusionment and moral lassitude, like the decaying Roman Empire.

Paton's description of a compartmentalized secularized world is very apposite today when one considers the ravages caused in education by overspecialization, the schizophrenia of people whose home life cannot be synchronized with their business or professional lives, the multiplicity of conflicting roles forced upon women, and the tendency to abdicate all decisions in whatever field to a specialist, whether a doctor, a politician or a priest. The description of religion in a secular world is unfortunately exactly what has happened as the Church sinks daily further into the ghetto. Paton is right to say that what is required of a religion is that it should present a world view in which everything can be integrated. If it fails, it will be superseded. Paton therefore calls on every Christian to play his part in formulating a Christian world view. His call should still be repeated today. Canon Quick's analysis, deriving from his understanding of the significance of the Incarnation, is similar.[47]

Paton's analysis of secularism is consistent with his demand that Christianity be applied to all spheres of life and to all areas where social reform is necessary.

David Gill summarizes the debate on secularism at Jerusalem. While delegates were agreed about the crucial importance of meeting the challenge of secularism, there was no agreement on how it should be met. John McKenzie, a great friend of Paton's, denounced it as the greatest enemy to Christian mission among students in India, and Hocking called for a new alignment of world religious forces against 'scientific materialism or naturalism', a position which has brought much notoriety to the Jerusalem meeting unfairly.[48] Many others, both missionaries and nationals of China and Brazil and other countries, echoed the condemnation without finding any redeeming points. The Anglican theologians from England were more positive, adopting an attitude similar to Paton's, that is, they found positive values in it. Temple himself predicted that all non-Christian religions are doomed to crumble before the secular view of life. Christianity alone can survive because it can adapt to such ferment and change. He even pointed to the way in which science would be reconciled with Christianity and strengthen it, because of the origins of scientific inquiry in Christian culture.[49]

As David Gill demonstrates, Oldham and Paton were not consistent in their views. Paton's article 'Jerusalem and After', written in 1928 is much stronger in its condemnation. This is hardly surprising in view of the newness of the subject and the amount of work needing to be done, when even definitions of the phenomenon were open to question and change. A consensus among such a diversity of delegates would have been unlikely, considering the number present who had probably never considered the subject before. Oldham realized how crucial the issue was. Not, as he claimed to Richey Hogg when interviewed by him in July 1948, that he had perceived the significance of the subject before the Jerusalem meeting, but when he returned from Africa in 1928 he seized on the question of the Christian message in a secular world and devoted all his energies to it.[50] Since Paton, Oldham and Warnshuis had their own 'comity agreement' whereby they divided up the work of the I.M.C. among them, it is not surprising that Paton ceased to write much on the subject for a decade, while Oldham engaged Brunner and many other theologians to write on the subject for the Oxford Life and Work conference preparations. For Paton the subject became secondary to his considerations of the implications of modern nationalist and totalitarian states' ideology.

The logical consequence of Paton's definitions of social evil and of secularism was his sensitivity to the ethical side of many of the issues of his day. It is not possible to examine in detail the development of his understanding of all such issues on which he wrote and spoke, but his campaign against opium, the forced labour system and his concern with the whole question of freedom of religion and the principle of human rights involved in this issue have already been discussed. However, it is interesting to take one such issue, that of racism, as a paradigm of his thought, and the way in which it developed. Paton did not always succeed in submerging his personal prejudices. For example, he was vehemently opposed to any form of birth control and rejoiced to see Marie Stopes prosecuted. As Dorothy Mackie wrote in March 1942 after meeting Paton in Toronto, 'I felt more than ever that it is very odd for a man with his advanced views to have put six children through the most expensive schools and Oxford. Not that they didn't turn out well of course. He naturally told me how brilliant they all were'.

Paton was usually involved personally: for example he was not only concerned about industrialism and the exploitation of the working classes, but his furlough in 1926 coincided with the General Strike, and he was to be found addressing the striking railwaymen, arranging a lecture programme to relieve their boredom and keep up their morale, and finally organizing a service for the strikers in St Albans' Cathedral, a step which in 1926 was a small social revolution in itself. His concern about racism sprang directly from his experience in India in 1918, since in one of his first letters home he writes of the prejudiced attitude of members of the Indian Civil Service whom he met on the voyage out, and of his shock and horror at seeing missionaries beating their servants.

Paton's first attempt to write systematically about race relations in May 1919 appeared as an article in the I.R.M. after discussion in the I.R.M. Group,[51] but his own ideas stand out clearly in very uncompromising language about the effect of race prejudice on the successful evangelisation of India and the much lauded and much neglected idea of the devolution of responsibility from missions to the churches. If the aim of mission is to build up a living Christian fellowship rather than to promulgate abstract ideas, then the relations between a missionary and the people around him are almost as important as the actual preaching of the Word. His remarks bear on the state of race relations everywhere where the Christian community is being weakened by racial differences.

The first danger is that of the paternal attitude, of missionaries who have laboured long to build up a Christian community, but cannot acknowledge that their converts have achieved spiritual maturity, and that their criticism of missions may be justified. Another tendency he analyses occurs when Indians are treated as 'mission fodder' and not as persons, brothers for whom Christ died. French Protestants complain about the same attitude prevailing among the American Y.M.C.A. which has arrived to 'do good' in France without a Christian understanding of the French personality being built up first. At the root of this feeling is complacency about one's own attitude. In its missionary manifestation racism is closely allied to these two tendencies.

> 'The feeling of racial superiority on the part of the white man to the coloured man, in its more blatant expression, is not a thing to which anyone who wants to be a missionary is likely to be tempted. The view in which all Indians are subsumed under the category of 'damned niggers', or, more briefly, 'dagoes', is not appropriate to the missionary temper. Nevertheless, racial feeling is an astonishingly subtle thing, and may easily poison relations between men of different races unless either they are constantly on the look-out for it, or, which is the Christian way, they forget their race altogether in the constraining unity of a common allegiance'.

Racial feeling in India is much inflamed by the fact that one race rules another so that race and class prestige are combined. In his letters home Paton had complained of the aloofness of missionaries. Now he explains that when a man is told that intimacy with Indians 'lets the white man down', he must realize that this form of racial superiority not only destroys personal friendship, but is dependent for its existence on an air of mystery and aloofness surrounding the privileged nation.

Paton then examines the criticisms of missions raised by educated Indian Christians, who compete for jobs in the Y.M.C.A., but will not work for missions. There is, he acknowledges 'a large element of irresponsibility and of sheer wrong-headedness' in this, because it is the ecclesiastical equivalent of the upsurge of nationalism. Like Farquhar, he states that much of the criticism falls on the ears of sensitive missionaries who least deserve such mistrust, because the Indian Christian would not voice such sentiments to the real offenders. Nevertheless it cannot be dismissed as a student outpouring since some of the ablest and most responsible Indians sense the need for a re-statement of missionary plans and methods to correct the situation. Most mission boards completely fail to appreciate the urgency of the question. Others ignore or pour scorn on the Indian viewpoint, as the leader-writer in 'The Harvest Field' had done recently. One meets Indians who had never known a European Christian intimately even though they may have official relations with them. Some missionaries will not allow Indians to sit in their presence. The majority simply fail to make the effort to form friendships across the divide. 'One knows of missionaries who have worn themselves out in the service of India and yet they had not love'. Would race consciousness be overcome if Europeans adopted Indian food and dress? (Paton only tried the former, and gave up after six months because it was making him ill.) He found that the conclusion of Indian Christians was that it was their spirit which mattered, not the style in which they lived. The greatest cause of strife is the failure to apply the same standards to ourselves as we do to Indians.

Paton's conclusion, after pointing to the causes of offence which should be removed was to demand the abolition of the 'philanthropic' motive, whereby a man tolerantly and patiently waits for the Indian to 'come round' to his view point as though he were a child:

> 'There is a real difference between going to the Indian with a message you want him to receive and even friendship you would like him to share, when at the bottom of your heart you can get on quite well without him, and going to him because you need him. . . . Can it not be said truly that we touch here something vital to the very nature of God? The Incarnation must surely mean that God needed man and yearned over him and sought him. The sending of Jesus is not an accident in the life of God, it is of his very essence, and the going forth of the missionary is in the same spirit, according as God may give it to him'.

In view of the Amritsar massacre shortly after this article was written, Paton's words acquire a tinge of prophecy. It is very difficult to establish how accurate his observations are, because the missionaries whom I have interviewed were devoid of prejudice themselves, and most worked in schools where there was very little prejudice between European and Indian members of staff, or in the Y.M.C.A. But from those who worked in the church in India it is clear that massive discrimination did exist above and beyond that which was inherent in a colonial system, though it was more of the paternalistic variety than of anything resembling race hatred. Paton found it very difficult to avoid being treated as a 'padre sahib', apart from the fact that the enormous differences in personal wealth made equality almost impossible. One of the most telling incidents in Paton's letters is when he recounts going to a party held by an Indian friend and meeting all sorts of interesting educated Indians, but no white person who was socially acceptable in Calcutta.[52]

Paton is very fair in discussing the racial element in Indian nationalism. It seems to him a justifiable patriotic reaction to the sight of India ruled by an alien race of much less ancient cultural and religious traditions. To describe such Indians as 'disloyal' or 'seditious' for voicing aspirations inspired by western ideas of liberty and democracy is short-sighted. 'Social Ideals in India' was written at the same time as the I.R.M. article, but is more critical of Indian attitudes. He describes how the race issue is used as a stick to beat the missionary and yet refuse responsibility in church government. Since Paton was never minister of a congregation in England or in India, he tends to underestimate the capacity of the average Christian to carry on feuds in the church council with pleasure.[53] He defends the missionary because he is usually judged by the infinitely high standard of Christ's example, he is doing more than anyone else in India to promote inter-racial brotherhood, and he is less guilty of arrogance than most Europeans are in their relationship to their servants, and those of a lower social class. So his plea to those in the East and West is to guard against patronizing the Indian.

On the other hand he describes in detail how the Church in India may enrich the universal Church with its own insights and how important it is to allow Indians to develop a simpler and more spontaneous system of church organisation.[54] These pages are important when one attempts to answer the question whether Paton's belief that all non-Christian religions were inadequate and in some aspects positively evil was not in itself a form of racism. Paton's unconsciously patronising attitude at Tambaram has already been discussed, but I think that on balance, considering his criticisms of the 'Christian' society and civilization which he knew and his many friendships with Indian nationalists, he generally succeeded in overcoming whatever innate prejudices he may have had.

In 'The Highway of God' Paton and Harnett explain the Indian reaction to the Amritsar massacre, and how they interpret the European failure to condemn it, as 'an attitude of contempt for India and Indians, of denial to the Indians of the rights of human beings, and determination to put the security of the British Raj before any consideration for India herself. Violence has been done to the soul of India . . . we can understand any Indian patriot feeling that Amritsar expresses more truly than Westminster the attitude of the British to India'.[55]

The writers have clearly perceived that both Amritsar and the Khalifat question are more significant in racial than in political terms, which is a point some secular historians obscure. In this book, it is race relations in Africa which receive fullest treatment since African countries are traded like pawns among the European powers and ruthlessly exploited commercially. He protests against the view that there is anything simple and unsophisticated about tribal life, but insists on the serious effects of the process whereby it is broken down.[56]

Paton devotes a chapter of 'A Faith for the World' to the Christian opposition to racism, because: 'The Christian religion brings a message of fullness of life, the fruits of the Spirit are love, joy, and peace, and the coming of the Kingdom of God in the world is the exact antithesis of the spirit which it generated among the peoples by racial and international antagonism'. He justifies taking nationalism and racism together because they are so closely akin though the former is an ideologically inspired thing, the latter stems from physical differences.[57]

In the case of India Paton now believes that the tension is entirely because of the political situation, not the racial one, and that the solution lies in self-government for India. In spite of a more hostile atmosphere in India than has previously existed, inter-racial friendships are easily possible. Paton attributes the communal riots between Muslim and Hindu to the socio-economic background of the two communities, and not to any racial difference. This analysis shows that Paton's views have changed considerably since 1919. What he condemns as racist is the 'white Australia' policy on immigration to Australia, and the restrictions on immigration to Canada and the United States. In China the insolence of the British has fanned racial tension. He has not changed his analysis of the South African situation except to commend the patience and dignity of black South Africans.

Whether nationalism, economic or social rivalry or colonialism are the grounds of the tension, Paton describes the difference of colour as being the factor which leads white races into an attitude of unjustified superiority, 'until many people . . . are convinced beyond redemption that their feeling of antagonism is based on a primeval instinct entitled to the same respect as the major instincts of human life'.[58]

There is, Paton writes, no simple solution to this situation. In some cases a political settlement is necessary, in some, social justice. There is a need of study groups and action groups. The Church has no clean record, but it could transform the situation. The only way forward for the Christian is to encourage bold inter-racial experiments. Ultimately, as Dr Hope, an American black, and Miss Tilak of India said at the Jerusalem meeting, it is a question of applying the principle that in Christ there is neither Jew nor Greek.

After 1929 Paton treated the question of racism in a strictly political or ideological context, that is, he urged self-government for India as soon as possible, in the former context, and he studied the significance of 'volkische' teaching in National Socialism. It is another example of the way in which Paton's thinking was translated into the context of its political significance. The final stage can be seen in the writings of 1940-43. In the case of racism, he drafted a pamphlet as a sequel to 'The Church and the New Order' in which he argues entirely from a political framework, concerning the post-war reconstruction, the treatment of Germany and of former colonies using Christian principles of justice, but stating them in secular terms.[59]

Paton's last word is to be found in a broadcast he prepared in July 1942, on the subject 'What is man?' Looking at the state of the world at war, he attributes it to the false doctrines of man developed by both sides, because both exalted the idea of man and his capacity for infinite progress from the time of the Renaissance onwards. Fascism is simply a further perversion of this, but in proclaiming the glory of men, man has become further enslaved by his nation, his race or his class. This is a complete departure from Christian teaching, which has contributed a great deal to human freedom, but starts with God and the divine creation, not the goodness of man. He proceeds to a classical statement of creation and atonement and the love of God, then asks what follows from such a belief.

'First, a radical view about man's sinfulness and his desperate plight. There is nothing of the cheery optimist about the Christian, so far at least as his insight into man is concerned. He knows quite well that man has within him the possibility of incalculable evil, and that he cannot do that good which he wants to do because of an inner infirmity and corruption. But it does not stop there. It goes on to say that God loved man so greatly that the indescribable sacrifice of the life and death of Christ was given for man, that he might be brought back to God . . . If you believe this then you cannot believe that man is just a sample of racial bloodstream, or that he is just the plaything of economic forces, or that he is only an atom in national life. For man on this showing has his roots in the eternal, his dependence is his glory, his weakness is his strength. You assert the dignity of man . . . because God made him and God loves him and God gave Christ to save him'.

Paton was, according to David Paton, much influenced by C.H. Dodd and probably derived a 'semi-realized' eschatology from him. He was much more concerned with the past, with God's redeeming acts which had already taken place rather than any future consummation. His scepticism of an entirely futuristic eschatology can be seen in the various passages quoted in this chapter, and he was very far from accepting what he believed to be the Lutheran position, of acting as though the Kingdom would come, but never as though your actions had any bearing on whether it came or not. Paton talked about 'acted prayer' with regard to the words 'Thy Kingdom come, thy will be done', and that there was no point in praying those words and then sitting back and waiting for it to happen in God's own good time. He was cautious about the phrase 'building the Kingdom', but he did not entirely reject it.[60] This is consistent with what we know of Paton as a practical administrator, not a mystic or speculative thinker. His hopes are most typically expressed in the closing paragraph of the 'Highway of God'.

> 'It is sometimes difficult to maintain hopeful enthusiasm for the 'new world' of which so many have dreamed and died without beholding it, when we look at half Europe famine-stricken, at race riots in America and political tension in India, at the world-wide ramifications of commercial enterprise and the new slavery of the black peoples. But the Christian has looked into the face of a more terrible scene, a more complete denial of God and of goodness than even our world today. He has looked at Jesus Christ put to death on the cross, and found there with amazement and gladness, that 'the victory remained with Love'.'

Chapter X

The Genesis of the World Council of Churches

Just as the Continuation Committee of the World Missionary Conference was formed in time to save missions from the worst ravages of the first World War, so the World Council of Churches was declared to be 'in process of formation' and its staff were appointed only two years before the outbreak of hostilities in 1939. The World Council of Churches in process of formation (W.C.C.F.) had a baptism of fire, in which it was shaped and developed on an experimental basis to meet the needs of ecumenical co-operation and relief in wartime. Its ministry was of such significance, and Paton played such an important part in it, as part-time general secretary of the W.C.C.F., that this chapter and the three following are devoted to a discussion of various aspects of its work.[1] As the W.C.C.F. achieved a more substantial shape, with the increasing weight of work, Paton displayed the psychological effect of this on himself and others in a curious way. As he ordered new batches of notepaper, the heading changed so that the words 'World Council of Churches' became progressively larger and the words 'in process of formation' shrank until they became insignificant.

The inauguration of the W.C.C.F. at the Utrecht meeting in May 1938 savours of a response to the 'kairos', of the right time having come for a particular decision, and of an event with a supra-historical significance. There was, however, very considerable opposition to the formation of the W.C.C.F., both from within the ecumenical movements involved, and from without. The Utrecht meeting in 1938 only happened as the result of years of preparation and several previous abortive attempts to form a similar body. So one must examine the coincidence of theological and non-theological factors which resulted in the successful initiation of the W.C.C.F. After nearly forty years of official and unofficial existence, it becomes difficult to realize that the justification for creating a World Council was far from clear then and that when its existence was questioned, the frame of reference for these questions was quite different.[2]

Paton emerges as one of the chief protagonists of the W.C.C.F., devoting ever more time to it, so that it is a reasonable hypothesis to suggest that had he lived to see the official founding of the World Council at the first World Assembly in 1948, he would have resigned from the I.M.C. whether he had brought it into the W.C.C. or not, and worked full-time for the W.C.C. This is also Dr Payne's view. This would have been consistent with the development in his theology from a response to missionary questions to a fully thought out ecclesiology, discussed in Chapter XIV and would have been easier to do when Mott, Oldham and Warnshuis had been replaced (1937-44). There is no dearth of books which include the subject of the

W.C.C.F. and there are the reports of the W.C.C.F. itself,[3] but it is necessary to turn to the archives of the W.C.C. to perceive the full complexity of the developments and the forces at work in the situation, and in particular the powerful British contribution of Temple, Oldham, Paton and Bell, of whom only Bell was active after the war.[4] I am particularly grateful to the W.C.C. for allowing me access to their confidential files, especially the original copies of Temple's correspondence, which contrasts with the decision of Lambeth Palace not to allow me to see their copies of this same correspondence even though Temple's executors supported my application.

In solitary witness, with all the documentary evidence against him, Tatlow maintains in 'The History of the Student Christian Movement', that there was a Continuation Committee appointed by the World Missionary Conference held in New York in 1900. In fact the period of continuous, organized ecumenical co-operation began in 1906 with the negotiations between the Presbyterian missionary boards in Scotland and those in the U.S.A. for another world missionary conference, that held in Edinburgh in 1910, and with the appointment of J.H. Oldham as conference secretary in 1908. The historic decision to retain Oldham as secretary of a Continuation Committee (which went through various changes of name and constitution before it was fashioned into the I.M.C. in 1920) meant that in all the negotiations described in this chapter, the I.M.C. was the senior body, and the most stable, with an aura of respectability which the other organisations, with the possible exception of the World Alliance for Friendship among the Churches (formed in 1912 and reformed in 1919), did not have.[5] Some of Paton's influence must derive from the resources which, in the I.M.C., he had at his behest. The I.M.C's relative financial stability has already been discussed. Robert Mackie is convinced that Paton was invited to be a general secretary of the W.C.C.F. in order to give the infant body a semblance of stability and to reassure the conservatives. Paton thought that he had been appointed to bring in the missionary contribution and to forge a link with the younger churches.[6] It is interesting to find letters to Paton emanating from China and India to the effect that the Christian churches there had confidence in the I.M.C., and whatever steps it might take for church unity, but not in the Life and Work movement or the Faith and Order movement, which were regarded by these correspondents as largely irrelevant.[7]

The growth and development of the 'grass-roots' of the I.M.C. in the N.C.C's of the various countries in Asia and Africa has already been described. These councils, composed principally of expatriate missionaries, were being converted into bodies whose membership contained at least 50% representation by nationals of the country, whether church leaders or mission employees. Each national body was supported by a network of provincial and local councils in a typical Presbyterian structure. Since 1922 these bodies had full-time secretaries, of whom Paton had been one, their own periodicals, research projects and so on. So one can see the logic of the representations which H.T. Hodgkin spearheaded at the I.M.C. meeting at Jerusalem for the formation of an international council of churches. Hodgkin argued that it was important to 're-christen' the I.M.C. and the I.R.M. and find a better word to express the larger field of the modern missionary movement than was implied in the word 'missionary'.

'Few things seem to me to be more important just now than the working

> out of fresh methods whereby the primacy of the church in the mission
> lands should be fully recognized and given effect. . . . How can we work
> out methods that correspond to the acknowledged fact that the Christians
> in a country like China have at least as much right as, and perhaps more
> than, those of the sending countries? The question of where authority lies
> and where it should lie . . . is one that needs to be faced in a fresh way. . . .
> To me it seems that some kind of grouping wider than denominational and
> in larger geographical units than are sometimes thought of, is needed if the
> voice of these churches is to be given in an effective way. It may be that
> such bodies as the National Christian Councils should be called in to
> perform a function for all the churches in certain executive ways not
> hitherto contemplated, or it may be that we must be content with
> functioning by national groupings of denominations or unions such as the
> Church of Christ in China. . . .'[8]

During the Jerusalem meeting the committee of the I.M.C. met frequently to discuss the questions of policy which would be brought before the main session, or to deal with business matters. Dr David Yui of the Y.M.C.A. of China raised the question of a change in I.M.C. name and structure to make it church-based. He was supported by a motion from the N.C.C. of Japan by whom it was claimed that some churches would not join the N.C.C. of Japan while it was mission-based. The change of name was opposed by representatives of the home boards, but the discussion did have the positive result in making the members aware of the dual nature of the I.M.C. Much consideration was given to the question of linking the organisation of the I.M.C. closer to that of the N.C.Cs without increasing the amount of administration and committee meetings, and changes were introduced into the I.M.C's constitution to bring this into effect.[9]

The committee was grappling with the basic problem which made the integration of the I.M.C. into any other ecumenical organisation so difficult. In the so-called mission field it was composed of representatives from bodies which combined church and mission elements, whereas in Europe and America the equivalent bodies, the C.B.M.S. and the Federal Council, were entirely missionary bodies with the occasional bishop or churchman being appointed because of his personal interest in missions and membership of a missionary society. In Germany and Scandinavia even this personal link with the churches was absent. Secondly, it is clear from the number of papers written in the period 1926-28 on the function and significance of the I.M.C. that there was so much uncertainty about its role that a radical change might have undermined it altogether.[10] There was a commendable fear lest the machinery of ecumenical co-operation should proliferate. If the Hodgkin-Yui proposals had been accepted, there would have arisen a type of World Council based in the East, with no balancing structure in Europe and America. It is characteristic of the entire movement towards Christian unity that the proposals should have come from China and Japan, because since Edinburgh 1910, the most powerful voices urging unity had come from the Chinese and Indian delegates.[11] Paton appears to have been most involved in the question of how to make the I.M.C. more representative of its constituency.

This abortive attempt to create a more fully ecumenical body demonstrates the enormous difficulties in the path of such an idea and how unprepared even leading churchmen were for such an idea. The ordinary church member or supporter of missions would be less comprehending. (900 members of S.P.G. presented a petition to the Society protesting against its participation in the Edinburgh conference in 1910.)

It was shown in the controversy surrounding the D.S.I.R. how fierce the demarcation disputes were in the ecumenical movements, and how a gentlemen's 'comity' agreement appeared to operate, which is probably the most adequate explanation of how the I.M.C. came to be responsible for the 'Fifth Section' of the Life and Work movement.[12] Although Söderblom suggested, in 1919, a council of religious bodies, nothing came of his idea, in fact the Life and Work movement is reputed to have rejected a suggestion that it and Faith and Order should plan a joint first conference with the view to amalgamation.[13] Members of the Life and Work movement held firmly to the slogan Söderblom invented, 'Doctrine divides, service unites' and were convinced that a closer association with theologians and churchmen would result in the movement stagnating in sterile doctrinal disputes. This was a prejudice which Oldham shared, according to Kathleen Bliss, so that unlike Paton who represented not only the I.M.C. but also the English Presbyterian Church at Faith and Order meetings, Oldham did not attend the Faith and Order conference and committee meetings in the 1930s. Being a layman himself, he had determined to maintain in the Life and Work movement a high proportion of laymen.[14]

Faith and Order, on the other hand, found the pronouncements of the Life and Work movement very irritating, not only in the 1920s, when they championed the League of Nations so uncritically, but also in the 1930s, when the question of the status and authenticity of the Confessing Church raised profound questions as to the nature of the true Church and the true Gospel for both movements, and when the political situation in Germany involved members of the Life and Work movement in a defence of their persecuted brethren. I have previously argued the thesis that the predicament of the Confessing Church forced the members of the ecumenical move-ment to re-define their position and produce a positive statement of the value of the Church in a manner analogous to the classical statements of Trinitarian theology which the great heresies evoked from the councils of the early Christian Church.[15]

The long road to unity between the Life and Work and the Faith and Order movements has been described in detail in my M.A. thesis. Gradually, as members of the various ecumenical organizations learnt to understand and trust each other as they pursued the same ends so the barriers between the movements came down. The Life and Work movement found that it could not ignore the theological commission in 1927.[16] The studies begun in 1934 on the theme 'Church, Community and State', not only overlapped with a considerable amount of I.M.C. work on the situation of the Church in the Far East, but also forced on the movement a thorough study of the nature of the Church. The areas of common interest began to be greater than the areas of different specialisations. Here Paton's habit of speaking all over Britain on the subject of the universal Church and its international significance cannot have been without effect in communicating an ideal to which the ecumenical organisations were tending in the practical expressions of their work. Neither did he have a monopoly of this theme.[17] However, there were important practical considerations which influenced the formation of the World Council of Churches.

Firstly, among the group of influential people involved in the 'ecumenical consultative group' from which the proposals for a World Council of Churches emanated, which was organized and chaired by Temple, there were a significant proportion of people like Paton and Temple who were involved in two or more of the ecumenical movements whose union was under discussion. Similarly a substantial proportion of delegates at the world conferences of the movements were accredited by their churches to attend more than one conference. Not only was this a more economical proposition for the sponsoring organisations, especially if a transatlantic passage was involved, but also it seems that Oldham, Paton and their colleagues did not distinguish very carefully which hat they were wearing when they were acting for the different organisations of which they were members. On the other hand, Paton at least had a fairly integrated vision of what he was trying to do in terms of Christian unity and mission whatever committee he was sitting on.

Apart from the increasing overlapping of function and personnel, there were compelling economic reasons for merging the movements. Because it drew so much of its support from the Continent, Life and Work was the most badly hit by the financial crises and the depression. Study programmes had to be cut back, and the trilingual periodical 'Stockholm' went out of circulation after only a brief three year existence.[18] When Bishop Bell became president of the Life and Work movement in 1931 his first task was to save it from financial collapse.[19] He was successful in raising a capital sum in matter of weeks, but it was partly for reasons of economy and partly because of the need for close liaison between the two movements that H.L. Henriod was appointed secretary of both Life and Work and the World Alliance, with his office in Geneva. In 1933 the financial crisis afflicting Faith and Order was so great that their Geneva office was closed. Their secretary, protesting fiercely about the cuts and the changes in policy, resigned. Leonard Hodgson, a canon on an inadequate stipend at Winchester Cathedral, became part-time secretary of Faith and Order. In short, the ecumenical organisations were stream-lined as much as possible. Their work became very dependent on voluntary contributions of time and money.

One reason for the financial difficulties of Faith and Order and Life and Work was that there was considerable confusion in the church-going public's mind about the various ecumenical organisations competing for donations. The formation of the W.C.C.F. meant a great simplification of finance, although there were initial difficulties which Paton had to deal with concerning the allocations of finance to the different 'offices' of the W.C.C.F. and the Faith and Order section of it from the churches' contributions. He also had to employ all his diplomatic arts to extract the promised contributions when they were needed.[20]

One cannot ignore the fact that there was a certain sociological common factor which may have helped the various meetings concerning the formation of the W.C.C.F. to 'gel'. Many of those involved had a connection with the S.C.M. or the Y.M.C.A., a classical, university education, and had been caught up in the ecumenical movement by John R. Mott. Whether they possessed private incomes or aristocratic connections, the Americans and Europeans were with few exceptions middle class, which the black American delegate at Utrecht considered a difficulty when he asked whom the proposed W.C.C.F. would represent.[21] This social cohesion can be seen in the pattern of meetings in August, in hotels in the Netherlands or Paris, or in St George's School, Clarens, Switzerland. However, it is easy to exaggerate this factor, and forget the important contribution of the Orthodox members, whose background was so different. It did mean that certain procedures, structures, language and priorities were automatically accepted, and that the question was more one of how to make the machinery which they would inevitably create fit the goal which they eventually agreed they all sought, rather than there being any radical questioning about the nature and function of ecumenical organisation. In fact as Hodgson admitted to Miss Sinclair:

> 'More than once the Archbishop of York has had to remind us that we are not a theological discussion society meeting for the purpose of enjoying theological discussions with one another, but a movement with a definite purpose of considering the differences between us which are a hindrance to unity'.[22]

Dr Ehrenström states that the ecumenical movement demonstrates the way in which churchmen who intensely disliked each other had to work together to achieve their common aim. He cites Niemöller and Würm, as an example of this but there are many other examples. Therefore, one must not over-estimate the importance of the personal friendships among those involved in the ecumenical movement. However, such friendships must have facilitated matters. Bell and Paton together on a committee, for example, have been described as a well co-ordinated tennis doubles partnership, placing the ball so that it would return exactly where the other could hit it.

In August 1935 after a period of informal co-operation in the planning of the 1937 conferences and the 1938 I.M.C. conference, in which arrangements were made to collaborate in study, to prevent overlapping and to share each other's organisational resources, Hodgson wrote a letter to Temple which reveals the difficulty of diverting the course of an ecumenical movement.

> 'While the Stockholm Movement is largely in the hands of a group of prominent people much engaged in international affairs, it has been repeatedly borne in upon me since I became secretary two and a half years ago how much the strength of Faith and Order lies in the interest in it on the part of numberless simple church people all over the world and in the support given to it by them . . . They have cherished whatever advance towards mutual understanding was achieved in 1927, they have gone on praying and giving and looking forward to 1937. Whatever decision we may arrive at we shall have to give an account of it to this constituency . . .'

> 'I think it is only fair to recall a little of the history of the movement of which Oldham may be ignorant as he only recently came into touch with them at all. As I understand the past, right from the beginning our only desire in Faith and Order was to go on quietly doing our own work. But the Stockholm Movement has repeatedly tried to draw us into the general current of 'an ecumenical movement'. The proposal to hold both conferences in one year came entirely from them . . . it was entirely in order not to appear non-co-operative that we agreed to this, and if now they wish to turn us out of the year which we had publicly announced as that of our next conference as early as 1930, there does seem to me to be something of the cuckoo about it.

> '. . . as I explained to Bonhoeffer, our movement is essentially a conference in which churches talk to one another. If there is to be an ecumenical movement which shall claim to speak for Christendom as a kind of super-church we shall have to be extremely careful not to get tied up in it or we shall compromise the guarantee given to all the churches we invited to be represented in Faith and Order that they shall not be committed by any

of our activities. I have no desire to try to compete with Life and Work in any way, all I wish to press for is that we should be allowed to go on quietly and steadily doing our own work and not be subject to continual attempts to divert us from it'.[23]

This letter has been quoted so extensively because it explains the reluctance of some members of Faith and Order to join in the W.C.C.F. when they felt this would be advancing further than their member churches had given them a mandate to go. Hodgson had no historical justification for these remarks, exasperated though he may have been by the practice Oldham had of forming an élite of philosophers around him, because the Life and Work movement in England had inherited the enthusiasm and impetus of the COPEC conference held in Birmingham in 1924 and the study and action programmes which followed it, now directed by the Christian Social Council. Hodgson also raises the principal difficulties, that the W.C.C.F. (or whatever body he thought was envisaged in 1935) would be a 'super-church'. This has been an abiding problem for the W.C.C. In all the early drafts of the constitution made during 1935-38 attempts were made to surmount it by stating that the W.C.C. has only authority to act in the way in which its member churches request it. Temple temporarily solved the other problem in 1938 by stating categorically that whatever statements the secretaries, chairman or the assemblies of the W.C.C.F. might make, they would not be in any way binding on members, and would only possess such authority as their contents merited. The signatories would not confer any authority on the statement.[24]

Nevertheless another motive for the formation of the W.C.C. was that a body was needed to act on behalf of the churches in the same way that the I.M.C. acted on behalf of the missions, to negotiate with governments and provide a united front when any external agency tried to manipulate, exploit or undermine member churches. This was very clearly stated in a statement made by the Utrecht conference which opens with the sentence: 'The Christian Church today finds itself face to face with problems, needs and forces which constitute a challenge to its principles and even a menace to its life'.

At the Oxford Life and Work conference, when unanimous consent was given to the idea of a World Council, and representatives were empowered to work out ways of implementing this idea, there was a very strong sense of the Christian Church being under attack, and the inability of a single denomination to withstand the challenge. In Chapter VI it was shown how the delegates meeting at Tambaram in December 1938, were confronted by similar hostile situations. The Protestant churches were well aware that they stood at a disadvantage in relation to the Roman Catholic Church. Pastor Hoyois told the Utrecht meeting that on the occasion of Oldham's visit to interview the Belgian Colonial Secretary, it had been very difficult to persuade the Colonial Office that he had any importance until he compared him with the Cardinal Secretary of State.[25] Although those involved in the discussions at the Utrecht meeting were fully alive to the dangers of creating a Protestant Vatican, nevertheless, it was recognised that some united authority was needed for negotiating with governments and for co-ordinating international joint action.

The statement quoted above continues: 'The Church possesses in the Gospel the word of healing for the ills of the world, but it is ill-equipped with resources required for exhibiting the relevance of the Gospel to many of these problems and for bringing it to bear effectively upon them' (war and social injustice). After calling for the whole church to repent and pray for God's help in a situation which only he can resolve, the statement concluded:

> 'The proposal to establish a consultative body representing all churches which accept its basis and approve its aims arises by an inevitable process from the development of various movements since 1910. But it comes before us at a moment when the need for a symbolic presentation of the unity of all Christians in face of unchristian and anti-christian tendencies in the world is of special importance. We hope that it may be considered in relation to the special tasks of the world-wide Church in the world today.[26]

It will be clear from what has already been written in this book, that there was no 'inevitable process' at all, unless one sees a supernatural agency at work forcing the churches together, but that would be a denial of the idea of free will. It is significant that whoever compiled this statement thought there was an inevitable process at work. A sense of the Church's failure and need to repent was present in ecumenical statements from the Stockholm Life and Work conference in 1925 onwards, but it was never accepted by Orthodox and Anglo-Catholic members. The idea of a 'symbolic presentation of the unity of all Christians' is valuable, and would allay the fears of those holding views similar to Hodgson's, but would be inadequate if subjected to strain in the way that the League of Nations was.

In spite of the Hodgson-Tatlow misgivings, it is significant that it was Life and Work and Faith and Order which came together, and not the former organisation and the World Alliance, which superficially seemed much closer together. It has already been noted that both organisations shared certain staff (Bonhoeffer was Youth Secretary for both in Germany), yet there was a great disparity between their relative strengths at national level. For example, the World Alliance predominated in England, to the almost total eclipse of Life and Work (thus Bell was the only English person present at the Life and Work meeting at Novi Sad in 1933), but the situation was reversed in Germany. Henriod produced a highly confidential memorandum for Bell and Bishop Ammundsen of the World Alliance in December 1936 on 'The Future of the Ecumenical Movement' in which he argued that the existence of several movements prevented any one of them being world-wide, describing the relationship between Life and Work and the World Alliance as an inadequate 'modus vivendi' at best. It is significant because he accepts representation based on the churches, when this was the chief stumbling block to union between the two bodies. Life and Work was closely linked to its church constituency, but the World Alliance was more of an association of friends and international figures, and it was not supported by grants from church bodies, as Life and Work was.[27] Many of those in it felt that a closer association with the churches would mean the sacrificing of the World Alliance's freedom to be a radical and prophetic body.

Henriod also adopts the idea of 'confessional representation' which was eventually rejected in the discussions concerning the formation of the W.C.C.F. The autocephalous Orthodox churches' representatives had rejected the idea as not providing adequate representation for the different Orthodox churches, and on the other hand, small churches would have suffered. At Utrecht, Mrs Pierce argued that to base representation on the world confessional bodies would tend to exclude women and lay people. Much time was given also at Utrecht to deciding how large a church had to be to qualify. From then until now the deciding factor has been whether a denomination has 10,000 or more members and shows reasonable signs of stability. A certain geographical element was incorporated instead. (Henriod's system was very heavily weighted against the Third World.)

The decision to make the World Council firmly based on the denominational churches, and not on national ecumenical societies or councils was probably the most important single decision made at the various planning meetings. Elaborate clauses were woven into the constitution to provide for the membership, representation and participation of the churches in decision-making. Judging by the time and energy which Paton and Temple devoted to the difficult task of getting churches to respond to invitations to join the W.C.C.F. in the years 1939-43, they were in full support of this principle. Demoralised by the second world war in a generation, superseded by the W.C.C's Commission of the Churches on International Affairs, impoverished by the withdrawal of its main source of income, the Christian Peace Union, the World Alliance collapsed. It had been represented at Utrecht, but an insuperable stumbling block was the doctrinal basis of membership.[28]

If one asks why the World Council was formed in 1938 rather than in 1928, when Hodgson and Yui raised the question of the I.M.C's structure, or why Söderblom's proposals came to nothing, the answer seems to lie in two directions. First, it took thirty years to acclimatize church leaders to the prospect of greater organizational unity and closer international co-operation and for the emergence of a new generation — Paton, Temple, Kraemer, Oldham, Henriod, Koechlin and so on who had grown up in the ecumenical movement, starting in the S.C.M. or the Y.M.C.A. in the period 1900-1910. In spite of the now annual weeks of prayer for Christian unity, there was no serious or systematic attempt to popularize the idea of a World Council or an international ecumenical movement among the British church-going population at large until the publicity for the 1937 conferences began. This was Kraemer's conclusion when he reported on the Oxford conference.[29] It was the 'Religion and Life' weeks held 1941-44 in association with the formation of the B.C.C. which signalled an effort at mass communication. So one cannot argue that this lapse of time was necessary to accustom church opinion to the idea of a W.C.C.F. Secondly, it was the crisis of the 1930s, because of both the ideological assault on the churches and the plight of the Evangelical churches in Germany,[30] and the financial difficulties which the various ecumenical organizations found themselves in, which provoked the ecumenical organizations into such a reaction.

It is now necessary to describe Paton's participation for, although some of the participants have written their autobiographies to cover this period, ranging from the exotic eccentricity of Marc Boegner, president of the Continental section of Life and Work, in 'The Long Road to Unity', to the informed precision of Dr Visser't Hooft's 'Memoirs', nevertheless it is instructive to trace one man's path through to the W.C.C.F.[31] One must also remember that there were the losers also, who dropped out of the ecumenical movement because they objected so strongly to the way in which it was going, and especially to its increasing institutionalisation and its collaboration with National Socialism, as they saw it. Wilfred Monod's autobiography 'Après la journée' is very illuminating concerning this point.[32]

It is impossible to establish when Paton first became involved with the Life and Work movement, but his involvement with it does seem to ante-date his participation in the Faith and Order movement. The development of his thought on social questions has already been described in the preceding chapter. He had fought vigorously to see the D.S.I.R. established as an independent bureau with no official connection with Life and Work in spite of protests from P.T.R. Kirk, the secretary of the British Section of Life and Work. However, in 1932 Paton was collaborating with Life and Work, perhaps more in a personal capacity than as secretary of the I.M.C. Schönfeld, the recently appointed director of the Life and Work Research Institute, sent him the papers and report of the Basel conference on unemployment (April 1932) inviting his comments.[33] Paton replied at length criticizing the actual economic analysis of the causes of unemployment on technical grounds, and complaining that the conference did not suggest what the churches or the nations might do in practical terms. The letter exuded good feeling towards the Life and Work department. Schönfeld replied that it was not the aim of the Basel conference to make specific proposals, but to educate public opinion. He announced that he was sending Paton 50 copies of the English report and 30 of the German version for Paton's committee, which seems a disproportionately high number. This seems to have been the beginning of a regular correspondence in which Schönfeld sought Paton's comments on Life and Work reports.

It seems as though Paton was rapidly becoming Schönfeld's London contact, to the exclusion of P.T.R. Kirk. Atkinson did suggest to Bell that Paton would be a useful collaborator in Britain. Schönfeld wrote to Paton asking if he could recommend an English research worker to be appointed to liaise between the churches and economists independently of the Life and Work educational programme. Paton suggested a former S.C.M. colleague, H.A. Mess, but said he was not in a position to advise Life and Work. Always a stickler for procedure, he informed P.T.R. Kirk of the correspondence, while arranging for Kirk to meet Mott to discuss collaboration between Life and Work and the I.M.C. Kirk replied that he was grateful for Paton's kindness. It was only another instance of the Geneva staff assuming a responsibility which rested with the Executive Committee of Life and Work. There was no likelihood of the appointment being made because of the financial situation. Kirk said that he was writing in confidence, but he was anxious to show him the difficulties they were up against in Geneva. This incident cannot have increased Paton's confidence in Life and Work. His reply to Schönfeld is interesting:

> 'I have felt from the beginning that the research department was starting before the committee responsible had thought out carefully and thoroughly what they believed to be its main functions and I believe that much of the troubles through which you have passed (and these are of course in no way due to you) are the result of this original mistake. I believe that the greatest thing for the Stockholm Institute is that it should give itself to very thorough, radical thinking as to the true place that it occupies in the whole international scheme. . . . '[34]

In spite of his sympathy with the Life and Work research department and in spite of a resolution passed at the I.M.C. meeting at Herrnhut in July 1932 authorizing closer contacts with Life and Work and Faith and Order, Paton was initially very suspicious when he was invited to join the first ecumenical consultation at Bishopthorpe, Temple's palace, in February 1933. He wrote very cautiously to Henriod, who was a close friend from S.C.M. days when Henriod worked among foreign students in London:

'I hope that you are not under any misapprehension as to the impossibility of the I.M.C. entering into any kind of merger at the present time. If nothing more is desired than purely informal conversation, that is all right, but I should be entirely opposed to the impression being given to the leaders of other organizations that we were beginning, even in an informal way to plan towards something in the way of organic union'.[35]

Henriod replied reassuring him that no integration of the organisations was intended, but an exchange of views on the planning of the proposed 1937 world conferences. The meeting would not be official because the members were being selected in an arbitrary way. Henriod's personal view was that the greatest harm would be done to organisations such as the I.M.C. which are free agents of Christian unity and understanding by relating them to the churches officially. Paton objected to this:

'No discussion in which we are concerned can be of any use unless it is recognized that the I.M.C. is not a centralized group only in a very slight degree responsible to anyone, but that it is built up from national organisations, all of them with their own life, and in some cases very powerful organizations representive of the missionary endeavours of the churches'.

Paton declared that Henriod's views on the aims of the talks were the same as his, but as Henriod was urging a union of Life and Work and the World Alliance, one must conclude that he was dissembling.[36] The moving spirit behind the Bishopthorpe meeting was Dr William Adams Brown, chairman in 1933 of the Administrative Committee of Life and Work, who describes the meeting in his book 'Towards a United Church'.[37] Judging by the resolutions agreed on at the meeting, it was a time of small beginnings, but very significant for a number of developments. First, a clear conviction emerged that the various movements were part of the total manifestation of the Church in its one service to the world and that it was vitally important for those concerned with the direction of these movements to meet frequently to assist each other. For the purpose of these consultations, members of the movements should be recognized officially or unofficially, as their representatives. Henriod and Temple were elected joint convenors of further meetings to achieve this. Secondly, it was decided to hold the two world conferences of Life and Work and Faith and Order so close to each other as to make possible a united witness.

Hodgson's letter concerning the second point has already been discussed. Despite the difficulties, the two conferences were planned to take place in the same month in Britain, in August 1937, with joint services in London and receptions, broadcasts, publicity and so on creating the desired effect of a united witness. There were also efforts to link them to Tambaram, though as has already been shown, the I.M.C. conference was much more than a translation of the British conferences into the situation in the Far East. After the Bishopthorpe meeting, Paton began to co-operate very closely with Henriod in the planning for the Oxford conference. He was invited to the Fano conference which Oldham attended, which was an historic confrontation with the German church problem and the beginning of the 'Church, Community and State' planning, but declined because it was the only time he could take his children on holiday.[38] Nevertheless the subject of co-operation with other ecumenical movements was thoroughly discussed at the I.M.C. committee meeting at Salisbury in July 1934 and the progress from the Bishopthorpe meeting explained. The I.M.C. officers were given a mandate to continue developing such contacts provided that 'the complete autonomy and liberty of independent action of the I.M.C. should in no way be impaired'.[39] So, simply in respect of Paton's activities alone it is not true to say, as it is stated in the Rouse and Neill 'History of the Ecumenical Movement', that there were no immediate practical results of the Bishopthorpe meeting.[40] A meeting in Paris in April 1934 of eight of the original collaborators produced a useful number of decisions on practical aspects of co-operation.[41]

Paton was absent in the Far East from September 1935 to April 1936, but while he was unable to participate in any discussions in England, he built up contacts for Life and Work and Faith and Order in the Far East.[42] Oldham, meanwhile, had produced a memorandum which inspired further action, including the formation of a 'Committee of Thirty-Five' of which Paton was a member, though most of its members had been appointed by the summer conferences of Life and Work and Faith and Order.[43] The committee was charged with reviewing what had been accomplished in terms of co-operation so far, and making fresh recommendations to the 1937 world conferences. A deliberate attempt was made to include lay people and members of the youth movements.

When the Committee of 35 met in October 1936, Paton and Oldham dominated the proceedings with a single closely reasoned argument. Paton opened by agreeing with Tatlow, Hodgson and those who opposed the idea of an ecumenical organisation which would make public pronouncements, not because he thought this was dangerous but because he thought it was useless. (As will be shown in Chapter XII, he apparently revised this view when he was actually secretary of the W.C.C.F.) He then launched out on the subject of the two possible lines of direction for the ecumenical movement, that of thought and that of action. He supported Oldham's arguments to the hilt for an ecumenical central research body to give systematic and continuous thought to the problems facing the churches and to the practical information necessary for the churches to make decisions on matters of policy, for example on relations between church and state. Oldham emphasized the difficulties of getting together a manageable and representative ecumenical group, and taking sufficient account of different national situations. The I.M.C. had a common goal of evangelism, but no such shared interest united the other bodies, in practical activities. He therefore suggested a small body drawn from the larger denominations meeting annually, and a larger conference meeting at intervals. Henriod then came up with ways of broadening out and uniting the existing structure to achieve this end.[44]

There is evidence that during these months until the 1937 conferences, Paton performed a very useful role, explaining the doubts of Faith and Order to Life and Work (usually in the shape of Henriod) since from 1935 he attended all the meetings of the Faith and Order Continuation Committee, and vice versa.[45] He was appointed to the sub-committee of the Committee of 35 which drew up the actual motion presented to the conferences at Oxford and Edinburgh. Shortly before the conferences, the Committee of 35 met at Westfield College, London, and achieved unanimity on the question of a body, to be called, at Dr Cavert's suggestion, the World Council of Churches, which would be representative of the churches and would continue the work of Life and Work and Faith and Order, in order to facilitate corporate action by the churches, to promote co-operation in study, to promote the growth of ecumenical consciousness in the churches, to consider the establishment of an ecumenical journal, to co-operate with the confessional alliances and to call world conferences on specific subjects as and when necessary. Only a general outline of the constitution of this body was drafted.[46] The final draft was completed by the Utrecht meeting.

At the Oxford conference the proposals met with no opposition, but at Edinburgh Bishop Headlam led a small resistance party. The crucial debate was late at night, but delegates felt a sense of urgency which would not permit them to consent to an adjournment. The vote was eventually taken with a few dissident voices, but the result of the amendments to the original action was that the Faith and Order department was incorporated into the W.C.C.F. as an independent department which could organize its own conferences, raise funds and have members who were not necessarily members of the W.C.C.[47] It led to a very anomalous situation as Life and Work handed over all its resources to the Provisional Committee. This was formed from the Committee of 14 which had been elected jointly by the two conferences. Temple was the chairman of the Provisional Committee, Boegner and Archbishop Germanos were vice-chairmen, and Visser't Hooft and Paton were officially appointed secretaries at the Utrecht meeting. Henriod found himself passed over and resigned the Life and Work secretaryship in 1937.[48] The Faith and Order conditions, concerning the definitions of the W.C.C.F's authority, the 'Basis' of the new organization, which Visser't Hooft also insisted must be undeniably Christological, and the independence of the Faith and Order Department, proved to be the most time-consuming questions at the Utrecht meeting, but in the 1950-68 period the provisions made for Faith and Order at Utrecht have proved to be very valuable in the W.C.C's approach to Orthodox and Catholic churches. The Committee of 35 and the Provisional Committee were fortunate in having Temple, with his unlimited patience and his drafting skill in the chair at these meetings.[49] Oldham, however, was driven to remark when he first read the conditions, that Faith and Order had got married, but wished to remain single.

Prospects concerning the idea of a 'Basis' were conveyed to the Utrecht meeting from the International Association for Liberal Christianity and Religious Freedom, the British Assembly of Unitarian and Free Christians, and the Czechoslovakian church. However, to Leonard Hodgson's amazement, for some time the debate centred on whether the Apostles' Creed or the Nicene Creed should be adopted as the basis of membership for the churches. The Orthodox insisted that there must be a statement of faith so that they could explain to their fellow Christians on what basis they were able to build friendships with other churches, but such influential figures as the Bishop of Novi Sad of Life and Work thought that since the Faith and Order basis had been used successfully for so long, it should be retained, and this view prevailed. Paton did not contribute to the debate, and I do not know what his view was, but probably he would have agreed with those who urged that the membership should be as wide as possible, and that the reasons for having a Basis of a doctrinal nature should be explained as carefully as possible. Interestingly, no-one raised the question which had troubled him so much in the S.C.M., that of member branches who originally adhered to the Basis of membership and then dropped it. Later in the W.C.C's history, there was a resolution that the W.C.C. would conduct no heresy hunt to determine whether members really held the Basis or not. If they had once subscribed to it that was sufficient.[50]

The discussion on the authority of the W.C.C.F. was inconclusive. Those present were opposed to general statements being issued, Temple insisted that conference resolutions of meetings be published, but they would not bind the churches to any particular action. A subject of much greater and profounder discussion was the task of the W.C.C.F., particularly relief work and study. The question of the authority of the W.C.C.F. was closely bound up with the question of representation. While various delegates spoke up for certain sections — women, young people, blacks, members of the 'younger churches', and minority churches, Temple and Paton spoke of the difficulty that appointment of delegates by the churches inevitably led to the selection of those 'in orders', advanced in age and occupied primarily with ecclesiastical administration, yet it would be impossible to secure agreement except on this basis of selection.[51] Paton proposed a quota of non-voting consultants in order to ensure both lay representation and an adequate number of scholars. Considering the analysis of the sections of the church which delegates at the Uppsala World Assembly of the W.C.C. in 1968 represented, his words were unfortunately prophetic.[52] Paton was secretary of the drafting committee of the constitution which had to grapple with all these problems. It was intended that this constitution should be the basis of the World Assembly to be called in 1941, which would ratify it. Because of the hostilities of the Second World War the assembly could not meet until 1948, by which time two meetings of the Provisional Committee had modified some of the details. In fact the constitution is remarkably uncluttered and flexible, though it could not provide for every contingency which arose.[53]

It seems from what evidence survives of Paton's contribution to the formation of the W.C.C. that his efforts were qualitative rather than quantitative. He did not produce a great number of ideas, but he concentrated on what were to him the vital issues and spoke to those. He was a useful mediator between those involved, and to some extent an independent party whom Life and Work and Faith and Order members turned to. In representing the I.M.C. he had his own unique element to bring, to remind delegates that the Oecumene is not confined to America and Europe, and neither he nor Oldham hesitated to put the experience of the I.M.C. at the disposal of the meetings with which he was concerned. One suspects that it was this 'backroom' activity which earned him the position of part-time general secretary. There was apparently much debate as to whether Visser't Hooft was not too young at 37 for the position, which Temple discounted in arguing his candidature.[54] Paton provided a balance, since he was closer to the generation of most of those involved in the discussions. In fact, the two men complemented each other very well, at this stage working together very effectively. With Henry Smith Leiper as associate secretary in New York the movement must have seemed well-balanced. The principal problem was that the little group who had been involved in the discussion from the beginning understood the significance of what was happening, but few people outside did. Neither was the national machinery very adequate to support the W.C.C.F. in all countries. In May 1938 the principal feeling was that it was remarkable that things had been settled so amicably, and there was much hope for the future.

The extent of Paton's conversion from caution to enthusiastic support for the W.C.C.F. can be measured from the address which Paton gave to the Tambaram

I.M.C. meeting.[55] He spoke about God's gracious purpose in allowing them to meet at all at Tambaram. The mystery of the divine grace seems greater as one contrasts it with human pride and the struggle for power. They were now seeing the reality of world community as he said:

> 'We do not begin to understand the meaning of the Church until it has dawned on our minds that the fellowship which we know and enjoy is not the expression only of a common purpose of our own, but it is rather the recognition that something has been done for us by God . . . we must begin from an act of God's grace, which it is right for us to humbly and gratefully acknowledge, the fact that in recent years there has been an increase in the degree to which the existence of a world Christian community is acknowledged'.

The proposals to form a World Council of Churches were, he continued, in some ways the most significant attempt to gather the various movements into a world Christian fellowship. The W.C.C. is a symbol of the Church within the churches, an acknowledgment of the existence of a universal fellowship in spite of the ecclesiastical divisions. The I.M.C. had something of priceless value to give to the ecumenical movement, the reminder of the Christian obligation to evangelize the world. Without this the ecumenical movement could hardly live. The pursuit of church unity should not be conducted for the sake of making the church respected, efficient or successful. There is no Church without the Cross. It was fashionable to stress the tension which exists between the temporal and the eternal, the practical exigencies of life and the Christian duties: 'If this notion is not deeply accepted in the innermost soul, the dialectical approach may come to mean nothing more than a pompous name for moral lethargy. It may become nothing more than a way of excusing to ourselves an attitude of armchair passivity. We, like most other Christians, are burdened by a sense of futility. We have not got clear answers and have a limited amount of sympathy. It is more important to recognize that we have not entered deeply enough into the distinctive Christian experience'. This must be the starting point, that the churches acknowledge their need for forgiveness and mediate it to others, the latter being impossible without the former step. It is time to acknowledge that we are not serious in our acceptance of it. Paton's judgment was that progress to church union would not be so slow if the churches took seriously their common fellowship in Christ.

This emphasis on the pain and difficulty of proceeding to union presumably springs from his experience of negotiations for the W.C.C.F., but his belief that accepting the forgiveness mediated by Christ and obeying him is consistent with what is known of his own conversion experience and the Gospel he learnt through the S.C.M. Unfortunately the outbreak of war prevented the development of a proper system of co-operation between the I.M.C. and the W.C.C.F. A joint committee was set up, but never met until the end of hostilities; co-ordination depended entirely on Paton, who wrote a number of letters during the war to Visser't Hooft raising the question of the participation of the younger churches in the W.C.C.F. He took care to see that Visser't Hooft and the other office-holders in the W.C.C.F. knew what was happening to the missions in wartime, but he died before a proper institutional relationship could be evolved. It seems the consensus of opinion of these whom I have interviewed, that, had he lived, he would have ensured a greater degree of participation from the younger churches immediately after the war.

Chapter XI

Allowing Christians in Germany to choose the date of their own crucifixion: Paton's Relationship to the Confessing Church

Hanns Lilje told an audience of English S.C.M. members, when a student was demanding that the Evangelical Churches take a stronger stand against Hitler, not to over-simplify the situation. The Evangelical Churches would oppose the interference in church affairs, but 'You must allow us the right to fix the date of our own crucifixion'; words which sum up Paton's attitude.[1] Paton, like many of the friends of the Confessing Church in England, listened sympathetically and did his best to protect those like Lilje who visited him and tried to keep him informed of the significance of the German Church struggle, but he did not actively intervene until it was a question of finding support for the Confessing Church in England, 1938-46. There is not the scope within one chapter to discuss fully the repercussions of the church struggle in Germany on the English churches or on the ecumenical movement, although the significance of the German Church struggle for the formation of the W.C.C.F. has been discussed in the preceding chapter and in my Master of Arts' thesis. Significant full-length studies have already been completed by J.S. Conway, Daphne Hampson and Armin Boyens, among others.[2] The amount of original documentation is vast, which is the more remarkable when one considers that it belongs to the genre of samizdat literature.[3] Yet from this sea of literature it is very difficult to make meaningful generalisations, to draw theological conclusions or to do more than protest about the romanticism which surrounds the names of a few and which ignores the dilemma of the many. As J.S. Conway remarked, the battlelines are still drawn in Germany and Switzerland. The controversy has by no means subsided, but has become institutionalized, with the setting up of institutes of 'Kirchliche Zeitgeschichte'.[4] This development does allow for the systematic treatment of material, but whether greater understanding will follow is difficult to say. In view of the nature of the subject, it is necessary to preface this chapter with a few general remarks, but basically one must discuss what Paton did, rather than the part which anyone else played in the drama, especially because it is so dangerous to stereotype the reactions to the Nazi assault on the German churches. There have been various attempts, now discredited, to show that the class element formed the basis of resistance to Hitler, particularly with regard to the attempts to assassinate him.[5] In actual fact, one finds aristocrats, professional soldiers, former trade unionists, university graduates and intensely conservative churchmen among those arrested and executed for supposed complicity. However, in a police state, the plotters naturally trusted their friends and families first, and this is presumably one of the reasons why Paton became involved. As early as 1939 he became aware of the possibility of a military coup. The first communication he received was from Adam von Trott zu Solz in September 1940, followed by Bonhoeffer's approach in October 1941. Both would have known of his access to many of the policy makers in Whitehall and Chatham House. Bonhoeffer would have known of his friendship with Lilje, Bell, Koechlin and Visser't Hooft, and according to Professor Fenn, had met Paton, though Bethege can find no proof of this. Adam von Trott knew Paton through Lindsay of Balliol, Toynbee and Zimmern. This is why Paton took the reports of a possible overthrow of the German government seriously, though he may have been too cautious because he disliked Schönfeld and distrusted his optimistic reports of widespread resistance, and imminent coups.[6] Similarly, the rebuff from Eden, the Foreign Secretary in 1941, to the request for encouragement for the German resistance may have been due to Eden's lack of personal contact with those involved as much as to failure of imagination or misguided policy. One striking factor is that throughout the period, Paton was dealing with Germans as decent and law-abiding as himself, also men of principle, who were as far removed from the I.R.A. or the international terrorist of today, as he himself was from shooting anyone in cold blood.[7]

One assertion which one hears frequently when discussing the position of Paton or Bell on the Confessing Church struggle, is that the situation was never understood in England. In view of the language difference, the difference in democratic and theological traditions, and the existence of numerous denominations as well as an established church in England, it would be surprising if this were not so. It is clear from Paton's writings on the Confessing Church struggle that he was acutely conscious of this difference. An examination of his broadcasts shows how much allowance he made for it, though one may always question whether he made sufficient allowance.[8] For example, knowing the teaching of the centuries of the Lutheran churches on the nature of obedience to the state, he was impressed that there should be signs of resistance from Christian circles. It would seem that his Presbyterian background and his theological standpoint were of considerable advantage to him in understanding the members of the Confessing Church. It is significant that, except on the question of the Peace Aims Group, his contribution to the series of Christian Newsletter Books and Karl Barth's were so close in their analysis of the German situation.[9] As a Presbyterian church leader, Paton could, like Micklem, come and go to Germany without attracting attention, or having his position exploited for propaganda purposes, as in the case of Bishop Headlam.[10]

Nevertheless, after perusing so many letters from those actually involved in the German church struggle, one wonders how many Germans understood the significance of what was happening themselves. Several times Paton was driven to comment about a particular German refugee, that although he was German, he no longer understood what was happening.[11] Paton was one of the few who saw the ecumenical significance of the church struggle. Most Germans did not, and judging by the enormous disparity between the vast number of books analysing the internal significance of the church struggle and the small number written on the ecumenical significance, few do yet. Nygren, Keller and Micklem wrote paperbacks on the subject in vain.[12]

Paton was concerned not only with the position of the German churches and the state, and the significance for the universal church, but also with the practical political questions of the relationship of Germany to Europe and her post-war position. Having shed his pacifism, and having opposed Bell's 'Peace at any price' attitude in November 1939, which will be discussed in the next chapter, Paton took a realistic line, while opposing those of his compatriots who sought the total destruction of Germany. He was seeking to relate the insight of Christian theology to the post-war political settlement, while refusing to allow himself to be swept into an anti-communist position. It will be shown in this chapter how this fundamental disagreement affected the relationship between the British sympathisers of the Confessing Church and Bonhoeffer, Adam von Trott, Leibholz and Visser't Hooft.

Confronted with the situation in Germany, Paton and his friends took certain steps: they kept an informed watch on the situation, they made diplomatic representations, they helped refugees, they gave spiritual support, and they supported the creation of the Confessing Church in England. One must assess how appropriate their action was, and what the alternatives would have been, and whether Paton did enough for Bonhoeffer and the German resistance.

Apart from his own links with German missionary leaders, with Dr. Iserland of the D.I.S.R., who continued in friendly contact with the I.M.C. after he became a Roman Catholic in 1936, and with the members of the I.M.C's sub-committee on Jewish Missions working with refugees, Paton's principal source of information concerning Germany was H.L. Henriod, secretary of Life and Work, and a friend. Henriod's files from 1933 onwards show his deep involvement with the members of the Confessing Church.[13] Whatever criticisms are made of Henriod's failure to adjust to the development of the W.C.C.F., the merit of his position and his attempts to get Life and Work to take an initiative, should not be overlooked.[14] Koechlin made crucial journeys to Germany to try and save the independent Christian youth work there (1934-37). Much has already been written about Oldham's understanding of the position of the Confessing Church at the Fano meeting of the Life and Work executive. As Paton's colleague, it is reasonable to assume that he was also an important informant, as Nathaniel Micklem was. The key person was Hanns Lilje, who deeply impressed Paton when he shared a tent with him at Mysore in 1929, and who was a frequent visitor to England on behalf of the D.S.C.V.[15] Paton himself visited Herrnhut in 1932 and the annual Bremen missionary conferences. When he was in India and Borneo he was given a rapturous welcome by German missionaries, as someone in the Anglo-Saxon world who understood their position and could help them in their isolation. It seems logical to conclude that he possessed a basic empathy with them which they rarely encountered.[16] Nevertheless, it must be admitted that Paton's knowledge was largely secondhand.

Paton did attempt to rectify this by arranging to go on a fact-finding party to Berlin at Easter 1938, organized as in previous years by Amy Buller. Unfortunately Lord Lothian was a key member of this mission, and he decided that as a member of the British government, he would compromise the government by going so soon after the German annexation of Austria. Without him the group fell apart. Behind the scheme was the idea that the group would meet top Nazi leaders and listen to them, while surreptitiously contacting members of the Confessing Church to be briefed on their viewpoint, so that they could ask awkward questions.[17] Would this scheme have worked? Bell encountered enormous difficulties arranging a post-Oxford goodwill visit to the Evangelical Churches, which Bishop Marahrens unsuccessfully tried to postpone. The visit by Bell, Koechlin, Oldham and Fuglsang-Damgaard was a very delicate operation, but much appreciated by German church leaders.[18] It might have benefited Paton to experience the Nazi propaganda vehicle personally. The problem repeatedly debated by English church leaders was whether their intervention would endanger the lives of the Christians in Germany. Frau Niemöller was adamant about the value of Bell's interest in her husband's case. It seems that as in the case of Soviet dissidents, knowledge and intervention by outside public figures did provide some measure of protection, though Paton did wonder if the reverse was true in Niemöller's case. The Confessing Church had its own system of praying for those pastors who disappeared or were swallowed up in concentration camps, whose numbers have never been counted; but in the absence of any organisation comparable to Amnesty International, there was very little that could be done directly by English churchmen. They were not even able to prevent Bishop Headlam writing to 'The Times' that Niemöller deserved his incarceration.[19]

It seems a faintly ridiculous and an inadequate way of conducting the debate, that so much importance was attached to the correspondence columns of 'The Times', especially since relatively few Germans would buy 'The Times'. Even though one may be tempted to believe that Paton bought 'The Times' solely for the crossword, since that was the first thing he looked at, 'The Times' was probably his most frequent secular source of information. 'The Times' had a social and political significance before the war which it has subsequently been forced to share with 'The Guardian' and 'The Daily Telegraph'. Paton used 'The Times' as an authoritative source of information, lunched with the editor periodically, and supplied information on the Far East.[20] It will be shown in the next chapter, however, that, in considering the most appropriate action for the executive of the W.C.C.F. in the time of war, he was very cautious about the use of 'The Times' for ecumenical statements. Paton had reservations about Bell's use of 'The Times' to champion the Confessing Church.[21]

Richard Crossman and Richard Gutteridge also supplied Paton with accurate and profound reports on Germany.[22] Paton developed contacts with the German Social Democrats in exile and received their newsletter and literature 1939-43. Paton was also the object of Mrs. Buxton's attentions, though it was Bishop Bell who was the principal victim of her agitation about 'atrocities'. Paton devoted much energy to explaining to Mrs Buxton that the leaders of the Confessing Church wanted support on religious and theological grounds, not political agitation from an outside power, and that they were fighting to maintain the purity of the Gospel, not the right of freedom of religion, since there was no evidence that Rosenberg was officially backed by the German government.[23] Therefore Paton, Elmslie, Garbett and Fenn discreetly collected a group of churchmen to study the German Church struggle informally and to activate the networks of church information in order to get the ordinary congregation praying for Christians in Germany in an informed way. Paton lobbied the episcopal bench discreetly. The entire discussion was closely linked with the question of practical help for refugees. Paton explained the idea in a lengthy letter to Alan Don, Archbishop Lang's senior chaplain.

The small committee, he wrote, had been chosen to include all kinds of people, from whom the suggestion had come that they frame a statement to focus on the central religious issues, and to separate them from the controversial political questions which fill most people's minds when they think about Germany. It would provide information for both prayer and preaching. Paton then explained how he proposed to get the statement to the maximum number of Anglicans possible, with the support of Bell and Garbett. To Garbett, who wanted a clause concerning the persecution of Christians in Russia, Paton wrote that the German Church Struggle raised special questions for our own Christian faith which the confrontation between Christianity and Communism in Russia did not.[24]

This approach of Paton's is derived directly from messages which W.T. Elmslie brought back from German Confessing Church leaders when he visited friends in Germany privately in March 1938. The consensus of opinion which he reported, was that political pressure would be useful if Germany were seeking an alliance with England, but this was doubtful. Non-political action, and friendly approaches by Lord Lothian or Lord Halifax would be appreciated, but the distinction must be made that the fight is for the purity of the Gospel, not freedom of religion. Böhm wanted frequent letters and messages to impress the government censors intercepting them, but the others wanted friendly letters only. Other suggestions including sending British students to the clandestine theological seminaries (similar to Finkenwalde which Bonhoeffer had directed). Above all, the British must strive to understand the situation.[25]

Two documents emanated from the group, both of which display signs of Paton's hand in the drafting.[26] The pamphlet 'National Socialism and the German Evangelical Church. What is the issue?' is an attempt to set out factually the criticisms made of the Christian Church by the National Socialist party and state, and the replies of the churches. Careful study of these suggests that 'there is an essential incompatibility between the Christian point of view and that of the National Socialist Party . . . that National Socialism is in itself a religion which is gradually enforcing its claim over the whole of life and cannot admit of any rival'. If this is the case, the pamphlet concludes, the Christian Church faces a grave responsibility because the cause of Christianity is one. (Professor Fenn remembers that Paton's chief concern in these discussions was to see the problem in the context of the universal Church.) The pamphlet explains the rise of the 'German Christians' and the 'Confessing Church', but concentrates on the position of Dr Zoellner, moderate president of the central 'Reich Church Committee', in resigning in protest at government interference in internal church affairs.[27] The pamphlet links the attack on the Church with the persecution of the Jews, a link which Paton had made as early as 1935.[28]

The other document is much longer although it covers similar ground. In 'The lessons and claims of the German Church conflict' it is also argued that the struggle is not political in the sense that that word is normally understood, but Micklem's summarization is quoted: 'The Protestants would have us understand that the integrity of the Christian Gospel is at stake; the Romans that Christian civilization is at stake. I think they are both right'. (Micklem had visited Germany privately on several occasions and had established close contacts with German Catholics.) Finally, it was stated that 'The Christian cause in the world is essentially one . . . the fate of the German Church will affect the witness of the Church at large, the particular witness made by the German church in this hour of crisis deserves the attention of all who have the Christian Gospel at heart'.

Unlike the first pamphlet, attention is given to the Roman Catholic position but for the sake of brevity there is more emphasis on the Protestant position. It is in fact a very good brief analysis which can be supported by what modern research has uncovered.[29] The various shades of opinion on tactics within the Confessing Church are described from Würm to Barth with sympathy and insight, but with the caution:

'Our sympathies easily go out to them (i.e. those inspired by Karl Barth) but much of our sympathy ignores the very vital differences between our own general theological views and theirs. For most British Christians their theological position would be foreign and repugnant, and their political views highly conservative. They themselves are aware that they are fighting that in Germany which has its counterpart wherever there is no clear frontier drawn between Christianity and culture. Their stand calls much of our own witness in question, no less than that of the German Christians. It is impossible to give them the sympathy we should extend unless it is based on understanding and recognition of these differences'.

This is an extremely important ecumenical statement, especially when one reads Dillistone's account of the sundering of the relationship between Raven and Hildebrandt (a non-Aryan pastor who had been in exile in Cambridge since 1937) over Hildebrandt's book 'This is the Message' (1944), which was an unsuccessful attempt to explain his position to a liberal Anglican.[30] Paton's group faced the difficulty, then faced Rosenberg's ideology and its implication, and finally listened carefully to the words of Confessing Church leaders: 'First be faithful to the Gospel in your own setting, second understand what we are contending for, then pray for us in such spiritual solidarity as God gives us', and this is said to be worth more than political demonstrations, and also to be much more difficult. This pamphlet has been quoted at such length, because however much Paton wrote of it, it gives the clue to most of his actions for the Confessing Church until Bonhoeffer and Adam von Trott moved ahead and demanded his help for their plots to overthrow Hitler. It explains Paton's emphasis on gathering as much accurate information on the German Church struggle as possible, and the steps which he took to strengthen the spiritual position of the Confessing Church. Hanns Lilje's influence is very great, which is not surprising since he and Pierre Maury came to England to spend a weekend with Amy Buller's frustrated expedition three months before this pamphlet was written. It can be detected by comparing the argument of the documents with Lilje's book 'In the Valley of the Shadow', in which he describes the reasons why he was not actively involved in the plots to assassinate Hitler, but concentrated on giving spiritual support in strictly non-political terms to those who were.[31]

Unfortunately, in spite of the importance of these documents, Lang refused to sanction their circulation in the Church of England because he said it would cause another flare-up of the Bell v Headlam controversy, and although he had already snubbed Headlam over his visit to Germany, he could not afford to be too partisan. Paton was very disappointed because he felt this missed the whole point of the statement, which called for prayer, not political action. He detected the hand of Alan Don in delaying the document and in creating difficulties for him at the printers, S.P.C.K. Lang's view was that his Council on Foreign Relations was the body which should act, rather than Paton's ad hoc group. Bell himself criticized the document as being too much of a manifesto and its publication as a waste of money when they should have been concentrating on an appeal for refugees. So the documents died an unnatural death, though the thinking behind them continued to motivate the group.[32]

The most significant steps taken by the group as a result of their thinking together were those to make arrangements for services in German and English for Confessing Church refugees and their friends. The importance of these services, held at St John's, Smith Square, is discussed by Jasper and by Bethge in their respective biographies of Bell and Bonhoeffer.[33] It took Paton and Garbett, who were backed by Fenn and Welch of the Religious Broadcasting Department of the B.B.C. and who ruthlessly exploited their contacts in the Ministry of Information, eighteen months to wear down the B.B.C's objections to broadcasting services in German to Germany. The official argument was that religion was not to be used as propaganda against Germany, and that Confessing Church leaders like Büsing, Rieger and Hildebrandt should not be exposed to the charge of being traitors in Germany. This sensitivity drew scepticism from Paton, who felt that the B.B.C. disliked broadcasting religious services, and that Rieger's choir singing Bach chorales could hardly be called political. Similarly he fought the Ministry of Information hard to get German pastors and refugees the opportunity to give spiritual talks, but the only concession in his lifetime was to allow sermons starting from August 1942 (cold feet at the B.B.C. prevented the Easter Message for 1942 being broadcast in German), and for Micklem to broadcast a weekly religious news bulletin in German which Paton helped to prepare. By wooing Crossman Paton finally won the case.[34]

Paton's difficulties with the B.B.C. should be seen in the context of the B.B.C's total broadcasting policy. The B.B.C. had been threatened with total closure in 1939 by Neville Chamberlain, who was not the only highly literate man who failed to imagine how vital the B.B.C. would become to the British propaganda effort. Then the government tried to subordinate the B.B.C. to the propaganda effort completely. Nevertheless the B.B.C., while under the control of Electra House (the Foreign Office), did genuinely strive to present factual news and a full broadcasting programme, as well as relaying messages to the various resistance movements. It is odd that Paton, whose broadcasts 1941-42 are so outspoken an attack on Nazi ideology, should have failed to see the difficulty about services and sermons in German. It is probably because he was so imbued with the religious approach to the problems of the Confessing Church as contained in the documents quoted, and because he saw the services as a medium of evangelism. Compared with the anti-German hysteria of the first World War, the fact that broadcasts were made in German was in itself remarkable. With religious propaganda in the hands of the Ministry of Information, Religious Affairs Division, the B.B.C. could afford to be more impartial.

Nevertheless, to revert briefly to the ban on pacifists discussed in Chapter III, such was the hold that the idea of a Confessing Church had got on the minds of Billy Greer and Alan Booth of the S.C.M., Eric Fenn and others, that they threatened to start a 'Confessing Church' (cutting across all the denominations) on the issue, and Paton had to work hard to dissuade them on the grounds that no theological issue was involved, and that they should hold their fire for an occasion when the State might, under the pressure of war, try and corrupt the Christian Gospel.[35]

Since Paton was a Christian very much involved in political issues such as independence for India, and who was fully prepared to involve the churches in political protest, as in the case of the B.B.C's absolute ban on pacifists, it is the more remarkable that he treated the Confessing Church issue as a religious issue (and therefore to him a more profound issue). Undoubtedly this was because he saw that the root of the problem was theological and ecumenical and much more than a question of an adjustment of Church-State relationships. The most commendable aspect of his attitude is his careful alignment with the desires of the Confessing Church leaders themselves, instead of imposing his own ideas on how the campaign should be conducted on the problem, or allowing his own personality to embroil him with any one adversary, to the detriment of the principle involved, as Bell did in his confrontations with Headlam.

After the outbreak of hostilities, Paton's sources of information were limited to the letters and news-sheets which Koechlin and Visser't Hooft sent him, based on W.C.C.F. and Resistance sources; the Ministry of Information's sources, apart from the news-sheets which they appropriated from Visser't Hooft; and Swedish sources.[36] Unlike his American colleagues who were responsible for two very dangerous 'leaks', Paton was scrupulously careful to re-process information so that clandestine sources would not be exposed to German retaliation.[37] In 1942 he wrote a little booklet 'Continental Christianity in Wartime', which is significant for the way in which he weaves together information from the three sources mentioned, for the way in which he avoids using Visser't Hooft's 'classified' information on Eastern Europe, and for the sympathetic way in which he attempts to understand the position of Christians in Finland and France who felt betrayed by the British, or of those who are retreating into religious life and ignoring the malevolence of the German occupying powers.[38] The purpose of the booklet is to demonstrate that the way of life in what is known as 'Christian civilization' is at stake, that even where it is under most pressure the Church (in the widest sense of the word) has shown remarkable resilience, and that in Europe a revival is taking place as the Church proves to be the only institution built on a rock.

Although much independent evidence could be marshalled in support of Paton's arguments, it is strange that though well-informed, Paton did not detect the ultimate aim of the Third Reich: the destruction of the Church.[39] He merely comments that this was the effect of the occupation of Posen and quotes the warnings of Peter Drucker and Hermann Rauschnig concerning the Nazi doctrine of nihilism. Instead his attention is drawn to the anti-Jewish measures and the growing unity of the Church in the face of persecution. The pamphlet is commendable for its brevity and measured understatement. Almost identical arguments were used in 'Christian Counter-attack', a book written by Martin, Newton, Waddams and Williams of the Ministry of Information Religious Affairs Division, but expounded at such length that they are by comparison clumsy and overstated.[40]

Paton's final position on the Confessing Church question can be seen in a letter he wrote to the Confessing Church news-sheet in February 1942 on the subject of peace aims.

> 'You are afraid that there will be a desire to overlook any contribution which the German churches can make to their sister churches, and that the Christians and the churches of Germany should be conceived of as just pawns to be moved on the ecclesiastical board, not as parts of the Church of God to whom God also speaks, and who, as listening to Him, have themselves the right to speak . . . it may be that British Christians have erred by lack of tact or sympathy in what they have said in conversation with the Christians of Germany . . . if this is so, we can only ask for your forgiveness, and for your belief that fundamentally we are in no kind of doubt of our fellowship with you in the universal Church'.

Acknowledging that he knows less than his friends about the German church struggle, he continues: 'The plain truth is that the entire Christian society throughout the world lies under a debt of gratitude to those Christians in Germany who at infinite cost to themselves, with complete disregard for their own personal future, and an entire reliance upon God, preferred to obey the word of God rather than the word of man'.[41]

If Paton's stand seems insignificant, then one must turn to the pages of the 'Volkische Beobachter', and the wrath which Paton attracted from its correspondent, Wilhelm Brachmann in March 1938.[42] Paton's speeches at Oxford are singled out as a 'collapse into liberalism', and as an example of the way in which the world ecumenical movement is fraternizing with 'Rome'. This can be seen, Brachmann argues, in the way in which both preach 'universalism' and a common 'humanity' instead of a racial philosophy.

> 'Mr Paton explained that the cause of the 'community' must render it a matter of reproach to those who want to separate off the life of a People on such grounds as Race, Soil, History and Spirit. The basis of the Church was not the Nation but Humanity, to which the Jews also belong, and Mr Paton expressed himself strongly on their behalf. Such ideas were continually heard at Oxford. . . . The conference indulged in dreams of a 'humanity' which does not exist at all when they imagined a universalistic world outlook in contrast to racial philosophy . . . '

It is evident from this that Paton had hit the target he was aiming at. As was stated in my M.A. thesis, there are considerable grounds for arguing that the significance of the Oxford Life and Work conferences was better understood by those who opposed it, than by the Christians who lived in the same milieu as the conference participants. In fact the Volkische Beobachter's attack on Paton became so vitriolic that it was mentioned in a B.B.C. news item the same month. According to Paton's family, he took great pride in the discovery by British intelligence that his name was on the list of those who were not to survive a Nazi invasion of Britain.[43]

Similarly, the W.C.C.F. may have seemed a very weak and new organization to support the Confessing Church, but a directive from an S.S. Hauptsturmfuhrer to the Sicherheitsdienst R.F.S.S. of Würtemburg/Baden/Pfalz/Saar dated 15.2.1938. shows that the ecumenical movement was equated with international Freemasonry, Jewry and Marxism as a dangerous and subversive organization to be undermined at all costs.[44]

Since Paton's approach was nothing if not practical, his embryonic W.C.C.F. office in London was engulfed in relief work for aliens, refugees and prisoners of war as soon as war broke out. In October 1940 he wrote to Visser't Hooft that half his time was spent on work for refugees.[45] He worked in close partnership with Bishop Bell, whose activities have been described by his biographer.[46] When Bell was arranging a lectureship for Leibholz in the United States, he explained that no decision could be made without Paton.[47] Paton's principal contribution was to be chairman of the Committee for Aliens, Refugees and Prisoners of War, which was formed in September 1939 to help German citizens interned under emergency regulations. It aimed to bring together all the welfare agencies, such as the Society of Friends, the Red Cross, the Y.M.C.A. and so on, in one committee, so that there was no duplication or overlapping, but a nationwide strategy. As with the C.B.M.S., a common front was formed in tackling the Home Office or the War Office. Paton worked as strenuously as Bell to get individuals released when they were intially interned in September 1939, when they were reinterned during a panic about quislings in May 1940, and in subsequent arbitrary rearrests. Like Bell he not only fought the red tape (he was very critical of the government's hasty deportation of a number of German refugees to camps in the West Indies in October 1939), but he exercised a real pastoral ministry in helping the German pastors of the Confessing Church reconcile themselves with their fate. His argument was that while they were imprisoned they had an excellent opportunity for ministry and evangelism of other Germans. His visits to the camps were very greatly appreciated by the internees, though it is doubtful whether they would have appreciated the rhyme he used to repeat in the office:

> 'Come to the beautiful Isle of Man —
> Do get interned if you possibly can!
> You can lie in the sun, and bathe in the sea
> Safely interned under Rule 18b'

(This was of course when the ordinary citizen could not bathe in the sea for barbed wire or travel restrictions.) His committee (which later divided itself into two halves, one half for aliens and refugees, the other for prisoners of war) was responsible for finding materials and means to enable the internees to relieve their boredom. Miss Morden remembers him joking that he had 'made a new Diehl' by visiting Pastor Diehl on the Isle of Man and cheering him up. He himself insisted that Confessing Church pastors should be interned in groups, and not be isolated among Nazi prisoners.[48] The wider ecumenical significance of Paton's work for refugees will be considered in the context of the W.C.C.F. ministry in wartime in the following chapter.

A typical Paton act of faith was his belief that ultimately the Allies would win the war. How many years the struggle would take, and how much devastation would have been wrought by the Nazis on the Christian Church before this victory, he did not know; and therefore his participation in the German Confessional Institute was part of his long-term strategy for the reconstruction of Christian institutes in Europe and his desire to help the Confessing Church survive.[49] Until his death he was chairman of the committee concerned with forming a Confessing Church Institute, and it was entirely due to his midwifery that the Institute saw the light of day, and that a group of highly individualistic German pastors were enabled to train ordinands and lay workers for Christian witness on their return to Germany.

The original plan as written down by Büsing envisaged using one of the colleges at Selly Oak, Birmingham, with a staff of two resident lecturers, one principal, and occasional non-resident lecturers. It would aim at producing not only German ordinands to replace the losses to the Confessing Church in Germany, but also at educating them in Anglo-Saxon theology and involving English students in the study of German theology, in particular, non-Aryan students. There was no question of founding another English denomination, but of helping those refugees who still felt themselves to be part of the Confessing Church. By the end of September 1942 Pastor Rieger had produced a highly practical version of these plans.[50] The committee sent a questionnaire to Christian German refugees, and were amazed to receive replies from 65 refugees committing themselves to study at the Institute, either full-time or part-time, if this could be arranged with the Ministry of Labour and National Service. In fact, it was not possible for the majority of postulant students to gain such release and the Institute was, at Paton's insistence, refashioned to provide evening classes and part-time study courses.[51] Bishop Bell gave the inaugural lecture on 2nd November 1942 on 'The spiritual situation on the European Continent. Impressions from a journey to Sweden'. This was the beginning of a programme on German literature, politics, sociology and so on by Ehrenberg, Leibholz and Rieger. In London under the blitz it was very difficult to find permanent accommodation for the Institute; ironically the first offer of a permanent home was received at the meeting at which silence was kept for several minutes in memory of Paton, and Bell was elected chairman in his place.[52]

The situation was in many ways comparable to the Paris Mission's London committee of which Paton was Chairman, mentioned in Chapter VIII.[53] The German pastors were inclined to behave like a government in exile, and argue the theory of the situation endlessly while failing to achieve anything practical. Paton wrote to Simpson.

> 'I am a little alarmed occasionally by the keen desire of the German pastors who are on the committee for our German theological institute to keep the whole thing very German, very confessional, and I wish I saw among them more dispositon to learn something from us poor Anglo-Saxon blighters! However, that will change, I think, so at least I confidently expect'.[54]

On the other hand, Paton received fierce criticism from Ehrenberg, a non-Aryan pastor from Heidelberg, to the effect that one could not transplant the illegal Confessing Church seminaries to England, although the Confessing Church spiritually must be maintained. He was also very opposed to the name of the Institute and the phrase 'Confessional' being used to cover a syllabus of secular subjects, even philosophy. There was very great tension between the majority of Paton's committee and Carl Schweitzer, another refugee scholar, who mistakenly thought he had been excluded from the committee and who set out to found a rival institute specifically for lay-training in Wistow, a country house in Leicestershire so remote that R.R. Williams was driven to declare that only students wishing to take the veil would study there. Paton had to reconcile the two factions, prevent Büsing resigning in protest and raise money and facilities for the London Institute. In April 1943 he wrote to Schweitzer:

> '. . . the patience of some of the committee is drawing near to an end (this is rather like Adolf Hitler) and if the whole matter (of the nature of the two institutes) is reopened I am afraid they will wash their hands of it . . . I shall myself be unable to give further time to the subject, I am terribly busy and have already spent a great deal of time in endless discussions. I have come to the conclusion that rightly or wrongly the only way forward is a modest beginning to be actually made. So soon as action begins, the realities of the situation can be tested, but so long as nothing is done, we are left with the endless bandying of theories'.[55]

Fortunately, Paton had found in Dr Emmerich a refugee scholar whose sanity and moderation impressed him and the whole committee, who had no hesitation in appointing him the first principal. Even though it was not entirely clear what he was to be principal of, he was a sterling character whose ordination in the Church of Scotland Paton was able to negotiate without difficulty. Dr Emmerich gave the whole Institute stability and status, particularly during the vicissitudes caused by Schweitzer's 'schism'. Paton himself repented of his loss of patience when he heard of the execution of five students in Munich (the so-called 'White Rose Conspiracy').[56] The heroism of these students, executed for distributing pamphlets critical of national socialism inspired his imagination and determination to get the Confessional Institute going. At the meeting in May, according to Schultz, a member of the Press Room at the Ministry of Information, who was on the committee, Paton and his British friends saved the Institute. Judging by the wealth of material concerning fund-raising and the eventual consensus among the German pastors as to the nature of the Institute, Paton not only saved the Institute by his skills as chairman, but by his practical efforts. His bull-dozing tactics were confined mainly to the dissident minority. In spite of the letter quoted above, he acted as an executive to get a German plan implemented, not a British one. Unfortunately he died before similar efforts were successfully made to start a theological college among prisoners of war in a P.O.W. camp near Nottingham, which was organized with the support of Mansfield College, Oxford, and Nathaniel Micklem, who was also on Paton's committee. Otherwise it would have been interesting to compare the two institutions.[57]

Probably the most controversial question of Paton's whole life will be his response to the plea for help which he received from Adam von Trott zu Solz in September 1940 and May 1942, and from Bonhoeffer in September 1941. The problem is to avoid considering the question retrospectively, or in one single context. I hold no brief for Paton's defence, but I do think that his actions and his assessment of the situation have been seriously underrated. Paton opened his book 'The Church and the New Order' with the confession that in the study of international politics he was an amateur, and in economic questions even less than an amateur. Therefore, one should not expect him to show greater wisdom than professional politicians or, in spite of the closeness of his relationship with Dr Visser't Hooft, to be able to imagine the complexities of the resistance movement in Germany. Visser't Hooft writes that after his visit to England in 1942 he was so appalled at the lack of information in London he sent everything he could to Paton from then onwards. However, reading their correspondence he seems oblivious to the strain and the effect on British morale of the blitz.[58] Therefore it is not surprising that the gulf between Paton and Bonhoeffer and Adam von Trott was even greater. Yet the gulf which preoccupied Paton during the whole sequence of events under discussion was that between England and America, which is why discussion of the 'Peace Aims Group' will be deferred and not considered in this context, where it is usually taken. Everyone whom I have interviewed who was involved in the group refuted Visser't Hooft's post-war argument that the Peace Aims Group was only significant in as far as it stimulated Bonhoeffer's circle. 'The Church and the New Order' and the discussion behind it had its own intrinsic value in British and American circles.

Secondly, it should be remembered that the initiatives from Germany took place when Britain's military position was extremely grave. When Adam von Trott's memorandum arrived in September 1940, the Battle of Britain was at its height, and all the subsequent communications were received before the battle of El Alamein in October 1942 marked the end of the British retreat in Africa. Therefore, had it become known that the British government was in communication with any section of the German government or a new German government, it would have seemed that there was something lacking in the British determination to win the war. Paton took very seriously the argument that all questions of the final peace settlement should wait until victory was won, but defended the discussion on the grounds that the aims of the war should be carefully thought out (as they were manifestly not in the first World War) and that the discussion was important for ridding the atmosphere of hatred and vindictiveness or any desire for vengeance. Already in July 1940 Paton and Temple were trying to manoeuvre Halifax into making a 'positive' statement of British war aims, without success because, they conjectured, Halifax did not want to bind himself to anything before the threat of invasion receded.[59]

To accuse Paton of complete lack of comprehension is unfair. In March 1939 he wrote to his colleague, Henry Smith Leiper, that there would either be a war or a revolution in Germany in the summer. 'The growing definiteness of commitment to one another of the powers which want to settle things by consent rather than by force may possibly give pause to the German leaders. I fear, however, that, as we are dealing with men who have no shred of ethical principle to guide them and are solely out for power for its own sake, it is little use expecting them to act rationally, still less on moral considerations'.[60]

A more remarkable letter to A.D. Lindsay, the Master of Balliol, concerns the German-Russian pact of 1939, and its significance as far as Russian intentions are concerned. He concludes:

> 'If we push on with a long war, the bolshevisation of Germany would seem to be the only certain result. Do you not think that we should now look for a definite movement of the Army, Foreign Office and old aristocracy to push the National Socialists down the hole and constitute the only alternative government to Communism?'[61]

Unfortunately it is impossible to ascertain whether this letter arises from enlightened guesswork or inside knowledge, because there is no written corroboration in any other letter Paton received.[62] However, the letter was written before Paton visited Copenhagen in search of a negotiated peace. It was probably through Lindsay that von Trott heard of or met Paton, as he had met Oldham at Balliol and in Liverpool. Paton had accurately perceived where the resistance to Hitler lay, and the importance of the fear in these circles of a repetition of the Munich Communist uprising of 1919. Through all the documents Paton received later from resistance circles there runs this thread; fear of Russia and fear of Communism in Germany.[63] Since, with certain exceptions, Britain has been allied with Russia since the reign of Ivan the Terrible, the fear of Russia was one which Paton and his friends could not share. Secondly, the lesson of the Treaty of Brest-Litovsk was interpreted differently in Germany and in Britain. For the Atlantic alliance, it meant that any peace settlement at the end of the war must be one in which all the Allies participated. There could be no separate negotiations by anyone of the Allied powers. A fatal miscalculation of both Adam von Trott and Bonhoeffer was that Britain would act independently of Russia in encouraging the formation of a new German government, and possibly negotiating with it. From the correspondence between Paton, Garbett and Rushbrooke, concerning Garbett's visit to Moscow in 1942, it is clear that they had their eyes open to the nature of Soviet oppression, but that with the majority of the British population, they believed Britain must remain allied to the Russian people in their struggle against the German invasion. Secondly, in the plans for social Communism in England and a welfare state, Temple even advocated economic (as opposed to political) Communism and this caused further differences between Paton and continental Christians. The Bell-Leibholz correspondence reveals that Leibholz caused Paton to modify his views slightly.[64]

Far from failing to react to Bonhoeffer's memorandum of September 1941, in January 1942 Paton was still beavering away, trying to make some impact on government circles and thinking about the implications of the proposed coup d'état. He wrote to his old friend from S.C.M. and I.M.C. days, Edwyn Bevan:

'. . . it is really impossible to make terms with a reformed army regime . . . from a number of quarters, including some of our best continental advisers, it is now plain that this kind of proposal is being put up. I believe it to be true (for I have checked this with some of the government people here) that there is what might be called a Christian-cum-army party growing up which certainly hates the National Socialists though whether it is likely to be strong enough to overcome the Gestapo I gravely doubt. It is further urged, especially by people who are afraid of the bolshevisation of Germany that the only bulwark against such a movement is the German army, and that we should therefore be wise to act on that view. To this I am at present inclined to reply a) for a variety of reasons I do not expect the bolshevisation of Germany, b) I do not see how, with the facts before us, any army regime could be trusted'.[65]

Bevan, Paton and Temple were agreed that the Allies would have to insist on the disarmament of Germany, the occupation of Germany for a set number of years and a definitive European settlement, none of which would be acceptable to the German resistance, but which would prevent the followers of Vansittart destroying Germany and make an economic restoration of Germany possible. Visser't Hooft argued that faced with the prospect of a complete loss of sovereignty, Germans of goodwill would grow desperate and 'escape to worse forms of revolution' since they were afraid of being at the mercy of vengeful nations.[66]

Paton's assessment of the power of the Gestapo was realistic, though obviously he could not have known about the bad luck which dogged the various assassination attempts. One of Paton's problems was that of convincing the British government that such a group existed. R.R. Williams of the Ministry of Information, Religious Affairs Division, did not believe it until a letter dated 30.9.41 between two German Swiss was intercepted which described the army resistance, as well as their own anguish about the silence of the Roman Catholic Church and the B.B.C. on the incompatibility of Hitlerism and the Christian religion.[67] It is clear, too, from an account of an interview which R.R. Williams had with Dr Koeppler of the Political Warfare Division in May 1942, that Koeppler could not be convinced of the strength of the resistance, nor of the importance of changing British propaganda in the direction indicated by Bonhoeffer and Adam von Trott.

To consider the various approaches made to Paton separately, the first direct contact was made by Adam von Trott zu Solz. Miss Gladys Bretherton, Tatlow's secretary from 1910-14, was not only a friend of Paton's while she worked for the S.C.M., but through her work for the Y.W.C.A. and the Girl Guides' Association knew Adam von Trott's mother. Probably this is why, when she was stranded in Geneva in September 1940, and decided to try and reach England, Visser't Hooft showed her a document by Adam von Trott, the contents of which she was to communicate to Paton, David Astor, and Russell Bretherton.[68] Everything was wrapped in great secrecy, she was not allowed to see Adam von Trott himself, or carry the actual document. Her journey was a very long and dangerous one, so that it was two months before Paton received her notes and her account of her conversations in Geneva. When she reached England, it was to a very hostile reception from Paton, who muttered that he wished Visser't Hooft would not play at politics. She was, therefore, indignant when she later learnt of Paton's meetings with Visser't Hooft, and the extent of his involvement in the German political question. She must have caught Paton before his transition from the purely religious and theological position outlined above. His reply to Visser't Hooft was:

> 'I imagine that you would now agree that some of the points then made (two months ago), are rather fantastic today. I wish you could be here for a week, it would open your eyes to a number of things. In saying this, of course, I do not for a moment doubt your own personal attitude, and I can well understand the effect of prolonged contact with the existing order of things around you'.[69]

The document reprinted by Armin Boyens' is an amalgamation of Adam von Trott's memorandum and Visser't Hooft's comments.[70] It is an accurate assessment of the problems of creating a resistance when the German government can claim such economic and military successes, and has achieved such propaganda successes among the younger clergy. Only a small élite motivated by high principles are likely to oppose the government while it is successful, but if the government suffers great reverses, and the war stretches into another winter, then the situation might change profoundly. In such circumstances a magnanimous peace offer might cause a new situation to arise. Such an offer would have to inspire German trust and be far removed from the Versailles treaty or any suggestion of 'doing Germany down', as well as giving Germany her ethnographical boundaries. The document concludes that the struggle is at rock bottom spiritual, and all who believe in law and liberty will have to stand together. It envisages co-operation between the resistance movements of different occupied countries and the German groups, which in fact proved impossible to achieve.

Viewed rationally from a distance of thirty years, the document seems fairly sensible. Yet since Paton was no idealist, as von Trott was, it appeared to him too vague and optimistic and completely unrelated to the British situation, which is probably best typified by the famous Low cartoon of May 1940. This shows Winston Churchill advancing on Europe from the shores of Britain, rolling up his sleeves for a punch-up, followed by a crowd of men doing the same over the caption 'We're right behind you, Winston'.

Visser't Hooft's second attempt on Adam von Trott's behalf was during his visit to Britain in May 1942.[71] Boyens summarizes the documentation in Geneva and in the Public Records Office, but is highly selective in his interpretation and citation of them. It seems from the Public Records Office that Paton and Toynbee had established Visser't Hooft's bona fides. This was quite an achievement in view of the fact that in October 1940 Visser't Hooft had tried to meet Paton in Lisbon using a German visa, which had caused Paton much difficulty, to explain away what a lonely Dutchman isolated in Geneva might do without intending to harm Allied interests.[72] Van Kleffens, a Dutch politician in exile, had influenced the Foreign Office against Adam von Trott's document, which this time did not pass through Paton's hands, though he may have seen it.[74] The principal proposals were that after a coup d'état, anti-semitism would be condemned, the German armies in western and northern Europe would be withdrawn, Austria's fate would be decided by plebiscite, but military guarantees would be necessary before German armies would retreat from the Russian front. Visser't Hooft did have an interview with the Foreign Secretary, Anthony Eden, but got no further than Paton had with Bonhoeffer's proposals. Eden's verdict was that until the plotters achieved something and gave visible signs of their activity they were of little use to England or Germany. The various Foreign Office memoranda collected a variety of comments indicating that the Foreign Office was prepared to exploit the overture for political ends while remaining suspicious of whatever spheres of influence were behind von Trott. Toynbee and Zimmern saw von Trott's memoranda, but they did not object to the conclusion that they were unrealistic, as indeed they were. Eden said he would welcome a change of regime, but would commit himself no further. There is no indication as to who arranged Visser't Hooft's interview with Eden, but one may assume that Paton had a hand in it. Eden's verdict on von Trott, that he was 'a curious mixture of highminded idealism and political dishonesty' is not too far from the truth, although it takes no account of his exceptional courage.

The whole course of Bonhoeffer's thoughts on the consequences of a coup d'état and the future foreign relations of the new state, the meaning of a 'new order' as postulated by Paton, and his attempts to communicate what was happening in Germany to Britain, with a request for encouragement, have been meticulously and systematically treated in Bethge's biography of Bonhoeffer, while there is a shorter summary in Boyens' second volume, and the actual document is published in Bonhoeffer's collected writings.[74] As Bethge points out, there was behind the document Paton received, another draft, closer to Bonhoeffer's own ideas but unintelligible to Anglo-Saxon thinking. Visser't Hooft's role as interpreter was crucial at this point, as in the whole period when he was corresponding with Paton and with contacts in occupied Europe. Nevertheless, this fact lays open the question, that had Paton and Bonhoeffer reached an agreement, the result might have been unacceptable in the unecumenical Confessing Church circles in Germany.[75] Bonhoeffer waited in vain for a response from Paton, but it is very difficult to see what the response could have been. Paton fed Bonhoeffer's ideas into the Peace Aims Group in England and America and Chatham House, but he could not move Eden at all. As in the question of the extermination of the Jews, it was not that he did not understand (the letters to Bevan quoted above remove that possibility) but that he could not do anything.

Boyens draws attention to a note of Churchill's to Eden of January 1941 forbidding any consideration of peace feelers.[76] A further fact which Kenneth Grubb emphasizes is that Churchill abhorred Temple and ignored Bell. Paton, as a close associate of both would not have received a sympathetic hearing, and the Christian nature of the German resistance would have drawn further scorn from that anti-religious aristocrat. Paton received Bonhoeffer's document shortly before another one brought by an American Quaker, Roland Elliott, which was based on Elliott's interview with two Germans in Geneva. The future strategy with regard to German withdrawals is similar to the von Trott proposals, but the document is marked by gross exaggeration of the amount of support in the army. 'They are convinced that there is leadership in the movement, that there may be a coup d'état, and Germans would wake up to find the heads of all the departments changed overnight'. Paton was singularly unimpressed by the document and by Roland Elliott, but its arrival may have blurred his appreciation of Bonhoeffer's efforts.[77]

Bell's encounter with Bonhoeffer in Sweden in October 1942 is too well-known to require description here. Taking the various initiatives as a whole, there are two problems. One is the competence of any of the resistance groups to form an alternative government. In Paton's time there were fewer army coups than there have been since the war. In Portugal, Greece and many African states we can now see what a few determined officers can achieve. But this was much less obvious in 1941. Secondly, would British support have aided the German resistance? Actual support of arms or supplies, or agents might well have been as disastrous as 'Operation North Pole', whereby 52 British agents, parachuted into Holland to aid the Dutch resistance, fell straight into the hands of the Gestapo. A more delicate question concerns that of national loyalty. There has been much emphasis on the revolution in Bonhoeffer's attitudes whereby he was forced to pray for the defeat of his own country.[78] The resistance would have lent itself to accusations of treachery if there had been a relationship with the British government. In the German film 'Die rote Kapelle' about the German Communist resistance, this point came over strongly, that the German Communist plotters found it very difficult to get support from people who hated National Socialism because the Communists were being directed from Moscow. Had it been a purely German movement it would have been more successful. Therefore the failure of the British government to respond may have been to the advantage of the July 20 plotters.

Paton's position is perfectly intelligible if it is compared with Hanns Lilje's and seen in the light of his desire to be of service to the Confessing Church. When Adam von Trott and Bonhoeffer approached him, the two politicians with whom he had most influence, Lord Lothian and Lord Halifax, were dead or in political disgrace respectively. If he had responded positively, he would have given hope where there was none. Asked in a television interview on the occasion of the publication of his memoirs, Otto John, one of the July 20 plotters and a close friend of Klaus Bonhoeffer, replied to the question as to why the assassination plot failed, that he thought now that a negotiated settlement with a new government would not have been the right answer. For National Socialism to be completely discredited and for a new Germany to be reconstructed it was necessary for Germany to suffer unconditional surrender and the terrible destruction of the closing years of the war. As a general he did not use theological language, but he was speaking of atonement. In view of the continuing controversy about Bonhoeffer's involvement in politics in Germany, this would seem to be the right answer, though obviously it is not one which a British person or a Scotsman can advocate.[79]

Chapter XII
An Ecumenical Ministry in Wartime

The work of the World Council of Churches in process of formation in wartime, and therefore of Paton as its joint secretary was a paradox. On the one hand it reached millions, through refugee relief, literature for prisoners of war, broadcasts, the Religion and Life weeks in England, study groups and ecumenical opportunities for prayer, but on the other hand the W.C.C. did not officially exist, and in questions of a message to all Christians or a peace initiative, everything had to be done to preserve the illusion of a temporary arrangement. Wartime austerity meant that the W.C.C.F. had to function with the barest minimum of administration even though ever-increasing demands were made upon it. In 1942 it absorbed the Bureau of Inter-Church Aid after a certain amount of friction with the director, Adolf Keller, so that the means were available after the war for a great intensification of the relief work.[1] The visit of Samuel McCrea Cavert to Geneva in September 1942 marked the beginning of concrete plans for the future work of the W.C.C., but throughout the war there was a regular traffic of churchmen across the Atlantic. Paton visited America for two periods of two months, February - April 1940 and 1942, but on both occasions was handicapped by becoming extremely ill with pneumonia.[2] On both occasions he was concerned to collaborate with van Dusen and a circle of scholars based on Princeton seminary in ecumenical study, though the attempts to stimulate ecumenical study in America and Europe met with mixed success. It is difficult in one chapter to discuss the pluriform manifestations of ecumenical life as stimulated by Paton and the W.C.C.F. and also to include the peculiar British creations in which Paton was heavily involved, the founding of the British Council of Churches and the Religion and Life weeks. This diversity is typical of Paton's many interests, and also of the attempts to make Christian witness relevant to all spheres of life, which was why Bishop Heckel's attempts to sabotage the W.C.C.F. in Europe were resisted.[3] It was not a continuous success story, but the failures themselves indicate something of the nature of what Paton was creating in the W.C.C.F's wartime ministry.

In two vital matters Paton and Visser't Hooft were agreed. First, that the main office of the W.C.C.F. should remain in Geneva. This decision of Dr Visser't Hooft's, taken in the face of Leiper's urgings that he evacuate the office to America, required great courage. Geneva became very vulnerable to enemy attack though, as the war continued, it also became an excellent terminal for resistance routes.[4] His position was different from that of Robert Mackie, who moved the W.S.C.F. office from Geneva to Toronto in 1940 because the latter had no money in Europe and the European universities were affected by mobilization. Students, as McCaughey shows, were very reluctant to cast off their isolationism and pacifism, whereas Paton, Visser't Hooft and their collaborators were, with certain notable exceptions, not pacifists and were determined not to allow the war to wash over them without making a positive contribution to the understanding of the situation.[5] As Paton stated in the Preface to 'The Church and the New Order':

> 'Christians . . . must face and answer the questions raised by the fact of power and the part it plays in human affairs, that the key to the future lies in the use we make of the present emergency and the instruments it calls into being, that within the human scheme of things an immense responsibility rests today upon the British Commonwealth and the United States of America, which they can only discharge by acting together as the leaders of those who agree with them; and that the Church of Christ (that word being used in the widest sense to include the whole community of those who believe in Jesus Christ) has a task of its own to fulfil, distinct from, though intertwined with, the efforts of statesmen to obey the ethical imperative in affairs of state'.

Paton's initiatives in the formation of the W.C.C.F's ecumenical ministry were essentially an attempt to apply these principles even at considerable risk to himself and his country, as will be shown in the discussion of the Berggrav peace initiative. The 'Peace Aims Group' implied less of a risk, though the spectre of a purposeless war or one motivated by a desire for vengeance and the destruction of Germany continued to haunt him. When Paton wished to broadcast on the subject of peace aims, there were objections from Electra House about clergymen meddling in international affairs.[6] Paton's untimely death in the middle of the war meant that much of his work was lost in the secular currents of the time, though some might judge that to be a sign of success of the 'Peace Aims Group', but also it meant a decline in the prestige of the ecumenical operation in Britain.

One interesting oblique commentary on Paton's work came from his cousin-in-law Van Dusen and his associates, who complained that the W.C.C.F. was dominated by Europeans, and that all its paid staff were 'Continentals'.[7] If Paton knew about this, he might have seen it as a sign that his idea of a European community in post-war Europe was beginning to take hold, though in fact he assiduously wooed American participation while remaining exasperatingly British.

The main outline of the W.C.C.F. policy in wartime, as it was carefully formulated at the meetings of the Provisional Committee at St Germain-en-Laye in January 1939, and at Zeist in July 1939 and of the Administrative committee at Appeldoorn in January 1940, and at various meetings concerning international refugee work, does not appear to have been seriously disputed.[8] Correspondence over draft plans tended to refine rather than correct the original ideas as to how the Christian community could be held together and welfare work advanced. There was, however, great controversy over the question of a joint statement before the outbreak of war. Visser't Hooft has described very vividly in his Memoirs the way in which he was caught in a cross-fire between Karl Barth, who was urging total committal to the onslaught on totalitarianism by the W.C.C.F., which would have cost the W.C.C.F. its remaining links with Germany, and those who were demanding the strictest neutrality of the W.C.C.F. Of the latter, Bishop Berggrav of Oslo was typical. Writing to Bell after a visit from Siegmund-Schultze, he objected to the plans for a statement because it would seem like a political encirclement of

Germany by the churches:

> 'Peace seems to be identified with the welfare of the entente powers, peace is the status quo, peace is our righteousness . . . but what does Christianity tell us about our enemies? Shall we encircle them and unite against them? They feel it as if we are condemning them without recognizing our own sins, and without recognizing the righteousness and justice in their claims. . . . Christ wishes us to cross human barriers, not to build a Maginot line of churches'.[9]

However, it proved impossible to secure Boegner's agreement to any statement which involved the acknowledgment that all nations had sinned, since he did not think that Germany's sins should be by implication equated with any alleged Czecheslovakian sin. Bell was sympathetic to Berggrav's argument, preferring an appeal for refugees, which Paton thought would confuse the issue at a time when people were looking for guidance in a sea of conflicting moral statements.[10] Visser't Hooft later admitted to Barth that he was very uncertain at this point. He wanted a statement about refugees, whereas Paton was convinced that the Word of God, not a word about refugees was needed.[11] In a letter to Temple Paton wrote:

> 'Surely it is possible, in view of the genuineness of ecumenical Christian conviction, to say some central Christian things and to believe that, if we say them truly, in the desire not simply to mobilize spiritual forces behind our arms, but to call people to remember the righteousness, the holiness and the redeeming love of God, to judge ourselves by those facts and to hold together in doing so, we need not greatly worry, spiritually speaking, whether the leaders of totalitarian governments think it is a democratic dodge or not. In any case, I have ceased to believe that any action of churchmen or the churches will have a direct effect upon the policy of totalitarian states (perhaps not very much on others) and I feel that any Christian statement or action must be made in faith that God will use it, and not made as a semi-political action'.

Karl Barth berated Visser't Hooft along similar lines, applauding the British attitude, and pointing out that the judgment of God was involved in a completely different context of justice and right than in the 1914-18 war.[12]

Berggrav had said that his objections to the political nature of any statement would be assuaged if it was made jointly with Roman Catholic church authorities. In spite of Boegner's protests, Temple did write to the Vatican, but received nothing but procrastination from officials who did not seem impressed by the fact that they were dealing with an Archbishop of York. However, this was the beginning of collaboration with the Cardinal Archbishop of Westminster, Cardinal Hinsley, not only on practical matters involving refugee relief, but in broadcasting series and evangelism, and public statements, so that Cardinal Hinsley's signature stood with those of Temple, Archbishop Lang and the Moderator of the Free Church Federal Council of Great Britain in a letter addressed to 'The Times' on 21st December 1940 on the subject of peace propsals.[13] Visser't Hooft was very suspicious of this collaboration with offical Roman Catholic circles, although he had his own unofficial contacts with French Roman Catholic theologians. Paton argued that although he and Temple were well aware of the political implications created by Roman Catholic associations, nevertheless, in England the Roman Catholic Church was less politically motivated. Hinsley and his assistant bishop, Bishop Matthew, were in fact genuine ecumenical Christians, but in 1940 Paton and Temple had still achieved a significant step forward in Christian unity.[14] They argued that to associate the W.C.C.F. with the Pope's appeals was a sign of Protestant strength, not weakness.[15]

To return to the first attempt at an ecumenical joint statement, at the beginning of May 1939, Paton stayed at Lambeth Palace to discuss the form of statement, helped draft a covering letter, and placed the materials in Temple's hands for the 'Form of Prayer' which was issued jointly. The 'Form of Prayer' was a liturgy for use in wartime, which had an important ecumenical significance, the attempt to issue a statement on the German Church situation to the churches in order to stimulate prayer. The liturgy took the form of a meditation on the Lord's Prayer, and is evidence that Temple's gift of the felicitous phrase could be used for prayer as well as for ecumenical conference motions. He ended it with a paragraph to the effect that 'the world having got into a mess by sin, wants the Church to provide a way out, other than by abandoning that sin', which Paton or Visser't Hooft cut out.[16] It is prefaced by an explanation that in a time of war Christians should be united in their prayers and avoid praying against each other (as happened in the First World War). They will be able to do this if their prayers conform to Christ's teaching 'for Christian prayer is not an attempt to use God for our purposes, but a petition that He will use us for His'. If Christians are truly praying for the doing of God's will, they are united at the deepest point. The 'Form of Prayer' was published at Whitsuntide with the backing of Eidem and Boegner, as well as the Church of Scotland.

An ill-considered speech of Lang's in the House of Lords on 20th March, which identified the Church of England too closely with the policy of the British Government, made a joint statement impossible in the eyes of Paton, Temple and Visser't Hooft. Nevertheless Paton did attempt to draft on the lines of recalling society to the fundamental truths of the gospel and the Christian understanding of man. Instead, Temple wove a draft statement on the task of the Church in the time of war into a covering letter. In July 1939 a group of distinguished clergy and laity gathered at the Hotel Beau Séjour in Geneva for a consultation on 'The churches and the international crisis'.[17] It resembled the pre-Oxford conferences on Church, Community and State. Paton was there. The consultation discussed their theological presuppositons, the causes of the present disorder, the application of Christian principles in government and the duty of Christians to contribute to political life. However, there was no agreement on the use of force for national protection so the conference fell back on the message of the Oxford conference. Unanimity was achieved not when the church leaders took the initiative, but when they felt compelled to react to a statement by eleven German church leaders which contained the sentences 'All supra-national or international churchliness of a Roman Catholic or World Protestantism type is a political degeneration of Christianity' and 'The Christian Faith is the unbridgeable opposite to Judaism'. Visser't Hooft harmonized drafts for Karl Barth and Temple to produce a declaration signed by Temple, Boegner, Paton and himself.[18]

In the whole attempt of the W.C.C.F. to find a common Christian attitude to the war, British churchmen played a very prominent role. This was most marked at the meeting of the Administrative Committee of the W.C.C.F. in Appeldoorn in January 1940, which was attended by Bell, Temple, Paton and Henry Carter, a Methodist involved in relief work. There are vivid accounts of the amount of subterfuge which surrounded the meeting in Boegner's and Visser't Hooft's memoirs, and in Bell's book 'Christianity and World Order'.[19] At the meeting Berggrav had assumed the Söderblom role of international conciliator, but found that the group could not agree on a statement (which he intended to take to Berlin). Temple and Paton drew up a statement of the conditions under which they thought negotiations for peace could begin, which they had prepared in London and smuggled through customs. They included the independence of Czechoslovakia and Poland, a plebiscite in Austria and a measure of economic justice, and on this they were as immovable as they judged the British people were. Bell, Eidem and Berggrav wanted the W.C.C.F. to issue a statement on freedom and aggression supporting the opening of negotiations regardless of conditions (they were perilously close to the doctrine of 'Peace at any price'). Paton's opinion of Bell, as expressed to Temple, was that he was frequently 'betrayed into actions whose full effect I do not think he quite understands'. Visser't Hooft, Boegner, Koechlin and Temple and two Dutch leaders, felt a statement should only deal with spiritual attitudes. Boegner opposed any direct intervention by the member churches of the W.C.C.F. because there were no representatives of the German churches present. Three documents of varying degrees of conciliatoriness were produced by Visser't Hooft, Temple and Bell, but no consensus appeared. Had they succeeded it is certain that Berggrav and his friends in the Moral Rearmament movement, who were the hosts at Appeldoorn, would have used any statement to do irreparable diplomatic harm to relations between the British and German churches and their respective governments. The stalemate illustrates the reason why no W.C.C.F. pronouncements were made on the war. Frustration at this meeting fueled Paton's determination to sustain a 'Peace Aims Group'.

Two consequences of this meeting can be seen to be of significance for the ecumenical movement. First, statements appeared over individual signatures, such as Temple's ill-fated 1941 goodwill message to the churches in Germany, which caused Paton much difficulty with the Ministry of Information because he had not seen it before it was posted, and it failed to pass the censorship.[20] Individual members and officers of the Provisional Committee who managed to meet in Geneva developed the habit of issuing letters or messages, especially at Christmas and Easter, though on occasions there was dissension, as when Eidem refused to sign the December 1942 letter.[21] Secondly, the content of these messages was 'spiritual' rather than 'political'. This coincided with the nature of the literature which the W.C.C.F. was distributing from London and Geneva. Because of the way in which the W.C.C.F. refugee and prisoner of war work was dovetailed to that of the Y.M.C.A. and the Red Cross, the W.C.C.F. was responsible for the distribution of Bibles and devotional material and ecumenical news, and suitable books for the growing congregations inside the P.O.W. and concentration camps. Paton was always a contributor to the W.C.C.F. brochure which was compiled by Visser't Hooft at Christmas and Easter. The 'message' of the W.C.C.F. therefore remained a 'spiritual' one, because of the failure to agree on the issue of war and peace, although its leaders were also inhibited by the difficulties in defining the nature of the authority of the W.C.C.F. Any 'political' statement in 1939 would have imperilled the Church of England membership of the W.C.C.F.[22]

A peculiar atmosphere prevailed in England after the Declaration of War at the beginning of September 1939 until the opening of the German offensive against France in April 1940. It was known as the 'phoney' war because in spite of the introduction of wartime restrictions, the reality of this war was unimaginable, Poland was too far away, rationing was barely necessary, but rearmament was accelerated and all the preparations were made for a static European land war. The Berggrav-Paton peace initiative was insignificant in the files of the Foreign Office because of the flood of similar efforts, by the royal families of Holland and Belgium, by various Scandinavian agencies and by the Society of Friends which flourished in this atmosphere. The Appeldoorn meeting was the turning point in Berggrav's effort when sympathy for his initiative seems to have ebbed away. Temple reported on the meeting directly to Halifax, the Foreign Secretary, that he had been non-committal; and he passed on remarks of Berggrav's about German reactions to British propaganda, which were considered helpful. Boegner also reported to the French Ambassador in London, who passed his memorandum to the Ministry of Information, declaring that Berggrav exploited the situation and that the meeting showed the lengths to which the German propaganda machinery would go. Boegner clearly thought that Berggrav was being used by Goering and Ribbentrop, his principal Berlin contacts. Paton, on the other hand, formed the impression that Berggrav and to some extent Fulgsang-Damgaard were acting as part of a co-ordinated Scandinavian effort by the governments of those countries to put pressure on France and England to negotiate.[23] From this situation it is clear that Paton, Temple and Bell were taking very considerable risks of being compromised politically when they entertained Berggrav when he came to England in October 1939 at Paton's invitation. In fact Temple eventually published that agreed 'note' about Appeldoorn in the 'Times', when Berggrav was 'misquoted' in a Scandinavian paper and gave the impression that Temple, Paton and Bell would support 'peace at any price'.[24]

There are two accounts of the initiative, one Paton's contemporary report, and one a retrospective 'Diary' which exists in Norwegian only, as Berggrav composed it after his long imprisonment by the Nazis.[25] The former is full of terse comments, Paton with his ear to the ground as he visited the Scandinavian capitals, reported on his meeting with the primates of Norway and Denmark, Ehrenström and Schönfeld. He was suspicious of Gerstenmaier, which is significant in view of Gerstenmaier's subsequent record, even though he was inclined to disbelieve Siegmund-Schultze's allegations that Gerstenmaier was a Gestapo agent. He would only shake hands with him.[26] He accomplished what he wanted in terms of getting Scandinavian church leaders committed to the idea of peace aims discussion groups and the ecumenical study programme, and in working out a policy for refugees and chaplains to camps. The very considerable financial support which the Scandinavian governments in exile and the Swedish government gave to the W.C.C.F. and the I.M.C. might have been stimulated by Paton's approach. He also extracted important information from Schönfeld about the church situation in Germany. Berggrav begins his account by describing the thunderstorm through which the aircraft taking him to the Beau Séjour conference flew, comparing this storm with the outbreak of war. He asks if it was not madness to try and create a peace in those months, even if they could not have foreseen the subsequent pattern of hostilities. His decision is that they were compelled to try.

One mistake Berggrav made, according to Paton, was that he did not perceive that the W.C.C.F. united the Anglo-American, French, Dutch and Belgian churches, but the World Alliance united only the Germans and Scandinavians.

Berggrav should not have tried to use the World Alliance network ubiquitously, particularly, in England where it was very weak. For a leader of the World Alliance, Berggrav's comments about the politicians whom he met seem naïve, especially when compared with Paton's. Paton was determined that Berggrav should see all aspects of British life during his visit and organized a lightning tour which included visits to Birmingham factories as well as Scottish universities.[27] This had its impact on Berggrav who at this time was oblivious to the reality of life in Germany under Hitler. The significance of Berggrav visits to England in October 1939 and February 1940, and of Paton's visit to Copenhagen in November 1940 lies more in the way in which a precedent was set for the visits of Scandinavian church leaders to Britain during the war and for British leaders being granted permission to travel abroad and so maintain ecumenical fellowship, than for the political objective.[28] The Foreign Office persisted in seeing all the attempts at mediation as a 'peace offensive' and Paton himself was fully alive to the dangers of another 'Munich', while it seems a reasonable judgment that Berggrav over-estimated the influence of the German officials whom he saw. There is no reason to believe that Hitler's foreign policy would have admitted of peace with England, though Berggrav did observe with perspicacity the effect of Hitler's pact with Stalin on German opinion. For a biography of Paton, it is interesting to note from Berggrav's account, how Paton's attitude changed between October 1939 and February 1940. As Dr Payne says, it hardened, and Berggrav noted that his proposals were treated with markedly less cordiality and sympathy on his second visit. On his first visit he noticed how well-oiled all the doors of Whitehall were as Paton opened them for him.

In Paton's report of his conversations in Copenhagen, one interesting comment concerns the statements of British Church leaders about the war, which seemed to the Scandinavians to breathe the spirit of ecumenical fellowship and contain the right note of penitence. Paton's principal argument concerned the Scandinavian contention that the W.C.C.F. was rendered ineffective by containing so many representatives of the belligerent powers. The Scandinavians thought that the Provisional Committee should now be run by neutrals, which Paton rightly objected would make it unecumenical and unrepresentative. As Paton observes, the whole incident was symptomatic of an attempt by the Scandinavian churches to take the lead in the ecumenical movement.[29] Paton was shown a 'Form of Prayer' for use in wartime which had evolved among Confessing Church leaders and typically, he seized on it, took a copy to England, and began to use it and to quote it as proof of where the real Christian spirit resided in Germany.[30]

Allusion has already been made in several contexts to the formation of the 'Peace Aims' discussion groups. The origins of these groups are to be found in the personal and international circumstances of Paton's life. In 1938 Oldham had gathered up the most congenial spirits who had been involved in the Oxford Conference, intellectuals and poets such as Karl Mannheim and T.S. Eliot, and formed 'The Moot', a select discussion group which almost verged on a tertiary religious order (there was a precedent in the Tatlow-Temple 'Collegium' 1910-1919). Paton was deeply hurt to find himself excluded from this group, because he did not acknowledge any social or intellectual difference between them and him. One may argue that even if he would not have 'fitted in', he should have been allowed to participate because he would of his own accord have dropped out when he saw the abstract and totally theoretical nature of the subjects chosen for discussion. However, this thesis concerning class differentiation is invalid because the other person excluded was the aristocrat Archbishop Temple, who had a distinguished academic record as a philosopher before his episcopal elevation. It seems more likely that Temple and Paton were excluded because of their association with the ecclesiastical establishment. A key figure in the Moot was Eleanora Iredale who dominated J.H. Oldham at this point in his life, and was financial officer for the newly formed 'Council for the Christian Faith and the Common Life'. Her antipathy to any form of church organization as represented by its clergy is notorious. A brilliant but unhappy woman, she became an officer of the W.S.C.F. after Paton went to India. No-one knows when her feud with Paton began. Paton, in forming the 'Peace Aims' group with Temple seems to have almost deliberately created a group which, although also a select band, was firmly tied to practical schemes and to people with power and influence in church and state. For example, John Foster Dulles, the American secretary of state, and his brother Allen Dulles, were both involved in the group, which they would never have been in the 'Moot'.[31] There was a certain overlap between the two groups in that members of both were among Oldham's advisory group for the Christian News Letter, and took part in the discussions behind some of the issues of its special supplements.

The international origins of the 'Peace Aims' Group' lie on the one hand in the anguish of the Tambaram and Oxford conferences and on the other, in the unsuccessful attempts of the W.C.C.F. to formulate a statement. One finds members of the I.M.C. staff involved in the 'Peace Aims' discussions. Paton was responsible for attention being paid in a constructive way to the problem of colonies, not merely with reference to India, but also in the context of Chinese-Japanese-American relations.[32] When Paton wrote to Temple to explain how a relationship could be forged between the government's advisers in Oxford (the so-called Chatham House Group), he said that they wanted to use the link to help bring international Christian thinking to bear upon the problems of war and peace.[33] Paton responded to the cordial reception he received from Lindsay, Sir John Hope Simpson, Arnold Toynbee, H.J. Paton and Sir Alfred Zimmern by suggesting an international group with separate sub-groups kept in touch by visitation. The basis would be the Beau Séjour conference document. The Oxford scholars thought this would be an excellent way to get serious Christian thinking taken seriously at least by the British government. They emphasized the problem which always remained with the 'Peace Aims' groups, that of mastering highly technical material, but promised to put their resources at Paton's disposal. All of them seemed to value a specifically Christian contribution, believing that outside the common Christian bond there is no hope for the renewal of European civilization.

Sir John Hope Simpson shared his problem with Paton, that he is now head of the peace aims section of Chatham House, with the responsibility of collecting all such information as may be of value to the British government at the time of the eventual peace conference whenever it takes place. This seems to him an enormous task, but he would like W.C.C.F. material, although they do not intend to adopt any specified declaration, such as President Wilson's 'Fourteen Points'. The interests of Europe as a whole would be their over-riding consideration.

Paton gave his interpretation of the problem in his reply

> 'From all sorts of quarters, proposals come, from church people mainly, but also from others, for some kind of conference of churches about peace

terms. The latest is a rather half-baked proposal from Scandinavia. I do not myself feel that the time has come for this, but it is the kind of thing which I would tremendously like to talk over with you. The issues at stake in this business are so tremendous that one is almost equally afraid of optimistic rashness and over-calculating caution'.[34]

Paton succeeded in forging such good relations with a wide cross-section of government advisers, that when eventually signatories were needed for a Peace Aims statement in 1943, to match a declaration issued by the Federal Council of Churches entitled 'The Six Pillars of Peace' in March 1943, it proved very difficult to find lay people who were members of the Peace Aims Group in Britain, but not connected to government, and therefore obliged to be anonymous. At the inception of the Peace Aims Group in Britain, Paton was gratified to receive encouragement from Halifax and there is little doubt that Paton and his colleagues could not have received such preferential treatment in the granting of travel facilities to the U.S.A. if they had not had a considerable amount of governmental support. According to Bishop R.R. Williams, who negotiated many of these visas when he was in the Ministry of Information, a person of Paton's convictions moving independently in America, but undermining isolationism with almost every word he spoke, was very useful precisely because of this fine balance of independence from and support for the British Government which he achieved in America. His church contacts in Sweden were also useful to the Ministry of Information trying to cultivate public opinion in Sweden.[35] It is significant that when Paton's 'opposite number' in the American Peace Aims Group, H.P. van Dusen, came over in October 1941, he was able to spend two evenings with the Minister of Information, Brendan Bracken, to have a prolonged interview with Sir Stafford Cripps and Anthony Eden (Colonial Office and Foreign Office) and was given red carpet treatment for his B.B.C. broadcast. 'Influence', especially on governments, is something very difficult to measure, but it is significant that the 'Peace Aims Group' had this intimate connection with the government planning. Paton reciprocated by criticizing government propaganda eclectically. For example, he used statements from ministerial speeches in the House of Commons to define the beginning of the discussion on 'peace aims', but he condemned the propaganda directed to Germany to exhort Christians who did not need exhortation but only information so that they could maintain a sane and balanced viewpoint amid all the Nazi propaganda. He was as much opposed to Vansittart and his notorious speeches against all things German as Bell was.[36]

Amid the vast quantities of study material which was generated by the 'Peace Aims' groups in Britain and America, and the individual papers from the Continent, there is much which is analytical of public opinion in the way which 'Christianity in the Eastern Conflicts' was. Those papers are interesting for indicating the state of morale and public awareness of the crucial issues during the war.[37] The problem is to know how accurate they were. For example, in 'Notes on the attitudes of Christians to this war' written in November 1939, Visser't Hooft paints a picture of France prepared for war which is totally at variance with Sartre's final volume of 'Chemins de la Liberté' and which, if it were accurate, would make the fall of France inexplicable.[38] The confusion in England which he reports is completely different from the picture one gains from Paton's letters, and was probably a generalization from the confusion which did exist in English universities.[39] The papers Visser't Hooft produced in May 1940 are profoundly affected by his depression at the military situation, but whereas Visser't Hooft's papers are always redeemed by his firm grasp of the theological issues at stake, and his ability to distinguish God's cause from the Allied cause (a point Paton was always scrupulous about), nevertheless a sensitive knowledge of public opinion is important.[40] If Visser't Hooft's and van Dusen's letters of October 1941 could both be taken as accurate, then there would be reason to think that 'The Christian Newsletter' and the 'Peace Aims' discussion had been an important influence in the framing of public understanding of the issues involved. However while van Dusen was writing of the high morale, purposefulness and positive attitude to Germany of the British he encountered, Eric Fenn was writing a very private letter in blackest hues to Robert Mackie from the wilderness to which the B.B.C. had been evacuated.[41]

The situation is clearer in America, where the overwhelming majority of the churchmen involved in the ecumenical movement found in 1939 that they could not share the isolationism and pacifism which prevailed in the United States. They felt intimately involved in the fate of the church in Europe, and they had a world view which went beyond the negative attitude of the average American who did not want to see Britain crushed, but did not want her to be victorious in view of her iniquitous imperialism etc.[42] Van Dusen and his friends in the American 'Peace Aims' group were bitterly attacked by the 'Christian Century', a supposedly 'radical' magazine which performed a complete volte face after Pearl Harbour. John Bennett noted in 1943 that few theologians had been pacifists, and his assumption is that the practice of theology had benefited their understanding of the international situation.[43] One suspects that this may be due to their better grasp of ecclesiology. Since the concept of the united church as a divine reality was firmly held by them, they perceived more clearly the responsibility of the Church and of individual Christians to the international order. This is certainly true in the case of Paton's theology, as will be shown in the next chapter. Van Dusen himself became involved in the 'Lend-Lease' negotiations, whereby the American government supplied military aid to Britain for nominal sums in comparison with the actual value of the ships and aircraft given.[44]

Beyond the question of the sensitivity of the group members to public opinion, their desire to educate it in respect of seeking a post-war settlement in accordance with Christian principles, and the way in which they reflected values proven in the ecumenical movement rather than national sentiment, there is the high quality of the study documents produced. One cannot read them quickly, nor are they cliché-strewn, even though it is clear from 'The Church and the New Order' and the similar books produced by Bell, Temple, Beales, Baker and van Kirk, that their authors are aiming at a popular audience.[45] Temple's famous words concerning his attitude as a churchman to the men in the street: 'I do not ask: "What will Jones swallow?" I am Jones demanding what there is to eat', could well apply to the Peace Aims Group. Although meetings and conferences in Britain and America tended to be semi-private affairs arranged by invitation with limited numbers allowed, much of the 'Peace Aims' groups' best thought was disseminated in popular lectures and broadcasts, the Christian Newsletter, and subsidiary regional conferences. The W.S.C.F. and the S.C.M. took up the issues. Naïve and unclear documents there were — Foster Dulles produced one of the worst in late 1942, — but by the time a document had been read and discussed by the original discussion group for whom it was prepared, and by twin groups on the other side of the Atlantic or on the Continent, the worst excesses had been rounded off. The whole Peace Aims Group exercise across all continents can be seen as an example of 'consensus theology' as well as Christian planning. It would be invidious to select any one document as an example of this high quality. It is unfortunate also that the size and scale of the study group material is such that any summary is impossible in this book.

Paton's book 'The Church and the New Order' is to some extent a personal work: he wrote it in great trepidation, but he did not flinch from giving a carefully considered judgement on many topical questions in a more unequivocal way than in 'Christianity in the Eastern Conflicts'. Nevertheless, it is basically the product of the Peace Aims Group. The Peace Aims Group were sensitive to the charge that they were imposing answers on other people. Therefore they were prepared to criticize their own presuppositions radically. For example, they took seriously the claim of ecumenical documents such as 'Germany and the West', in which it was argued that the democracy was not the automatic political solution to Germany's problems, and that the tradition of democracy was foreign to Germany.[46] Paton himself wrote in terms of the need to find a political machinery appropriate to the evident skills of a people who had shown themselves pre-eminent in science, economics, literature and philosophy but who, because of the late date of German reunification and the imperial tradition, lacked political maturity.

One significant tendency, which Paton developed, though not without criticism, was support for an eventual form of world government or for a European community of states who agreed to limit their sovereignty in the interests of the whole, and who accepted Germany as an equal partner in this. N.A.T.O. and the E.E.C. do not fulfil this ideal completely, but one should see in the Peace Aims Group some of the ideological support for these groupings. The United Nations was a more obvious target for their plans, although one does not find the same heady idealism and tendency to equate it with the Kingdom of God as one who finds among American churchmen at the Stockholm conference in 1925, when they declared their support for the League of Nations. Paton's particular contribution was to examine the Anglo-American relationship which, in his visits to America in 1940 and 1942, and his invitations to American theologians and churchmen such as Reinhold Niebuhr and van Dusen, J.W. Decker (Warnshuis' successor) and Walter van Kirk, he had been at pains to foster. He wrote pamphlets on the Anglo-American relationship and on features of British church life for circulation in America. At a time when the Atlantic alliance and the 'special relationship' was embryonic, he advanced the hypothesis that the future policy stability of Europe would depend on the peace-keeping forces of the United States and Britain. He believed also that American economic aid would be a powerful political bargaining counter in the political settlement in Eastern Europe.[47]

Bishop Bell argued that the Peace Aims Group ought to concentrate on the economic aspects of reconstruction rather than the political aspects. Paton himself saw that for Britain the war had brought a social revolution. For example, as the Ministry of Supply had control over food and materials and was distributing them equally in the rationing system, the population had never been healthier because most people were receiving a balanced diet. Paton envisaged an extension of this system in peace-time not only for the population of Britain, or as a short-term expedient for the countries of occupied Europe, when they were recovering from the effect of the economic blockade, but as a permanent means of redistributing wealth fairly to end famine and exploitation in the Third World. The 'Peace Aims' Group became the focus of church-based demands for greater social and economic justice.

William Temple had always been a campaigner for social and economic justice, a controversial figure attacked by bankers and businessmen, who maintained that their professions should be inviolate from criticism by churchmen. In 1940 he presided over a three day conference at Malvern, whose 400 participants were dazed by papers from Middleton Murry, T.S. Eliot, Dorothy Sayers, Sir Richard Acland, D.M. MacKinnon, V.A. Demant, H.A. Hodges and Maurice Reckitt. Fortunately the 'follow-up' programme was better organized than the actual conference itself, but its resolutions were very controversial. In particular, in describing the stumbling blocks which make living the Christian life more difficult, the conference declared: 'we believe that the maintenance of that part of the structure of our society, by which the ultimate ownership of the principal industrial resources of the community can be vested in the hands of private owners, may be such a stumbling block'.[48]

The controversy over this resolution ensured maximum press coverage for many months to come, and stimulated the Industrial Christian Fellowship to organize on a scale parallel to C.O.P.E.C., culminating in a rally in the Albert Hall in September 1942.[49] In 1942 the Beveridge Report was published which laid the foundations for the plans for social services after the war. For the 'Peace Aims' Group and the conferences of the Industrial Christian Fellowship, the Religion and Life weeks organised by the British Council of Churches, and the statements issued by the Commission on International Friendship and Social Responsibility did not happen in a vacuum, nor was their influence confined to church circles. It is one of the most remarkable features of the Second World War, that while citizens of the British Commonwealth were intent on winning the war with a decisive victory, (the idea of a negotiated peace disappeared abruptly in Spring 1940), the most comprehensive plans for social reconstruction were conceived and discussed, and some of the enabling legislation, such as the 1944 Education Act, was passed before the end of hostilities. There was a keen sense that the promises of 'a land fit for heroes' should be honoured, not set aside as in 1919. The Peace Aims Group, therefore, had a relevance which few church-based phenomena have (it was formally organised under the aegis of the W.C.C.F. Provisional Committee). Yet all the thought and energy which went into the Peace Aims Group, the Malvern follow-up and the Religion and Life weeks disappeared from church life after the end of the war. One cannot attribute this simply to the death of those inspiring or organising the movement: Temple, Paton and Elmslie. No institutionalised forms were proposed. No recurring phenomena appeared as in the Lay Institutes in Germany or the Kirchentage, which would be the closest to the Religion and Life weeks.[50] Instead, it seems a reasonable explanation that the phenomena became secularized, that the common Christian thinking of Paton's era became absorbed into the idealism behind the creation of the welfare state in 1948, and probably contributed to the Labour Party victory in 1945. Although the whole discussion was an assertion of the Church's responsibility in international affairs and social welfare, and of its duty to speak out, nevertheless it would seem that the majority of those involved immersed themselves in the appropriate secular agency, and, being lay people, concentrated on Christian witness in their careers. The other possibility is that the Peace Aims Group did not develop a sufficiently 'Christian' critique of society for it to maintain a distinctive entity.

In Paton's life, the 'Peace Aims' Group was significant as providing a vehicle for an extension of his thought on social issues and international affairs, and as furnishing intellectual muscle for all the refugee and relief work which he was involved in. He was able to help the churches find the means to achieve what the W.C.C.F. had failed to do, to speak together. By this is meant that in the publication of the pamphlets 'Social Justice and Economic Reconstruction' and 'The Christian Church and World Order', by the Commission of the Churches for International Friendship and Social Responsibility (C.I.F.S.R.), which were adopted by the commission and by denominational bodies, a way was found to produce statements which were more relevant and had more impact than letters to the 'Times' appealing for peace, or, according to Bell, than papal pronouncements at Christmas, which everyone ignored in spite of the distinctive ethical pre-suppositions behind them.[51]

The problems surrounding the birth of the British Council of Churches were completely different from those surrounding the 'Peace Aims' Group, and yet its inception and work was equally vital to the wartime ministry of the W.C.C.F. According to A.C. Craig, the first secretary of the B.B.C., it was Paton who single-handedly changed the original scheme radically, and then pushed it through, removing the chief obstacle, J.H. Oldham, in order to do so. This was, according to Dr Craig, because Temple had a certain opaqueness where the Apostolic Succession was concerned, and could not judge what should be done in relation to the Free Churches, and because Lang, as Archbishop of Canterbury, was too preoccupied, although he was very keen on Paton's scheme, which would relieve him of the chairmanship of a commission whose name he could never remember (the (C.I.F.S.R.).[52] The problems were therefore both organisational and personal, and it took Paton from 1936-1942 to solve them.[53]

The establishment of the Continuation Committee of the World Missionary Conference in 1910 had led to the founding of national missionary councils (later the National Christian Councils of India, China, Japan and so on) and in Britain to the formation of the C.B.M.S. The problem created by the formation of the W.C.C.F. was that in England, Scotland and Wales, no national body existed which embraced the activities of the W.C.C.F. There was Paton's office, representing the British section of the Provisional Committee, the Council of Christian Faith and Common Life, founded after Oxford and commonly known as 'Joe's Council' because Oldham dominated it, and the British sections of the Life and Work movement and the World Alliance which had merged into the Commission, of which Paton had been a co-opted member since its inception. In addition, there was the British section of Faith and Order, which Temple and everyone else seem to have forgotten about until 1941, but whose members, led by Tatlow, were obstinately determined that 'Joe's Council' should not usurp Faith and Order functions, and who were so deeply suspicious of the W.C.C.F., the proposed B.C.C. and all its works that they refused to make any financial contribution. This was in contrast to the American section of Faith and Order who, under Floyd Tomkins, did their best to help Visser't Hooft financially.[54] Consequently, there was not only a hiatus between the international organisation of the W.C.C.F. and the British churches, but, because the formation of the C.I.F.S.R. had been made in anticipation of the World Alliance becoming part of the W.C.C.F., there was a difficult area caused by the C.I.F.S.R. dealing with non-W.C.C.F. activities. Visser't Hooft had difficulty corresponding with the secretaries of so many different organisations though he tended to concentrate on Paton, Craig (C.I.F.S.R.) and Tatlow. He faced a complete log-jam with regard to

Oldham, who never passed anything on, and was obstinately opposed to the formation of the B.C.C. and the evolution of the W.C.C. from a select band of experts to a practical organisation preoccupied by refugee relief.[55]

In the discussions on the C.I.F.S.R. concerning the proposed formation of a B.C.C., Paton stressed that the argument that there was no British agency to mediate W.C.C.F. ideas comparable to the Federal Council of Churches in America was not the strongest argument. He insisted that whatever organisational structure was adopted, it should reflect the British situation, and British needs. (There was already a United Christian Council of Ireland.) However, such a multiplicity of organisations did confuse the outsider, and as none were very strong financially or administratively, their powers of effective action were limited. Further confusion stemmed from the fact that the Council arose from the Oxford conference, and was a new creation, involving many people newly interested in the ecumenical movements' potential for Christian witness and study, whereas the C.I.F.S.R. had a disproportionately high number of septuagenarian members whose experience began with C.O.P.E.C. or even with the World Alliance before the First World War.[56] Temple himself was impressed with the N.C.C's and wanted to see one in Britain. In 1939 the C.I.F.S.R. gained a full-time secretary when Craig was appointed. Paton spent much time inducting him into the job, which impressed Craig when he considered how much international work Paton had, but the weaknesses of the system were very evident.[57]

The main obstacle to the formation of the B.C.C. was Oldham. Eric Fenn worked for him for two years, and describes how he was detailed off to prevent the formation of the B.C.C. He worked in vain to reconcile Oldham and the church leaders diplomatically.[58] In February 1939 Paton complained to Visser't Hooft that the Finance Committee of the Council was a 'pretty hopeless' body. The Oxford conference follow-up was on very questionable lines. Everyone admired Oldham so much that no-one had the courage to tell him that his scheme was defective. There was almost no money in sight and no way of raising it apart from Eleanora Iredale's efforts. Paton attempted to do this in September 1939. He reported to Visser't Hooft: that he had had a long talk with Oldham and Iredale:

> 'I urged upon them, and I think they fully agree that the present emergency gives the new British Council of Churches a first class chance to become effective before the public and to perform a really valuable common service which can be easily understood by all Christians. It seems to me quite clear that, without deserting their profounder work with scholars, they ought now to become a regular consulting group of the British churches. They are adequately supported by the Churches in every formal way. . . . I very much hope that out of this terrible situation in which we are now the specific functions of Joe's body may become plainer. . . . If it should be the case, it is going to make the position of the W.C.C. much easier'.[59]

This letter hinted at the major difference between Paton and Oldham. Oldham kept procrastinating and writing further memoranda on the role and purpose of the proposed body, which he would revise as soon as anybody adopted them. This infuriated Bell, Burlingham (the other newly appointed C.I.F.S.R. secretary) Urwin and others. However, the import of all the memoranda was that he envisaged a small prophetic band of scholars similar to 'the Moot' which would advise the churches on social, political and economic questions. All the various structural alterations — making the C.I.F.S.R. responsible to the council, for example, — could not conceal the fact that Oldham opposed a close association with the churches since they represented to him 'the establishment'. He was more interested in 'the frontier', among lay people, where people were on the borderline between Christianity and secularism. Hence his preoccupation with 'The Christian Newsletter' and a movement known as 'The Christian Frontier' which sprang from the subscribers to the Newsletter. Originally the Newsletter was subsidized and supported by the Council. Craig agrees that the difference between Oldham's concept and Paton's democratic principle of a council representing the churches directly was like that between a small family business and a public corporation accountable to its shareholders. Paton deserves the credit for creating the B.C.C. and making it a catholic body, while preserving its functions for study and for publishing informed statements as guidelines for the churches.

In 1941 Paton engineered a crisis, forcing Iredale to resign after he had systematically gathered her financial responsibilities into his hands, and persuading Oldham to retire.[60] In June 1941, Paton became secretary to the Council. He was very keen to become secretary to the C.I.F.S.R. with the appointment as secretary of the B.C.C. confirmed later, but the Council decided to appoint Craig instead. However, Paton did much secretarial work during the time of transition. Finally the plans for the B.C.C. were adopted and ratified by the churches very rapidly after Oldham's departure, with the inaugural service for the B.C.C. taking place in September 1942.[61] Kathleen Bliss's only explanation for Oldham's behaviour is that he was continually ill during this period, and secondly, that he could never understand that it was not possible to form the B.C.C. simply by getting the general secretaries of the main denominations together for a cosy chat with Temple. He could not understand that the B.C.C. would not be an ecumenical 'club' with the members proposing others for membership and deciding the rules. Even in 1949 he was trying to undermine the B.C.C. and expressing his disapproval.

Membership did cause one difficulty. The doctrinal basis of membership of the British branches of the ecumenical movements had become very vague and all inclusive. Even Unitarians were active members, and the Society of Friends protested vigorously against any step to limit their participation. However, the Utrecht meeting had adopted a definite Christological formula as the basis of membership of the W.C.C.F. and obviously, there would be something anomalous in churches being members of the B.C.C. and not the W.C.C.F. even though that was precisely the position of the Baptist Church of Great Britain at that time. Paton admitted that the Basis of membership for the W.C.C.F. would be reviewed at the next world conference, so that it was not a permanent guideline for the B.C.C. but the Bishop of Bristol was very firm that the basis should be trinitarian so as to attract the broad mass of Anglicans. At one meeting of the C.I.F.S.R. Unitarians were effectively excluded, but W.T. Elmslie campaigned against this so furiously that at the next meeting, when Paton was absent, G.F. Fisher's compromise was adopted, namely that the basis of the B.C.C. should remain as for the W.C.C.F., but that any churches who were former members of any of the constituent bodies merging in the B.C.C. should also be members even if they did not accept the Basis. This, it was decided, would include the Unitarians and the Friends, but exclude Jehovah's Witnesses, Spiritualists and Christian Scientists. Paton knew when the battle was lost, and worked to persuade the Anglican members to accept this.[62]

Partly because of Temple's oversight, the British section of Faith and Order was not sufficiently consulted about the moves to form the B.C.C. Tatlow was very recalcitrant, but was eventually persuaded to allow the Faith and Order movement to merge with the B.C.C. though he protested that there ought to be a separate department for its concerns.[63] The Youth Department was a new creation which brought together youth movements and youth workers among the churches. It soon had its own secretary. Study was an important function inherited from the C.I.F.S.R., with topics such as evacuation and gambling forming part of the projects undertaken. However, evangelism played the principal role in the creation of the B.C.C. The Religion and Life weeks have already been mentioned several times. Paton, Temple, Craig, Bell and many local church leaders were heavily involved in these week-long civic evangelistic campaigns (which often included 'Peace Aims' topics) and which were designed to reach every section of the population. They were described as civic 'Swanwick Conferences', although they more resemble S.C.M. 'Religion and Life' Missions to the Universities 1919-20. The first was held in Bristol in 1940, followed by very successful weeks at St Albans, Newcastle, Manchester, Bolton, Sheffield, Glasgow and so on. Special campaigns were held among army camps. Based on local initiative, the local organisers could call upon the C.I.F.S.R./-B.C.C. for resources and speakers. There has been nothing to compare with the Religion and Life weeks since, with the possible exception of the 'People Next Door' campaign. Conducted in a 1940 idiom, there were none of the evangelical theological overtones of individual salvation, but it was more of a rallying of all Christians and any who cared to join to tackle social problems and christianize society. The way in which people were forced to work together to win the war may have been reflected in these co-operative efforts, but they reflect a spontaneous spirit which went much deeper. The curious ecumenical phenomena of local councils of churches in 700 towns in Britain may also stem from this unleashing of local initiative.[64] For once the ecumenical movement reached the proverbial 'grass-roots'.

One could write a great deal more about the ecumenical ministry of the W.C.C.F. in wartime, even if one confined oneself to Paton's activities. One of the most important aspects of the P.O.W. work has not been discussed: by frequent exchange of letters, Paton and Visser't Hooft kept each other informed of conditions in the opposing belligerent country and used a doctrine of 'reciprocity' to wring concessions out of the other side. Similarly, when rumours of atrocities on prisoners threatened to sever the Geneva Convention, Paton provided evidence that it would not be abrogated in Britain, and put strong pressure on the British authorities not to retaliate in kind for such things as the shackling of British prisoners in Germany. Visser't Hooft was less successful, but he did manage to get access to the P.O.W. camps for neutral W.C.C. representatives. However, the ministry of the W.C.C.F. is thoroughly well chronicled in Visser't Hooft's contemporaneous reports, and in 'The History of the Ecumenical Movement'.[65]

Margaret Sinclair argues that the effect of the outbreak of war was to limit Paton's activities to Great Britain. Yet his correspondence with Visser't Hooft shows that the boundaries of his concern were not limited to British problems, and he strove hard to build up a relationship between American and British churchmen. Significantly Paton's ministry involved him in secular problems, government planning, P.O.W. camps, peace initiatives and so on. In spite of the churches' limited ability to speak together on the implications of the war situation, the W.C.C.F. and the B.C.C. enabled them to work together effectively and creatively, though how much they would have achieved without Paton's driving energy and impatience with inadequate machinery and procrastinating septuagenarians, is open to question.

Chapter XIII
A Labour of Compassion and a Labour of the Gospel : Paton's Work among the Jews

It is very difficult not to write a chapter such as this anachronistically, now that the full horror of the holocaust in Nazi-dominated lands is known, and it can be seen how centuries of anti-semitism made such a crime possible. The modern state of Israel has been established since Paton's death, after the ending of the British mandate in Palestine, while the radical political changes have been accompanied by equally radical theological changes in the understanding of the relationships between Jews and Christians for which one could use the term 'ecumenical' if one joined those scholars who argue that the first great schism in the Church was between Jews and Christians.[1] In Paton's lifetime, however, it was legitimate for him to characterize the situation as 'dialectical', as he compared the theological imperative to evangelize the Jewish people, and their immediate need to be saved by all means possible from extermination. In the work done by the International Christian Council on the Approach to the Jew (I.C.C.A.J.), Paton strove to maintain the balance as the crisis in Europe worsened. Therefore the major questions which must be asked concern not only Paton's understanding of the theological significance of mission to the Jews and anti-semitism, but also his practical efforts through the machinery of the I.M.C. and the W.C.C., by co-operation with independent agencies such as the Büro Grüber in Berlin or simply by helping individuals. The difficulty is the same today as it was for Paton and his friends and colleagues, namely to appreciate the enormity of the dilemma and reduce it to the terms of individual human suffering. It is impossible to answer the question (in moral terms) of whether enough was done by Paton and his colleagues, however certain one may be that governments failed in their humanitarian responsibilities. Dr Visser't Hooft writes in his Memoirs that not enough was done, and the guilt will always remain with him. The Revd Robert Smith, who worked in Prague 1935-39, and for the I.C.C.A.J., believes nothing more could have been done by the I.C.C.A.J. or the Church of Scotland.

As in the question of Christian resistance to Hitler, the crucial issue is one of communication and public indifference. Robert Smith and his wife are convinced that they realized from what Jewish refugees in Prague told them in 1936 and from studying 'Mein Kampf' that the Jews were doomed; and Conrad Hoffman's reports from Autumn 1935 onwards show vividly the harassments, persecution and murders of Jews unable to emigrate. By 1939 Paton writes so unequivocally that clearly he had no doubts. Probably he perceived the danger as early as 1934. The only unanswered question in Paton's mind was how, given existing technology, several million Jews would perish. This chapter will also expose the extent of Christian indifference to the plight of Jewish and Jewish Christian refugees and discuss the reasons for this indifference and its implications. Paton linked this indifference to the unpopularity of missions to the Jews, accusing his compatriots of practising a more subtle form of discrimination. By denying the Jews the right to hear the Gospel, they were implying that the Jews were not good enough for the Gospel.[2]

Paton was greatly exercised in his mind about the 'final solution' of the Jewish problem. He envisaged the assimilation and conversion of the Jews, not to the existing feeble Christianity, nor at the cost of forgetting their social customs, but to a new creation. He had doubts about a Hebrew Christian Church, but he was firmly convinced that mission to Jews was the responsibility of ordinary church congregations. His views, if taken to their logical conclusion, would have meant the abolition of special missions to the Jews, which may be why he encountered such difficulties with the member missionary societies of the I.C.C.A.J. in the period 1941-43. His highest diplomatic skills were required to conciliate feuding missions and factious Hebrew Christians. As with his pacifist principles in the First World War, Paton was not afraid to champion unpopular causes, but not being a theologian, he did not think the subject through as thoroughly as Bonhoeffer did in 1933.[3] Bonhoeffer considered that the exclusion of the Jews from the Church was so important morally and theologically that the Church could no longer be considered to be the Church. Paton approached the question from the opposite end, insisting that one could not exclude mission to Jews from the evangelistic task of the Church. Otherwise the entire Gospel was called into question.

Unfortunately there were many shortcomings in Paton's understanding of Judaism, due it would seem to his early encounter with Hinduism before he encountered Judaism, and his tendency to under-estimate the importance of the historical significance of Judaism.[4] His involvement in the I.C.C.A.J. also meant that he left a trail of turbulent relationships behind him, which must be examined if one is to understand either the significance of his theology of mission or the extent of his practical efforts on behalf of Jewish refugees.

Paton's induction into mission to the Jews

The question of mission to the Jews was discussed at the I.M.C. meeting at Jerusalem in 1928, but Paton did not become actively involved in the problem until it was decided at the I.M.C. committee meeting at Williamstown in 1929 to set up the I.C.C.A.J. It was intended to function as a separate department of the I.M.C. in the same way as the D.I.S.R., also instituted at this meeting, as a result of a request from the Jerusalem meeting.[5] Initially the two departments differed little in their structure, purpose and financing. The I.C.C.A.J. however, had only one full-time secretary, who was expected to divide his time between London and New York, but was not expected to raise a proportion of his own salary, as Merle Davis was. Its similarity of aims, that is, of educating public opinion, advising missions, acting as a catalyst in the formation of a common missionary policy and gathering information, might have sustained the resemblance beyond 1932, if it had not been for the direct action necessary to meet the challenge of anti-semitism. The principal difference between the I.C.C.A.J. and the D.S.I.R. was that the I.C.C.A.J. itself was a committee of 15, divided into three continental sub-committees, for America, Britain, and Europe. Appointed by the I.M.C., they were responsible for policy decisions, finance, and finding contacts for the I.C.C.A.J's director. Unfortunately, although a good cross-section of scholars, members of mission boards and pastors involved in work in Poland and Hungary were nominated, their average age was over seventy, reflecting the average age of workers in missions to the Jews, but creating a built-in cause of friction for younger men such as Paton and the director, Conrad Hoffmann. This factor probably protected the I.C.C.A.J. from the controversies and difficulties of the D.S.I.R., since the support of such important Scandinavian missions as the Svenska Israel Mission never faltered. Instead, hostility lurked in the 'progressive' church circles in America. The Federal Council of Churches of the U.S.A. was particularly antipathetic, especially the chairman of the American section of Faith and Order, Dr Parkes Cadman. Considerable obstacles were therefore placed in the way of Hoffmann's work and efforts to raise funds.[7]

Significantly, the original contributors to the I.C.C.A.J's separate budget were the Anglican members of the I.M.C., the northern Presbyterian Church of the U.S.A. and the Church of Scotland, who provided a substantial proportion of the salaries of the I.C.C.A.J. staff seconded by these denominations.[8] The I.C.C.A.J. was continually hamstrung for lack of funds, a symptom of church indifference on the one hand and the instability of the Hebrew Christian organisations on the other, since they made promises of support they did not always fulfil. Even in the first two years there were considerable arrears.[9] This deficit was erased by a single private donation, which was no solution to a continuing problem. Hoffmann attributed the difficulty in raising money in America to the American preference for giving to projects designed to halt starvation. After the Americans entered the war in Europe, they preferred to give money for comforts for the troops or to the emerging United Nations. In January 1940 Paton wrote to Miss Bracey of the Society of Friends:

> '. . . what I have recently heard about the state of affairs in America from the point of view of giving, is extremely unfavourable. It seems to me that the moral condition of the belligerent countries is better than that of the neutrals, but I can hardly expect you, as a Quaker, to believe that'.[10]

A theme which runs through the I.C.C.A.J. appeals, the European Bureau for Inter-Church Aid, and Life and Work appeals, is that when American Jews are giving so much for European Jews, and are even assisting Christian Jews,[11] the Christian Church ought to be ashamed that it is neglecting its own people, the Christian 'non-Aryans', who in Germany outnumbered the practising Jews by about 3:1, and were equally threatened.[12] Paton thought the reluctance to help stemmed from theological uncertainties about missions to the Jews, but it cannot be said that Bishop Bell's appeals were more successful, except on the occasion when Lord Baldwin lent his name and energies to an appeal.[13] When Paton died, Smith was very doubtful whether the I.C.C.A.J. could continue to raise money, so much had depended on his personal authority. So although there probably was a theological element in the reluctance to support the I.C.C.A.J., one is driven to conclude that anti-semitism, passive rather than overt, lay behind the problem.[14]

The practical work of the I.C.C.A.J. or the Anglo-Saxon section of Life and Work was never endangered by theological disputes to the extent which the work of a collaborating body, the Schweizerisches Evangelische Hilfswerk für die Bekennende in Deutschland was. From May 1940 to January 1941, the Barth and Brunner factions of the committee insisted on spending much time hearing papers on whether the committee should endorse the Barmen church declaration (1934) or not. This was at a time when the situation of Jewish and German refugees in Switzerland was critical.[15]

278

The theological implications of the Christian approach to the Jews

In what is described in his memoirs by Dr James Parkes as a piece of ecumenical imperialism by Mott, Conrad Hoffmann, a secretary of the International Student Service, who had particularly good relations with impoverished Jewish students in Europe, was persuaded to accept the post of director of the I.C.C.A.J.[16] Paton wrote him many letters urging him to accept on the grounds that work among the Jews was intimately related to the very heart of the Christian movement, and that in the New Testament the Gospel was brought to the Jews first and then the Gentiles. When Hoffman described his difficulties with pastors and Y.M.C.A. workers who referred to the rabbis in their communities as far better Christians than most professed Christians, Paton replied expounding his view:

> 'I have always felt quite clear that the whole-hearted Christian position, if fearlessly stated and separated from any kind of racial, national or group superiority, must ultimately win people's respect, and that there is no other possible way for us but to stand firm on that position. Any sort of hedging merely creates a suspicion and does not disarm hostility'.[17]

Paton took his stand on the motion proposed at the Digswell Park meeting of the I.C.C.A.J. in 1932, which he supported by a paper, now lost, on 'The Ground of the Christian Approach to the Jews'.[18] The motion declares that the duty of Christians to approach the Jews with the Christian message is based on exactly the same grounds as the proclamation to all other races, namely the universality and sufficiency of the Christian Gospel. The responsibility is especially great because Jesus was a Jew by race. In the I.C.C.A.J. documents very little allowance seems to be made for the theological developments in Judaism since the first century, and insufficient attention to the weight of Christian guilt for spreading anti-semitism, though it is exaggerating to call Paton's attitude bureaucratic, as Dr Parkes does.[19] It was somewhat inflexible, but it does not seem to have prevented him enjoying good relations with Jews whom he met socially, such as his daughter's parents-in-law and the five rabbis present at his memorial service.[20]

The members of the I.C.C.A.J. found that the theology of mission to the Jews was intricately bound up with the question of the appropriate evangelical approach. In North America there was arising spontaneously a sincere interest among intellectual Jews in the founder of Christianity, which is reflected in Klausner's widely read book 'Jesus of Nazareth', originally written in Hebrew from the Hebrew University of Jerusalem, and Sholom Asch's books.[21] Paton was right to think that Christianity could only meet such intelligent investigation, and maintain its claims, if it was presented honestly and without the vagueness and uncertainty which characterized a great deal of Anglo-Saxon theological and apologetic thought at this time. This demanded a high standard of scholarship and intellectual honesty to understand Judaism, and also keen observation of the extent to which those of Jewish descent still adhered to Jewish belief, a constant theme of I.C.C.A.J. reports. A man such as A.E. Garvie typified this approach. He once convinced a protesting rabbi of the justification for mission by saying that if he, Garvie, had a priceless treasure, a gift he valued above all else, what was more natural then that he should want to share it with his Jewish friends?[22]

It was, however, recognised from the beginning that in the evangelization of the Jews the relationship differed in certain respects since they were not a dormant or decadent people who needed educational stimulus or philanthropic help. Religious Jews and Christians were held to have much in common, since the Christian heritage had been immeasurably enriched by Jewish spiritual treasures. Only Christ himself stood as a barrier between the two peoples, but it was now their privilege to interpret him to them.[23]

It cannot be said that the I.C.C.A.J. always escaped from attitudes of cultural superiority; for example, Hoffmann's reports on the plight of East European Jews do not mention their heritage of Yiddish oral and literary tradition, but their poverty and deprivation. Nevertheless, this difference is significant, and effectively prevented any of the theology of the 'Social Gospel' merging into the theology of mission to the Jews. The I.C.C.A.J. could maintain this position in 1931, but by 1939 the situation was complicated by the position of destitute Jews whom the stations of the missions were feeding and providing with material aid. This had begun in 1920 in Vienna, Budapest and Bucarest, with the result that it was a common belief among central European Jews that missions were bribing Jews to be baptized. One mission attempted to curb any possible abuse by refusing to baptize any Jews without independent means, but worsening conditions made this impossible. Jewish refugees mistakenly believed that a certificate of baptism would help them emigrate, and in their compassion some priests connived with this, giving certificates to the un-baptized, which caused further confusion for missions trying to identify genuine converts. It is against this background that one should read Paton's letter to Warnshuis discussing whether Hoffmann should come to Europe to work among refugees. He wrote that he would have to seek the answer by prayer, since he could see that both sides of the case could be backed by rational argument.

> 'There is a tendency for Christians to try now to offer a Christian witness through refugee work as if that could be a final and complete substitute for the evangelical witness. I hold myself that the Christian Church has no greater duty at the present moment in regard to the Jews than is constituted by refugee work. At the same time all Christian history goes to show that Christians can never render a Christian witness except on the basis of a full Christianity and any Christian work done on a half-hearted basis is always doomed to failure'.[24]

The second half of this chapter will be devoted to a discussion of the practical work of the I.C.C.A.J. and the W.C.C., but it is necessary to indicate here how extraordinarily complicated the issues of the relationship between the theology of mission to the Jews and relief work was.

The mature expression of Paton's theology is to be found in the foreword to Kosmala and Smith's book: 'The Jew in the Christian World'.[25] It can be shown how many of his ideas are derived from his correspondence, particularly his polemics concerning Henry Carter.[26] He considers the subject 'one of the most important in our contemporary world', but one which is not adequately examined by most Christians, who ignore the religious question in discussing the economic and political problems. Paton is convinced that the ultimate barrier is that of religion, since however many secularized Jews there may be, they are 'the covenant people'. Equally, Christianity is not a mode of culture, but a religion of revelation. Some thoughtful Christians, ashamed of the 'unchristianity' of the Christian world before the moral dignity of the Jews, are reluctant to admit the duty to bear witness to the

Jews. Yet what is involved is not the claims of a superior competing culture, but the unmistakable revelation in the New Testament of Christ, which confronts the Jew who reads the New Testament for himself, whether the Christian upholds it or concedes the Jewish case instead. Similarly, Judaism can be equally intransigent, but both parties can only benefit from honesty and frankness. No real meeting of minds is possible unless both Judaism and Christianity are taken in their fullness.

Paton does not comment on Kosmala's assertion that much anti-semitism stems from people failing to recognize the significance of the Jews' religious and spiritual heritage to them, and supplying tales of 'international conspiracies' and 'magical rites' to explain their cohesion as a people. He repeats instead Smith's assertion, if it was not his idea originally, that the refusal to present the Gospel may be a subtle form of anti-semitism.[27] The problem is really one of diluted values — a weak, uncertain Christianity, Judaism reduced to social rites which differentiate one human group from another. Paton is searching for the essence of each religion so that 'deep can speak unto deep'. It is a very Protestant approach, going back to the fundamentals of the Christian faith, and seeking to obliterate any religious differentials so that all are considered equal before the truth; and secondly, in basing his appeal unconditionally on the New Testament as an independent witness, which will bear the revelation of God, whatever wayward Christians do.

Since the I.C.C.A.J. derived so much support from the Continent and since Paton, Smith and Hoffmann were Presbyterians, it may be relevant to compare their theology with that of Karl Barth, especially as there are some points of contact. However, for Barth, a theology of mission was not axiomatic, whereas the I.C.C.A.J. proceeded from such a presupposition; secondly, he wrote on the subject of the relationship of Jews and Christians many years after the holocaust, and his own experience in the campaign to pressurise the Swiss authorities to allow Jewish refugees from occupied Europe into Switzerland, instead of sending them back to the concentration camps from which they had escaped, as happened before 1942.[28]

Barth admitted that witness is owed to the synagogue, which is both a promising and an alien field, but there is no question of proclaiming the Gospel, in fact mission to the Jews is an insult. This is because there is no question of proclaiming a true faith in place of a false one. The Jews are the natural historical monument to the love and faithfulness of God, a living commentary on the Old Testament and proof of God outside the Bible.[29] In the I.C.C.A.J. approach there was also no question of replacing a false religion with a true one, but this view is even more defective than Paton's, in as much as the Jews seem to be relegated to a museum, crystallized in one moment of history. In contrast to this, there were in the I.M.C. Indian and Chinese members who equated their pre-Christian heritage with the Old Testament.

Secondly, Barth considers that the implication of the Jews rejecting the Messiah, who became the Saviour of the World, is that the synagogue has an empty future, waiting without the grace manifested to the heathen. Therefore, we should fear God's judgment in love. A Jew cannot go back on his former repudiation without an exceptional intervention by God. (This is diametrically opposed to C.S. Lewis's belief that it is the Gentiles who are saved by an exceptional intervention, and his Jewish wife's conversion was the natural working of grace.)[30] The only way to fulfil the ministry of witness to the Jews is to make Israel jealous, as Paul advocates (Romans 11 v 11), and make Jesus dear and illuminating and desirable. The life of the Church, therefore, should be that of a community before Jesus Christ, which it has failed to be in Western Europe. The absence of Israel from the modern ecumenical movement is more damaging than the absence of Rome, since the Christian Church must live with the synagogue not as with another religion but as with the root from which it sprang.

Barth would therefore use the same arguments as Dr Parkes for including the Jews in the ecumenical movement. Barth seems to be ignoring the racial, social and economic factors which so perplexed the I.C.C.A.J., but he does give a positive value to Judaism. Like the fundamentalist missions to the Jews and the Hebrew Christians, Barth bases his eschatology on Romans 9-11, with which Paton had so little sympathy. To assert that the Jews have rejected their Messiah for all time unless God intervenes is coming close to the principle behind the former Roman Catholic charge of deicide, which has fostered so much anti-semitism, as Catholics frequently held that present-day Jews were responsible for the crimes of a small mob centuries earlier. In the work of Forell of Vienna or the Hungarian pastors associated with the Church of Scotland, to cite two well-documented cases, the I.C.C.A.J. would point to the successful evangelisation of those who were certainly not repudiating the Messiah, apart from those Jews assimilated unnoticed into German society before 1914.[31] The I.C.C.A.J. based its theology on general New Testament principles rather than on one passage and its possible interpretation. However, in all its statements, the I.C.C.A.J. emphasized the person of Christ to virtually the complete exclusion of everything else. Both Barth and the I.C.C.A.J. in the later period emphasized the importance of the role of the Christian Church.

When Robert Smith was appointed associate director of the I.C.C.A.J. in 1940 he and Paton exchanged many letters on the policy of the I.C.C.A.J. since Paton was supervising his work.[32] Paton justified Smith's appointment by arguing that the most alert and resourceful thinking available to the Church should be applied to the condition of the Jews 'as changed by revolution and secularism' (a constant concern of the I.C.C.A.J.) Smith agreed with Paton that the Christian approach to the Jews must be laid on the leaders of the Church as their responsibility, but restated the problem that Christians were prepared to accept the Jews' evaluation of the situation, and tolerate a 'laissez faire' attitude. Significantly, Paton considered that when Smith was studying the question of aiming for the conversion of individuals or of society, he did not sufficiently consider the significance of the strong family sense of Jewish society. This is consistent with Paton's understanding of the mass movements in India, where whole families, and social groups were admitted into the church together, in a way natural to the organisation of Indian society where the individual is sub-ordinated to his caste group or family.

The great weakness of the traditional organisation of mission to the Jews, in Paton's eyes, was that they had concentrated on inner city areas, which were now being vacated by Jews in Britain and America. The missions to Jews fought each other for converts and then used them for ministers, but the I.C.C.A.J. was not concerned with improving the efficiency of missions but of changing the fundamental theology of this approach. Previously only the Church of Scotland had involved itself directly in mission to the Jews, and in its work in Hungary had established good relations with local Reformed congregations, who absorbed the Jewish converts.[33] Working from this precedent, but also from sound theological principles, Hoffmann sought to direct the entire programme of evangelism into being a church responsibility, whether as that of the local congregation welcoming the Jews in their midst, or in terms of the national church leadership sponsoring conferences, training for clergy and so on. This was a radical departure, but was consistent with all that Paton and the I.M.C. were doing in India to encourage the movement from missionary society to church evangelism; it had its justification in the Tambaram findings. In other words, seen in the context of developments in other fields, it was not an original development. Hoffmann was probably encouraged by Paton's experience, because otherwise the link between mission to Jews and other types of evangelism is very tenuous indeed.[34] Nevertheless, it is the most important single contribution to the understanding of evangelism.

By placing the responsibility for mission to the Jews on the local congregations wherever Jews and other unchurched people were living, Hoffmann was anticipating the 1968 W.C.C. study, 'The missionary structures of the congregation'. He argued, and Paton agreed with him, that the existing missions to Jews were so fundamentalist and independent of church control as to be more of a hindrance than a help to evangelism.[35] He even discussed starving out all agencies not accredited with churches. His attempts to educate American congregations in their responsibilities were so conspicuous that it is not surprising that there was friction with the older missions to Jews, though Hoffmann and Paton at times expressed admiration of their work. Successfully carried to its logical conclusion, this aspect of the I.C.C.A.J's policy would have led to the demise of such societies.[36]

Paton's theological position was the cause of much misunderstanding and argument when the Council of Christians and Jews was formed. The incident does not show Paton in a very attractive light, but it is significant for illustrating the depth and passion, as well as the inflexibility of his convictions. In Chapter XII the role of the 'Peace Aims Group' was discussed, in which Paton was endeavouring to match his exploitation of government policy makers with his efforts to stir up church people into some form of forward planning. He was also very concerned, as in the case of the Cloister Group discussed in Chapter IV to maintain the dialogue between groups with diametrically opposed views on the same vital subject. So in April 1941 he took typical steps to form a little group with the blessing of the I.C.C.A.J. 'to get some thinking done.' No papers survive relating to this group, unless articles by Dr. Garvie, Dr. Hans Kosmala, a refugee scholar of Jewish problems, and one of the non-Aryan W.C.C. scholarship holders, Dr. Hans Ehrenberg in the April and July issues of the I.R.M. in 1941 relate to this. It can also be proved that Paton was circulating the archbishops of Canterbury and York, Bell, Hutchison Cockburn, Berry and Aubrey of the Baptists with documents describing the conditions of the Jews in Europe. These, however, were his colleagues in the formation of the B.C.C. and the Peace Aims Group, so the group might simply have been a sub-group of the Peace Aims Group.[37]

According to Dr. Parkes and W.W. Simpson, Mrs. Freeman and Dr. Parkes first thought of the idea of a council of Christians and Jews, so it is very strange to find Paton taking up cudgels on behalf of Mrs. Freeman, an English Hebrew Christian he much admired for her ability and intelligence, when it transpired that both of them had been excluded from a 'Joint Council of Jewish-Christian Relations'. This body had been formed in November 1941 after a meeting which they had both attended, at which it had been decided to 'take appropriate action', though Paton considered it to have been an 'extremely floppy, ineffectual meeting'. Paton correctly concluded that it was their connection with the I.C.C.A.J. which had led to this discrimination against them. He perhaps did not know what Parkes and Simpson both recall, that the Chief Rabbi was as suspicious of the Council as a Roman Catholic hierarch about the W.C.C.F. and that any hint of 'proselytism' would have made co-operation impossible. Paton thought, perhaps, that his W.C.C hat entitled him to participate, since he was undoubtedly involved in the same concerns as the Council of Christians and Jews, namely: the promoting of positive relations between the two communities, especially in areas receiving Jewish refugees; co-operation between Jewish and youth organizations so that youth can be educated out of prejudice; public statements to combat prejudice; and joint study on a new order. Beeley of the Chatham House Group thought that there would be little overlapping and competition with Paton's approach to the subject.[38] Paton consequently became involved in a vitriolic correspondence with the Revd Henry Carter, a doctrinaire Methodist pacifist many years older than Paton, who was a Methodist representative on Life and Work and also part of the Bloomsbury House organization for aiding refugees. He rejected any suggestion that he was beholden to Paton for an entrée into the W.C.C.F. and stoutly maintained his independence of Paton.

The correspondence with Carter turned on the point that Paton believed that all Christians involved should be committed to the New Testament principle of evangelizing the Jews.[39] To be committed to less was to hold the Jews to be unworthy of the Gospel. He wrote to Cooper of the Home Office that he was pleased at any effort to get Jews and Christians together, but doubted if much would be achieved because of the similarity between this movement and the 'goodwill' movement in the United States. However, at the end of December 1941 Paton's reaction to Smith's inquiry about what the attitude of the I.C.C.A.J. should be to the formation of a body in Scotland on similar lines, with the purpose of discussing anti-semitism and common questions without compromising the mission issue, was to reply that he saw no objection to an attempt to do this, provided that co-operation was tied to specific topics. He compared it to the situation in the relationship to the Roman Catholic renewal movement 'The Sword of the Spirit' where both sides respected the other's position.[40] It is absurd to think that co-operation should be taken to imply a retreat from the Christian claims to the Gospel imperative. Paton called this attitude 'dialectical', that is holding in tension the Gospel imperative to evangelize and the desire for practical co-operation with the Jews on reconstruction. Whatever the true explanation of events, Paton felt martyred for a view very close to his heart, despite the I.C.C.A.J's stand against anti-semitism and support for relief work. The way in which he 'threw the Bible' at Carter was identical to the full-scale row he had in 1930 on Geneva station platform with Dr Parkes who was then working for the I.S.S. in Geneva and endeavouring to combat anti-semitism in Switzerland.[41] It was unfortunate that Paton could not recognize that at this point he could not be a chameleon, and that the sensitive situation in Jewish-Christian relations was such that it was not possible to co-operate in quite the same forthright terms as he could with Indian nationalists seeking an independent church and state for India. The cause of the dispute was at root theological, and in this instance Paton only barely modified his views over a decade, and not significantly enough to make a new relationship possible. W.W. Simpson admits that his own theology was very woolly at this point, as Paton thought it was, but he was open to learn about Judaism to a degree which Paton was not.[42]

In May 1940 Robert Smith was surprised to hear that Paton had been making informal inquiries about a position at the headquarters of the Church of Scotland, as secretary of the Jewish Missions Committee, but Macanna had already been appointed assistant secretary with a view to succeeding the venerable Dr Webster as secretary the following year. It would have meant moving to Edinburgh and accepting a lower salary, but Robert Smith deduces that it is evidence of the seriousness with which Paton regarded mission to the Jews in 1940, since had the post still been vacant, he would have undoubtedly been appointed. Robert Smith may be right about this aspect of the significance of his request for the post, and therefore the incident has been taken as a conclusion to this discussion on Paton's contribution to the work of missions to the Jews. It should also be remembered that by 1940 Paton was secretary of the W.C.C.F. and moving in a churchward direction. A position in the Church of Scotland administration would have been a stepping stone in the direction of a church-based position.[43]

Preparing the churches and missions to meet the emergency

In his efforts to make mission to the Jews church-centred, Hoffmann observed a very significant tendency among the members of American congregations who had formerly supported the traditional missions to Jews. They were prepared to approve of such activity when it was conducted in distant Europe, but not when it was happening on their doorstep. This reaction sprang from none of the theological principles discussed above, but from anti-semitism. In discussing the work of Paton, Hoffmann and his colleagues in attempting to arouse the churches to the dire predicament of Jews in Europe, the question of anti-semitism assumes central importance. Whatever may be written to demonstrate that anti-semitism was incidental to Hitler's ideology, or that he was exploiting for his own ends a mass psychosis, the fact remains that he was able to re-animate and systematize a centuries' old tradition sustained by popular religion and economic tensions.[44] Undeterred by crushing military defeats on the Eastern front, Hitler continued the programme of extermination regardless of the military resources it absorbed. In view of the British habit of ignoring unpleasant facts until they are hit on the head by them, one must ask: to what extent did the I.C.C.A.J. endeavour to make the churches aware of the root cause of the emergency, whether it was appreciated how anti-semitism strikes at the roots of the Christian faith, and what practical steps were taken? The degree of Paton's personal involvement is again hard to establish, but Catherine Paton remembers 'anti-semitism' being one of the topics ardently debated in the Paton household as 'totalitarianism' and 'fascism' were. The Paton children tried to undermine Mrs Paton's belief in the infallibility of Chesterton and Belloc by pointing to the blatant anti-semitism in their writings.[45]

In the early reports of the I.C.C.A.J. one finds that the subject is being tackled in two ways. First, as in the motion of the Chicago conference of May 1931, a positive statement was made of the social and cultural benefits which Jewish citizens bring to society.[46] To a certain extent, this is a more effective rebuttal of passive anti-semitism than a direct condemnation of it, such as one finds at later conferences, for example, the Oxford Conference on Church, Community and State. The Jewish presence is considered a privilege rather than an economic liability. Secondly, much of Hoffmann's work was educational, in an attempt to correct prejudices and misinformation, whether he was working among Sunday school children in England or exposing the harsh facts of the impoverishment by legal restrictions of Jews in Germany and Poland, and the plight of those attempting to flee. He considered then that although the outbreaks of anti-semitism have brought the problems of Jews to the attention of many in the West for the first time, and in some respects have been counter-productive in terms of sympathy aroused, the most important development caused by prejudice was the growing consciousness of Jews of their heritage. Mission to the Jews must take account of this new awakening.

The I.C.C.A.J. inevitably responded with a motion passed at the I.C.C.A.J. meeting at Digswell Park in 1932, which had the value of stating clearly where the I.C.C.A.J. stood on the question in unequivocal terms. While stating that the causes of misunderstanding and prejudice did not rest entirely on one side, it continued:

> 'Discrimination against any race is utterly contrary to the mind and example of Christ, and the situation throws a special responsibility on Christian people to show the love of Christ in their attitude to the Jews . . . on the Church rests the urgent duty of doing everything possible in the Spirit of Christ to remove causes of misunderstanding, hatred and prejudice'.[47]

The I.C.C.A.J. recognised that anti-semitism was deeply rooted in the Christian Church. Therefore, Hoffmann worked with Hanns Lilje of the D.C.S.V., though Parkes' memoirs show how difficult such work was because of the total absence of unbiased Aryan speakers. Richter, the I.M.C's elder statesman in Berlin, organized a seminar attended by about 40 Fascist students on anti-semitism, in which Jews participated, but this hopeful omen was a small flicker of light in the darkening political scene.[48] One has to turn to Heinrich Grüber's memoirs 'Erinnerungen aus den sieben Jahrzehnten' for a full description of the corruption of the Evangelical Churches by anti-semitism.[49] A particularly unsavoury set of writings are those of Otto Dibelius, dating from 1928, before the Evangelical churches came under pressure from the Nazi party.[50] After the 'Nazi organised' lynchings and burnings in April 1933 Otto Dibelius broadcast a report to America that there had been no bloodshed in this boycott of Jewish shops and that all was quiet in his diocese. Peace in Germany depended on whether the agitation against Germany continued or not, so he appealed to friends in America to see that the situation in 1933 was a return to good German traditions, and trust the Germans to solve their own problems. (People whom I have interviewed say that the attitudes and discrimination bore a great similarity to much of what one knows is happening in South Africa.) Dibelius' reaction shows that protests by Life and Work and the I.M.C. were having some effect, but neither organisation was a giant-slayer.

The dismal history of the Evangelical churches' adoption of the Aryan paragraph excluding Jews by race from office in the church has already been effectively and accurately chronicled.[51] Paton was fully informed because of the activities of his two friends in the Basel Mission, Hartenstein and Koechlin. In 1933 representatives of the Herrnhut, Basel, Berlin, Barmen, Leipzig and Hermannsburg missions (all members of the I.M.C.) issued a 'Barmen Declaration' rejecting the Aryan paragraph and authorizing the German Evangelical Missionary Council (D.E.M.R.) to make representations to the church administration through the channels which supported the missions and directly to diocesan rulers, laying down the exact boundaries of the missionary constituency, and rejecting any interference in it by the state and the advocates of the 'New Order'. The missions rejected a philosophy which would contravene the principles of the Reformation, the idea of the universal Christian Church manifested in the ecumenical movement, and the teaching of Christ. The statement is not as theological nor as profound as the second Barmen Declaration in which Bonhoeffer was involved in 1934, but is essentially a conservative reaction to preserve the Gospel. Nevertheless Paton applauded the statement.[52] Only after the war did Hartenstein manage to work out the theological implications of anti-semitism properly.[53]

Paton agreed with Hoffmann's statement in his 1935 report:

> 'Increasingly Christendom needs to realize that consistent anti-semitism such as the present German government is now fostering, cannot tolerate the Christian religion with which it is irreconcilable and against which it must therefore fight. It is ominous that Christians both within Germany and abroad so largely fail to recognize this fact'.[54]

If Paton saw that anti-semitism struck at the heart of the Christian Gospel, it is doubtful whether he ever asked the question which Bonhoeffer wrestled with in 1933, that is, whether the Church could be considered to be the true Church which discriminated against Jews.[55] In England, whatever the extent of popular sentiment against Jews, there was no official discrimination, and therefore discrimination tended to be 'passive', rather than 'active', except for such manifestations as Oswald Mosley and the marches and counter-marches in the East End of London. In fact the proportion of Jewish to non-Jewish members of Parliament was and probably is higher than the proportion of Jews among the population. The Church of England and the Presbyterian churches re-employed most of the refugee non-Aryan clergy from Germany, and from the documents emanating from Kosmala and from the people whom I have interviewed it would seem that middle-class Christians made a special effort to welcome Jewish refugees. Moving in the circles that he did, Paton would therefore not find the question so urgent, apart from the fact that in 1933 he was only beginning the transition from a mission-based theology to an ecclesiological one. It should be added that as a participant in the Life and Work movement and as a friend of Bishop Bell's, Paton must have known how the Universal Council of Life and Work was avoiding taking any decision on Bonhoeffer's claims as to whether the Church Office in Berlin or the Confessing Church Synod at Barmen represented the true Church in Germany, whatever they thought privately.[56]

Paton's solution was a very middle class one. He arranged for the transfer of the 'Leipzig Delitzschianum' to London via Vienna, and scraped together a salary for the director, Hans Kosmala, for whom he then arranged lecturerships, lecture tours, and the publication of the book 'The Jew in the Christian World'. Kosmala's work was on the same subject as Dr Parkes', the historical development of anti-semitism and was intended as a way of breaking the intellectual block which exists concerning most forms of racism. 'The Institute of Jewish Studies' was entirely the product of his energies, though it remained very small in wartime conditions.[57] A question to which there is no answer, is whether there was in Paton's mind any distinction between anti-semitism and racism. What is certain is that the study of anti-semitism provided a bridge between Paton's concern for mission to the Jews and practical relief work.

Practical help for Jewish people

The missions to Jews in Central Europe could not cope with the crisis of 1933 when more than 500,000 non-Aryans became destitute. Until the last depot was forced to close, the missions did what they could with their slender resources, but more powerful organisational aid was needed. Consequently the I.C.C.A.J. instructed Paton to collaborate with Henriod of the Geneva Life and Work office. Paton was anxious not to duplicate another organisation's efforts, and to get accurate information on the situation. He had justifiable doubts about supporting the High Commissioner for Refugees coming from Germany's office (which was a League of Nations office not supported by the League of Nations budget but by contributions coming in theory from the governments receiving refugees). Henriod replied to his query in February 1934 that it was the policy of Life and Work to support existing organisations, and stimulate the churches into sending money especially for Hebrew Christians. The I.C.C.A.J. seems to have adopted this policy.[58]

Hoffmann's visit to Germany in the summer of 1935 marks the transition to increasing involvement in relief work. The report Hoffmann produced in September 1935 shows him concentrating his imagination and the reflections from his encounters with hundreds of pathetic cases to suggest sweeping improvements in the woefully inadequate aid which was trickling through. With great command of language he contrasted the Germany which the tourist and such apologists for national socialism as Bishop Headlam and the Dean of Chicester saw, with the hell two million Jews were living in. Paton had no direct contact with Keller, the Director of the European Bureau of Inter-Church Aid, and deeply mistrusted him.[59] To Paton and Hoffmann there was no question of the problem being solved by other than government action. Paton himself vigorously supported the lobby trying to persuade the British and American governments to ease immigration procedure to allow whole families to enter instead of isolated and affluent individuals. The High Commission and the European Bureau also saw this as being the central issue. Paton and Hoffmann corresponded much on the prospects for the two conferences held to stimulate government action, the Evian conference of 1938 and the Bermuda conference of 1943, which were complete failures, even in the direction of making it possible for refugees to apply successfully for the limited number of visas available, apart from the question of enlarging the quota.[60]

As secretary of I.M.C., Paton was active in only one aspect: that of endeavouring to find employment with missionary societies for non-Aryan doctors who were forbidden to practise in Germany and Austria. However, Continental medical degrees were not recognized within the British Empire for doctors applying for government work, so further training in England was necessary. Secondly, British missionary societies were experiencing difficulties in finding the salaries of their existing staff. A handful of people were enabled to come to Britain to study and I think three or four went straight out to the field.[61] There is one letter to indicate, perhaps, that Paton took action on his own account.[62] There were an estimated 30,000 Jewish and non-Aryan refugees in Belgium, and unlike those in Holland, they were not interned anywhere. Paton wanted help organised for them and found that Anet, the I.M.C. correspondant in Belgium, was creating difficulties about this, while his fellow clergy were very reluctant to accept any responsibility. Paton refuted Anet's objections that the Jews were scroungers or spies: he said that he had never, in all his experience, met deception such as Anet suggested, a statement which the archived dossiers of personal cases amply support. Paton suggested a hospitality committee of Jewish missions at work in Belgium, which would include the several Dutch missionaries doing good work in Brussels. It would be interesting to know if Paton tried to activate the I.M.C. machinery in any other country. In Holland Dr Slotemaker de Bruine, an I.M.C. collaborator, was a member of the efficient hospitality committee, and was collaborating closely with the Büro Grüber. It was he who received Robert and Ethel Smith when they brought 70 Jews from Prague to London in March 1939 in a dramatic flight Mrs Smith initiated by refusing to move from the city commandant's office until he signed the exit visas.[63]

In 1938 Hoffmann made a journey across Europe which convinced him that a new initiative in refugee relief desperately needed making on a very large scale, and that he was the person to head a Berlin office to do this. In his anguish he drew up a comprehensive plan for relief for starving Jews in Germany based on the First World War P.O.W. programme he had experience in, training for settlement in Palestine or areas where they would need English, actual emigration and resettlement. Drastic action was needed by the churches to force governments to admit settlers. He concluded that action to save the Jews has become a touchstone of the sincerity of Christians and that if they act as their beliefs demand, recognition of the validity of these beliefs will follow, not that the Jews should be helped in order to win more converts.[64]

Paton's reaction was at first very cautious. It might prove right for Hoffmann to devote all his time to the refugees' problems, but he hopes nothing will prevent him from carrying out the British I.C.C.A.J. programme. In the end Paton wrote to support Hoffmann's case to the Northern Presbyterian church, who were still finding the larger part of his salary. Warnshuis was much more cautious, and maintained that his place was raising money in America, since nothing could be done without funds. It would be better to set up a campaign to arouse the conscience of Protestant Christendom and so insist on the strengthening of the President's committee on refugees. However, in view of what Warnshuis says Cavert was already doing, it seems probable that Hoffmann would have duplicated his efforts.[65]

The outbreak of war necessitated a complete change of the W.C.C's staffing arrangements and caused an acute financial crisis. In December 1939 Hoffmann reported to Paton that he had drawn a complete blank on the Inter-governmental Committee on Refugees, which had been set up by the Evian conference in 1938. Not only could Hoffmann not raise fresh money, Paton became seriously alarmed that the I.C.C.A.J. would not be able to carry on at all, and was surprised that Mott and Warnshuis should allow this to happen after all Hoffmann's work. He deprecated the idea of Hoffmann starting P.O.W. work in Europe as Visser't Hooft and Freudenberg were doing this, as well as Kraemer, Koechlin and the Scandinavians.[66] Paton's activities on behalf of non-Aryan refugees seem mainly to have been directed towards money-raising and spreading information. Paton was responsible for the appointment of Dr Freudenberg, himself a non-Aryan refugee, as the W.C.C.F. worker for refugees. He was also from 1938 a member of the International Christian Committee, which was Bishop Bell's relief committee. The conference he attended in Geneva in March 1939 inspired plans for a W.C.C. refugee office to be centred in London, with the functions of liaison work, stirring up support, and inventing emigration possibilities. Paton was charged with finding transatlantic support and the medical placements.[67]

As secretary of the W.C.C.F. Paton was involved in the decision to bring four refugee non-Aryan scholars to Britain, and had much correspondence with at least one of them, Hans Ehrenberg, who was living in a remote area of Cheshire. Neither he, Kosmala nor Leibholz could manage on the £250 per year which Paton had arranged to have paid to them, so Paton tried to find them additional sources of income. Paton helped to find positions in the Presbyterian churches for some of the non-Aryan pastors whom Bell arranged to come to England. Pastor Hildebrandt cannot remember a direct relationship with him, but Rieger and Büsing, both pastors of German congregations, were particular friends, and involved him in the Council of the Confessing Church pastors, which met as a church synod in Cambridge. He made financial and literary contributions to their magazines. For various reasons the pastors became embittered and suspicious of the staff of the Geneva Office, since Schönfeld had passed on information about them to Heckel, and Freudenberg was still managing to travel to Germany. Visser't Hooft seemed to them to be out of touch with the political realities of the situation and too much under Schönfeld's influence. Paton stoutly defended the Geneva Office.[68] One should also note here that Paton was active on behalf of the non-Aryan pastors as well as other refugees interned under the May 1940 internment measures.

In conclusion, it seems that Paton did not drift into involvement in refugee relief, but was drawn in because of the demands made on Jewish missions and because of his position as I.M.C. and W.C.C.F. secretary. Through the work of Hoffmann, he learnt of the terrible sufferings of individuals, and applied his organisational skills in disseminating information, raising money and finding opportunities for individuals to the limit of what was possible with his slender resources. He urged government action as the only practical solution. His friendship and counsel were greatly appreciated by the refugees he knew, but neither he nor Hoffmann were able to mobilise public opinion to any great extent. He was very anxious not to duplicate any other organisation's work. I do not know that he ever reflected on the theological implications of what he was doing but he was concerned that justice should be done as in the case of the refugees in Belgium, whose presence was so unwelcome.

Witness to a massacre

The shadow of the terrible deaths of six million Jews, victims of national socialist racial policies and the indifference of Allied governments, lies across any discussion of refugee work 1930-45. The extermination policy did not begin with Auschwitz, but with smaller massacres, and constant harassment of Jews so that many were driven to take their own lives. The inexorable question as far as the terms of reference of this book are concerned are simple; how much did Paton perceive of the situation, and how soon? Given the responsibility which was his when he possessed information about the massacres, how does one assess his reaction? Paton is not one of the very few people of whom one can say that they did all they could, but he did show remarkable sensitivity when he could have abdicated responsibility in a question too grave for the individual churchman. An example of Paton's reactions is the Lublin concentration camp.

The first report of these transportations was published by the 'Neue Zürcher Zeitung' on 1.11.39. All male Jews were being sent from Poland and occupied Baltic countries to a reserve near Kattowitz. An American, Miss Pohek from Vienna, checked the story and reported that 2,000 Jews had been transported from Vienna. Freudenberg wrote urgently to Hoffmann about this, requesting more money if they were to do anything, and saying that there could be no doubt that their fate would be comparable to the Turkish massacres of Armenians. Hoffmann responded by calling the American committee immediately, and writing to Sweden with specific financial requests. His efforts were being nullified by the labour regulations which forbade organisations from paying emigrés' fares. Freudenberg wrote to Paton at the same time begging him to get permits for those with British relatives, and to mobilise Christian opinion. Readers of the Christian Newsletter were alerted to the situation by a bluntly realistic 'Supplement' written by Dr Parkes on December 6th, 1939, in which he described in grim detail the entire plight of the Jews in Europe.

On 12.11.39 Paton met Norman Bentwich, a leading British Jew, Miss Bracey of the Society of Friends and Miss Livingstone of the Y.W.C.A., Bishop Bell's sister-in-law, to discuss the 'desperate situation in Poland'. Paton had learnt from Freudenberg of the transportation of Jews to an area near Lublin in Poland where they were forced to live without shelter or adequate food, and were dying of exposure.[69] It was reported that in England it was impossible to raise fresh money, and with war regulations it was unlikely that it would be possible to transfer it. Bentwich said: 'It is no good arguing about whether the area is 40 square miles or 40 miles square for the plain object of the plan is to kill off the Jews'. So Paton added when he wrote to Hoffmann:

> 'Unless the conscience of America can be moved by what is one of the greatest tragedies in all history we shall simply watch the slow massacre of several hundreds of thousands of people. I learnt from Visser't Hooft that in answer to his appeal you could only reply that you had already had to borrow. If that really does represent the attitude of Christian America on the subject, I am afraid we must resign ourselves to the massacre to which I have referred. I can only beg you to do all you can to get people in America to see that there is in progress, if this plan of the reserve at Lublin goes through, a comprehensive massacre'.

There was a public outcry about Lublin, and at the end of December news filtered through of a postponement of the plan, but according to Freudenberg this was the result of Nazi disagreement with their Soviet friends, while the intention to exterminate the Jews had not changed at all. Paton was insisting that utmost energy be devoted to pushing emigration from Germany. Kullmann of the League of Nations' High Commission was to question the accuracy of the reports because of the known breakdown in transportation from Stettin, but Visser't Hooft, who uncovered this 'official' incredulity in March 1940, said Kullmann saw the need for getting people out of Germany.

The question of the Lublin reserve is a paradigm for the question of W.C.C. and the League of Nations' officers receiving information and acting or not acting upon it, as far as it would have been possible for them to do so. Paton's sources of information through government channels were good, and for much of the war he was receiving weekly letters from Visser't Hooft, but those working in Switzerland were in an incomparably better position, not only for access but also for organizing relief.[70] The question, however, is not merely one of whether adequate and accurate sources of information were available to the W.C.C., but whether the recipients were able to comprehend its significance. Dr Visser't Hooft writes in his memoirs that the full horror did not strike him until a Swiss business man who had been to Russia, apparently late in 1942, described the work of one of the Einsatzgruppe, who had rounded up Jewish men, women and children, forced them to lie down in mass graves and machine-gunned them. Yet in the W.C.C. archives there are the letters of individual non-Aryans who relate harrowing experiences; for example, a woman wrote in September 1939 of how 64 people in her village, including the clergy, had been slaughtered, others taken hostage in a five day episode of organised terrorism.[71] Another letter came from a Jewish Christian assistant of the Büro Grüber after Grüber's arrest in 1942, describing how her family is being harassed and members of it are disappearing in the deportations.

Although the tenor of Nazi propaganda ought to have alerted observers to the ultimate fate of the Jews, the enormity of the intended crime was too great to be imagined for many. Until one can break down the numbers into eye-witness accounts such as those quoted above, or those received from Auschwitz 1942-44, statements such as Freudenberg's to Karl Burckhardt of the 'Mixed Commission' of the Red Cross, that a high-ranking German, whose good faith they have no reason to doubt, says that 6,000 Jews a day are being shot in Poland, remain anonymous facts.[72] Another element to be taken into consideration is the degree to which Jews and resistance workers who were surrounded by the evidence did not realize what was happening. Visser't Hooft writes of Dutch resistance leaders who did not equate Auschwitz with death and Jeanne Merle d'Aubigné of Jews whom she could not persuade to take the danger to themselves seriously, sometimes giving themselves up voluntarily.[73]

It is the systematic, scientific mechanical nature of the extermination pro-gramme which was the most difficult thing to comprehend. We know now that delays in the programme were due to technical difficulties, but that once begun even the most urgent demands of the military situation were sacrificed to it. While the war on the Russian front was lost for lack of transport along over-extended lines of communication, the vitally needed wagons were being used to transport Hungarian Jews to the extermination camps. Paton was certain of the fate of the Jews in 1939, but he could not see how it would be done.[74]

The problem resolved itself into three points. Getting suitable information on which to base an appeal in America and Great Britain, raising money from a very reluctant public and getting it converted into a usable currency, and exploitation of the opportunities Grüber was using throughout 1941 to help Jews emigrate. The spread of warfare meant the gradual closing of these avenues. Dr Visser't Hooft prosecuted all these points during his visit to England via France in March 1940. His subsequent report to Freudenberg is full of optimism concerning the rehabilitation and settlement of refugees in England, but he found that although everything was being done to campaign for more humane immigration regulations, nothing was being achieved. In his memoirs he recalls how Temple was still campaigning in the House of Lords in March 1943 without success.

Freudenberg was exchanging letters with Gerhard Rieger, general secretary of the World Jewish Congress in Geneva, at times on a daily basis. Rieger recalls that Visser't Hooft and the W.C.C. were instrumental in convincing Swiss authorities of the threat to the Jews in occupied countries and trying to obtain from them a more liberal attitude in their policy of not admitting refugees who were the victims of racial, as opposed to political, persecution. This only happened at the end of 1942 after some particularly outspoken sermons from Karl Barth and a diplomatic manoeuvre by Koechlin to ensure the entry of fugitives who were smuggled in by the Comité Inter-movementale auprès des Evacuées (C.I.M.A.D.E.), whose names C.I.M.A.D.E. had communicated to Bern previously.

Bringing Jews across the Swiss border was a feat of great heroism especially in the severe winter of 1942, since, when Boegner protested about the deportation of Jews from France, Laval, Petain's most powerful minister, told him that the strength of the border guards had been trebled. It is the heroism of CIMADE more than anything else which vindicates the efforts of the W.C.C. Founded by French S.C.M. members on an ad hoc basis to help Protestant evacuées from Alsace-Lorraine settle among the Catholic population of Southern France, CIMADE became the 'Aide Protestante' in the internment camps in Southern France, working very closely with the Y.M.C.A. Appalling conditions reigned in these camps, particularly after the fall of France, when they were filled with Jews. CIMADE was gradually driven under-ground as the Vichy regime became more oppressive, and the workers of CIMADE realized the danger to the Jews who had not yet been interned. CIMADE was supported by Boegner, President of the Federation of Reformed Churches, who made some notable approaches to the Vichy Government in unison with other religious leaders, and by Visser't Hooft, who found them finance, gave counsel and received the exhausted smugglers in Geneva.

In February 1942 Donald Lowrie of the Y.M.C.A. overheard a conversation between Laval and the German Commissar for Jewish Affairs which led him to suspect that deportation lists were being prepared. Five months later he extracted the necessary information from the Chief of Police that 10,000 would be deported in August. The American Quakers were alerted, and they and Cardinal Gerdier inter-vened. Tracy Strong saw Pétain himself and stressed the effect this action would have on American opinion. Pétain temporized, saying it was necessary to allow foreign Jews to go to save French Jews. The papal nuncios secured a delay in which CIMADE as well as catholic organisations helped about 5,000 Jewish children to disappear. News of this reached Paton via Geneva. In his report Tracy Strong drew his own conclusions, that the camps were being used as reservoirs in repeated round-ups and that as no Jewish Labour was used in German factories something sinister was intended which the official explanation of a 'reservation' in Poland did not cover. It must be part of a programme of 'purification' which is being kept to schedule in spite of military setbacks. Lowrie reported to Mott enormous ecumenical action to save the Jews, especially children, and the outrage expressed by the French. It is a strange coincidence that both ends of the Nazi plan were reported to Geneva at the same time, that Lowrie, Strong and the CIMADE workers struggled against the deportations at the same time as the first heavily disguised message about the Auschwitz extermination machinery came through in September 1942 to the World Jewish Congress in Geneva.

Rieger alerted the U.S. State Department, who told Rabbi Wise of New York, but then did nothing but demand 'verification'. Rieger informed the English Jew, Sidney Silverman, M.P., when the first reports came in, and the American church leader, Samuel McCrea Cavert, when he visited Geneva in September for a meeting of the Provisional Committee to plan reconstruction work. However, Visser't

Hooft's note in the archives (3.3.65) is that although more reports reached Geneva in the following months it was striking that for a long time the impression in Geneva and other well informed circles was that only a certain number of Jews were being killed, but that many others were put to work. Freudenberg's appeal to Burckhardt, of December 1942, was the third that he had made, and did not elicit much response. In December 1942 also Barou and Easterman of the W.J.C. in London sent out a letter on the action attempted so far, exhorting a general rallying of support, with approaches to all political and spiritual leaders and anyone whose broadcasts over Europe are likely to be of influence. Consequently at a rally held in Smith Square, London, by the International Federation of Trade Unionists, a strong resolution was passed condemning 'these monstrous atrocities' as it 'was time for trade unionists in Germany to do something or assume complicity'. Temple's reaction was different. Replying perhaps to a letter sent out to all religious leaders in Britain by the W.J.C. appealing for help and demanding denounciation and retribution on the Nazis, he said to Easterman that what he says will have no effect on German leaders as they know the game is all up with them when they are defeated anyway, but he will continue to express his views in the House of Lords for the sake of justice. This view of Temple's seems more reasonable than that expressed by many historians, that the Allied Government should have uttered dire threats and warnings on behalf of the Jews. The British Press began reporting the atrocities in November 1942, which is when Garbett made a famous speech on the subject.[75]

Nevertheless, Temple criticized the Evangelical churches in Germany in a sermon on Niemöller for not making any specific protest against the treatment of the Poles and Jews, although he told Paton he did it with some hesitation as he had not thoroughly checked the point. His justification was that the German pastors thanked him for saying it because they said it had been much on their consciences and yet they as people living in safety could not say it themselves. Paton thought he ought to have worded it differently, and replied: 'It was not only true but needed saying . . . I suppose my feeling is that these poor devils are having such a rotten time that if they do have the guts to go for the Gestapo in public they should get the credit for it'. I suppose this is a reference to the actions of the South German bishops in protesting against euthanasia, implying that a positive reference to ecclesiastical action ought to have been coupled with the reproach.[76] Unfortunately, Temple was saying this ten years too late.

Eventually in March 1943 an 'Aide Memoire from the secretariat of the World Council of Churches and the World Jewish Congress' was sent to the High Commissioner for Refugees of the League of Nations, Sir Herbert Emerson, with copies for the British and American governments through the British Embassy in Bern. Paton met one of the Commissioner's staff three weeks later and was amazed to hear of the document which he deduced must have emanated from Visser't Hooft. One can imagine his embarrassment at having to ask for a copy, especially as he was as much 'the secretariat of the W.C.C.' as Visser't Hooft. He became more indignant when he saw the document because he disagreed strongly with several points, and when he circulated it to Carter, Temple and Bell, he complained about the way in which 'my colleagues in Geneva' had 'swallowed Zionist proposals neat'.

The full text of the aide memoire can be found in Visser't Hooft's memoirs. Paton dismisses the W.J.C. as per se Zionist, but it is difficult to see the justification for Paton's protests, since the document states the obvious, that Jews should be admitted en bloc to North and South America and Palestine in exchange for German civilians held in those countries. Carter tried to allay his fears by pointing out that a suggestion could hardly be Zionist when the government had confirmed through a minister (Eden) that there were plans for receiving 33,000 Jews into Palestine from South East Europe. In fact the activities of the papal nuncio in Istanbul, Roncalli, and others were producing the effect of breaking the log jam in British colonial bureaucracy and the number of Jews allowed to enter was rising by a steady 9% on the pre-war flow, apart from a special block of visas allowed under the Evian promises, of 75,000 visas.[77] However, this was not enough for certain very vocal elements in New York, who influenced American opinion against British policy while ignoring the obstructionist policy of the State Department. Paton's judgment was coloured by his proximity to the Foreign Office, which apart from having to suppress the Grand Mufti's German-inspired agitations, feared a serious revolt of inflamed Arab opinion. In view of the outbreak of the Israeli war of independence in 1947-48 when the Jewish and Arab populations achieved parity, their caution was well-founded. They had no desire to face a war in Mesopotamia at the same time as a European war as happened in 1916-18. Paton was privy to Foreign Office thinking because he told Smith confidentially in 1942 that H.M. Government was asking the American government to quieten the Zionist agitation in New York.

Paton had a long interview with the High Commissioner for Refugees, Sir Herbert Emerson, on 20th April which he related to Carter, but not Visser't Hooft.[78] Emerson was very critical of the proposals, especially on the grounds that special attention directed at the Jews while such a large proportion of refugees were not Jewish was inviting anti-semitism. He said the only exchanges feasible would be of British P.O.Ws and wounded for German civilians but British public opinion would never tolerate wounded British being left in Germany while Jews were exchanged. The suggestion that security screening of applicants be dropped was impossible, and various other means of succour were not mentioned, such as the plan to allow Jews through Spain to North Africa. However, his chief point was that sufficient assurances had already been given to neutral countries and that proposals for rehabilitation had already been forwarded to the coming Bermuda conference. The aide memoire lies in the Ministry files 'pending' with no official comment attached to it, under Sir Antony Eden's instructions.[79]

Bell and Paton were agreed with the point that re-emigration as opposed to re-patriation should be open to refugees. In this Jews, Germans and Austrians were expected to proceed elsewhere. At the beginning of the war Paton had heard the assurances given that refugees in England would not be expected to leave — in fact large numbers of P.O.Ws and servicemen from Eastern Europe remained, but the decision should be contrasted with the British government's inhuman decision to hand over Russians fighting in the German forces to the Soviet government.

The Bermuda conference in April 1943 did not result in any increased activity to save Jewish people. The Secretary of State, Cordell Hull, justified his government's policy as liberal and humane when the British Ambassador in Washington made representations as a result of parliamentary agitation. Paton finally received a communication from Visser't Hooft in May 1943, which of course he had already received from other sources. Possibly, had Paton lived, he would have undertaken more diplomatic activity for Jews, for example on his planned visit to Sweden in September 1943. Possibly he compromised himself by being too close to the Foreign

Office, yet the man who successfully fought to have the ban on Lutheran missionaries 1942-43 lifted, and who effectively used his 'hot-line' to the India Office, was surely capable of wielding more muscle in government circles if he had been fully informed. Therefore, it becomes legitimate to ask what he would have done if he had been fully informed of all that was known in September 1942 and asked to act. At the time of his death he had just begun inter-governmental strategy to try and achieve an easing of religious persecution in Russia. He had the vision capable of initiating action on a similar scale for Jews. It would have been necessary to convince him that special rescue operations were necessary for Jews, and that mention of Palestine did not necessarily mean complicity with Zionism. However, had Visser't Hooft briefed him with more than generalities, he could have done more. In the Annual Survey of the I.R.M. for 1940 he stated that Jews were being exterminated in Germany, without giving any qualification or elaboration. He may not have known more, but had more been written it would of course, have affected the sending of the I.R.M. by indirect means to Germany. It is possible, too, that with better information, Paton might have been more successful in raising money for relief work. He was hardly in a position to argue effectively with Emerson because he did not know what exactly had inspired the aide memoire. As it was, by maintaining payments to the W.C.C.F. in Geneva, Paton was indirectly helping support CIMADE.

In his memoirs, Dr Visser't Hooft reproaches himself for not having done more to arouse the churches from their apathy and blindness. It is difficult to know what more an organisation as small and weak as the W.C.C.F. could have done when the institutional might of the Roman Catholic Church was unavailing, and only the resourcefulness of individual Catholics taking in small groups of refugees was successful. It was ultimately the small illegal underground escape chains organized by CIMADE which were most effective, though CIMADE itself was at one point torn by divisions. Boegner and Koechlin did their utmost on a diplomatic level, for which the only Catholic parallel would be the action in April 1941 - April 1944 to save Hungarian and Rumanian Jews. Again it was a question of individuals' initiative. The most obvious and suitable organisation, the Red Cross, which had much greater resources than the W.C.C.F., was hopelessly compromised. The crime committed by the National Socialist government will remain one which casts guilt on Christendom. The exchange with Emerson does not show Paton in a good light, but the purity of his motives in the I.C.C.A.J. work does redeem his record somewhat. On the outbreak of war it was estimated that 10,000 children and 60,000 adult refugees of Jewish extraction had entered Britain, 1933-39, albeit on transit visas in many instances. Turning to the lack of righteousness of the British government, what they declared to be impossible then, in terms of admitting Jewish refugees to Britain after the outbreak of war, has been demonstrated to be perfectly possible with the action taken by the British government in September 1972 to admit 27,000 Ugandan Asians who were under a similar threat of extinction, imperfect though that settlement has been. There is very little to mitigate the condemnation of their policy, except that the U.S. government was much worse, and took proportionately fewer refugees in the years 1933-39.

Chapter XIV
Paton's Discovery of the Church

'The rediscovery of the Church' is the convenient label given to the development in ecumenical theology which began with the flowering of ecclesiology at the Oxford conference on 'Church, Community and State', and which continued until the Montreal Faith and Order conference in 1963. The catch-phrase suggests the recovery of an ancient truth which had been submerged, whereas in Paton's theology it was an entirely new departure, based on his reflections on the new developments in missionary expansion since 1800, which had resulted in the planting of churches all over the world. The ecumenical context of Paton's theology of the Church is important, but the development was due to more profound causes than a desire to adapt to prevailing ecumenical fashions. This can be shown by the fact that in 'World Community', a book based on lectures given in Princeton and Cambridge in 1937, Paton has made the theological evaluation and practical application of a doctrine of the Church into an integral part of his theology, and has become as much of an apologist for the Church as he was for mission. As in Paton's thought on mission and his approach to social questions there is a close correlation between Paton's experience and his reflections on that experience. His approach is practical, not abstract, and the resulting theology sustained him in his work for the I.M.C. and the W.C.C.F.

Paton's vision of a 'world-wide Church under God' was one which he was most successful in communicating, especially to student audiences who grasped the feel of the universal Church with as much fervour as their predecessors had the idea of 'The Evangelisation of the World in this Generation'.[1] Since Paton had always been something of a hawk in an ecclesiastical dove-cote, his championing of the idea of the Church might seem to be the conversion of the reprobate, but in fact taken to their logical conclusion his ideas would completely undermine the ecclesiastical establishment as he knew it, and they made him very impatient of the failures in church unity. No amount of argument from Orthodox, Roman Catholic or Anglican friends would persuade him that any one historical denomination was the Church as Christ intended it to be, much less the manifestation of the Kingdom of God.[2] However, his appreciation of the idea of the Church, and what the historical approximations to it have achieved, leaves him with the concept of a unique, divinely-created and sustained fellowship without which the world cannot be saved.

Neither in the original 1916 edition of 'Jesus Christ and the World's Religions' nor in the 1927 revised edition is there any use of the concept of the Church, even though each chapter ends with a description of how Christianity can supply what is lacking in other religions. The sole reference to the Church comes in an exhortation, that it is all or nothing for Christianity, and that the only safe task for the Church is to undertake a task which seems impossible, in other words, the evangelisation of the world.[3] Unfortunately this is such a fleeting reference, that it is impossible to infer what his definition of the Church was, beyond that of being an instrument of God's will for the evangelization of the world. It is unlikely that he had already progressed so far as to be able to see mission as the task of the Church directly and not specialist missionary societies. One cannot cite passages in 'The Highway of God' (1921) because it was written jointly with Kathleen Harnett, but in 'Social Ideals in India' there are a few passages describing the growth of Christian communities in Indian villages. Paton's first glimpse of the Church would seem to have been the occasion when he conducted his first baptism, of an English-speaking convert at a Presbyterian mission on the Ganges, in Bengal, when it seems that he was as moved as the convert who was making public profession of his faith.[4] In fact one could argue that the reason why he found it so difficult to understand his wife's entry into the Church of England was because he failed to appreciate the significance to her of the idea of the Church. In 1918 Grace Paton was writing furious letters to Tatlow, and presumably to Paton, about the failure of the Church to overcome the barriers of class privilege and wealth.[5]

The reasons for this complete absence of an ecclesiology derive from Paton's position as a convert, as he described it himself when he was pleading for a non-theological Basis to the S.C.M. Paton's thought has been shown to develop in a logical fashion. If, as was argued in Chapter I, it took five or six years for Paton to begin to mature his Christological ideas, it plainly would be many years before he came to have a mature view of the Church. In addition to that, his membership of the S.C.M. would insulate him from the issue, especially since his ordination was postponed from 1911 to 1917. Judging by Skinner's writings, the subject would not be given much prominence on the Westminster College syllabus, and although Paton preached regularly in Presbyterian churches, the question would not present itself to him with any urgency. Here one sees again a marked contrast between Paton's position and that of Neville Talbot, the bishop's son who was also converted within the S.C.M. Tatlow was extremely careful not to allow the S.C.M. to become an alternative to the churches, and to encourage church membership, but there is little to indicate that the average S.C.M. member thought of the Church as more than a fellowship of individuals who were committed to serving Christ. From the keenness of church leaders to come to Swanwick, it is clear that the churches had little hold on students, whether they had been reared in their Sunday school systems or not. One suspects from the enthusiasm with which Paton's friends and contemporaries organized evangelistic campaigns through the churches that they saw the churches as a convenient base from which they could evangelize Christians to arouse in them a proper fervour for mission. Paton was probably too pre-occupied with missions and with evangelizing his fellow students to concern himself with questions of the nature of the Church.[6]

'A Faith for the World', which Paton wrote in 1929 in the aftermath of the Jerusalem meeting of the I.M.C., is directed to the average church member in an attempt to get him to join the tiny minority of the Church who support missions. The question is whether the whole Church is to be involved, or merely an enthusiastic minority. He devotes a chapter to consideration of the Church as the divine community, the Body of Christ, but he does so from the viewpoint of it being a deployable factor in missionary strategy. He now emphasizes the importance of building up churches, not mission stations, in the mission field and the significance of national leadership of these churches. He quotes the views of church leaders who want more missionaries, not fewer, and who want them for evangelism, not administration. The racial discrimination and disunity among the churches threaten to prevent the indigenization of the churches, but he is hopeful of the various schemes being evolved such as that for a Church of South India. In this context he discusses the problem for church leaders of choosing between international fellowship on a confessional or denominational basis, and national church unity schemes. The chapter reflects Paton's encounter with Asian and African churchmen who were concerned for the decolonization of their churches and their strengthening and expansion as the pre-requisite of mission. There is nothing in the chapter which cannot be traced back to the debates at Jerusalem and nothing which suggests Paton's own theological reflection on the question of the Church.[7]

Paton's address to the Mysore meeting of the W.S.C.F. in December 1928 contains a definition of the church which is significant.

> 'The Church is not a human creation. It is not like a club which people have invented and in which they amuse themselves to forget their weary hours. It is the Divine Society; it is, with all its historic faults — and nothing that is not divine could have survived the leadership the Church has sometimes had — with all its faults it is a Divine Society, an order of human living set in the world by God, something which, in His infinite Grace, Jesus Christ has used and is using as the vehicle of His spirit and mouth-piece of His will. And when you think of our world drawing closer together by mechanical means and yet not drawing closer together in the things of the Spirit, you will see what the Church might be as a truly spiritual supernatural fellowship in which every kind of man or woman can find himself or herself at home'.[8]

Although this passage comes in a speech on 'Federation and Internationalism' Paton does not make his doctrine of the Church the basis of his understanding of true internationalism in the way that he was to do in 'World Community' and 'The Church and the New Order' ten years later. Apart from the wry comment about the Church needing divine help to sustain it during periods of indifferent leadership, which was not repeated in later writings, the passage contains the kernel of his later ideas, namely that the Church is the creation of the divine will, not human inclination, and that it exists to obey God. Secondly that in the Church all differences of race and class are transcended by the value which God sets on every mortal whom He has redeemed.

It is obvious therefore from the chronology of Paton's writings that there is again in operation the slow maturation of his thought over a period of years. It is difficult to isolate any single experience as inspiring it, though probably the Jerusalem I.M.C. meeting, with so many representatives of the younger churches present, and with the unique experience of a united communion service was crucial, even though his immediate reaction was to think in terms of missionary strategy, not theology.[9] In 'The Faiths of Mankind' (1932) Paton is still thinking in terms of the individual's salvation, not of the corporate life of the Church, but in a chapter on the Christian life and Christian discipleship he does make the point that the Christian does not have to struggle in isolation, but has the support of the Christian congregation. He defines the Church then as being the earnest of the Kingdom of God, and the place where the Kingdom of God should be manifest, ideally. What he meant by this is uncertain because Paton's eschatology, such as it was, was not futurist, but seems to have been closer to the concept of realized eschatology, though he was always careful not to pre-empt God's future judgment.[10] The term 'earnest of' meaning a 'token of' first came into English theology from the writings of Calvin concerning the sacrament, but he had appropriated the term from Zwingli. It is a term which Paton would have encountered in his Presbyterian background.

One of Paton's strongest arguments, he considers, for the universal Church is the fact that it actually exists, planted throughout the world as a result of the modern missionary movement, and now through the grace of God, growing with its own roots in the lives of the people to which it was taken. The preparations for Tambaram and the actual conference itself are evidence to him of the universal nature of the Church as a Christian fellowship in which the members of the colonial powers and the nationalists, the members of warring nations and women released from centuries of social bondage, former beggars and Brahmin nobles can meet together, all redeemed by the same love of God in Jesus Christ. The empirical argument from the fact and texture of this fellowship is enough for him, although he does not gloss over the racism and prejudice which can exist in the Church, and he is particularly scathing about the Church's failure to welcome Christian Jews.[11] Paton's experience as I.M.C. secretary has produced this development in his theology and not any pre-existent intellectual conviction.

It is important to consider in which respects Paton's developing ecclesiology reflects the contemporary developments in the ecumenical movement. It is necessary to use conference reports and statements to do this since they represent a minimum consensus, though individual theologians advanced further. The First World War forced churchmen to rethink the whole question of the nature of the Church and its role in international affairs, since the churches seemed to have been gravely compromised by their association with the belligerent powers. The conference of neutral churchmen began this process when they met in Uppsala in December 1917, but in 1940, when writing 'The Hour and its Need', Paton was expressing his anxiety lest the churches should fail again in wartime, believing that the wrong actions by the churches would do irreparable damage.[12]

A further step was taken at the Stockholm Life and Work conference in 1925, when several delegates called upon 'the Church' to give a 'Christian soul' to the League of Nations. 'The Church' seems to be envisaged as a temporal institution with a prescribed sphere of action, of which individual denominations were part, but intoxicated though the delegates might have been by the display of Christian unity at the Stockholm conference, no indication is given as to how 'the Church' might do this, when it is so divided. Paton displays in 'World Community' and 'The Church and the New Order' a more sophisticated version of this idea when he argues that since the western world lost the coherent Christian world view which it had in the mediaeval concept of 'Christendom', civilization has disintegrated because there has been no undisputed motivating force.[13] In order to establish international law and an agreed framework of reference for national states and individuals it is necessary to return to the Christian ethic. This is an extension of Paton's earlier argument in his missiological writings that the Christian Gospel was necessary for nation-building in China, India and Japan.

The second report of the Stockholm conference on 'The Church and Economical and Industrial problems' produced a more adequate definition of the Church: 'The Christian Church has not by herself to carry out programmes of reform, but to impart the life-giving spirit to them, and take part in them where desirable. It is not required of her that she should furnish economic systems or technical details or political programmes, but it is expected of her to regenerate with the power which comes only from on high'.[14]

Some of the delegates at the Jerusalem conference displayed a tendency to assume that all Christians must support certain types of schemes of rural uplift, co-operative ventures, rural credit funds and so on, and to confound other delegates who did not possess their technical knowledge, but wished to query this attitude.[15] One cannot discern from surviving records whether Paton stood aloof from this or not, but in all his writings on the Church he does warn against the tendency to align the Church with any particular form of government or social programme for even 'western democracy' is expendable, particularly since in its present manifestations it had become separate from the Christian principles of the equal rights of all men which had given rise to it.

The third report of the Stockholm conference introduces a controversial view of the Church as God's instrument to hasten the coming of the Kingdom of God, first by converting individuals, but then to guarantee the revelation of God to all men and secure their 'right to salvation'. Apart from the eschatological expectation in this definition it is significant that the Church is seen in universalistic terms, as Paton always described it. Paton believed that it was the duty of the Church to carry on the work of God, confident that this was contributing to the Kingdom of God without giving the work a direct casual link to the coming of that Kingdom. Otherwise there was no point in praying 'Thy Kingdom come'. However, this point was fully discussed in Chapter IX.

Through the agency of William Temple, the message of the Lausanne conference on Faith and Order had much influence on the I.M.C. meeting at Jerusalem the following year. Since the I.M.C. was under a self-denying ordinance not to discuss theology, especially in the realms where denominational differences were rampant, the Lausanne report on 'The Nature of the Church' was less influential.[16] The report itself reveals all the difficulties involved in seeking an agreement on such a subject, since it gives a list of characteristics of the Church which appears to be an agglomeration of each denomination's definition of what these should be. Delegates were divided when they tried to explain the relationship of the denominations to each other. The Protestant view was that all the various denominations were members of one Church like the members of a body, even if the limbs were not very well co-ordinated. This would seem to have been Paton's usual shorthand definition in later years. To him, the Christian Church embraced all who acknowledge Christ and join together with other Christians in worship.

Has the Church a visible or an invisible nature? Can it be identified with any single existing body? Paton would answer that its nature was invisible, and it could not be identified with any existing body, but at Lausanne the full spectrum of opinion was displayed from the extreme Protestants who interpreted the term entirely spiritually, to others who thought it to be partially visible in the denominations, though its bounds go beyond the conventional denominational structures. The Orthodox and Söderblom drew an analogy between the body and the soul, the visible and invisible nature of the Church, defining the nature of the Church in the language of the Incarnation. It is unlikely that Paton would have gone as far as that.[17]

The real awakening to the problem of the nature of the Church came through the Oxford conference, which was a response to the problems for the ecumenical movement of the German church struggle. The debate the conference stimulated had a very profound impression upon Paton, as can be seen by the extensive use which he makes of Oxford conference material in 'World Community'. The Oxford conference delegates sought to clarify the question of the Church's duties in a totalitarian state, a matter of great interest to Paton after his visit to Japan, Korea and Manchuria. He agreed with J.H. Oldham's words: 'In the question of the Church are centred many of the problems that concern mankind, not Christians alone, but modern man'.[18] The Church militant was submitted to close scrutiny. Had the Church done enough to proclaim the Gospel and match it with costly deeds? Too often it has compromised its standards with those of the surrounding society. The Church must confess its failures and try again. The Church must serve the community, but not be subordinated to the state.[19] In Paton's writings it is clear that although he accepted the question of the Church's need to repent of its past failures, nevertheless, he would not permit the Church the luxury of wallowing in such statements of self-accusation, but saw them as a reminder that the Church as well as society stood under God's judgment, and could not adopt a stance of righteousness when urging society to repent. He criticized the Oxford report for putting 'penitence in every paragraph'.

The Oxford conference saw the birth of the oft-misunderstood slogan 'Let the Church be the Church', which Paton does not utilize as often as one would expect. The phrase was interpreted as meaning not that the Church should live for itself in a selfish way, in a self-imposed ghetto, but that it should be free to be the Church which its Master intended, untrammelled by political tradition, social convention or state control. In preparation for the debate on the nature of the church, Oldham and Visser't Hooft produced a book: 'The Church and its Function in Society', which Paton read carefully.[20] It contained a survey of denominational teaching on the Church, but the authors concluded that there was no 'ecumenical' definition which could be accepted by the denominations, and that 'the Church' does exist among the denominations but that one cannot say how or where it exists.

Paton attended the Edinburgh Faith and Order conference in 1937, at which the delegates were not merely exploring their differences as at Oxford, but were trying to go beyond this to a new understanding of the Church. However, the second section on 'The Church of Christ and the Word of God' was unable to delineate the bounds of the Church satisfactorily, though no-one would go to the extreme of excluding the 'communion of saints' or the struggling sinners here on earth. Protestant delegates were forced to take the idea of 'the communion of saints' seriously for the first time at Edinburgh, and probably Paton among them.[21] In 'World Community' Paton could write:

> 'Because the membership of the Church is based upon God's loving act, the relationship cannot end with death. In its belief in the Communion of Saints the Church has held to the truth that its members are not only those who live on earth, for they are one in fellowship with the 'glorious company', the 'goodly fellowship', 'the noble army' sung in the Church's great hymn of praise, Te Deum Laudamus'.[22]

There is no indication that Paton was in any way affected by the other major ecclesiological debate at Edinburgh, which concerned the relationship between the Holy Scripture and tradition and the Church. It took the form of a 'hen and egg' argument, which Bishop Talbot caricatured by saying that the Lutherans seemed to be arguing as though the Word of God dropped from the skies like a meteorite, and that the Church was then an appendix to the Word of God. In his view, if there were no Church, the Gospel could not be preached.[23] This question of whether the Word of God or the Church took precedence in evangelism was not resolved. However, the effect of the discussions was a call for a conference exclusively on the problem of the nature of the Church. The W.C.C.F. responded to this by devoting its study resources to consideration of 'The Ethical Nature of the Church' and the idea of 'Ecclesia Militans'.[24]

Paton does not seem to have contributed a paper to this study, perhaps because he was pre-occupied with the Peace Aims group study on the Church and international order, but he did offer his suggestions in 1941. He warmly supported Visser't Hooft's plans but he wanted to see the problem of the Church in mass society considered.

> 'At the Oxford conference, in the book that you and Oldham wrote and in several of the speeches delivered, there was reference made to the fact that the Christian fellowship of the Church in western urbanized society tends to be more and more a fellowship simply in terms of worship and that it is evacuated of the rest of the content which in a simpler phase of human society church life possesses. I remember in the address I gave at the conference drawing a contrast between the Indian mass movement type of community, where the church life means education, medicine and economic help as well as worship, and our western, urban church life. The point I wish to make is that this tendency for the Christian fellowship to lose its grip on the texture of human living is going to be accentuated in coming years if the tendencies which not only were growing before the war, but show every sign of increasing afterwards continue. There will, for instance, be large scale economic and reconstructive planning done on lines which must necessarily cut across the bounds of nations. It will be necessary that this should be done if human affairs are to be organized at all, but it is surely manifest that in proportion as this large scale planning succeeds church life will be affected and that Christians will either have to think out new ways of preserving the reality of Christian fellowship or be swamped'.[25]

Paton continued by describing the Church as the bulwark of personal freedom against the impersonal decisions of those planning the economics of mass society. Paton's prophecy concerning the effect of mass society has certainly been realized.[26] Unfortunately, I do not know whether Visser't Hooft acted on Paton's suggestions.[27] In general, it would seem that Paton was eclectic in his use of ideas concerning the nature of the Church when they were under discussion in the ecumenical movement. He was most influenced by the Oxford conference on Church Community and State, as his use of conference material in 'World Community' shows. Paton used ideas which were current in the mainstream of ecumenical thinking, but did not actually put them into print immediately after the respective conferences except in the case of the Oxford conference. Judging by his interest in the study on

'The Ethical Nature of the Church' it is fair to assume that had he had the time and the opportunity he would have contributed especially as his concern about the evolution of mass society would have been so relevant to post-war society.

Paton began his book 'World Community' by taking as his text a friend's remark that he felt that the Church was a completely hopeless organisation and that it was the hope of the world. He claims to be honest about the failings of the Church (although in fact he does not dwell very much on this point) while committing himself unreservedly to the latter conviction. In the book the term 'The Church' is used to denote 'that wide and actual fellowship of Christians, in some measure comprising and comprised in the divided communions which more and more we all recognise bind us together'.

Society has lost its inner unity of philosophy, morals and education which it possessed in the Middle Ages, when the idea and standards of 'Christendom' prevailed, whether individuals obeyed or disobeyed the Church, its authority was unchallenged until the Reformation and the growth of national churches. Paton attributed the mediaeval church's decline to the fact that a clerical caste were laying down rules for the laity, which is similar to Bonhoeffer's complaint about the double standards of morality in the Middle Ages.[28] Paton is no Anglo-Catholic seeking to restore the mediaeval position of the Church. He sees both Fascism and Communism as an attempt to reintegrate society and provide a soul for a spiritless society. They give a sense of meaning to life while claiming the whole person, so that he no longer has any freedom. He does not consider that western democracy as it stands is any more inspiring to young people.

After criticizing the Oxford conference report for over-emphasizing the need for a penitent Church, Paton then sets out to show how the Church is relevant to our need, and our frantic searching after community. There would be no point in doing this if the authentic Christian life and word were not found in the Churches. In the bewildering clamour of the new absolutes, Paton asserts that the key to community lies in the recognition of something that transcends human community.[29] This is the Church which can trace its ancestry back to the call to Abraham, and being in its essential nature chosen by God, claims to be Israel. One is brought into the Church by the love of God and not by human volition. The Church grew as the disciples went around doing what they believed to be God's will, convinced that whatever persecution might befall them, they were on the side of the Eternal. Consequently there is no activity of the Church which is quite as fundamental as its worship. The life of Christian society begins and ends with adoration. It is not possible to adore God in Christ and compare that revelation with that of other religions. The worship of God is crucial to this fellowship with Him, a point which Paton has not made so clearly or so strong in any of his previous books.

Central to the life of the Church is the Lord's Supper, which commemorates what in human terms was failure and betrayal. This paradox may explain the unpopularity of the Church; where it is unpopular, it shows that the foundation on which the Church is built is forgiveness. 'The Church is not only a society believing that God called it into being and seeking to put Him first in its life and thought, it is specifically a society based on the recognition that in the Cross of Jesus Christ the very life of God breaks forth into the world'.[30]

Because of God's action, the Church is a place where forgiveness is known. It is the Christian valuation of man, redeemed at such a price from the consequences of his sinfulness which makes human freedom so valuable to the Church. If God values man so much, what human society has the right to curtail his freedom? Paton elaborates these ideas more fully at the conclusion of 'The Church and the New Order' when he is describing post-war Europe. There is hope that society, corrupted by national socialism and by the war, will be redeemed, while the Church has already proved the value of this appreciation of its position by its stand in the different occupied countries for human freedom. Courage, constancy and succour for the persecuted and the refugees have been the hallmarks of the European churches, but hope for the future is not based on the Church's past record during the war, but on the Easter Gospel. Christ's terrible suffering and atonement for our sin, his identification with human predicament and his victory over death are the basis of the Christian hope.

> 'Forgiveness and power — they go together. The release from the bondage and fetter of sin by the knowledge of the divine forgiveness is the beginning of power for the Christian. He can make his own, as God gives him grace, that which Christ has already done. He is not going into an uncharted waste of waters as he faces the world of human sin, for in a deep and true sense Jesus has been there before him. He is not to offer mere good advice or moral counsel, admirable as these things are, he is to offer to desperate men the knowledge that a victory has been won, and that in repentance and faith they may make it their own'.

The Church has no other message for the world, and this is the real difference between state action and the work of the Church. If Christians in England can convey to Christians in Germany their sense that they both stand under the judgement of God, then reconciliation will be possible and new life. The work of the Church is, therefore, an acted prayer to God that they may be used in the doing of His will.[31]

This distinction which Paton made is of fundamental importance, because it provides a theological barrier to any confusion between the Church and a welfare organisation, a social club or a political power. It also links Paton's concept of the Church firmly to his Christology, or, as he would say, to the central redeeming action of God. He specifically rejects concepts of the Church based on Platonic concepts as being inadequate.[32] It is also typical of Paton that having arrived at a definition of the Church he immediately applies it to a burning issue of his time, the re-establishment of relations with Germany. This question is itself an illustration of the continuous process which he envisages joining God's work in reconciling the world to Himself and the Christian's action. The passage is also very significant as giving some indication of the theology which sustained Paton when he was working for Jewish refugees, German pastors, prisoners of war and other victims of the darker side of man's nature.[33]

In 'World Community' Paton proceeds to discuss the meaning of community. He describes the Church as the 'household of God', hence the high place given in it to love.[34] Love among men reflects and has its origin in the love of God. To be a Christian means to be reborn into a new order of existence in which reign love and freedom. The Church is a fellowship of all who enjoy a personal relationship to God of love. Although derived from a passage in 'The Church and its Function in Society', the way Paton works out the implications of this is very reminiscent of passages in Bonhoeffer's 'Cost of Discipleship'.[35] The Church is a universal fellowship because the possibility of such a relationship to God is open to all. Hence the proclamation 'Sirs, ye are brethren', not 'ye will become brethren'. This is not an invitation to a vague cosmopolitanism, nor is it the automatic erasure of racial and political differences between men or between men and women, but it is an assertion of the value of all individuals to God and therefore to Christians. Unfortunately the Church has not always remembered this and has allowed distinctions of race and class to creep into the Church. To prove his assertions about the nature of the Church when he asks if there is anything which actually exists which corresponds to this divine promise of world community, Paton embarks on a 'missionary survey' of the results of the expansion of the Church due to the nineteenth and twentieth century missionary movement. In the West, Christians are accustomed to thinking of the Church in retreat, but this is the only part of the world where there is a decline to be seen. The Church can now be said to be ecumenical because it is found in all the inhabited earth. He also stresses the significance of the transition from missions directed from Europe to Church-based mission in the Third World, which was discussed in Chapter V. This argument from the actual existence of a world-wide church is the basis of Paton's other systematic treatment of the question of the Church, 'The Hour and its Need' (1939).[36]

Since the growth of the Church is dependent upon evangelism, Paton proceeds to justify evangelism by considering all the objections to the Church's intransigent and exclusive attitude which many of a more tolerant disposition would claim disqualifies it as a world community. His apologia for evangelism does not differ significantly from that rehearsed in previous books. The essential message of redemption in the Gospel makes evangelism not an optional extra, but obligatory. In addition Paton claims that he can show that it really works by citing cases of successful evangelism by the churches, though he admits that he is highly selective in his choice of examples.[37]

In considering 'The Church and National Life' Paton confronts the problem of the separate churches and communities which are stained by human sins, pride, cowardice, and sloth, and which exhibit many of the characteristics of any major human institution. However within these fallible bodies is the Body of Christ. There is something more behind the institutional aspect and within the great variety of ordinary bewildered mortals, namely the revelation of God in Christ, and through professing this, they are the Church.[38] From here he argues the relevance of the Church today, though the kind of service to the nation which is appropriate will vary in each country. His central ideas on the Church and the Nation are drawn entirely from the Oxford conference, in accepting the nation as a God-given arrangement, but protesting against the elevation of the idea of the nation to the point where it becomes absolute. He is prepared to allow nationalist leaders in the Third World considerable licence in their statements because they have been denied nationhood for so long. Without Christianity, he asserts there is no way of limiting the powers vested in the nation. In a similar fashion Paton argues for radical economic change, though he sees the difficulty of introducing a permanent socialist order in a democracy of frequently changing governments. This is where the Church should get to work on its own members because if they were to abandon their vested economic interests, they would set a powerful example for the state to follow.

'Surely it is not just wishful thinking and evasion of reality if we urge that from within its (the Church's) own fellowship there should be a possibility of the Church bringing forth understanding and reconciliation. It is at such junctures that one wakes up to realize how pernicious is the clericalization of our thought of the 'Church'. The Church's efforts in this field ought not to be primarily those of the clergy. They ought not to be primarily displayed in the passing of somewhat general resolutions in assemblies. They ought to be the efforts of Christian men and women who are deeply immersed in the work of the world, who know the technique of industrial, commercial and financial life, whose 'shop' it is, as it is not and cannot be that of the clergy'.[39]

There is also an element of prophecy in these words, inasmuch as the tendency to clericalization in the churches has not been reversed, and consequently efforts to encourage social justice by the churches have been nullified. 'The Church' remains identified with the clergy in the popular mind. It should also be noted, in view of what has been written in Chapter XII about the Peace Aims group and the Moot, that at this point Paton was in agreement with Oldham.

In discussing the 'Church and the World of Nations' Paton is careful to distinguish between the universal nature of the Church and the international character of the League of Nations. Christians all over the world are not united by common aspirations or objectives as the nations who were members of the League of Nations were, but by an act of God. From this unique position they approach such questions as racism, international peace, law and order and so on. What Paton writes on race is really enlightened common sense. He does not mince his words about the prejudice which obstructs attempts to help Jewish Christians, though he does not accept Dr Parkes's accusation that anti-semitism resides in the Christian interpretation of the crucifixion as being the responsibility of the Jews.[40] He was brought up in the Evangelical school which insisted that it was his sins, not the activities of the Jews which nailed Jesus to the Cross. On the subject of war he explains the complexities of the Oxford conference debate. The Church has a special responsibility in the protection of minorities.[41]

In describing the churchman's responsibilities he places much emphasis on Reinhold Niebuhr's speech at Oxford.[42] He warns of the dangers of self-righteous pietism on the one hand and of compromise with the world's standards on the other. In comparing the two extremes of 'building the Kingdom' and abdicating responsibility for social conditions because God alone can inaugurate the Kingdom of God, Paton criticises both viewpoints.[43] The Church, he says, works under the shadow of the Kingdom, looking always for a full manifestation of it. Therefore, the Kingdom will transcend the best that man can achieve in society. The Christian cannot escape from the imperative of the law of love and therefore must act. This is the true way, that of alignment with the Kingdom, which will enable the Christian to avoid disillusionment which will result from identifying the eternal with some human social project, and yet involve him in 'the aspirations and labours of a needy world'. He must put the Christian house in order by working for Christian unity, not for the sake of increased efficiency but as an act of obedience to Christ. As with virtually all Paton's books, he ends with a call to action on behalf of the Gospel.

In 'The Church and the New Order' Paton does not go much further in principle than in 'World Community' though he demonstrates the application of his theology of the Church in more detail. His ecclesiology is therefore strictly transcendental, yet closely linked to his understanding of the work of Christ in the world. It is sharply differentiated from secular considerations. Paton did not aspire to be a theologian and consequently there is very little reference to metaphysical concepts in his books. His ecclesiology depends on a strong belief in God, and on placing obedience to God as the first priority of Christian life. In questions of eschatology and the Kingdom of God, he seeks a via media between the various contemporary positions. The whole structure of his theology was tested by the content of his faith. If it did not work for him, or if it had no relevance to what he was trying to do, then he rejected it. Although the idea of the Church arose in his thought c 1929 and increased in prominence and originality until the time of his death, he did not relinquish his passion for mission. The defence of evangelism and the praise of missionary endeavour still occupied a place of honour in his theology, but it was deepened by his new understanding of the nature of the Church. This is very clearly demonstrated in a book such as 'The Hour and its Need' or 'The Message of the world-wide Church'.

Paton was fortunate in being able to start from scratch with no presuppositions about Apostolic Succession or the validity of orders to encumber him. His wife's Anglicanism and subsequent Roman Catholicism seems to have had little effect, for his concept of the 'communion of saints' is a logical sequel to his belief that church membership depends on a living relationship to God, which death could not sever. Since so many of his letters about church unity, particularly those relating to the Church of South India, are full of arguments on the practical advantages of unity, or the lowest common denominator which all parties would accept, it is significant that Paton now stresses the theological reason for Christian unity.[44]

A short paper which Paton wrote in 1942, 'The Christian Church and the International Order' is a good example of the way in which Paton was using theology rather than common sense or his own opinions to work out an ethic applicable to the international situation.[45] His aim in writing this paper is to set out the central truth about world order which Christian revelation contains and the bearing of this truth on the actual situation, as well as the distinctive role of the Church. He begins with the divine rule of God as the inescapable reality to which all humanity belongs. Therefore, knowledge of God's will is not an ornament to be added to one's structure of thought. One can never impress too strongly upon man the consequences of breaking the law of God, since it results in sin and death. Christ, however, has appeared as the restorer of the divine order giving dignity to man in that God was prepared to die for him, working into the texture of human life the principle of brotherly love which is implied in a common sonship to God. The Church is the herald of the divine order. In the Church there is given to man a society both human and divine which is in itself the earnest of a re-constituted society. The Church is a divine society because it was constituted by Christ and is dependent on his spirit, but it is also a human society in which the pride and stubbornness of some churchmen has actually hindered the Gospel. Nevertheless it is the one society in which the principle is to transcend human divisions. The principles implied by the Church's position have a wider validity for society, that is the dignity of man as the child of God, the fact that no nation has the right to exploit another, and the principles of economic justice. Paton then works this out in detail in the context of the issues raised by the peace aims discussions, stressing the dangers of

Britain identifying moral right with national advantage. The Church's distinctive task is to call for repentance and reform. It shares human guilt because even when it has got the message right, it has failed to convince people of the relevance of the Church. It has especially failed to condemn racism and economic injustice. Its task is now to evangelise the younger generation, which the Confessing Church will be able to do in Germany after passing through the fire, with the support of other churches. It must proclaim the Gospel and build up the ecumenical fellowship. Its reward will be a world order which has foundations and whose builder is God.

The principal advantage of Paton's approach is that it is distinctively Christian, rather than liberal humanitarian, and that the tenets of orthodox Christian faith are its warp and woof. It is the reverse of Paton's own definition of secular, as given in Chapter IX. The statements which Temple drafted for the C.I.F.S.R. use exactly the same methodology. There is no question of flavouring the message to suit the palate of the modern world. In a war situation, there is a value in such an uncompromising position, and it would be of benefit to encourage Christians to think out their own ethics. It would be of limited appeal to the non-Christian, except that the breadth and comprehensiveness of his vision was very appealing.[46] A.C. Craig selects a passage from an address which Paton gave at a Religion and Life Week to illustrate the dimension which appealed so much to him. These world horizons and the authority with which he spoke, as well as his iconoclasm made him a very popular S.C.M. speaker at this time also.

> '. . . The nature of the Church is universal — not first national and then international, but first an universal fellowship as wide as God's mercy and only secondly national or interdenominational or local. Such a unity, if really believed and practised, would be a mighty bulwark to international peace. We do not mean that the unity of the Church in the world should be thought of as a tool for creating political concord. The life of the Church is for the glory of God, not for a political end, but just in as far as the Church realises in its own life the unity that Christ has given, passing the bounds of race and culture and nation and wealth, just in so far will the Church create that ethos, that moral unity, which is the only true foundation of international law'.[47]

This was a theme that Paton reiterated in broadcasts, in other Religion and Life Weeks and in his contributions to the Peace Aims Group, and the testimony of virtually everyone whom I have interviewed is that he was very successful in conveying his vision.[48] The one exception was the Bishop of Worcester who said it was above the heads of the men in his camp, when he got Paton to address them, but was appreciated by the officers, who could think in terms of strategy.

One virtue of Paton's ecclesiology is that it is so clearly his own homegrown brand. He may quote Oldham, Middleton Murry, Schweitzer or Kraemer, but it is only because they express what he wants to say, and perhaps because he wants to exploit their authority, being a diffident theologian, in the same way that he would 'name-drop' the names of prominent politicians who had expressed themselves to him on the subject he was discussing. It is an intrinsic part of his rock-like faith. It is not necessary to demonstrate with chapter and verse how profoundly Biblical it was, but there is a correlation between this type of ecclesiology with its heavy emphasis on God's action in redeeming man, and his final missiological stance with Kraemer. It may be argued that he is reverting to English Calvinism, but this is unlikely after such a long pause without any formulation on the Church (1904-29/35) and with such an uncharacteristic emphasis on worship, and the communion of the saints. On the other hand, his thoughts do display a certain amount of eclecticism of thought current in the ecumenical movement, suggesting that he formulated his thoughts by discussion rather than by study. His idea of the Church is essentially one related to action: God's action and man's response. It is not for meditation but is a call to obey the will of God with costly service, which was precisely what Paton was trying to do himself.

Chapter XV
Conclusion

Massive though this biography is, only a small fraction of the total amount of material available has been utilized, and of the thousands of letters which Paton wrote, only a very few have been quoted, although the majority of these letters have not been read or studied before. Similarly, although the cross-section of Paton's work which has been discussed in this book includes the most important aspects of his work, still much of great interest has had to be omitted or compressed: for example, his participation in the 'Advisory Council on Christian Education Overseas', which held a conference in 1931 at which Paton delivered a paper on sex education (then known as 'moral hygiene').[1] There has been no space to discuss his contribution to the W.S.C.F. and its international fellowship.[2] His action to alert mission boards to the conditions of White Russian refugees in Manchuria in 1927, his correspondence with Bishop Hall about child slavery in Hong Kong, and in particular the action he orchestrated between Archbishop Davidson and the C.B.M.S. when they made representations to the League of Nations concerning religious liberty in mandated territory might have been discussed in the context of his concern for human rights and the alleviation of poverty throughout the world.[3] Much more might have been written analysing his broadcasts, since he was not slow to see the potential in religious broadcasting for reaching the unchurched millions. Many of those who have written to me consider that his chairmanship of the Committee for Aliens, Refugees and Prisoners of War, which was briefly mentioned in Chapter XII, was one of the most important things he did because he was able to hold together representatives from widely different organizations.[4] The elaborate process of integration of Faith and Order and Life and Work has been much compressed, though Paton's participation in Faith and Order was increasing, and the ecclesiological subjects of the post war studies by the Faith and Order department would presumably have invoked a greater contribution from him after the war. With his phenomenal energies and catholic interests, Paton succeeded in achieving more in his shortened life-span than many achieve with another twenty years. It can be argued, as some have argued concerning William Temple, that he spread himself too thinly, and that he should have concentrated on pursuing fewer issues. Temperamentally this would have been impossible for Paton. In this he was quite unlike Oldham and Visser't Hooft, who moved methodically from one job to another, swerving neither to left nor right. The scale of Paton's work, covering several continents, enabled him to synthesise ideas, and bring together disparate facts in order to present a world view which he would not have been so well equipped to do if, for example, he had limited himself solely to educational work.

When Paton died in August 1943 he was going at full tilt. He was maintaining the elaborate machinery necessary to succour 'orphaned missions' and was wringing money out of the British Churches for the Geneva office of the W.C.C.F. He was helping Archibald Craig work himself into the secretaryship of the British Council of Churches, and was speaking on Religion and Life platforms all over England and Scotland. The Peace Aims Group was particularly active, with the arrival in England of the American 'Six Pillars of Peace' statement. Paton had set up a special sub-group with Kenneth Grubb, Archbishop Garbett and Rushbrooke of the Baptist World Alliance on religious freedom in Russia, with a view to making representations to the government about the situation. The political situation in India was causing him grave concern, so the previous year he had organized an initiative from British Christians after the failure of the Stafford Cripps mission which had done much to soothe troubled relations between Indian and British Christians.[5] Two books lay in embryonic state on his desk, a biography of C.F. Andrews, who had died in 1940, which was completed by Nicol MacNicol, and a sequel to 'The Message of the World-wide Church', on missionary policy. Most significantly, he was due to fly to Sweden in September to discuss the reconstruction of Europe with as many of the Provisional Committee of the W.C.C.F. and staff as could manage to get there. A new director of Inter-Church Aid, Theodore Hume, had been appointed, and after staying with Paton a fortnight before his death, had flown to the Stockholm meeting and died himself when the aeroplane was shot down. Paton had organized a committee on the reconstruction of Christian Institutions in Europe, and it is reasonable to assume that after the war much of his energy would have been given to Inter-Church Aid.

It is not only the work which Paton was doing at the time of his death, but his potential contribution to the ecumenical movement which underlines the tragedy of his death. In the same letter which was quoted in the introduction to this book, David Paton remarks that his father had achieved everything which he was going to achieve, that after 50 a man does not do anything new, but that it was sad that his father had died before he accrued the honours due to him. In this he was mistaken, though in fairness it should be said that David Paton had not seen his father for four years. In his thought on the Church discussed in Chapter XIV and his experiments with the 'Peace Aims' Group Paton was still ploughing new fields. Since Paton had consented to the request made by the W.C.C.F. in 1938 for his full-time services, and then had applied for a position with the Church of Scotland Board of Jewish Missions in 1940, it is a reasonable conjecture that after the war he would have eased himself out of the I.M.C. as Oldham had done, and worked full-time for the W.C.C. There is little doubt that he would have secured much better representation at the Amsterdam World Assembly and on the Central Committee of the W.C.C. for representatives of the 'younger churches', though opinion is divided as to how soon he would have brought the I.M.C. and W.C.C together. At the time of his death their union was achieved in his person, because of his dual role, and not in any formal way, because the committee on co-operation which had been set up at Tambaram and Utrecht would not meet in wartime. Some, for example Charles Ranson, Max Warren and Oliver Tomkins, feel that he was stampeding the I.M.C. and the W.C.C. into a shotgun marriage, which both parties would have resented if it had been achieved in 1948, but it seems reasonable to assume that he would not have tolerated the delay until 1961 when integration did in fact take place. To go beyond this is to enter the realms of speculation. One honour which Paton desperately coveted was an honorary doctorate from Oxford, though he was very proud of the Edinburgh doctorate conferred in 1939. Although he would have been 78 in 1964, it is not beyond the bounds of possibility that he would have been made a Life Peer when Harold Wilson embarked on a policy of elevating non-conformist church leaders to balance the Anglican bishops in the House of Lords, and such an honour would have given him immense pleasure.[6]

It has already been shown in Chapter XIV how closely Paton's theology followed that of the general pattern of development in the ecumenical movement. It is fair to assume that after the war he would have been affected by the developments around the World Assembly at Amsterdam, when Barth and Hromadka (whose exit from Czechoslovakia and sojourn in the United States during the war Paton had helped to organise) had such influence. There is also a sense in which the post-Tambaram meetings of the I.M.C. were a regression from the radical position adopted at Tambaram. Whether Paton could have prevented this by a different choice of experts to attend the Whitby and Willingen conferences, is not clear, but it should be remembered the extent to which he was responsible for the sponsorship of Kraemer's book for the Tambaram meeting.

One sign of how far Paton had moved since Tambaram is the rift in his relationship with John R. Mott. Robert Mackie was extremely close to Mott during the war. When the I.M.C. offered him Paton's job in 1943 it was Mott who persuaded him not to accept when he was very torn between the I.M.C. and the W.S.C.F. He thinks that it was a subtle alienation from the I.M.C. and from Paton which caused Mott to give him this advice. There is also the extraordinary fact that Mott did not write a letter of condolence to Mrs Paton, which greatly hurt her. Paton himself had been very hurt by the fact that Mott did not write to him until more than six weeks after the outbreak of war, in spite of the fact that he was worried about how missions would survive, and would have welcomed some words of reassurance. In his days with the S.C.M., Mott had been Paton's 'guru'. Even in the late 1930s, Paton defended Mott from criticism, though he felt that definite arrangements must be made at Tambaram for Mott's retirement from the I.M.C. chairmanship. Robert Mackie is probably right to attribute the rift to Paton's concern with the idea of the Church and with church unity, which Mott never really understood. He was a Methodist, but at heart he was undenominational, he ignored denominational boundaries, and although he had to be invited to be chairman of various W.C.C.F. committees, he accepted with a great show of reluctance. Mackie does not think he comprehended the significance of the W.C.C.F., and he probably resented Paton's devoting so much time to it. One might also add that there is every sign that Mott remained stuck in the same groove intellectually from about 1928 onwards,[7] whereas Paton grew and matured, and eventually outgrew Mott, as he had outgrown Tatlow, who, I suspect from Kathleen Witz's evidence, regarded Paton in the same light that Henry IV regarded Prince Hal. Paton never made the mistake of outstaying his usefulness in the one organisation.

Was Paton's death avoidable? He was first taken ill in Edinburgh, when he was staying with Professor Sinclair and his wife Margaret (not to be confused with Paton's assistant, Margaret Sinclair), but he pretended it was nothing and ignored Margaret Sinclair's urging that he go to the doctor. He then broke his holiday to return to London and clear off some work, then he went on to the S.C.M. conference at Cheltenham. He seemed to be desperately tired, and looked very grey, but that was not unusual for him. The next attack came when he was in the hills above Rydal Hall. It took four hours to get down, and another four hours to get him to hospital, before he could be operated on for a perforated ulcer. He was too weak to survive the operation and died four days later. The ulcer could have perforated any time, because apparently he must have been suffering from it for some time. He would have stood a better chance if it had happened in London, though there is no reason to suppose that there was anything lacking in the medical care at Kendal General Hospital. As it was, there was time for some of his family to reach him, and for them to write to his friends, requesting their prayers, a request that greatly moved Garbett. Grace Paton had gone to Mass when the end came, but the hospital staff managed to fetch her back in time, and he died as she murmured 'Jesus, Jesus' over and over again.[8]

Grace Paton had chosen the one word which sums up Paton's life. All his books and all his theology, his worship and his missionary efforts had centred on the person of Christ, and the love of God which he reveals. Paton expressed his own deep faith in the final broadcast which he made of 'Some principles of reconstruction — The proposals of the American churches' which was transmitted after his death.

> 'As we look at all these gigantic tasks, we need to remember that God has set us in this particular historic moment, and that we are in the hands of His providence. What nations can do for good or evil, in modern conditions of organized power, is greater than in past ages. But we are not in a world of chance, we're in our Father's house, and we need to rise to the height of the historic moment in which we are set, not trusting only to our own cleverness and skill in devising, but far more to His love and guidance'.[9]

Paton had been entrusted with the final address at the S.C.M. Cheltenham conference, but to the surprise of Billy Greer, the General Secretary, John Stewart of Manchuria and other old friends listening, he did not speak about peace aims, or reconstruction or the world mission of the universal church or any of his other world-embracing themes. Instead, he spoke very quietly and sincerely of prayer, and how one lives the Christian life. Since he was usually so reticent about his personal religion, one cannot help wondering if he had a premonition of his death, since these were the most important subjects to him. Unfortunately he spoke ex tempore and no record was made of his address, but his audience were impressed by the concluding words 'If you put your life into the hands of God, he will never let you go'. Alan Booth wrote to Grace Paton that he seemed to cast off the weight of his responsibilities and become 'Bill Paton of the S.C.M.' again: 'we were never more conscious of the greatness of God's gift to us in him — his simplicity and his knowledge of the goodness of God'.

Grace Paton received literally hundreds of letters of condolence written in tribute to William Paton, but only one will be quoted here because it illustrates the point that the element of tragedy in Paton's death lies on the side of the bereaved and not on Paton's side since for him, as for Bonhoeffer, death was but the transition to life. Hutchinson Cockburn of the Church of Scotland wrote:

> 'It is catastrophic, his outlook was so sane, his mind so well informed, his consecration so complete. We shall not look upon his like again. He

was so variously gifted. We had learned to trust him utterly and I greatly valued his friendship . . . and now he serves the Church in heaven, which will be richer for his coming. We grope, he sees. In our darkness we must seek more earnestly the source of all light. . . . '

Paton was buried in St Albans after a simple Presbyterian service at which Bishop Hunter preached. The memorial service held a month later in St Paul's Cathedral resembled a repeat performance of the Tambaram conference except that the secular professions were better represented as well as the governments of several nations. (Similarly after the memorial service for Archbishop Temple in October 1944 it was possible to hold a meeting of the Provisional Committee of the W.C.C.F.) Temple gave the address, and afterwards wrote down what he thought he had said for circulation. He spoke of the challenge to faith presented by Paton's death, both because Paton seemed indispensable and was needed so much to solve so many different questions, and because Paton's own faith was a challenge to everyone else's. Instead of relying on him to do the task single-handed, all must co-operate to do together the unfinished work, in such a way that the burden is more evenly distributed.

> 'In some such way I think we may see how it is possible that this, which seems to us so purely loss, may be gain even for the Church on earth; we who believe in the resurrection to eternal life may never suppose that the purpose of God is limited to what we can see of it here ourselves, and we believe with all our hearts that if God has called him hence, it is for wider service in another sphere. Yes, Paton had that kind of assurance which made faith almost matter of fact in its impact, so that in the judgment of those with whom he worked there was nothing that made it seem remote or aloof, something to which he might have recourse in mystical moments; it was a practical guide and a practical energy in the daily affairs of life, it was the appreciation of the things of earth in the light of the righteousness and love of God; and it is as we face the work that he had left for us to do in that spirit that we shall find the inspiration of his example'.[10]

In the Sinclair biography of William Paton it is argued that in some respects Paton's death was providential, that he would have hated being an invalid, and a special diet would have been difficult to manage with war-time rationing. As it was he died amid his beloved hills and not in a distant country. This is to underestimate Paton's powers of adaptation, since he seems to have borne cheerfully his enforced convalescence after both attacks of pneumonia in America (1940 and 1942 — either attack could have been fatal). He did tell Muriel Underhill the last time he saw her that he dreaded retiring in eight or ten years, and not being at the heart of things, but I suspect that like some of his colleagues, he would merely have switched his activities to another field when he was forced to retire from the I.M.C. and the W.C.C.F. No-one seems to have considered how much he would have enjoyed his grandchildren and great grandchildren. One can appreciate that the older members of Paton's family would comfort themselves in this way, and it is better that he should have died when he did than in the aeroplane crash with Theodore Hume, as he might have done with the Ministry of Information system of granting passages. However, this does not solve the problem of why the ecumenical movement was bereft of one of its leaders.

Temple hints at an answer when he says that Paton's death should result in an increase of faith so that they can all work together to finish Paton's work. Oldham and Visser't Hooft were the two colleagues who felt most bereaved because they had been working so closely with Paton for so long. On the morning of Paton's funeral, Oldham wrote a letter of sympathy to Visser't Hooft in which he struggles to find an answer to the problem of Paton's death:

> 'On every front the position is seriously weakened. I think we must accept the fact that there are important things which he could have made possible and will in fact in the future remain undone. God does not take Christians or Christian causes out of the tragic setting of life in which catastrophic consequences may follow on such incidents as these. The lesson we are doubtless meant to learn is that our sole trust must be, not in human supports, however indispensable they may seem to us, but in God's everlasting mercy and in His truth which endures from generation to generation'.[11]

When Visser't Hooft replied he agreed with Oldham's judgement. Perhaps some of Paton's friends and colleagues had relied on him to fix everything too often, and had not taken the responsibilities themselves which they should have done. Paton's death is perhaps also a judgment on the ecumenical movement for relying too much on personal contact. Far too many areas of the W.C.C.F. constitution had been left vague and woolly, for example the question of how a general secretary should be appointed, or how the W.C.C. and the I.M.C. should work together. All Paton's carefully nourished church and government contacts fell to earth, and his successors, Oliver Tomkins in the W.C.C. and Norman Goodall in the I.M.C., had to start again from scratch. Paton obviously did not send himself memoranda when he was wearing both his hats at once, and his secretary Miss Morden had great difficulty reconstructing his intentions. She managed to hold the 'peace aims' group together, but found he had arranged many things verbally. It is actually a sign of Paton's efficiency in training his secretaries that the three secretaries — Miss Gibson, Miss Morden and Miss Standley managed to run things for a year after his death before his successors took up office.

Both A.S. Kydd and J.W. Decker wrote to Mrs Paton that they had realized that Paton was overworking and had long conversations about how they could lighten his load, without ever finding an answer. Mott said that Paton could never refuse a job. This, however, is not true. Paton could refuse jobs, as when he said that he could only work for the B.C.C. when he was not required to travel for the W.C.C. or the I.M.C. Similarly, he did not involve himself with social questions when he was having to devote all his time to missionary problems. The case of the secretaryship of the B.C.C. is a case where Paton actively sought additional work, even though, after so many attacks of pneumonia, he must have known that he was endangering his health. He wrote to David Paton: 'I seem to have a finger in every godly pie there is. One risks much loss of depth, but one can't shirk things because one is busy'. However, the vital clue comes in an earlier letter: 'Mummy is very busy with her British restaurant. It is most valuable work, but it does take the jam out of her. But it helps to bear the worries about you and James and Michael and we both feel that the only tolerable thing just now is to be desperately busy'.[12] In other words, Paton deliberately worked at the limit of his powers in order to blot out the worry about David in China, James in the Navy and Michael on the North West frontier in India.

Paton's death alone would not have been so catastrophic if it had not been followed thirteen months later by that of William Temple, the causes of whose death were similar: exhaustion and strain aggravating an existing complaint which ought not to have been fatal. Then when London was blitzed by V2 rockets in Spring 1945, one landed on the English Presbyterian Church headquarters where the British section of Faith and Order were meeting. Among the dead were W.T. Elmslie, who had done so much for the B.C.C. and Father Tribe, S.S.M., a useful Anglo-Catholic theologian. Leonard Hodgson himself was very severely injured, but survived. The noise of the bomb landing could be heard in the offices of the Ministry of Information. Hugh Martin exclaimed angrily to Williams: 'If Hitler's got Willy Elmslie, I'll believe in a personal devil', implying that with the deaths of Temple and Paton it was too much. It was not only the Confessing Church which yielded up its martyrs in the Second World War. Not by torture, by lonely execution in humiliating circumstances, or by the frustration of years of imprisonment, but by ceaseless work beyond the limits of human endurance to organize relief work and spiritual comfort for prisoners and refugees, by incessant travel in war conditions (delays, cold and overcrowding) and by the nagging fear that whatever is done it will not prevent the Jews being massacred or civilians bombed. Temple and Paton poured out a stream of books and pamphlets, broadcasts and addresses all in the attempt to maintain a Christian witness in England amid the passions of war. They will not receive a martyr's crown because they died without glory, the victims of their everyday life.

One of the most significant features of Paton's life was his involvement in questions of Church-State relations. This began when he was involved in pacifying Indian Army Officers and State Governors who suspected the Y.M.C.A. of India of subversion, and Paton hired a servant so that he could stay with this class of person. He then found himself intervening in the attempts to induce the colonial authorities to allow German missionaries to return to the British Empire, and get their property restored to them. He failed to get the difficult district commissioner at Madura removed, but after the unhappy results of the Keithahn case, he did find a means of protecting missionaries from arbitrary expulsion. He devoted a great deal of study and research to the question of religious liberty in non-Christian countries such as the Islamic countries of the Middle East, Turkey, Japan and China, where the minority Christian Church either had no freedom to evangelize or was restricted in the fields of education, youth work and so on. He did all he could to support the Confessing Church and to prevent it being excluded from the ecumenical movement, but his most effective work was with the British government. Paton believed in a discreet word in the right ear, in lunching with the Under Secretary of State for India, in placing memoranda in the hands of Lord Halifax, the Foreign Secretary, which would contain information not available to him from any other source, in liaising very closely with the Ministry of Information, and if necessary as a very last resort, threatening an all-out confrontation, as in the case of the ban on pacifists by the B.B.C. It was the tactics of the stream of water wearing away the rock, as in the case of the religious broadcasts in German. It meant reticent use of letters to the 'Times' and very few statements, in a style quite different from that adopted by the B.C.C. and the W.C.C. today. Bishop Williams saw both Bell and Paton at work when he was working for the Ministry of Information. He thinks that Paton was more effective because he was a strategist, and knew when to compromise, and when to push something so far and no further. Bell was completely oblivious to the antagonism he created, and in his opinion would have been a disastrous Archbishop of Canterbury (not that it ever came in question) because he was so partisan. It should be added that Bell had an advantage in being a bishop with a place in the House of Lords. Paton possessed no such automatic platform. The degree of influence he achieved was the more remarkable because he was a member of a very small English denomination and yet could not claim to represent the English Free Church tradition in the sense that a Methodist or a Congregationalist could,

The basis of his position was his wisdom. He was incredibly well-informed, sane and sensible, able to give sound advice to archbishops and members of parliament alike. He could transmit this quality to others. According to Carol Graham, most commissions in India, whether government or missionary, were 'innocents abroad'. The Lindsay Commission was able to avoid the usual pitfalls because of Paton's brilliant stroke in securing Lindsay as chairman, and because he had made them do their homework first, so that they were well-informed before they came. She attributes the success of the Lindsay Commission to this. The other factor was Paton's ability to make friends with those who had no church connections. Richard Crossman explained his connection with the Life and Work movement, and hence presumably with Paton, as being due to this interest in the overall German situation and the fact that he acted as Bishop Heckel's interpretor. Paton's friendship with Antony Wedgwood Benn's father, also a Labour politician and Under Secretary of State for India, was an interesting 'secular' friendship. These personal links gave him a wider perspective on Church-State relations, and enabled him to see both sides of the question. It might be argued that in the period 1940-43 he got too close to government and that he should have done more for Adam von Trott and Bonhoeffer. Yet he had no sympathy with Churchill and Eden's policy, apart from the ultimate imperative to win the war, and it would have been wrong for him to encourage hope where none could exist. Even in this period he could get tough with the government, as in the case of the attempt to exclude Lutheran missionaries from the British Empire, described in Chapter VIII. In this case he could use leverage which in the instance of the German resistance he did not possess. Paton was shrewd enough to know the limits of church power. In this book the aim has been to show the complexity of church-state relationships as they affected the ecumenical movement (how they affect the Church of England is an entirely different question). Paton was on the side of compromise and co-operation, and in the terms of what he achieved, he was justified. The missionary enterprise was very vulnerable, and a confrontation would have helped no-one. It could also have led to a dangerous confusion of politics and religion if the I.M.C. had been openly and officially identified with the Indian nationalist struggle.

David Paton has thrown serious doubts on the soundness of his father's political judgement, and A.C Craig is very critical of the way he would announce in Religion and Life weeks that there were more Christians in the Chinese Nationalist government than the British government. It is true that like most church leaders Paton was completely 'taken in' by Chiang Kai Shek. However, statements like the latter (he had an equivalent for Japan) should not be taken at face value. Paton was really saying 'If so many patriotic Japanese/Chinese are involved in their national governments, you ought to get involved in politics too'. He does seem to have assumed that a Christian politician was bound to be a better politician than a non-Christian one, which is a very dubious assumption, and presumably one which he might have revised if he had lived to see the post-war Christian Democratic parties in action. As in the case of German politics, he was influenced by the opinions of Christian nationals, such as T.Z. Koo, the assistant general secretary of the W.S.C.F., which surely is better than depending on the commentaries of European observers. Most of his contemporaries credit Paton with sound political judgment, though some say that his own transparent honesty and 'guilelessness' meant that he imputed good motives where there were none. This might be true in his attempts to be fair to the Japanese in 'Christianity in the Eastern Conflicts', but is not true when he was castigating American-isolationist-liberal-pacifist opinion and American business interests in 1940, nor is it true of his shrewd comment that the reason for the breakdown of the Stafford Cripps talks in 1942 was that the Indian nationalists wanted to be on the right side in the event of an Axis victory.[13]

David Paton is certainly right to say that his father never appreciated the intellectual challenge of Marxism. When Paton first came in contact with the Chatham House group he was reproved for imagining that Communism could be defeated by a military victory or by political means, when it was an ideological challenge.[14] He did avoid the mistake of many of his contemporaries in England of underestimating Russia as a military power. He commented to David Paton about Visser't Hooft's visit to England in 1942: 'We had Visser't Hooft over here. I hope he learnt something. He was certainly told. He still takes far too much a continental Christian attitude to Russia — though we may have gone too far, but what has happened is at bottom not just setimental but an appreciation that there are things to be understood'.[15] It is difficult to assess the extent to which Paton perceived that Russian Communism was Russian nationalism rather than Marxism, but he thought there was room for dialogue, and he tried to explain to Visser't Hooft that British sympathies lay with any country fighting for survival when invaded, apart from their gratitude that someone was diverting the German attack.[16] This difference with Visser't Hooft might have led to friction after the war, and it probably stemmed from the different cultural background of the two men, but also from the fact that Paton was above all else a realist in politics. He had abandoned pacifism because it was unrealistic in a sinful world. He would probably have found cold-war attitudes equally unrealistic.

Why did Paton want to be a bishop? The sacerdotal aspects of the role would not have appealed to him, even if he had tried to evangelize confirmation candidates. It might be because he felt his basic impotence in the question of church-state relations, and felt he would be able to do more as a leader of the established church. It might be that he unconsciously sought the authority vested in a bishop's position even if such a concept of authority was anathema to him intellectually. Kenneth Grubb has commented that Paton would have preferred to command in situations when the weakness of his power base meant that he had to persuade, while his family referred him as a benevolent dictator.[17] There were even occasional jokes about him being the 'protestant pope'. The reasons why Paton did not become an Anglican in 1918 were discussed in Chapter I and Chapter III. A further reason might have been the feeling among pioneers in the ecumenical movement that it was not 'playing the game' to change denominations, and that it would undermine one's integrity to do so, when charges of 'proselytism' were rampant. Dora Pym related the substance of a conversation she had had with him on a walk over Helvellyn in 1942.

'He was also talking of the attitude of the official Presbyterian Church to him and his work and I said 'Do you still feel yourself to be a Presbyterian?' 'Well, not really', he said. 'To be quite honest I belong to the world church'. He then asked me rather surprisingly whether I thought he would have been a bishop if he had been an Anglican! He seemed quite gratified — again surprisingly — when I said he had far more official power than any bishop'.[18]

Dora Pym's last comment was quite true. If one examines the Ministry of Information files, he appears to have had better access to diplomatic facilities than Temple. Garbett, as was shown earlier, considered that had Paton been an Anglican he would have been an archbishop. Presumably he meant in place of himself at York (1942-56) which would have meant a formidable combination with Temple at Canterbury. However, I think the clue lies in the remarks he was evidently making about the official Presbyterian church, which had become too narrow for him. Not that Paton had ceased to be highly critical of individual Anglicans. The staff of the Abbey in St Albans continued to exasperate him. In the same month as the walk over Helvellyn he wrote to David Paton: 'Most of the Abbey clergy are pathetic. What do some of these parsons and congregations think God allows them to exist for? The cultivation of an inherited chicken run apparently'.[19]

Paton did not believe that the world-wide Church was an ideal for which all ecumenically-minded Christians should strive. He believed that it actually existed because of the existence of flourishing churches in what was formerly known as 'the mission field', and he identified himself with it. The proof of the reality of the world-wide Church he sought in such diverse things as his friendship with Karl Hartenstein, the successful operation to rescue missions cut off by the hostilities from their home base, the formation of the W.C.C.F., and the growth of indigenous church leadership. Since he considered that all denominations were branches of the true Church, he could speak of the under-lying unity created by faith in Jesus, compared with which the denominational boundaries were relatively superficial. This would explain his confrontation with Amy Buller when she was going through an Anglo-Catholic phase. She had organised a reunion of former S.C.M. secretaries for a week-end retreat. She then at one point said a few words about the Sunday communion service, to the effect that they were at an Anglican Church and that only the Church of England members could participate, but the others would be welcome to attend the service. Paton muttered loudly to Kathleen Witz that he would be an Anglican tomorrow. Amy Buller overheard and repeated what she had said, and that to do otherwise would offend the Church authorities. Paton ignored her and took communion at the early celebration every morning because he believed that he was a Christian in the House of God, and that was more important. If challenged, he was prepared to say that a gathering of S.C.M. secretaries was an exceptional occasion and that he felt at one with it.[20]

It was this attitude which led him to write in his pamphlet on church unity in India in 1942, that the churches should act as though they were united already — an impossible statement according to Michael Hollis and A.J. Boyd because no two societies paid their missionaries the same salary, which caused havoc with a united venture such as the Vellore Hospital. It seems as though Paton was so imbued with the ecumenical spirit that he could not appreciate the difficulties of others. However, that does not detract from his contribution to Christian unity in bringing the missionary movement firmly into the mainstream of 'organized' ecumenism and seeing that the experience of the younger churches were brought to the attention of the European churches. The I.M.C. continued to pioneer methods of ecumenical conferences and generally achieved in his lifetime a better cross-section than Faith and Order and Life and Work. While he lived the subject of evangelism was never far from the minutes of the C.I.F.S.R. and the B.C.C. When Oldham became involved in the Life and Work movement he shed his attachment to the I.M.C. but when Paton became involved, he took his responsibilities with him, to the benefit of both movements.

It is very difficult to assess how much of a contribution to 'grass roots' ecumenism Paton made. He assiduously organised 'follow up' programmes after the major I.M.C. conferences, and although the outbreak of war meant the end of many projects, one still finds German and Dutch memoranda on the Tambaram themes being compiled in 1943.[21] Paton himself was tireless in the amount of public speaking which he did, not only in the Religion and Life weeks which were discussed briefly in Chapter XII, but generally in speaking engagements all over England, apart from his annual appearances at Swanwick. The B.B.C. told him in 1942 that the audience for one of his broadcasts was two million, but he thought that was an over-estimate. As national secretary of the N.C.C. of India Paton was better able to organise at the 'grass roots', with conferences for rural experts, members of theological colleges, and other special interest groups. The effect of the Lindsay Commission report, where it was implemented, was also in the direction of increasing Christian unity among ordinary church members rather than at top-level administration.

It is difficult to summarize Paton's contribution to India, extending as it did from his work for the Y.M.C.A. of India in 1918, when he experienced what was to him the joy of taking the Gospel to villages where it had never been heard before, to his fund-raising for the Vellore hospital in America in 1942. In organisational terms, his role was that of providing support for those working in the field, whether European or Indian, and protection from excessive government control. In political terms, he was concerned that the American and European public should be better informed and less biased about the situation. He believed that in spite of the extremists on both sides, a peaceful transition to self-government was possible, and he also foresaw what a disaster the creation of Pakistan would be.[22] He came to believe that Christian missions would flourish better in an independent India because the innate racism involved in the colonial system of government would cease to exist. This did not prevent him defending the British Empire as being the best organized colonial system compared with the French, the Dutch and the Portugese. However, Paton's chief contribution was in practical terms, in the number of educational institutions rebuilt and strengthened by his recruitment of S.V.M.U. volunteers, and later by the sums he raised in the India Colleges Appeal and other funds, and by the better planning and co-ordination of educational facilities in the different language areas, though much was left to be desired in planning terms. Charles Ransom criticized Paton for not being aware of the importance of theological education for the building up of the Indian Church.[23] It is true that the subject was left entirely to William Adams Brown in the Lindsay Commission and that this chapter was the least satisfactory. Paton did nothing about the tendency in the I.M.C. to treat theological education very cautiously, as a subject only for specialists to discuss. It is also strange that so much attention was given to the question of indigenous forms of worship and very little attention to the question of indigenous theology, probably because missionaries were so terrified of the accusation of syncretism.

Eric Fenn's comment in his letter of condolence to Grace Paton sums up Paton's predicament with regard to India as well as being a general comment on him. He said he felt that they had lost a good solid rock . . . 'I always felt he paid a terribly high price in having to deal so much with organisation and strategy when he wanted to preach the mercy of God'.

Throughout this biography, in almost every chapter, the traces of this tension have been found, from Paton's first conflict with Tatlow over the Basis of the S.C.M., which he argued was too theological for the newly converted, but which had been used to exclude Unitarians and define the membership of the S.C.M., although it was causing chaos where office-holders could not subscribe to it (before 1911). In the W.S.C.F. he was also involved in conflict over the Basis of member-ship. In India there was the problem of the attempt of Government to control missionaries as symbolized in the 'Memo. A' system and the principle of freedom to evangelize. The whole of his I.M.C. career could be summed up under Eric Fenn's epitaph, and though he was more successful in preaching the Gospel in the B.C.C., he might have suffered the same tension in the W.C.C.F. There were always com-plaints about the conferences which he organised that too much business was crammed into them, and there was not enough time for prayer and reflection, and the agenda was a rigid discipline which should have been broken more often. The answer to the question why he allowed himself to be caught in this tension would seem to be that he felt it was his duty to use the considerable talents for administration and strategy which God had given him in the most effective way.

Perhaps the most impressive feature of Paton's ability was the way in which he would make things cohere. He would associate phenomena or ideas drawn from very different situations and show their inner unity. The impetus of the I.M.C. con-ferences could easily have become dissipated in the detail of the different fields; but instead the general principles such as spiritual values in non-Christian religions, or 'Das Wunder der Kirche' emerged. The 'international zoo' aspect of such a meeting was lost in the united worship and keenness on evangelism. One can see the same process at work in the formation of the B.C.C. from so many diverse organizations. Conversely he could envisage the massacre of the Jews because of other massacres and persecution in the Far East and in Armenia. Both the Kingdom of God and the world under God's judgment had an order and coherence in his eyes which made him unafraid to draw comparisons and generalize.

Finally one must ask what the significance of Paton's life was in theological terms. Concerning his death, it has already been argued that it was in some sense a judgment on the W.C.C.F. and the I.M.C. for the way in which they had depended too much on one person, and had left too many questions of organization and representation hanging in the air, or had temporarily resolved them by making Paton play a dual role. Secondly, there is a sense in which the deaths of Temple and Paton were martyrdoms, because they were the victims of the strain of life in war-torn England, and their attempts to maintain a Christian witness there. Paton's whole life was one of witness, whatever his particular failures.

Succeeding generations in the ecumenical movement have forgotten Paton or confuse him with his son, David Paton. He is not revered in Germany as Bishop Bell is, and churches are not named after him, as they are dedicated to the memory of

William Temple. This may be because he had shared the fate of all saints and prophets worthy of the name, that they are not honoured in their own countries nor among their own people. Certainly Paton's remarks to Dora Pym quoted above suggests that the English Presbyterian church hierarchy did not appreciate him. The reason may however be due to the decline in British leadership in the ecumenical movement. Dr Visser't Hooft says that before the war, whenever he had a problem, he had only to come to England and consult Temple, Paton, Bell and Oldham for the problem to have been solved by their wisdom, combined or singly. It has been argued that the Anglo-Saxon monopoly should have been broken, but circumstances made it impossible for the German churches to contribute adequately, and German students were strangely reluctant to join the W.S.C.F. However, a closer examination of the history of Life and Work makes the 'Anglo-Saxon monopoly' theory untenable. There may be a connection with David Edwards' thesis concerning the decline in the calibre of the clergy of the Church of England since the war, that has been reflected in a decline of those interested in the ecumenical movement, and here the collapse of the S.C.M. would be a relevant factor.[24] However, another element is the fulfilment of Paton's prophecy concerning the clericalism of the Church. Until the Fifth Assembly at Nairobi in 1975 the numbers of lay people and in particular laywomen involved in the W.C.C. had been steadily declining. It is significant that Oldham and Mott were merely the most eminent laymen in the ecumenical movement, and Paton was only ordained to save him from conscription, and he never held a pastoral charge, In tolerating this trend to clericalism the ecumenical movement has brought judgement upon itself.

There seems to be an inner logic in Paton's life, as he progressed from the student movement to missionary work in India and from the experience of ecumenical co-operation on a national scale to the same problems on an international scale in the I.M.C. and from the I.M.C. to the W.CC.F. His thought also develops logically in one direction. I hope that is a reflection of his character and of the way in which the will of God was leading him, and not any superimposed anachronistic pattern. There was a catchphrase in the S.C.M. c 1905-15 which was used at the conclusion of a committee meeting or an address in which the speaker attempted to lift the whole debate onto a spiritual level. Paraphrased a little, it was 'And if the spirit of God catches hold/ we open ourselves to Jesus/ seek the will of the Lord, *anything can happen*'. Wilder and D.S. Cairns used to resort to it frequently, but it became a habit, and the uninitiated complained that in using this tactic committees were avoiding difficult practical decisions, or taking a vote, or that speakers were evading the question of the individual's specific responsibility. However, in the case of William Paton, it was a question of 'anything can happen', given the sort of rock-like faith which he possessed.

For Paton was not educated at a famous public school, and went to one of the more obscure Oxford colleges, handicapped by being a 'scholarship boy'. He did not get a first class degree, and did not possess a brilliant, original mind. He was a member of a minority Protestant denomination, when the Church of England possessed prestige and power to dwarf the Presbyterian Church of England. He was a pacifist, in many people's eyes in the First World War, an unforgivable sin. His books are boring in patches, and are not spiritual classics. Only one was really a 'best-seller'. He was a blunt and forthright character with few social graces. He was always embarrassed by personal financial difficulties. Yet with all these disadvantages he achieved all that has been described in this book, in terms of personal influence with civil servants, politicians, archbishops and so on, and in terms of getting ideas translated into practice. At rock bottom, the reason for this was his unshakeable faith and sheer nerve in attempting the impossible, fortified by the belief that it was not possible for the purposes of God to be ultimately thwarted. In his case one can say that with faith in God 'anything can happen', though it is not proposed to write a discourse on the nature of faith to prove this assertion.

Paton's life does exhibit the extraordinary scope of the Gospel, and how it can be applied on a world-wide basis. It shows the grace of God working in a great variety of situations through a very fallible man. Above all, it shows, in the successes and failures of the international missionary movement and the World Council of Churches, the judgment of God on the household of God.

Notes

Note: Sources can be identified from the list of archives in Appendix A. Full bibliographical details if not given in the footnote, are to be found in the bibliography.

Abbreviations: CR   cross reference within this book.

cp	compare
cf	consult
E.H.	Edinburgh House
E.H.P.	Edinburgh House Press
Paton Papers:	Documents emanating from Paton held in the W.C.C. archives, Geneva.
M.A. thesis:	Master of Arts thesis submitted to the University of Birmingham, October 1972.

Notes to Chapter I

1 'Temple Gairdner of Cairo' by Constance Padwick p.2. p.36. 'History of the S.C.M.' by Tissington Tatlow for a description of the beginnings.

2 Interview Elizabeth Montefiore.

3 Tatlow p.33. Most of the Unions had formed 1885-93 as a result of the campaigns of Moody, Sankey and Henry Drummond.

4 S.C.M. archives: Memoranda produced by B.C.C.U. 1900-04 filed 'B.C.C.U. 1888-1904'. Scrapbooks on the campaigns.
'John R. Mott: World Citizen' by Basil Matthews.

5 Dorothy L. Sayers: 'Gaudy Night' and 'Murder at Pentecost' pub. by New English Library, illuminate the sociological point.

6 Kathleen Witz tried to dry them out and sort them out. Floyd Tomkins re-raided them in 1952 but couldn't remove all he wanted because of the chaos.

7 Founding of the N.U.S.: 'Voyages of Discovery' by James Parkes, Gollancz London 1969.

8 Interview Nathaniel Micklem. Sinclair Ch.I.

9 Unlike the 'Modern Churchman's Union' which flourished then, or the present S.C.M., the 1904 S.C.M. was neither 'liberal' nor 'radical' and cherished its links with the Churches. The continuity of S.C.M. organization was broken at the 1970 General Assembly of the S.C.M. (cf 1970 G.A. minutes, S.C.M. archives).

10 C.I.C.C.U. file. S.C.M. archives; Interview R.L. Pelly.

11 'And at first, whilst I remained thus so obstinately addicted to the superstitions of the papacy that it would have been hard indeed to have pulled me out of so deep a quagmire by sudden conversion, (God) subdued and made teachable a heart which, for my age was far too hardened in such matters'. Preface to the 'Commentary on Psalms' of 1557 quoted by Wendel: 'Calvin', Fontana 1963 p.37.

12 'Cosmo Gordon Lang' by J.G. Lockhart, Hodder & Stoughton, 1949.

13 Wilder considered Oldham a pernicious influence in the S.C.M. cf. Wilder correspondence with Tatlow filed 'Wilder' S.C.M. archives 1909-11. R.L. Pelly testified to Wilder's charm and influence. Biography by his daughter, Ruth Wilder Braisted (cf bibliography).

14 Sinclair p.14.

15 Scene witnessed by Rev Robert Hughes, University of Birmingham.

16 Interviews Elizabeth Montefiore, David Paton. Quotation from letter of 17.11.33 to Banninga of the Madura American Mission. E.H. archives. Box 410.

17 Lenwood was appointed foreign secretary of the L.M.S. in 1912 and by 1915 had wiped off their deficit. Forced to resign because of heretical Christology (cf Sinclair) he took a slum parish in the East End of London. Killed in a climbing accident in 1934. Interview Miss Bretherton.

18 Miss Bretherton and Miss Witz dissent on this question of Mott's 'manliness' cf Mott campaign letters filed under W.S.C.F. 1909 S.C.M. archives Paton to Grace MacDonald 24.12.10. Montefiore Papers.

19 Norman Grubb: 'C.T. Studd: pioneer missionary and cricketeer'.

20 Kathleen Ferguson to Paton. 19.7.17. 'I could think "This isn't words, Mr Paton said that. He's a real living thinking man and he absolutely believes it" '. Montefiore Papers.

21 Documents filed under 'Aim and Basis' 1900-1912. S.C.M. archives.

22 James Denney 1856-1917. Professor at Glasgow United Free Church College 1897-1917. Refused invitation to address S.C.M. saying that he had his sphere and Tatlow had his. Purely substitutionary theory of the Atonement which influenced Paton. cf 'Death of Christ', Hodder and Stoughton, 1902.

23 A memorandum by Douglas Thornton of 1900 fully justified his claim. S.C.M. archives cf the Report of the Commission of 1912.

24 Interview Mrs Kingsley Smith (née Lilian Paton) and Rev John Hood, Church of Scotland, Geneva.

25 Sinclair p.11. The prizes for Sunday School essays were not remarkable. Paton had nothing else to do on Sundays.

26 William James 1841-1910. Pragmatist philosopher. Gifford Lectures 1902 'The varieties of religious experience' for the origin of the distinction between the 'once-born' and 'the twice born'.

27 Paton to Grace Paton 15.5.18 and 25.7.18. Montefiore Papers CR p.111-2.

28 Paton to Grace Paton 4.5.18 Montefiore Papers.

29 From Paton's Essay on Genesis I, c.1910 Montefiore Papers, we know that Paton was familiar with modern Old Testament Form Criticism. The S.C.M. of 1913 had already adapted itself to biblical criticism which makes the low standard of 'The Missionary Motive' the more surprising.

30 Probably the book should be seen as a clumsy attack on von Harnack, cp Lietzmann 'A History of the Early Church' vol.II pub. 1938 Lutterworth.

31 'The Missionary Motive' ed. W. Paton, pub. for S.C.M. 1913 p.222 Professor Paton thinks that the analogy about muscles is so awkward that Paton must have borrowed it from someone else.

32 After his wife's early death Colonel Oldham retired from the Indian Army and devoted himself to church work. cf also 'Edward Stuart Talbot' by Stephenson, S.P.C.K. 1936.

33 Tatlow p.389f; cf policy document 'The interdenominational position of the S.C.M.' S.C.M. archives. Tatlow was furious when a 1919 group of students petitioned against the rigid rules excluding members of one church from taking communion in another. Interview Robert Mackie cp. Talbot/Tatlow correspondence 1908 S.C.M. Inter-communion was allowed at the smaller Bible Study conferences at Swanwick.

34 William Temple wrote in 1915: 'Members of the S.C.M. ought to know that without their movement there would never have been held the Edinburgh conference which was the greatest event in the life of the Church for a generation'. Tatlow threatened to stop recommending students to work for S.P.G. if they did not participate in the conference cf Tatlow 'History of the S.C.M.'

35 Kenneth Grubb, Margaret Sinclair. Kathleen Witz remembers Christopher Paton coming down to breakfast and being sent back because he had not said his prayers. He was absent for 15 minutes.

36 Tatlow p.225f on the prayer at the 1904 Conishead Priory conference and the prayer meeting which had no ending.

37 'The Book of Prayer for Students' compiled by Leslie Solomon, Malcolm Spencer and Tatlow. cf Tatlow p.461.

38 Letter filed under 'Oldham/World Missionary conference' c.1912 S.C.M. archives.

39 In 1922 H.A. Mess was appointed social studies secretary. He had more success than Malcolm Spencer in changing the individualism of the S.C.M. members into a corporate consciousness. A few students began to vote Labour but the vast majority were 'true blue' conservatives. 'Christ and Human Need' pub. for the S.V.M.U. 1912.

40 Tatlow p.355-63.

41 Tatlow p.261. Hodgkin to Tatlow 4.8.06 under 'Hodgkin/S.V.M.U. Tatlow to Warner 3.6.08 under 'Bible Study'.

42 'The relationship between Bible Study and apologetic study' R.H. Lomas September 1912; Lawson to Tatlow 6.12.09 under 'Bible Study' S.C.M. archives. Report of the sub-committee on Bible Study Easter 1914.

43 Memo on 'The relationship between Bible and Apologetic Study' R.H. Lomas September 1912. Ibid. D. Warner's undated criticism of text-books. Report of a conference of officers 26-29.11.09. 'The Bible should become a living book through the study of which both individually and collectively we gain an ever deepening sense of God'.

44 cf minutes of the Executive meetings 1908-1911. R.L. Pelly was secretary 1911-1914, L.S. Hunter 1914-18. Decay: cf Pelly circular Feb. 1912.

45 Wilder to Tatlow 25.2.10 filed under 'Wilder', S.C.M. archives. Tatlow p.60, 220, 260, 543f.

46 Undated letter in the Montefiore Papers. CR p.132-139.

47 D.S. Cairns to Grace Paton 28.8.43. Montefiore Papers. For what the S.C.M. meant to Cairns cf his autobiography. S.C.M. Press London 1950.

48 Interview Miss Bretherton, who was at the camps 1908-1914.

49 Bretherton, Pelly, Micklem, Haile.

50 Unsigned memo. dated Dec. 1906. T.C.D. Box.

51 cf 2 articles by Tatlow pub. in 'The Student Movement' describing Edinburgh University C.U's objections and the Matlock conference in 1901. Also 'The Basis and the Gospel' by Malcolm Spencer written before 1904 describing it as a call to arms, an invitation to fellowship and a challenge to convert others.

52 Tatlow p.192f.

53 Undated MS sent by Paton to Mott annotated and signed by Tatlow. Written on 1912 note-paper, it probably dates from 1913.

54 The difficulty was over the equation of Jesus with God. There was also the question of associate membership or non-voting membership for those who could not bring themselves to sign cp. controversy over membership of the B.C.C. p.434, 498.

55 Southwell to Tatlow. 13.7.13. 'Aim and Basis' S.C.M. archives.

56 Report of the sub-committee appointed by the General Committee of the W.S.C.F. to consider the question of the Basis which summarises the pre-history of the debate. cf Appendix in Rouse on the changes in the W.S.C.F. Aim and Basis.

57 Filed under T.C.D. S.C.M. archives. (chronological order)

58 Paton's participation of reports by Trafford 4.5.09; E. Murray Page Autumn term 1910; George Ewan, and L.S. Hunter. Feb. 1914 for the decline at Westminster College after Paton left.

59 Documentation filed under C.I.C.C.U., S.C.M. archives; interview with R.L. Pelly.

60 Correspondence re R.D. Rees; W. Dyson, Tatlow to Moulton 12.7.14. Whyte to Tatlow 19.7.14. S.C.M. archives, Whitehorn to Tatlow 29.12.21 S.V.M.U. files Tatlow p.578.

61 J.H. Oldham file, S.C.M. archives. Papers B.C.C.U. 1888-1904.

62 Description supplied by A.J. Haile 26.9.75 and 30.9.75. Yeo to Grace Paton 6.9.43; J.C. Harley to Grace Paton 23.8.43. Jack Hoyland 29.8.43, Frank Cheshire 7.8.43, Robert Richards 12.11.43 on his contribution. Started by Lenwood and H. Carter and supported by the Free Church public schools. A dozen undergraduates were in charge of 80-100 boys at each camp. Their main purpose was to train the boys in Christian living.

63 CR p.112, p.252-4.

64 Interview Robert Mackie. General Secretary of the W.S.C.F. 1938-46. It is significant that most of the people whom I interviewed knew virtually nothing about the W.S.C.F. unless they were staff members.

65 Mackie considers the figures too optimistic. First decennial report filed under W.S.C.F. in S.C.M. archives (no copy in Geneva).

66 'The World's Student Christian Federation' Ruth Rouse. S.C.M. Press 1948. Tatlow p.413f., 677f., 773f. and Hans Mayr 'Einheit und Botschaft' (W.S.C.F. History 1895-1939) University of Tübingen 1975.

67 Letter to Grace Macdonald undated. Montefiore Papers.

68 Tatlow to Mott 8.11.11. S.C.M. archives.

69 John 17vll. Had a special significance for members of the W.S.C.F. In a sense it replaces the Watchword, and was inscribed on a banner to hang behind the platform at the conference.

70   Rouse p.155-6, p.317.

71   'Beatenberg 1920' by William Paton in 'The Student World' p.144 October 1920. Quoted by Rouse p.231.

72   Paton to Grace Paton 2.6.13. Montefiore Papers. Rouse p.174.;'John R. Mott: World Citizen' by Basil Matthews p.303f.

73   Tatlow p.680; p.719. Rouse reports filed by country in the early W.S.C.F. boxes in the W.C.C. archives, Geneva. Filed W.S.C.F. and the date in S.C.M. archives. CR Ch. XIV. 'Voyages of Discovery' by James Parkes. Gollancz, London 1969.

74   W.S.C.F. Lake Mohonk conference 1913. Report published for the W.S.C.F. New York.

75   Ibid.

76   cf Rouse history. Work of Bidgrain and Suzanne de Dietrich.

Notes to Chapter II

1 Interview with Dr Ernest Payne. 1949 is the last year in which figures for new volunteers survive. Numbers had dwindled to 25 from 259 in 1912 at the peak and 191 in 1896 when the record begins.

2 Tatlow p.6-7; 'In this generation' by Ruth Wilder Braisted; 'John R. Mott: World Citizen' by Basil Matthews. Tatlow always refused to accept that the S.V.M.U. was a purely American creation.

3 Tatlow p.33; S.C.M. archives for Byrde's correspondence. At the first executive committee meeting 223 were already held with 69 more on Byrde's list.

4 'Four years' retrospect' Report presented to the S.V.M.U. Quadrennial held in London in 1900 p.124 pub. by the S.V.M.U.

5 Tatlow p.119f.

6 CR p.33-4. It is impossible to tell from the figures whether there was an increase of theological students volunteering or of volunteers deciding to be ordained, as Paton did.

7 Financial Reports filed under S.V.M.U. 1894-1904. S.C.M. archives.

8 Ibid. 'Report of the S.V.M.U. for the four years ending 31.12.03.'

9 Dec. 1910. Men: women: theologicals. 38:73:45 as opposed to 41:34:30 in 1909 (S.V.M.U. figures).

10 e.g. Miss Witz signed the S.V. Declaration in 1915 and was accepted by the C.M.S. after an abstruse theological examination. She began training at her own expense, passed two medicals and was then abruptly dropped for having a supposedly weak heart in 1922. Dental treatment cured her the same year. Welsh Calvinist Methodist S.Vs were rejected in 1910 and there were similar cases of English Presbyterians being rejected. In 1895 most societies foolishly turned down medical students only to be short of them in 1900.

11 Interview. Miss McNair of Queen Margaret's College, Glasgow where there was a particularly strong C.U. cp. Miss Brockway (35 years' service in India) and Bishop and Mrs Hollis. The S.V.M.U. was claiming a monopoly over missionary candidates in a document c 1900.

12 'The Holy Spirit and Missions' Address to the 1900 Quadrennial in 'Students and the missionary problem' Addresses delivered at the international student missionary conference London, pub. for the S.V.M.U. 1900. The same argument appeared in 'The Christian Message' at the I.M.C. conference in Jerusalem 1928 at which Speer had great influence CR p.276.

13 'The missionary motive' p.213. cp. an undated memo in the S.C.M. archives c1913. Filed S.V.M.U. which elaborates the last point.

14 Cairns to Grace Paton 28.8.43. Montefiore Papers.

15 'Students and the missionary problem' Addresses by the Rev Owen, R.T. Campbell and Alexander Connell.

16 Missions inspektor Axenfeld's address at the 1912 Quadrennial Conference report 'Christ and human need' pub. for the S.V.M.U. 1912.

17 Ibid. 'The problem of society' by William Temple.

18 Tatlow to Flint 9.3.22 quotes Paton's attitude. Filed under 'Finance' Undated 'Suggestions and recommendations to the General Committee from the S.V.M.U.' c1918/19. Suggested abandoning the Watchword. cp. Paton's memo to the S.V.M.U. committee June 1921.

19 Letter quoted in full in original thesis, University of Birmingham, May 1976. Talbot to Tatlow 2.3.08. S.C.M. archives 'If God permit' covering a multitude of circumstances: pamphlet dated July 1919.

20 Davies to Tatlow 23.1.19; Paton commented to his wife that Davies' great personal wealth was not resented in India because of his loving personality 30.11.17. Montefiore Papers.

21 Miss Craig to the missionary retreat sub-committee: 'Analysis made of the remarks at the committee by W. Paton' 1915. Filed S.V.M.U. 1915 D. Thornton: 'Tatlow' p.119-134, etc. Padwick biography of Temple Gairdner.

22 Talow's correspondence concerning Lettice Shann 1914-16. S.C.M. archives. Interview Kathleen Witz. Memo on the work of the S.V.M.U. by Paton c1912.

23 Memo of 1900 in 'The Declaration'. From all the letters sent to Tatlow by S.Vs withdrawing on the grounds that they signed in haste it is clear that this danger was not avoided. On the other hand, one girl was incarcerated in a vicarage and not allowed to return to college because her father objected to a further committment before she had finished her training.

24 cf letters written to Paton by S.Vs in the trenches, especially from W. Dyson, T.C.D. secretary died of wounds 1916. Filed 'Y.M.C.A.' 1915/16.

25 Ida de Charevoic — S.V.M.U. executive 10.1.12 filed under 'Liverpool 1912' in S.C.M. archives.

26 Letters to Grace Macdonald, undated. Montefiore Papers.

27 'Some notes on the missionary policy of the Student movement with special reference to the S.V.M.U.'; June 1921.

28 Tatlow p.92; Denton Lutz 'The evangelisation of the world in this generation'.

29 J.M. Maclean to Tatlow 13.1.09 on the history of the controversy. Filed 'Watchword', S.V.M.U., S.C.M. archives.

30 Minutes of the meeting 22.12.06 with R.K. Evans in the chair. Tatlow, Watson, Garfield Williams, Lenwood, Louis Byrde, C.W.G. Taylor, Grant, S.K. Datta, Malcolm Spencer, Robert Wilder, W. Seton, McLeod Campbell, W.G. Hardie, Ruth Rouse, Winifred Sedgwick & Misses Barrow, Stevenson and Margaret Bretherton present. Filed under S.V.M.U. 'Watchword'.

31 cp. Lenwood's speech 22.12.06 and letter of 7.1.12 saying that the Watchword was irrelevant in Benares, where he was working. Agnes de Sélincourt, writing from Allahabad 24.1.09 gave the opposite testimony about its effectiveness.

32 Oldham to Tatlow 8.11.06; 3.11.06; (wrongly dated 07), quoted by Tatlow p.314.

33 A.G. Fraser, Oldham's brother-in-law, later of Trinity College Kandy, and Achimota. Letter to Tatlow 18.12.06. He was afraid that if people observed the demise of the Watchword, they would lose the accompanying sense of urgency.

34 This book was briefly accepted as the official interpretation 1900-1 in 'The past policy of the S.V.M.U.' Tatlow p.314 on how Mott's address at the 1904 Quadrennial quelled a rebellion temporarily. In December 1914, in a memorandum, Wilder demanded that Mott should update his ideas.

35 'Randall Davidson' by G.K.A. Bell p.572-74.
'History and records of the Edinburgh 1910 conference' vol IX pub. Oliphant Edinburgh 1910. It seems from evidence culled from the Whitgift School magazine that Paton first heard the Watchword when Randall Davidson addressed his school's prize-giving in 1903. (original Ph. D. thesis. Ch.I)

36 Even more significantly, a speaker at the 1900 Quadrennial said the Watchword was defensable and had much meaning left in it.

37 Dr Warneck's objections which Oldham repeated to Tatlow in his letter 3.12.06. Tatlow p.109-10.

38 Lenwood's evidence to the 1906 committee. Hodgson to Tatlow on Lenwood's objections 11.3.09.

39 Tatlow to Wilder 8.8.21 that Paton's report was not of a decisive character because hardly anyone was interested enough in the Watchword to reply to his questions. They were simply clearing out lumber. The 1918-19 S.V.M.U. Commission decided it was completely dead and that it would be pointless to try and revive it.

40. S.K. Datta. Son of a Bengali freelance evangelist, later headmaster of a school in Peshawar. S.K. went to Glasgow University to study medicine 1899-1906; m. Rena Carswell whom he met while working for the Y.M.C.A. in France in 1915. Worked for the W.S.C.F. in Geneva. 1928-32, head of Forman College 1932-42. A great friend of Paton's.

41 Tatlow to Charles Flint (filed under S.C.M. Finance) 9.3.22.

42 Tatlow p.345; Paton quoting D.S. Cairns in a memo on the proposed retreat January 1916.

43 Introductory pamphlet. This and other documents are filed under 'Swanwick 1910', S.C.M. archives. The missionary commission of 1918-19 found the same attitudes still prevailing among students.

44 K. Witz's recollections.

45 cp with William Dempster's remarks to the missionary retreat sub-committee 'Foreign missions and the Gospel' Impressions of the S.V.M.U. retreat held at Swanwick by Paton pub. by the S.C.M.; circular of the S.V. executive 19.1.16. Memorandum the S.V.M.U. campaign March 1918 by Lettice Shann. Robert Mackie and many others consider 1919-22 the golden age of the S.C.M. and S.V.M.U.

46 'Ein Leben für Kirche und Mission' ed. by W. Metzger. Ev. Missionsverlag Stuttgart 1955; George Bell/Alphons Koechlin Briefwechsel 1933-54 ed. Andreas Lindt p.17. Ev. Verlag, Zürich 1969.

47 Minutes of the preliminary meeting of the commission 29.11.18. S.V.M.U. files.

48 14.2.19 L.S. Hunter to Tatlow filed under 'Y.M.C.A.' 1914-19.

49 Opening assessment of the problem in 'The Report of the third commission appointed by the executive of the S.C.M. September 1913 to consider the missionary work of the movement'. The commission included Paton, Tatlow, Fairfield, Cockin, Grace McAuley, Olive Moberly, J.H. Oldham, Dora Pym, Lettice Shann and reported in 1919.

50 Undated memo c 1909 on S.V.M.U. policy; Spencer's memo 13.10.08.

51 Filed 'S.C.M. Finance' Tatlow to Flint 24.5.11; Tatlow to Connell of the English Presbyterian Church Foreign Mission Committee 20.1.13.

52 S.V.M.U. files 1908-11. The first approach was made to a candidate in 1908.

53 Undated letter from Westminster College c Feb. 1911. He insists that he is not haggling, but is making a point which may not have occurred to the committee. He communicated his worries to Grace Macdonald.

54 Undated letter to Grace Macdonald.

55 Lenwood to Monk 28.12.11, explaining the justifiable illogicality of the S.V. Declaration, and of missionary service in general.

56 Undated Memo. on the work of the S.V.M.U. c1912; cp. with his circular of 1.11.12 on the state of play re recruiting for the S.V.M.U. and his description in 1917 of the qualities of the ideal S.V. member.

57 This was Oldham's idea c 1908, but was first used systematically by Paton as a means of educating students re missionary needs and of stopping a student losing his vision in general aspirations by focussing his attention on specific opportunities.

58 Circular of October 1913 explaining the policy of making the C.U. responsible for missionary study instead of the S.V.M.U., with instructions to implement this.

59 Filed under S.C.M. : Swanwick 1913, Missionary Retreat Sub-Committee : 'Analysis of remarks of executive members by William Paton'.

60 Tatlow's correspondence with T.C. Lunt of C.M.S. : 'Relations with Missionary societies 1914'.

61 cf. E.T. Stevens' letters to Tatlow 1912-14 filed 'Correspondence with missionaries', complaining about the discrimination against women in the Madras Representative Council. Mrs Hollis supported this.

62 Report of the annual conference of the U.C.M.E. 6-8.3.14.

63 'Some notes on the missionary policy of the student movement with special reference to the S.V.M.U.' June 1921.

64 Filed under 'Relationships with missionary societies'. The S.C.M. received £1,885 in 1915 and £1,392 from donations. The L.M.S. gave £10 per year for work among foreign students.

Notes to Chapter III

1 Cyprian op. 8.9.20, cf 7.14.1 cited Lietzmann 'The Founding of the Church Universal' p.227 Lutterworth Press 1938.

2 Interview Catherine Paton, who was embarrassed as a child by this, that her parents were different from other people's.

3 Tatlow p.506f. Tatlow's sources for these figures are unknown, but he repeated them in virtually every letter he wrote. In the W.S.C.F. annual report, it is stated that 60% of German students enlisted immediately, but all French students were automatically conscripted in 1914.

4 cf. Zoë Fairfield's collection of essays on the subject of women's suffrage. S.C.M. Study book 1912; Howard Houlder's study books ; CR p.375-377.

5 Grace Paton knew Keir Hardie from childhood (Memoirs.,Montefiore Papers) Tatlow's report : 7.11- 7.12.12, on a dinner held for S.C.M. secretaries to meet Ramsay MacDonald. S.C.M. archives.

6 Although the actual outbreak of war was unexpected, tension had been mounting since 1911. From MSS in the German Imperial war archives, it is clear that war could have been declared in 1905, 1909 and 1911. 'The Origins of the First World War' ed. H.W. Koch, Macmillan 1972(Koch) and 'The Home Fronts Britain , France and Germany 1914 -18 ' by John Williams pub. Constable, London 1972(Williams).

7 Grace Paton to David Macdonald, Easter Day 1915 or 1916, and 22.1.17., Montefiore Papers; Paton to Tatlow 14.8.17. S.C.M. archives. Lloyd George : M.P. for Caenarvon from 1890. Minister for War 1916. P.M. 1917 after ousting Asquith. Returned at the head of a national coalition government in 1918.

8 Skinner to Paton 15.2.12. Context unknown. 'The more I think of your affair the more I sympathise with you and understand how the misunderstanding came about. . . . I hope you understand how truly my sympathies are with you, and how gladly I would do anything to bring things right.' Montefiore Papers.

9 'Social dynamism as a factor in the new imperialism' H.W. Koch, Zeitschrift für Politik XVII 1970. This philosophy, observed by Koch, regarded war as the natural outcome of human evolution.

10 Skinner to Paton 20.9.14. Montefiore Papers.

11 Quoted in Tatlow p.578; Filed T.C.D. : Dyson 1914-15. S.C.M. archives cp. letters Dyson to Tatlow 2.9.14; 7.9.14; 14.12.14.

12 The canonization process can be seen in Tatlow's 'History'. Tatlow came into conflict with Dyson's sister, who also wrote a Memoir of him. Tatlow is mistaken about the circumstances of his death. CR p.57; Chapter II footnote (24).

13 John A. Forrester-Paton of the United Free Church of Scotland was a liberal and a pacifist, later president of the World's Y.M.C.A.s and an M.P. A generous donor to Paton's projects. His brother Ernest went to India and lived in holy poverty, often in trouble with the police for demonstrating on behalf of Indian nationalists. E.H. Box 415.

14 Quoted 'George Bell : Bishop of Chichester' by R.C.D. Jasper p.294; cf Chapter XII

15 Tatlow p.524. CR p.38,41-42.

16 Rouse and Neill p.523; Tatlow p.514f; 'The Ecumenical Movement in World Affairs' by Darrill Hudson, Weidenfeld and Nicolson London 1949.

17 'Goodbye to all that', autobiography of Robert Graves, pub. Jonathan Cape, London 1929.

18. 20.8.15. S.C.M. archives; W.W.'s identity is unknown.

19 'The Home Fronts' by John Williams. The Pankhurst family was split. Williams confused Mrs Pankhurst with her daughter Sylvia who opposed the war, and was a founder member of the British Communist party.

20 Williams p.68; 'Conscription and Conscience' by John Graham p.71. One C.O. tried to quote from the Greek N.T. 'Greek!' shouted the chairman of the tribunal. 'You don't mean to tell me that Jesus spoke Greek. He was British to the backbone.' Graham p.43.

21 See file 'Relations with other bodies 1914-18' Letter to F.J. Tritton 15.4.16. S.C.M. archives.

22 Ibid. Tatlow to a Mr Shakespeare 8.1.17.

23 Ibid. Letter to a Mr Hill 21.10.18.

24 At one point there were only two male secretaries, the rest being in prison or at the front. Most of the office staff were called up.

25 'Deutsche Weihnacht' pub. by the D.S.C.V. and distributed to 40,000 soldiers. Christmas 1914, summarised in 'Student Movement' Vol XVII p.115. The German articles call for repentance by Germany and an end to hatred of England.

26 'Student Movement' Vol XVII p.31.

27 'The Home Front': Williams.

28 Letter dated 21.12.41. in the possession of Michael Paton.

29 'Student Movement' Vol XVII p.44.

30 'Church and Nation' The Bishop Paddock Lectures 1914-15, Macmillan, London 1915.

31 Paton met Temple at Oxford, where he was a Fellow of Queen's College. He was a popular summer camp speaker for the S.C.M. and toured Australia on their behalf in 1910. 'William Temple' by F.A. Iremonger O.U.P. 1948 is not a very satisfactory biography.

32 This Act effectively removed a pacifist's civil rights. Graham p.140,164.

33 Graham p.69; 'Twentieth Century Pacifism' by Peter Brook, van Northand Reinhold Company 1970 p.42; 'Conscience and Pacifism. The British Government and the Conscientious Objector to military service 1916-19' John Rae O.U.P. 1970(Rae): 'The Rebel Passion' by Vera Britain. George Allen Unwin 1964.

34 Graham p.54,p.110.

35 Ibid p.74. Snowden's speech to the Commons. 17.2.16 published as 'British Prussianism. The scandal of the tribunals'.Paton's views: Paton to Elmslie 3.10.39; Paton to Raven 6.10.39. Paton Papers Box V WCC archives, Geneva.

36 Graham p.78,p.158. Men who volunteered for the R.A.M.C. were liable to be transferred to combatant units.

37 Ibid p.113, 'Objection overruled' by David Boulton. MacGibbon and Kee, London 1967. p.66f also gives figures of 16,000 C.O.s, 34 sentenced to death, 73 deaths in prison and 31 driven insane.cf. Appendix in Graham; Williams p.76.

38 Undated letter, Montefiore Papers, cp. with the C.O.s' letters printed in Graham.

39 'Apparently the S.C.M. and Mr T regard him as absolutely indispensable. In any case he would not serve in a combatant corps and unless they change the arrangement, not in a non-combatant one.' Letter written before May 1916; Montefiore Papers. Similar arguments in her letters of Easter Day 1916 and 22.1.17.

40 Tatlow p.529f. The 'zweites examen' corresponded to the General Ordination Examination but is taken at university. cp Grüber : 'Erinnerungen aus sieben Jahrzehnten'.

41 Tatlow p.577 Documentation in the S.C.M. archives. Held on 20.11.15.

42 Graham on the 'Non-conscription Fellowship.'; Bertrand Russell's autobiography; Tatlow/-Grensted correspondence, filed M.I.C.C.U. 1917 S.C.M. archives.

43 Letter filed: 'Paton and the Y.M.C.A.', Tatlow to Gillie of the English Presbyterian Church 9.6.17.

44 Paton to Grace Paton October 1917 Montefiore Papers.

45 'The Importance of being Ernest' Act I.

46 Grace Paton to David Macdonald 13.2.17. Montefiore Papers: Tatlow to Neville Talbot 28.12.18. is a fairer assessment of the Y.M.C.A.'s shortcomings. Carter/Tatlow exchange Dec. 1916 on the terms of Paton's employment. Paton to Tatlow 26.8.19. and 11.8.19. on the failings of the Y.M.C.A. Filed Y.M.C.A., S.C.M. archives.

47 Interviews : John and Gwen Lewis, Kathleen Witz, Tatlow letter re Thomson 3.2.16. whose cardinal sin was to wear plimsolls in the Quadrangle. Filed 'Cambridge'; L.S. Hunter to Paton 28.3.18. filed 'Y.M.C.A.'; Tatlow/Grant correspondence 1918; CR p.9.

48 Paton to Tatlow 19.1.13. S.V.M.U. files S.C.M. archives.

49 Tatlow to Connell 20.1.13. Oldham first suggested the idea of an assistant for Tatlow in 1908 (filed Edinburgh W.M.C. 1910) Tatlow declared that the S.C.M. had been searching for a suitable man for four years. CR p.74.

50 Tatlow to Garnett of Manchester, Manchester Inter-Collegiate Christian Union finances, blaming Paton for not writing memos on what he was doing 30.3.20; Tatlow to Maclean of the C.B.M.S. 3.5.22 : 'I find that some of our people think Bill filled the picture a little too much from the S.C.M. point of view, and they would like me to pick up a certain measure of contact with the societies again.' Filed 'Relations with other societies' S.V.M.U. 1920-21.

51 Paton to Grace Paton 24.10.17; 20.10.17; 'Farquhar is a lovely person to travel with'; 'Not to destroy but to fulfil. The theology of J.N. Farquhar' by Eric Sharpe.

52 Sources : Paton to Grace Paton 14.11.17; 24.3.18; Montefiore Papers; Paton to Tatlow 22.1.18; 12.6.18; circular of 12.6.18. Paton file Y.M.C.A. papers S.C.M. archives.

53 Paton to Grace Paton 24.3.18. partly illegible. Montefiore Papers.

54 Ibid Paton to Grace Paton 24.3.18.

55 Ibid Paton to Grace Paton 27.4.18.

56 Ibid Paton to Grace Paton 15.5.18.

57 CR p.8, p.14-15.

58 Ibid Paton to Grace Paton 27.4.18.

59 Ibid Paton to Grace Paton 6.7.18.

60 Garbett: Diary 21.8.43. quoted by Charles Smyth in his Life of Garbett. Hodder and Stoughton 1959 p.460.

61 Graham p.204f; 'The Rebel Passion' by Vera Brittain is a history of the F.o.R.

62 Cambridge and St Thomas's Hospital. Served in West China 1905-1910; Secretary of the Friends' Foreign Missionary Association 1910-20. One of the very few Friends exempt from military service. Secretary of the N.C.C. of China 1922-29.

63 'H.T. Hodgkin : a memoir' by H.G. Wood. S.C.M. Press 1937.

64 CR p.475; In 1939 Quakers tried to act as mediators.

65 I.M.C. Box 117 WCC archives Geneva.

66 Paton circular 6.1.22. 'Race hatred is pretty bad in India, and in spite of Gandhi's personality, high character and disinterested love for India one cannot acquit him of having set going methods and ideas which inevitably breed both race hatred and violence.' Y.M.C.A. papers, S.C.M. archives.

67 'Adnotationes ad dies poenitentiae et spei' by Karl Hartenstein. Written in 1946, original in Stuttgart, Basel Mission archives. Copy at the Basel Missionshaus. Hartnestein's report to the Basel Mission committee 15.3.34 I.M.C. Box 330, Geneva.

68 Tambaram Series Vol. VII p.84f.

69 Founded c 1936 from those who voted not to defend King and country. Many subsequently volunteered for the Armed Forces as soon as war broke out.

70 Paton attributed American isolationism 1939-41 to business interests : businessmen who believed they would make a fortune out of sales to both sides, and could thus weaken their commercial rivals.

71 Paton to a B.G. van Groningen 5.1.42. Paton Papers VIII, WCC archives Geneva.: 'I have found certain aspects of the life and practice of the Group very undesirable and I think they habitually exaggerate their achievements . . . I cannot help noticing the enormous extent to which the Group now goes in for this kind of propaganda and I do not think it is spiritually very healthy.'

72 From an unpublished rough draft of the Oxford conference debates compiled under Hugh Martin's directions. WCC archives, Geneva.

73 'The Churches survey their task' ed. J.H. Oldham Vol VIII pub. 1937 George Allen Unwin.

74 Visser't Hooft : Memoirs, p.72.

75 cp 'World Community' (1938) and 'The Message of the world-wide Church' Christian Newsletter series 1939.

76 Paton to Muir 15.9.38. I.M.C. Box 42; to Palmer undated letter I.M.C. Box 117; to Grace Paton 24.11.38 Montefiore Papers, very significant because he expresses fears re fate of Jews in Czecheslovakia, very anti-Chamberlain.

77 'Charles Raven : Naturalist, Historian, Theologian,' by Dillistone Hodder and Stoughton 1975 p.303f.

78 Interview Alan Booth. Paton gave Booth the impression that he thought that they were making a lot of fuss about nothing.

79 Smyth p.298f. Garbett had been chairman of the Religious Advisory Committee since 1923.

80 Interview Eric Fenn. Garbett had an hour and a half long lunch with Sir Alan Powell, Director of the BBC and achieved nothing. Lang thought it pointless to try. Garbett admired Fenn's non-conformist conscience.

81 There are conflicting oral traditions as to who this was, and how it happened. Iremonger nearly resigned because he was expected to review a biography of H.R.L. Sheppard without mentioning that he was a pacifist.

82 CR p.248.

83 See appendix. Paton Papers IV, WCC archives, Geneva.

84 Interview Dillistone. Canon Dillistone could not find the records of the Cloister Group, which are filed under Paton Papers IV, and copies are in the Selly Oak Colleges' archives (SOC).

85 Letter to Visser't Hooft. Paton Papers II, WCC archives, Geneva.

86 B.B.C. sound archives; Copies : Paton Papers IV; SOC archives.

Notes to Chapter IV

1 The Dillistone definition is good (p.303, 'Charles Raven'), cp Dr Parkes' struggle for a liberal theology in 'Voyages of Discovery'. Briefly, 'Liberal theology' emphasizes the revelation of God in the natural world, progressive revelation, the Incarnation. It tends to see man as inherently good rather than thoroughly corrupt. Sometimes includes proofs of God's existence. Flourished in the Church of England 1850-1940. Illustrated by Dyson's reports of visits to Oxford theological colleges in 1915 and Paton to David Paton 19.4.42 that he is distressed at the narrow romantic Anglo-Catholicism R.O. Hall is propagating in America, but R.O. Hall's problem is that he only did one year's serious intellectual work at Oxford.

2 Interview David Paton.

3 'A Faith for the World', Cargate Press 1929, p.10 and p.47.

4 Jerusalem Series Vol I, Stanley Jones on Secularism. CR p.279, p.389.

5 'Jesus Christ and the World's Religions' U.C.M.E. imprint 1916 Eleven impressions 1916-26, when it was revised for a second edition.

6 Preface of 'A Faith for the World'; William Paton gave Michael Paton a copy of Rudolf Otto's 'Idea of the Holy' and told him it was gold, pure gold.

7 CR p.217ff.

8 'Randall Davidson : Archbishop of Canterbury' by G.K.A. Bell. O.U.P. third edition 1952. Bell wrote this while he was Dean of Canterbury. The 'Penguins' are listed in the General Bibliography.

9 Dr Craig. Secretary to the Churches' Commission on International Friendship and Social Responsibility. First Secretary of the B.C.C. Letter to Miss Morden March 1973.

10 'A Faith for the World' p.39 is lifted from 'Jesus Christ and the World's Religions' p.89. Unconscious plagarism?

11 Paton to Grace Paton 17.9.18 and 10.1.36. Montefiore Papers.

12 'Rethinking missions. A layman's inquiry after 100 years' ed. W. Hocking Harper Bros. London and New York 1932. CR p.188.

13 'A history of the expansion of Christianity' Vol VI by K.S. Latourette. pub. Paternoster Press 1971. pp.114-117, 145; 'The Life of Alexander Duff' 2 vols by George Smith 1870. Duff arrived in India in 1829 and with the help of Ram Mohun Roy founded Duff College, and a second college when he had to relinquish the original college after the Disruption.

14 cp. Farquhar's reservations about apologetic discussed by Eric Sharpe in 'Not to destroy but to fulfil. The contribution of J.N. Farquhar to Protestant missionary thought before 1914.' Stud. Miss. Upsalensis V pub. in Uppsala in 1965. p.16f, p.231, p.301.

15 R.O. Hall remembers that Kraemer insisted on writing and thinking in unintelligible English instead of Dutch. 'Hendrik Kraemer : Pionier der Ökumene' by Dr A. Th van Leeuwen. Basileia Verlag Basel 1962; 'Kraemer towards Tambaram' C. Hallenkreuz Stud. Miss. Upsalensis Stockholm 1968.

16 Fragments found in the Montefiore Papers.

17 'J.N. Farquhar' by Eric Sharpe. Y.M.C.A. Press Calcutta 1963.

18 cp 'The Faiths of Mankind' p.152 in which he attributes much of the tension between Hindu and Muslim in India to the tension between the ideas of God who is and God who acts.

19 A verse from Revelation was inscribed in her wedding ring.

20 'The quest of the historical Jesus', a translation of 'Von Reimarus zu Wrede' by A Schweitzer was the only work in English available to Paton at this time.

21 Paton was always weak on the subject of apocalyptic. cp A.G. Hogg : 'Redemption from this world' p.65 pub. by T.T. Clark 1922.

22 Paton does not use source criticism to consider the authenticity of this speech, but accepts it at face value.

23 'Not to destroy, but to fulfil' pp.272f,312,327.

24 CR p.164,222-3.

25 'Not to destroy but to fulfil' p.63; CR p.212; K.S. Latourette : 'A history of the expansion of Christianity' Vol VI p.167f; J.W. Pickett: 'Christian Mass Movements in India. A study with recommendations' Abingdon Press 1933.

26 'Alexander Duff: pioneer of missionary education.' S.C.M. Press 1923 p.137f.

27 Roland Allen : 'A Church Policy for North China' (1902), quoted by David Paton in 'Reform of the Ministry' Lutterworth Press 1968. Paton and Allen both knew Herbert Kelly who was interested in Allen's ideas, but did not like Paton. There is no evidence to connect them directly.

28 CR p.178; Jerusalem Series Vol I.

29 'The Rebuke of Islam' by Temple Gairdner C.M.S. imprint 1920, originally pub. by U.C.M.E. as 'The Reproach of Islam' 1909.

30 'Jesus Christ and the World's Religions' p.28-29 (second edition).

31 Mt 5 v 20.

32 cp explanation by Nirad Chaudhuri : 'The Continent of Circe' Chatto and Windus, London 1964.

33 'The Christ of the Indian Road' E. Stanley Jones. Hodder and Stoughton London 1925.

34 Ram Mohun Roy was the founder of a reforming movement in Hinduism, the Brahmo Samaj. cf 'Alexander Duff' for Paton's tribute to him.

35 'Not to destroy but to fulfil' p.327ff.

36 'Alexander Duff' p.47.

37 Ibid p.206. Latourette Vol VI p.116. Duff was convinced that Christianity and science were compatible. Nehru is an example of Duff's fears.

38 Mott. Addresses and Papers Vol VI p.238, p.391.

39 'Jesus Christ and the World's Religions'. p.88. Second edition p.90.

40 CR p.154.

41 'A Faith for the World' p.38.

42 Paton to Grace Paton 27.8.18. Montefiore Papers.

43 'Jesus Christ and the World's Religions.' p.93f.

44 When taught about the Reformation, Victoria noted in her diary her resolve to be good.

45 'The Faiths of Mankind' p.134, 149; 'Jesus Christ and the World's Religions' p.94-95.

46 'Jesus Christ and the World's Religions' Final chapter. cp Visser't Hooft : Memoirs p.46.

47 cf the cartoons reproduced in Iremonger's biography depicting the resentment caused by Temple's pronouncements.

48 cp the preface of 'A Faith for the World' with 'The Christian Message in a non-Christian World' (Kraemer).

49 'Not to destroy but to fulfil' p.167.

50 'The faiths of Mankind' p.157 Parallels in Kraemer.

51 Ibid p.152. Communalism with its demand for separate electorates for the different religious groupings in India was the scourge of Indian politics 1920-47.

52 Ibid p.52.

53 IRM Vol XXVII p.333, p.338 (1938).

54 MacNicol to Grace Paton 26.11.43. Paton was always friendly with C.F. Andrews despite their theological differences. cf Daniel O'Connor : 'The testimony of C.F. Andrews', Bangalore and Calcutta 1974.

55 Uncatalogued pamphlet in the WCC archives, Geneva, copy SOC.

56   'Missions and the post-war world' I.M.C Box 113; 'The future of the missionary enterprise' IRM Vol XXXI p.385, October 1942. Bonhoeffer's plan for a book is appended to 'Letters and Papers from Prison' Fontana paperbacks 1963.

57   Paton to Grace Paton 24.10.17; 20.10.17. Montefiore Papers.

58   Kraemer's papers were preserved in Oestgeist, Holland. Complete bibliography available from the WCC. Kraemer's I.M.C. related papers are in Geneva, Box 994, Confidential files.

59   Summary of Kraemer's position : Tambaram Series Vol I 'The Authority of the Faith' O.U.P. 1939.

60   Kraemer/Barth relationship : 'The Christian Message in a non-Christian World' p.115-20, 130; Visser't Hooft : Memoirs p.59.

61   His family and Margaret Sinclair believe that this was a powerful motive.

Notes to Chapter V

1   The Khalifat volunteers were a band of Muslim Indians organised to restore the Caliphate, which Britain had permitted to be abolished in 1919. Backed by the Congress Party, they revolted in the 'Moplah Uprising'. Michael Edwedes; 'British India', Sidgwick and Jackson, London 1967 p.157f, 199f, 218; 'Muslims and the Kaliphate' article by Paton IRM Vol XII p.83.

2   'An advanced History of India' by R.C. Majundar Part III, p.959, 'India and the Common-wealth' by S.R. Meprotra, Allen Unwin 1965 p.192.

3   Paton circulars 6.1.22, 25.5.22 etc. filed 'Y.M.C.A. 1919' in SCM archives and Montefiore Papers. Paton to Tatlow 2.8.22.

4   Circular 5.1.22 cp. 'Social Ideals in India', Chapter XI.

5   The reason perhaps lies in his sympathetic attitude re the difficulties of being baptised at a time of anti-western unrest.

6   'Christian Literature in India' I.M.C. Box 103; I.M.C. Box 306 Statement by Paton 1.4.30. Memo from Dr Shonie Oliver of the Canadian Presbyterian Medical Mission to Margaret Sinclair, Montefiore Papers. Copy SOC.

7   cp. 'Christianity in the Eastern Conflicts' and repeated annual surveys in the IRM. CR 72f. p.164, p.165, p.171, p.199f, p.242f.

8   'Ecumenical Foundations' by Richey Hogg, Harper Bros. New York 1952, p.33, 152, 213; Rouse and Neill p.364, 388; M.A. Thesis Chapter III.

9   Confidential Oldham circular to colleagues 19.1.22. D.W.M.E./I.M.C. Box 30 WCC archives, Geneva.

10 Ibid.

11 S.P.G. archives. Paton used to take his family to stay in the Metropolitan of Calcutta's bungalow at Shillong. Paton to Oldham 29.6.22. on the resolutions of the meetings at Shillong.

12 Paton to colleagues. 25.5.22. D.W.M.E./I.M.C. Box 30.

13 E.T. Stevens to Tatlow 7.12.13 S.V.M.U. files. Wives were not allowed to stand unless they had their own work and most women could not pass the language requirements.

14 Datta to Oldham 4.11.20. E.H. Box 414.

15 Warnshuis to Turner 19.5.22. D.W.M.E./I.M.C. Box 30.

16 See Bishop Hall's writings in the bibliography.

17 Oldham to Miss Hunter 16.1.23. E.H. Box 393.

18 Government of India Act 1919 enacted 1921.

19 'Minutes of the N.M.C. Meeting at Poona' E.H. Box 385, D.W.M.E./I.M.C. Box 30.

20 Proceedings of the All-India conference of Indian Christians 1914-31 E.H. Box 414.

21 Paton to Tatlow 18.1.23; Y.M.C.A. files S.C.M. archives.

22 Lenwood to Oldham 4.4.22.

23 Datta to Oldham 4.10.20. E.H. Box 414; Oldham to Miss Hunter 15.1.23, E.H. Box 393.

24 Banninga to Warnshuis 19.1.22. 'Even though the problems and their solutions had not been of such far-reaching consequences, the mere sight of Oldham and his way of doing things would have been a fine psychological study. I haven't the slightest doubt that Oldham is a man of the most transparent sincerity, but I can't help feeling that he is also a diplomat of the highest order.' D.W.M.E./I.M.C. Box 30.

25 Minutes of the Ninth Meeting of the N.M.C. at Ranchi E.H. Box 385.

26 'Correspondence with Canada' E.H. Box 393 and D.W.M.E./I.M.C. Box 30.

27 Precis of the meeting of the executive committee of the N.M.C. 1922, E.H. Box 393, MacNicol (letter of 23.3.22.) thought that his being a new man would be an advantage.

28 Minutes of the eighth Meeting of the N.M.C. at Poona. p.10.

29 Paton to Grace Paton 18-25.1.22. Montefiore Papers.

30 Paton to Oldham 5.4.22. D.W.M.E./I.M.C. Box 30 Oldham's assertion that 'Paton feels that it is clearly God's call' (19.1.22 circular) is a figment of his imagination.

31 S.C.M. archives Filed under 'Paton : Y.M.C.A.' 16.1.19.

33 All correspondence relating to the boards is in E.H. Box 393. See MacNicol's letter of 23.4.22.

34 Maclennan to Oldham pointing out the error of his letter 12.3.22. Ibid Oldham to Paton 12.3.22. reassuring him that he was writing a letter which would be 'a corker': Paton to Maclennan 4.5.22. on failure E.H. Box 394.

35 Oldham to Paton 18.5.22. E.H. Box 393.

36 Paton Papers 1922-26 E.H. Box 394.

37 'The East and the West' Vol XXI pub by S.P.G.

38 Paton to Oldham 28.6.23. E.H. Box 394.

39 Paton to Oldham 30.4.25. E.H. Box 394; Richey Hogg p.237.

40 Paton to Oldham 14.4.25. Ibid.

41 Minutes of the N.C.C. Meeting at Calcutta. November 1926; Minutes of the Meeting at Waltair November 1924; reports on the N.C.C.s E.H. Box 385.

42 Sinclair p.101f; The conference on Citizenship, Economics and Politics under the chairmanship of William Temple was held as the climax of two years' intense ecumenical activity at grass-roots level. Archbishop Söderblom was very impressed, and copied aspects of the conference for the first Life and Work conference at Stockholm in 1925. Its leaders became involved in Life and Work, the grass-roots in COPEC Housing Association work, and the Christian Social Councils. CR p.179, 284, 417, 487f, 489.

43 cf bibliography for Paton's writings on opium. Richey Hogg p.234; 'Charles Brent, Crusader for Christian Unity' by Zabriskie, Westminster Press U.S.A. 1957.

44 Bishop Pickett : 'Christian mass movements in India', New York 1933.

45 Benares United Mission : E.H. Box 409. Paton attended a few meetings of the London committee 1941-43.

46 Michael Edwardes : 'British India' p.251.

47 Interview Miss McNair and Miss Mangat Rai; 'The Indian Muslims' by M. Mujeeb, George Allen Unwin London 1967. Paton to Oldham 21.7.24. and Paton to MacNicol 6.4.27. E.H. Box 394.

48 L.E. Browne S.P.G. archives Box 'C.B.M.S. and I.M.C.'; cf van Leeuwen biography of Kraemer.

49 Paton to Oldham 18.8.22; 23.8.23. E.H. Box 394.

50 Ibid Correspondence with MacNicol.

51 I.M.C. Boxes 370, 371 WCC archives, Geneva. The hostility arose from the antagonism of the China Inland Mission and the Lutheran Missions to the Chinese theologians of the Church of Christ in China.

52 Paton to Oldham and to Maclennan 19.11.24. Paton to Oldham 14.5.25. E.H. Box 394.

53 i.e. 1928/29, 1930/31, 1935/36, 1938/39. It was resented by his children. Testimonial: Minutes of the N.C.C. Meeting at Calcutta, E.H. Box 395 K.T. Paul's letter is preserved in the Montefiore Papers.

54 Die ökumenische Diskussion im Banne der Weltwirtschaftkrise und des ostlichen Nationalismus' p.46f Chapter of a thesis submitted to the University of Heidelberg 1972 : Die Ökumene in der Entwicklungskonflikte'

55 CR p.182f, p.193f, p.195f, p.344f.

56 CR p.218; 'The Theology of the Laymen's Inquiry' by John Mackay, IRM Vol XXII 1933; 'The Christian Message in a non-Christian World' p.47.

57 'Report of the Commission on Higher Education in India' ed. A.D. Lindsay O.U.P. 1932.

58 'The Laymen's Foreign Missions Inquiry' by K.S. Latourette. Concluding sentence. IRM Vol XXII 1933.

59 Minutes of the Williamstown Meeting p.36, I.M.C. Box 24, WCC archives Geneva S.P.G. archives, box labelled 'C.B.M.S. and I.M.C.'; Paton to Stacy Waddy 14.1.30; D.W.M.E./-I.M.C. Box 38 Folder (1); correspondence with J.Z. Hodge E.H. Box 395

60 Correspondence with J.Z. Hodge, E.H. Box 394; Circular from Salem 19.2.31. I.M.C. Box 91.

61 McDougall to Paton 16.2.29.; 10.10.29. E.H. Box 427.

62 Letter: 23.10.30. I.M.C. Box 316; An estimated half million dollars were probably spent. A letter (25.9.30) shows Paton trying to save them £25, which they resented.

63 Ibid exchange Paton/John Mackenzie of Wilson College, Bombay, 5.11.31.

64 Ibid. from Rangoon 11.6.31.

65 Paton to Hodge 2.2.32. E.H. Box 394.

66 Paton/Davies correspondence E.H. Box 395.

67 Paton to Hodge 2.2.32. E.H. Box 394.

68 Paton to Mackenzie 23.11.31. I.M.C. Box 316.

69 Hodge to Paton 30.10.31.; Reply 10.12.31. E.H. Box 395.

70 'The Christian Message' Jerusalem Series Vol I, p.383f.

71 According to M.M. Thomas, 30,000 men and women were in prison for political offences, the Viceroy, Lord Irwin, was ruling by special decrees and the Round Table conference delegates were arriving in India to treat with Gandhi.

72 'The Laymen's Foreign Missions Inquiry' by K.S. Latourette, IRM Vol XXII, 1933.

73 CR 209f. Contrast this with R.R. Keithahn, who would admonish an Indian for wearing sandals with plastic straps, and then preach the Gospel whereby salvation depended on every village having a telephone installed, according to Bishop Hollis.

74 India Colleges Appeal E.H. Box 428.

75 Joint Appeal Correspondence D.W.M.E./I.M.C. Box 38(4), Paton to Mott 28.5.31. in particular. Distinct coolness from Mott and Warnshuis exuded in the letters from Mott to Paton 12.10.31; Warnshuis/Paton 9-22.10.31. I.M.C. Box 30; Fund-raising in America : D.W.M.E./-I.M.C. Box 31(2) and Box 38(1).

76 Folder : 'Central Board on Higher Education in India 1934-37'. Paton to P.O. Philip 28.3.34. E.H. Box 428.

77 Paton's letter of 31.12.31., E.H. Box 394; Bishop Newbigin's recollections.

78 I.M.C. Box 303; Correspondence with T.W. Gardiner E.H. Box 424.

79 CR p.189f.

80 Robert Speer : elder statesman at the I.M.C. Meeting at Jerusalem. Objections November 1932 issue of 'The missionary review of the world', subsequently published in book form.

81 Initial favourable reaction : 10.11.32., I.M.C. Box 95, later reaction : Paton to the Bishop of Salisbury 27.3.33. I.M.C. Box 316.

82 Westman on Torm April 1933 I.M.C. Box 316.

83 'Consultation with the chairman of the I.M.C.' D.W.M.E./I.M.C. Box 35(7).

84 Philip to Paton 13.1.33. E.H. Box 394.

85 Paton to Grace Paton 11.3.18. Montefiore Papers.

86 Richey Hogg p.185; 'Randall Davidson' p.926-34; Darrill Hudson : 'The Ecumenical Movement in World Affairs' Weidenfeld and Nicolson 1969.

87 Bishop of Chota Nagpur to Pascoe of S.P.G. 19.3.15. 'Chota Nagpur correspondence 1914-15, S.P.G. archives.

88 I.M.C. Box 4; confidential material supplied by Hirtzel of the Foreign Office after a bomb trial in Zurich in 1919. I.M.C. Box 124.

89 'atrocities' : undated letter Oettli to Oldham in 1914, Oldham to Würz re sending cuttings from 'The Times' to show that the conditions of the troops were worse than those of the missionaries Book 49, Cupboard 11, Basel Mission archives. Box of pamphlets in the Basel Mission archives. Exclusion of the B.M.S. : I.M.C. Box 136.

90 Bishop of Calcutta to Foss Westcott of Chota Nagpur 9.6.15. Confidential report to Bishop Montgomery 3.6.15. The Bishop of Chota Nagpur urged the government to believe that not all Germans hate England, and that they should return: 'Daily Telegraph' 6.1.22; Folder 'Misc.'(1) I.M.C. Box 153, WCC archives, Geneva; Whyte confidential report on the Basel Mission I.M.C. Box 153; Oldham to Secretan of the K.E.M. Ibid.

91 Oldham to Paton 7.3.24. I.M.C. box 153; Resolution of the L.M.S. that the Basel Mission should return 24.9.19. I.M.C. Box 325.

92 '1922 Madras Govt. Notes from an interview with Sir Lionel Davidson. Madras 1922', I.M.C. Box 127.

93 I.M.C. Boxes 152 and 153, folders labelled 'German Missionary Property' and 'Commonwealth Trust'. Paton's correspondence with the Government of India I.M.C. Box 127; Letter to Oldham 9.8.24. on the opposition from traders; Hartenstein to Phillips 23.11.29. Book 45 Basel Mission archives.

94 Interview with Dr Rossel of the Basel Mission; with Paul Jenkins of Basel; Koechlin's letter of 10.11.39. on the situation in Basel. Book 53, Basel Mission archives.

95 Geschichte der Baselen Mission 1920-40. Band V p.46f; cp. Oettli to Oldham 30.7.23. I.M.C. Box 324, WCC archives, Geneva, and I.M.C. Box 153 Folder : 'de Benoit. India 1916-17, 1922-25'.

96 Book 46, Basel Mission archives; cp Oldham to Axenfeld, March 1915; Oldham to Würz 15.1.15; Oldham's speech to the Church of Scotland Assembly 1917, I.M.C. Boxes 4 and 325.

97 Lenwood to Würz, Book 45 Basel Mission archives.

98 Mott to Tatlow 16.4.15. SCM archives; Mott/Oldham correspondence I.M.C. Box 4.

99 Public Records Office : 07239/6759/36 Paton's approach to the Foreign Office, 11.6.40; 08813/679/36 Visit to Portugal; 0689/689/36 Position of the Church in Portugese colonies.

100 'Britain and China' by R.O. Hall S.C.M. Press 1926.

101 Strong to Warnshuis 23.5.30.; Memo to Emerson protesting over the delays 27.12.30. Details of cases in which Paton failed, I.M.C. Box 124.

102 Paton to Moss 15.9.39; Paton to Westman 3.9.39; Paton to Miss Gibson 1.3.36 that 1½ tons of paper had been expended on the issue. I.M.C. Box 125.

103 Copies deposited in SOC; I.M.C. Box 128.

104 Paton to Sloan 4.4.22 I.M.C. Box 127; cf also individual cases I.M.C. Boxes 124 and 125.

105 Paton to Oldham 3.4.24. I.M.C. Box 149.

106 E.H. Box 409 contains documentation relating to several instances, and an illustration of the continuing power of the I.M.C. when a disreputable mission collapsed.

107 Poona Minutes. Resolution on German Missions E.H. Box 385.

108 Reynolds of the Friends' Service Committee to Paton I.M.C. Box 127A; Paton's reply 28.7.30; Dawson of the India Office to Paton 6.9.30. with the facts on Reynolds.

109 Correspondence with the Madura Mission to establish facts : I.M.C. Box 127A Paton's correspondence with J.Z. Hodge: E.H. Box 395; with Leslie Moss of the F.M.C., I.M.C. Box 126; to allay Banninga's fears : E.H. Box 410, letter dated 30.5.32; Protest over Hall's letter from the F.M.C. 26.9.30 I.M.C. Box 127A.

110 Paton to J.Z. Hodge 22.4.31; I.M.C. Box 127A; Paton to Alden Clark 21.4.31. I.M.C. Box 126, 'Christian Century' article I.M.C. Box 127A.

111 I.M.C. Box 153.

112   Sinclair p.160f; Holmes Smith and Templin affair 1940, Buell and Baker 1942 I.M.C. Box 127A.

113   pub. 1937 Edinburgh House Press p.155.

114   Interview Leonard Schiff; N.C.C. action on political issues : E.H. Box 395 and 414.

115   Paton described these reforming movements in 'Social Ideals in India'. The fundamentalist Arya Samaj was founded in 1875 with the watchword: 'Back to the Vedas' by Dayanand Saravati, who wrote 'The light of truth' published in 1946. The Brahmo Samaj, founded in Ram Mohun Roy, was liberal. Both were a reaction to Christianity and imitated western methods of organisation.

116   Paton circular 1.5.24. Montefiore Papers.

117   e.g. Paton to Grace Paton 2.12.38. Montefiore Papers.

118   Paton/Koechlin correspondence E.H. Box 415. The S.C.M. looked after Gandhi and organised meetings for him. Robert Mackie used to convey him round London by taxi to see that he got to Round Table Conference meetings on time.

119   Letter dated 29.4.31. E.H. Box 415.

120   Datta to Paton 4.5.31. E.H. Box 424. 'I would like to be in the position to say to Mr Gandhi that as an Indian I shall stand for the liberty of Christian work being carried out. I do hope that the question of the status of Christian missions is not going to be bracketted with safeguards for European commerce'.

121   'Christianity in the Eastern Conflicts' p.95.

122   E.H. Box 416.

123   Until this meeting, Paton shared H.M.G.'s view that Nehru was a dangerous revolutionary. Circular letter 21.9.35. Nehru was released 4.9.35, E.H. Box 416. Ralla Ram introduced him. Appreciation of Nehru: 'Christianity in the Eastern Conflicts' p.68.

124   I.M.C. Box 82 with notes on it by the IRM Group.

125   Part of a long memo by J.N. Farquhar. E.H. Box 414 c 1920.

126   'Preliminary statement regarding the forthcoming meeting at Williamstown' 17.5.29, I.M.C. Box 30; Jerusalem Series Vol I 'The Christian Message' p.15, p.452.

127   'The problem of religious freedom in the mission field' April 1935.

128   cf 'Adaptation or Revolution' by Karl Hartenstein, WSCF Box 220A, WCC archives, Geneva, or his 'Bericht über die Internationale Studentische Missionskonferenz in Basel' Book 59, Cupboard 11, Basel. Wilfred F Butcher to the Canadian SCM, WSCF Box 220A.; Dr Hans Mayr : 'Einheit und Botschaft, das oekumenisches Princip in der Geschichte des christlichen Studentenweltbundes 1895-1939' Thesis submitted to the University of Tübingen 1975 Copy SOC.

129   'Christianity in the Eastern Conflicts' p.17, p.40.

130   cp. 'Lutheran missions in a time of revolution. The China experience 1944-1951' Jonas Jonson Stud. Miss. Upsalensis. 1972.

131   'Christianity in the Eastern Conflicts' pp.157-161.

132   'God speaks to this generation' ed. Hugh Martin S.C.M. Press 1937 p.64.

133   'The world mission of the Church' pub. for the I.M.C. 1939, p.146; Tambaram Series vol VI 'The Church and the State'.

134   I.M.C. Box 83 c 1919 cf. Bibliography.

135   The Germans attacked the American and British members of Life and Work for identifying the Kingdom of God with the League of Nations. Stockholm Conference Report ed. G.K.A. Bell, O.U.P. 1926.

136   Paton circular 1.5.24. Montefiore Papers.

137 'Nehru : a political biography', Michael Edwardes, Allen Lane, London 1971; and 'British India'; Interview M.M. Thomas.

138 cp p.388 of Nehru's autobiography.

139 Paton circular letter 27.3.36. David Paton's papers.

140 'Jawaharlal Nehru ; an autobiography' Bodley Head, India 1936, p.283; Paton on the I.C.S. : circular 26.2.31. I.M.C. Box 91, re Lord Willingdon 31.3.31, E.H. Box 409.

141 Letter to Forrester-Paton 10.11.32. E.H. Box 415.

142 Paton to Grace Paton 1917-18; national aspirations : 'Christianity in the Eastern Conflicts.' p.153f; Correspondence with J.Z. Hodge E.H. Box 396.

143 Letter in the possession of Bishop Newbigin 28.9.39; Correspondence with Azariah : E.H. Box 410, Folders 2 and 3.

144 'Christ and Human Need' ed. Hugh Martin S.C.M. Press 1921 p.117.

145 'Azariah of Dornakal' by Carol Graham. Religious Book Club 1949.

146 E.H. Box 408 Devolution of Mission Property. Paton papers relating to this problem.

147 Paton/K.T. Paul correspondence E.H. Box 415.

148 Also Dr Shonie Oliver's MS : Montefiore papers. This time Paton told missionaries they should defend themselves in the face of Indian criticism.

149 'Christianity in the Eastern Conflicts' p.176f.

Notes to Chapter VI

1 Iremonger biography of Temple p.386; Robert Mackie's complaints and others. Mott to Oldham 19.11.27. I.M.C. Box 20 on his need to have Mrs Mott with him to provide support.

2 Schlunk 'Das Wunder der Kirche' pub. Ev. Missionsverlag. Stuttgart and Basel 1939.

3 Paton to Mott 13.4.27. I.M.C. Box 21(1); Paton's address : 'Authority of the Faith' Tambaram Series Vol I O.U.P. 1939.

4 'The churches in council : Oxford, Edinburgh, Hangchow' IRM Vol XXVI p.296; 'The Madras meeting and the ecumenical movement' IRM Vol XXVII, p.153.

5 Paton to Mott 19.12.27, I.M.C. Box 21; correspondence I.M.C. Box 49.

6 I.M.C. Box 20 Folder 2; 'By Kenya possessed. The correspondence between Norman Leys and J.H. Oldham 1918-26' ed and with an introduction by John W. Cell. The University of Chicago Press. 1976; Oldham to Paton 25.11.35 summarising how far he has got in arousing American interest, money and study, for Paton to take over. I.M.C. Box 43.

7 I.M.C. Box 19 Committee Meetings : Atlantic City and Rättvik.

8 Oldham's objections: to Warnshuis 15.4.26 I.M.C. Box 19; Meeting of the C.B.M.S. with Mott 18.3.27, I.M.C. Box 20. Gibson correspondence with Germany 16.10.25. Ibid; Oldham/Schlunk correspondence ibid.; Oldham/Warnshuis 27.7.25. I.M.C. Box 22.

9 Oldham to Thompson 10.1.27 I.M.C. Box 20 Folder (4), cp. Hodgkin to Oldham 14.12.26. I.M.C. Box 20 (3) and Oldham to Schlunk on the W.M.S. 10.2.27. ibid.

10 No copy survives. Reference Mott to Paton 27.6.27. I.M.C. Box 21.

11 Mott to Paton justifying his choice 24.6.27. I.M.C. Box 21; Würz's comment 16.10.25. I.M.C. Box 20; Schlunk : 'Von den Höhen des Olberges' Ev. Missionsverlag, Stuttgart 1928.

12 Minutes of the I.M.C. Meeting at Salisbury p.8; Paton's memo. 'On the business before the Ad Interim Committee of the I.M.C.' I.M.C. Box 33; Paton to Hawkins, 27.4.37. I.M.C. Box 37.

13 Japanese enthusiasm : document presented to Mott I.M.C. Box 363. Harikari remark : Paton circular 5.11.35. I.M.C. Box 91.

14 Paton to Mott 19.11.35 and reply 18.12.35. I.M.C. Box 37.

15 Minutes of a meeting held in New York 2.11.37. Azariah invited the I.M.C. to India at that meeting. Ibid.

16 Paton's correspondence 'African delegates', I.M.C. Box 40: M.A. Thesis p.123; Armin Boyens : 'Kirchenkampf und Ökumene' Vol I p.154f.

17 Hall to Paton 7.3.38. and 14.1.38. I.M.C. Box 37.

18 Interview Bishop Hall September 1973.

19 Axeling to Paton 15.9.37. I.M.C. Box 37.

20 I.M.C. Box 20.

21 Hodgkin to Warnshuis 23.1.28. I.M.C. Box 371.

22 'China and Britain' by R.O. Hall. S.C.M. study book 1928.

23 Summary of the Continental delegates' objections 16.3.28. Paper delivered by Knak at the meeting 17.3.28. I.M.C. Box 24.

24 Paton circular 22.10.35. I.M.C. Box 91.

25 Sixth meeting of the N.C.C. of China, sub-committee on studies 17.12.35. I.M.C. Box 44 Folder 'China'; Davis to Mott 8.12.36. I.M.C. Box 42.

26 Hall to Paton 14.1.38. I.M.C. Box 37.

27 I.M.C. Box 44. 'The faith by which the Church lives' by Dr J.H. Bavink, 'The Gospel and the Muslim' by E.G. van Kekem; 'Church and People' by Dr Müller-Krijn; Paton circular I.M.C. Box 91.

28 Paton to Hodge 15.10.36. and 23.10.36. I.M.C. Box 44; cp the proposals made at the Old Jordans meeting of the I.M.C. in 1936, which indicate Paton's understanding of the significance of the life of the Church.

29 'Questions for the I.M.C. at Madras, India. Dec. 13-13. 1938' pub for the I.M.C. London 1938. Correspondence in I.M.C. Boxes 38 and 43.

30 Hartenstein/Miss Gibson correspondence I.M.C. Box 44.

31 Interview Dr Visser't Hooft December 1973.

32 cf. the Oxford conference volumes 'Church, Community and State', George Allen and Unwin, 1937 and the vast number of preparatory documents in the WCC archives, Geneva.

33 Consensus opinion of virtually everyone I interviewed including Bishop Woods, Robert Mackie and Bishop Hall.

34 Kraemer to Visser't Hooft. 5.12.39. Box D994. Box 1 Kraemer WCC Geneva confidential files. 'The Christian Message in a non-Christian world' p.120.

35 M.A. Thesis p.133, p.135, p.136 CR p.373, p.382-4.

36 I.M.C. Box 40 : 'African delegates'; and Scholten's chapter in 'Das Wunder der Kirche' ed. Schlunk.

37 Paton's preface to the Tambaram Series Vol I, and correspondence with Watson of Cairo, October 1938, Box 994(1).

38 Essay in 'The Authority of the Faith' p.148.

39 IRM July 1938 Vol XXVII. Articles by both.

40 'The Authority of the Faith' p.7.

41 Paton to Mott 16.2.28. I.M.C. Box 21.

42 Correspondence in I.M.C. Box 40.

43 Weber p.185, Footnote 2 on 'Daughter of Africa' by Seabody.

44 6.1.37. I.M.C. Box 40(2) Folder 'Colombo conference'. It looked bad that Couve's son-in-law was sent by the Paris Mission, though he was said to be the best man available.

45 Correspondence scattered in I.M.C. Boxes 37,38,40 and 145, WCC archives, Geneva, and E.H. Boxes 1223-1226. Letter by Miss Gibson on the causes of its collapse 12.7.40; and Dexter, the Treasurer 12.12.40, I.M.C. Box 145. The council was almost exclusively a white Dutch Reformed effort, very inefficient and dependent on a grant from Mott, who founded it.

46 Smyth on Garbett; Bishop of Worcester's diary (kindly lent by the owner) Miss Gibson 18.1.39.

47 Miss Gibson to 'Margaret' 18.1.39. Copy in SOC.

48 Kenneth Grubb : 'Crypts of Power', Hodder and Stoughton 1971.

49 Paton had the same row with Mott at the Tambaram conference, I.M.C. Box 38 Tambaram Press arrangements I.M.C. Box 49.

50 Letter dated 5.9.38. E.H. Box 396, third folder.

51 Paton to Warnshuis 29.9.27. I.M.C. Box 95.

52 Correspondence I.M.C. Box 95.

53 Jerusalem Series Vol I 'The Christian Message' p.341.

54 Article in Box 994(1) Kraemer WCC confidential files, Geneva.

55 As per Chapter VII Footnote (161); Dejung p.32; Visser't Hooft : 'Memoirs' p.27 on his doctoral thesis; pub in English 1963 on 'The background of the Social Gospel in America' CR p.380f.

56 'The Christian Message' p.355.

57 Lukas Vischer : 'Documentary History of the Faith and Order Movement', Bethany Press, Missouri, p.29.

58 'The Christian Message' p.478f.

59 See Paul Ramsey : 'Who speaks for the Church?', Abingdon Press, Nashville Tenn. 1967. The currency has been devalued by overuse.

60 'The World Mission of the Church : Tambaram 1938' I.M.C. imprint London 1939 p.12 Statement signed by Mott, Warnshuis and Paton, edited by Paton, written on board ship 26.1.39.

61 'The World Mission of the Church' p.18; 'The authority of the Faith' p.185, p.191f, p.193.

62 Ibid p.212; Kraemer p.328f.

63 Ibid p.203f.

64 'Das Wunder der Kirche' ed. Schlunk Chapter II.

65 Ibid Chapter IV.

66 CR p.144.

67 Jerusalem Series Vol III. The drafts are missing from I.M.C. Box 26.

68 cp the 'Findings' of Tambaram Section XII 'The economic basis of the Church' and Section XIII 'The Church and the changing social and economic order' Tambaram Series Vol IV.

69 Mission of Fellowship : Paton's idea E.H. Box 395; Paton to Mott 16.12.32 that the mission was such a success that one ought to think in terms of sending Chinese to India and Asians to Africa, and so on. I.M.C. Box 96.

70 'Von den Höhen des Ölberges' Chapter 5. Account of the debate by Henry Silcock : Jerusalem Series Vol III.

71 'Das Wunder der Kirche' p.57.

72 Ibid p.54.

73 Conference on Politics, Economics and Citizenship as per Chapter V, footnote (42). Conference Volumes I - XII ed. by Lucy Gardner, Longman, Green and Co. London 1924.

74 Jerusalem Series Volume V 'The Christian Message in relation to the industrial problem'.

75 Jerusalem Series Vol VI p.275f. Rural reconstruction follow-up : E.H. Box 395. Correspondence with Hodge 1929-1933.

76 Schlunk felt this to be a great problem. 'A German view of the Jerusalem meeting. Review of Von den Höhen des Ölberges' by M. Underhill, IRM Vol XVIII 1929.

77 Memo on 'Patrouilles' which impressed Paton I.M.C. Box 42. Minutes of a meeting on Roman Catholic affairs. I.M.C. Box 43. Underhill to Paton 18.12.30. on the system in New Guinea which Missionsdirektor Eppelein of the Neudettelsau Mission wanted investigating. I.M.C. Box 83.

78 'Das Wunder der Kirche' p.136. Carl Ihmels was the son of Bishop Ihmels of Saxony and of the Life and Work movement (b.1890 - d.1970).

79 Dillistone p.154.

80 R.E. Reports, drafts etc. I.M.C. Box 24; correspondence re the book I.M.C. Box 25(4).

81 Oldham's obsession with religious education led to his concern with secularism. Paton's interest was mainly with the context of church/state relations, and whether the Church has a right to insist on R.E.

82 'Days of vision' by Cheng Ching-yi. I.M.C. Box 33. Mott foiled Lyon, an old China hand, who wanted to reduce it by 30%. pub. Jerusalem Series Vol VIII; Ibid p.98 for Datta's speech.

83 Tambaram Series Vol VI pp.17, 23, 28.

84 'Das Wunder der Kirche' p.59.

85 Tambaram Series Vol VII Quoted by Paton in 'The Hour and its need' p.19.

86 cf the 'double issue' of the IRM July 1937; Paton bibliography; post Tambaram articles I.M.C. Box 50.

87 Dillistone p.156. His principal source was E.F.F. Bishop, a missionary in Jerusalem.

88 Rouse and Neill p.337, 447.

89 'The theology of Hogg' by Eric Sharpe, Christian Literature Society, Madras 1971 p.81.

90 I.M. Box 41; 'The World Mission of the Church' p.11; Heinrich Scholten : 'Das innere Leben der Kirche' in 'Das Wunder der Kirche'.

91 'Von den Höhen des Ölberges' p.59.

92 I.M.C. Box 24; Boxes 49 and 51.

Notes to Chapter VII

1 Apart from Oldham's attempt to resign in 1922, letters of resignation exist dated 5.11.26. I.M.C. Box 280.26; 19.12.27, I.M.C. Box 20; 17.2.31. I.M.C. Box 99; German missionary leaders talked him out of resigning at Herrnhut; 20.9.38. I.M.C. Box 48; 'Memorandum on the I.M.C.' re 'a certain paralysis in regard to the I.M.C. and a feeling of hesitation in regard to the task which the future holds in store'. I.M.C. Box 84.

2 Paton to Mott 8.5.28. I.M.C. Box 83A.

3 Paton to Hodge 19.7.32. E.H. archives Box 395.

4 e.g. in prodding the IMC/CBMS to do something about Christian literature.

5 Letter from Miss Morden 6.4.73.

6 as per (3).

7 Bishop Newbigin recalls how he would refuse an invitation from van Dusen only to receive a letter back offering double the fee. Inverted racism : Paton to Dixon 28.1.38. I.M.C. Box 48.

8 Circular letter 5.12.35. Paton also wrote to 'The Times' about 50 Manchurian pastors who had been imprisoned. I.M.C. Box 91; 'Christianity in the Eastern Conflicts' p.46.

9 Kenneth Grubb : 'Crypts of Power' p.140; cp Norman Grubb; 'C.T. Studd Cricketer and pioneer' Lutterworth Press 1933, and 'After C.T. Studd' Lutterworth Press 1939.

10 CR pp.228 -234; Minutes of the Ad Interim Committee of the I.M.C. Salisbury 1933 p.6.

11 Rouse and Neill, p.390-391; Paton circular 16.1.36 on Slotemaker de Bruine and van Randwijk I.M.C. Box 91; Folder 'Netherlands Indies' in I.M.C. Box 44; Letter dated 14.11.30, I.M.C. Research Box 23.

12 Her papers are in the I.M.C. Boxes 43, 50 and 90: Meetings at Kasteel Hemmen : I.M.C. Box 77.

13 Knak : Westman/Paton correspondence I.M.C. Box 90; Koechlin to Warnshuis 9.2.40 and Koechlin to Paton 9.2.40 I.M.C. Box 131; Koechlin to Oldham 15.8.33 that he must write via Switzerland because the Nazis are opening Schlunk's mail I.M.C. Box 165; McCaughey on the D.C.S.V. p.44f; Opinion of Gerold Schwarz on the narrow base of German missions.

14 Iserland's report to Mott : 23.9.30, I.M.C. Box 83.

15 Oldham/Torm/Lundahl correspondence re Rättvik I.M.C. Box 19; Paton to Rees 2.2.32., 26.4.32; Lobenstine to Paton 1.4.32. I.M.C. Box 371; Jonas Jonson 'Lutheran Missions in a time of revolution'; Activities of Augustana Synod missionaries I.M.C. Boxes 138 and 139.

16 Correspondence in I.M.C. Boxes 87, 91-96.

17 In I.M.C. Box 280.26 and I.M.C. Box 83B; Discussion editorial notes Oldham/Underhill/- Paton 19.4.27 I.M.C. Box 82.

18 First meeting 6.12.19 I.M.C. Box 82; CR 268f, p.272.

19 Meeting on the theme 'The Christian explains himself' 6.12.19. I.M.C. Box 83 Discussion October 1920 and 3.12.20. I.M.C. Box 82; IRM Vol IX p.281-88; Bevan's article : IRM Vol X p.207f; Lenwood's article IRM Vol X p.351f.

20 Paton to Oldham 3.3.30. I.M.C. Box 83.

21 Underhill to Paton 24.10.33 I.M.C. Box 83A.

22 Paton to Mott 15.10.31 on having to sacrifice the IRM's unique bibliography Paton to Mott 6.11.31 on reducing the length, I.M.C. Box 280.26; Restoration Paton letter 10.11.32. I.M.C. Box 82.

23 Correspondence with P.O. Philip E.H. Box 394; Minutes of a meeting on Roman Catholic affairs at Tambaram I.M.C. Box 43; cp correspondence with Gooch of the World Evangelization Alliance I.M.C. Box 117.

24 Underhill to Paton 15.1.31. I.M.C. Box 82.

25 Paton to Underhill criticising an article on R.C. Missionary methods I.M.C. Box 83A.

26 Minutes of a meeting of Findlater Stewart, Lord Hailey and Maclennan with representatives of the missions 14.9.39. P.R.O. Inf. I/401.

27 Latourette was very critical, but Paton retorted that he could not make American writers produce articles. Paton to Latourette 6.7.34; 9.11.36 Latourette to Paton 25.11.39. I.M.C. Box 280.26.

28 Analysis of the IRM, I.M.C. box 48; It was said of Kraemer at the meeting 20.12.27 that he had not produced an article promised two years previously I.M.C. Box 82.

29 Gibson correspondence I.M.C. Box 331.

30 Paton to Latourette. 30.3.43. I.M.C. Box 280.26.

31 Minutes of the I.R.M. Group 18.12.29; 17.11.30; 29.11.31; 28.11.33; 10.12.34 I.M.C. Box 82.

32 Torm : 'The place of social questions in a missionary's work' IRM Oct. 1930 p.593; Anet : 'Protestant Missions in Belgian Congo' IRM July 1939, p.415.

33 Underhill to Paton 21.12.39; Paton to Underhill 24.12.39 I.M.C. Box 83A Underhill was furious because Mott failed to thank the donor properly.

34 Interviews with Margaret Sinclair, Professor Paton and Sigrid Morden.

35 Interviews David Paton, Elizabeth Montefiore, Dora Pym.

36 Warnshuis to Paton 3.10.28. with a letter from Mott attached, Paton to Warnshuis 26.10.28. and 31.10.28 I.M.C. Box 87.

37 I.M.C. Box 89. Folder 'Correspondence with Continental bodies' 1920-28 CR p.188, p.183.

38 Budget for 1929; Extract from C.B.M.S. Minutes 15.6.28; British shortfall: Maclennan to Speers 23.3.31. I.M.C. Box 87.

39 Quarterly accounts : I.M.C. Box 86; German contributions : I.M.C. Box 89; Emergency arrangements : I.M.C. Box 327; General decline : Warnshuis to Paton 3.2.38. I.M.C. Box 88.

40 Letters 28.7.38; 12.7.38; 'Comments to accompany fund-raising for Tambaram' I.M.C. Box 42.

41 Warnshuis to Paton 23.10.28.; Paton to Warnshuis 26.10.28. I.M.C. Box 87; Oldham to Warnshuis 20.11.28 on Africa I.M.C. Box 94.

42 Mott raised money for South Africa; E.H. Boxes 1223-6; I.M.C. Boxes 38-41 re Tambaram; N.E.C.C.; Mott circular 9.7.31; Wilder to Flint 4.11.31; Paton to Mrs Flint 29.4.29. I.M.C. Box 86.

43 Mackie, McCaughey, e.g. 'The Christian Century's ill-informed onslaughts'.

44 Paton to Warnshuis 26.10.28. I.M.C. Box 87.

45 D.W.M.E./I.M.C. Box 38(2) Paton to Warnshuis 28.11.28 etc.

46 Correspondence : I.M.C. Box 87. Folder 'Third Secretary Fund'.

47 Ibid Warnshuis to Paton 27.11.28. and reply 31.10.28.

48 Ibid Oldham to Paton 27.11.28; to Paton 31.12.28 I.M.C. Box 94.

49 Paton to Warnshuis 23.4.37 I.M.C. Box 88.

50 Ibid Warnshuis circular 2.3.38; Warnshuis to Paton 14.6.38.

51 I.M.C. Box 32 'Finance'.

52 as per (42); M.A. Thesis Chapter IX.

53 McCaughey p.50; p.143; Tatlow p.667.

54 Mysore Minutes and memo of Dr H.C. Rutgers on Finance 12.10.28 W.S.C.F. Box 122, Geneva; Visser't Hooft Memoirs p.43-44; W.S.C.F. Report : 'Students find the truth to serve' 1931-35.

55 Richey Hogg p.421 reproduces the Mott/Oldham exchange on this.

56 Interview Eric Fenn. Visser't Hooft could not understand why he had taken a 'secular' job. Paton Papers II 1939 correspondence.

57 Minutes of the I.M.C. meeting at Herrnhut 1932 p.53.

58 I.M.C. Box 42 Folder 'Finance'; Interview with Bishop Woods who remembers the scene in Woodbrooke when Paton explained his plans for Tambaram and Cadbury wrote a cheque for £2,000, with tears streaming down his face and Paton glowing with gratitude.

59 I.M.C. Box 88. Paton/Warnshuis correspondence October 1939.

60 Rouse and Neill p.555.

61 Jerusalem Series Vol V 'Christianity and the growth of industrialism in Africa, Asia and South America'.

62 K.L. Butterfield; 'The Christian Mission in rural India', New York, 1930; Schweinitz de Brunner : 'The rural mission of the church in eastern Asia', Jerusalem Series Vol VI; Latourette's reports : E.H. Box 395.

63 Minutes of the Executive Committee meeting of the Netherlands Missionary Council 14.11.30. I.M.C. Research Box 23.

64 I.M.C. Research Box 23. Two copies dated 5.7.28. and 18.9.28. Mott's replies have not survived in Geneva.

65 The I.L.O. was set up in 1920 as an independent agency of the League of Nations.

66 Ibid letter dated 12.6.28. but probably written 12.7.28; Comment in a wodge of undated material : 'Mr Grimshaw was willing to give us a great deal of help and his sudden death has gravely affected our plans'.

67 Ibid and D.W.M.E./I.M.C. Box 44(4) 8.5.28. Paton to Mott on possible sources of grants and personnel. The woman would have received the same salary as Grimshaw, but for full-time, not part-time work.

68 I.M.C. Research Box 23. Mott/Paton correspondence re Davis. The salary was higher than Paton's, and so high that there was little left for Iserland and a secretary. D.W.M.E./I.M.C. Box 38(1) Minutes of the Standing Committee, p.4 29.5.30.

69 Paton to Mott 9.9.30. Paton persistently championed Iserland's case as a man with a young family. I.M.C. Research Box 23.

70 Interview with Dr Ehrenström.

71 'World Religious Peace' was a group similar to the Theosophists.

72 Memo. circulated 6.6.29. Minutes of the Williamstown Meeting I.M.C. Box 30.

73 Paton's documentation : I.M.C. Box 114.

74 Interview V.A. Demant December 1971; 'Christian sociology' in Paton's view seems to have been the discipline of radical criticism of existing social structures by the application of Christian principles.

75 I.M.C. Research Box 24; 'John Merle Davis. An autobiography' Kyo Bun Kwan Press.

76 United Mission to the Copperbelt : Records in the C.B.M.S. archives, Edinburgh House.

77 I.M.C. Research Box 24.

78 I.M.C. Research Box 23 'Records of an informal meeting held at Edinburgh House 19.4.32. Present Mott, Merle Davis, Iserland, Maclennan, Oldham, Paton and Miss Standley.; 'Minutes of the I.M.C. Meeting at Herrnhut. Appendices A - B; Paton to Hodge 19.7.32. E.H. Box 395.

79 'Records of an informal meeting' p.5 as per (78).

80 I.M.C. Research Box 23 Paton to Mott 2.10.31.; Audited Accounts Ibid; Correspondence with Schram D.W.M.E./I.M.C. Box 44(4).

81 Ibid Paton to Warnshuis 3.2.33.

82 Paton to Mott 2.10.31. I.M.C. Research Box 23.

83 Warnshuis to Paton 18.5.28. and 30.5.28. I.M.C. Box 95.

84 CR p.187, p.274.

85 cf Kirk to Paton 4.2.29. I.M.C. Research Box 23 Folder 'Life and Work'.

86   Alphons Keller was Director of the European Bureau of Inter-Church Aid from 1922. A Swiss, he was a good lecturer and writer but Paton criticised his administrative abilities. Keller : 'Vom Geist und Liebe' Leopold Klotz Verlag. Gotha 1934; CR p.462f.

87   Paton to the Bishop of Salisbury 11.6.29. I.M.C. Research Box 23; cp Bell to Oldham 20.8.30. and Paton to Bell 18.9.30. on co-operation.

88   Paton to Mott 28.6.28. D.W.M.E./I.M.C. Box 35(1).

89   Bell to Oldham 20.8.30. I.M.C. Research Box 23.

90   Oldham to Hickman-Johnson 19.2.31. I.M.C. Research Box 23.

91   'Scandinavian' denotes the member countries of the Northern Missionary Council, Norway, Sweden, Denmark and Finland, who sent a statement of protest to the Herrnhut meeting of the I.M.C.

92   Iserland to Oldham 25.9.32. I.M.C. Research Box 23.

93   Lundahl sent these resolutions to the I.M.C. 22.10.30. D.W.M.E./I.M.C. Box 44. cf his letter 16.12.29. in I.M.C. Box 32.

94   'Christianity in the Eastern Conflicts' p.53; Paton to Rees 2.2.32. I.M.C. Box 371.

95   'The place of social questions in missionary work' F. Torm I.R.M. October 1930 p.593 Tawney at Jerusalem : Jerusalem Series Vol V.

96   Siegfried Knak : 'The discussion on the Department of Industrial and Social Research'. I.M.C. Box 32.

Notes to Chapter VIII

1 Paton to Dibdin 25.9.39, I.M.C. Box 134. cp 'The Hour and its need' p.21.

2 Minutes of the British sub-committee on German missions. Monthly meetings November 1934-1936. I.M.C. Box 327.

3 This was discussed at the German missionary societies' conferences at Barmen in 1933 and 1934 when they were under pressure from so-called 'German Christians'. cf Miss Gibson's account of an interview with Knak, 24.10.33; Koechlin's account of the 1934 conference in the University of Basel archives; Hartenstein to Oldham 6.10.34. Basel Mission archives Book 49; Paton to the German societies : Keithahn correspondence I.M.C. Box 126, Geneva; Koechlin to Oldham 15.8.33. I.M.C. Box 165, asking Oldham to send a warning to Schlunk re neutrality for the benefit of the police intercepting the mail.

4 Memorandum on aid to the German societies February 1935, I.M.C. Box 327.

5 The Anglicans at Ranchi took over some of the Gossner Mission's work, but the mission's difficulties were not so much financial as the result of a feud dating back to 1914 between all the missionaries except Stosch and the Church Council. Memo McLeish to Gibson I.M.C. Box 134.

6 Paton to Temple 20.9.39. I.M.C. Box 51; Paton to Koechlin 11.9.39. I.M.C. Box 131; Ibid Koechlin to Paton 16.12.39.; Ibid Warnshuis to Paton 1.9.39. on the Kasteel Hemmen plans.

7 Paton to the MOI and the Colonial Office re Danish missionaries 16.4.40. I.M.C. Box 132; Maclennan to Dibdin 17.4.40 P.R.O. Inf. I/410; Re the Finns, Paton to Westman 8.12.42. I.M.C. Box 90.

8 Warnshuis' tables : I.M.C. Box 145; Correspondence N.Z. Hodge/Warnshuis I.M.C. Box 147.

9 Gibson/Paton correspondence I.M.C. Box 145; Paton to Warnshuis re the Wallace case 3.11.39. : 'Your handling of this matter has not been such as to increase my sense of unity in the I.M.C.' I.M.C. Box 131.

10 Ibid. July 1940. The B.M.S. asked the Southern Baptists for a financial guarantee for Serampore in case it became impossible to remit money from London. To their embarrassment the money arrived immediately. Norman Goodall : 'Christian Ambassador : A Life of A.L. Warnshuis'; Channel Press New York 1963. This book is of limited use because sources are not cited and there are no footnotes.

11 I.M.C. Box 131 Paton/Koechlin correspondence October - February 1939-40. Since the German government had made it as difficult as possible for German missions to continue 1934-36, Paton found this solicitude very exasperating. Koechlin to Warnshuis 9.2.40. Basel Mission archives Book 53 'I do not doubt a moment that Knak and others have mentioned to the Government the high political interest existing for the German Reich to maintain Germans on the mission fields, to avoid a financial appeal for German missionaries which would be humiliating for the German Reich'. As a 'neutral' society the Basel Mission could not accept this money.

12 Paton to Maclennan asserting that it was organised out of loyalty to the British Government 7.2.40. I.M.C. Box 131.

13 Koechlin to Warnshuis 18.4.40 Book 53 Basel Mission archives.

14 Paton to Westman 8.12.42 I.M.C. Box 90.

15 Box 266.200 'Orphaned Missions' Confidential files, WCC archive, Geneva.

16 Total American gift sent to the British Churches by September 1941 : $1.5million; Canada : £6,000; Indian churches : Rs300,000; China : £1,000; Congo : £700; Syria : £550, and Cameroun : £125.

17 e.g. Bishop Leonard Wilson; Interview Herr Göttin.

18 Paton to Westman 21.1.41. I.M.C. Box 90.

19 I.M.C. Box 131, dated 19.9.40. cp also Knak to Kraemer 8.2.40.; Freudenberg to Visser't Hooft (Freudenberg files, Geneva).

20 Book 53, Basel Mission archives; Hartenstein to Paton 26.10.39. that the first edition of 'Das Wunder der Kirche' was sold out.: 'We are and remain one in Christ and saw a manifestation of real unity of the Church at Tambaram which will give us strength to get through this dark patch' I.M.C. Box 131.

21 Book 53 Basel Mission archives Paton to Hartenstein 25.9.39.

22 'Notes on the post-war missionary situation' by A.S. Kydd August 1942 I.M.C. Box 192; Memorandum compiled by the society secretaries in the C.B.M.S. April 1942 and 'Extract from the minutes of the executive committee of the Bengal Christian Council 28.8.41'; 'Confidential statement on the stage reached by the N.C.C. of India in discussions' I.M.C. Box 113.

23 P.R.O. C14658/14658/62 Documents concerning the arrangements made for liaison between government offices when confronted by a united front of Paton and the C.B.M.S.

24 P.R.O. C8813/6759/36 24.8.40.; Bishop Williams recalls the difficulty he had in getting a visa for John Baillie to visit the USA. So he told the Foreign Office that he was the greatest living British philosopher.

25 Warnshuis to Paton 1.9.39 I.M.C. Box 131.

26 P.R.O. C14658/14658/62 Foreign Office Minute (Mr Baggallay).

27 Foreign Office opinion that missionaries would not prove to be useful agents : 19.9.39.; Lord Hailey's memo. 13.9.39 P.R.O. Inf. I/401 Lambeth Palace meeting Inf. I/403.

28 Minutes of the Missionary War Emergency Committee P.R.O. Inf. I/412.

29 Minutes of the meeting of 14.9.39 P.R.O. Inf. I/401.

30 Halifax's letter : 17.8.40. I.M.C. Box 131. Paton also wooed Malcolm MacDonald for support.

31 Publications had to be drastically reduced. The Christian Newsletter bought in stocks of paper which it was unable to use owing to the regulations.

32 Paton/Hodge correspondence I.M.C. Box 139.

33 Interview Bishop Williams, By June 1941, 106 passages had been obtained but a further 300 were waiting to sail. Report to the War Emergency Committee P.R.O. Inf. I/412.

34 Note of an interview at the Colonial Office with Robinson and Major Vischer 12.10.39. P.R.O. Inf I/408; Paton/Maclennan correspondence I.M.C. Box 131; Reaction in the India Office 1.10.39. P.R.O. Inf I/410.

35 Dibdin to Frampton 2.1.40. P.R.O. Inf I/410.

36 Halifax to the Foreign Office 26.9.39 P.R.O. C14658/14658/62.

37 Memo by Miss Gibson 1.10.39. I.M.C. Box 136.

38 Interview Herr Raaflaub.

39 Documents : I.M.C. Box 131; Liaison with the India Office P.R.O. Inf. I/40.

40 Interview given by Sandegren to Kristelist Dagblad. Copenhagen 19.11.39 I.M.C. Box 134. Paton's counter-offensive when the MOI showed him the article 6.12.39. I.M.C. Box 147.

41 I.M.C. Box 131; cp Das Schwarze Korps 23.11.39 Book 53 Basel Mission archives and the identical problem with the Christian Century's deliberate misrepresentations.

42 I.M.C. Box 324 The Press was at Bangalore. The material concerned is in Box 328. When war broke out, Matthews of the M.M.S. took over.

43 Paton to Koechlin 8.12.39. Book 53 Basel Mission archives; Paton to Warnshuis : 16.1.40. I.M.C. Box 147.

44 Knak also got 9 Canadians released. I.M.C. Box 137; Return of the Americans in July 1941 I.M.C. Box 139; Letter of 4.4.41. in I.M.C. Box 147.

45 Paton to Warnshuis 16.1.40. I.M.C. Box 147.

46 e.g. Wiegrabe, unjustly suspected of being a Nazi spy, and Hagele of the Bremen mission, who were impoverished. I.M.C. Box 137. Since two Moravians were Nazis, all were interned in Tanganyika. Paton fought against this. I.M.C. Box 138.

47 Letters to Westman 21.7.42; 8.12.42. I.M.C. Box 90.

48 Paton to Gibson 19.8.41 and to L.S. Amery 4.9.41.

49 Needham to Warnshuis/Paton 5.11.40. I.M.C. Box 147.

50 Paton to Rev. Jesse Arrup 9.12.40. I.M.C. Box 133.

51 Material in I.M.C. Boxes 138, 139, 145.

52 I.M.C. Box 139 Folder 'I.M.C. efforts for outside help' Letters to Kellerhals of the Basel Mission 1941-42.

53 I.M.C. Box 138.

54 Bishop Asgaard was an American Norwegian Lutheran. Correspondence in I.M.C. Box 132.

55 Bishop Neill to Paton 11.9.39 and 19.9.39 I.M.C. Box 134 : 'They are mostly refugees — that is to say, they loathe Hitlerism, while remaining utterly German'.

56 Basel Mission archives Room 120 Book labelled Ind. Korr. Koechlin-Streckeisen.

Notes to Chapter IX

1 Walter Rauschenbusch : 'The Theology of the Social Gospel' p.23 etc.

2 'The White Man's Burden' pub. for the Social Service Lecture Trust by the Epworth Press 1939 (Beckly Lecture).

3 'The Secular City' by Harvey Cox Pelican Books 1968.

4 CR p.154f, p.166f, p.243, p.245.

5 Paton circular to S.V.s 12.6.18. SCM archives, cp 'Social Ideals in India' p.97f.

6 Beckly Lecture p.17-19; 'Social Ideals in India' p.100-101 etc.

7 This is David Paton's considered opinion.

8 Minutes of the W.S.C.F. meeting at Lake Mohonk pub. for the W.S.C.F. New York 1913. cp Minutes of the W.S.C.F. meeting at Oxford 1909 which received the full impact of the Matlock conference. The Decennial Report reveals that social questions had been discussed since 1904.

9 Many universities and colleges had these centres in slum areas which were manned by enthusiastic students in the vacations, and combined some of the functions of present day playgroups, citizens advice bureaux, youth clubs and so on, as well as being centres for the distribution of food and clothing.

10 Beckly Lecture p.13, CR p.44-5.

11 'Social Ideals in India' p.44-52.

12 Beckly Lecture p.13, CR p.51, p.53.

13 Beckly Lecture p.33.

14 'Social Ideals in India' p.98f.

15 Ibid p.15-16 cp his broadcast July 1942 on 'What is man?' Copy SOC archives.

16 'Social Ideals in Idea' p.99f.

17 For example : General Booth encountered great hostility from Free Church leaders 1865-1905.

18 Beckly Lecture p.19, p.30-32.

19 'Social Ideals in India' p.83.

20 'The Stockholm Conference on Life and Work' edited by G.K.A. Bell O.U.P. London 1926.

21 'Social Ideals in India' p.72-74.

22 'The Church and its function in society' p.147f; 'Church Community and State' Series (CCS) Allen & Unwin 1937.

23 'The Highway of God' p.79.

24 IRM Vol IX April 1920 p.281-88.

25 Temple was won for the SCM at the 1907 Conishead Camp, being most impressed by Canon Scott Holland on the power of Christ to regenerate society. He was at the Matlock conference in 1909. Iremonger p.125, p.328f, p.381, p.581, p.188.

26 SCM Press 1916. Deals with the question of the deprivation of normal children and the local government statutory obligations.

27 CR p.61, p.81; p.250.

28 Niebuhr wrote in his letter of condolence to Grace Paton : 'I had, beside a common faith, also many common social and political convictions with your husband, and therefore feel his loss particularly keenly.' 29.8.43. Montefiore Papers.

29 Beckly Lecture p.15-17.

30 'The World Mission of the Church' pub for the I.M.C. 1939, p.180-1.

31 'Social Ideals in India' p.1, p.67.

32 'The Highway of God' p.24.

33 D.S. Cairns : 'From Edinburgh to Jerusalem' IRM Vol XVIII 1929.

34   CR p.143f; p.161-2; p.175.

35   'Secular civilization and the Christian task' in 'The Christian Message' Jerusalem Series Vol I p.284.

36   'What is secularism?' IRM Vol XVII 1929 - p.346.

37   Paton to Warnshuis 29.9.27. I.M.C. Box 95 WCC archives.

38   Paton to Mott 9.5.27. which ought to be in Box 95, quoted by David Gill IRM Vol LXVII 1968, p.347. Minutes of a meeting on 6.5.27. at Bible House London. A scientist was sought. Hocking, Raven, Tawney and Burgh were suggested. I.M.C. Box 20; cp 'Social Ideals in India' p.36-7.

39   The servants of India Society were a society of reforming Hindus who campaigned for social progress and lived a life of personal austerity. They might be considered Hindu Quakers.

40   'What is secularism?' IRM Vol XVIII p.351.

41   'A Faith for the World' p.50.

42   'The Christian Message' p.27; Paton on Kraemer's understanding of secularism ; 'A Faith for the World' p.241.

43   'The Christian Message in a non-Christian World' p.129.

44   as per (40).

45   Ibid p.354.

46   In 'World Community' (1938), Paton links this kind of secularism, especially the exclusion of religion from politics, with the decay of western civilization. p.20-22.

47   'The Christian Message' p.356.

48   Ibid p.369, 363, 373.

49   Ibid p.377.

50   Oldham to Mott 14.11.34. Quoted by Richey Hogg p.422; Interview p.284.

51   Written May 1919. I.M.C. Box 9 Copy SOC.

52   Paton to Grace Paton 15.5.18 on an all-European conference on education Paton to Grace Paton 31.3.22 Montefiore Papers.

53   M.M. Thomas/Dr Rossel interviews. Hartenstein and Koechlin correspondence with Streckeisen in the Basel Mission archives.

54   'Social Ideals in India' p.38, p.84-89.

55   'The Highway of God' p.20.

56   Ibid. p.114f, p.142f.

57   'A Faith for the World' p.215.

58   Ibid p.229.

59   Draft of a pamphlet proposed as a sequel to 'The Church and World Order' B.C.C. archives SOC.

60   Beckly Lecture p.30-32.

Notes to Chapter X

1   Oldham to Visser't Hooft, July 1937, that Cavert is urging a strong effort to get Paton as executive officer. Oldham Papers, WCC General Correspondence Temple to Mott 19.9.38 I.M.C. Box 48.

2   The WCC existed unofficially from August 1938 when the Utrecht proposals were accepted by the executive committees of Life and Work and Faith and Order. The constitution had to be submitted to a World Assembly to become 'official'.

3   'The Ten Formative Years. The World Council of Churches in process of formation. Report to the Amsterdam Assembly' ed. by W.A. Visser't Hooft. WCC Geneva 1948; War-time reports in the possession of Miss Guittard. Listed in 'No man is alien' ed. Robert Nelson, Brill, Leiden 1971 as nos 341, 363, 376, 395, 413, 432.

4   Dr Visser't Hooft says that before the war he had only to go to London, to consult the combined wisdom of Temple, Bell, Paton and Oldham to get any problem solved.

5   WCCF Box XI (WCC archives) 262.54 Karlström/Oldham correspondence 1952 in which Oldham claims that the I.M.C. antedates Life and Work by eight years. Complete set of World Alliance Minutes 1912-48 SOC.

6   Interview Robert Mackie. Letter to the author from Charles Ranson.

7   Interview Bishop Hollis. Paton's correspondence with N.C.C. of India secretaries e.g. Paton to P.O. Philip July 1932 E.H. Box 394; Folder 'Meetings in America' I.M.C. Box 102 Meeting 17.12.41.

8   Hodgkin to Warnshuis 23.1.28. I.M.C. Box 371.

9   Minutes of the sixth session of the I.M.C. Committee 2.4.28 and the seventh meeting 4.4.28. 'Report of the Committee of Council on the future organisation of the I.M.C.' I.M.C. Box 24.

10 'The future of I.M.C. co-operation' by Oldham, I.M.C. Boxes 20 and 21; Paton to Bell 18.3.30. I.M.C. Research Box 23; 'Memorandum on the I.M.C. : Notes of a statement made at the meeting held at Chipstead 13.9.22.' by Oldham is crucial. I.M.C. Box 84.

11 Timothy Lew's speech at Edinburgh 1910 : Vol VIII, Edinburgh conference series; Azariah's speech : 'The Second World conference on Faith and Order held at Edinburgh 1937' p.42, p.268; 'Asia and the ecumenical movement' by Hans-Ruedi Weber S.C.M. Press 1966.

12 CR p.188f; Henriod to Bell 4.10.34. WCC General Correspondence Box 8.

13 WCCF Box XI (262.54) Folder 1917-19; Rouse and Neill p.533.

14 Oldham had studied theology, and was licenced once, but was never called to a church. Henriod to Oldham 7.10.36 on the difficulty of implementing this policy. WCCF Box XI (262.54).

15 M.A. Thesis Chapter VI; Armin Boyens : 'Kirchenkampf und Ökumene' (Vol I) In the third part of his work he gets half-way towards this thesis. Temple/Hodgson correspondence re the implications for Faith and Order 1935-1939. WCC General Correspondence. Hodgson's memo. to the executive Council of Faith and Order 27.6.39 WCCF Box I.

16 Rouse and Neill p.557. Bell's commission produced 'Mysterium Christi : Christological studies by British and German theologians', London 1930; A joint project Paton was involved in was a study of the concept of revelation filed under Life and Work, Geneva; Temple to Hodgson 6.8.34; Oldham to Temple 25.8.34. Temple Correspondence, Geneva.

17 cp Chapter XIV with Faith and Order pamphlet No 73 (First Series).

18 Rouse and Neill p.556.

19 WCC General Correspondence 'Henriod'; Ibid 'Henry Smith Leiper' papers 1932-35 re October 1932 crisis and October 1935 when Henriod had Sw Fr 15 in cash.

20 A continuing saga in the Paton/Visset't Hooft correspondence, Paton Papers II, WCC, Geneva.

21 Bishop L.S. Greene. Utrecht Minutes p.16 WCCF Box II, Geneva.

22 5.10.36 WCC General Correspondence Box 50.

23 Hodgson to Temple 1.8.35. 'Hodgson' WCC General Correspondence. By resolution of the Faith and Order Continuation Committee at Majola in 1929, all overtures were rejected in principle.

24 Rouse and Neill p.704. Explanatory Memorandum quoted. This idea was enshrined in the Toronto Declaration 1952 : 'The Churches, The Church and the World Council of Churches'.

25 Utrecht Minutes p.18; CR p.166f, p.199f.

26 Utrecht Minutes Appendix D.

27 'Memorandum presented to the officers of Life and Work and the World Alliance for their discussion in February 1937' Henriod papers, WCC General Correspondence cp Bell to Henriod 1933 General Correspondence Box 8; Oldham to Henriod 30.8.36. that the Alliance is taking itself too seriously, and that he won't be dictated to by a small clique. WCCF Box XI(262.54).

28 Rouse and Neill p.566.

29 'Stellungnahme zu den Ergebnissen von Oxford' by Kraemer Box 994(1), Geneva.

30 Church leaders were slow to realise what was at stake. Bell to Leiper 14.12.34. on the resolution of the Upper House of the Church Assembly drawing attention to the warning in the Barmen Declaration. 'Henry Smith Leiper' WCC General Correspondence.; Ibid Bell to Leiper 9.12.35 that he did not think that Hitler was trying to destroy the Church. Oldham was aware of this danger at this time. Bethge p.288, 298, 306 etc.

31 'The Long Road to Unity' by Marc Boegner pub. Collins 1970; Visser't Hooft's 'Memoirs' SCM Press 1973; G.K.A. Bell: 'Christianity and World Order' Penguins Harmondsworth 1940.

32 'Après la journée' by Wilfred Monod. Paris 1938; Élie Gounelle papers in Geneva; Rouse and Neill p.576; Siegmund-Schultze whom Paton rebuffed. Paton to Visser't Hooft 9.2.40. Paton Papers II; cf. forthcoming biography of Siegmund-Schultze by J.S. Conway.

33 Paton Papers I, WCC, Geneva. Folder 'Correspondence with Schönfeld' Paton to Schönfeld 31.5.32.

34 Ibid Paton to Schönfeld 20.7.32.; Atkinson to Bell, September 1932, Bell correspondence, Geneva.

35 Ibid. Paton to Henriod 15.2.33.

36 Ibid Henriod to Paton 18.2.33.; Paton to Henriod 21.2.33; The 'we' in Paton's letter of 15.2.33. might refer only to I.M.C. leaders.

37 William Adams Brown : 'Towards a United Church' pub. Charles Scribner and Sons, New York 1946 p.34-37. Rouse and Neill p.699.

38 M.A. Thesis Chapter V; Bethge p.301f; Paton Papers I Paton to Henriod 25.6.34.

39 Minutes of the I.M.C. Meeting at Herrnhut 1932 p.29; Minutes of the I.M.C. Meeting at Salisbury 1933 p.6 cp Paton to Baroness Boetzelaer 12.9.34 I.M.C. Box 90; Paton/Oldham memo. 'The Relation between the I.M.C. and other ecumenical movements' I.M.C. Box 33.

40 Rouse and Neill p.699.

41 Hodgson to Temple 14.4.34. filed 'Temple' WCC General Correspondence Two letters to Bell 17.4.34; 18.4.34. WCC General Correspondence Box 8.

42 Correspondence with Henriod, Paton Papers I and VIII (previously Box D219 Box 2).

43 They were M.E. Aubrey, C.M. van Asch van Wijk, Bishop James Baker, Albert Beaven, Y. Brilioth, M. Boegner, W. Adams Brown, Walter T. Brown, S. McCrea Cavert, G.K.A. Bell, Hutchinson Coburn, Archbishop Germanos, F.F. Goodsell, L.Hodgson, Eleanora Iredale, Koechlin, Henriod, Lilje, W.F. Lofthouse, Lewis Mudge, Walter Moberly, Mott, Oldham, G. Ashton Oldham, E.L. Parsons, Paton, Schönfeld, Tatlow, von Thadden, Visser't Hooft, Temple, S. Zankow, F. Zilka, Dr. Zoellner. Paton to Henriod 14.6.36. re his standing, Paton Papers I.

44 Aide Memoire of the meeting of the ecumenical consultative group. London October 20-21 1936. WCCF Box I.

45 Paton Papers I Correspondence 1936-37.

46 'The churches survey their task' CCS Vol VIII p.276; 'Edinburgh 1937' ed Hodgson p.270-4.

47 Visser't Hooft 'Memoirs' p.82.

48 Visser't Hooft was unofficially selected at the Oxford conference. Oldham went to great lengths to conceal this. It was decided that Henriod would not adapt to the new situation. Oldham correspondence, WCC General Correspondence.

49 Iremonger p.403.

50 Visser't Hooft to Floyd Tomkins 1.3.39. WCC General correspondence 'Floyd Tomkins'; M.A. Thesis Chapter IV p.70.; 'Die Trinitarische Basis des O.R.K.' by P. Wolfdieter Theurer, Bergen-Enkheim 1967; 'Das "Was" und "Wie", Inhalt und Austrichtung der ein Botschaft' in Hollenweger : Theologie der Tagesordnung der Welt Sequenzen und Konsequenzen, Zurich 1972/73.

51 Leiper to Paton 13.9.38. on the difficulty caused because the Presbyterians would not appoint van Dusen as their representative, although he had been co-opted chairman of the Administrative Committee. WCC General Correspondence 'Leiper'.

52 See Table in M.A. Thesis. 'The sociology of the Uppsala World Assembly' by R. Dickinson, Ecumenical Review July 1969.

53 Utrecht Constitution : Report on the First World Assembly at Amsterdam Vol V ed. Visser't Hooft SCM Press 1949; one painful discovery in 1965 was that there was no procedure laid down for the appointment of a General Secretary.

54 Iremonger p.411, Visser't Hooft Memoirs p.82.

55 Tambaram Series Vol VII p.121f.

Notes to Chapter XI

1   Recalled by Robert Mackie; McCaughey p.44f, p.47-9, 73-76 on Lilje's contibution to the British S.C.M.

2   'The Nazi persecution of the churches' by J.S. Conway, Weidenfeld and Nicolson, London 1968; For Daphne Hampson's thesis, application must be made to the author c/o The University of St Andrews, Armin Boyens: Kirchenkampf und Ökumene : Band I 1933-39; Band II 1939-45', Chr. Kaiser Verlag, Munich pub 1971 and 1973 respectively.

3   e.g. Martin Neimöller Archiv in Bielefeld.

4   I am indebted to Dr Nicolaisen of the Kirchliche Zeitgeschichte Institüt in Munich for ideas, encouragement and criticism.

5   'The German Resistance to Hitler' by Gramml, Mommsen, Reichhardt and Ernst Wolf, pub. B.T. Batsford Ltd London 1970, and under the title 'Der deutsche Widerstand gegen Hitler: vier kritische Studien' ed. Walter Ivanmittlernner and Hans Buchheim by Kiepenheuer and Witchi, Köln/Berlin.

6   Paton to Toynbee 10.11.39. WCCF Box IX Ibid to Bell 16.10.39. Visser't Hooft agreed with Paton's view of Schönfeld, who was torn between his employer, Bischof Heckel's, demands and his sympathy for the Resistance. As a result his health and sanity were ruined.

7   I.M.C. Box 127/127A. Reacting to Hall's command that all missionaries should carry arms, Paton told a worried American missionary that he would rather be murdered by Indian insurgents than be identified with the occupying forces in a manner contrary to the Gospel.

8   'The Church calling' Six broadcasts by Paton E.H.P. 1942.

9   'The Message of the world-wide Church' Sheldon Press, London 1939; 'A letter to Great Britain from Switzerland' by Karl Barth, Oct. 1941.

10   'Arthur Cayley Headlam' by R.C.D. Jasper O.U.P. 1960 p.290-301; 'Das politisches Tagesbuch Alfred Rosenbergs' 1964 p.65.

11   e.g. Paton to Visser't Hooft 9.2.40 on Siegmund-Schultze Paton Papers II, WCC Geneva.

12   Vol XXVII : 'Arbeiten zur Geschichte der Kirchenkampfes' Vandenhoeck and Rupprecht, Göttingen; 'Church and State on the European Continent' by Adolf Keller, London 1936; 'National Socialism and the Roman Catholic Church in Germany' by Nathaniel Micklem, Oxford 1939; 'The Church Controversy in Germany' by Anders Nygren S.C.M. Press 1934.

13   D212 Box 15 World Alliance, re refugees : Henriod's memoranda : Box 284.43. WCC Confidential files.

14   Criticism from Bliss and Visser't Hooft; Paton refused to countenance Atkinson's attempts to remove him from the secretaryship of the World Alliance in 1941. Paton Papers II; Henriod worked for the British S.C.M. 1917-20 and belonged to Paton's generation. CR p.237f. Chapter X Footnote (48).

15   Hanns Lilje : 'Memorabilia : Schwerpunkte eines Lebens', Laetare Press 1974, p.238; Paton to Betty Gibson 5.12.28, I.M.C. Box 124 Folder : 'India Office : No objection certificates'.

16   Letter to Grace Paton 30.12.35 Montefiore Papers.

17   Interview Eric Fenn; Paton to Oldham 10.9.35. Filed 'Oldham' WCC General Correspondence.; Paton Papers V; correspondence with Amy Buller.

18   Bell Papers Box 3 'Oxford conference'; Lambeth Palace, WCCF Box VI.

19   Bethge p.501; Paton to Harris, editor of 'The Spectator' 12.4.38. that it is important to keep Niemöller's name in the news and not be distracted by the Anschluß as the German government wants. Paton to Garbett 20.4.38. that fervent protests from Bell were not the right Paton Paters V.

20   Paton to his children about the Manchurian situation, and the arrest of 50 pastors 17.11.35. Montefiore Papers; Requests to the N.C.C. of Japan to bring pressure to bear on the Japanese Government I.M.C. Boxes 363 and 364; Paton wanted a discreet but influential account to appear in 'The Times'.

21 Paton to Fenn and Garbett April - August 1938 Paton Papers V; Oldham to Lang 6.9.35; 'Oldham' WCC General Correspondence; Jasper : 'George Bell' p.237.

22 Richard Crossman : young Labour politician who acted as Heckel's interpreter at the Fano conference; Richard Gutteridge was Professor of International Law at Cambridge. Paton Papers V.

23 Mrs Buxton, wife of the M.P. Noel Buxton, was a 1935 Peter Hain type but less intelligent according to Professor Fenn. Bell Papers, Lambeth Palace; J.S. Conway 'Nazi persecution of the churches' p.249f.

24 Paton to Garbett 27.6.38; to Alan Don 23.6.38. Paton Papers V.

25 Ibid Elmslie's report on a visit to Germany 22-28.3.38.

26 Ibid Minutes 24.5.38.

27 cf J.S. Conway's excellent definitions of the groups The 'German Christians' attempted a synthesis between German Lutheranism and National socialism, and were exploited by the Nazis in their attempt to gain control of the churches 1933-36. The Confessing Church took its name from the Barmen Confession, issued by the synod of Barmen in imitation of the Confession of Augsburg.

28 CR p.523 cp Bethge p.240.

29 It is unfortunate that Daphne Hampson gives so little space to the Roman Catholic reaction.

30 Dillistone biography of Raven: 'This is the Message: A Continental Reply to Charles Raven' by Franz Hildebrandt, Lutterworth Press, London 1944, which is a reply to Raven's book 'The Good News of God' and joint lectures on Romans 1 - 8 pub. Autumn 1942.

31 'In the Valley of the Shadow' by Hanns Lilje, S.C.M. Press 1950, pub originally as 'Im finstern Tal' pub Laetare Verlag, Nürnberg 1947.

32 Jasper : 'George Bell' p.219f; cp 'Arthur Cayley Headlam' by the same author. Headlam and Bell were successively chairmen of Lang's Committee on Foreign Relations. Paton Papers V.

33 Jasper: 'George Bell' p.146f. Held at Holy Trinity, Holborn, later. Tatlow refused the use of his church unless the services were conducted by an Anglican: Bethge p.833.

34 Paton Papers IV; Paton to Crossman 15.12.41, 11.1.41. etc. Fenn had the idea originally although Barth was demanding something of the sort. Fenn to Visser't Hooft 8.9.39. Paton thought it was a gesture the BCC ought to make as a reminder of the true international nature of Christianity. Paton's scepticism : Letter to Garbett 12.12.40. MOI documents : P.R.O. Inf. I/788.

35 Paton to Bartlett with a message to Raven 29.1.41. Paton Papers IV; Alan Booth remembers Paton's dampening effect. See Appendix D for Paton to Fenn on the folly of this idea.

36 Miss Morden remembers the excitement when a dispatch arrived in the office, having come 'in the bag' and then had to be cyclostyled for selected church leaders, the MOI etc. The entire operation was under surveillance by the MOI.

37 Bell correspondence Box 8 General Correspondence, Geneva. Leiper was responsible for the 'leak' over Fano. Paton to J.R. Temple of the B.F.B.S. July 1943. Someone leaked the document Mackie brought back from Sweden, endangering Confessing Church leaders.

38 WCCF Box XIV (New style), Box X (Boyens). Paton did not see Ehrenström's confidential reports on his visits to Hungary.

39 J.S. Conway ('The Nazi persecution of the churches') proves this. Paton knew of the imprisonment of Asmussen, Gunther Dehn, Albertz and Böhm for conducting theological examinations of candidates for the ministry in the Confessing Church. Box 284.43 WCC archives.

40 'Christian counter-attack' by Martin, Newton, Waddams, Williams, SCM Press 1943.

41 Paton Papers IX Much correspondence concerning this newsheet.

42 English translation dates 6.3.37, probably a mistake for 6.3.38. since it reviews the Oxford conference volumes. Copy SOC.

43 Story by David Paton and Elizabeth Montefiore.

44 Box 284.43. 'Germany' labelled 'from Boegner 30.11.45.' Visser't Hooft : 'Memoirs' p.130f; in Berlin it may have been thought that Schönfeld was a double agent.

45 Paton to Visser't Hooft 13.10.40. Paton Papers II.

46 Jasper : 'George Bell' p.147f.

47 'An der schwelle zum gespaltenen Europa' (Bell - Leibholz Briefwechsel) edited by Eberhard Bethge and R.C.D. Jasper, Kreuz Verlag, Stuttgart. p.24. Paton was also involved in getting Hromadka to the United States.

48 Correspondence with Visser't Hooft, Paton Papers II; Interview Sigrid Morden; Paton to son William : 'The P.O.W. committee was a biggish job, because they have interned, wisely on the whole, all the Class B refugees and all who live on the south coast of any class. Therefore the chaos in the camps and prisons is baddish, but due to unavoidable haste'.

49 'Christian Newsletter Supplement' no 176 : 'The Reconstruction of Christian Institutions in Europe'.

50 Paton Papers VII (also labelled D219 Box 1) Questionnaire sent out 5.11.42. and processed 23.11.42. Half the candidates wanted to study theology.

51 Ibid 14.12.42. Paton's report to the committee; cf Minutes 25.1.43. re the Ministry of Labour and the syllabus.

52 Minutes 17.11.43. Money came from the L.M.S., the Women's Missionary Society of the Presbyterian Church of Canada, the Christian Council for Refugees and from Lord Barwick.

53 The Paris Mission Committee's average age was 80, they were consumed by feuds and were making the society's secretary's life impossible. There was a suspicion of racial prejudice against the committee member who was coloured. I.M.C. Box 133 and 320, Paton was chairman. CR 207.

54 Paton to John Hope Simpson of Pembroke and the Peace Aims Group 13.1.43 Paton Papers VII.

55 Ibid. April 1943. Schweitzer lobbied Bell. 'An der Schwelle' p.136; Bell to Paton 3.5.43.

56 Ibid Schultz 1.5.43. The execution of Professor Huber of Munich also much moved him. Letters to Schultz 3.5.43, 5.5.43 etc.

57 Information from Pf. Dr Müller, German Lutheran chaplain in Birmingham.

58 Interview Dr Visser't Hooft; Paton's comment on Visser't Hooft's lack of understanding : Letter to David Paton 10.8.42. Karl Barth (to Visser't Hooft 7.10.39) seems to have more insight into the issues.

59 'The Church and the New Order' p.8; Paton to Leiper 31.3.39, Paton Papers II; Temple/Paton correspondence July 1939, BCC archives SOC.

60 Paton to Leiper 31.3.39. Paton Papers II.

61 Paton to A.D. Lindsay 13.10.39. Paton's hesitation was due to the fact that he thought it was a negative reaction, and there was no positive programme.

62 von Dohnanyi and Bonhoeffer were not involved at this time. Bethge p.575. However, the MOI had received reliable information about a plot from their agent in the Vatican, which it is conceivable they might have told Paton about. P.R.O. C19745/13005/18 The Source, Msr Kaas, gave the same motivation for the plotters.

63 'Germany and the West' WCCF Box VII (old style); von Trott memoranda : Boyens Volume II p.325, Notes on the situation in September 1940', P.R.O. 70371/30912/9135.

64 'An der Schwelle'; Paton to Leibholz 26.10.41., Leibholz to Bell 2.9.41. and reply p.29.

65 Letters 12.1.42; 13.1.42. Paton Papers III. Paton to Crossman 15.12.41. Paton Papers IV; 'Paton does not understand' Bethge p.645.

66 Vansittart, Home Secretary : 'An der Schwelle' p.34, Jasper : 'George Bell' p.260, 272f, 282. Paton also considered him a menace. Held a similar outlook to Enoch Powell. Visser't Hooft to Oldham 18.6.41. Paton Papers II.

67 P.R.O. C11033/61/8. Interview with Bishop R.R. Williams.

68 The Hon David Astor, editor of 'The Observer' 1946-75, b1912, educated Eton and Balliol, had trained as a journalist and was now in the Royal Marines.

69 Paton to Visser't Hooft 1.11.40. Paton Papers II.

70 'Kirchenkampf und Ökumene' Vol II pp.152 and 325.

71 Adam von Trott zu Solz (1909-1944) was the son of a former Prussian Kultusminister. Studied law in Munich, Berlin and Göttingen. Rhodes Scholar 1936. Travelled to the Far East and the USA. Employed in the Foreign Office, Berlin (1940) Member of the Kreisau circle. Met Chamberlain and Halifax, July 1939 and advocated a strong policy with Hitler. Used international contacts on behalf of the Resistance. Elizabeth Wiskemann British agent in Bern was an important contact. 'Das Gewissen steht auf' by Annake Leber, Mosack Verlag, 1954; 'Cornishman Abroad' by A.L. Rowse, Cape 1976.

72 P.R.O. C9731/6789/836. Paton's rebuke to Visser't Hooft is heavily disguised.

73 There is no evidence in the Foreign Office files to support Jasper's claim that Stafford Cripps showed the document to Churchill. Jasper: 'George Bell' p.270f; Bethge p.666. Cripps' brother, Lord Parmoor, was very active in the Life and Work movement.

74 Visser't Hooft : 'Memoirs' pp.152-155, Bethge p.645, 'Gesammelten Schriften' p.361.

75 Visser't Hooft disputes this although he acted in a similar fashion, supplying von Trott with the Christian Newsletter in 1941. Visser't Hooft to Oldham 18.6.41. Paton Papers II.

76 Paton Papers II 'Notes on a talk with A.R. Elliott' by Visser't Hooft. Paton sent Visser't Hooft's memorandum on 'The Church and the New Order' to Fenn, which he acknowledged 16.10.41. P.R.O. Inf I/785. Bonhoeffer's ideas were discussed by the American Peace Aims Group March 1942. Paton/Visser't Hooft correspondence. Letters 8.9.41; 27.2.42; and 30.9.41; cp Visser't Hooft to Bell 19.3.42. WCC General Correspondence Box 9.

77 'I knew Dietrich Bonhoeffer' ed. by Wolf-Dieter Zimmermann and Ronald Gregor Smith, Collins 1966. Biography by Mary Bosanquet, Hodder 1968; cp 'Der 20 Juli; Alternativ zu Hitler?' ed. Hans - Jurgen Schultz, Kreuz Verlag, Stuttgart p.105 and p.120.

78 Bethge p.834; Paton in a letter to the editor of 'The Christian Fellowship in wartime'.

N.B.   Since I worked through the WCCF series of boxes in Geneva, they have been re-organised. Where possible I have tried to give the old and the new numbering.

Notes to Chapter XII

1 Visser't Hooft/Paton correspondence 1939-43 reveals continuous difficulties. e.g. 30.10.42. and 21.1.43. Both condemned his prolonged stay in America during the war.

2 7-29.3.40. extremely ill; 5.4.40 left hospital. Resumed engagements 21.4.40. He caught pneumonia through showing off as a hardy Briton who did not need a heavy overcoat in a New England winter. (Margaret Sinclair) In 1942 he was ill for most of March and was only saved because the Americans were already using M and B sulfa drugs.

3 Visser't Hooft; 'Memoirs' p.87; Boyens Volume II p.387 and 84; WCCF Box VI Old style/IX; Visser't Hooft to Boegner 7.4.39. WCC General Correspondence 'Boegner'. Bishop Heckel, a church administrator, whose nefarious activities are chronicled by Bethge, was attempting to make the WCCF pull out of Europe. He had already prevented the German delegation attending the Oxford conference in 1937. Now he tried to sabotage the WCCF appointments and to control their contacts with Germany. 'Memorandum concerning relations between the Provisional Committee and the German Evangelical Churches' by Visser't Hooft. June 1939, Copy SOC.

4 Visser't Hooft to Paton and Leiper, 'Memoirs' p.125-6. Visser't Hooft to Paton 8.12.39. Paton Papers II.

5 McCaughey p.13-15; The exceptions were Bell, Carter and Craig. cp Visser't Hooft to Temple 26.4.39. applauding the introduction of conscription to Britain. In 1940, 27 American church-men including Mott and van Dusen signed an open declaration supporting the Lend-Lease policy. Most of the signatories were members of Life and Work or Faith and Order. Reuter Survey 415, New York 23.3.40. WCC archives, copy SOC.

6 As a result of a 'peace aims group' broadcast, Lord Crichton Stuart complained to the MOI about the left wing bias of the BBC. P.R.O. Inf I/785.

7 van Dusen to Visser't Hooft 15.6.39; 27.9.39.; 1.11.39. and 7.11.39. van Dusen was chairman of the WCCF study commission and very critical of the study programmes. cp CR p.240.

8 Visser't Hooft : 'Memoirs' p.110f; Boyens Vol II p.295; Rouse and Neill p.707; 'Memorandum of a conference on the co-ordination of Christian refugee work throughout the world' WCCF Box V(O.S); Bell to Jonkheer Baud 28.3.39. WCC General Correspondence Box 9; Paton/-Visser't Hooft correspondence on the various statements of it. Paton Papers II.

9 Berggrav to Bell 25.5.39. WCCF Box VII(O.S.)

10 Ibid Bell to Berggrav 30.5.39.; Visser't Hooft 'Memoirs' p.106; WCC General Correspondence files 'Boegner'.

11 Paton to Temple 3.5.39. and 9.5.39. Paton Papers V. Paton acknowledged the difficulty, but insisted that the Word of God was not the same as a word on refugees. cp Visser't Hooft to Temple 1.5.39. It is clear that he had not understood Paton's point. 'Temple correspondence' Geneva.

12 Paton declared one should not seek rational meaning in Hitler's speeches, they were actions in themselves. Paton to Temple 7.5.39. WCCF Box VII (O.S.) Karl Barth to Visser't Hooft 7.10.39 etc. Barth/Visser't Hooft papers, Geneva.

13 Ibid Paton to Temple 3.5.39; Visser't Hooft : 'Memoirs' p.107; Jasper : 'George Bell' p.245f.

Bishop Mathew was a member of the Council of Christians and Jews CR p.283-5.

15 Paton Papers II. Paton to Visser't Hooft 22.5.39.

16 Temple to Paton 1.5.39. WCCF Box VII(O.S.) The paragraph is not in the published version, reproduced by Boyens, Vol I p.381-384. A paragraph echoing the preface was the only state-ment accepted at Appeldoorn. Minutes of the Administrative Committee Meeting at Appeldoorn. Jan. 1940.

17 Boyens Vol I p.271f; Papers in SOC.

18 Published in 'The Times' 10.5.39; Visser't Hooft : Memoirs p.95f; Boyens Vol I p.380f; Documents in Geneva and Selly Oak. Heckel threatened to break off relations because of its publication.

19 'The Long Road to Unity' by Boegner p.140f; Visser't Hooft : 'Memoirs' p.116; 'Christianity and World Order' by Bell, Hammondsworth, London 1940 Documentation in Boyens Vol II Appendix. The meetings were merged because Temple could only be present for a few days. cf Paton's correspondence, BCC archives.

20 Paton Papers III. The Foreign Office kept it for two weeks. It should have gone through the 'diplomatic bag' to Sweden, but eventually it went by ordinary post to Visser't Hooft. Paton accused the MOI of dictating what the churches should say. (R.R. Williams)

21 'Messages' are filed in WCCF Box III(O.S.) and WCC General Correspondence under 'Eidem'.

22 Headlam was contesting this on the grounds that the WCCF was too political Visser't Hooft to Eidem 27.4.39. on the probable consequences in the C of E to a response to the Swedish demand for a statement. There was also a hostile reaction from Eidem, who was much influenced by Berlin according to Koechlin 11.7.40. WCCF Box IX.

23 'Attitudes of the Protestant churches to the peace offensive', P.R.O. 875/87562; 'The Long Road to Unity' p.141f; Box labelled 'Bishop Berggrav's visit to Scotland' WCC confidential files.

24 Paton to Berggrav to explain Temple's decision arising from a report in the 'Aftenposten' about the 'common clerical peace front'. Suggested Berggrav ought not to say anything to the Press. 8.2.40. Box labelled 'Berggrav's peace action. Zilven 1940.' WCC confidential files.

25 Ibid. Report sent to Geneva from the Norwegian Economic Institute. Kindly summarised for me by Livberit Tallakson; 'Notes on a visit to Denmark' WCCF Box IX, Boyens Vol II p.309, MOI Inf I/722.

26 'Gerstenmaier' by Paton WCCF Box IX, Visser't Hooft : 'Memoirs' p.94, 96, p.116, 127, 160 cp Gerstenmaier/Demant meeting July 1939. Paton Papers V. Like Schönfeld, Gerstenmaier was involved in both sides. He was director of the Inter-Church Aid in Germany after the war.

27 Berggrav's Diary. Box labelled 'Visit of Bishop Berggrav to Scotland' Paton to Hutchison Cockburn 6.12.39. Letter of invitation 28.11.39. Paton to Bell 9.12.39. on the World Alliance.

28 Meeting of the British members of the Provisional Committee with Bishop Brilioth 23.11.42., which formulated plans for post-war meetings of the WCC and heard an address by Brilioth. Notes by Craig.

29 MOI Inf I/773 Koechlin was of the same opinion. To Visser't Hooft 11.7.40. WCCF Box IX.

30 Paton to John Hope Simpson 12.1.40. Paton Papers IX; 'Continental Christianity in wartime' E.H.P. World Issues series.

31 Sources for this paragraph : Mrs Montefiore, David Paton, Eric Fenn, Kathleen Bliss, Oliver Tomkins.

32 Peace Aims Group Minutes Paton Papers IX, 'The Church and the New Order' SCM. Press 1941.

33 Paton to Temple 23.11.39. Paton Papers VIII; Paton to Demant 21.12.39. Paton Papers VIII.

34 John Hope Simpson to Paton 15.11.39. Reply 17.11.39. Paton Papers IX.

35 P.R.O. Inf I/773.

36 'The Church and the New Order' p.72, Letter to John Hope Simpson. 12.1.40. Paton Papers IX.

37 *Peace Aims Bibliography.* (more significant works only)
    'The Church as an ecumenical society in time of war.' Undated. pre Sept 1939
    'The work of the Provisional Committee in time of war' Sept 1939
    'Notes on the attitudes of Christians to this war', Visser't Hooft Nov. 1939
    'The Responsibility of the churches for a new international order', Visser't Hooft Dec. 1939
    'The churches and the international situation. Report of the findings of the national study conference held in Philadelphia Feb 27-29 1940'
    'Germany and the West', Visser't Hooft March 1940;
    'Stellungnahme zu die Verantwortung der Kirchen für die internationale Ordnung' Anon? Leibholz May 1940.

'The ecumenical Church and the international situation' April 1940 Visser't Hooft;
'Principles of Reconstruction' Temple April 1940
'Peace Aims as seen from Great Britain' May 1940
'Is the Church the Church in wartime?' Visser't Hooft May 1940
'Anonymous comment on the Peace Aims Group in America' June 1941
'Notes on the possibility of national sacrifice with reference to British history in the nineteenth century' Dr G.F. Barbour April 1940
'First notes on the question of communion and international order' by Paul Anderson Paris 1940
'The problem of war aims from the point of view of the Church' Paton Dec 1940
'Notes on the responsibility of the Churches for international order by an English collaborator'
'Protestantism and world cultures' Anon
'The real questions concerning the future. Minutes of the Poughkeepsie Meeting' Feb 1942 W.S.C.F.
'Is it possible to create an enlightened public opinion under Nazi tyranny?' (Norway)
'The English situation' by Maurice Reckitt c 10.40;
'A message from the national study conference on the churches and a just and durable peace' Delaware March 1942;
'Social justice and economic reconstruction' C.I.F.S.R. 1942
'The Church and world order' May 1942 C.I.F.S.R.
'The attitude towards Germany' Dec 1942
'The Church and international reconstruction' Jan 1943
'American Christians and the war' John C Bennett April 1943
'American Christians and the European war' Henry van Dusen 1943
'Christian principles and reconstruction' Meeting 5.2.43. on the Delaware Report'
'Report of the commission on international study in the S.C.M.' July 1943
'Post war relief and rehabilitation' B.C.C. meeting July 1943
'The reconstruction of the international order' C. of S report August 1943
'Comments on the six pillars of peace' November 1943 (also in German)

38 'Notes on the attitudes of Christians to this war' November 1939 SOC Visser't Hooft : 'Memoirs' p.114.

39 McCaughey p.13-15 cp Paton/Warnshuis correspondence I.M.C. Box 95 and Miss MacCurchy's attitude. She invited Paton to 'drink a cup of tea to victory' I.M.C. Box 133.

40 'The Church and the New Order' p.32. The nobler cause is not always victorious : the Church may be driven into the catacombs again.

41 Van Dusen circular letter 10.10.41; Fenn to Robert Mackie Box 241.172(42) WCC archives.

42 'The Church and the New Order' p.25; Canon Iddings Bell to Bell 30.12.39. Box labelled 'Visit of Bishop Berggrav to Scotland'; cp Visser't Hooft to Paton 8.12.39. on the lack of comprehension in America. All they can suggest is that the WCC withdraws to America. BCC archives.

43 'American Christians and the war' by John C Bennett. 'Student World', Second quarter 1943. Statement by 27 Protestant church leaders as per (5).

44 Williams Adams Brown to Visser't Hooft 17.5.40. WCC General Correspondence 'William Adams Brown'.

45 e.g. 'Towards a Christian Britain' by Temple 1940, or the best sellers written by Dr Parkes under the pseudonym 'John Hadham'.

46 Paton Papers IX. Paton/van Dusen discussion, and Leiper's protest against 'Germany and the West' WCCF. Box VI; 'Ein Beitrag zu dem Gespräch über Kirche und neue Weltordnung' 1942 in the Ehrenström Papers. 'Internationalism and oecumenicity' by W. Menn c 1939.

47 'The Church and the New Order' p.88f; 'America and Britain' October 1942; 'William Temple' mimeo. March 1942. David Paton recalls that the Paton household was one of the few in which America was not spoken of with hostile comment.

48 Malvern 1941. 'The Life of the Church and the Order of Society' Longmans 1941.

49 CR p.179; p.284; p.330f; M.A. Thesis.

50 Organised after the war by a remarkable layman, Reinhold von Trieglaff-Thadden. cf 'The Ecumenical Advance' by Harold Fey.

51 Pamphlets published by the SCM 1942; BCC archives. Bell to Paton 27.1.43 Bell also protested in this letter that Paton should concentrate on economic and spiritual issues Paton Papers IX.

52 Interview Dr Craig. cp Lockhart biography of Lang.

53 Paton was co-opted onto the Council February 1939, according to Dr Bliss at Oldham's suggestion. First co-opted onto the Commission 21.1.36 and again July 1940. There were 89 members.

54 cp Visser't Hooft's correspondence with Tatlow and Floyd Tomkins. WCC General Correspondence; Paton with Tatlow and Tatlow with Craig 1941-42 BCC archives.

55 J.H. Oldham file 1940-49 BCC archives.

56 Paton to Craig 10.11.41. on Faith and Order relationships; Item 68, Minutes of the Council 3.2.42. + Oldham's memo. 23.3.39. 'A policy for the Council'; Visser't Hooft to Craig 26.3.40. on the difficulty of dealing with a joint World Alliance/Life and Work organisation. Craig to Paton 22.4.40. on how the World Alliance felt ignored. Elmslie to Visser't Hooft on the attitude of the British Section, the World Alliance to Inter-Church Aid. 12.7.43 WCC General Correspondence and BCC archives.

57 Meeting of the Commission 29.7.41.

58 Interview with Eric Fenn, who was on the Oxford conference staff. Oldham's aide de camp. 1937-39.

59 Paton to Visser't Hooft 27.2.39., and 7.9.39 Paton Papers II.

60 Oldham's resignation : 29.7.41. when Iredale's future was discussed. Resignation 3.2.42. received by Council.

61 Minutes of the Commission, December 1941 - September 1942 BCC archives.

62 Interview Sigrid Morden, Paton correspondence with the Bishop of Bristol, BCC archives; Minutes of the meeting 15-17.4.42 Motion proposed by Fisher and seconded by A.E. Garvie.

63 Paton to the Bishop of Bristol 29.4.42. BCC archives.

64 See R.M.C. Jeffery's report on local councils of churches, pub by the B.C.C. in 1973.

65 Rouse and Neill p.698 and the first chapter of 'The Ecumenical Advance'.

Notes to Chapter XIII

1 e.g. Karl Barth; 'Where two faiths meet' by W.W. Simpson pub. by the Council of Christians and Jews. London 1955.

2 Paton to E.N. Cooper of the Home Office 10.12.41. Box labelled 'Jewish Christian relations' WCC archives.

3 Bethge p.240; Bonhoeffer 'Gesammelten Schriften' p.44-53; 'No rusty swords' Fontana 1970, p.218-225.

4 Interview Dr J Parkes CR p.26, p.89.

5 'Minutes of the IMC meeting at Williamstown 1929' pub for the IMC New York and London 1929 CR p.163.

6 Paton to Hoffmann 7.11.32.; but the opposite is implied in a letter of 28.7.38 DWME/IMC London files Box 32; Mott and Paton were responsible for raising his salary. 'Minutes of the I.M.C. Meeting at Old Jordans' 1935 p.2.

7 By 'progressive' is meant those circles which regard themselves as ' "enlightened, modern and liberal" (and subscribed to The Christian Century') Hoffmann to Paton 3.10.30 and 25.4.32 D.W.M.E./I.M.C. London files Box 32.

8 Ibid. Letter of 16.6.30. They agreed to provide £500 for the next 5 years. The other churches provided a substantial part of the secretaries' salaries.

9 Ibid. Miss Standley's correspondence 1930-32 chasing up pledges. Parry of the London Mission to the Jews was a bad offender in 1940.

10 Paton to Miss Bracey 23.1.40. Paton Papers III.

11 Hoffmann to Paton 24.1.40. re $125,000 the American Joint Relief committee was giving to Catholic and Protestant agencies. When CIMADE managed to spirit away a number of French Jewish children, it contributed to their keep.

12 Estimates of the number of Jewish people at risk vary greatly. The High Commissioner for Refugees coming from Germany underestimated with 500,000. A more accurate estimate would be two million German citizens and refugees from Poland and Russia with Jewish connections.

13 Life and Work appeals : Box D994.494. Box I World Alliance Box D212 Box 15, WCC archives.

14 D.W.M.E./I.M.C. London files Box 33 Folder 'Robert Smith', Letter of 27.8.43; Hoffmann to Visser't Hooft 30.6.42. WCC General Correspondence Box 51.

15 WCC Box 284.43 Folder 'General Reports 1935-45', Protokoll der Sitzung des Sch. Ev. Hilfswerkes 8.5.40.'

16 'Voyages of Discovery', Victor Gollancz, London 1969. Many of these Jewish students regarded his acceptance as a betrayal.

17 Paton to Hoffmann 17.2.30. cp 3.5.32. D.W.M.E./I.M.C. London files Box 32.

18 ICCAJ Box 3 WCC archives.

19 Interview and 'Voyages of Discovery'.

20 Interview Elizabeth Montefiore. There are five letters of condolence in the Montefiore Papers from them. They were his colleagues in refugee work.

21 Klausner's book had an extraordinary influence, and is sound scholarship showing how Jesus was a typical Rabbi of his time. Unfortunately he starts the final chapter on the Resurrection with the presupposition that it could not have happened. Sholom Asch's most famous book was 'The Nazarene', a novel based on the life of Christ. Trans. Maurice Samuel Routledge London 1939.

22 Speech by A.E. Garvie. 'Christians and Jews'. Minutes : Atlantic City conference May 1931. pub IMC New York 1931; 'Minutes of the special meeting of members of the ICCAJ' 15.5.31.

23 Report : 'The first six months' by Hoffmann. D.W.M.E./I.M.C. Box 32 London files.

24 Paton to Warnshuis 5.9.39. Ibid.

25 'The Jew in the Christian World' Smith and Kosmala. March 1942 SCM Press.

26 Box : 'Jewish - Christian Relations' November 1941, WCC archives.

27 'World Community' p.150 and as per (2).

28 'God's Underground' ed by Emile C Fabre. Bethany Press, St Louis, Missouri 1970 p.55.

29 Church Dogmatics p.72, Vol IV/3, p.876-878; Vol II/2 para 34.4. It appears that 'proof of God' is a mistranslation of the German.

30 'Smoke on the Mountain' by Joy Davidman, preface by C.S. Lewis, Hodder and Stoughton 1955.

31 Paton condemns 'deicide' charges : 'The Church and the New Order' p.133 Forell of Vienna had been driven out of Prague. Not to be confused with the Swede 'Birgen Forell'. As a result of ICCAJ intervention, he was sent to New York, where he enjoyed great success.

32 Paton to Hoffmann re the appointment. 19.1.40. Box 32 (London files). Paton to Smith 2.10.40.; 16.12.40.; 18.12.42. Box 33 (London files).

33 This mission began by accident when two Church of Scotland ministers got stranded in Budapest on their way to the Middle East, and has been operating for over 100 years. It continues today.

34 Box 33 London files Folder 'Correspondence with Robert Smith September 1939' Webster of the Church of Scotland complained that the C.B.M.S. never gave attention to mission to Jews, and they never got anything out of the C.B.M.S. conferences at Swanwick. Smith felt the same.

35 'The Church for Others' and 'The Church for the World' Final Report of the western European Working Group and the North American Working Group of the Department of Studies in Evangelism. ed. W.J. Hollenweger WCC Geneva 1967.

36 The societies resented the threat to their independence created by the churches' renewed interest. The final rupture between the ICCAJ and the International Hebrew Christian Alliance came when the Alliance accused Hoffmann of doing direct evangelistic work among students.

37 Deduction from the state of Paton's files, and the section on anti-semitism in 'The Church and the New Order' p.127-134. The documents he circulated are also in Box 284.43. 'Germany', WCC Confidential files. See also Standley to Hoffmann 5.5.41. Box 32 (London files).

38 Box 'Jewish - Christian relations' Beely to Paton 27.11.41.

39 Ibid. Paton to Carter 26.11.41.

40 Ibid. Smith to Paton 17.12.41. and reply 22.12.41. cf Paton to Smith 5.10.42 in Box 33 London files.

41 Paton to Carter 26.11.41. '. . . I am still awaiting evidence, not based on what the Jews think, but on what the New Testament says, which will show me that I am wrong'. Box labelled 'Jewish - Christian Relations'.

42 Interview with W.W. Simpson. Standley to Hoffmann 4.12.41. re Simpson's defection because of his weak theology.

43 CR p.308-9.

44 See James Parkes' writings and 'While six million died' by Arthur Morse Seckar and Warburg 1968; 'The Sunflower' by Simon Wiesenthal W.H. Allen London 1970.

45 Interview Catherine Paton.

46 'Modern Jewry and Christian responsibility' Report of the ICCAJ 1.6.32.-1.9.33. Box 32 London files.

47 Minutes printed for private circulation ICCAJ Box 3.

48 Report of the First Five Years of the ICCAJ, 1935, ICCAJ Box 3.

49 pub. Berlin/Köln 1968.

50 Die nach Amerika gerichtete Rundfunk Rede des H. General-Superintendent Dibelius. Box 284.43. 'Germany', which differs from the English text given as an appendix in J.S. Conway 'The Nazi Persecution of the Churches' cp 1929 statement quoted in my M.A. Thesis.

51 J.S. Conway, Armin Boyens, Bethge.

52 CR Chapter VIII, footnote (3). Statement on the church situation by Knak in the Berliner Missionsberichte June 1933, I.M.C. Box 333; Paton to Schlunk 22.11.33. : 'May I say how very thankful I am for what was done at Barmen. It has been very difficult for people like myself, who are in profound sympathy with the struggle that is being waged for full religious and missionary freedom to know whether we help or hinder more by statements that may be made publicly. I hope that you and your friends do realise the great volume of prayer and sympathy which is going out to you from all over the world. I do not know of anything in recent years which has so much displayed the true spiritual character of the Church of Christ as the movements in German Christianity during these last months for safeguarding true spiritual freedom'.

53 Interview Gerold Schwarz, Hartenstein's biographer.

54 Hoffmann's report, September 1935, Box 32 London files.

55 as per (3) cp 'The Church and the New Order' p.133.

56 Bethge p.301; 'The Christian Newsletter' Supplement by James Parkes no 6 6.12.39; No 102 8.10.41. 'The Jewish Question Today'.

57 The translation of Delitzschianum adopted. Kosmala was director and was paid the same as the WCC refugee scholars Correspondence Box 32 London files.

58 Paton Papers VIII (formerly D219 Box 2) Paton to Henriod 6.2.34., reply 8.2.34.

59 From a letter of Levison to Keller 12.10.33. Box 'Germany Studienabteilung' WCC Confidential files, it would seem that Hoffmann corresponded with Keller. The Dean later recanted.

60 I.M.C. Box 330; 'While six million died' Arthur Morse.

61 I.M.C. Box 144. Case of Dr Otto Piper; Paton to Hoffmann re a letter from Grüber 9.11.39. Box 32 London files.

62 Paton to Hoffmann 18.9.39. Box 32 London files.

63 Ibid Paton to Hoffmann 5.9.39. Interview Robert and Ethel Smith.

64 15.10.38. Box 32 London files; also Paton to Warnshuis 5.9.39. on Hoffmann's future.

65 Ibid Warnshuis to Hoffmann 23.8.38.

66 Ibid Hoffmann to Paton 2.12.39; Reply 20.12.39. and 28.12.39.

67 Freudenberg's appointment : Paton Papers II March - May 1939; Details of the refugee conference : Bell papers, WCC General Correspondence Boxes 8-9.

68 Büsing to Paton 1.9.42. Paton Papers III. Büsing was secretary of the refugee conference : Bell Papers WCC General Correspondence Boxes 8-9.

69 Box 32; Visser't Hooft to Paton 24.11.39. Paton Papers II; Correspondence with Miss Livingstone, Paton Papers III. Paton was very upset because he could not get any response from America.

70 P.R.O. MOI Inf I/409; Contact with Grubb MOI Inf I/770. 'General policy re Jews'. There is nothing in this file about extermination.

71 16.9.39. File 'Freudenberg' from a box labelled 'General Correspondence Malagnou staff' cp chapter by Freudenberg in 'God's Underground'.

72 Freudenberg to Burckhardt 3.12.42. Box 'WCC action at the time of the extermination of the Jews'.

73 Visser't Hooft : 'Memoirs' p.166; 'God's Underground' p.77, p.92, p.175.

74 11.12.39. Hoffmann compared the massacre of 681,000 Jews to that of the Armenians by the Turks. Paton (12.11.39.) on his convictions.

75 Box 261.1 contains material on which the preceding two pages are based. WCC reaction and Visser't Hooft's note in 'WCC action at the time of the extermination of the Jews'.

76 Ibid. 26.1.43. (Temple to Paton 22.1.43).

77 Visser't Hooft : 'Memoirs' p.168f; 'God's Underground' p.41; 'The last three popes and the Jews' by Pinchas Lapide Souvenir Press London 1964.

78 Paton correspondence with Carter, Bell and Temple, April - May 1943 Box labelled 'WCC action at the time of the extermination of the Jews'.

79 P.R.O. 5/04/49/48 Help for Jews in Europe 29.3.43.

Notes to Chapter XIV

1   Interviews David Paton and Alan Booth; cp Visser't Hooft: 'Memoirs', and Jacques Rossel: 'Découverte de la Mission' (1946).

2   Preface to 'World Community', Religious Book Club edition No 6. SCM Press.

3   'Jesus Christ and the World's Religions' revised edition 1927, p.100.

4   Paton to Grace Paton 30.11.17. Montefiore Papers.

5   Grace Paton to Tatlow 18.8.18. SCM archives filed under 'Paton : Y.M.C.A.' Her letters to Paton have not survived.

6   e.g. Tatlow to Fr. Kelly 6.6.19 on the isolation of the upper echelons of the C of E from lay people; 'Minutes of a conference on recruiting for the mission field. '30.10.19 Compiled by Paton, illustrate the SCM's attitude exactly.

7   'A Faith for the World' Cargate Press 1929.

8   'The Federation and Internationalism' 15.12.28 Box 122, WSCF files, WCC archives, Geneva.

9   CR p.167-8.

10 'The Faiths of Mankind' p.104-5.

11 'World Community' p.18; 'The Church and the New Order' p.49.

12 Sundkler : 'Nathan Söderblom, his life and work', Lutterworth Press, London 1968, p.189-205; Rouse and Neill p.523f; 'Introduction to the official report of the Universal Christian conference on Life and Work held in Stockholm in 1925' ed. G.K.A. Bell O.U.P. 1926; 'The Hour and its need' p.70-71.

13 'World Community' p.18; 'The Church and the New Order' p.127f.

14 Stockholm Report p.193f.

15 Schlunk : 'Von dem Höhen des Olberges'; Underhill review thereof, IRM Vol XVIII 1929.

16 Ev. Miss. Mag. 1928 vol 72 Karl Heim : 'Die Tagung des erweiterten Internationalen Missionsrates'; Vischer : 'Documentary History of the Faith and Order Movement' p.30.

17 Lausanne Report p.321.

18 cf Oldham's article in 'The Student World' October 1935 and his pamphlet 'The Question of the Church in the World Today'.

19 'The Churches survey their task' p.69; 'World Community' p.37.

20 'The Church and its function in society' CCS series George Allen and Unwin 1937. Sole reference to 'Let the Church be the Church': 'World Community' p.141.

21 Vischer p.50.

22 'World Community' p.56.

23 'Edinburgh 1937' ed. Leonard Hodgson SCM Press 1938 p.70-71.

24 cf WCCF Study Department files, and Ehrenström Papers, WCC archives, for a complete set of papers.

25 Paton to Visser't Hooft 15.1.41. Paton Papers II; Paton quoted Maritain and Mannheim in support of the argument that small groups could defend human freedom.

26 Harvey Cox : 'The Secular City' cp 'The Church and the New Order' p.114, p.154f.

27 Judging from 'No man is alien', the bibliography of Visser't Hooft's writings by Robert Nelson, it would appear not.

28 'World Community' p.20; 'The Cost of Discipleship' SCM Press 1966 p.38f.

29 'World Community' p.39.

30 Ibid p.45.

31 'The Church and the New Order' p.171-188; 'The Hour and its Need' p.75.

32 'The Church and the New Order' p.184.

33 'The Hour and its Need' p.67-68.

34 The broadcasts of Paton's on the theme are dated 19.4.34. a sermon on Eph. 2 v 29 introducing the ideas of the Oxford conference and 17.11.40 on the Church and the New Order.

35 'World Community' p.52; 'The Church and its function in society' p.160; 'The Cost of Discipleship' p.86.

36 'The Hour and its Need' October 1939. E.H.P.; describes the work of the world-wide Church.

37 'World Community' p.78f, p.86, p.118.

38 'World Community' p.128 Heavy dependence on John Middleton Murry 'New Statesman' 5.2.38.

39 'World Community' p.139.

40 Ibid p.126, p.149. 'The Church and the New Order' p.133. Paton does not actually attribute this idea to Dr Parkes, but it is the view he holds to this day. Quotes Parkes with approval p.132, that the Jews are always oppressed when the State tries to create an homogeneous society. Parkes now traces anti-semitism to the Gospel writers.

41 The WCC has taken on this responsibility : 'World Community' p.15f.

42 Ibid p.165. No printed records survive of the debates at Oxford but Hugh Martin produced a mimeographed MS which survives in fragments.

43 'World Community' p.117, p.169f 'Beckly Lecture' p.25.

44 'Towards Unity in India' IRM Oct. 1941 reprint. Paton to Maclean 28.7.39. Letter in the possession of Bishop Newbigin. That if the S.I.U.C. insists on lay celebration of holy communion, the Anglicans will not agree to the C.S.I. scheme. The Anglicans are getting more reasonable on inter-communion, before union, but one cannot expect them to adopt a practice neither the Methodists nor the Presbyterians have.

45 Only one extant copy in the BCC archives, c 1942.

46 cp 'The political importance of origin sin', a BBC broadcast by Dr E.R. Norman, Fellow of Peterhouse, 12.4.76. Recording No BLN 11/027J102.

47 'Religion and Life' Essays edited by Paton p.82 pub by King and Staples 1942.

48 e.g. 'God's call in the present crisis' given at St Andrews 24.7.41. P.R.O. MOI : Inf I/769.

Conclusion

1. I.M.C. Box 158. Kathleen Bliss considers this council to have been of great significance.

2. Sinclair biography.; 'The World's Student Christian Federation : A History of the first thirty years 1895 - 1924' by Ruth Rouse SCM. Press 1948; Visser't Hooft : 'Memoirs'.

3. I.M.C. Box 114 : 'Industrial and Social Questions'; I.M.C. Box 111 : 'Missions and Government'.

4. Visser't Hooft underlined the importance of this committee in his letters to Paton. Paton Papers II. Papers of the committee itself Paton Papers III.

5. 'Thirty years of the British Council of Churches 1942-73' by Dr Ernest Payne p.8-9 pub. by the BCC.

6. Fenner Brockway, a courageous pacifist in the First World War, and a socialist writer, was given a life peerage at a similar age in 1964. Autobiography : 'Towards tomorrow', Hart-Davis MacGibbon, London 1977.

7. From the evidence of Vol VI of his addresses and papers, one is tempted to say, not since 1904.

8. Details from Miss Potts, who was in the house-party at Rydal Hall, and from the circular letter Grace Paton sent out after his death.

9. 'Some principles of reconstruction. The proposals of the American churches' pub. in 'The crisis of the western world' by Allen Unwin London 1944 p.42-48.

10. Report of the address given by the Archbishop of Canterbury at the memorial service for Dr William Paton, at St. Paul's Cathedral 28.9.43 Text from the final verses of 1 Corin. 15. Copy SOC.

11. Oldham to Visser't Hooft 25.8.43.; Visser't Hooft to Oldham 30.8.43. Copies SOC.

12. Paton to David Paton 28.3.43 Montefiore Papers.

13. Ibid Paton to David Paton 22.11.42.

14. Correspondence with Chatham House Paton Papers VIII, Geneva.

15. Paton to David Paton 13.4.42. and 10.8.42 Montefiore Papers.

16. Paton to David Paton 4.10.42. Correspondence with Visser't Hooft Paton Papers II.

17. Letter received 16.3.73.

18. Letter to Grace Paton 25.8.43. Montefiore Papers.

19. Ibid Paton to David Paton 10.8.42. He also remarked that Kenneth Oxon had become a fully-fledged fool.

20. Interview Kathleen Witz and Eric Fenn.

21. 'Was kann die Gemeinde tun, um ihrer missionarischen Verantwortung gerecht zu werden?' December 1942 Box 284(43) 'Germany'; 'To our friends in Great Britain and the United States' Uit Trouw, December 1943, Basel Mission archives, dossier Oek Rad. der Kirchen, Genf, Duplicating Room.

22. Interview Osyth Potts.

23. Letter received September 1974.

24. Robert Smith felt that with the death of Paton and Temple the light went out of the ecumenical movement, and was not re-kindled. David Edwards: 'Leaders of the Church of England 1828-1944' pub. O.U.P. 1971 p.335.

Bibliography

Official reports and conference volumes.

1 'Students and the Missionary Problem'. Addresses delivered at the international student missionary conference. London January 1900'. pub. for the S.V.M.U. 1900.

2 'Addresses and Records of the World Missionary Conference held in New York 1900' pub. Harper Bros. New York 1900. Copy in Edinburgh House. 2 vols.

3 The World Missionary Conference held in Edinburgh 1910. Titles for eight volumes as per the eight commissions. 'History and Records of the Edinburgh World Missionary Conference' vol. IX pub. Oliphant, Edinburgh 1910.

4 'Christ and Human Need' Records of the S.V.M.U. Quadrennial held in Liverpool 1912. pub. for the S.V.M.U. 1912.

5 'Christ and Human Need' Records of the S.V.M.U. Quadrennial held in Glasgow 1921, pub. for the S.C.M. 1921.

6 Report of the Conference on Politics, Economics and Citizenship. 12 volumes edited by Lucy Gardner. Longmans, Green and Co. London 1924.

7 Conference on Christian Politics, Economics and Citizenship. Handbook. edited by Lucy Gardner, Longmans, Green and Co. London 1924.

8 Minutes of the International Missionary Council (including Minutes of the Committee of Council and of the Ad Interim Committee) as per place and date, all published under the I.M.C. imprint in the same year: Oxford (1923), Atlantic City (1925), Rättvik (1926), Williamstown (1929), Herrnhut (1932), London (1933), Salisbury (1934), Northfield (1935), Old Jordans (1936), Kasteel Hemmen (1937 and 1939).

9 Minutes of the International Christian Council on the Approach to the Jews, as per place and date of meeting. Digswell Park (1932), Old Jordans (1935), Kasteel Hemmen (1936), Bucarest (1937). pub. under I.M.C. imprint.

10 'The Stockholm Conference on Life and Work 1925' edited by G.K.A. Bell. Oxford University Press. London 1926.

11 'Faith and Order. Proceedings of the World Conference: Lausanne 1927' edited by Canon H.N. Bate S.C.M. Press London 1927.

12 'Convictions: Responses to Lausanne 1927' edited by Leonard Hodgson S.C.M. Press London 1934.

13 The International Missionary Council meeting at Jerusalem. Series edited by Paton, see under 'Bibliography of Paton's writings'.

14 'A Documentary History of the Faith and Order Movement 1927-63' edited by Lukas Vischer. Bethany Press. St. Louis U.S.A. 1963.

15 'The Second World Conference on Faith and Order, Held at Edinburgh 1937' Edited by Leonard Hodgson. S.C.M. Press London 1938.

16 'God speaks to this Generation' S.C.M. Quadrennial 1937. edited by Hugh Martin. S.C.M. Press 1937.

17 'The Churches Survey their Task: the report of the Conference at Oxford on Church, Community and State, July 1937' edited by J.H. Oldham. George Allen and Unwin. London 1937.

18 'The Church and its function in society' Vol I of the Church Community and State series, by W.A. Visser't Hooft and J.H. Oldham. George Allen and Unwin London 1937-38.
N.B. There are seven other volumes in this series.

19 Records of the International Missionary Council meeting at Tambaram 1938 Series of Volumes edited by Paton. See 'Bibliography of Paton's writings'.

20 'Christus Victor: Report of the world conference of Christian youth, Amsterdam, Holland, July 1939' edited by Denzil Patrick. Geneva 1939.

21 'The Ten Formative Years. The World Council of Churches in process of formation'. Report to the First World Assembly, Amsterdam 1948. edited by W.A. Visser't Hooft, W.C.C. Geneva 1948.

22 'The Church for others', 'The Church for the world'. A quest for structures for missionary congregations. Final report of the West European working group and the North American working group of the Department on Studies on Evangelism. Edited by W.J. Hollenweger, W.C.C. Geneva 1967.

Books written for Student Christian Movement study groups.
(published under the imprint of the S.C.M., S.V.M.U. or U.C.M.E.)

23 'The Evangelisation of the World in this Generation' by John R. Mott. S.V.M.U. New York 1900.

24 'The Decisive Hour of Christian Missions', by John R. Mott, U.C.M.E. 1910.

25 'The Rebuke of Islam' by Temple Gairdner. C.M.S. imprint 1920, originally 'The Reproach of Islam' pub. under the U.C.M.E. imprint 1909.

26 'The Desire of India' by S.K. Datta, U.C.M.E. imprint 1908.

27 'Asiatic Asia' by S.K. Datta. Faber and Faber Ltd., 1932.

28 'The Uplift of China' by Houlder, U.C.M.E. 1908.

29 'The Outcastes' Hope' by Godfrey Phillips, U.C.M.E. 1911.

30 'The Crown of Hinduism' by J.N. Farquhar, U.C.M.E. 1915.

31 'The Child and the Nation' by Grace Paton, S.C.M. 1916.

32 'The World and the Gospel' by J.H. Oldham U.C.M.E. 1916.

33 'Christ and the World at War' by Basil Matthews (editor) pub. Clarke London 1917.

34 'China and Britain' by R.O. Hall, Edinburgh House Press 1927.

35 'The Church controversy in Germany' by Anders Hygren, S.C.M. Press 1934.

36 'The Book of Prayer for Students' ed. Leslie Salomon, Malcolm Spenser, Tatlow. S.C.M. Press 1912.

37 'The Art of a Missionary' by R.O. Hall, S.C.M. Press 1942.

38 'T.Z. Koo: Chinese Christianity speaks to the West', by R.O. Hall, S.C.M. Press 1950.

39 'The Renaissance in India' by C.F. Andrews, U.C.M.E. 1912.

40 'Reinhold Niebuhr. An introduction to his thought' by D.M. Paton, S.C.M. 1937.

General histories and interpretations, theses etc.

41 'A History of the Ecumenical Movement 1517-1948' edited by Ruth Rouse and Stephen Neill. S.P.C.K. London 1967.

42 'The Ecumenical Advance: A history of the Ecumenical Movement vol II 1948-68'. Edited by Harold Fey, S.P.C.K. London 1970.

43 'The Story of the Student Christian Movement' by Tissington Tatlow, S.C.M. Press London 1933.

44 'The World's Student Christian Federation: A History of the First Thirty Years 1895-1924' by Ruth Rouse. S.C.M. Press 1948.

45 'Asia and the Ecumenical Movement 1896-1961' by Hans-Ruedi Weber, S.C.M. Press 1966.

46 'Christianity in a Revolutionary Age' K.S. Latourette Vol. III Ch. 15 and Vol. V Ch. 18. Harper Bros. New York 1952-62.

47 'The Evangelisation of the World in this Generation' by Denton Lutz. Thesis presented to the University of Hamburg 1972.

48 'Christian Obedience in the University'. J.D. McCaughey, S.C.M. Press 1958.

49 'Learning Wisdom. Fifty years of the Student Christian Movement' by Eric Fenn, S.C.M. Press 1937.

50 'Church Unity: Studies of its most important problems' by C. Briggs, New York 1909.

51 'Brève Histoire de L'Oecumènisme' by Paul Conord. Paris 1958. From the collection 'Les Bergers et les Mages'.

52 'Christendom' by Einar Molland. First edition 1959. Mowbray. London 1959.

53 'Ecumenical Foundations' Richey Hogg. Harper Bros. New York 1952.

54 'Ein Gespräch beginnt: die Anfänge der Bewegung für Glauben und Kirchenverfassung in den Jahren 1910-20', by Karl-Christoph Epting. Theologischer Verlag Zürich 1972.

55 'The Quest for Christian Unity' by Robert Bilheimer. Association Press, New York 1952.

56 'The Ecumenical Movement' Three lectures given at the University of the South, Sewanee, Tenn. March 1950 by Leonard Hodgson. University of the South Press 1951.

57 'Fifty years of Faith and Order' by J.E. Skoglund and J.R. Nelson. Bethany Press, St. Louis 1964.

58 'The Ecumenical Movement in World Affairs' by Darrill Hudson. Weidenfeld and Nicolson, London 1969.

59 'The Social Thought of the World Council of Churches' by Edward Duff S.J. Longmans, Green and Co. London 1956.

60 'COPEC Adventure. The work of the Birmingham COPEC Housing Trust', by Margaret Fenter. Obtainable from the Birmingham COPEC Housing Trust.

61 'Christian Citizenship: The story of COPEC' by Edward Shillito. Longmans, Green and Co. London 1924.

62 'Life and Work: Stockholm 1925' by Edward Shillito. Longmans, Green and Co. London 1926.

63 'Die Weltkirchenkonferenz in Stockholm' by F. Siegmund-Schultze. Ev. Pressverband für Deutschland. Berlin 1926.

64 'Die Stockholmer Bewegung: die Weltkirchenkonferenzen zu Stockholm 1925 und Bern 1926' by Adolf Deissmann. Furche Verlag Berlin 1927.

65 'Anglicans et Catholiques' by Jacques Bivort de la Saudée. 2 vols Lyons and Paris 1949 (Le problème de l'union anglo-romaine 1833-1933).

66 'The Conversations at Malines, 1921-25: original documents' by Lord Halifax. Philip Allan and Co. London 1930.

67 'Recollections of Malines' by W.H. Frere, Centenary Press, London 1935.

68 'Lausanne 1927: an interpretation of the World Faith and Order Conference' E.S. Woods S.C.M. Press London 1927.

69 'Lausanne: the Will to Understand' by Edmund Soper. Doubleday, Doran & Co. New York 1928.

70 'Von den Höhen des Ölberges' (Die Tagung des erweiterten internationalen Missionsrates, Jerusalem 1928) ed. M. Schlunk Ev. Missionsverlag Stuttgart 1928.

71 'Christian Education in India. The report of the Commission on Higher Education in India' ed. A.D. Lindsay, Oxford University Press 1932.

72 'Rethinking Missions. A Layman's Inquiry after 100 Years', ed. W.E. Hocking. Harper Bros. London and New York 1932.

73 Laymen's Foreign Missions Inquiry: Fact-finders' Reports 6 vols, New York 1932.

74 'Die Ökumene in der Entwicklungskenflikt' by Karl-Heinz Dejeung. Thesis submitted to the University of Heidelberg 1972 and subsequently published by the Friedensforschungabteilung of Heidelberg. 1973.

75 'Kraemer towards Tambaram' by C. Hallenkreuz. Studia Missionalia Upsaliensis Stockholm 1968.

76 'The Nazi Persecution of the Churches' by J.S. Conway. Weidenfeld and Nicolson London 1968.

77 'Kirchenkampf und Ökumene' Band I 1933-39 by Armin Boyens pub. Chr. Kaisar Verlag, Munich 1969. Band II 1939-45 pub. Chr. Kaisar Verlag 1973.

78 'Ökumene und Katholismus' Chapter by Klaus-Martin Beckmann in 'Volk Nation and Vaterland' Edited by Horst ZilleBen. Guerlocher Verlag 1970.

79 'George Bell-Alphons Koechlin Briefwechsel 1933-54' ed. Andreas Lindt. EV2 Verlag Zurich 1969.

80 'An der Schwelle zum gespaltenen Europa' Briefwechsel zwischen George Bell und Gerold Leibholz. ed. by Eberhard Bethge and R.C.D. Jasper Kreuz Verlag Stuttgart 1974.

81 'The Relationship between the English Churches and the German Evangelical Church 1933-39' by Daphne Hampson. Bodleian Library, Oxford. Thesis submitted to the University of Oxford 1973.

82 'En marche vers l'Unité chrétienne' by Marc Boegner. Tierage au part du cahier du 'Christianisme Sociale' Jan-Feb. 1937.

83 'Sommaire des grandes conferences d'Oxford et d'Edimbourg' in 'Le Prevue du Christianisme Sociale Aout-Dec. 1937, ed. by Élie Gounelle.

84 'Church and State in Europe' by Adolf Keller, Epworth Press, London 1936.

85 'National Socialism and the Roman Catholic Church in Europe' by Nathaniel Micklem, Oxford University Press, London 1939.

86 'Das Wunder der Kirche' ed. by M. Schlunk. (Series of essays on the I.M.C. Meeting at Tambaram 1938) Ev. Missionsverlag Stuttgart 1939.

87 'Kirche und Volk in der deutschen Missionswissenschaft' by J.C. Hoekendijk Chr. Kaiser Verlag Munich 1967.

88 'Das trinitarische Basis des Ökumenischen Rat der Kirchen' by Wolfdieter Theurer, Verlag Gerhard Kaffke, Bergheim, Enkheim bei Frankfurt am Main 1967.

89 'Towards a United Church' by William Adams Brown. Charles Scribner and Sons New York 1946.

90 'God's Underground. The story of CIMADE' collected by Jeanne Merle d'Aubigne and Violette Mouehon, edited by Emile Fabre. Bethany Press St. Louis 1970 originally published as 'Les Clandestins de Dieu' by Librairie Artheme Fassard 1968.

91 'Lutheran Missions in a time of revolution': The China experience 1944-51' by Jonas Jonson. Studia Missionalia Upsalensis. 1972.

92 'The Kingship of Christ. The Story of the World Council of Churches' by G.K.A. Bell. Penguin Books Harmondsworth London 1954.

Personal accounts, popular works, theological studies.

93 'Edinburgh 1910: an account and interpretation of the World Missionary Conference' by W.H.T. Gairdner, Oliphant Anderson and Ferrier Edinburgh 1910.

94 'If not a United Church — What?' by Peter Ainslie. S.C.M. Press London 1920.

95 'Karma and Redemption' by A.G. Hogg. pub. Christian Literature Society, London and Madras 1909.

96 'Redemption from this World' by A.G. Hogg. T.T. Clark London 1922.

97 'Not to Destroy but to Fulfil: The Contribution of J.N. Farquhar to Protestant Missionary thought before 1914' by Eric Sharpe. Studia Missionalia Upsalensis. Stockholm 1965.

98 'The Missionary Spirit and the Present Opportunity'. H.T. Hodgkin Swarthmore lecture 1916. pub. by Headley and Sons, London 1916.

99 'Church and Nation' The Bishop Paddock lectures 1914-15, by William Temple, Macmillan 1915.

100 'Strategic Points in the World's Conquest' by J.R. Mott 1897. James Nisbet and Co. London.

101 'Christian Fellowship' by Nathan Söderblom. S.C.M. Press London 1923.

102 'Understanding: being an interpretation of the Universal Christian Conference on Life and Work, held in Stockholm 1925' by Charles Brent.Longmans, Green and Co. New York 1925.

103 'The Church and Peace' The Burge lecture 1929, by Nathan Söderblom Oxford University Press London 1933.

104 'The Present Day Summons to World Mission' John R. Mott, New York 1932.

105 'Addresses and Papers of John R. Mott' Vol VI Association Press New York 1947.

106 'Co-operation and World Mission' by John R. Mott pub. for the I.M.C. by the Rumford Press New York 1935.

107 'The Christ of the Indian Road' by Stanley Jones. Hodder and Stoughton London 1925.

108 'That they go forward' by Eric Fenn. S.C.M. Press London 1937.

109 'Edinburgh 1937' by Hugh Martin. S.C.M. Press London 1937.

110 'Ten Minutes to Twelve' by Adolf Keller. Nashville; Cokesbury Press 1938.

111 'Christianity and World Order' by G.K.A. Bell Penguin paperback Harmondsworth, London 1940.

112 'The Christian Message in a non-Christian world' by Hendrik Kraemer Kregel publications, Michigan, U.S.A. 1955 (fifth edition).

113 'Malvern 1941' (The papers of the Archbishop of York's conference) Longmans, Green and Co. London 1941.

114 'And other pastors of thy flock. A tribute to the Bishop of Chicester' ed. by Franz Hildebrandt, Cambridge 1942.

115 'This is the message: A reply to Charles Raven' by Franz Hildebrandt Cambridge 1944.

116 'The Jew in the Christian World' by Smith and Kosmala, pub. S.C.M. Press 1942.

117 'World encounter. To Amsterdam and beyond' by James Kennedy. Morehouse Gorham and Co. New York 1948.

118 'The British Council of Churches, The First Thirty Years 1942-72' by Ernest Payne. pub. for the B.C.C. 1972.

119 'German Catholics and Hitler's wars' by Gordon C. Zahn. Stagbooks, Sheed and Ward London 1963.

120 'The German Church Struggle, Tribulation and Promise' Lectures given in Oxford and Birmingham by Karl Barth. pub. Kulturkampf Association, Hinckley. 1938.

121 'Barmen' Beitrage zur Evangelischen Theologie Theologische Abhandlungen ed. by Ernst Wolf. Chr. Kaisar Verlag Munich 1957.

122 'The Significance of the Barmen Declaration for the Ecumenical Church' Foreword by G.K.A. Bell. Theology Occasional Papers. New Series V. pub. S.P.C.K. London 1943.

123 'Die Gnade in Gottes Gericht' by Edmund Schlink. pub. C. Bertelsmann Verlag, Gütersloh 1946.

124 'Der Ertrag des Kirchenkampfes' by Edmund Schlink pub. C. Bertelsmann Verlag, Gütersloh. 1947.

125 'Who speaks for the Church' by Paul Ramsey. Abingdon Press Tenn. 1967.

126 'The Church in South Africa' by Peter Hinchliff S.P.C.K. London 1968.

Biographical Studies

127 'The testimony of C.F. Andrews' by Daniel O'Connor. Christian Literature Society, Bangalore and Madras 1974.

128 'George Bell, Bishop of Chichester' by R.C.D. Jasper. Oxford University Press London 1967.

129 'George Bell' by Kenneth Slack. S.C.M. Centre Books 1971.

130 'The Long road to unity' by Marc Boegner, Collins London 1970.

131 'Dietrich Bonhoeffer' by Eberhard Bethge (original German pub. by Chr. Kaiser Verlag Munich 1967) Collins London 1970.

132 'Dietrich Bonhoeffer' by Mary Bosanquet, Hodder London 1968.

133 'I knew Dietrich Bonhoeffer' edited by Wolf-Dieter Zimmermann and Ronald Gregor Smith, Collins London 1966.

134 'Charles Brent, Crusader for Christian Unity' by Zabriskie. Westminster Press U.S.A. 1957.

135 'David Cairns: an autobiography' S.C.M. Press London 1950.

136 'Randall Davidson. Archbishop of Canterbury' by G.K.A. Bell, Third edition Oxford University Press London 1952.

137 'John Merle Davis An autobiography:' Kyo Bun Kwan Press, Japan.

138 'J.N. Farquhar' by Eric Sharpe, Y.M.C.A. Press 1963.

139 'Temple Gairdner of Cairo' by Constance Padwick, S.P.C.K. London 1929.

140 'Cyril Foster Garbett, Archbishop of York' by Charles Smyth, Hodder and Stoughton London 1959.

141 'Crypts of Power' by Kenneth G. Grubb pub. Hodder and Stoughton 1971.

142 'Erinnerungen aus den sieben Jahrzehnten' by Heinrich Grüber. Kiepenheuer and Witschi Berlin/Köln 1968.

143 'Arthur Cayley Headlam' by R.C.D. Jasper, Faith Press London 1960.

144 'Karl Hartenstein: Ein Leben für Kirche und Mission' ed. by W. Metzger Ev. Missionsverlag Stuttgart 1953.

145 'Henry T. Hodgkin: A memoir' H.G. Wood, S.C.M. Press 1937.

146 'The theology of Hogg' by Eric Sharpe. Christian Literature Society, Madras 1971.

147 'Hendrik Kraemer: Pionier der Oekumene' by Dr A. Th. van Leeuven Basileia Verlag Basel 1962.

148 'Cosmo Gordon Lang, Archbishop of Canterbury' by J.G. Lockhart. Hodder and Stoughton 1949.

149 'The valley of the shadow' Hanns Lilje, S.C.M. Press 1950. First pub. as 'Im finstern Tal' by Laetare Verlag. Nürnburg 1947.

150 'Memorabilia: Schwerpunkte eines Lebens' Hanns Lilje Laetare Verlag Nürnberg 1973.

151 'An irenic itinerary' by Silas McBee. Longmans, Green and Co. London 1910.

152 'Après la journée' The autobiography of Wilfred Monod, Paris 1938.

153 'John R. Mott — World Citizen' by Basil Matthews. S.C.M. London 1934.

154 'Voyages of discovery' by James Parkes. Victor Gollancz London 1969.

155 'William Paton' by Margaret Sinclair, S.C.M. Press London 1949.

156 'Charles Raven. Naturalist, Historian, Theologian'; by F.W. Dillistone, Hodder and Stoughton, London 1975.

157 'Nathan Söderblom: Prophet of Christian Unity' by Peter Katz. James Clarke and Co. London 1949.

158 'Nathan Söderblom: his life and work' by Bengt Sundkler, Lutterworth Press London 1968.

159 'Von Geist und Liebe' (A tribute to Söderblom) by Adolf Keller. Leopold Klotz Verlag. Gotha. 1934.

160 'C.T. Studd: pioneer missionary and cricketer' by Norman Grubb. 9th impression Lutterworth Press 1939.

161 'After C.T. Studd: Sequel to the life of the famous pioneer missionary' by Norman Grubb. Lutterworth Press 1939.

162 'Edward Stuart Talbot' by D. Stephenson. S.P.C.K. Press London 1936.

163 'William Temple. Archbishop of Canterbury' by F.A. Iremonger, Oxford University Press London 1949.

164 'Memoirs' by Dr W.A. Visser't Hooft. S.C.M. Press London 1972.

165 'Christian Ambassador. A life of A.L. Warnshuis' by Norman Goodall. Channel Press New York 1963.

166 'In this generation. A biography of Robert Wilder' by Ruth Wilder Braisted pub. for the S.V.M.U. by the Friendship Press New York 1941.

167 'Ökumenische Profile' Ev. Missionsverlag Stuttgart 1961.

168 'Men of unity' by Stephen Neill, S.C.M. Press London 1960.

169 'Leaders of the Church of England' 1828-1944 by David L. Edwards, Oxford University Press London 1971.

170 'Das Gewissen steht auf' by Annake. Leber, Mosack Verlag Berlin 1954.

Secular histories and general works, arranged in the order they are referred to

171 'Half Angels' by Elisabeth Montefiore, Faith Press London 1961.

172 'The Origins of the First World War' ed. by H.W. Koch, Macmillan 1972.

173 'The Home Fronts: Britain France and Germany 1914-18' by John Williams Constable London 1972.

174 'A History of the First World War' by A.J.P. Taylor, Macmillan 1974.

175 'Goodbye to all that' Autobiography of Robert Graves, Jonathan Cape London 1929.

176 'Twentieth Century Pacifism' by Peter Brook, Van Nortrand Reinhold Co. New York 1970.

177 'Conscience and Politics. The British Government and the conscientious objectors to military service 1916-19' John Rae. Oxford University Press London 1970.

178 'The Rebel Passion' by Vera Brittain. George Allen Unwin and Co. 1964.

179 'Objection over-ruled' by David Boulton. MacGibbon and Kee London 1967.

180 'Conscription and Conscience' by John Graham. George Allen and Unwin 1922.

181 'The Continent of Circe' by Nirad Chaudhuri. Chatto and Windus London 1964.

182 'The autobiography of an unknown Indian' by Nirad Chaudhuri. MacMillan London 1951.

183 'British India' by Michael Edwardes. Sidgwick and Jackson London 1967..

184 'Nehru: a political biography' by Michael Edwardes. Allen Lane London 1971.

185 'Saint on the March (Vinoba Bhave)' by Hallam Tennyson, Victor Gollancz London 1955.

186 'An advanced history of India' by R.C. Majumdor Part III, Macmillan 1940.

187 'India and the Commonwealth' S.H. Mehrotea. Allen Unwin and Co. 1965.

188 'The Indian Muslims' by M. Mujeeb, George Allen and Unwin London 1967.

189 'Gandhi in South Africa' by Robert Huttenback, Cornell University Press U.S.A. 1971.

190 'Jawaharlal Nehru: an autobiography' Bodley Head India 1936.

191 'India: Mirage and reality' Peter Schmid. Harrap and Co. London 1961.

192 'Mahatma Gandhi' by C.F. Andrews, George Allen Unwin and Co. London 1929.

193 'Beggar among the dead' by Hans-Ulrick Rieger, Rider and Co. London 1960.

194 'British foreign policy since Versailles 1918-63' by W.E. Medlicott. University Paperbacks no. 280, Methuen and Co.

195 'Hitler's rise to power: The National Socialist movement in Bavaria' by Geoffrey Pridham, MacGibbon London 1973.

196 'The German resistence to Hitler' by H. Gramml, Mommsen, Reichardt, Ernst Wolf. B.T. Batsford Ltd London 1970 pub. originally as 'Der deutsche Widerstand gogen Hitler' ed. by Walter Ivanmittlerner and Hans Buckheim Kiepenheuer and Witschi, Köln, Berlin.

197 'Der 20 Juli. Alternativ zu Hitler?' ed. by Hans-Jürgen Schultz Kreuz Verlag Stuttgart and Berlin.

198 'When six million died' by Arthur Morse, Secker and Warbung London 1968.

199 'The last three Popes and the Jews' Pinchas Lapide. Souvenir Press London 1964.

200 'By Kenya possessed. The correspondence between Norman Leys and J.H. Oldham 1918-1926' ed. and with an introduction by John W. Cell. The University of Chicago Press Ltd 1976.

Bibliography of Paton's published and unpublished writings.

(SM = The Student Movement : IRM = International Review of Missions)

1909-1911

1 'So each of us shall give account of himself to God' Exposition of Romans 14 v 10. Unpublished notes.

2 Commentary on Revelation 1v3-2v9 Notes in the form of a letter.

3 'The tree of knowledge and the tree of life'. Exposition of Genesis 3. 36 page handwritten essay.

1911

4 'St. Paul's missionary methods' 12 page handwritten essay.

1913

5 'The missionary motive' (edited) S.C.M./U.C.M.E. study book.

6 'The Renewing of our Covenant' (a discussion of the Aim and Basis of the S.C.M.) SM vol XVI, p.31 1914.

7 'The Missionary Policy of the Christian Union' SM vol XVI p.184 1914.

1914

8 'Foreign missions and the war'. Article in 'The Student Movement' December 1914. SM vol. 17 p.44f.

9 'The finality of Christianity' S.C.M. apologetics pamphlet.

1915

10 'Ideals of ministry' S.C.M. apologetics pamphlet.

11 Letter to Student Volunteers on the effect of the war on foreign missions. Signed by William Paton, Ronald Rees, Tissington Tatlow and Lettice Shann SM Vol XVII p.33.

12 'Foreign Missions and the War' SM Vol XVII p.43.

1916

13 'Jesus Christ and the World's religions' U.C.M.E. imprint. Reprinted 1916, Jan. & April 1917, Jan. & August 1918, 1921, 1923, 1925, 1926. Second revised edition 1927 by Edinburgh House Press (E.H.P.)

1918

14 'The Student Movement and the Church' SM Vol XVIII p.178.

1918

15 Letter from Calcutta dated 16.11.17. SM Vol XX p.79 pub. February 1918.

16 Letter from the North West Frontier dated 13.212.17 SM Vol XX p.112, pub. April 1918.

17 Letter from Bombay dated 20.2.18. SM Vol XX p.148 pub. June 1918.

Date Uncertain

18 'The Student Volunteer in College' S.C.M. pamphlet.

1919

19 'The new world' mimeographed article produced for the I.R.M. group.

20 'The place of missions in the world today' Discussed by the I.R.M. group April 1919. I.M.C. Box 83. W.C.C. archives, Geneva.

21 'The Indian Christian and the missionary' Discussed by the I.R.M. group May 1919.

22 'Personal relationships between Europeans and Indians' Article in the I.R.M. October 1919 vol. VIII p.522-530.

23 'Social ideals in India' U.C.M.E. imprint.

24 'A missionary policy for the Christian Union' Article in 'The Student Movement' SM vol. XXII p.59. Jan 1920.

25 'What a missionary is for' Glasgow Quadrennial papers No. 2 pub. S.C.M. Press imprint.

26 'A plea for a fresh study of missions to the Muslim world' mimeographed article. I.M.C. Box 82 W.C.C. archives, Geneva.

27 'Age-long principles and modern life' article in the I.R.M. vol. IX, p.281-288. I.M.C. Box 83 W.C.C. archives, Geneva.

28 'Beatenberg 1920' in 'The Student World' October 1920 issue.

1921

29 'The Highway of God' (jointly with Kathleen Harnett) U.C.M.E.

30 'The missionary task of the Movement' SM Vol XXIII p.132 June 1921.

1922

31 'A letter from India' SM Vol XXV p.55 Dec 1922.

1923

32 'The National Christian Council of India' article in 'The East and the West' vol. XXI pub. by

1923

32 'The National Christian Council of India' article in 'The East and the West' vol. XXI pub. by S.P.G.

33 'Muslims and the Khalifate' I.R.M. vol. XII p.83.

34 'Alexander Duff, pioneer of missionary education' S.C.M. and U.C.M.E. series of missionary biographies.

1924

35 'Opium in India' An Inquiry by the N.C.C. of India (81 pages) printed by the N.C.C. in Calcutta.

36 'Tidings from India' SM Vol XXVI p.82 Jan 1924.

37 'The opium trade and India. The next step' N.C.C. Review.

38 'The work before the N.C.C. of India' I.R.M. vol. XIII p.84.

39 'Industrial education in India' I.R.M. vol. XIII p.403.

1925

40 'India and opium' I.R.M. vol. XIV p.116.

1926

41 'India and opium. The present situation'. N.C.C. Review January issue.

42 'Concerning evangelism in India' I.R.M. vol. XV p.161.

1927

43 'The indigenous church' I.R.M. vol. XVI p.46.

44 'Eastern Industrialism and Christian missions' I.R.M. vol. XVI p.542.

1928

45 'The Jerusalem meeting of the I.M.C.' editor of the series of eight volumes pub. by the Oxford University Press, 1928. Author of 'Industrialism in Asia and Africa': vol. V.
Vol. I The Christian Message in relation to non-Christian systems of thought and life.
Vol. II Religious Education.
Vol. III The Relation between the younger and elder churches.
Vol. IV The Christian Mission in the light of race conflict.
Vol. V The Christian Mission relation to industrial problems.
Vol. VI The Christian Mission in relation to the rural problem.
Vol. VII International missionary co-operation.
Vol. VIII Addresses and other records.

46 'The Jerusalem Meeting of the I.M.C.' I.R.M. vol. XVII p.3.

47 'The Jerusalem meeting and after' I.R.M. vol. XVII p.435.

48 Entry on mission in the 'Encyclopedia Britannica' 1928.

49 'Federation and internationalism' paper delivered to the W.S.C.F. General Committee meeting Mysore. Summarized in the Mysore minutes.

1929

50 'What is secularism?' I.R.M. vol. XIX p.340.

51 'A Faith for the world' Cargate Press 1929.

52 An appreciation of Zoe B Fairfield, Twenty Years in the S.C.M. SM Vol XXXI, p.206 June 1929.

53 Chapter on co-operation in 'The Christian task in India' by J. Mackenzie. Macmillan 1929.

1931

54 'Christian missions in India today' I.R.M. vol. XX p.381.

*56 Article on religious liberty. N.C.C. Review July 1931.

55 'Kanakarayan Tiruselvam Paul 1876-1931. An obituary.' SM Vol XXXIII, p.199 June 1931.

57 'Moral hygiene and education' Council on Christian Education conference paper No. 2 April 1931, I.M.C. Box 158.

1932

58 'The faiths of mankind' S.C.M. study book.

59 'The Herrnhut meeting of the I.M.C.' I.R.M. vol. XXI p.489.

1933

60 'The Indian mission of fellowship' I.R.M. vol. XXII p.215.

1934

61 'Christian missions and religious liberty' I.R.M. vol. XXIII p.489.

62 'The new era in missionary work; next steps'. C.B.M.S. pamphlet.

63 'Must it be retreat?' (on the financial problems of missions) SM Vol. XXXVII p.50 Dec 1934.

1935

64 'The problem of religious freedom in the mission field' Written in April 1935, translated into German for the German version of the 'Church, community and state'. 'Totalitarische Staat und Christliche Freiheit in dem Missionsfeld'. ed. Gerstenmaier Band VII pub. Geneva 1937 by the Life and Work Research Department.

65 'Prayer and the Indian crisis' SM Vol XXXVII p.147 April 1935.

66 'Christianity and the modern east' Address given to the joint W.S.C.F. and I.M.C. held in Basel in August, published in 'The Student World' vol. XXVIII No. 4.

1936

67 'The I.M.C. and the future' I.R.M. vol. XXV p.106.

68 'Our missions in the modern East' under the imprint of the Foreign Missions' committee, Presbyterian Church of England.

69 'A five years' plan' pamphlet pub. by the Edinburgh House Press.

1937

70 'The Far East' address given to the S.C.M. Quadrennial January 1937, pub. by S.C.M. in the conference volume 'God speaks to this generation' ed. Hugh Martin p.64f.

71 'Notes on the Far East' preparatory material for the S.C.M. Quadrennial. pub. for the S.C.M. by the Talbot Press, Saffron Waldron.

72 'The churches in council: Oxford, Edinburgh, Hangchow' offprint from the article in the I.R.M. vol. XXVI p.296.

73 'Christianity in the Eastern conflicts' pub. E.H.P., translated into German 'Das Christentum im Ringen des Ostens' pub. Verlag von Huber Frauenfeld und Leipzig 1938 under the imprint of the I.M.C. and Forschungsabteilung des Oekumenisches Rat für Praktisches Christentum Kirche und Welt Studien und Dokumente Band II.

1938

74 'The Madras meeting and the ecumenical movement' I.R.M. vol. XXVII p.153.

75 'World Community' S.C.M. Press Religious Book Club edition No.6.

76 'Letter to Robert Mackie', pub. in 'The Student World'.

1939

77 'The meeting of the I.M.C. at Tambaram I.R.M. vol. XXVIII p.161.

78 'Looking forward from Tambaram' I.R.M. vol. XXVIII p.490.

79 'Studies in evangelism' (circulated privately under I.M.C. imprint).

80 The Tambaram series following the meeting of the I.M.C. at Tambaram. edited by Paton pub. Oxford University Press vol. I
Vol. I 'The authority of the Faith'.
Vol. II 'The Growing Church'.
Vol. III 'Evangelism'.
Vol. IV 'The Life of the Church'.
Vol. V 'The Economic basis of the Church'.
Vol. VI 'The Church and State'.
Vol. VII 'Addresses and other records': including 'The Church and World community', an address by Paton, p.119.

81 'The world mission of the Church' (the I.M.C. meeting at Tambaram summarized) I.M.C. publication, London.

82 'The message of the world-wide church' Sheldon Press, London Christian Newsletter books series No.4.

83 'The white man's burden. The Beckly social service lecture' Epworth Press, London.

84 'The spiritual significance of Father Kelly' to the S.C.M. printed in 'Theology' Oct. 1939.

85 'The hour and its need' E.H.P. London (October 1939).

1940

86 Foreword to the English edition of 'Spiritual revolution in the East' by Walter Freytag.

87 'The churches as an ecumenical society in the time of war' written jointly with Visser't Hooft mimeographed W.C.C. archives, Geneva.

88 'Christianity and civilisation' I.R.M. vol. XXIX p.486.

89 'The problem of "war aims" from the point of view of the Church' 31.12.40. Paton papers Box VI. memograph.

3.1.40.

90 The Christian Newsletter Supplement No. 10 'The world-wide Christian society'.

12.2.41.

91 'War and peace aims and the Church's task' Christian Newsletter Supplement No.68.

92 'The Church and the World Order' (including a review of Bishop Bell's book 'Christianity and World Order') SM Vol XL p.63 February 1941.

10.9.41.

93 Christian Newsletter Supplement No. 98 'Britain and India'.

94 'Towards unity in India' I.R.M. vol. XXX p.501. Also an I.M.C. off-print.

95 'The Church and the new order' S.C.M. Press Religious Book Club edition No.23.

1942

96 'Continental Christianity in wartime' E.H.P. London, World issues. Series 5.

97 'The Russian Alliance' SM Vol XLIV June 1942.

98 'The Church calling' (6 broadcast talks) E.H.P. London.

99 'America and Britain' mimeograph, pub. October 1942 in the 'World issues' series Morrison and Gibb and E.H.P.

100 Article sent in the form of a four page letter to the editor of 'Christian fellowship in wartime' February 1942 issue. Paton Papers III. The newspaper of the English Confessional Synod, February 1942 on 'peace aims'.

Bibliography

101 'A plan for a British Council of Churches' mimeograph. March 1942 Paton Papers Box VIII.

102 'The prospects of international order' Paton Papers Box VIII.

103 'William Temple' written in America in March 1942, only mimeographed copy (14 pages long) in W.C.C. Archives, Geneva.

104 Preface to 'The Jew in the Christian World' by Hans Kosmala and Robert Smith. pub. S.C.M. London, 1942.

1942

105 Draft of a pamphlet proposed as a sequel to 'The Christian Church and world order' B.C.C. archives.

106 'The Churches help each other' 800 words mimeograph. Paton Papers II.

107 'The ecumenical church and world order' pub. in a volume of addresses after the Delaware conference. Delivered at Ohio 4.3.42. Box VIII Paton Papers.

108 'Religion and life' Collection of addresses ed. by Paton, King and Staples 1942.

109 'The future of the missionary enterprise' I.R.M. vol. XXXI p.385.

110 Four page letter to the editor of 'The Christian Fellowship in wartime'.

111 'An open letter from William Paton'. 'Student World' vol. XXXV 1942.

1943

112 'Christian voices in India' I.R.M. vol. XXXII p.272.

10.3.43.

113 Christian Newsletter supplement No.176 'The reconstruction of Christian Institutions in Europe'.

21.8.43.

114 *Unfinished* = * fragments for a biography of C.F. Andrews. Plan for a book on the significance of missionary policy in wartime. I.M.C. Box 113.

* Indicates that a reference to this work exists, but no copy of the actual document. Conversely, owing to the disappearance or non-availability of full sets of 'The Student Movement', 'The Guardian' and other religious periodicals of Paton's era, it cannot be said that this is a definitive or exhaustive bibliography, but only the best possible in view of the fragmentary nature of the surviving archives.

Appendix A
Archives consulted in the course of this research

The Baptist Missionary Society archives, 93/97 Gloucester Place, London W.1.: Gaps 1917-27 because of material lost in the blitz, but committee minutes intact. Barth archives, C/o Professor Stoevesandt, Basel: Barth's letters to Visser't Hooft are an important source. Basel Missions Archiv, Der Baseler Mission, Missionstr.2, 4 Basel 3: Correspondence with the I.M.C. and with their own missionaries 1914-44. University of Basel archives: Koechlin reports and correspondence. British Council of Churches, 12 Easton Gate, London S.W.1.: C.O.P.E.C. material, World Alliance, and from the bodies which formed the B.C.C. 1924-42. (B.C.C. archives. Transferred to Selly Oak Colleges' archives, Birmingham 29.)

Edinburgh House archives, 2 Eaton Gate, London S.W.1.: I.M.C. papers relating to India and Africa, C.B.M.S. papers. (Now divided between W.C.C. archives and Centre for Oriental and African Studies, University of London. Some copies in Selly Oak Colleges' archives.)

Ehrenström papers: (now with the W.C.C. in Geneva). Lambeth Palace archives: George Bell's papers are available. 1933-39. 'Montefiore Papers': in fact the Paton family papers, in the care of Mrs Elizabeth Montefiore, Bishopscroft, Harborne Park Road, Birmingham 17. Public Records Office: Ministry of Information files 1939-44. (A permit for this archive also permits one to consult the Foreign Office, India Office and Colonial Office papers, as well as the Chancery Lane deposits).

Soest: Okumenisches Archiv. Siegmund-Schultze papers.

The Revd Robert Smith, 2 Moungan, Station Road, Ellon, Aberdeenshire, holds many I.C.C.A.J. papers. Society for the Propagation of the Gospel archives. U.S.P.G., 15 Tufton Street, London S.W.1. (Bishop Montgomery's papers, and the society's records.) Student Christian Movement papers, C/o Selly Oak Colleges' Library, Bristol Road, Selly Oak, Birmingham 29.

The Whitgift School archives, Haling Park, South Croydon, Surrey.

World Council of Churches archives, 150 Route de Ferney, 1211 Geneva 20: contains International Missionary Council papers from London and New York.

Department of Industrial and Social Research papers.

Life and Work (including study department)

Faith and Order (principally on microfilm)

Paton Papers (London Office of the W.C.C.)

World Alliance for Friendship among the churches

World Council of Churches in process of formation

World Council of Churches General correspondence (confidential)

World Student Christian Federation files 1921

The principal ecumenical and missionary periodicals.

Appendix B
List of people interviewed, 1973-1976

* 27. 6.74   Dr. Kathleen Bliss. Missionary in India. Colleague and biographer of J.H. Oldham, 1940 onwards.

10. 2.75   The Revd Alan Booth. Assistant General Secretary 1942-44. General Secretary of the S.C.M. 1944-51.

22. 9.75   Dr Alec Boyd, b.1896. S.C.M. 1919-22, Principal of Madras Christian College 1938.

24.10.75   Miss Gladys Bretherton, b.1885. Tatlow's secretary 1908-14 World's Y.W.C.A. 1930-36.

12. 8.75   Miss Nora Brockway. Taught at the Women's Christian College, Madras, and St Christopher's College 1920-54.

2. 2.76   David Cairns. Professor of Divinity at Aberdeen University. Son of D.S. Cairns.

24. 5.75   Dr A.C. Craig, b.1890. First secretary of the British Council of Churches, 1942-46.

19. 4.75   Professor Prakash Datta. Brought up in Geneva. University College, London.

10. 4.75   Mrs S.K. Datta, b.1886 (née Rena Carswell). Secretary to Ruth Rouse of the W.S.C.F. 1911-19. Returned from India 1945. Wife of S.K. Datta of Forman College, Lahore.

6.11.75   Canon F.W. Dillistone. Charles Raven's biographer.

24. 5.75   Dr J.W.C. Dougall. Oldham's secretary on the Stokes-Phleps Commission, 1926-7. Secretary of the C.B.M.S. 1936-40.

20.12.73   Dr Nils Ehrenström. Life and Work research institute 1930-38 W.C.C. Study Department.

6. 6.75   Dr J. Eric Fenn. S.C.M. staff 1930-35. J.H. Oldham's assistant 1936-38. Assistant Head B.B.C. religious broadcasting 1939.

11.10.74   Miss Jean Fraser. W.S.C.F., Youth secretary of the W.C.C. etc.

10. 9.74   Herr Göttin. Basel missionary in Borneo 1933-57.

12. 9.73   Sir Kenneth Grubb. Freelance missionary in Latin America. Ministry of Information 1939-45. Member of the World Dominion Press.

9. 9.73   Bishop R.O. Hall, 1895-75. Paton's successor in the S.C.M. 1921-5. Bishop of Hong Kong 1932-66.

26. 7.75   Mrs C.M. Hogg. Married Laurie Hogg of the Y.M.C.A. in Calcutta, 1922. Went out 1920.

1. 9.75   Bishop Michael Hollis and Mrs Hollis of the Church of South India 1931-60.

6. 9.73   Bishop L.S. Hunter and Mrs Grace Hunter (née McAulay d.1975) S.C.M. secretaries 1914-19.

2. 9.75   The Revd Philip Lee-Woolf. General Secretary S.C.M. 1948-52.

6. 9.75   John and Gwen Lewis (née Owens). Travelling secretaries of the S.C.M. 1921-23.

* 25. 5.75   Dr Robert C. Mackie. Gen. Sec. S.C.M. 1929-38, Gen. Sec. W.S.C.F. 1939-46.

9. 9.74   Archdeacon Mara of the Church of South India.

31. 5.74   Miss McNair and Miss Probala Mangat Rai, principals successively of Kinnaird College, Lahore. 1928-67.

19. 9.75   Dr Nathaniel Micklem, b.1887. d.1976. Knew Paton from 1907-43. Principal of Mansfield College, Oxford.

13. 9.73   Miss Sigrid Morden. Paton's secretary 1940-43. Previously secretary to Betty Gibson.

23. 8.75   Bishop J.E. Lesslie Newbigin of the Church of South India. First sailed 1932.

7. 9.75   Dr Cecil Northcott. Secretary of home missions of the L.M.S. 1935-50.

3.10.75   Dr James Parkes. Secretary of the S.C.M. and I.S.S. 1922-31.

* 3. 9.73   Canon David M. Paton. S.C.M. Secretary 1936-39, Y.M.C.A. in China 1939-44, and Mrs Paton (née Alison Stewart) S.C.M. Secretary 1944-46.

6. 9.75   James Christopher Paton. Colonial Service, Warden of International Student House, London. 1964.

*   9. 8.74   Professor Sir William Paton, Department of Pharmacology, Oxford.

*   13. 9.73   Mrs Elisabeth Montefiore (née Paton), Medical Social Worker.

2. 5.75   The Ven. Michael Paton, formerly of the Diplomatic Service.

13. 2.75   Miss Catherine Paton. Manager of Paton Books, St. Albans, Herts.

23. 4.75   Dr Ernest A. Payne. B.M.S. 1932-40. Member of U.C.M.E. with Paton. President of the W.C.C. 1968-75.

5. 9.75   Canon R.L. Pelly, b.1887, d.7.4.76. Last chairman of the undivided C.I.C.C.U.; Missionary in India.

6.11.75   Miss Osyth Potts, friend of Lorna Southwell's. St George's School, Clarens Switzerland and Rydal Hall.

13. 9.73   Mrs Dora Pym (née Ivens). Chairman of S.C.M. 1917-18, friend of Paton family.

9. 9.74   Praeses Raaflaub, formerly of Basel Mission. Cameroun 1939.

4. 9.73   The Revd Ronald D. Rees, b.1888, and Mrs Rees (née Janet Edminson, d.1974) Lingnan University 1922-30 Canton. Secretary of the N.C.C. of China 1930-47.

6.12.73   Dr Jacques Rossel, Director of the Basel Mission. Missionary in India.

17. 7.75   The Revd and Mrs Leonard Schiff (née Satterthwaite). S.C.M. secretaries and missionaries in India.

10. 4.75   The Revd W.W. Simpson, sometime Chairman, Council of Christians and Jews.

11. 2.75   Miss Margaret Sinclair, Secretary, Life and Work 1933-40. Assistant Editor, I.R.M. 1940-43.

25. 5.75   Mr and Mrs Kingsley Smith (née Paton, b.1892).

25. 5.75   Dr Colin Kingsley (Smith), Paton's nephew. Professor of Music, Edinburgh.

28. 5.75   The Revd and Mrs Robert Smith, formerly I.C.C.A.J. 1939-46. Church of Scotland missionaries to Jews, Prague 1935-39.

14. 4.75   The Revd Vernon Sproxton, B.B.C. Religious Broadcasting.

10. 9.74   Professor Ernst Staehlin (emeritus). Basel. At Edinburgh 1937 conference.

11. 5.74   Professor M.M. Thomas of Union Theological College, Bangalore.

18. 3.74   Bishop Oliver Tomkins and Mrs Tomkins (née Ursula Dunn), both secretaries of the S.C.M. 1935-40.

7. 9.75   Miss Mary Trevelyan. Warden International House (S.C.M.) 1932-46, friend of Paton's.

28.11.73   Dr Visser't Hooft. General Secretary W.S.C.F. 1929-38, and W.C.C. 1938-66.

20. 5.74   Dr Marcus Ward. S.C.M. member, missionary in India, sailed 1932.

6. 5.75   Bishop R.R. Williams of Leicester. Ministry of Information 1940-45.

22.10.75   Miss Kathleen Witz, S.C.M. secretary 1917-21, Tatlow's secretary 1927-29.

12. 5.75   Bishop R.W. Woods of Worcester, Missionary Secretary of S.C.M. 1938-40.

25. 5.75   Dr Ruth Young (widow of C.B. Young), St Stephen's College, Delhi, Principal of the Lady Hardinge School of Medicine, Delhi, returned in 1940.

N.B.   This is only a list of those whom I interviewed who knew Paton or his friends first-hand. It does not include colleagues and acquaintances with whom I have been collaborating.

*   Indicates that I have worked particularly closely with these people.

Appendix C
Chart of Paton's illnesses reconstructed from his letters.

His sister remembers him as a healthy child, who was excused the usual Victorian dosages of malt extract etc.

1911   April. Ill during the W.S.C.F. conference at Constantinople.

1912   September. In bed with unspecified illness.

1915   January? date of attack of influenza Mrs Pym remembers vividly.

1916   January. Influenza (3-17.1)

1917   March, unspecified illness. April another illness.

1918   January, throat infection, 28.7-21.8 Dengue fever.

1919   January/February. Influenza.

1923   November, throat infection.

1930   December. Influenza followed by malaria.

1931   Ill for most of July; Christmas and most of January 1932 in bed with influenza.

1935   June 'a bout of fever'; November unspecified illness.

1936   April, exhaustion. December bad attack of pneumonia.

1937   Effects of the pneumonia lasted until March. Severe cold October.

1938   Undated attack of influenza. August exhaustion.

1939   14.2.-21.3 influenza (very much weakened afterwards). April bronchitis and lumbago.

1940   March-April, near fatal attack of pneumonia.

1941   January severe cold. April chest trouble affecting his voice. September severe cold.

1942   17.2-20.3 further attack of pneumonia.

1943   February in bed with unspecified illness.
           14.8.43 first attack of severe stomach pains, which he ignored.
            9.8.43 Observed to be looking very tired indeed.
           18.8.43 Emergency operation for stomach ulcer.
           21.8.43 Died of peritonitis and post-operative pneumonia.

Appendix D

'I cannot say that the main arguments of your memo carry my assent. A large part of the argument, and especially the whole analogy with the German Confessional Church, really presupposes that what is at issue is the freedom of pacifists to preach pacifism on the wireless as a part of the Christian Gospel. You use for instance on p.3 the phrase 'a man is invited to preach, not his own views, but the Gospel of God'. In fact you are not making that case, and you are not pleading the right of the pacifist as a part of the total witness of the Church, to utter pacifist views as a part of the Gospel. Once the pacifist has agreed that for obvious reasons he cannot ask the B.B.C. to allow him to preach pacifist views during war time, the analogy to some extent breaks down. I feel that some of the ground taken in your memorandum is really too high a ground and there is some truth I think in my more or less jocular suggestion that the fight was about the right of pacifists not to preach pacifism on the B.B.C. I feel this also about your paragraph 4 on the same page 3. This is quite definitely an argument for the preaching of pacifism on the wireless, but that, I understand, is not really asked. Again, on page 5, you say that the Confessional Church fought against the principle of subordinating the preaching of the Gospel to a national criterion, whereas the Gospel itself stood superior to such criteria and itself judged the life of nation and state. I doubt if this paragraph holds unless we are to go further and say that a man who believes that pacifism is a part of the Word of God shall be free to broadcast it and that any interference with that right is fighting against the purity of the Word.

We are, in fact, dealing with something a little lower down the scale than these high ideas and the two solid points that come out for me are these: (a) if the B.B.C. should pursue this policy so far as to ban all people who profess pacifist views, then I think the Church should act, not because it claims the sacred right to preach pacifism as a part of the Word of God, but because it desires to maintain in the Broadcast Church, so to speak, the unity between pacifist and non-pacifist, and can say to the State that the pacifists in question recognize the situation and would not abuse the privilege; and (b) on entirely other grounds I think that the B.B.C. would then be performing an act of extreme silliness in that they would be greatly increasing the tendency, now widespread among thoughtful people of all kinds, to regard everything that is said on the wireless as propaganda. An intelligent and imaginative handling of this question would be of great practical value to the B.B.C.

Yours affectionately,

Chapter III

Paton to Fenn 25.3.41. Paton Papers Box IV. W.C.C. Geneva

My Dear Eric,

Thanks for your letter. I am sorry that I have failed to make clear my point in contesting the analogy which you draw with the situation of the German Church. It seems to me that if once it is granted, as it is on all hands in this controversy, that the B.B.C. are right in refusing to allow pacifism to be preached on the wireless, then the analogy with the German Church and the arguments by which you support that analogy must be abandoned. If once you are going to say that the Church should claim on the wireless to preach the Word of God without conditions as something which judges man and is not judged by him then you must stick to that line. You cannot say the Church claims to preach the Word of God without conditions, but is agreeable that pacifism shall not be preached even by those who believe it to be a legitimate inference from the fundamental Gospel. In taking this sensible and practical line you and the leaders of the Church have recognised that what is at issue is not strictly speaking the freedom of the Gospel. Freedom of the Gospel would be at stake if an ecclesiastical body forbade a minister to preach pacifism or if the State forced a minister in his church to preach pacifism. My contention is that in this particular controversy the acceptance by the pacifists concerned of a ban on the preaching of pacifism makes it impossible to use the arguments which have been advanced.

The musicians have a simpler case. Apart from Churchill's gibe to the effect that they were not to sing 'Deutschland Uber Alles' there is no real connection between their musical performances and their views. In the case of the pacifist clergy there is such a connection and, as I understand the case, the pacifist clergy agree to this diminution of their freedom in that, if they did broadcast, they would not preach what are commonly called pacifist views, though no doubt they would preach the Gospel from which they believe those views to be a proper deduction. The musicians therefore can say quite properly that this mixing up of our political views and our music is mere persecution. The church can say to the B.B.C. (a) we think it all wrong that Christian ministers who have a Gospel to preach and who are willing to accept the general conditions which govern broadcasting as an instrument of State in war time, should be prevented from doing so. We desire to maintain as great unity as possible between pacifists and non-pacifists and we regret that this unity shall not be sampled on the air. (b) The Church can say to the B.B.C. you are being extremely silly and offending against your own interests by taking action which must be seen as the general credibility of all speaking on the wireless.

My only difference from your memorandum is on the one point that I do not think that you can use the argument about the primacy of the Word of God unless you are prepared to urge that Christian pacifists should preach pacifism on the wireless should they be moved by the Spirit of God to do it. That is the proper conclusion from the arguments of your memorandum.

Yours affectionately,

Chapter IV
S.C.M. Archives, Selly Oak
Memorandum on the Christian Message to Non-Christians
W. Paton

If I begin what I have to say on this subject with the remark that what I most felt in India in dealing with educated non-Christians was that I wanted to 'introduce them to Jesus' I hope that I shall not seem to be using a mere phrase. It expresses as well as anything else the thing that I most felt, and as I look back on my short experience in India it is still what I feel most. In making speeches and in private conversation with men I felt myself all the time to be labouring, often very unsuccessfully indeed, to get men into the realisation of a personal existence of which one was conscious oneself, and to get them to open their minds and spirits to the influence of a Person who both incarnated certain general principles, and also has an effect on human personality when it is exposed to His influence. I would begin, therefore, with this, that we want to get people to understand Who and what Jesus Christ is, to get to know Him, and to let Him do His work upon their own spirits.

The things which are involved in this stated as ideas I think I would put somewhat as follows:—

1) The knowledge of God as a Father, with a definitely knowable character of holiness and love, quite distinct on the one hand, from the pantheistic conception of God as merely Reality, and on the other hand, equally distinct from the Deistic conception of God which is the faith of Islam. I suppose that in dealing with primitive peoples the thought of the Fatherhood of God would be, perhaps, the greatest immediate message one could give, and I found that present in the minds of those who were dealing with the outcastes.

2) A raised and purified standard of human life, morality and conduct. I am sure that the effect of contact with the Person and Spirit of Christ is not only to raise and purify men's thought of God, but also to transform their conception of what human nature ought to be, of how life ought to be lived, and of the ideals of human conduct. This is true along the whole range of ethics and is just as true, neither less or more, of such questions as sexual ethics as it is of the subtler principles which ought to animate society as a whole.

3) Following on 2. comes the sense of sin and of the need and possibility of forgiveness. I am not particularly concerned with the question which of these comes first. I think that to some people there comes first the sense of sin, that is of failure and worthlessness, when life is viewed by the standard of Jesus; while to others the love of Christ as shown supremely in the Cross first arouses the soul to the sense of its own sinfulness. To minds which are habituated to the doctrine of Karma and which, in consequence, are either deadened to the sense of the urgency of the moral struggle, I believe this message, that sin is an affair between man and God and that reconciliation with God is both necessary and possible, is one of the things that has to be preached if Indian life is to be redeemed from its moral nervelessness.

4) I am sure that one most important element in the missionary message is the idea of moral and spiritual power in religion as distinct from the view of religion which represents it as being merely an ethic. How far we are any of us succeeding in preaching this, either at home or abroad, I should not like to say. Certainly the idea that Christianity means a series of negatives is quite as prevalent in the Indian Church as it is at home. All the same, that is not Christianity, and one large part of the influence of Jesus on men's lives is to assure them of the existence and power of the life of God in the world and in men, and of the possibility of doing things for Him and of achieving holiness.

I think I will add to this — and perhaps it ought to be a separate point — that the thought of the Church not so much as an institution, as the necessary expression of the social nature of the Gospel. I am sure it is one of the vital things which the Spirit of Christ does when it touches people, that it unites them into a brotherhood which transcends the limits of private and personal affinities and is really a fellowship constituted by the Spirit of God.

I suppose that theologically these things involve the Christian doctrine of God, of man, of the Person and the work of Christ, of sin and forgiveness, and of sanctification, but I don't wish to treat the matter from that end. Indeed, I should like to stress the idea that we have got, somehow, or other, to help the Christians in the mission field to formulate things for themselves. S.K. Rudra of Delhi said to me that to his mind the really distinctive thing which missionaries had to preach was the historic Jesus. "We have", he said, "a long philosophical tradition in India and we naturally wish to work out the Christian theology in view of that philosophical background which is different from that of the West". I know that this rather a platitude in advanced missionary circles, but I think it needs far more attention to be given to it, and that we shall not make progress with it unless we send out more missionaries who are quite clear, both as to what they do want to preach and as to what they don't want to preach.

I confess to two things that make me more convinced of the difficulty of doing this than I was before I went to India. The first is that I saw, I think I may say, no signs whatever in any Indian Christian of what is so often talked about by theological students who are interested in missions, i.e. the distinctive Indian contribution to Christian theology. I found a great deal of the distinctive Indian method in propaganda and a distinctive emphasis on aspects of the Christian ethic, and also a general tendency to a pantheistic interpretation. Apart from this I cannot say that I found anything in the way of a distinctive Indian interpretation of Christian thought, and I tried hard to find it both from Indian Christians themselves and from those who were teaching Indian theological students.

The other thing which I think has to be recognised is the extreme difficulty of drawing a line between the historic revelation of Jesus and the interpretation of His Person and work. The eschatologists like Schweitzer have effectually delivered us from the idea that you can extricate from the Gospels and particularly from St. Mark a Jesus who utters nothing but moral precepts. They have at least shown that on any honest reading of the story the question of His relation to the ultimate nature of the universe and to world judgment arises. Attempts such as that made by the author of "By an Unknown Disciple" have shown quite recently how an attempt to retell the story as a plain historic narrative must end in throwing into relief the great questions which have got to be answered, of the relation of Jesus Christ to God, and of His own attitude towards His death. To start on these questions is to start on theology and you are landed in the difficulty to which I have referred of giving any message at all about Jesus Christ without dealing to some extent with a theological interpretation of His Person. However, this is simply stating the problem and while one cannot expect the average Student Volunteer to worry much about it, I am sure it is a question to which the abler ones have got to give their minds.

I would also add, in parenthesis, that one cannot assume that every intellectual background is equally suitable for Christianity. Pantheism to my mind is incompatible with the Christian conception of God, and one has to recognise the danger of a preaching of the historic Jesus which will be only too easily fitted into a pantheistic view of the universe. On the other hand there is a half truth in pantheism which has been a good deal lost in the over-emphasis on personality which distinguishes a good deal of modern thought. There are three general principles I would add:—

1) I want to attack the idea that Christianity is simply abstract moral and spiritual truths, e.g. the Fatherhood of God, and the brotherhood of man. These truths are part of the Christian message, but we not only do not exhaust Christianity when we have stated them, but we have not conveyed the Gospel, the apprehension of which will alone make men believe these things. One has, of course, to allow for exceptional spirits, such, perhaps, as the father of Rabindrinath Tagore, who seemed, judging from his writings, to have got hold of something remarkably like the Christian view without conscious indebtedness to Christ. Broadly speaking, however, I think that one can defend the thesis that a really living belief in the Fatherhood of God and the brotherhood of man is the fruit of belief in Christ, is mediated to men through the historic events of His life and death and resurrection, and apart from those events and belief in them is not likely to subsist with compelling force among men. I found Brahmins everywhere who would cheerfully agree to the doctrine of the Fatherhood of God and the brotherhood of man; the trouble was that they had never been got into contact with the shattering personality of Jesus and were using words which had a meaning for them, and doubtless a good and useful meaning, but the thing that was in their minds was not that conviction which it is the distinctive work of Christ to produce.

2) I agree in the main with the position taken up by Mr. Bevan in his paper which I think, Mr. Oldham is supplying for the Commission, i.e. that Christianity is rooted in certain acts of God and cannot be understood apart from these historic acts. I do not wish to press the distinction between general truths and historic events illegitimately; it is a part of the Christian message to say what God is, but I feel that to the Christian God is known as being what He is because of what He did and does and that it is distinctively in what He did and does in Christ for us that we know Him as Father and as Love.

3) I think we ought to emphasize the place of the Christian community, that is of the Church, in the missionary message. There is perhaps no way so successful in the end of getting people to know what Christianity is as to introduce them to a Christian society, and this is essential and not accidental, because Christianity is a religion of fellowship. Perhaps our greatest obstacle in the mission field is that the

native Church sometimes exhibits so little real fellowship that to introduce a man to it is not necessarily to bring Him within the compelling power of the spirit of Jesus. All the same, this is what has to be done. It is, I think, the strength of the Roman point of view all through that it stresses this side of things, and while I do not for a moment plead for its methods or its theology, I think it is true that, if not the best, at least one of the best, ways of getting anybody to know Jesus is to get him inside or into contact with a society of people who believe in Him and are trying to live like Him.

Chapter V
Paton circular written for Salem, India. I.M.C. Box 91. 19.2.31.

An ancient strife now does seem to be within reach of settlement, unless I am too optimistic. The causes of dispute are too long even to summarise, but they go back to a visit of a previous Patriarch of Antioch who excommunicated Mar Dionysius, desiring to exercise control himself over the temporalities of the Church. (There are 400,000 Romo-Syrians using the Syrian rite but obeying the Pope; 200,000 Jacobites in communion with Antioch [now Mosul]; and 100,000 Mar Thoma or reformed Syrians.) The strength of the Jacobites has been for over a generation wasted in litigation, enriching the Brahmin lawyers and destroying the Church. There are two parties of the Jacobites, pro and anti-Patriarch, and Mar Dionysius, an aged man, is the Metropolitan of Malabar acknowledged by the majority or anti-Patriarch section. I came into this matter by the accident that when I last left India I was to travel through Iraq and was asked by a number of my friends among the Syrians to see the Patriarch and try to get him to see the grievous state of the Church and to use his power for a settlement. This I did (two years ago) and did actually get the old gentleman to agree to make the Anglican Metropolitan (Dr. Westcott of Calcutta) an impartial chairman of a conference of the two sides. But he didn't get his bishops to agree, and nothing came of it. Recently the Syrians, led by Chacko, asked the Viceroy, who had shown much kindness to the different sections on his visit to Travancore, to cable to the Patriarch suggesting that he should allow him, the Vieroy, to appoint impartial assessors. The Patriarch replied that he was coming to India himself. He had shown no sign of accepting the suggestion that any impartial element should be supplied to help him, but I have recently learned that he is shortly coming to India, landing at Karachi and going to Delhi first to see the Viceroy. I have ventured to suggest that the Viceroy might ask the Patriarch to let *him* call the conference, inviting the two parties and also nominating some impartial persons such as Bishop Gore, now in India, who has offered to help in the matter if desired. We shall soon know what is to happen. The importance of these events may to some seem exaggerated. In part it lies in the fact that a section of the Jacobites, despairing of settlement have gone over to Rome headed by an able bishop. The Roman Catholics are as in the Near East making very strenuous efforts to win over the members of the ancient churches, and I was told in Travancore that offers of money to say masses for the departed are made all over the state to Jacobite priests. When I think of the splendid Jacobites, such as K.C. Chacko, that I know, and of the ring-fence that surrounds the convert to Rome, I do greatly desire that the strength, latent if you like, of this ancient Church should be released for wider service.

Chart showing the number of new Student Volunteers per year
1896-1946

New Volunteers

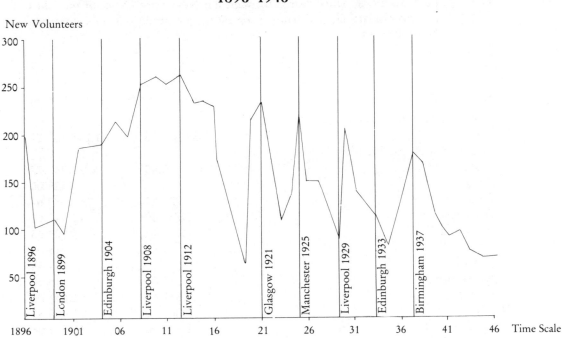

Time Scale

'Aid to orphaned missions' (Chapter VIII)

N.B.   These are the amounts cleared through the New York Office of the I.M.C.
They do not include assistence given by neighbouring missions. Data from
I.M.C. Box 145.

Sent   from   :

Sent from :	Total 31.6.41.	Total 31.12.43.
United States, for Continental missions.	$659,623.55	$3,238,163.02
United States, for British missions.	$502,000.00	$921,357.77
Angola		425.00
Argentina	232.81	89.67
Australia	3,744.00	10,440.61
Bermuda		929.33
Brazil	10.00	15.03
Burma		1,194.44
Cameroun	515.00	515.00
Canada	27,611.10	91,637.00
China	4,000.00	4,460.83
Congo	2,843.00	11,444.63
Denmark	6,705.00	6,705.00
Great Britain	34,575.00	79,164.00
India	9,584.00	16,396.00
Japan	100.00	(100.00*)
Kenya		530.44
Madagascar		235.00
Mexico		(27.57*)
New Zealand	1,250.50	17,036.70
Norway	8,149.00	11,956.00
South Africa	17,505.00	35,498.46
Straits Settlements	180.00	180.00
Sweden	24,000.00	45,324.00
Switzerland	6,878.00	5,358.00
Syria		2,200.00
Totals	$1,315,918.96	$2,977,254.21

(*)   indicates that these items were cleared by the I.M.C. in London

These figures are given as an indication of the size of the operation to save the
'orphaned missions', and the distribution of effort.

Index